SOCIETY OF BIBLICAL LITERATURE

1984 Seminar Papers

SOCIETY OF BIBLICAL LITERATURE
SEMINAR PAPERS SERIES

Editor, Kent Harold Richards

Number 23

·

Society of Biblical Literature
1984 Seminar Papers

Editor, Kent Harold Richards

SOCIETY OF BIBLICAL LITERATURE
1984 SEMINAR PAPERS

Editor, Kent Harold Richards

One Hundred Twentieth Annual Meeting
December 8–11, 1984
The Palmer House
Chicago, Illinois

Scholars Press
Chico, California

SOCIETY OF BIBLICAL LITERATURE
1984 SEMINAR PAPERS

Editor, Kent Harold Richards

©1984
Society/of Biblical Literature

ISBN: 0-89130-810-5
ISSN: 0145-2711

Printed in the United States of America

Contents

Introductory Note

The papers in this volume were prepared for discussion at the One Hundred Twentieth Annual Meeting of the Society of Biblical Literature convened at The Palmer House Hotel, Chicago, Illinois, 8-11 December 1984. The papers are printed in the order of their presentation in the program of the meeting. They represent, in most cases, experimental and initial work on a subject. Therefore, they should not be considered finished works but works in progress. The Society encourages this type of publication to stimulate discussion which may lead to the refinement and precision necessary in a journal article or monograph.

The Society's publication program has generated research among its members. Younger scholars and the veteran are able to prepare papers for discussion. This dispenses with time allotments for the reading of papers and permits significant debate at the Annual Meeting.

The Editor expresses appreciation to Drs. Maurya Horgan and Paul Kobelski for their able preparation of the text of this volume. The Editor also takes this opportunity to thank the chairs of all Annual Meeting program units for their assistance in developing a stimulating program.

Kent Harold Richards, Editor
The Iliff School of Theology

The Gospel of Truth:
Witness to Second-Century
Exegetical Traditions

Jacqueline A. Williams

The College of William and Mary

The Gospel of Truth (hereafter GTr) stands out among extant Christian literature of the mid-second century[1] as striking because of its exegesis of Christian texts rather than Jewish Scriptures. Although this fact has been tacitly acknowledged since the earliest publications dealing with GTr,[2] its implications remain largely unaddressed. Such an unfortunate gap in scholarship may stem in part from a common approach to the study of Gnostic literature in general, i.e., that it is inferior to its non-Gnostic counterparts either theologically or in a literary sense. An approach to the study of ancient Christianity which acknowledges its diversity is not only historically accurate but also allows scholars to incorporate much of the early Christian literature that has been discovered in the last hundred years into their investigations.[3]

A detailed analysis of the way the author of GTr incorporated early Christian texts into his own composition has only recently been undertaken.[4] Such an analysis leads to the observation that the author of GTr used three broad groups of writings: Matthean, Johannine, and Pauline. Moreover, the author has integrated specific texts into his presentation of the gospel[5] in such a fashion as not simply to allude to them but rather to

---

[1]The two manuscripts of GTr which were found at Nag Hammadi can be dated to the early fourth century; these are Coptic translations of a Greek original which is not extant. External (patristic) evidence suggests that GTr is a product of early Valentinianism, particularly since a mythological superstructure may not be present (see Tertullian, *Adv. Val.* 4.2). It is quite likely that Valentinus himself wrote GTr; B. Standaert (" 'L'Evangile de vérité': critique et lecture," *NTS* 22 [1976] 243-75) presents a rhetorical and stylistic comparison of frgs. 1, 2, 5, and 8 from Valentinus with GTr 17:5—18:10 which makes a convincing case for Valentinus's authorship.

[2]W. C. van Unnik did an early study of this in which he listed many possible references and discussed a few; see "The 'Gospel of Truth' and the New Testament," *The Jung Codex*, ed. and trans. F. L. Cross (London: Mowbray, 1955) 79-129.

[3]H. Koester ("Apocryphal and Canonical Gospels," *HTR* 73 [1980] 105-30) addresses this problem by paying specific attention to the contents of non-canonical gospels in relation to canonical gospels. He also points to the prejudices and presuppositions that have haunted his specific area of research (p. 106).

[4]See my dissertation, "The Interpretation of Texts and Traditions in the Gospel of Truth" (Ph.D. diss., Yale, 1983).

[5]The question of whether "gospel" should be understood as referring to genre in the title of GTr was debated in the earlier publications on GTr, but this discussion generally confused the question of genre with the question of the title of Gtr. Certainly GTr does not share the form of the canonical gospels, but its claim to being a "gospel" should not be dismissed thereby since it is still possible to understand "gospel" in its earliest Christian sense ("good news").

interpret them. Three examples, one from each category, will suffice to illustrate this statement.[6]

Matt 18:12-13 is clearly used in GTr 31:35—32:4; this was first recognized by van Unnik.[7] By placing the two passages side by side one can readily see the careful use of Matt by the author of GTr.[8]

GTr 31:35—32:4~Matt 18:12-13

He (the beloved Son) being the shepherd	12 ... ἐὰν γένηταί τινι ἀνθρώπῳ ἑκατὸν πρόβατα καὶ πλανηθῇ ἓν ἐξ αὐτῶν,

who left behind the ninety-
    nine sheep
which had not gone astray,
    came, (and) he searched for
the one which had gone astray.
	οὐχὶ ἀφήσει τὰ ἐνενήκοντα
	ἐννέα (cf. πρόβατα above)
	ἐπὶ τὰ ὄρη
	καὶ πορευθεὶς ζητεῖ
	τὸ πλανώμενον;
	13καὶ ἐάν
	γένηται εὑρεῖν αὐτό . . .

He rejoiced when he found it because the ninety-nine ...	χαίρει ἐπ' αὐτῷ (cf. ἐὰν above) γένηται εὑρεῖν αὐτό μᾶλλον ἢ ἐπὶ τοῖς ἐνενήκοντα ἐννέα τοῖς μὴ πεπλανημένοις.

Subachmimic text

35ⲉⲛⲧⲁϥ ⲡⲉ ⲡϣⲱⲥ 36ⲉⲩⲧⲁⲍ ⲕⲱⲉ ⲛⲟⲩ⳿ ⲙⲡⲓⲡⲥⲧⲉ¹ϥⲓⲥ

ⲛ̄ⲉⲥⲁⲩ ⲉⲧⲉ ⲙ̄ⲛⲟⲩⲥⲱⲣⲙ̄ ²ⲁϥⲉⲓ ⲁϥϣⲓⲛⲉ ⲛ̄ⲥⲁ ⲡⲉⲉⲓ ⲛ̄ⲧⲁϥ ³ⲥⲱⲣⲙ ⲁϥⲣⲁϣⲉ

ⲛ̄ⲧⲁⲣⲉϥ⁴ϭⲓⲛⲉ ⲙ̄ⲙⲁϥ ϫⲉ ⲡⲓⲡⲥⲧⲉⲩⲉⲓⲥ

---

[6]See pp. 263-68 of my dissertation for a complete list of passages used and their relative degree of certainty of use.

[7]Van Unnik, pp. 112-13.

[8]Explanation of the sigla: Solid underlining (_____) indicates verbatim parallels; broken underlining (_ _ _ _ _) indicates nearly verbatim parallels. The tables in this article appear on pp. 173, 30, and 249, respectively, of my dissertation. The translations are my own. The Coptic (Subachmimic dialect) given is from a collation of *Evangelium Veritatis: Codex Jung f. VIIIv-XVIv, XIXr-XXIIr*, ed. and trans. M. Malinine, H. C. Puech, G. Quispel (Zurich: Rascher, 1956), and *Evangelium Veritatis (Supplementum): Codex Jung f. XVIr-XVIIIr* (Zurich and Stuttgart: Rascher, 1961), ed. and trans. M. Malinine, H. C. Puech, G. Quispel, and W. Till, which was done in Cairo under ultraviolet light by S. Emmel. The Sahidic fragment from Codex XII can be found in *The Facsimile Edition of the Nag Hammadi Codices*, Codices XI, XII, XIII (Leiden: Brill, 1973); all attempts to fill in the lacunae have been controversial, including the one here, due to the poor state of the manuscript. A more detailed analysis of these passages can be found on pp. 173-78, 30-33, and 249-51, respectively, of my dissertation.

Sahidic fragment

$$^{25}ⲡⲗⲉⲓ \ ⲡ[ⲉ \ ⲙ̅ⲱ̅ⲭ] \quad ^{26}[ⲉϥⲕⲱ \ ⲉ_2ⲡ]ⲁ̣[ⲓ̈] \ ⲙ̅ⲛⲓϥ̅ⲧⲁⲉ ⲓⲟ̣[ⲩ$$

$$ⲙ̅ⲛ̅ \ ⲯⲓⲥ] \quad ^{27}[ⲛ̅ⲉⲥⲟⲟⲩ] ⲛⲗⲉⲓ \ ⲉⲧⲉ \ ⲙ̅ⲡⲟⲩⲟⲱ[ⲣⲙ̅ \ ⲗ̣ϥ̣] \quad ^{28}[ⲱ]ⲓⲛⲉ \ ⲛ̅ⲥ]ⲁ$$

$$ⲡⲗ̈ⲓ \ ⲛ̅ⲧⲗ̣ϥⲥⲱⲣⲙ̅ \ [\qquad]$$

The authors of both Matt and GTr present a parable about a shepherd who leaves behind ninety-nine sheep in his flock so that he can search for one that has strayed from the others. Finding it is an occasion for rejoicing. That the author of GTr has used Matt is clear from the large number of verbatim or nearly verbatim parallels.[9] The rhetorical structure of this passage in GTr differs from that in Matt due to the author's desire to identify Matt's shepherd with "the beloved Son." The major difference is in the interpretation of the two prables, however. The parable as told by Matt's Jesus emphasizes that the Father wants all believers to be saved, whereas the parable as told in GTr emphasizes the unity and completeness of all those who comprise the Father.

The author of GTr has shifted the reader's focus of attention to an epistemological level. In general, the author has restricted all intellectual activity to that which occurs within the deity,[10] most often called "Father" (much as Matt's Jesus refers to God as "Father"). This restriction enables the author of GTr to ignore material reality and to reinterpret texts so as to reflect this shift in focus. Thereby, the readers of GTr may understand that this parable is to be understood on the epistemological level as referring to all those who are predestined to salvation.[11] All those persons who know their origin and destiny[12] know that they came from and will return to the Father and, thus, that they comprise the deity.

A clever use of allegory has enabled the author to effect this surprising change of focus. The allegory is introduced by a subtle change from "more than" to "because" in the explanation given for the shepherd's rejoicing. Of course, the reader is prepared for the allegory because of the earlier identification of the shepherd with the beloved Son (i.e., Jesus). Thus, an apparently minor substitution of "because" in GTr for "more than" in Matt enables the author of GTr to explain that the shepherd's reason for rejoicing had something to do with a deficiency inherent in the total number minus the one sheep who had strayed (i.e., 100 - 1 = 99).[13] In the finger-reckoning system widely used in antiquity,[14] one counts up to ninety-nine on the left hand (the deficient side), but with the addition of one to ninety-nine the counting shifts to the right hand (the propitious side).[15]

Not all of the details of the allegory are clear, although that an allegorical

---

[9]There is, of course, a parallel passage in Luke 15:3-7, but there is little evidence that the author of GTr has used Luke in his composition. The parable as told by the author of Luke has special Lukan features which are absent in both Matt and GTr, as noted by C. I. K. Story, *The Nature of Truth in "The Gospel of Truth" and in the Writings of Justin Martyr* (Leiden: Brill, 1970) 21.

[10]E.g., GTr 18:31-35.

[11]E.g., GTr 20:3-14, 25:25—26:6, and 36:35-39.

[12]E.g., GTr 22:2-15.

[13]GTr 32:4-6.

[14]See van Unnik, pp. 96-97, 113; K. Grobel, *The Gospel of Truth* (Nashville: Abingdon, 1960) 129, 131, 133, nn. 353-58; and especially H.-I. Marrou, "L'Evangile de vérité et la diffusion du comput digital dans l'antiquité," *VC* 12 (1958) 98-103 for discussion of this system.

[15]GTr 32:4-17.

interpretation is intended is stated in GTr 32:16-17. The sheep, of course, are people whose names have been spoken, i.e., who have been called.[16] These predestined ones are also identified with numbers whose total is one hundred. One suspects that the emphasis is not so much on ninety-nine as one hundred because the author is interested in the unity which is the perfection of all[17] (i.e., all those who know their origin and destiny and can thereby achieve the latter). Ninety-nine is important because it signifies the deficiency of those whose perfection has only been imperfectly realized.[18] The conversion of those persons will bring about the unity which must occur within the Father.

The interpretation of this passage from Matt takes place on two levels, the macro (the general interpretation given to the parable) and the micro (changes made in retelling the parable). On the macro level, extensive use of allegory is made. This in itself is not surprising because Christians in the second century frequently used both allegory and typology, a related method of exegesis,[19] but these methods were used with Jewish Scripture as a way of retaining its validity for Christians. Not until Irenaeus and Clement of Alexandria was allegory used with New Testament material[20] if one does not include Gnostic literature. Indeed, among both Gnostic and non-Gnostic Christian material, GTr is apparently the earliest example of allegorical exegesis of New Testament material.

On the micro level, alteration of rhetorical structure in GTr from that in Matt, mentioned earlier, results in the recasting of a saying (more specifically, a parable) of Jesus by the author of GTr. This level of interpretation has largely been ignored by scholars, who prefer to speak of allusions,[21] but it is especially important because close examination of the use of Matt in this passage shows an interpretive use by the author of GTr. This is, again, a departure from typical Christian practice in the mid-second century. Free sayings of Jesus circulated along with written gospels for much of the second century,[22] and, indeed, only toward the middle of the second century did written gospels

---

[16]As the reference in GTr 32:17 to the spoken form of the numbers suggests.

[17]GTr 18:36-38.

[18]GTr 31:34-36.

[19]R. P. C. Hanson (*Allegory and Event* [Richmond: John Knox, 1959] 7) draws a clear distinction between typology and allegory. Briefly, typological interpretation focuses on the fulfillment of Scripture, whereas allegorical interpretation relates the original text to an object or person at a later time without attempting to draw a logical connection between the two. *The Epistle of Barnabas* is a good example of an early Christian writing which uses both methods of exegesis.

[20]Hanson (pp. 112-13) draws attention to Irenaeus's allegory of the parable of the Good Samaritan in *Adv. Haer.* III.18.2. He includes a thorough discussion of allegory in the writings of Clement of Alexandria (and Hippolytus) on pp. 113-20. More recently, H. von Campenhausen (*The Formation of the Christian Bible* [Philadelphia: Fortress, 1972] 302-5) has discussed allegorical exegesis of New Testament writings in the second century.

[21]Van Unnik (pp. 115-21) gives a list of parallels as does J.-E. Ménard (*L'Evangile de vérité,'* [NHS 2; Leiden: Brill, 1972] 3-8) but neither gives a detailed description of the author's use of texts in these passages. The synopsis format used in this paper allows one to see precisely where changes have been made.

[22]Pioneering work in this area was done by H. Koester (*Synoptische Überlieferung bei den apostolischen Vätern* [TU 65; Berlin: Akademie, 1957]), who demonstrated that sayings collections, rather than one or more of the synoptic gospels, may have been used in the writings of the apostolic fathers. In addition, von Campenhausen (pp. 118-21) summarizes the secondary literature and briefly analyzes the primary evidence for the use of both oral and written traditions of the words of Jesus in the first and second centuries.

begin to be used in Christian writings.[23]

GTr, then, is noteworthy because it shows the literary use of Matt in the mid-second century and also because it does not simply cite Matt but alters it in an interpretive manner. In so doing, the author feels free to recast sayings of Jesus.[24] Moreover, the preceding example is typical of the exegesis of Matt in GTr. Whenever Matt is interpreted in GTr, either a saying or a parable of Jesus is recast so that it fits naturally into the current argument and overall message of GTr.

Identification of those passages from the Johannine literature which are used in GTr is more problematic because the Johannine literature contains thematic material which is continually reworked. Nevertheless, it appears certain that the author of GTr has used John, 1 John, and Rev.[25] The use of John 14:6 in GTr 18:18-21 demonstrates the extent to which Johannine theology has been incorporated and reinterpreted in GTr. Again the relationship between the two passages can be seen most clearly when they are placed side by side.

GTr 18:18-21 ~ John 14:6

(Jesus Christ)	^{6}λέγει αὐτῷ [ὁ] Ἰησοῦς·
he enlightened them;	(cf. ἡ ζωή below)
he	ἐγώ
gave them	εἰμι
a way,	ἡ ὁδὸς
and the way is the truth	καὶ ἡ ἀλήθεια
about which he taught them.	
	καὶ ἡ ζωή.

Subachmimic text

^{18}ⲁϥ ⲟⲩⲁ^{19}ⲉⲓⲛ ⲁⲣⲁⲩ ⲁϥϯ ⲛ̄ⲟⲩⲙⲁⲉⲓⲧ· ⲡⲓ^{20}ⲙⲁⲉⲓⲧ· ⲛ̄ⲁⲉ ⲡⲉ ϯⲙⲛ̄ⲧⲙⲏⲉ

ⲉⲛ^{21}ⲧⲁϥⲧⲁⲙⲁⲩ ⲁⲣⲁⲥ·

The passage in John is an enigmatic "I am" saying, which the Johannine Jesus characteristically uses as a means of self-revelation, whereas GTr describes the salvific activity of Jesus. As with the passage from Matt, the number of verbatim or near-

---

[23]H. Koester ("Apocryphal and Canonical Gospels," pp. 108-10) lays out the evidence especially clearly by using a table format.

[24]This is very common in GTr, both with the Matthean and Johannine writings. Moreover, recasting of material is not uncommon in other literature which is roughly contemporaneous. For example, the Qumran Temple Scroll, recasts quotations of the Pentateuch from the third person singular to the first person singular, as Y. Yadin noted in "The Temple Scroll," *BA* 30 (1967) 136. Moreover, as is well known, Philo in *De Vita Mosis* frequently recasts his narrative source. Indeed, the practice may have been widespread.

[25]There are few scholars today who would maintain that the same person actually wrote these three books, but the question of authorship was not as acute in the second century as in the present one. The authorship of Rev was questioned by Gaius, as Dionysius Bar Salibi (*Comm Apoc.* CI, 1 f.) relates. Von Campenhausen (pp. 237-42) gives a brief description, but the most thorough investigation has been done by J. D. Smith ("Gaius and the Controversy over the Johannine Literature" [Ph.D. diss., Yale, 1979]).

verbatim parallels makes the use of John here in GTr convincing. Again, as with the passage from Matt, words of Jesus have been recast into narrative form; thus, the author of GTr has put John's saying of Jesus into third person singular, indirect discourse. In the process of recasting, however, modifications of terminology have been made which affect the Christology of the passage in GTr. GTr says that Jesus Christ enlightened those who desire knowledge of the Father.[26] While attaining knowledge of the Father is part of the context of this passage in John also,[27] the chief difference between the two passages hinges on whether Jesus *is the* way to the Father (John) or whether Jesus *gives a* way to the Father (GTr). It may have been the case that the self-predication of the Johannine Jesus was considered to be ambiguous by later Christians, including the readers of GTr; if this is so, then the author of GTr has simply resolved the ambiguity.

The use of "way" in both John and GTr is clearly metaphorical. The term had been used figuratively at least as far back as Xenophon, who used the already familiar metaphor of the two ways (paths, i.e., virtue and vice) open to Heracles at the crossroads.[28] In early Christian literature, the term continued to be used metaphorically, sometimes qualified by the term "life."[29] In both John and GTr, however, "way" refers not simply to a path that one may choose to take in life but rather to the choice of life itself. In John, Jesus is the way to life,[30] whereas according to GTr, Jesus has enlightened those who have knowledge of the Father. Although the two passages do not look very similar on the surface, the author of GTr has implicitly identified light with life on the basis of the prologue to John's gospel (cf. John 1:4, "the life was the light").[31]

The interpretation of John 14:6 continues with an explication of "way." In fact, "way" and "truth" are identified. Again, this may resolve an ambiguity in John, which takes "way" and "truth" as parallel self-predications of Jesus. In GTr, the way is said to be the truth about which Jesus taught. "Truth," of course, occurs frequently in both John and GTr.[32] Moreover, in both John and GTr, truth is closely associated with knowledge.[33] For the author of GTr, however, "truth" is part of an exegetical presupposition, i.e., that God is the Father of truth[34] and that Jesus Christ brings that truth, which is knowledge of the Father. Thus, "truth," which is descriptive of Jesus and parallel to "way" in John, is part of the functional role performed by Jesus in GTr, that is, his teaching.[35] Jesus is understood to be the dispenser of truth, which is knowledge of the Father.

From this example of the interpretation of John 14:6 in GTr, it is clear that the general method of incorporating texts in GTr from John is much the same as the way Matthean texts were incorporated. The situation is complicated by John's own recasting of words of Jesus in the composition of his gospel.[36] Moreover, both John and GTr lend

---

[26]GTr 18:16-18.

[27]John 14:7.

[28] *Memorabilia* 2,1,21 ff.; Xenophon credits Prodicus the Sophist with this metaphor.

[29]E.g., *Didache* 1:2; *Barnabas* 19:1. Examination of the syntax in these passages does not warrant a suggestion that they too are dependent on John.

[30]Literally, of course, "and the life."

[31]See also GTr 32:21, where "give life" is interpreted allegorically as "impart knowledge" and 32:31-37, where "enlighten" means "impart knowledge." Thus, one may infer that GTr is internally consistent in identifying "light" with "life."

[32]E.g., John 1:14, 17; 17:17 and GTr 16:31, 33; 17:17-18; 26:28.

[33]See n. 27 above.

[34]GTr 16:33.

[35]GTr 16:33.

[36]R. Bultmann called attention to this issue in *The Gospel of John* (Philadelphia: Westminster, 1971, pp. 3-5), where he noted that, in contrast to the synoptic gospels, the narrative and sayings material cannot easily be separated from the editorial framework

themselves to motif-oriented study,[37] and comparison of these motifs, such as "truth" above, yields insight into the theological presuppositions and views of both authors. Yet, what stands out most clearly is that the author of GTr used exegetical presuppositions which can be (and may have been) derived from John to further explicate texts from John itself.

Interpretations of the Pauline literature are somewhat more difficult to evaluate than those of John. The method of incorporating the Pauline texts into GTr, however, is the same as for Matt and John. In this respect the interpretation of Rom 3:23 in GTr 42:3-4 is a typical example. Again, a side-by-side comparison clearly shows the use of Rom in GTr.

GTr 42:3-4 ~ Rom 3:23

. . . nor have they (the parts)	[23] πάντες γὰρ ἥμαρτον καὶ
fallen short	ὑστεροῦνται
of the glory of the Father	τῆς δόξης τοῦ θεοῦ

Subachmimic text

[3] ΟΥΤΕ ΜΠΟΥϢϢΤ· ΜΠΒΑΥ [4]ΜΠΙϢΤ·

These lines in GTr are virtually a paraphrase of the Pauline passage, although the resulting interpretation is quite different from the intended message of Rom. Four changes have been made. First, the subject has been changed from "all" to "parts."[38] Second, "God" has been changed to "Father"; this is a typical interpretive alteration.[39] Third, "nor" has been added. This addition transforms the meaning of the Pauline passage from an assertion that all humanity has fallen short of God's glory to a statement that those who comprise the Father have *not* fallen short of his glory. Fourth, Paul's reference to sin has been omitted. Although this is not the only time the author of GTr has omitted

---

in John. This, of course, makes the question of the relationship of John to the synoptic tradition virtually impossible to answer. R. E. Brown (*The Gospel According to John (i-xii)* [AB 29; Garden City, NY: Doubleday, 1966]) discusses the question of John's dependency on the synoptics on pp. xliv-xlvii and gives a pertinent bibliography on p. li. A more recent article by D. M. Smith ("John and the Synoptics: Some Dimensions of the Problem," *NTS* 26 [1979-80] 425-44) contains an extensive review of the literature and concludes that there was probably no extensive contact either in the narrative or sayings tradition, although the complexity of the issue makes an easy solution impossible.

[37]The classic study of C. K. Barrett ("The Theological Vocabulary of the Fourth Gospel and of the Gospel of Truth," in *Current Issues in New Testament Interpretation: Essays in Honor of Otto A. Piper* [ed. W. Klassen and G. F. Snyder; New York: Harper & Row] 210-23, 297-98) exemplifies this approach. Barrett's study concentrates on comparing the respective worlds of ideas and themes of John and GTr. By not adopting an approach which allows one to demonstrate the literal use of John in GTr, however, the danger of losing sight of the reason for comparing the two in the first place exists.

[38]The "parts" comprise the Father; thus, the "parts" are the Gnostics, who, in an epistemological sense, *are* the Father.

[39]E.g., GTr 18:15 (Col 1:25) and 34:3 (2 Cor 2:14).

a reference to sin in his exegesis,[40] Paul's reference to sin has probably been omitted in GTr due to the context, which refers to the Father's parts, who of course could not be sinful. Because sin is connected with forgiveness in GTr 35:25-29, it is unlikely that GTr is unconcerned with ethics.

This example of the exegesis of Pauline material leaves little doubt that Paul's writings have been used in GTr, but the fact that the meaning of this passage has been changed so drastically raises a question about how to evaluate the use of Pauline material in GTr. Was Paul "the" apostle for the author? Although the issue of Paul's authority in the second century has been prominent in recent years,[41] a study of the interpretation of Pauline writings in GTr adds little that directly contributes to that discussion. Nevertheless, it is clear simply from examining the means of incorporating Pauline writings into GTr that the author does put the Pauline writings on a par with those of Matt and John. This contrasts sharply with Justin Martyr's reluctance to use Paul's writings, even though he knows them.[42]

From the three examples discussed above, both exegetical changes that occur throughout GTr and exegetical methods used in GTr can begin to be explored. Exegetical changes that have been noted include the change from God to Father[43] and the shift from an ethical to an intellectual plane.[44] Other changes which occur in GTr have also been mentioned in discussing the three examples; these include an increased focus on predestination and a redefinition of salvation in terms of one's origin and destiny (i.e., both are within the Father).

Such changes are characteristic of the author's technique, but they also give clues to the presuppositions underlying GTr. These presuppositions include an all-encompassing Father who is removed from human activity on earth, no unlike the God or Nous of Middle Platonism.[45] Moreover, salvation, which was brought by Jesus the illuminator to those who were predestined, is to be apprehended on an epistemological level. In this way, all those who are saved (through knowledge of their origin and destiny brought by Jesus through his crucifixion)[46] can participate in the Father, much as the Ideas in Middle Platonic thought may be contained in the mind of God.[47] Since intellectual

---

[40]See also the interpretation of Rom 8:3 in GTr 31:4-6.

[41]A thorough study has recently been done by A. Lindemann (*Paulus im ältesten Christentum: Das Bild des Apostels und die Rezeption der paulinischen Theologie in der frühchristlichen Literatur bis Marcion* [BHT 58; Tübingen: Mohr-Siebeck, 1979]). D. Rensberger, in his review of Lindemann (*JBL* 101 [1982] 287-89), however, draws attention to factors which should be given more weight than Lindemann does, particularly chronology. The general conclusion, however, is clear, namely, that the Pauline letters were used throughout the second century, not only by Marcion and Gnostics but also by those segments of ancient Christianity later recognized as mainstream. The Pauline letters, in fact, appear never to have been the main source of ancient Christian theology, but they were an important part of ancient Christian tradition.

[42]T. Stylianopoulos (*Justin Martyr and the Mosaic Law* [SBLDS 20; Missoula: Scholars Press, 1975]) argues, convincingly, that Justin's anti-Marcionite feelings limit his use of Paul.

[43]Exegesis of Rom 3:23.

[44]Again, exegesis of Rom 3:23.

[45]This is also very similar to John, for whom the Father is so removed from "the world" that only his Son, Jesus, can bring light to the darkness of this world. As is also the case in GTr, the Johannine Father and Son are so closely connected that Jesus says in John 10:30, "I and the Father are one" (cf. GTr 39:19-20).

[46]See GTr 18:24-27 (Gen 2:17; 3:7) and GTr 20:23-27 (Col 2:14).

[47]J. Dillon (*The Middle Platonists* [London: Duckworth, 1977] 29) says that the

reality has been restricted to events that occur within the Father, GTr shows little interest in ethics;[48] one should not infer from this that GTr denies material reality but rather that material reality is unimportant when compared to epistemological reality.[49]

Just how the author's presuppositions were formed is an exceedingly difficult problem which has invited speculation.[50] While it may not be possible to delineate comprehensively what is behind the general outlook of GTr, the example of the exegesis of John 14:6 discussed above may give a clue. This passage[51] contains three Johannine themes, way, truth, and light (the last in verb form, enlighten). Moreover, the most likely explanation for the presence of "light" instead of "life," as in John 14:6, is that the Johannine identification of life with light (John 1:4) is presupposed here in GTr. It is just possible, then, that some of the author's presuppositions may come from a close reading of the early Christian writings, particularly John, that he used in his own composition.

The preceding examples have raised the question of exegetical methods in a particularly acute manner. Of course, one exegetical method used in GTr is allegory.[52] The example of exegesis of Matt 18:12-13, discussed above, contains allegorical interpretation (shepherd = beloved Son; sheep = people = numbers) and undoubtedly introduces further allegories in the long interpretation of the Matthean parable as incorporated into GTr. The initial allegorical interpretation does not seem particularly arbitrary, although as the interpretation progresses, the allegory seems less obvious. The reader of GTr is prepared for the use of allegory because much of GTr must be understood figuratively in that the readers must realize that all activity takes place on an epistemological level. Indeed, the most striking fact about this particular allegory is that it uses Matt 18:12-13.

A more intriguing aspect of the author's exegetical methods centers on the manner in which texts are incorporated into GTr. To say that GTr merely alludes to texts is misleading. Rather, as the texts are incorporated into GTr, they are changed and interpreted. This general method is familiar in early Christian literature, for example, in Rev. There, however, a similar method of incorporating references to Jewish Scripture has been adopted.[53] GTr may be the earliest treatise extant in which Christian texts are

---

notion can be traced to Xenocrates (frg. 15). G. C. Stead ("The Valentinian Myth of Sophia," *JTS* n.s. 20 [1969] 90-98) has suggested that Valentinus's presuppositions may be reconstructed by paying careful attention to some of Philo's presuppositions, particularly the contrast between the ideal and material worlds and the necessity for an intermediary between God and this world. This emphasizes the connection of GTr to the Middle Platonic thought-world.

[48]There is a paraenetic section in GTr 32:35ff., which does appear to exhort the readers to ethical behavior, although it is probable that much of the passage should be understood allegorically as an exhortation to convert non-Gnostics (see especially GTr 33:7, those who sleep = the ignorant).

[49]A similar explanation may be offered for the shift in emphasis away from the eschatological, which also occurs in GTr (e.g., GTr 20:28-32, 21:10-14, 25:15-19).

[50]Most speculation itself has arisen out of presuppositions about what Gnosticism is. Ménard (pp. 17-37), for example, works with a broad view of Gnosticism as those religious traditions which are concerned with self-knowledge in relation to God. Ménard and others presume that GTr belongs to this broad type of Gnosticism before they discuss it. The suggestion presented here is that GTr is Gnostic, but one must understand what this means by focusing on GTr's own depiction of Gnosticism.

[51]GTr 18:18-21.

[52]GTr is also firmly in line with contemporaneous early Christian tradition by including a typological exegesis of Gen 2:17; 3:7 in GTr 18:24-27 (cf. *Diognetus* 12 for a similar exegesis).

[53]This is much like the well-known practice of Paul when he quotes Scripture. For

used in this manner. One is hard pressed to label this method of interpretation, but perhaps it comes very close to midrash. In fact, one insightful probe into the nature of midrash has yielded four characteristics of midrash: that it begins with Scripture, is homiletical, pays close attention to the text, and adapts the text to the present.[54] Each of these characteristics is present in GTr, and hence one might reasonably refer to the general method of incorporating texts as midrashic. The first of these characteristics should be emphasized, namely, that midrash begins with Scripture. It is certainly likely that the author of GTr considers the texts that he uses to be Scripture.

In conclusion, the present study suggests that GTr should be viewed as a remarkable witness to Christian exegesis of the mid-second century. The author uses Matthean, Johannine, and Pauline writings as Scripture.[55] This is a departure from the usual practice of contemporaneous Christians for whom Jewish Scripture was still retained, sometimes through creative exegesis, as the sole Christian Scripture. There is, of course, no way to be certain that GTr was the first writing to interpret Christian Scripture to this extent.[56] Nevertheless, the present study of this homiletical,[57] midrashic treatise known as GTr calls for more careful studies which will both identify this type of interpretive writing in other early Christian literature and then determine its place in the history of early Christian exegesis.

---

example, in Gal 3:10, he cites Deut 27:26, which, oddly enough, makes the opposite point from the one Paul makes. Paul's exegetical technique, however, turns the citation to his own advantage. W. Meeks gives a concise discussion of the problem of Gal 3:10 in *The Writings of Saint Paul* (New York: Norton, 1972) 16-17 n. 5. Paul may be using a midrashic technique in which two contradictory passages are cited which must be resolved by a third. On this, see N. Dahl, "Contradictions in Scripture," in *Studies in Paul* (Minneapolis: Augsburg, 1977) 159-77.

[54] R. Bloch, "Midrash," in *Approaches to Ancient Judaism,* ed. W. S. Green (Brown Judaic Studies 1; Missoula: Scholars Press, 1978) 31-33.

[55] Scripture and canon are not the same thing. The process of canonization was a lengthy one which involved many factors. "Scripture" denotes authoritative status which in every case was attained earlier than canonization.

[56] Of course, GTr was not the first Christian writing to use other Christian writings (see the synoptic gospels!). Nevertheless, its sophisticated exegesis is striking.

[57] Justin, 1 *Ap.* 67 says that the "memoirs of the apostles" were read at worship services and then expounded by the "president" of the congregation. Perhaps this refers to the use of homilies based on Christian writings in worship services. A. J. Bellinzoni, (*The Sayings of Jesus in the Writings of Justin Martyr* [Leiden: Brill, 1967]) has proposed that Justin's sources for his sayings of Jesus (the "memoirs of the apostles") were *written* and included the synoptic gospels as well as harmonizations based on them for catechetical purposes.

Ramism as an Exegetical Tool for English Puritanism as Used by William Perkins

Donald K. McKim

University of Dubuque Theological Seminary

The influence of the French philosopher-logician Pierre de la Ramée (Peter Ramus; 1515-1572) extended in many directions throughout the sixteenth and seventeenth centuries.[1] As a University Professor in Paris, Ramus and his associate Amdomarus Talaeus (Omer Talon; ca. 1510-1562) wrote prolifically.[2] Their major thrusts were toward educational reforms centering on the reorganization of dialectic and rhetoric. Ramus is chiefly known for his "Ramist logic" which in the tradition of Renaissance humanism sought a simplified logic to replace that of the reigning scholastic logic built on the works of Aristotle. To carry out his goal of subjecting all the liberal arts to the rules of logic, Ramus needed a logic that could be taught quickly and grasped easily by young students. His resulting system was applied by his followers throughout the catalogue of the liberal arts. Ramus's conversion to Protestantism gave special impetus to applying his system to theology. In particular, his system was useful for many English Puritans who found it ideally suited as a method for carrying out their theological aims.[3]

One way that Ramism benefited Puritans was as a framework through which biblical exegesis could be done. Ramist Puritans such as Laurence Chaderton (1536?-1640), William Perkins (1558-1602), George Downame (1565?-1634), Paul Baynes (d. 1617), Arthur Hildersham (1563-1632) and William Ames (1576-1633) used the Ramist philosophy and logic not only for presenting their systematic theological writings but also as a method of approaching and exegeting Holy Scripture. As such, Ramism proved a powerful exegetical tool. It provided a theoretical background and sanction for Puritan practices in exegeting Scripture as well as helping to shape those practices through the insights it provided for how a text (or a subject) should be "logically analyzed," "resolved," or "unfolded" (frequent Ramist terms).

To understand better how Ramism was appropriated as an exegetical method by English Puritans, it is important to look at the backgrounds of Ramism. Then one highly

---

[1] The major treatment of Ramus is Walter J. Ong, *Ramus, Method, and the Decay of Dialogue* (1958; rpt. New York: Octagon Books, 1974); hereafter cited as *Ramus*.

[2] Ong, *Ramus,* p. 5. Cf. Walter J. Ong, *Ramus and Talon Inventory* (Cambridge, MA: Harvard University Press, 1958) for a catalogue of these editions.

[3] The connection of Ramus with the Puritans was pointed out and elaborated upon by Perry Miller in *The New England Mind: The Seventeenth Century* (1939; rpt. Boston: Beacon Press, 1954); hereafter cited as *NEM*. Cf. Donald K. McKim, "The Functions of Ramism in William Perkins's Theology," *The Sixteenth Century Journal,* forthcoming; and Donald K. McKim "Ramism in William Perkins," (diss., University of Pittsburgh, 1980; University Microfilms ù8112622); hereafter cited as "Ramism."

influential English Puritan, William Perkins, who advocated the Ramist principles and practiced them in his approach to exegesis will be examined. From this, certain conclusions about how Ramism functioned as an exegetical tool for English Puritanism can be drawn.

L. BACKGROUNDS OF RAMISM

Ramus stood in the stream of the Renaissance humanist logical reforms of Lorenzo Valla (1407-1457) and Rudolph Agricola (1444-1485).[4] He sought relief from the vast complexities of the scholastic logic as taught in the *Summulae Logicales* of Peter of Spain (1210/1220-1277; Pope at his death as John XXI).[5] To simplify logic the humanists and Ramus taught that the major divisions of dialectic were "invention" (*inventio*) and "judgment" (*judicium*). These served to "discover" and "dispose" arguments. They did so by drawing on the "topical" or "commonplaces" tradition developed by the ancient rhetoricians. Rhetoric itself was to serve as only a means for ornamentation and delivery of what logic had produced. Thus logic was not to be separated into a logic of science and a logic of opinion. For Ramus there should be only one logic for both. "Method" was the key for organizing all that logic discovered. Thus the logician and rhetorician were equipped to give full expression to human thought.

According to Ramus, with the art of dialectic divided into invention and judgment, invention had the function of arranging individual concepts or arguments by which discourses were constructed and judgment served to join these arguments. Judgment proceeded by three steps. The first of these was related to the syllogism, the second was concerned with the linking together of arguments (out of which Ramist "method" came) and the third judgment was related to religion.[6]

Ramist Method

Ramus' development of "method" from his second step in the judgment process became his most important and influential contribution to communication theory and to the application of his logic to written texts.[7]

For Ramus the joining together of arguments to form an intelligible discourse occurred principally by definition and division. To him, a sentence was considered to have emerged from the sentence before it, either by defining something which was there or by dividing something there. He wrote that "the principles of the arts are definitions and divisions; outside of these, nothing."[8] While syllogisms were helpful, they did not function

---

[4]See Lisa Jardine, "Lorenzo Valla and the Intellectual Origins of Humanist Dialectic," *Journal of the History of Philosophy* 15 (1977) 143-64; and Wilbur Samuel Howell, *Logic and Rhetoric in England 1500-1700* (1956; rpt. New York: Russell & Russell, 1961) as well as Ong, *Ramus*, chap. 5.

[5]See Joseph P. Mullally, ed. and trans., *The 'Summulae Logicales' of Peter of Spain* (Notre Dame, IN: n.p., 1945) and Ong, *Ramus*, chap. 4.

[6]A full discussion of the Ramist philosophy is given in Ong, *Ramus*, Book III, and McKim, "Ramism," chap. II.

[7]See Howell, p. 160.

[8]Ramus, *Aristotelicae animadversiones* (Paris, 1543; rpt. Stuttgart-Bad Cannstatt: Friedrich Frommann Verlag, 1964) fol. 58. See Ong, *Ramus*, p. 188.

as they did in scholastic logic, namely, to clinch the truth.[9] Instead the syllogism for Ramus was to solve doubts when questions arose in matters of definition and division. The syllogism was not so much an argument in itself as a way of arranging an argument.

"Method" for Ramus meant basically the proper arrangement of propositions or axioms. True method was to move from "universals" to "singulars," from the general to the specific.[10] This procedure of organization moved forward by definitions and divisions. By applying this method, any discourse could be either constructed or analyzed. The prime illustration of method for Ramus was the arts. He wrote:

> The chief examples of method are in the arts. Here, although all the rules are general and universal, nevertheless there are grades among them, insofar as the more general a rule is, the more it precedes. Those things which are most general in position and first in order which are first in luminosity and knowledge; the subalterns follow, because they are next clearest; and thus those things are put down first which are by nature better known (*natura notiora*), the less known are put below, and finally the most special are set up. Thus the most general definition will be first, distribution next, and, if this latter is manifold, division into integral parts comes first, then division into species. The parts and species are then treated respectively in this same order in which they are divided. If this means that a long explanation intervenes, then when taking up the next part or species, the whole structure is to be knit back together by means of some transition. This will refresh the auditors and amuse them. However, in order to present things more informally, some familiar example should be used.[11]

Thus Ramus moved from a reliance on the syllogism which was the hallmark of scholastic logic to a dependence on the right ordering of self-evidencing axioms or propositions which were the components of discourse.[12] The ultimate goal of all dialectic for Ramus was discourse. The task of combining propositions (whether self-evidencing axioms or the conclusions derived from syllogisms) was given to method. The proper method of discourse was also for Ramus the best method of teaching. He wrote: "Method is the intelligible order (*dianoia*) of various homogeneous axioms ranged one before the other

---

[9]See Ernest A. Moody, *Truth and Consequence in Medieval Logic* (Amsterdam: North-Holland Publishing Company, 1953); and J. Maritain, *Formal Logic*, trans. Imelda Choquette (New York: Sheed & Ward, 1946).

[10]See Ramus, *Dialectici commentarii tres authore Audomaro Talaeo editi* (Lutetiae, 1546), p. 83, cited in Ong, *Ramus*, p. 245.

[11]Ramus, *Dialectica* (Basle, 1569), Bk. II, cap. xvii. pp. 542-43 as given in Ong, *Ramus*, p. 249.

[12]Miller wrote that for Ramus, "the stuff of judgment is not the syllogism but the axiom; the aim of an orator or preacher is a succession of sentences, not a display of deductions. When he has laid out the arguments and combined them into several axioms, he then ought to perceive from the axioms themselves what are their interconnections and what is their order; he should use the syllogism only when in doubt about formulating a particular proposition, or when incapable of recognizing the order of precedence among several statements" (*NEM*, p. 134). Alexander Richardson, a follower of Ramus wrote that "syllogisms serve but for the clearing of the truth of axioms," (*The Logicians School-Master: or, A Comment upon Ramus Logick* [London, 1657] 335).

according to the clarity of their nature, whereby the agreement of all with one another is judged and the whole committed to memory."[13]

The procedure by which method moved, namely, by definition and division, makes it possible to lay out a Ramist treatise in the form of a bracketed chart. A Ramist "analysis" which was an "unweaving" or disentangling of the various strands or threads of argument that ran throughout a discourse reduced discourse to its simplest components. To Ramus this reduction showed the true meaning of the discourse. Divisions or linaments on which the discourse was built were what stood and these could easily be diagrammed and their form exposed. The result was a bracketed outline which spread in a geometrical pattern of bifurcation since most often Ramus found that divisions of an axiom could be made into dichotomies. The chart shows how one division could be subdivided, divided again and thoroughly "analyzed" down to its smallest unit or most particular member. The chart spread horizontally across a page as opposed to the vertical or downward-like thrust of the syllogism in scholastic logic. The task of the logician for Ramus was classification. The job was to arrange everything under proper headings or rubrics and thus ultimately to lay bare the basic propositions or self-evident axioms of which true discourse was composed.[14]

It was this "logical analysis" that was the trademark of the Ramist handling of a text. A text was reduced to its simplest divisions. Then the process could be reversed. By "genesis" the parts could be reassembled to produce the discourse. The spatial diagrams or charts that Ramist method produces became the most obvious sign that a writer was a Ramist. If a discourse could be outlined in the bracketed fashion, it was certain that the Ramist method of composition had been employed. Indeed, the term "logical analysis" in the sixteenth and early seventeenth centuries was a term "so unmistakably partisan that no one but a professing Ramist or one intellectually descended from a professing Ramist would use it."[15]

II. WILLIAM PERKINS' USE OF RAMISM FOR BIBLICAL INTERPRETATION

William Perkins, Fellow of Christ's College, Cambridge, and preacher at the Great St. Andrews Church from 1584 until his death in 1602 was one of the most respected and influential Puritan leaders during the reign of Queen Elizabeth I. His *Works* were widely read and in the three volume edition published between 1616-1618 total 2,736 pages.[16] Many of these pieces had their origins in sermons. Collectively they include polemical,

---

[13]Ramus, *Dialecticae libri duo* (Lutetiae, 1574; same text as 1572), Bk. II, cap. xvii., pp. 72-73 as translated in Ong, *Ramus,* p. 251. Cf. Ong's chap. 11, "The Method of Method."

[14]Ong reproduces some charts from Ramus's works in *Ramus,* pp. 181, 200-202 as does Miller, *NEM,* p. 126. McKim ("Ramism," pp. 443-502) produces over 50 Ramist charts from Ramus or his followers.

[15]Walter J. Ong, "Johannes Piscator: One Man or a Ramist Dichotomy?" *Harvard Library Bulletin* 8 (1954) 153.

[16]All citations from Perkins are from this edition: *The Workes of that Famovs and Worthy Minister of Christ in the Vniuersitie of Cambridge, Mr. William Perkins,* 3 vols. (Cambridge: John Legatt, 1616-1618); hereafter cited as *Workes* or by volume and page number.

theological, and exegetical works as well as "cases of conscience" which were Christian ethical teachings centered on specific pastoral issues.

Perkins imbibed his Ramism at Cambridge University, most probably from his tutor Laurence Chaderton, one of the important leaders of the Elizabethan Puritan movement.[17] Recent study has shown that Ramism was pervasive in nearly everything Perkins wrote and in every category of his writings. This is so much the case that nearly all his works can be diagrammed as Ramist charts.[18] Perkins thus is a most appropriate person to examine for discerning the use and importance of Ramism as an exegetical tool for English Puritans.

Ramist Biblical Exegesis

Perkins' biblical commentaries followed the Ramist pattern or method. Earlier commentators had most often exegeted texts in a straightforward fashion proceeding verse by verse.[19] Occasionally these commentators digressed into some discussion of doctrine.[20] Some Continental commentators such as Johannes Piscator (1546-1625) had begun to employ "logical analysis" in the tradition of Ramus to the books of the Bible.[21] Others such as Francis Junius (1545-1602) and Lambert Daneau (1530-1595) did the same.[22] In addition they frequently used their knowledge of rhetoric when they commented on Scripture. Often they very carefully analyzed various figures of speech in what can be called "rhetorical exegesis."[23] This approach was complemented by their

---

[17]On Chaderton see Patrick Collinson, *The Elizabethan Puritan Movement* (1967; rpt. London: Jonathan Cape, 1971); and Peter Lake, *Moderate Puritans and the Elizabethan Church* (Cambridge: University Press, 1982). On Chaderton's Ramism see McKim, "Ramism," pp. 118-21. A sermon attributed to Chaderton on Romans 12:3-8 has a Ramist chart at its beginning. It is reproduced in McKim, "Ramism," Figure 5.

[18]See McKim, "Ramism."

[19]Luther's and Calvin's commentaries were set up in this way as were Nicholas Ridley's. See Ian Breward, "The Life and Theology of William Perkins" (diss., University of Manchester, 1963) 70.

[20]Breward points to Peter Martyr's *Commentaries,* particularly pp. 41a-44b where Martyr discussed the Mass. Breward writes: "This was the Protestant counterpart of the medieval scholion, and occurs frequently in Luther's commentaries," p. 70.

[21]On Piscator see Ong, "Johannes Piscator" and *Ramus, passim.* Ramist-style charts appear in Piscator's *Analysis logica Epistolarum Pauli* (1591).

[22]Francis Junius (DuJoy) was Professor of Divinity at Leiden. For his "logical analysis" see his *The Apocalyps* (Cambridge, 1596) p. 26 and the Table in the English translation of his *Apocalypsis* entitled *A Briefe and Learned Commentarie Upon the Revelation of Saint John...* (London, 1592). This is reproduced in McKim, "Ramism," Figure 21.

Lambert Daneau was an associate of Theodore Beza in Geneva and became a well-known Calvinist theologian. Some of Daneau's Ramistically styled charts are reproduced in Olivier Fatio, *Méthode et Théologie: Lambert Daneau et les débuts de la scolastique réformée* (Geneva: Droz, 1976). Cf. Daneau's *Twelve Small Prophets,* trans. J. Stockwood (Cambridge, 1594), pp. 228-41 and John Platt, *Reformed Thought and Scholasticism: The Arguments for the Existence of God in Dutch Theology, 1575-1650,* Studies in the History of Christian Thought, ed. Heiko A. Oberman (Leiden: E. J. Brill, 1982) 119-22.

[23]See Daneau, *Twelve Small Prophets,* p. 270.

studies of individual words and terms. This was frequently called "grammatical exegesis."[24]

In England, Dudley Fenner (1558?-1587) published a small Ramist commentary on Philemon.[25] In 1591, Richard Turnbull of Oxford used the Ramist logic to set forth *An Exposition of the Book of James*. This was complete with "the Tables, Analysis, and resolution both of the whole Epistle, and euerie Chapter thereof: with the particular resolution of euerie singular place." Turnbull claimed this was the most ample exposition available and "also more orderly then by any heretofore." He further asserted that he was the first to use the logical method on Scripture "in such a methode, as (to my knowledge) none hath laboured, eyther in this, or other like places of the Holy Scripture."[26] But despite these precedents, none of the English predecessors of William Perkins used the Ramist logical method to the same extent he did for biblical exposition.

Perkins' biblical commentaries show that he approached the scriptural books with the tools of the Ramist philosophy firmly in hand. Some of his biblical expositions have Ramist charts at their beginnings so the whole scriptural book is already "methodized" or "analyzed" or "resolved" according to Ramist method.[27] Others were clearly drawn according to the method.

Perkins wrote clearly of how he justified his approach to Scripture through the use of "the art of Logicke" (which for him was apparently synonymous with "Ramist logic") in his commentary on the first three chapters of the Book of Revelation:

> Hence obserue, the lawfulnesse of the art of Logicke: for diuisions are lawfull, (else the holy Ghost would not here haue vsed them) and so by proportion are other arguments of reasoning: and therefore that art which giueth rules of direction for the right vse of these arguments, is lawfull and good. Those men then are farre deceiued, who account the arts of Logicke and Rhetoricke to be friuolous and vnlawfull, and in so saying, they condemne the practise of the holy Ghost in this place.[28]

Perkins not only believed the exegete needed to use the arts of logic and rhetoric, but also that the Bible itself contained the natural divisions which it was the exegete's job to

---

[24]Breward, p. 70.

[25]Fenner became pastor of the Reformed Church in Middelburg, The Netherlands, after a stormy English pastorate. He translated Ramus and Talon's works into English in 1584 as *The Artes of Logike and Rethorike* and in 1585 published *The Sacred Doctrine of Divinitie Gathered out of the Word of God*, a Ramist systematic theology. See McKim, "Ramism," pp. 128-31. Ramist charts for his *Oeconomie (The Order of Householde...)*, *Epistle to Philemon*, and *The Sacred Doctrine of Divinitie* are found in McKim, "Ramism," Figures 8-10.

[26]See Richard Turnbull, *An Exposition Upon the Canonicall Epistle of Saint James* (London, 1591), "To the Reader." Turnbull's chart is reproduced in McKim, "Ramism," Figure 22.

[27]See the charts at the beginning of Perkins' *Exposition upon the whole Epistle of Jude* (III, 479) and *Commentiarie upon the Three First Chapters of the Revelation* (III, 207).

[28]*Workes*, III, 259. See also II, 650 and III, 95é (from the first 264 pages of Volume III) where Perkins approves the study of logic so that "false collections" of doctrines would be avoided.

uncover using the tools of logic and rhetoric. In this sense Perkins perceived the task of the logician and the scriptural exegete to be exactly as Ramus had said: to discover and dispose of matter.[29] The logician's job was to define, divide, and classify so the thought of the discourse might become clear. To Perkins the task of the biblical exegete was precisely the same.

Perkins' Use of Ramism for Exegesis

William Perkins produced a wide range of exegetical works. He wrote commentaries on complete books such as Galatians and Jude, parts of books such as the first three chapters of Revelation and Hebrews 11 as well as expositions of individual texts of Scripture. Often these textual treatments served as springboards for Perkins to launch into a further treatment of a particular theological issue such as witchcraft (Exod 22:18), idolatry (1 John 5:21) or Christian equity (Phil 4:5).[30]

A full survey of Perkins' use of Ramism in his biblical exegesis cannot be undertaken here. But several examples are instructive and indicate how Perkins worked with Scripture as one committed to the Ramist method and how that method functioned for him as a biblical exegete, theologian, and preacher.

The Ramist charts connected with Perkins' expositions are the clearest sign of his Ramism. Perkins' general Ramist procedure can be seen in its basic form in his exposition of Philippians 3:7 *The Trve Gaine: More in Woorth Then All the Goods in the World* (*Workes* I, 647-658). This exposition was prefaced with a Ramist chart which showed Perkins' basic procedure with the text.[31]

Perkins divided his text into two main parts. They were named "protasis" or "proposition" and "apodosis" or "assumption" though the terms were used only in the chart of the work. He then expounded these points according to the chart showing the Ramist order. For example, in his early discussion of the "meaning" that Paul counted as "dung"—the privileges, virtues, and works done before his conversion—Perkins expanded on five things that "may bee learned" from this. In his discussion of the "fellowship with Christ in vertue of his death," he divided the theme into the sufferings of Christ in his person and those of his members *and* fellowship either with us *or* without us. With Christ's "resurrection," Perkins listed eight effects of the doctrine.[32] Yet Perkins always returned to his main points and moved to his next division by noting what point he had just been expounding and what head he was beginning to discuss next. Thus the movement through the chart can be clearly and accurately followed. When Perkins finished discussing the main heads in order, he posed three final questions with various divisions of them. His movement here was from the most general to the most particular: "What shall cease in this estate? What we shall haue? What we shall doe?"[33]

---

[29]See above, note 8.

[30]See Perkins' works: *An Exposition vpon the fiue first chapters of the Epistle to the Galatians* (II, 153-343); *An Exposition of the three first Chapters of the Reulation of S. Iohn* (III, 207-370); *A Commentarie upon the 11. Chap. to the Hebrewes, containing the Cloud of faithfull Witnesses* (III, 1-206); *A Discourse of the Damned Art of Witchcraft, grounded on Exod. 22.18* (III, 607-652); *A Warning Against the Idolatry of the Last Times* (I, 669-716); *Epieikeia, or A Treatise of Christian Eqvity and Moderation* (II, 434-452).

[31]See the chart in Figure A.

[32]See I, 665, 664.

[33]I, 667.

In terms of form, the Ramist charts of Perkins' biblical expositions are composed of headings or terms that signify the subject of a division of the text. These divisions and heads were not arbitrarily chosen. Perkins' main divisions and the different sections of the chart would be set off by paragraphs in his works themselves. When Perkins partitioned a subject according to Ramist method, he named his divisions and the parts of them in such a way that each point most always had a paragraph devoted to it. Perkins began with a topic sentence which served in a chart to name or define a division. The heading of a division when it was not a single word could most always be captured in a short phrase which came right from the text of Perkins itself.

While a scholastic logician or exegete could adopt a similar style, there are significant differences between scholasticism and Ramism here. The scholastic moves toward a conclusion by deriving points from a proposition and from the point derived immediately prior to it. The Ramist would not do this. Each of the points Perkins listed for either a "doctrine" or a "use" would be points he apparently perceived to spring directly and immediately from his major proposition itself. He did not deduce them through a number of intervening propositions. He did not constantly use syllogisms to prove the truth of one point before moving on to the next. He did not construct a logical platform from which to display a final conclusion. Perkins did not so much seek to *prove* his points as simply to "unfold" them or draw them out directly from his text.

The use of Ramist method for exegesis here by Perkins fit precisely with Perkins' own theological understanding of the nature of Holy Scripture. For Perkins, the Bible was God's written Word inspired by the Holy Spirit.[34] In a sense the mind of God stood behind the writings of the Scriptures both as they were originally written and as they were exegeted and preached in the present time. The work of the Holy Spirit was operative in both inspiration and illumination of readers and hearers. The presupposition of Ramus was that by proper method a discourse may be analyzed, its component parts made clear and the whole "interior logic" of an art or a discourse will thus become plain for all to see. The Ramist chart epitomizes this. The way all parts of a discourse or art are arranged, put together and inter-related becomes apparent at a glance.

Ramism as an exegetical tool for the Puritans and for Perkins provided exactly what theologians, exegetes and preachers needed to interpret or "unlock" the Scriptures. It gave a method of approach which promised to lay bare the very mind of God which stood behind the texts of Scripture themselves. Perkins and other Ramist Puritans believed that as they applied Ramist method to biblical texts and the texts were "analyzed," their various components became clear and they could thus perceive how the Holy Spirit had framed the texts of Scripture. The texts of Scripture were to be exegeted and the results to be properly arranged according to Ramist principles moving from the general to the specific. The job of the Puritan scriptural exegete and the Ramist logician were the same: to discover and dispose of matter; to define, divide, and classify.

---

[34]Perkins wrote: "The Scripture is the word of God written in a language fit for the Church by men immediately called to be the *Clerkes*, or *Secretaries* of the holy Ghost," II, 647. On the nature of Scripture among the Puritans, particularly in the Westminster Confession of Faith see Jack B. Rogers and Donald K. McKim, *The Authority and Interpretation of the Bible: An Historical Approach* (San Francisco: Harper & Row, 1979) 200-223.

Yet when coupled with this theological concern to unlock the mind of the Holy Spirit, it is apparent how powerful a weapon the Ramist method was in the Puritan arsenal. When applied to biblical interpretaion, the Ramist system was classificatory logic but even more. For it was an attempt to perceive the logical plan in the mind of God that expressed itself through the flow of the Scriptural material. If this plan was uncovered it could therefore in addition reveal the true hermeneutics for Scriptural interpretation. The exact meaning of a text would be ascertained with certainty if the procedure used was able to uncover the mind of God behind the text. All other methods of interpreting that text would thus be false.

At times Perkins mentioned rules for proper hermeneutics. His *The Arte of Prophecying or, A Treatise Concerning the Sacred and Onely Trve Manner and Methode of Preaching* gave examples of good hermeneutical practice for certain scriptural difficulties.[35] But at the most basic level, William Perkins apparently did not doubt he was able to peer into the Holy Spirit's mind because he was "properly dividing" the scriptural texts that the Spirit caused to be written. Perkins gave a proper place to the use of logic and to human reasoning rightly applied.[36] But the goal of it all was to see clearly how the Spirit had constructed this pericope of Scripture. By laying out his "analysis" in biblical exposition according to Ramist method, Perkins was making plain how the specific parts of Scripture—parts of verses, verses, or chapters, were related to a broader whole. By giving each of these small pieces a heading or "key-word," Perkins could diagram the Scripture section or book. Thereby he laid out clearly for all to see what the Holy Spirit actually had in mind as the Spirit inspired Scripture's writing. Applied to biblical exegesis, the Ramist philosophy had far-reaching theological and metaphysical implications.[37]

III. RAMISM AS AN EXEGETICAL TOOL
FOR ENGLISH PURITANISM

From this survey of Ramus and William Perkins' use of Ramism for biblical interpretation, the relationship between Ramist philosophy and the English Puritans' appropriation of Ramism as an exegetical tool becomes plain.

Ramism provided Puritanism with tools of logic to be applied in the grammatical, rhetorical, and logical analysis of Scripture. These tools of "analysis" helped Puritans to a "resolution" of a passage of Scripture. A text was placed in its context, the words of the text were defined and then the process of dividing or "distributing" the text was begun.

The Puritan exegete and the Ramist logician both sought to discover and dispose of matter. Ramist method taught that proper procedure included defining, dividing and classifying from general to specific. The result was a Ramist chart. The "branches" or divisions of this chart served as the exegete's "arguments" in the Ramist sense of being the "topics" or "commonplaces." When arranged according to proper method, these

---

[35]II, 642-673. See pp. 650ff. This work is analyzed in McKim, "Ramism," pp. 195-217. Cf. John G. Rechtien, "The Visual Memory of William Perkins and the End of Theological Dialogue," *JAAR* 45/1 Supplement (March 1977) 69-99. *The Arte of Prophecying* itself was constructed Ramistically. See McKim, "Ramism," Figure 34.

[36]See *Workes* III, 259; III, 95é; II, 650.

[37]See McKim, "Ramism," pp. 298-305 for other philosophical implications of the use of Ramism by English Puritans.

provided one-word summaries or textual divisions so that one could see the basic outline or subject of a division at a glance. When preached, these commonplace heads were the key-words that triggered the preacher's memory.

The Ramist-Puritan approach differed markedly from the practices of Protestant scholastic theologians. Perkins and his colleagues did not use the Aristotelian categories and language of the scholastics. Their goal in scriptural interpretation was to discover the "arguments" already present in the text. The exegete "uncovered" and classified these as Ramus taught. The scholastic method (and the view of logic that Ramus opposed) was based on deductions that could be made "logically" from the texts. The supreme weapon for arriving at truth for the scholastics was the syllogism. Proper inference based on the process of deduction yielded truth in the scholastic view. Ramist-Puritans in the humanist tradition did not rely on the syllogism as the master instrument for making truth compelling. Ramus taught that the first step in judgment was either syllogism or method. It was method that was used most. Ramists believed texts could be "unfolded" (as some of their charts literally had to be folded to fit into their books) by the proper method. When this was completed, the interior logic or thought pattern of the author could be plainly shown. All inner-relationships of a discourse became immediately visible. William Perkins never attempted to justify or prove the division he made. To him these divisions had yielded self-evident axioms, the validity of which was beyond question. It was only when dealing with "crypticall" places where the "plain meaning" of Scripture was not readily apparent that Perkins resorted to the use of syllogisms.

Thus Ramism was an attractive and powerful tool for English Puritans looking for a key to the right understanding of Holy Scripture. Besides providing tools of logic, right method and a way of directly perceiving the mind of the Holy Spirit behind the texts of Scripture, Ramism as an exegetical tool helped keep theology itself and the exegesis of Scripture from becoming a purely theoretical discipline. Ramus had stressed the practicality and "use" of each art. When applied to theology and to biblical interpretation the theologian and exegete asked both what is the *doctrine* taught here and what is its *use*. This had the effect of tying together theology and ethics. As such it was attractive to Puritans bent on the reform of the English church yet who had a passion for this reform to be theologically grounded. Ramism provided a method of doing theology and approaching Scripture that maintained the unity of theolgoy and ethics while also providing a theoretical framework whereby the application of scriptural principles to the lives of people could be part of every sermon. This was most valuable for those who wished for the spiritual reformation of the English church. Scriptural interpretation and theological reflection were not ends in themselves for Ramist Puritans. Instead, biblical exegesis and theological thought served a more vital and practical purpose. They were to function as ways for William Perkins' definition of the purpose of theology to be realized: "to liue blessedly for euer."[38]

---

[38]*Workes*, I, 11. Peter Ramus had said theology was "the art of living well" (*bene vivendi*). See Peter Ramus, *Commentariorum de religione Christiana, libri quatuor* (Frankfurt, 1576; rpt. Frankfurt: Minerva Gmbh., 1969) 6: *Theologia est doctrina bene vivendi*.

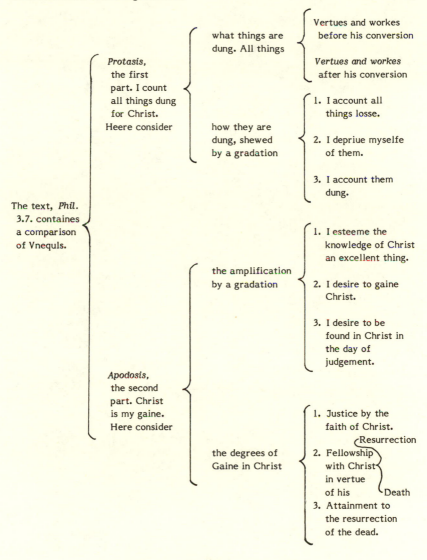

Figure A. William Perkins, *The True Gaine*.

Jesus-Paul, Peter-Paul, and Jesus-Peter Parallelisms in Luke-Acts: A History of Reader Response

Susan Marie Praeder

Boston College

Scholarly interest in Jesus-Paul, Peter-Paul, and Jesus-Peter parallelisms in Luke-Acts is at least as old as critical study of the plan and purpose of Acts. Nineteenth century tendency criticism linked the parallel roles of Peter and Paul in Acts to its claims about the apologetic purpose of Acts. Since the nineteenth century Jesus-Paul, Peter-Paul, and Jesus-Peter parallelisms have been catalogued or cited in passing in commentaries and special studies. From time to time twentieth-century redaction criticism has looked to Jesus-Paul, Jesus-Peter, and other parallelisms in Luke-Acts for clues to the literary plan and theological purpose shared by both books.[1]

The purpose of the present study is to review as reader responses representative nineteenth- and twentieth-century studies of Jesus-Paul, Peter-Paul, and Jesus-Peter parallelisms in Luke Acts. There are four parts to my study. In part one I survey the parallelisms proposed in a selection of twelve studies. Part two concerns the various types of parallels and the criteria for parallelism in these studies in relation to the practice of parallel reporting and the process of parallel reading. In part three I present my critical response to the proposed parallel miracles of Jesus, and trials of Jesus and Paul. Part four contains some conclusions, questions, and suggestions pertaining to parallelisms in Luke-Acts, reader responses, and critical responses.

I. PARALLELISMS IN LUKE-ACTS

The twelve studies that I have selected for my survey of parallelisms in Luke-Acts represent tendency criticism, radical criticism, literary criticism, typological criticism, and redaction criticism of Acts or Luke-Acts. My survey concentrates on nineteenth-century tendency criticism, as represented by the studies of M. Schneckenburger,[2] F. C.

---

[1] For the history of research see W. W. Gasque, *A History of the Criticism of the Acts of the Apostles* (BGBE 17; Tübingen: Mohr-Siebeck, 1975) 21-54; F. Neirynck, "The Miracle Stories in the Acts of the Apostles," in *Les Actes des Apôtres: Traditions, rédaction, théologie* (ed. J. Kremer; BETL 48; Gembloux: Duculot, 1979) 169-213; W. Radl, *Paulus und Jesus im lukanischen Doppelwerk: Untersuchungen zu Parallelmotiven im Lukasevangelium und in der Apostelgeschichte* (Europäische Hochschulschriften 23/49; Bern/Frankfurt: Lang, 1975) 44-59.

[2] *Über den Zweck der Apostelgeschichte: Zugleich eine Ergänzung der neueren Commentare* (Bern: Fisher, 1841).

Baur,[3] A. Schwegler,[4] and E. Zeller,[5] and twentieth-century redaction criticism, as represented by the studies of C. H. Talbert,[6] A. J. Mattill, Jr.,[7] R. F. O'Toole,[8] W. Radl,[9] and G. Muhlack.[10] Nineteenth-century radical criticism of Acts, twentieth-century literary criticism of Luke-Acts, and twentieth-century typological criticism of Luke-Acts are represented in order by the studies of B. Bauer,[11] R. Morgenthaler,[12] and M. D. Goulder.[13]

Tendency Criticism

According to tendency criticism, Peter's miracles in Acts 1-12 parallel Paul's miracles in Acts 13-28, and this Peter-Paul parallelism is related to the apologetic purpose of Acts. Schneckenburger argues that Acts is an apology for Paul addressed to an audience of Jewish Christians. He explains the parallel miracles of Peter and Paul as part of Luke's apologetic strategy; they are evidence that Paul was an apostle the equal of Peter. Baur, Schwegler, and Zeller are also of the opinion that Acts is an apology, an apology for Gentile or Pauline Christianity, and that the parallel miracles are part of the author's apologetic strategy. Although these critics agree that Acts is a *Tendenzschrift*, Schneckenburger is alone in his interpretation of Acts as a first-century apology and in his allowance for its historical reliability. Baur, Schwegler, and Zeller place Acts in the second century, and Schwegler and Zeller, in particular, refer to the parallel miracles so as to impugn its historical reliability.

Schneckenburger lists six parallel miracles and mighty works of Peter and Paul: Peter's healing of a man lame from birth and Paul's healing of a man lame from birth (3:1-10, 14:8-13), Peter's punishment of Ananias and Sapphira and Paul's punishment of Elymas (5:1-11, 13:6-12), the healing power of Peter's shadow and the healing power of Paul's clothing (5:15, 19:12), Peter's triumph over Simon Magus and Paul's triumph over Elymas, the slave girl, and the Ephesian exorcists (8:9-24; 13:6-12, 16:16-18, 19:13-19),

---

[3] *Paulus, der Apostel Jesu Christi: Sein Leben und Wirken, seine Briefe und seine Lehre: Ein Beitrag zu einer kritischen Geschichte des Urchristentums* (Stuttgart: Becher & Müller, 1845; 2d ed., ed. E. Zeller; Leipzig: Fues, 1866).

[4] *Das nachapostolische Zeitalter in den Hauptmomenten seiner Entwicklung* (2 vols.; Tübingen: Fues, 1846).

[5] *Die Apostelgeschichte nach ihrem Inhalt und Ursprung kritisch untersucht* (Stuttgart: Mäcken, 1854).

[6] *Literary Patterns, Theological Themes, and the Genre of Luke-Acts* (SBLMS 20; Missoula: Scholars Press, 1974).

[7] "The Jesus-Paul Parallels and the Purpose of Luke-Acts: H.H. Evans Reconsidered," *NovT* 17 (1975) 15-46.

[8] "Parallels between Jesus and His Disciples in Luke-Acts: A Further Study," *BZ* 27 (1983) 195-212.

[9] See n. 1.

[10] *Die Parallelen von Lukas-Evangelium und Apostelgeschichte* (Theologie und Wirklichkeit 8; Frankfurt: Lang, 1979).

[11] *Die Apostelgeschichte: Eine Ausgleichung des Paulinismus und des Judenthums innerhalb der christlichen Kirche* (Berlin: Hempel, 1850).

[12] *Die lukanische Geschichtsschreibung als Zeugnis: Gestalt und Gehalt der Kunst des Lukas* (ATANT 14-15; 2 vols; Zurich: Zwingli, 1949).

[13] *Type and History in Acts* (London: SPCK, 1964).

Peter's healing of Aeneas and Paul's healing of Publius's father (9:32-35, 28:7-10), and Peter's raising of Tabitha and Paul's raising of Eutychus (9:36-43, 20:7-12). Other Peter-Paul parallelisms include the respect and reverence that are shown to them on several occasions (5:13, 10:25-26; 14:15, 28:6) and their laying on of hands in connection with receptions of the Holy Spirit (8:14-17, 19:1-7).[14]

Baur compares six sets of passages that are said to contain Peter-Paul parallelisms. Three sets correspond to the parallel miracles listed by Schneckenburger (3:1-10, 14:8-13; 5:14-15, 19:11-12; 9:36-43, 20:7-12).[15] Baur's comparisons of the remaining three sets modify, slightly or significantly, some of Schneckenburger's suggestions. Schneckenburger mentions in passing that the apostles and Paul are released from prison, but Baur specifically states that these miraculous releases are part of the Peter-Paul parallelism in Acts (5:17-26, 12:1-19, 16:25-34).[16] Baur considers one of Schneckenburger's three parallels to 8:9-24, Paul's cursing of Elymas, as a parallel to Peter's confrontation with Simon Magus.[17] Schneckenburger claims that Peter's laying of hands on the people of Samaria parallels Paul's laying of hands on the disciples of John the Baptist. Baur compares Paul's conversion of the disciples of John the Baptist to Pentecost and Peter's conversion of Cornelius and concludes that the references to speaking in tongues (2:4, 2:11; 10:46; 19:6) set up a parallel series of passages and a Peter-Paul parallelism.[18]

As evidence that Acts is a *Tendenzschrift*, Schwegler and Zeller offer systematic summaries of its Peter-Paul parallelisms. Schwegler summarizes the parallelisms under four headings: "Thaten und Wunder," "Berufung und Würde," "Begabung und Befähigung," and "Verhalten."[19] His list of parallel miracles and mighty works of Peter and Paul corresponds to Schneckenburger's list.[20] Continuing to follow Schneckenburger, Schwegler claims that Peter and Paul are portrayed as parallel apostles to the Gentiles. Their apostolic calling rests on visionary experiences as the result of which Paul is sent to the Gentiles and Peter is sent to the Gentile centurion Cornelius.[21] Both share in the apostolic power of laying on of hands. Schwegler sums up the portrayal of Peter as his "Paulinization" and "dejudaization" and the portrayal of Paul as his "Petrinization" and "judaization."[22]

Zeller summarizes the Peter-Paul parallelisms under six headings: "Wunderthätigkeit," "Leiden und Widerwärtigkeiten," "Lehre," "Verhalten," "Befähigung," and "Beziehungen." His list of parallel miracles and mighty works of Peter and Paul contains some of those suggested by Schneckenburger and Baur (3:1-10, 14:8-13; 5:1-11, 13:6-12, 19:13-19; 5:15, 19:12; 8:9-24, 13:6-12, 19:13-19; 9:36-43, 20:7-12) and the exorcisms of Peter, his circle, and Paul (5:16, 8:7; 16:16-18, 19:11, 19:13-19). The imprisonments of the apostles, Peter, and Paul are listed among their parallel sufferings. In his summary of the

---

[14]Schneckenburger, *Zweck*, 52-58. Throughout I have tried to correct, standardize, and supply verse references for the passages cited in nineteenth-century studies.

[15]Baur, *Paulus*, 95-97, 188-89, 191-93; 2d ed. 108-10, 214-15, 218-20.

[16]Schneckenburger, *Zweck*, 60; Baur, *Paulus*, 157; 2d ed. 179.

[17]Baur, *Paulus*, 91-92; 2d ed. 104-5.

[18]Ibid., 182-87; 2d ed. 208-13.

[19]Schwegler, *Zeitalter*. I have taken the headings from the table of contents (2. iv-v) and the chapter on Acts.

[20]Ibid., 2. 76-77.

[21]Schneckenburger, *Zweck*, 170; Schwegler, *Zeitalter*, 2. 77-81.

[22]Schwegler, *Zeitalter*, 2. v, 81, 99.

parallel teachings, powers, and general portrayals of the apostles, Zeller follows Schneckenburger and Schwegler.[23]

Radical Criticism

Bauer refers to Jesus-Paul, Peter-Paul, and Jesus-Peter parallelisms in his chapters on the portrayal of Paul in Acts. He sees Paul as the principal pawn in the second-century author's account of the origins of Gentile Christianity. As a radical critic, Bauer attacks the historical reliability of the account, and his references to the parallelisms are part of his attack.

The starting point of his chapter on Paul "Der Wunderthäter" is a catalogue of previously suggested Peter-Paul parallelisms (3:1-10, 14:8-13; 5:15, 19-12; 5:16, 16:16-18, [19:13-19]; 5:1-11, 8:9-24, 13:6-12; 9:32-35, 28:7-10; 9:36-43, 20:7-12). Then he proposes that the synoptic portrayal of Jesus as a miracle worker is the model for the twin portrayals of the miracle workers Peter and Paul in Acts and proceeds to cite synoptic parallels to the miracles in Acts. Most of these parallels come from Mark. Jesus' healing of the paralytic (Mark 2:1-12) parallels the healings of men lame from birth, his healings and exorcisms (Mark 3:10-11, 6:55-56) parallel the healings and exorcisms in Acts, Jesus' healing of Simon's mother-in-law and the multitudes (Mark 1:29-34) parallels Peter's healing of Aeneas and Paul's healing of Publius's father, and Jesus' raising of Jairus's daughter and his raising of the widow's son (Mark 5:21-24, 35-43, Luke 7:11-17) parallel Peter's raising of Tabitha and Paul's raising of Eutychus. No parallel is cited for the triumphs and punishments (5:1-11; 8:9-24, 13:6-12).[24]

In the chapter "Paulus als Apologet" Bauer claims that the circumstances of Paul's trial in Acts parallel those of Jesus' trial in Matthew, Mark, and Luke. Jesus is heard before the Sanhedrin, Pilate, and Herod in Luke, and Paul is heard before the Sanhedrin, Feliz, and Agrippa in Acts. Jesus and Paul are bound and delivered up (Mark 15:1, Acts 21:11), slapped (Mark 14:65, Acts 23:2), declared innocent (Luke 23:15, Acts 23:9, 26:31), could have been released (Luke 23:16, 20, 22, Acts 26:32), and are delivered up (Luke 23:25, Acts 27:1). Pilate and Felix try to put off the Jews (Mark 15:10, Acts 24:22). Pilate's wife shows interest in Jesus' case (Matt 27:19), and Felix's wife Drusilla shows an interest in Paul's case (Acts 24:24). Herod is in Jerusalem, has had an interest in seeing Jesus for a long time, and is in the company of soldiers (Luke 23:7, 8, 11), and Agrippa is in Caesarea, interested in hearing Paul, and in the company of military tribunes (Acts 25:13, 22, 23).[25]

Literary Criticism

Morgenthaler cites parallel passages from the trial of Jesus in Luke and the trial of Paul in Acts in his study of the governing literary principle of Luke-Acts. He is convinced that Luke-Acts is governed by a *Zweiheitsgesetz* and catalogues parallels representing all levels of composition—single words, phrases, sentences, paragraphs, and sections—to

---

[23]Zeller, *Apostelgeschichte*, 320-35. The headings are taken from these pages and the table of contents (xi).

[24]Bauer, *Apostelgeschichte*, 9-21.

[25]Ibid., 105-9.

prove his point. The *Zweiheitsgesetz* is itself a literary realization of Luke's theology of witness and its requirement for "two or three witnesses."

Morgenthaler proposes a compositional plan for Luke-Acts that consists of four parallel Jerusalem scenes (Luke 1:5-4:13, 19:45-24:53, Acts 1:4-7:60, 21:18-26:32) and three travel narratives (Luke 4:14-19:44, Acts 8:1-21:17, 27:1-28:31). The parallel passages from Jesus' trial and Paul's trial are cited in connection with his comments on the third and fourth Jerusalem scenes. Parallelisms are found in the charges against Jesus and Paul (Luke 23:2, Acts 24:5), the shouts "Away with him!" (Luke 23:18, Acts 21:36), their hearings before the Sanhedrin (Luke 22:66-71, Acts 22:30—23:10), the slappings (Luke 22:63, Acts 23:2), the three declarations of their innocence (Luke 23:4, 14, 22, Acts 23:29, 25:25, 26:31), the remarks about their release (Luke 23:22, Acts 26:32), and their long and involved trials: Jesus is sent from Pilate to Herod and back to Pilate, and Paul speaks before Lysias, Felix, Festus, and Agrippa.[26]

Typological Criticism

Goulder constructs a typology for Acts from the life of Christ in Luke. The theological point of his typology seems to be that the life of the Christian community and the lives of its leaders are a reliving of the life of Christ. According to his typology, there is a point-by-point correspondence between the life of Christ and the structure of Acts. Acts is structured in four sections, and one of these sections, the Pauline section, is similarly structured. The sections of Acts parallel one another as well as the structure of the life of Christ in Luke.

The four sections of Acts are the apostolic section (1:1—5:42), the diaconal section (6:1—9:31), the Petrine section (9:32—12:24), and the Pauline section (12:25—28:31). These sections follow a compositional plan of nine parallel points that, in turn, correspond to the compositional plan of Luke: choosing (Luke 1—2, Acts 1:15, 6:1, 10:9, 13:1), descent of the Holy Spirit (Luke 3:1, Acts 2:1, 8:14, 10:44, 19:1), kerygma and baptism (Luke 4:16, Acts 2:14, 3:2, 8:26, 10:34, 13:16, 17:22, 28:17), mighty works (Luke 4:33 *et passim*, Acts 3:1, 6:1, 11:29, 14:8), persecution (Luke 5:21 *et passim*, Acts 4:1, 6:8, 12:1, 14:19), church gathering (Luke 5:16, 6:12 [prayer] , Acts 4:23, 8:14, 11:1, 15:1), false disciple (Luke 22:3, Acts 1:16, 5:1, 8:18, 12:20, 13:8, 23:1), passion and death (Luke 22—23, Acts 5:17, 7:54, 12:3, 27:1), and resurrection (Luke 24, Acts 5:18, 9:1, 9:32, 9:36, 12:7, 28:1).[27]

Redaction Criticism

The redaction critical studies of Talbert, Mattill, and O'Toole all contain large collections of parallelism in Luke-Acts. Talbert's collection is the starting point for his consideration of the pastoral and literary contexts of Luke-Acts. He concludes that the parallelisms are linked to Luke's pastoral concern to trace "the true Christian tradition" and his literary choice of biography to portray Jesus, Peter, Paul, and others who are in

---

[26]Morgenthaler, *Geschichtsschreibung*, 1. 163, 182-83.

[27]Goulder, *Acts*, 65-66, 72-97. The verse references are taken from the chart (74) or from the headings throughout the chapter on Acts.

the line of the true tradition.[28] Mattill presents a collection of Jesus-Paul parallelisms in his reconsideration of H. H. Evans and this nineteenth-century scholar's suggestion that Acts is an apology for Paul. O'Toole concludes that the parallelisms serve as an apology for Peter, Paul, and others, as a call to imitation of Christ, and, most importantly, as a sign of the continuity between Jesus in Luke and his followers in Acts.[29] The redaction-critical studies of Radl and Muhlack are limited to select parallelisms in Luke-Acts. Radl reviews the parallel sufferings of Jesus and Paul, and Muhlack compares five sets of parallelisms in Luke-Acts.

Talbert summarizes and supplements the findings of nineteenth- and twentieth-century research on the parallelisms in Luke-Acts. He catalogues Jesus-Peter parallelisms (Luke 4:16-30, 5:17-26, 7:1-10, 7:11-17, 7:36-50, Acts 2:14-40, 3:1-10, chap. 10, 9:36-43, 11:1-19), Jesus-Paul parallelism in their journeys to Jerusalem (Luke 9:51—19:28, Acts 19:21—-21:17), in seven references in these journey sections (Luke 9:51 and 9:53, 13:22, 13:33, 17:11, 18:31, 19:11, 19:28, Acts 19:21, 20:22, 21:4, 21:11-12, 21:13, 21:15, 21:17), in their stays in Jerusalem and Paul's stay in Caesarea and sea voyage (Luke 19:37, 19:45-48, 20:27-39, 22:19a, 22:54, 22:63-64, 22:26, 23:1, 23:8, 23:13, Acts 21:17-20a, 21:26, 23:6-9, 27:35, 21:30, 23:2, chaps. 23, 24, 25, 26), in their trials, Jesus' death, and Paul's sea voyage (Luke 23:4, 23:14, 23:22, 23:6-12, 23:16, 23:21, 23:18, 23:47, Acts 23:9, 25:25, 26:31, 25:13—-26:32, 26:32, 21:36, 27:3, 27:43), and in the conclusions (Luke 24, Acts 28), and Peter-Paul parallelisms in sequence (2:1-4, 13:1-3; 2:14-40, 13:16-40; 3:1-10, 14:8-13; 3:12-26, 14:15-17; chaps. 10-11, 13-21; chaps. 12, 21-28) and in no particular sequence (8:9-24, 13:6-12; 9:36-43, 20:9-12; 10:25-26, 14:13-15; 12:6-11, 16:24-26; 18:14-17, 19:1-6; 6:1-6, 14:23).[30]

Mattill and O'Toole organize their articles according to themes that repeat themselves in the parallelisms in Luke-Acts. Mattill organizes his Jesus-Paul parallelisms under three headings: "The Unity of the Christian Church with the Traditions of Israel" (with the subheadings "The Law," "Preaching in Synagogues," "Affirmation of the Pharisaic Doctrine of the Resurrection," and "Fulfillment of Scripture"), "God's Plan of Salvation" (with the subheadings "God's Servants," "Divine Necessity," "Spirit, Revelations, and Angels," "Signs and Wonders," and "Turning to the Gentiles"), and "The Journey Toward Jerusalem and Passion."[31]

O'Toole organizes his Jesus-Paul, Jesus-Peter, and other parallelisms under six headings: their activities and experiences (baptism, travel, prayer, signs and wonders, breaking of bread), their association with Jerusalem, the temple, Samaria, and Gentiles, the characterization of their preaching, the content of their preaching (repentance, kingdom of God, reference to scriptures), their general characterization (full of spirit and wisdom, possessing power, grace, joy, subject to divine necessity, etc.), and their passions or sufferings.[32]

Radl's dissertation is the only full-length study of the parallel sufferings of Jesus and Paul in Luke-Acts. He compares the prophecies about them and their sufferings (Luke 2:32, 34b, Acts 9:15-16), their inaugural sermons (Luke 4:16-30, Acts 13:14-52), the beginning of their journeys to Jerusalem (Luke 9:51, Acts 19:21), their farewell addresses

---

[28]Talbert, *Patterns*, 141-43.
[29]O'Toole, "Parallels," 209-11.
[30]Talbert, *Patterns*, 16-18, 23-24.
[31]Mattill, "Parallels," 21-37.
[32]O'Toole, "Parallels," 197-209.

(Luke 22:21-38, Acts 20:18-35), the passion predictions (Luke 9:22, 9:44-45, 12:50, 13:32-33, 17:25, 18:31-34, Acts 20:22-25, 21:4, 21:10-12), the passages set "in the face of death" (Luke 22:39-46, Acts 20:36-38), their trials and a related passage (Luke 22:47—23:25, Acts 21:27-26:32, 28:17-19). There is also a consideration of Paul's sea voyage in Acts 27-28 as a parallel to Jesus' death and resurrection.[33]

Muhlack's five sets of parallelisms are the healings of the lame by Jesus, Peter, and Paul (Luke 5:17-26, Acts 3:1-10, 14:8-18), Jesus' healing of the centurion's slave and Peter's conversion of the centurion Cornelius (Luke 7:1-10, Acts 10:1-48), the raisings of the dead by Jesus, Peter, and Paul (Luke 7:11-17, 8:40-56, Acts 9:36-43, 20:7-12), the meals in Luke-Acts, and the inaugural sermons of Jesus, Peter, and Paul (Luke 4, Acts 2, 13).

II. PARALLELISMS AND READER RESPONSES

Throughout the twelve studies there are references to "Parallelen," "Parallelisierung," "Parallelismus," "intentional parallelism," "parallelisms," "parallels," and the like in Acts or Luke-Acts. It is only recently, however, that anyone has reflected on the criteria for parallelism and tried to sort out the various types of parallels.[34] Thus, this part of my review contains a survey of the types of parallels in nineteenth- and twentieth-century studies as clues to their criteria for parallelism.

The primary criterion for parallelism in the twelve studies is textual similarity. Similarities in content, language, literary form, sequence, structure, and theme found in two or more places are seen as the stuff and proof of parallel passages, portrayals, and compositional plans. Parallel content is a catch-all type of parallel; even the least and less obvious textual similarities can be seen as parallels in content. Parallel language is a much more precise type of parallel; only verbal repetitions or similarities qualify as such. Parallel literary form refers to the like classification of two or more passages. In the twelve studies this reference is more often than not to two or more miracle stories in Luke-Acts. Parallel sequence covers the similar ordering in passages or sections and the corresponding order of passages or sections in larger sequences. Parallel structure is a special type of parallel sequence that concerns the similar patterns of passages, sections and larger sequences. Parallel theme is a special type of parallel content, the correspondence of the central points of two or more passages. In the twelve studies these points are sometimes seen in relation to the central themes of Luke-Acts.

The secondary criteria for parallelism include the relation of particular textual similarities to the historical, literary, or theological concerns of the twelve studies and the redaction-critical status of these similarities. Thus, in tendency criticism similarities pertaining to the portrayals of Peter and Paul are seen as Peter-Paul parallelisms, and in the studies of Mattill and O'Toole similarities that fit into their thematic organization of Luke-Acts qualify as parallels. Talbert and Radl are inclined to accept as parallels all similarities that can be assigned to Lukan redaction.

My criticisms of these criteria are reserved for part three of this study. My concern in this part is to sketch what these criteria, reported and unreported, and the reporting of types of parallels reveal about the reader responses preserved in the twelve

---

[33]Radl, *Doppelwerk*, 68-297.
[34]Ibid., 346-51; Talbert, *Patterns*, 77-82.

studies. The comments on the parallelisms in Luke-Acts in these studies are themselves parallel reports. Whether in the form of charts, collections of quotations, columns, lists, short comparisons, or summary stories (some with titles and subtitles), these reports place side by side and in point-by-point correspondence passages and references that are not so closely connected in Acts, Luke-Acts, or other texts. In a sense, the scholars who compose these reports offer their readers short, highly selective, and parallel versions of the texts under consideration, and records of their own parallel reading.

Parallel reporting follows on parallel reading, and, I suggest, reflects the process of parallel reading of Luke-Acts. Parallel reports are short forms of Luke-Acts, and it seems that parallel reading leads to close study of certain parts of the text. The selectivity of parallel reports suggests that parallel reading is a process of remembering and forgetting. Parallels are remembered, and the rest is forgotten or remembered in connection with the parallels. In parallel reports similarities scattered throughout Luke-Acts are placed side by side for comparison. From this fact it seems that parallel reading is a long and painstaking process, requires a command of the full range of the text, and is not a strictly linear process.

Schneckenburger, Baur, Schwegler, and Zeller[35]

Schneckenburger's parallel report is in the form of a list that summarizes the miracles and mighty works of Peter and Paul. There seems to be no particular design in the order of the list; all that can be said is that it departs from the order of Acts. In his sets of parallelisms he usually introduces Peter's miracle first and then Paul's parallel miracle. He is selective in reporting similarities only and in reporting only a selection of similarities. It seems that his parallel reading of Acts was a process that involved multiple matchings of Peter and Paul.

His Peter-Paul parallelisms largely rest on similarities in content and literary form. He states that Peter and Paul possess the same healing powers, triumph over magic and superstition, and perform punishment miracles and raisings of the dead. His comments on 3:1-10 and 14:8-13 point to similarities in content, language, and sequence. These healing miracles are the first miracles of Peter and Paul, feature a man who was "lame from his mother's womb" (*chōlos ek koilias mētros autou*) and lept up and walked around, and are confirmed by the reactions of the crowds. No reason is stated for the Peter-Paul parallelism in 9:32-35 and 28:7-10.

Some of Baur's parallel reports take the form of short comparisons and collections of quotations in Greek. His parallel reading was a process of selecting similarities from passages that are both alike and unlike. He compares similarities in content and sequence in his comments on 8:9-24 and 13:6-12. On his first journey Peter thwarts the magician Simon, and on his first missionary journey Paul thwarts the magician Elymas. Moreover, Paul's curse recalls Peter's speech, and Elymas, the opponent of Christianity who is punished, contrasts with Simon, the Christian convert who is not punished. He collects three similarities in language from 3:1-10 and 14:8-13: "lame from his mother's womb" (*chōlos ek koilias mētros autou*), "Peter looked at him . . . and said" (*atenisas Petros eis auton . . . eipe*) and "he [Paul] looked at him . . . and said" (*atenisas autō . . . eipe*) and

---

[35]See nn. 14-33 for the basic page references to the studies of these authors and the other studies reviewed below.

"he leapt up, stood, and walked around" (*exallomenos estē kai periepatei*) and "he leapt up and walked around" (*hēlleto kai periepatei*). He concedes that the miracles are not completely parallel; one lame man is a beggar, and the other is a man of faith. In a footnote Peter's raising of Tabitha is compared by quotation to Jesus' raising of Jairus's daughter in Mark and his raising of the widow's son in Luke.

Schwegler cites Schneckenburger as the source for his list and follows him point by point. Zeller continues Baur's practices in his short comparisons and collections of quotations. He compares the circumstances and content of the miraculous releases from prison in 5:17-26 and 16:25-34. In both cases miracles lead to imprisonment, there are double releases, a supernatural release (which turns out to be unnecessary) and a natural release (which is unrealistic), the prisoners are beaten before or after their imprisonment, and security is tight. Among the features of Zeller's study of Acts are his appeals for the literary origin of the parallelisms. At the conclusion of this short comparison he wonders (still in the same sentence) how anyone can believe that these parallels owe to historical occurrences or to accidents of tradition.[36] It seems that he conducted his parallel reading and constructed his parallel text so as to set up this conclusion. He passes over the elements in these passages that are not of service to his point. He collects parallel quotations from 3:1-10 and 14:8-13, 9:36-43 and the NT, and 20:7-12 and the NT and OT. These quotations are set in footnotes, and those for 3:1-10, 14:8-13, and 9:36-43 are set in parallel columns.[37] His parallel reading looked beyond Acts and Luke-Acts for similarities in language.

Bauer

Bauer's comments on the parallel miracles of Jesus, Peter, and Paul contain short comparisons and collections of quotations. Some of his comments suggest that he sees his parallel reading as a higher authority than the evidence of Mark and Acts. He recognizes that some of his parallel miracles are not all that similar. Instead of questioning their qualifications as parallel miracles, he simply states that some parallels are closer than others or criticizes the author of Acts for "unhappy copying" of Mark.[38] Thus, he concedes that Peter's miracle in Acts 3:1-10 is closer to Mark 2:1-12 than is Paul's miracle Acts 14:8-13 and that Paul's miracle in Acts 28:7-10 is closer to Mark 1:29-34 than is Peter's miracle in Acts 9:32-35.

His comparison of the parallel trials of Jesus and Paul takes the form of a summary story composed of similarities in content and language. The similar sequence of Jesus' trial in Luke and Paul's trial in Acts serves as a prologue of sorts to his story. Then he compares the trials in Mark and Acts and, following this comparison, the trials in Luke and Acts. The order of the comparisons from Mark and Acts is not exactly that of Jesus' trial or Paul's trial. The comparisons from Luke and Acts are in sequence.

Morgenthaler

Morgenthaler sets similarities in content and language from Jesus' trial in Luke and

---

[36]Zeller, *Apostelgeschichte*, 326-27.
[37]Ibid., 177, 214, 269.
[38]Bauer, *Apostelgeschichte*, 15.

Paul's trial in Acts in parallel columns. His comments on the parallels highlight the charges (Luke 23:2, Acts 24:5) and declarations of innocence (Luke 23:4, 14, 22, Acts 23:29, 25:25, 26:31). The fact that there are three declarations of innocence is interpreted as a sure sign of parallelism, and the fact that the charges against Jesus are Lukan special material seems to be interpreted as such a sign.

Goulder

Goulder's chapter on "The Fourfold Structure of Acts" touches on similarities in content, language, literary form, sequence, structure, and theme. His parallel report takes the form of a summary story in nine parts and with titles corresponding to the nine points shared by Luke and the four sections of Acts. In turn, this summary story is summarized in a chart of the nine points of Luke and the four sections of Acts. Here typological reading is in complete control of the text of Luke-Acts, the reader, and the parallel report.

Talbert, Mattill, O'Toole, Radl, Muhlack

Talbert's parallel report contains similarities in content, language, literary form, sequence, structure, and theme set in columns. The columns include quotations and are accompanied by short comparisons. His report is the result not only of parallel reading of Luke-Acts but also of the long process of reading and studying other parallel reports. Evidence for Jesus-Paul, Peter-Paul, and Jesus-Peter parallelisms is accumulated from the similarities and their redaction-critical status. Again and again Talbert concludes that they are products of Lukan redaction and, therefore, products of intentional parallelism on Luke's part. Supporting evidence for intentional parallelism is offered from the first-century literary context of Luke-Acts.[39]

Mattill's parallel report is a summary story of Luke-Acts. It is ordered by theme, titled, and subtitled. An interesting feature of this parallel report is its use of "both" and "each" to summarize the separate stories of Jesus and Paul as one story. Their parallel stories become simultaneous stories or the same story:

Both are divinely sent . . . as servants to bring light to those in darkness. . . . Both are to be lights revealing salvation to the world. . . . Both are to open the eyes of men. . . . Both are to bring remission and release. . . . Both are to travel.[40]

Only Jesus and Paul deliver farewell addresses. . . . In his last words . . . before his passion proper . . . , each admonishes his hearers to "take heed" . . . and "watch" . . . ; believes his end is near . . . ; speaks of his coming sufferings . . . ; notes that he has served . . . ; recalls his testings . . . ; anticipates the blessings of the Kingdom . . . ; and realizes that his role in God's plan is being fulfilled. . . .[41]

---

[39]Talbert, *Patterns*, 18-23, 24-26, 67-82.
[40]Mattill, "Parallels," 25.
[41]Ibid., 32-33.

relation is the point of the Peter-Paul parallelism. The content and sequence of the miracle stories parallel the thematic sequence of Luke-Acts. Salvation is sent first to the Jews and then to the Gentiles. Similarly, Peter performs a healing miracle in Jerusalem and in the presence of Jews, and then Paul performs a healing miracle in Lystra and in the presence of Gentiles.

The similarities in language, sequence, and theme can be used to make a strong case for parallelism in the two miracle stories. Nevertheless, several questions remain. The similarities in language are striking. Literary form is not a clear-cut criterion; it could be part of the parallelism or the source of the similarities.[53] Since Luke is responsible for ordering the miracle stories and speeches, it is possible, but not necessarily so, that he set out to compose parallel sequences. The strength of the proposed parallel in theme is that it makes sense of the parallelism, but it remains to be seen whether or not making sense is a strong criterion for parallelism.

The requirements for parallel reading of the two passages correspond to the criteria for parallel composition. Parallel reading requires close reading of the passages, sensitivity to similarities in language and sequence, and knowledge of the literary and theological character of Luke-Acts. If the two miracle stories are parallel passages, then it should be observed that the point of the parallelism is not limited to the portrayals of Peter and Paul. The most striking similarities in language refer to the lame men, not to Peter and Paul. The parallelism calls not only for comparative reading but also for contrastive reading, in particular, in relation to the settings in Jerusalem and Lystra and the reactions of the Jewish and Gentile crowds.

Acts 5:12-16, 19:8-12. The references to the healing power of Peter's shadow and the healing power of Paul's handkerchiefs and aprons are parts of passages that map out two stages in the theological geography of Luke-Acts. Luke 6:17-19 and Acts 8:4-8 are two other such passages and stages. The four passages are similar in content, language, literary form, and theme. Similarities in content and language include the references to preaching, hearing, and healing and curing of the sick and those who are troubled by unclean spirits. The references to Peter's shadow and Paul's handkerchiefs and aprons perhaps have some relation to the healing power that comes forth from Jesus (Luke 6:19, Acts 5:15, 19:12). The passages are summaries and mention among other things, the ministries of Jesus, Peter and the apostles, Philip, and Paul to people of various places and the success of their healings and exorcisms of these people. The people mentioned can be said to correspond to the theological geography summed up in Acts 1:8, "you will be my witnesses in Jerusalem, in all Judaea and Samaria, and to the end of the earth." Jesus ministers to people from Judaea, Jerusalem, Tyre, and Sidon (Jews and Gentiles), Peter and the apostles to the people of Jerusalem, men and women, and people from the surrounding cities, Philip to the people of Samaria, and Paul to "all those residing in the province of Asia, both Jews and Greeks" (19:10).

With respect to parallel composition the central question is whether the similarities in content and language are related to literary form, parallelism on Luke's part, or both. Is this simply the way that Luke constructs his summaries or has he composed these summaries to correspond to the theological geography of Luke-Acts? If the latter

---

[53]The influence of literary form is not recognized in nineteenth-century studies. As a result, textual similarity is traced too quickly to authorial intention.

solution seems more satisfying, is it simply because it makes more sense of the proposed parallelism? Whether or not Luke composed the summaries as parallel passages, it is well within the rights of readers of Luke-Acts to take them as such. These reader rights are set by the text, not necessarily by the author who set the text, and in this case the text lends itself to parallel reading. Since there are four summaries, the focus of parallel reading should not be limited to the persons of Peter and Paul.

Luke 4:38-41, Acts 28:7-10. Jesus' healing of Simon's mother-in-law and Paul's healing of Publius's father are similar in content, language, literary form, and sequence. Simon's mother-in-law is suffering from a fever, and Pulius's father is suffering from fevers and dysentery (Luke 4:38 *synechomenē pyretō megalō*, Acts 28:8 *pyretois kai dysenteriō synechomenon*). These healing miracles and the related passages in Matt 8:14-17 and Mark 1:29-34 are the only NT passages that contain healings of individuals followed by healings of the sick (Luke 4:40 *asthenountas*, Acts 28:9 *astheneias*). Jesus lays his hands on the sick multitudes, and Paul lays his hands on Publius's father (Luke 4:40 *tas cheiras epititheis*, Acts 28:9 *epitheis tas cheiras*), but there are other such references in Luke-Acts.[54]

These two miracle stories are more likely a case of parallel composition than an occasion for parallel reading. It seems that Luke modeled one story on the other or shaped them from the same mold. The sequence of the two passages in Luke-Acts is a serious obstacle to parallel reading. Is it possible that readers of Luke-Acts remember Jesus' healing of Simon's mother-in-law by the time they reach Paul's healing of Publius's father? Are the similarities so striking that reading of one passage necessarily recalls the other passage? What is the point of reading the passages as parallel passages?[55]

The Journeys of Jesus and Paul to Jerusalem

The journeys of Jesus and Paul to Jerusalem are parallel in theme (Luke 9:51—19:28, Acts 19:21—21:17). Their journeys are journeys to passion, and this fact is reflected in the passion predictions that are made in the course of these journeys (Luke [9:22, 9:44-45] 12:50, 13:32, 17:25, 18:31-34, Acts 20:22-25, 21:4, 21:10-12).[56] These predictions are somewhat similar in content and language. The proposed seven parallel references to journeying to Jerusalem have their problems (Luke 9:51 and 9:53, 13:22, 13:33, 17:11, 18:31, 19:11, 19:28, Acts 19:21, 20:22, 21:4, 21:12, 21:13, 21:15, 21:17).[57] The counting of Luke 9:51 and 9:53 as one reference hides the fact that these verses contain two separate references to journeying. Two references in Acts are open to challenge. Acts 19:21 comes before the beginning verse of Jesus' journey in Luke 9:51, but Paul's journey begins in Acts 20:1. In Acts 21:17 Paul and his companions have completed their journey to Jerusalem. Thus, by other counts, there are eight references in Luke and five references in Acts. A separate question is whether these references bear any relation to parallel composition or are a sufficient basis for parallel reading.

---

[54]Luke 13:13, Acts 6:6, 8:17, 8:19, 9:12, 9:17, 13:3, 19:6.

[55]Elsewhere I have tried to make sense of Acts 28:7-10 by setting it in the context of the last two chapters of Acts; see "Miracle Worker," 127-28, and "Acts 27:1-28:16, Sea Voyages in Ancient Literature, and the Theology of Luke-Acts," *CBQ* (forthcoming).

[56]Radl, *Doppelwerk*, 133-58.

[57]Talbert, *Patterns*, 17, 20.

parallelisms in Luke-Acts make sense. They fit together, and they fit the concerns and themes of Luke-Acts. Sometimes textual similarities seem to make sense as parallelisms. They can be made to fit together and to fit the rest of Luke-Acts, and it seems necessary to take the risk of making sense of the text by calling them parallelisms. Certain similarities, however, cannot and should not be made to make sense.

Author, text, and reader should be recognized as separate elements and as equals, each with her, his, or its own realm, in the communication of Luke-Acts. Parallel composition is the realm of the author, textual similarities are in the realm of the text, and parallel reading is the realm of the reader. Textual similarities need not represent parallel composition (the redaction-critical fallacy) or parallel reading (the reader-oriented critical fallacy). Furthermore, critical responses should not be confused with authorial intention, the text, or readerly inference. Thus, as far as the new temptation is concerned, I would like to hear less about "the almighty reader" and more about "my reading," its strengths and weaknesses, the risks taken and not taken, and its relation to other readings.

Eschatology and "Platonism" in the Epistle to the Hebrews

Lincoln D. Hurst

University of California, Davis

In Memoriam **George B. Caird**

The background of the Epistle to the Hebrews[1] continues to be a storm-center of debate in New Testament studies. Early Jewish apocalyptic, Philo, the Dead Sea community, Gnosticism, the Samaritans and Merkabah mysticism are among milieus which have been advanced in the last thirty years as the "key" which unlocks the mysteries of the epistle's logic.[2] One area of crucial importance is that of the eschatology of the epistle, and in particular the context of *Auctor*'s remarks about the heavenly city and temple which are "greater and more perfect" than their earthly counterparts.

The claim of R. S. Eccles[3] that "the clearest evidence of the influence of Hellenistic thought patterns" is *Auctor*'s heavenly tent, and the view of C. K. Barrett[4] that the heavenly tent "is not the product of Platonic idealism, but the eschatological temple of apocalyptic Judaism" express the two main approaches which may be taken in interpreting one of the epistle's central concerns. "The fact that such completely different interpretations are perpetuated must give ground for reflection ... they are symptomatic of the fundamental cleavage in the interpretation of Hebrews, namely whether the predominant background is Alexandrian/Philonic or Palestinian/apocalyptic."[5] Despite the work of Barrett and R. Williamson,[6] the recent publications of L. K. K. Dey[7] and J. W. Thompson[8] indicate that there is no immediate promise of this cleavage being healed. One of the most confusing—and confused—chapters of biblical interpretation thus

---

[1]Referred to hereafter as "*Auctor.*"

[2]For a helpful survey of the question, cf. J. C. McCullough, "Some Recent Developments in Research on the Epistle to the Hebrews," *Irish Biblical Studies* 2 (1980) 141ff.

[3]R. S. Eccles, "The Purpose of the Hellenistic Patterns in the Epistle to the Hebrews," in *Religions in Antiquity,* Festschrift for E. Goodenough, ed. J. Neuser, 215.

[4]C. K. Barrett, "The Eschatology of the Epistle to the Hebrews," in *The Background of the New Testament and Its Eschatology,* Festschrift for C. H. Dodd, ed. D. Daube and W. D. Davies (Cambridge, 1956) 389.

[5]G. W. MacRae, "Heavenly Temple and Eschatology in the Letter to the Hebrews," *Semeia* 12 (1978) 186.

[6]R. Williamson, *Philo and The Epistle to the Hebrews* (Leiden, 1970).

[7]L. K. K. Dey, *The Intermediary World and Patterns of Perfection in Philo and Hebrews* (Scholars Press, 1975).

[8]J. W. Thompson, *The Beginnings of Christian Philosophy: The Epistle to the Hebrews* (CBQMS; Washington D.C., 1982).

continues. If the cleavage is to be narrowed, it will be necessary to pose a number of sub-questions which have yet to be *clarified,* much less answered.

I
Is a "Vertical" Dimension Necessarily "Greek" or "Philosophical?"

The view that Hebrew thought deals in time and Greek thought deals in space[9] reflects a viewpoint which has had considerable influence upon the interpretation of Hebrews. The caricature has in recent years been attacked,[10] and some now feel that a dichotomy in which a "horizontal" (temporal) framework is Jewish and a "vertical" (cosmological) framework is Greek is oversimplified. Thus, even if Hebrews *could* be shown to contain a "vertical" correspondence between heaven and earth, there is nothing in such a view which would compel one to think that *Auctor* has stepped out of mainline Jewish thought to the point where it is necessary to posit a specifically Alexandrian or philosophical orientation. There are several indications pointing in this direction: (a) The notion of an earthly temple built according to a god-given plan goes back as far as Gudea of Lagash (c. 3000 B.C.) and is reflected in the Code of Hammurabi.[11] Nineveh and Asshur, as well as their temples, were built according to heavenly patterns. In a notable *tour de force* G. B. Gray[12] argued that none of these Near Eastern texts indicates the existence of heavenly temples, only divinely given patterns (cf. a similar debate over the interpretation of Exod 25:40 within Judaism).[13] But it must be noted that much more work has been done in this field since Gray wrote, and it is now fairly certain that in the ancient Near East, rivers, fields, cities, and temples had heavenly counterparts.[14] (b) A great deal of "vertical" heaven-earth language exists in the OT itself. In Gen 11:5 God "comes down" from heaven to see the tower of Babel; Jacob's ladder reaches "upward" into heaven (Gen 28:12); and God's dwelling is repeatedly seen as "above" in heaven (e.g., Ps 24:4; cf. also Gen 18:21, Exod 20:22, etc.). Of particular interest is Ps 102 (101LXX):19: "For he looked out from the height of his sanctuary; the Lord looked upon the earth from heaven" (v. 19). Here is a statement which, occurring almost immediately before a passage quoted by *Auctor* (cf. Heb 1:10ff), depicts God's sanctuary (ἅγιος; cp. Heb 9:12) *as over the earth.* Is this "Platonic"? It is sterile to argue whether or how much

---

[9]Cf. O. Cullmann, *Christ and Time* (London, 1951). Cullmann makes a hard distinction between the "Greek" and "Hebrew" views. On p. 54 he says that the "Greek" view does not show up in Hebrews; the invisible is not thought of in terms of space, but in terms of time.

[10]Cf. Paul Minear, "The Cosmology of the Apocalypse," in *Current Issues in New Testament Interpretation,* Festschrift for Otto Piper, ed. W. Klassen and G. F. Snyder (London, 1962) 23ff.

[11]Cf., e.g., James Moffatt, *A Critical and Exegetical Commentary on the Epistle to the Hebrews* (Edinburgh, 1924) 106; C. T. Fritsch, "ΤΟ ᾽ΑΝΤΙΤΥΠΟΝ," *Studia Biblica et Semitica,* Festschrift for T. C. Vriezen, ed. W. C. van Unnik (Wageningen, 1966) 102 n. 3; R. J. McKelvey, *The New Temple* (Oxford, 1968) 25; H. Montefiore, *The Epistle to the Hebrews* (London, 1964) 135; and MacRae, "Heavenly Temple," 180.

[12]G. B. Gray, "The Heavenly Temple and the Heavenly Altar," *Expositor* 8 (1908) 394ff.

[13]Cf. ibid., 532, 542ff.

[14]Cf. M. Eliade, *Cosmos and History* (New York, 1959) passim; and K. Schmidt, "Jerusalem als Urbild u. Abbild," *Eranos-Jbch.* 18 (1950) 207ff.

such statements in the OT are indebted to Babylonian influences, and equally sterile to argue whether NT statements indicating a heaven-earth correspondence come from the Babylonian/OT branch or the Hellenistic branch.[15] The question should not be pushed to a choice between stark alternatives. There is probably *some* Greek influence at work in these texts. To argue that there is none would be equivalent to arguing that, because angels appear in the early strata of the OT, there is no Persian influence.[16] The problem is more complex than that of simple alternatives. It is more likely that some amount of Greek influence has come into play, but it came into ground which was already prepared for it in which there was no great contrast between the two traditions. Thus any NT writer who deals in "above" and "below" had not *a priori* stepped out of the Hebrew world into that which is exclusively "Greek." To this it must be added that the introduction by Christianity of the notion of two ages overlapping would make it virtually impossible to *avoid* speaking in terms of "above" and "below." Paul Minear[17] has demonstrated that in a thoroughly Jewish-Christian apocalyptic work such as Revelation one can find spatial categories which have nothing overtly to do with Platonism, and which, as neither timeless nor time-bound, do not conform to the usual caricatures of "Greek" and "Hebrew" thought:

> His city is devoid of neither time nor space, since it binds together acts of obedience and of sovereignty. Yet that city is neither bounded by space nor regulated by time. It comes down "from heaven from God."[18]

Since for John of Patmos things on earth have their corresponding entities in heaven, heaven itself is in one sense affected by time, yet it is not bound by time. Minear concludes by calling for a detection of "similar cosmological attitudes in other New Testament books."[19] Hebrews is certainly a likely candidate for this more sophisticated approach. For *Auctor* the future is in some sense also present; the two ages, as it were, "overlap." This could be one place where a certain amount of Greek influence has come into play; but it was the introduction *by Christianity* of the idea of two ages overlapping which had already provided the ground into which it came. Minear is correct to suggest that this is more widespread than is often thought. Col 3:1-4, e.g., says that

---

[15]As does, e.g., A. Cody, *Heavenly Sanctuary and Liturgy in the Epistle to the Hebrews* (St. Meinrad, 1960) 15, 24; and W. L. Knox, "Pharisaism and Hellenism," chap. II of *Judaism and Christianity,* ed. H. Loewe (London, 1937) 72ff. The latter, while he feels certain that "Hellenistic cosmology of the type" seen in Philo "has supplied the rabbis with abundant food for speculation" (75), admits that the divine pattern of the universe which is "clearly derived from the *Timaeus* . . . had affinities with the Jewish (and widespread Oriental) ideas of divine 'patterns' of which earthly sanctuaries were the copy," and says that "it would be hard to say whether the pattern of the temple in Wisd. ix.8 is drawn from the Greek or the Oriental source" (76). (On Wis 9:8, see below, n. 81.) The latter statement is oversimplified, since by the time Wisdom was written the two traditions had probably already been fused.

[16]On the early development of the belief in angels and its relationship to later Persian influences, see W. O. E. Oesterley, *The Jews and Judaism During the Greek Period* (London, 1941) 266ff.

[17]"Cosmology of the Apocalypse" (see above, n. 10).

[18]Ibid., 35.

[19]Ibid., 37.

> If you have been raised with Christ, seek the things that *are above*, where Christ is, seated at the right hand of God. Set your minds on things that *are above*, not on things that are *on earth*. . . . When Christ who is our life appears, then you will appear with him in glory.

Here one finds the dichotomy of "the things that are *above*" and "the things that are *on earth*," but it is nonetheless set in an eschatological framework (note particularly "you will appear with him in glory"). Even the Fourth Gospel, which is felt by many to depend heavily upon Platonic categories, sets "above" and "below" in an eschatological framework.[20] The more widespread this trend can be shown to be, the stronger becomes the argument against any *conscious* dependence in Hebrews upon "Platonic" categories in the juxtaposition of heavenly and earthly.

II
How Does the "Vertical" Dimension Operate in Hebrews?

With the above considerations in mind one must look to the most "vertical" sounding passage in Hebrews—8:4ff.:

> Now if he were on earth, he could not be a priest, since there are priests who offer gifts according to the law. They serve an outline and a shadow of the heavenly sanctuary; for when Moses was about to erect the tent, he was instructed by God, saying, "See that you make everything according to the τύπος shown to you on the mountain."

In this passage one is confronted with an initial question: what is the meaning of the present tense (λατρεύουσιν, "they serve")? Had *Auctor* said that OT priests *had* served a preliminary outline of the heavenly (which has now arrived), it would be easy to understand 8:5a in a time perspective of "then-now." A statement, however, that in *Auctor's own time* priests serve a shadowy outline of the heavenly does sound distinctly "vertical." But there is more than one way the present tense may be understood: (a) If the heavenly tent is "heaven" (cf. 9:24 as often interpreted), it would mean that priests during the entire OT age served[21] an outline and shadow of a reality which has always been there. This *could* be a Platonic/ Philonic model. (b) If the primary background of the heavenly tent is the eschatological temple of Jewish apocalyptic (as Barrett suggests), a vertical dimension is necessary *only* during the time when the two sanctuaries "overlap."

---

[20]For a helpful discussion of the essentially "realized" eschatology of the Fourth Gospel, cf., e.g., W. H. Cadman, *The Open Heaven: The Revelation of God in the Johannine Sayings of Jesus*, ed. G. B. Caird (Oxford, 1969); and C. H. Dodd, *The Interpretation of the Fourth Gospel*, passim.

[21]That *Auctor* can use the present tense to stand for events which are past is well known. B. F. Westcott, *The Epistle to the Hebrews* (London, 1889) 219, commenting on the fact that in Heb 8:5 Moses *is* warned, says "the direction of God is still present in Scripture." Cf. also A. Nairne, *The Epistle to the Hebrews* (Cambridge, 1917) cxlviif. (". . . often a present is due to the author's habit of referring to what stands written in books or pictured in history"); G. Milligan, *The Theology of the Epistle to the Hebrews* (Edinburgh, 1899) 41f.; and K. J. Thomas, "The Old Testament Citations in Hebrews," *NTS* 11 (1964-65) 311 (commenting on the use of λέγει in Heb 8:9f. and 10:16).

Thus the "they" of "they serve" are only those priests who continue to serve on earth once the new sanctuary has come. (c) The "they" of "they serve" involves the priests of the entire Jewish age, but in this case what is being said is simply that they have always served, not the finished work (which has finally arrived and into which Jesus has entered), but merely the preliminary sketch (which is now due to be discarded). This would not be a vertical framework at all; it is a horizontal framework of "then-now" (the earthly priests serve the sketch meant for "then," while Christ serves the finished work meant for "now"). The three approaches may be diagrammed:

(a)

"Platonic"
"eternal" sanctuary
(i.e., "heaven itself"?)

"they (= priests of entire Jewish
age) are serving a shadowy outline
of the heavenly

Moses ———————————————— Auctor ———— A.D. 70

(b)

"Apocalyptic"
sanctuary of new age ⟶

"they (= only priests
serving during the period
of the New Covenant) are
serving a shadowy outline
of the heavenly (which has
now come)

Moses ——————— A.D. 30 ———— Auctor ——— A.D. 70

(c)

"Apocalyptic"
sanctuary of new age ⟶

"they (= priests of entire Jewish
age) are serving a shadowy outline
of the heavenly

Moses ——————— A.D. 30 ———— Auctor ——— A.D. 70

In theory, any of the three options is possible. But, assuming for the moment (c), i.e., that ὑπόδειγμα and σκιά in 8:5 and σκιά in 10:1 have a "horizontal," "forward" nuance, what is to be made of the apparent "vertical" dimension seen in 8:5b (Exod 25:40)? Did not the τύπος already exist in Moses' time, and is not the τύπος the counterpart of the ἀντίτυπος of 9:23? Here it is important to ask what *Auctor* understands the τύπος to be. τύπος may mean "pattern," "blueprint," "original," *or* "copy." Because this is the only occurrence in the epistle of τύπος, it is usually taken to be the precise counterpart of ἀντίτυπος, i.e., Moses saw the "original" or "archetypal" sanctuary.[22] It is seldom stated that there are *two* possibilities: (a) It is not certain that *Auctor* focuses on the τύπος of Exod 25:40 as a *terminus technicus*, the precise antithesis of the antitype mentioned in 9:24. In the quotation it could simply bear its non-technical meaning of "pattern." It would be difficult to prove how logical he was being at this point. If the τύπος of Exod 25:40 was for him merely a pattern, model, or blueprint given from heaven which Moses reproduces (as was probably the original meaning of Exod 25:40),[23] it may have been *associated by him with the heavenly tent* so that, in a sense, both may be covered by the term τύπος without implying strict equivalence (although, it should be noted, *Auctor* never uses τύπος outside of the quotation in 8:5). The τύπος given on the mount, in other words, although only a blueprint or model, falls for him on the heavenly side of the ledger because, like the true sanctuary itself which comes later, *its origin is heaven*. (b) *Auctor* takes the τύπος of Exod 25:40 to indicate the actual heavenly tent and not its blueprint or model. It is usually assumed in this case that actual pre-existence or eternity is required for the heavenly tent.[24] Yet this is not the case. Ezekiel, e.g., was given a prophetic vision of a temple-city in explicit architectural detail without the implication being attached that it already actually existed. It is possible for biblical writers to depict future entities as apprehended in the present because they already exist invisibly in God, i.e., within his purposes. It should be remembered that for *Auctor* (11:1, 7, 13) OT men of faith are those who "see" the future as though it were present.[25] In 3:5 Moses is a "witness" (μαρτύριον) of things to be spoken in the future (τῶν λαληθησομένων). It is quite possible that *Auctor* interprets Exod 25:40 to mean that Moses, as a man of faith, "sees" the future sanctuary, one of "the good things to come"; then, in accordance with God's command, he makes a "shadowy outline" of what he "saw."[26] John of Patmos (also bearing some affinity with the Ezekiel account)

---

[22]Cf., e.g., M. Barth, "The Old Testament in Hebrews," *Current Issues in New Testament Interpretation*, Festschrift for O. Piper, ed. W. Klassen and G. F. Snyder (London, 1962) 269 n. 28; "In Heb. 8:5 'type' means archetype; the antitype mentioned in 9:24 corresponds to it."

[23]Cf. Gray, "The Heavenly Temple and Heavenly Altar," 533: "Neither Ezekiel nor Moses is represented in the Old Testament as having seen a temple in heaven."

[24]See W. Michaelis, "σκηνή, κτλ.," *TDNT* 7. 375: "The fact that the heavenly σκηνή pre-dated the tabernacle as its τύπος is used in Hb. as evidence of the high antiquity and indeed the pre-existence of the heavenly σκηνή before all times."

[25]It is, however, probably going too far to say with Strathmann ("πόλις, κτλ.," *TDNT* 6. 531) that because Abraham "looked for a city with foundations" (11:10), "the patriarchs already knew about the heavenly Jerusalem."

[26]Philo interprets Exod 25:40 as the giving to Moses of a mystic vision of the whole realm of incorporeal ideas (De vit. Mos. II. 74; Quest. in Exod. II. 90; Leg. all. III. 96-103; De somn. I. 206; De plant. 27). What is also interesting is that for Philo Moses' obedience to the command produced what were in themselves the "archetypes" (Leg. all. III. 102).

similarly depicts, through prophetic vision, things to come. Are they for him *already* present in heaven? Or are they entirely future (chaps. 21f.)? Such questions may be ultimately unanswerable. Yet 1 Pet 1:4f. ("kept in heaven . . . ready to be revealed in the last time") shows how common is the idea within Jewish-Christian circles *which have no demonstrable contact with current philosophical systems* that things may "exist" in heaven while awaiting the actual manifestation in history.[27] Heb 8:5b (Exod 25:40) could be said to contain *both* horizontal and vertical modes, but this needs to be defined very precisely. Both types of thinking are ways of relating the transcendent to the earthly, and in a mature theological perspective it may be that both are necessary. Based upon the other evidence for ὑπόδειγμα and σκιά, Heb 10:1 ("the law has a shadow of the good things to come") *and* Heb 8:5a ("they serve a shadowy outline of the heavenly") could provide the "horizontal"; Heb 8:5b (Moses' vision on the mount) then forms the point where "vertical" and "horizontal," as it were, intersect. The τόπος on the mount may well be considered "vertical" because, even in Moses' time, it existed within God,[28] and "horizontal" because it is yet substantially future. It would be impossible to reduce both frames to a single scheme which does justice to both without at the same time giving one or the other primacy. *Auctor* probably is sophisticated enough to know the value of including both. Thus his claim that Moses made an outline and shadow of the heavenly good things to come (temporal frame) is *based upon* the fact that, even in OT times, the τόπος existed within God because it was destined by him to be the place of Christ's self-offering. There is nothing *necessarily* "Platonic" or "philosophical" in this. Like John of

---

Bezalel produced *copies* (μίμημα) from, as it were, a shadow (σκιά). "For Philo Exod. 25:40 said something not about the relationship between a heavenly tabernacle and an earthly tabernacle copied from it, but about archetypal images, themselves copied from a heavenly pattern, which form the realities which the objects of the phenomenal world only imperfectly reflect (Williamson, *Philo and Hebrews*, 561). Philo thus uses Exod 25:40 for a positive purpose, to show the heavenly status of Moses, while *Auctor* uses it negatively to show the inferiority of the earthly sanctuary to the heavenly. It would be difficult to imagine how *Auctor* could be further removed from Philo at this point. It is characteristic of *Auctor* to take OT events interpreted by Philo in spatial terms and make them refer primarily to questions of present and future.

[27]"When the Jew wished to designate something as pre-destined, he spoke of it as already existing in heaven" (E. G. Selwyn, *The First Epistle of St. Peter* [London, 1946] 124). "The notion of blessings kept in reserve in heaven (Mt xxv.34), to be brought out at the decisive moment, was thoroughly Jewish, being familiar both to apocalyptic (I En. xlvii.7; lviii.5; Asc. Is. viii.25f.) and to the rabbis (SB, III, 762; IV, 1146f.; 1156f.)" (J. N. D. Kelly, *A Commentary on the Epistles of Peter and Jude* [London, 1969] 51f.). On 1 Pet 1:20—"predestined before the foundation of the world, but made manifest at the end of times for your sake"—cf. J. D. G. Dunn (*Christology in the Making* [London, 1980] 236f.) who argues against Kelly that the idea is not so much that Christ was actually pre-existent but that certain things were pre-destined for Christ. Cf. also 4 Ezra 7:28, 12:32, 13:32, 51f., etc. In 13:35 reference is made to "the Messiah whom God Most High has kept until the end of days, who will arise from the posterity of David." It is probable that here one sees a thoroughly Jewish description of eschatological realities which "pre-exist" within God's purposes while awaiting appearance in actual history. There is nothing distinctly "Greek" or "philosophical" in such a view.

[28]Cf. Barrett, "The Eschatology of Hebrews," 381; and W. F. Howard, "The Epistle to the Hebrews," *Int* 5 (1971) 82 ("The eternal realities are in heaven in the mind of God").

Patmos and other NT writers who are sensitive to the problem of integrating time and eternity, *Auctor* needs no recourse to Plato's solution. John of Patmos likewise can speak of things happening "from the foundation of the world" (13:8) in what appears to be a thoroughly Jewish context. With this in view it becomes easier to admit that apocalyptic writers and rabbis may similarly have thought in terms of "a tent prepared from the foundation of the world" (see below) while at the same time knowing that, in a time framework, the manifestation of such things is put off until the future.[29] In Hebrews what Moses "sees" may thus have been both "vertical" (existence within God's purposes) and horizontal ("the good things to come"). There is nothing in either approach which cannot be explained from what are essentially Jewish ideas. To attempt to emphasize a "horizontal" approach to the exclusion of a "vertical" approach, or vice verse, would be futile, unnecessary and damaging.

III
What Is Auctor's "True Tent"?

The answer to this question has in general followed two main approaches: (a) those scholars who view the heavenly tent as a metaphor for something else, such as (1) the whole cosmos;[30] (2) heaven;[31] (3) the eucharistic body of Christ;[32] (4) the glorified body of Christ;[33] (5) the church as the body of Christ;[34] or (6) an event or events, such as the death of Christ on earth and his ministry in heaven;[35] (b) those scholars for whom the heavenly tent is not reduced to mean something else, but for whom there is in heaven an actual tent, which in essence was what Moses was permitted to see on the mountain (whether in blue print or in substance). This group itself may be divided as follows: (1) There are those such as Farrar[36] who interpret the tent Platonically ("the ideal or genuine Tabernacle is the *eternal uncreated archetype* as contrasted with its antitype (or 'imitation') made with hands"). (2) There are those such as Windisch,[37] Barrett,[38] and Michel,[39] who claim that the heavenly tent is the eschatological sanctuary of Jewish

---

[29]It is difficult at times to know whether such statements refer to the earthly sanctuary or to their heavenly counterparts (see below, n. 81).

[30]Cf. Cody, *Heavenly Sanctuary and Liturgy,* 18, who, assuming that the "holy tent" of Wis 9:8 is "the whole cosmos," claims that "Wis. 9:8 affords the best background for an understanding of the notion of the heavenly sanctuary in Hebrews."

[31]See below.

[32]Cf. James Swetnam, "On the Imagery and Significance of Heb. 9,11," *CBQ* 38 (1966) 153ff,; and "'The Greater and More Perfect Tent.' A Contribution to the Discussion of Hebrews 9,11," *Biblica* 47 (1966) 91ff.

[33]Cf. A. Vanhoye, "'Par la Tent plus grande et plus parfaite . . .' (Hé 9,11)," *Biblica* 46 (1965) 1-28.

[34]Cf. e.g., Westcott, *Hebrews,* 260.

[35]See below.

[36]F.W. Farrar, *The Epistle of Paul the Apostle to the Hebrews* (Cambridge, 1902) 145.

[37]H. Windisch, *Der Hebräerbrief* (Tübingen, 1913) 113 ("Hebr hält an dem Realismus der Apokalyptik fest").

[38]Barrett, "The Eschatology of Hebrews," 383ff.

[39]O. Michel, *Der Brief an die Hebräer,* 12 Auflage (Göttingen, 1966) 285f., passim.

apocalyptic (although for apparent tensions in Barrett's position, see below); (3) There are those such as Fritsch,[40] who claim that *Auctor*'s arguments need not be explained by *any* current tradition but are simply the result of the typology found in the priestly sections in the OT (in which the view prevailed that earthly things have their corresponding heavenly entities).

Such divergent options are hardly a recent development. In some quarters of the Graeco-Roman world there was a clearly defined movement towards a spiritualization of the concept of temple (e.g., Philo), while in others the emphasis remained upon an actual temple (whether "new," "heavenly," or both).[41] Accordingly, views of a "heavenly" temple followed one or the other line; for some it must be a symbol for something else (e.g., the cosmos), while for others it meant that there was an actual temple *in* heaven which corresponds in most or all details to the earthly temple.[42] Today one is faced with the choice of which background best interprets Hebrews. Should his "true tent" be reduced so that it is a metaphor for yet something else (as in the case of Philo and other "Hellenistic" Jews)? Or, when *Auctor* says that Jesus has entered a tent which is "not of this creation" (9:11), does he mean that heaven itself contains its own sanctuary? This choice will ultimately determine which background, the Philonic or Jewish-apocalyptic, will best explain what *Auctor* means when he speaks of "the true tent." In order to evaluate which option is the more likely, further points will need to be clarified.

(a) A "reductionist" approach to the heavenly sanctuary is often assumed without argument. For many it is unthinkable that what corresponds to *Auctor*'s earthly tabernacle could be located in any place, even if that place is within heaven.[43] It must, therefore, be a "correspondence of the idea embodied, not of the form of their embodiment. All types are the shadowing forth of something that *cannot be grasped.*"[44] In this case Moses' tent is actually a symbol of a symbol. Such an approach is more conducive to a background of Philo than to the apocalyptic and rabbinic traditions. While Philo's view of the true temple is difficult to pin down (his writings reflect both Platonic and Stoic

---

[40]Fritsch ("ΤΟ 'ΑΝΤΙΤΥΠΟΝ," 106 and n. 1) claims that the typology of Heb 8-10 rests "not in Alexandrian philosophy" nor "apocaylptic visions," but rather in the Near Eastern heavenly-earthly correspondence brought into the OT through the Babylonian exile.

[41]On the notion of the new temple in the OT, apocrypha and pseudepigrapha, cf., e.g., McKelvey, *The New Temple*, 9ff.; and A. B. Kolenkow, "The Fall of the Temple and the Coming of the End: The Spectrum and Process of Apocalyptic Argument in 2 Baruch and Other Authors," *SBL 1982 Seminar Papers* (Chico, CA, 1982) 243ff. On the existence of a temple *in heaven* in the pseudepigrapha, rabbis, and Qumran, cf. McKelvey, 28ff.

[42]"There were thus opposing tendencies in the Judaism of Jesus' time: the spiritualizing of the cultus, and the belief in a restored or new cultus, with the latter acting as a kind of brake on the former" (McKelvey, 56f.).

[43]Cf. Westcott, *Hebrews*, 258f., for whom "it is obvious that all images of local circumscription must be laid aside. . . . The spiritual Tabernacle must not be defined by the limitations which belong to 'this creation.' . . . We must look for some spiritual antitype to the local sanctuary." Westcott subsequently defines this "spiritual antitype" as the body of Christ in heaven in which "the redeemed and perfected hosts [are] made one in Christ as His body." This, of course, is a Paulinizing of *Auctor*'s argument, importing as it does Pauline notions of the church as the body of Christ and the particular use of "tent" made in 2 Cor 5:1ff.

[44]E.C. Wickham, *The Epistle to the Hebrews* (London, 1910) 167 (italics mine).

influences), it is the Stoic spiritualizing tendencies which predominate. Thus the "pattern" on which the earthly temple is modeled can be either the soul[45] or the universe (cf. De somn. I. 215: "For there are, as is evident, two temples of God: one of them this universe . . . and the other the rational soul. . . ."). His favorite use of the temple, however, is as a symbol of the universe (cf. De spec. leg. I. 66, where the whole universe is God's temple, with "the most sacred part of all existence, even heaven" as its sanctuary (cf. also De vit. M. II. 101f.; Qu. in Exod. II. 91f.). Within this sanctuary or upper part (νεώς) are placed immortal beings (De somn. I. 34), with angels for priests (De spec. leg. I. 66) and the Logos for high priest (De somn. I. 215). Such cosmic symbolism for the earthly temple is by no means restricted to Philo, however; it is seen also in Josephus (Ant. III. 123, 180ff.; War V. 212f.), with details so different as to indicate that the interpretation was both widespread and independent.[46] A number of interpreters, including G. B. Gray,[47] Eccles[48] and Montefiore,[49] have argued to varying degrees for such a cosmic allegorizing in Hebrews (see below).

Any "spiritualized" interpretation of the true sanctuary in Hebrews, however, inevitably rests upon a particular exegesis of four extremely ambiguous passages: (1) 9:8, where, as just noted, "the outer tent" is symbolic of an entire age; (2) 9:11, where "the greater and more perfect tent" is viewed as a symbol for yet something else (e.g., the body of Christ, the church, etc.); (3) 9:24, where the sanctuary seems to be explained, not as an actual structure *within* heaven (or the heavenly city) but as "heaven itself"; and (4) 10:20, where the curtain of the heavenly tent is felt by some to be spiritualized as the flesh of Jesus. These will be briefly treated in turn.

(1) The statement of 9:8f. that the first tent is a "parable of the present time" has often been taken to indicate a spiritualized or cosmic temple in Hebrews. Sowers,[50] again, claims that behind it stands Philo, for whom the holy of holies is "heaven" and the Jewish priest's entrance is "the mystic soaring of the mind into heaven" (De somn. II. 231-33; De gig. 52; De mig. Abr. 104). MacRae,[51] on the other hand, along with Montefiore,[52] interprets the passage as *combining* "an apocalyptic time scheme with the

---

[45]"Apart from the κόσμος, the λογικὴ ψυχή, the νοῦς, the λογισμός, the διάνοια of the wise are called the θεοῦ οἶκος, the ἱερὸν ἅγιον, Som. II.248; I.149; Virt. 188" (G. Schrenk, "ἱερός, κτλ.," *TDNT* 3. 241).

[46]Josephus (III.181) focuses on the three parts of the tabernacle constructed by Moses: the first two are the earth and sea, accessible to men; the third is reserved "for God alone."

[47]Gray, "The Heavenly Temple and the Heavenly Altar," 538.

[48]Eccles, "The Purpose of the Hellenistic Patterns," 216.

[49]Montefiore, *Hebrews*, 136f.

[50]S. G. Sowers, *The Hermeneutics of Philo and Hebrews* (Zurich, 1965) 106 (cf. also 94f.).

[51]MacRae, "Heavenly Temple and Eschatology," 189.

[52]Montefiore, *Hebrews*, 137. On Heb 9:9, see below. For Sowers, *Hermeneutics*, the phrase ἅγιον κοσμικόν in Heb 9:1 "suggests the writer was thinking of the cosmic symbolism of the temple as expounded by Josephus and Philo." The phrase, however, probaby means, simply, "earthly temple." Cody, who elsewhere thinks the heavenly tent of Hebrews to be closer to the apocalyptic and rabbinic schools (*Heavenly Sanctuary and Liturgy*, 36), is appalled by "the anthropomorphisms and phantasies" of the latter (26) and feels that one can "find echoes" of the "world temple" in Hebrews (35).

Hellenistic mode of heavenly temple symbolism" in which the inner shrine equals "heaven" and the outer shrine equals "this age":

> By this the Holy Spirit indicates that the way into the sanctuary is not yet opened, as long as the outer tabernacle (τῆς πρώτης σκηνῆς) is still standing (which [ἥτις, i.e., ἡ πρώτη σκηνή] is symbolic [a παραβολή] for the present age).

For MacRae and Montefiore Moses' tent, rather than pointing to any actual sanctuary in heaven has a dual function: it is a "parable" or "symbol" of heaven and earth *and* the old and new ages. Yet, as with the other three passages to be considered, *any* interpretation of 9:8f. is dependent upon certain crucial decisions. (a) There is ambiguity in the use of πρῶτος in chap. 9. In v. 1 it is used for the first and second σκηνή, whereas in vv. 2, 6 the first and second σκηνή must mean the outer and inner tent. Which idea controls the sense of πρῶτος in v. 8? Is the "first tent" the entire Mosaic structure, or is it only the outer court? Sowers, Montefiore, MacRae, Westcott, Nairne, Peake, Buchanan, McKelvey and Michaelis[53] all assume it to be the latter, while Moffatt, Cody, Bruce and Héring, among many others, assume it to be the former. Westcott feels it is outrageous to suppose that *Auctor* suddenly changed his meaning from vv. 6f. to v. 8; Héring, on the other hand, claims that "this takes no account of the facility with which our author sometimes manipulates expressions with various senses." On Westcott's reckoning, as long as the outer court is recognized as the proper place of priestly activity (i.e., "has its standing") the people remain barred from the goal of worship; in Héring's understanding, the ascension of Christ into the true sanctuary robs the entire old center of worship of it "standing." In theory *either* interpretation is possible. But there seems something forced about the Westcott logic in this case; elsewhere when *Auctor* juxtaposes the old with the new, he deals with entire entities, whether priesthood (7:11), earthly sanctuary (9:24) or covenant itself (8:13). This seems to suggest that in v. 8 he does the same; i.e., he is looking back to the usage of 9:1 and signifies the passing away of the whole structure, the "first tent." This interpretation of 9:8 would involve no necessary relation to the cosmic temple symbolism of Philo. (b) The meaning of the phrase "which is a parable for the present age" is likewise ambiguous. As with the use of μέλλω in 2:5, is it "the present age" from the standpoint of *Moses* ("the time then present"—AV) or of *Auctor* ("the time now present"—RSV, NEB)? In the former case it would mean that the barrier between the two tents (or the entire tent itself) symbolized Jewish lack of access to the presence of God; in the latter it is a symbolic pointer ("prefiguration") to the future work of Christ as the high priest who achieves *real* access. It should be observed, however, that in neither case is the existence of a sanctuary *in* heaven precluded.

(2) The interpretation of 9:11 is so contentious that it would be hazardous to build *any* theory of the heavenly tent upon it. The old view of Oecumenius that the "greater and more perfect tent" is the body of Christ, the sacrifice of which allows him (διά) to enter the presence of God (9:12), has been almost universally rejected by all except

---

[53]Michaelis, "σκηνή, κτλ.," 376.

Roman Catholic scholars.[54] An equation of the true tent with the church[55] is likewise difficult. A much more serious proposal concerns the apparent division, if the διά of 9:11 is taken *locally*,[56] of the true tent into two sections. This could be used, however, to argue in several directions: (a) It could show that the true tent is spiritualized as the heavenly world in general. No actual tent *in* heaven is meant. Christ passes through the outer tent (the cosmological "heavens" of 4:14) and enters the holy place (the "axiological"[57] heaven of God's presence, 9:12). The true tent is thus a symbol for the upper regions. This comes close to Philo's cosmic allegorizing of the temple, in which the outer precincts represent the sense-perceptible (αἰσθητός) realm (including "the heavens"), while the holy place is the unchanging heavenly realm of ideas where God properly dwells (Qu. in Exod. 91-96).[58] (b) The twofold division of 9:11 indicates that for *Auctor* there exists in heaven an actual tent which corresponds structurally to the twofold tent built by Moses.[59] Thus "the heavenly sanctuary, too, has a front part which is greater and more perfect as compared with the tabernacle, but which is still to be distinguished from the true sanctuary, the holy of holies."[60]

These somewhat clear-cut options are complicated by a third possibility. If the διά is taken not locally, but instrumentally,[61] the thought of 9:11 would be more general. Christ enters the presence of God, not *by means of* any earthly tent, but *by means of* the true tent.[62] This would provide no actual information as to what the true tent *is* or which tradition *Auctor* reflects. Heb 9:11 is thus shaky ground upon which to mount any particular case.

---

[54]For this interpretation see Cody, *Heavenly Sanctuary and Liturgy*, 158ff., and the articles by J. Swetnam (see above, n. 32). Michaelis, "σκηνή, κτλ.," 377; J. Héring, *The Epistle to the Hebrews* (London, 1970) 77 n. 21; and R. Williamson, "The Eucharist and the Epistle to the Hebrews," *NTS* 21 (1975) 305, argue against this view.

[55]Cf. e.g., F. F. Bruce, *The Epistle to the Hebrews* (London, 1964) 199f., and "The Kerygma of Hebrews," *Int* 23 (1969) 3-19, 10. Bruce connects the "tent" of Heb 9:11 with the "house" of 3:3ff., noting that the consciences of the people of the house and the true tent are both connected with the term καθαρίζω (cp. 9:14; 10:2 with 9:22f.), but this does not necessarily require equation, especially if καθαρίζω in 9:23 means "inaugurate" (see below). L. Floor, "The General Priesthood of Believers in the Epistle to the Hebrews," *Neotestamentica* 5 (1971) 75, likewise argues that the true tent is redefined as a house (10:21), a meeting (10:25), and a city (12:22), leaving the conclusion that the congregation "is another name for the heavenly sanctuary."

[56]For the local interpretation of διά in 9:11, cf. Héring, *Hebrews*, 176, and MacRae, "Heavenly Temple and Eschatology," 187.

[57]Using Cody's well-publicized distinction.

[58]Cf. MacRae, "Heavenly Temple and Eschatology," 185.

[59]See, e.g., Michaelis, "σκηνή, κτλ.," 376f. Michaelis carries the correspondence between the two tents to the point of denying that God is actually "present" in the heavenly holy of holies, since it does not contain his throne (377)! This, of course, is an error, since in Judaism God's throne is always symbolically present in the sanctuary.

[60]Ibid., 377.

[61]Westcott, *Hebrews*, 258; cf. Montefiore, *Hebrews*, 151f.

[62]Just as, in 1:1f, God speaks *by means of* (instrumental), not *in* (local) his Son.

(3) The wording of 9:24 is also ambiguous. This text is commonly used as proof that for *Auctor* the heavenly tent = heaven: "For the first time the heavenly sanctuary is identified with heaven itself, a key point for understanding our author's argument."[63] Bruce[64] draws a parallel with Rev 4-7, where "heaven itself is the temple of God." Barrett, who has chosen to trace the true tent of Hebrews to the eschatological temple of Jewish apocalyptic,[65] does not make this equation (although he does say that the sanctuary has existed eternally *in* heaven). The problem of whether a heavenly temple is *in* heaven or is to be equated *with* heaven is not confined to the interpretation of Hebrews; it confronts one as well in the Near Eastern texts.[66] An equation of the heavenly tent in Hebrews with "heaven itself" is based solely on the assumption that in 9:24 *Auctor* intends this phrase to be the precise equivalent of the heavenly tent. It is more probable, however, that, rather than defining what the tent is, the phrase indicates the general realm in which Christ ministers *as opposed to* the earthly priests. *Auctor* may well be looking back in this verse to his earlier statement in 8:4: "Now if he were *on earth* he would not be a priest." "On earth" and "heaven itself" would be synecdoche in which the whole ("earth," "heaven") stands for the part (the earthly and heavenly sanctuaries).[67] This explanation would render 9:24 a dubious text to use against the existence for *Auctor* of a tent *in* heaven.[68]

(4) As W. G. Johnsson[69] has put it, if "flesh" defines "curtain" in 10:20 so as to read "through the curtain, that is, through his flesh" (RSV), one will have "unambiguous evidence of a 'spiritualizing' intent on the part of the author" regarding the heavenly tent. This is what Moffatt claims: "He *allegorizes* the veil here as the flesh of Christ."[70] The difficulty with this assertion is that there is no consensus among scholars as to how 10:20 would be translated. Should the phrase τοῦτ ἔστιν τῆς σαρκὸς αὐτοῦ attach to the term ὁδός, or should it attach to καταπέτασμα? Various grammatical and

---

[63]Montefiore, *Hebrews*, 160. Cf. also Eccles, "Purpose of the Hellenistic Patterns," 215; L. Goppelt, "τύπος, κτλ.," *TDNT* 8. 258 n .69; H. Traub and G. von Rad, "οὐρανός, κτλ.," *TDNT* 5. 528; McKelvey, *The New Temple*, 149; and R. Williamson, "Platonism and Hebrews," *SJT* 16 (1963) 420.

[64]Bruce, *Hebrews*, 166f. n. 32. G. B. Gray, on the other hand, uses Rev 4-7 as evidence (against Philo and Hebrews) for a temple *in* heaven!

[65]Barrett, "Eschatology of Hebrews," 386.

[66]Cf. e.g., Gray (396 n. 2), who, in interpreting the Code of Hammurabi, points out that the phrase *šu-ba-at ša-ma-i* may mean wither "dwelling *in* heaven" or "dwelling place which *is* heaven."

[67]The phenomenon of synecdoche or "enlarged reference" is a common occurrence in the NT. Cf. Matt 26:12, where "body" stands for "head"; Acts 21:28, where "temple" means only that part of the temple forbidden to Gentiles; and Heb 13:24, where "Italy" probably means "Rome." In Hebrews one of the clearest uses of this occurs in 7:11, where the "levitical priesthood" stands for the entire OT system.

[68]Williamson ("Eucharist and Hebrews," 36) seems to admit this possibility as well (". . . The greater and more perfect tent which is (in?) heaven itself. . . ."). Cf. also Traub and von Rad, "οὐρανός, κτλ.," 528: it "does not clearly say whether one enters God's presence in the heaven or whether this heaven is in some sense identical with God's presence. . . ."

[69]W.G. Johnsson, "The Cultus of Hebrews in Twentieth-Century Scholarship," *ET* 89 (1978) 107.

[70]James Moffatt, *A Critical and Exegetical Commentary on the Epistle to the Hebrews* (Edinburgh, 1924) 143 (italics mine).

theological points have been argued on both sides. The *grammatical* problem of taking "flesh" with "way" (i.e., the distance between the clauses and *Auctor's* apparent habit in τοῦτ' ἔστιν clauses elsewhere of matching his cases)[71] must be regarded as powerful. Yet the *theological* problem of taking "flesh" with "curtain" is perhaps even more formidable. It is often noted that this would involve the notion, unprecedented in the NT, that Christ's flesh forms a barrier to the presence of God. But the problem is greater than this, for it also requires the grotesque corollary that Christ's flesh is a barrier which *he himself had to penetrate, and which he helps others to penetrate.* Although the evidence is thus somewhat ambiguous, it remains difficult for many to overcome the theological and logical dilemma of taking "flesh" with "curtain."[72] In any case 10:20 is too uncertain to be used to argue for any "mystical-allegorical"[73] approach by *Auctor* to the heavenly tent.

A notably elaborate spiritualization of the heavenly sanctuary in Hebrews is provided by U. Luck.[74] For Luck the heavenly tent involves both Calvary and the priestly ministry in heaven (and hence spans "heaven" and "earth"). Luck's view has been accepted by, among others, McKelvey[75] and Floor.[76] Floor goes on to assert that "the church on earth forms together with the 'throne of grace,' or the inner sanctuary, the true tent into which believers can enter. . . ."[77] Again, such an interpretation would be similar to that of Philo, for whom the true tent is composed of two parts, earth (the outer court) and heaven (the holy place). This could make *Auctor's* view an interesting modification of the cosmic temple of either Philo or Josephus. But inevitably much of Luck's exegesis depends upon his interpretation of the four ambiguous passages above. To this it should be added that it is very difficult for anyone to relate what happens in the heavenly tent to what happens at the cross. Simply stated, the problem is that, if the atonement is transacted in the heavenly sanctuary "once and for all," one is dealing at that point with time and not eternity. But what relation is there between that and the *cross?* Does Christ

---

[71]Cf. 2:14, 7:5 and 13:15 (accus.-accus.); 9:11 and 11:16 (gen.-gen.).

[72]Those who *disassociate* the veil from Christ's flesh include Westcott, *Hebrews,* 322; Nairne, *The Epistle of Priesthood* (Edinburgh, 1913) 381; Sowers, *Hermeneutics,* 108 n. 50; Williamson, "Eucharist and Hebrews," 307 n. 1 (although cp. his earlier *The Epistle to the Hebrews* [Epworth, 1964] 100, where he connects "veil" with "flesh"); C. Spicq, *L'Épitre aux Hébreux,* II (Paris, 1952) 315f.; C. Mauer, "πρόσφατος, προσφάτως," *TDNT* 6. 767; A. H. McNeile, *New Testament Teaching in the Light of St. Paul's* (Cambridge, 1923) 229; and the NEB. Among those, in addition to Moffatt, who feel that the veil *is* Christ's flesh are F. F. Bruce, *Hebrews,* 247f.; McKelvey, *The New Temple,* 150; N. H. Young, ΤΟΥΤ' ΕΣΤΙΝ ΤΗΣ ΣΑΡΚΟΣ ΑΥΤΟΥ (Heb. X:20): Apposition, Dependent or Explicative," *NTS* 20 (1974) 100ff.; E. Schweizer et al., "σάρξ, κτλ.," *TDNT* 7. 142; W. Manson, *The Epistle to the Hebrews: An Historical and Theological Reconstruction* (London, 1951) 67f.; N. Dahl, "A New and Living Way. The Approach to God according to Hebrews 10:19-25," *Int* 5 (1951) 405; and E. Käsemann, *Das wandernde Gottesvolk* (Göttingen, 1961[4]) 146f.

[73]The phrase is that of W. Manson, *The Epistle to the Hebrews: An Historical and Theological Reconstruction* (London, 1951) 67.

[74]U. Luck, "Himmlisches und irdisches Geschehen im Hebräerbrief," *NT* 6 (1963) 207ff.

[75]McKelvey, *The New Temple,* 149, 154, 205.

[76]Floor, "Priesthood," 74-78.

[77]Ibid., 74f.

die on earth and *then, subsequent to his exaltation,* make the sacrifice in heaven? While this question is difficult to answer, the fact that for *Auctor* the death occurs outside the camp, and hence *outside the tent* (13:12f.)—with the blood subsequently brought in—makes it unlikely that in *Auctor's* understanding the true tent can be equated *even partly* with the sacrifice on earth.

Those approaches which view the heavenly tent in Hebrews as a symbol for something else therefore fall short of proof. Consequently one must look to the second possibility, that of an actual tent *in* heaven.

(b) Among those who argue that for *Auctor* there is an actual sanctuary in heaven, a thoroughgoing Platonic approach may be dismissed immediately. Farrar's statement that the heavenly tent is an *"uncreated* eternal archetype" which was copied by Moses is ruled out by 8:2: there it is said that at some point the true tent was "pitched" (ἔπηξεν, cf. Num 24:6LXX) by God. This could have been said by Philo, but not by Plato. It is equally unlikely, in the light of the evidence to be considered below, that *Auctor* is developing his thought in chaps. 8-10 solely from the priestly sections of the OT. It remains, then, to look at the evidence for the third option, the apocalyptic tradition.

It is not difficult to trace the Jewish belief in a new temple to its origins in the failure of the earthly temple.[78] Dan 8:14, 2 Macc 2:4-8 and Tob 14:5 show already the hope for a new, more glorious sanctuary to come. According to Jub 1:17, 28 God himself will build it in Zion, while in Sib 3:290 and Targ. Isa. 53:5 it is built by the Son of Man and the Messiah, respectively.[79] Eventually this hope for a new temple became fused with a growing interest in a heavenly temple. Now, perhaps under the influence of such OT texts as Isa 6 and Ezek 1, God is assigned his own temple in heaven. The earliest such reference is felt[80] to occur in T. Levi: "And thereupon the angel opened to me the gates of heaven, and I saw the holy temple, and upon a throne of glory the Most High" (5:1). Chap. 3 describes a heavenly cultus, complete with holy of holies and angels who minister (λειτουργοῦντες) and perform expiation (ἐξιλασκόμενοι) for the sins of ignorance of the righteous. In the book of Wisdom pre-existence may [81] also be ascribed to the heavenly sanctuary: "Thou has given command to build a temple on thy holy mountain, and an altar in the city of thy habitation, a copy (μίμημα) of the holy tent which thou didst prepare from the beginning" (9:8). This interest in a heavenly sanctuary was taken up by apocalyptic and fused to the notion of the new Jerusalem. According to 4 Ezra, "The city that is now invisible shall appear" (7:26); it "shall come and be made manifest to all men, *prepared and builded*" (13:36; cf. also 8:52, 9:26-10:57). Now the site of the old Jerusalem is no longer indispensable to the future salvation.[82] In 2 Baruch, likewise,

---

[78]Cf. McKelvey, *The New Temple,* 9ff., 40f.

[79]Cf. O. Michel, "ναός," *TDNT* 4. 889 n. 36.

[80]Cf. R. H. Charles, *The Apocrypha and Pseudepigrapha of the Old Testament* (Oxford, 1913) 2. 307; G. B. Gray, "Heavenly Temple and Sacrifice," 387; and Montefiore, *Hebrews,* 136. Charles, however, in *The Apocalypse of Baruch Translated from the Syriac* (London, 1896) 6, claims 1 Enoch 90:28 to be the oldest reference.

[81]Contra Sowers (*Hermeneutics,* 108), who implies that, according to Wis 9:8, the Jerusalem temple is a copy of Moses' tent. But Wis 9:8 is usually taken to refer to a heavenly tent. Cf. James Moffatt, *Hebrews,* 106 (it is "the eternal archetype"); MacRae, "Heavenly Temple and Eschatology," 182f.; and H. A. A. Kennedy, *The Theology of the Epistles* (London, 1919) 191.

[82]G. Fohrer and E. Lohse, "Σιών, κτλ.," *TDNT* 7. 326.

a "Jerusalem above" also appears to be "the Jerusalem to come" (4:1-7, 32:4): it is the city which was

> prepared beforehand here from the time when I took counsel to make Para-
> dise, and showed it to Adam before he sinned . . . and again also I showed it
> to Moses on Mount Sinai when I showed him the likeness of the tabernacle
> and all its vessels. And now, behold, it is preserved with me, as also Paradise
> (4:3-6).[83]

There are several especially interesting things about the 2 Baruch text: (1) It seems to reflect Ezekiel's vision of the temple-city, only now Moses is shown both the city and the tabernacle[84] (a transfer similar to what I have suggested for Heb 8:5a).[85] (2) Ezekiel said nothing about pre-existence; some form of this, however, is now attributed both to the city and the sanctuary. (3) The "city," "the tabernacle," and "Paradise"[86] all seem to be independent but related entities; they are prepared by God before or at creation (i.e., they were shown to Adam); yet they are in some sense "preserved" with God for a certain time. Here one has access to yet another thoroughly Jewish text which may shed light precisely upon those features of Hebrews which have previously been described as "Platonic."[87]

---

[83]The translation is that of Charles; cp. the translation of A. F. J. Klijn in *The Old Testament Pseudepigrapha: Apocalyptic Literature and Testaments*, ed J. H. Charlesworth (Garden City, NY, 1983) 622.

[84]Fritsch, "TO 'ΑΝΤΙΤΥΠΟΝ," 104.

[85]Cf. L. D. Hurst, "How 'Platonic' are Hebrews viii.5 and ix.23f.?" *JTS* n.s. 34 (1983) 156ff.

[86]But cf. Charles (*Apocalypse of Baruch*, 7), who is uncertain whether this "paradise" is a pre-existent heavenly paradise or the earthly paradise into which Adam is put.

[87]Although the limits of space do not permit it here, much more exploration needs to be done with regard to the parallels which seem to exist between Hebrews and 2 Baruch. Note, e.g., the following: (a) Baruch speaks of God making angels "of flame and fire" (2:16; cf. Heb 1:7), and of "innumerable angels" (48:10, 59:11; cf. Heb 12:22); (b) Baruch speaks of God calling "from the beginning of the world that which did not yet exist" (21:4; cp. Heb 11:3); (c) God is repeatedly called "Most High" (17:1, 64:8, 67:7, 69:2, etc.; cp. Heb 7:1); (d) Baruch depicts God as "shaking" the created universe (32:1 and 59:3; cp. Heb 12:26ff.), a process which will culminate in the revelation of the new Jerusalem, "renewed in glory and perfected forevermore" (32:4); (e) Baruch uses a Syriac phrase for "the consummation of the age" which might be rendered into Greek as συντελεία τῶν αἰώνιων (59:4, 8; cp Heb 9:26); (f) Baruch speaks of land which fails to produce vegetation (22:5f.; cp. Heb 6:7ff.); (g) Baruch speaks of the souls of the elect gathered in a great multitude (30:2; cf. Heb 12:1, 23); (h) Baruch makes a distinction between that which "abides" and that which "passes away" (44:11ff.; cp. Heb 12:26ff.); (i) Baruch says "the judge will come, and will not tarry" (48:39; cp. Heb 10:37); (j) Baruch, as noted above, speaks of God showing to Moses the heavenly Jerusalem (4:3-6) and "the pattern of Zion and its measures, which was to be made in the pattern of the sanctuary of the present time" (59:4; cp. Heb 8:5 as understood in my article "How 'Platonic' are Heb viii.5 and ix.23f.?" 162ff.; (k) Baruch speaks of the dedication of the sanctuary through many blood offerings (61:2; cp. Heb 9:23 as interpreted above); (l) Baruch shows an interest in God's throne (54:13, 59:3, etc.; cp. Heb 1:8, 4:16, 8:1 and 12:2); (m) Baruch speaks of the recipients of salvation as those who "inherit" it (44:13; cp. Heb 1:14, 9:15),

Such texts as 2 Baruch, Wisdom and 4 Ezra indicate a process at work in which "Old Testament texts which state that the tabernacle and the temple of Jerusalem were built according to a pattern are now taken to imply the existence of a heavenly archetype."[88] As time went on, this heavenly counterpart became increasingly "realistic."[89]

It is possible that this belief in a heavenly sanctuary was further stimulated by popularized Platonic notions in addition to early Jewish interpretations (or misinterpretations)[90] of texts such as Isa 6 (which were now felt to refer to a temple *in heaven*).[91] But this would be very difficult to *prove*. MacRae hesitates "to minimize the extent of hellenistic influence upon all forms of ancient Judaism, including the apocalyptic tradition,"[92] but McKelvey observes somewhat more cautiously that "the literature of Palestinian Judaism bears little if any trace of Platonism."[93] The central point to be made is that in the apocalyptic tradition one has access to literature which, coming from roughly the same period as Hebrews,[94] speaks of a "pre-existent heavenly Jerusalem" in a milieu which *at that time* was probably having little or no direct contact with Platonism. To this should be added perhaps the most important piece of evidence. Ethiopian Enoch speaks of a new Jerusalem and temple (14:16-18, 20, 26:1f.; chaps. 85-90), but in 90:28 it is made clear that this city and temple do not actually pre-exist: "All its pillars were *new*, and its decorations were new and greater than those of the old house which He had pulled down." According to Fohrer and Lohse,[95] "here the new Jerusalem is not depicted as a pre-existent city but there is reference to its origin in the act of God alone." In other words, the fact that it is built by God, not man, does not automatically mean that it already actually exists in heaven; its creation is put off to the future. Such texts show that during this period (1 Enoch, except for the Similitudes, is normally viewed as pre-Christian), there was something of a ferment in which opinions differed as to how the heavenly city and temple should be understood: before its consummation, does it "pre-exist," or is

---

and their inheritance is defined as "the world to come" (44:15; cp. Heb 2:5); the enemies of God, on the other hand, are "burned" (44:15, 48:39, 64:7; cp. Heb 6:8, 12:29); and (n) Baruch distinguishes between that which is present (which is "nothing") and that which is future, which shall not pass away: "that is what we shall hope for" (44:11; cp. Heb 11:1ff., which R. Williamson correctly interprets as indicating primarily faith in the unseen future (*Philo and the Epistle to the Hebrews* [Leiden, 1970] 309ff.). Such parallels are not of the same weight, and in no case is the wording close enough to suggest literary dependence. However, they do indicate that such texts as 2 Baruch (and 4 Ezra) constitute an extremely important—and neglected—Jewish apocalyptic background of Hebrews which might explain many features previously thought to be "Hellenistic" and "philosophical."

[88]McKelvey, *The New Temple*, 33 n. 1.

[89]Cody, *Heavenly Sanctuary and Liturgy*, 21.

[90]Cf. G. B. Gray, "Heavenly Temple and Altar," 545f.

[91]Ibid.

[92]MacRae, "Heavenly Temple," 184.

[93]McKelvey, *The New Temple*, 27. Yet McKelvey's supposition that "the NT writers were influenced" by Platonic ideas is prompted largely by his quasi-Platonic reading of Hebrews (cf. especially 206, where he rejects Barrett's arguments for the role of apocalyptic influences in Hebrews in favor of Platonic ideas).

[94]4 Ezra and 2 Baruch are often dated at about the end of the first century or early in the second century.

[95]"Σιων," 326.

it an entirely "new" entity? "On the one hand Jerusalem at the end of the days is the city of David built again with glory and magnificence, on the other hand Jerusalem is thought of as a pre-existent city which is built by God in heaven and which comes down to earth with the dawn of a new world."[96] It could be said that 4 Ezra and 2 Baruch are examples of an early Jewish apocalyptic strain in which the motif of the heavenly and earthly city is developed according to a "vertical" frame; Enoch 90:28, on the other hand, reflects what may be termed an entirely "horizontal" approach to the heavenly[97] Jerusalem. *That these differing approaches existed even within the apocalyptic tradition at the time when Hebrews was written* is a fact of paramount significance.[98]

The rabbis likewise believed a heavenly Jerusalem and temple to exist which parallel their earthly counterparts (B. Ta'an 5; Gen. R. 55.7; Mekl. Ex. 15:17).[99] In some cases this extends even to the vessels of the two sanctuaries. But even after A.D. 70 the rabbinic tradition, unlike the apocalyptists and NT writers, could not bring itself to see the earthly Jerusalem actually being superseded by the heavenly city. The first occurrences of such a view are found in the later midrashim,[100] where the heavenly Jerusalem finally comes down to earth. Yet McKelvey[101] uses the midrashim as further evidence of views current in the first century, and Barrett[102] cites Paul and John of Patmos, the other two NT writers besides *Auctor* who speak of a "heavenly Jerusalem," as proof that the notion of a heavenly Jerusalem was early. Paul speaks of the "Jerusalem above" as existing already (Gal 4:26)[103]—it is our "mother"; for John of Patmos it "comes down out of God" after the destruction of the old heaven and earth (Rev 21:1f.). Hebrews reflects both ideas. God has built the city (11:10) and prepared it for the saints (11:16); in one sense it can be approached now (12:22, "you have come"). On the other hand, it is still "to come" (13:14).

Auctor has been contrasted with the "crass literalism" of the rabbis (and presumably the apocalypticists):

---

[96]Ibid.

[97]McKelvey (30) states that the Jerusalem of 1 Enoch 90 appears to be the heavenly Jerusalem come to earth, although he admits this is not completely certain.

[98]Cf. Klijn, "2 Baruch," in Charlesworth (617), who says that within 2 Baruch itself are to be seen "conflicting" traditions about the Temple. "In chapter 4 the author used a tradition in which a new, already existing Temple from heaven will appear on earth. This differs from the tradition used in chapter 6 in which angels are sent from heaven to take away the vessels from the Temple in order to preserve them in the earth 'until the last times, so that you may restore them when you are ordered' (6:8). Here a restoration of the second Temple is supposed. Both traditions about the Temple have parallels in Jewish literature before A.D. 70. They show that in the Jewish world many ideas existed with regard to the future of the Temple."

[99]See S-B, 3. 701, 848-52, etc.

[100]S-B, 3. 796.

[101]McKelvey, *The New Temple,* 35.

[102]Barrett, "Eschatology of Hebrews," 375.

[103]But cf. Charles (*Apocalypse of Baruch,* 6), who thinks that in Gal 4:26 the Jerusalem above "is a symbol of the spiritual commonwealth of which the Christian is even now a member," whereas in Revelation it is "an actual city, the counterpart of the earthly Jerusalem, with its own building and vessels."

> We must not imagine that our generation is the first to appreciate the neces-
> sity of "demythologization" or to realize the inadequacy of the image of
> "God up there" . . . . The Writer to the Hebrews is the last person in the NT
> to be suspect of envisaging the sanctuary and throne as a superior but
> equally material counterpart of the wilderness tent.[104]

Such statements are usually accompanied by an insistence that the heavenly tent for *Auctor* could never be envisaged as a *locality*.[105] This approach, in addition to using the question-begging term "material," is unfortunate in two respects: (1) Linguists observe that it is possible to *visualize* an entity as concrete or local without necessarily *conceiving of it* in that way. 1 Kgs 8:13 depicts Solomon as, in a sense, "visualizing" the temple as God's dwelling, "a habitation for thee forever," while knowing that God transcends any limits of space and time (v. 27). Plato's language about the heavenly world of ideas (ὑπερουράνιους τόπος) likewise seems at times to imply that it exists in some "place" (ἔν τινι τόπῳ, Tim. 52b, c), but this is only "because of our finite understanding."[106] It is improbable that 1 Kings and Plato are isolated cases. John of Patmos, e.g., depicts events and entities in "local" terms on both the earth and in heaven without *confining* them in absolutely local terms.[107] (2) It is possible to employ images without any need to "envisage" them. All images involve comparison, but sometimes the comparison is *non-visual*.[108] Unlike John of Patmos, *Auctor* is not a particularly visual writer.[109] 6:19, where an anchor (hope) is found entering within the holy of holies, shows a striking lack of concern with the visual impact of the language about the heavenly tent; *Auctor* appears simply to be verbalizing. Yet this does not mean *a priori* that *Auctor's* images cannot be those of the rabbinic and apocalyptic traditions. For him the point of comparison with those images may be that of *function* rather than that of appearance. Both the earthly and heavenly tents, so to speak, function as the place where the sacrifice is made effective, and both function as the place where the presence of God is centralized. The heavenly Jerusalem of Rev 21, with its lack of any temple, is the exception which proves the rule[110] that, within primitive eschatology, even heavenly cities require a functioning temple or shrine; i.e., they require a place for both sacrifice and a centralization of the presence of God.[111] Apart from certain clues given by *Auctor* (see

---

[104]F. F. Bruce. "The Kerygma of Hebrews," *Int* 23 (1969) 9f.

[105]In addition to the comment of Westcott above, cf. Milligan, *Theology of Hebrews*, 175 ("the idea of *locality* is to be removed as far as possible from the epithet 'heavenly'. . . .").

[106]McKelvey, *The New Temple*, 39.

[107]Cf. Minear, "Cosmology of the Apocalypse," and Traub and von Rad ("οὐρανός, κτλ.," 528), who helpfully note that in Hebrews, "God is high above the heavens, and yet He is in the heavens."

[108]Cf. G. B. Caird, *The Language and Imagery of the Bible* (London, 1980) 149ff.

[109]Contra, e.g., G. J. C. Marchant ("Sacrifice in the Epistle to the Hebrews," *EQ* 20 [1948] 199), who claims that *Auctor* "fills out one pictorial idea from another." Cody rightly observes that *Auctor* differs in one respect from the apocalyptic and rabbinic traditions in that he does not "depict" nor does he paint "any detailed scene of the sanctuary precisely as sanctuary."

[110]Cf. Barrett, "Eschatology of Hebrews," 383 n. 2.

[111]"The future Jerusalem without a temple is an impossible thought for the

below), it is difficult to determine whether the "true tent" of Hebrews is the shrine of the heavenly city or whether for him it is an independent entity. The crucial point is that *Auctor* could have borrowed his images from the apocalyptic/rabbinic traditions without the need either to visualize them or to transform them into symbols for yet something else.

The nature of the above evidence must lead one to the conclusion that it is indefinite at this point which particular tradition *Auctor* reflects in his argument regarding the heavenly cultus. It could be claimed that there is a *cumulative* argument for a Philonic-type orientation. The four texts examined (9:8f., 9:11, 9:24, and 10:20) are ambiguous and, in theory at least, could go either way. This fact, coupled with the Platonic-looking σκιά in 8:5a and *possible* meaning of "copy" for ἀντίτυπος in 9:24, does make a case for Philo at this point feasible. The evidence, however, could go equally in the other direction when one adds up the points in favor of the apocalyptic tradition, and we shall call attention to further pointers in this direction in the discussion to follow.

IV
In What Sense Is the True Tent of Hebrews "Eternal" or "Pre-existent"?

This has already been partially considered, but there are further considerations made necessary by recent treatments of the eschatology of Hebrews. As has been seen, for Barrett the true tent is not the product of Platonism but is the eschatological sanctuary of Jewish apocalyptic. Consequently his assertions that "the new high priest requires a new sanctuary"[112] and the sanctuary exists in heaven in order that it may be manifested on earth[113] seem straightforward in the light of that background. The picture becomes blurred, however, when it is added that "the true tabernacle exists *eternally* in heaven, whither Jesus has ascended (vii.1), but the ministry exercised within it took its origin in the fulfilment at the appointed time of O.T. prophecy. . . ."[114] Does Barrett at certain points give back with one hand what he takes with the other? This question incubates when one reads that "the heavenly tabernacle and its ministrations are from one point of view eternal archetypes, from another, they are eschatological events";[115] that *Auctor* uses "philosophical language" and has written a "Christian approach to philosophical discourse"[116] in terms which would have been "understood" by Plato and Philo;[117] and that he may have read "Plato and other philosophers."[118] These statements by Barrett raise yet more unanswered questions. (a) What is meant by "from one point of view [they are] *eternal archetypes*"? This *could* mean that the sanctuary always pre-

---

ancient Synagogue" (O. Michel, "ναός," 889); cf. also Cody, 22f.; Barrett, "Eschatology of Hebrews," 374.

[112]Barrett, "Eschatology of Hebrews," 384 (italics mine).

[113]Ibid., 389.

[114]Ibid., 384. Cf. also F. F. Bruce (*Hebrews*, 374), who claims that the new Jerusalem in Rev 21:2 which comes down out of God has "existed eternally in heaven" without any clarification of what is meant.

[115]Barrett, "Eschatology of Hebrews," 385.

[116]Ibid., 393.

[117]Ibid.

[118]Ibid.

existed within the purpose of God. Elsewhere this seems to be Barrett's meaning—he states that *Auctor* is developing the idealist element in Jewish apocalyptic, and this seems a sufficient—and illuminating—explanation. But that this development is accomplished in a way that Plato or Philo would have "understood" (see below) or that *Auctor* would have felt his language to be "akin" to theirs, are more shadowy assertions. When stating the argument of Hebrews it is common practice to use loaded terms such as "copy," "archetype," and "eternal," terms which have inevitable associations with Plato.[119] This, however, serves only to prejudice the argument. The term αἰώνιος is used six times in Hebrews: 5:9 (of "salvation"), 6:2 (of "judgment"), 9:12 (of "redemption"), 9:14 (of "spirit"), 9:15 (of "inheritance") and 13:20 (for "covenant"). Except for possibly 9:14,[120] all these refer, not to any "timeless" sphere involving pre-existence, but to realities which come in time and are everlastingly valid.[121] Neither the heavenly city nor the sanctuary, furthermore, is referred to by *Auctor* as αἰώνιος. "Eternal" may thus be a misleading term to use for them.[122] If its use be insisted upon, however, it does not necessarily indicate a "Platonic" nuance. Truth which exists in the mind of God is, theoretically, "eternal." When, as we have seen, in a work not generally thought to have

---

[119]This extends also to the attribution to *Auctor* of Greek terms which he does not actually employ. A typical instance of this is Cody (*Heavenly Sanctuary and Liturgy*, 20f.), who, in comparing *Auctor* with Wis 9:8, speaks of "*their* views of μίμημα and παράδειγμα" (italics mine). Such lexicographic importation is the result of deciding ahead of time that the author's background is essentially Hellenistic and philosophical rather than letting the epistle speak for itself.

[120]It is not clear whether πνεύματος αἰωνίου in Heb 9:14 refers to the Holy Spirit (cf. the RSV) or the spiritual nature of the sacrifice (cf. the NEB).

[121]Sasse ("αἰών, κτλ.," *TDNT* 1. 209) illustrates the problem of language by claiming that αἰώνιος in Hebrews has "the full sense of divine eternity" (9:15) and "extends beyond the purely temporal meaning." But does "divine eternity" necessarily involve the notion of actual pre-existence?

[122]Contra Michaelis, "σκηνή, κτλ.," 375f. He admits that the tent is not called αἰώνιος or αἰώνια, but "it is called ἀληθινή (8:2) and fundamentally this can only mean that it is eternal in character." But ἀληθινή here, despite parallels which can be drawn with Plato, Philo, Plotinus and the Hermetic writings (cf. R. Bultmann, "ἀληθινός," *TDNT* 1. 250), occurs in a highly polemical context in which the term "true" has probably been given a specialized definition, i.e., the reality to which a symbol points. In this case a closer parallel than Plato would be Paul, who in Rom 2:28f. and Phil 3:3 speaks of "the true circumcision." Admittedly ἀληθινός does not appear in the Greek, but it is implicit in the point (well founded in the OT—cf. Deut 10:16, 30:6; Jer 4:4, 9:23ff., etc.) that fleshly circumcision is not the ultimate—it only points to the true thing, circumcision of the heart. In this case the Fourth Gospel, Paul and *Auctor* all reflect an *inter-Jewish debate* concerning the interpretation of certain OT legal institutions. In such "fighting" contexts words are given what is known as a "tactical definition" (cf. C. S. Lewis, *Studies in Words* [Cambridge, 1960] 19, who argues that words often are pre-defined in controversy to that no other meaning is possible: "They are attempts to appropriate for one side, or to deny to the other, a potent word. . . . You can see the same 'war of positions' going on today . . . the pretty word has to be narrowed *ad hoc* so as to exclude something he dislikes. The ugly word has to be extended *ad hoc* . . . so as to bespatter some enemy. Nineteenth century definitions of the word *gentleman* are also tactical"). Cf. also Caird, *Language and Imagery of the Bible*, 93.

been influenced by Platonic categories, John of Patmos speaks of "the lamb slain from the foundation of the world" (13:8), it is obvious that what is meant is an entity which "pre-exists" within God's purposes, i.e., it reflects the Jewish doctrine of predestination. Earlier this doctrine may have developed within Judaism with the help of some Platonic influence; but by the time John wrote, it was a thoroughly Jewish idea. "Eternal" could thus mean, simply, "predestined." The language used in discussions of the eschatology of Hebrews needs sharpening if distortions are not to result. Barrett claims that Hebrews contains *both* Platonic philosophical influences (albeit transformed) and primitive Jewish eschatology, but the eschatological imagery is primary, "as it must always be in any Christian approach to philosophical discourse." "The eschatology, though rough, crude and intractable,"[123] is essential. Yet there is no guarantee that such "rough, crude and intractable" eschatology (which includes, presumably, "the primitive sanctuary of Jewish apocalyptic") would have been understood *at all* by Plato or Philo. It is more likely that they would have *mis*understood *Auctor,* i.e., they would have read his eschatology in the light of their own philosophical categories, as numerous subsequent interpreters of Hebrews over the centuries have done. Williamson[124] points out that theologians have often read Christianity into Plato. But the reverse also applies: Plato (and Philo) probably would have read Platonism into Hebrews. (b) Barrett's language seems imprecise at points. He says, for instance, that "the heavenly tabernacle *and* its ministrations are from one point of view eternal archetypes, from another they are eschatological events." As with the interpretation of Luck, this seems to include the heavenly tent as, from one point of view, an "event." Elsewhere, however, Barrett distinguishes the tabernacle from events which occur *within* it. This is no pedantic distinction, for it is such lapses which lead to confusion regarding the referent of *Auctor's* language. (c) There is no basis for distinguishing, as does Barrett, the heavenly tent from eschatological events which take place within it by claiming that the former is "eternal." Once "eternal" is defined as "within the mind of God," "tent" *and* "events within it" are "eternal."

Although Barrett's study has done much to redress the balance of opinion on Hebrews towards Jewish eschatology and away from Platonic philosophy, one needs to ask whether he went far enough. Williamson, although he is deeply appreciative of Barrett's contribution, senses that it contains difficulties and attempts to come to grips with them. He reacts particularly to Barrett's statement that *Auctor* "may well have read Plato and other philosophers,"[125] and elsewhere revises Barrett so as to read "the activities of the heavenly tabernacle could not *become* 'eternal archetypes' until they had first *occurred* as 'eschatological events.'"[126] Yet *both* statements by Barrett and Williamson are in need of some scrutiny. In each much depends upon how the English terms "eternal" and "archetype" are construed. As noted above, the former may carry within it notions of pre-existence, or it may mean, simply, "everlasting." "Archetype" is similarly slippery. Like the Greek ἀρχέτυπος or ἀρχέ–τυπικῶς,[127] it may mean either "prototype" (i.e., the original pattern from which copies are made) or it may mean a perfect example or standard. In the latter case an entity may be an archetype *without*

---

[123]Barrett, "Eschatology of Hebrews," 393.

[124]Williamson, "Platonism and Hebrews," 423.

[125]Ibid., 424.

[126]*Philo and Hebrews,* 159 (italics mine).

[127]Cf. LSJ and G. W. H. Lampe, *Patristic Greek Lexicon* (Oxford, 1969) q.v.

being a prototype.[128] In Eusebius ἀρχέτυπος may even be *contrasted* with πρωτότυπον. [129] This is possible because in Greek the term ἀρχή, in addition to meaning "beginning" or "firstfruits" (i.e., that which precedes), may mean "rule," "sum-total," or "head."[130] What Barrett means by "eternal archetypes" seems fairly clear. He explicitly says that *Auctor* uses "philosophical" language akin to that of Plato and Philo in order to highlight the idealist element within Jewish apocalyptic, and that the Greek philosophers would have understood him. The truths to which *Auctor's* shadows point, in other words, are truths which exist *eternally* in the mind of God. This impression is strengthened if one compares Barrett's comment with a remarkably similar one made by Héring two years earlier: ". . . in the Alexandrian conception of the world, the heavenly tabernacle existed metaphysically from all eternity; but from the Religious point of view, it comes into reckoning only in 'our time' . . . that is in the era inaugurated by the ascension of Christ."

When Williamson speaks of things in Hebrews *becoming* "eternal archetypes," however, he seems to have changed Barrett's meaning, for if "archetype: is given Barrett's quasi-Platonic, philosophical nuance, the statement is simply not true. There is no way an entity can *become* an archetype which would have been understood by Plato and the philosophers by occurring in time as an "eschatological event." Neither can Williamson's statement refer to pre-existence within the mind of God (as does Barrett's), for it is equally untrue to say that such existence cannot be spoken of until the event occurs "in time"——there is no point logically at which something may "become" an entity within God's mind. Williamson must be thinking of archetypes as "ideal examples." In this case his statement makes complete sense and is quite valuable: "The activities of the heavenly sanctuary could not become permanently ideal examples of sacrifice and obedience until they had occurred once and for all in time." But in order to get this he has had to change Barrett's meaning, for Barrett clearly uses the term in question to admit a strand of semi-Platonic idealism into the scope of *Auctor's* thinking.

Williamson's revision of Barrett, however, relates only to the *events* within the heavenly sanctuary and leaves unresolved the question of whether the sanctuary itself bears any relation to Plato's "archetypes." A way forward may be the following. Rather than assuming, as does Sowers,[131] that "certain features of the earthly cult reflect prototypes in heaven while the sacrifices *within them* foreshadow features of Christ's work accomplished later in history," one could see the true tent in Hebrews as a basically *functional* entity. In other words, the sanctuary and the events within it are not to be *separated*. It is difficult to speak of anything (whether sacrifice or tent in which sacrifice occurs) which is so linked with humanity's sinfulness and its purgation as actually

---

[128]According to the *Oxford Shorter Dictionary* (93), "archetype" may be used of "a coin of standard weight," or, in comparative anatomy, "an assumed ideal pattern of each division of organized beings." In neither case is "prototype" synonymous (cf. also A. Baxter, "The Term 'Archetype', and its Application to Jesus Christ," *HeyJ* 25 [1984] 19ff.). Dunn (*Christology in the Making*, 120) speaks of Christ's work as "archetypal" in such a way that it clearly does not require temporal precedence, especially since his work is related to that of Adam.

[129]HE 10.4.55, cited in Lampe, *Patristic Greek Lexicon*, under "ἀρχέτυπος," q.v.

[130]Cf. Arndt and Gingrich, *A Greek English Lexicon* (Chicago, 1957) 111f.

[131]Sowers, *Hermeneutics*, 111. Cf. also Barrett, "Eschatology of Hebrews," 384.

"eternal." *Auctor* says that the earthly sanctuary was made on the pattern of what Moses saw (Exod 25:40), *but for him this may have included not only the physical structure, but everything which goes on there—i.e., the sacrifices.* Thus, before it is asked what the heavenly tent "is," or whether, as with 4 Ezra and 2 Baruch, it "pre-exists," a better question will be: what, according to *Auctor,* is the *sacrifice* of the heavenly tent? The answer to that question can only be the self-offering of Christ. If the sanctuary is thus viewed as a *functioning* institution and not just as an object, it becomes extremely difficult to suggest that *Auctor* thought that there was an "eternal archetype," whether "heaven itself" or something *in* heaven, beginning before Moses and going on afterwards, in which a heavenly sacrifice was eternally being offered or made effective. Once one is prepared to say with Sowers[132] and others that there is no eternal sacrifice going on within the sanctuary, and once one is prepared to admit that the "true tent" of Hebrews may be the functioning sanctuary of apocalyptic, it is but a short step to say that there is no actually "eternal" sanctuary in Hebrews. The one sense in which *any* functional entity which exists in consequence of human sin and finiteness could be said to be "an eternal archetype" would be within the destining purposes of God, but as noted, by the time *Auctor* wrote, this idea was thoroughly Jewish.

Two further observations may help to clarify this question:

(a) In addition to being "pitched" (8:2), the tent is said to have been *entered* at some point by Jesus. It has been observed[133] that this could not have been said by Philo, with his low regard for time and history. Such statements in Hebrews, however, may indicate not simply a difference of attitude from Philo; they may indicate *an entirely different background* for the heavenly tent of Hebrews. Within the apocalyptic tradition, the new temple no doubt *could* be entered by men, if only when ultimately the temple descends to earth. The unique contribution of *Auctor* would be his adjustment of this tradition so as to make the entry by men (i.e., Jesus) an event which has *already taken place.* In other words, its ultimate involvement in the affairs of mankind has begun "in these late days" (1:2).

(b) As was observed above, there was no consensus in the first several centuries as to whether the heavenly temple actually "pre-existed" or whether it was a new creation by God at the end of the age. There appear to be at least *four* different traditions which have survived as to "when" the heavenly sanctuary could have been built: (1) before the creation (Pesahim 54a, Nedarim 39b[134] Wis 9:8); (2) at the creation (Philo,[135] Bereshith Rabbah 1.4,[136] Wis 9:8);[137] (3) when the earthly sanctuary was built—whether Moses' tent (Num. Rabbah 12)[138] or the temple (Pesiqtha Rabbathi 5, Num. Naso. 12.12); (4) and

---

[132]Sowers, 111.

[133]Cf. Williamson's section on "Time, History and Eschatology," in *Philo and Hebrews*, 142ff.

[134]I owe some of these rabbinic references to Cody, 24.

[135]Although this might be classed with (a), since Philo's world of archetypes was created first as the blueprint.

[136]Implied rather than stated: "Six things preceded the creation of the world; some of them were actually created, while the creation of others was contemplated." The temple is among those things only contemplated.

[137]If ἀπ᾽ ἀρχῆς is taken to mean "from creation."

[138]"At the time when the Holy One, blessed be He, commanded Israel to set up the tent His words also included a command to the ministering angels that they should

at the end of the age (1 Enoch 90:28f.). The rabbinic references are late, but they may enshrine earlier traditions which show that in the first century questions about the origins of the heavenly temple were being asked. That such questions may never have occurred to *Auctor* needs no stating; but that such varied opinions existed demonstrates that there is more than one viewpoint from which scholars today must choose if they are to determine the kind of notions which surround the heavenly tent of Heb 8-9.

V
Is the True Tent of Hebrews the New Temple of Jewish Apocalyptic?

The groundwork for this possibility has been laid by emphasizing the ambiguity of such texts as Heb 9:8f., 11, 24 and 10:20 and by looking briefly at the evidence of the apocalyptic tradition. It remains now to look at several indications within the epistle itself upon which a case could be mounted which claims that *Auctor* stands firmly within the apocalyptic tradition, and that he is in line with the viewpoint represented by 1 Enoch 90:28f. that the heavenly Jerusalem and sanctuary are new entities built by God at the end of the age.

(a) *Heb 9:23.* A clue in this direction is provided by the singularly peculiar logic of Heb 9:23: "Thus it was necessary for the copies (ὑποδείγματα) of the heavenly things to be purified with these rites, but the heavenly things themselves with better sacrifices than these" (RSV). This text has caused interpreters enormous problems. Why do the "heavenly things" need "purification" at all? Moffatt[139] has called the idea "fantastic"; Montefiore[140] thinks it "an unhappy comparison"; Dods[141] calls it "poetry," not "theology." Attempts to relate the heavenly cleansing to the explusion of Satan from Heaven,[142] the notion of reconciliation found in Col 1:20,[143] or the cleansing of men's consciences[144] have not been convincing. What needs to be noted is that the context of 9:23 is not the annual Day of Atonement ritual but the initial purification of the newly built tabernacle at the inauguration of the first covenant. 9:6-14 does deal with the continuous atonement cycle, but the subject shifts at v. 15 to the manner in which a covenant is ratified. 9:15-18 describes the relation of the death of the victim to the institution of the covenant, while 9:19-20 reflects the aspersion of the altar (here substituted with "the book") and the people recorded in Exod 24:6-8. The sprinkling of the tent and vessels of 9:21 seems to be drawn primarily from the consecration of Lev 8:10f., 23f. (cf. Exod 29:12, 40:9-11) rather than the annual atonement ritual of Lev 16, only the sprinkling is now extended to the tabernacle and all its furnishings. Josephus (III. 206) also records the belief that at its inauguration Moses purified the tent and its vessels not only with oil but "with the blood of bulls and rams." Similarly, *Auctor* seems to say that, "just as it was necessary for the first tent to be inaugurated with blood, so it was necessary for the second tent." That the term καθαρίζω can be used interchangeably with

---

set up a tent on high" (cf. S-B, 3. 701f.; Michaelis, "σκηνή, κτλ.," 375 n. 38).

[139]Moffatt, *Hebrews*, 132.

[140]Montefiore, *Hebrews*, 160.

[141]M. Dods, "The Epistle to the Hebrews," *The Expositor's Greek Testament*, Vol. IV (London, 1910) 338.

[142]Cf. e.g., Héring, *Hebrews*, 82.

[143]Moffatt, *Hebrews*, 132.

[144]Montefiore, *Hebrews*, 160; F. F. Bruce, *Hebrews*, 219.

ἁγιάζω so as to mean "inaugurate" (cp. ἐγκαινίζω, 9:18)[145] is proved by Exod 29:36 and Lev 8:15LXX and especially by Josephus. The latter, in another passage clearly describing the inauguration (Ant. III. 197), states that "Furthermore, he sanctified (ἥγνιζε) both the tabernacle and the priests, accomplishing in such a way their purification (τὴν κάθαρσιν). . . . He anointed both the priests themselves and all the tabernacle, thus purifying (κεκάθαρκε) all."[146] One may speculate as to why for these writers the first tent needed *any* purifying at the inception of the covenant. The most likely answer is that it had been built by sinful human hands. Here, of course, *Auctor*'s analogy breaks down somewhat, for the heavenly tent, *not* built by human hands (9:11), would require no such rite; but that would be to press for an unnecessary logic. On this exegesis v. 22 needs to be viewed as neither parenthetical[147] nor the introduction of a new subject.[148] For *Auctor* the sacrifice of 9:15ff. is at the same time an inaugurative sacrifice *and* an atonement sacrifice. The death which is the initiation of the covenant (v. 18) has as its goal the forgiveness of sins under the first covenant (v. 15).[149] In Hebrews the maintenance of the covenant is subsumed in its inauguration. N. H. Young[150] is one of the few recent scholars to appreciate this and to note the inaugurative aspects of 9:23:

> If the old order required sacrifices to inaugurate it, the new order requires a better sacrifice, one that really is an act of ἄφεσις (9:22, 10:18). His sacrifice ushers in the new age and removes sin at the level of the conscience. . . ."[151]

Young, however, applies the inaugurative aspect only to the new age; he does not apply it to the sanctuary itself. This results from his equation of the true sanctuary with "heaven itself, the presence of God"[152] (and to his decision elsewhere[153] that the veil of the tent in Hebrews must be spiritualized to mean the flesh of Jesus). Yet it is certainly possible, if not probable, that what *Auctor* has in mind in 9:23 is the inauguration of the new

---

[145]Cf. Lünemann (344), who argues that καθαρίζειν "is an idea which entirely subordinates itself to the idea of the ἐγκαινίζειν, v. 18. . . ."

[146]Cf. also III.206: "He purified (ἐθαράπευε) the tabernacle."

[147]Cf. P. E. Hughes, *A Commentary on the Epistle to the Hebrews* (Grand Rapids, 1977) 380.

[148]Cody (183ff.) argues that 9:24-28 is a new section (based on Vanhoye's analysis of the structure of Hebrews) which is totally distinct from 9:15-22 and which looks back to the atonement ritual of 9:1-10. 9:22 thus acts as a "bridge verse" to the next section. This means that Cody denies that what is in view in 19:23 is the cleansing of a new sanctuary. "It is true that 9:18ff. have to do with an inauguration, but what is being inaugurated there is not the sanctuary but the New Covenant" (183). It is doubtful, however, that *Auctor* would have separated the two. In order to follow Cody one must have a lot of faith in Vanhoye's analysis of the structure of Hebrews. Cody himself admits that καθαρίζεσθαι "could refer . . . indirectly—by recall or association—to the idea of inauguration, with which he has been dealing," in which "the purification (καθαρίσμος) pertained to the sanctuary and was not sacrificial. . . ." (185f.).

[149]Cf. Kennedy, *Theology of Epistles*, 200 n. 2, 211f.

[150]N. H. Young, "The Gospel According to Heb 9," *NTS* 27 (1981) 205f.

[151]Ibid., 206.

[152]Ibid., 204f.

[153]"ΤΟΥΤ' ΕΣΤΙΝ."

temple (and *hence* new age) of Jewish apocalyptic. Such a view should be kept in mind in the light of Barrett's suggestions for the role of apocalyptic in Hebrews.[154]

(b) *Heb 9:8.* The possibility that *Auctor* thought of the true tent as the *new* tent is also raised by the language of 9:8. If *Auctor* in fact thought of the true tent as the "eternal prototype" of the earthly, it is doubtful that he could have referred to the earthly tabernacle as the "first" tent; it would have been more likely the "second" tent.[155] As was seen above, there is ambiguity with reference to *Auctor*'s use of πρῶτος in chap. 9, but if "the first tent" in 9:8 refers to the entire tabernacle structure, such a first tent-second tent schema would be unprecedented in any truly Philonic milieu. In this light it is interesting that Koester[156] (in discussing Heb 8:1ff.) can actually speak of "the prototypical *earthly* sanctuary." This is probably a more accurate way of depicting the argument of *Auctor* than speaking of *heavenly* prototypes. A closer parallel than Philo to this kind of thought would be 1 Cor 15:45-47, where Paul describes that which is "heavenly" as *second* rather than first in time. The "animal body" (NEB for τὸ ψυχικόν) is juxtaposed with the "spiritual body" (τὸ πνευματικόν), but the latter has not existed from all eternity, nor is "out of heaven" synonymous with "eternal"; "the man from heaven" is an *eschatological* entity. The point of departure of the physical and heavenly is not their natural status, but the relationship which each bears to "earth" and "heaven," respectively.[157] That which is "heavenly" (8:5, 9:23, 12:22) in Hebrews may be

---

[154]Williamson ("Platonism and Hebrews," 420f.) notes another interesting facet of this text, the relation of the two cleansings in 9:23 as "earthly" and "heavenly" without the use of a "vertical" scheme. The earthly cleansing comes *first*, the heavenly cleansing comes *second*. This is a further indication that when *Auctor* thinks in terms of "heaven" and "earth," he thinks not as a dualistic metaphysician, but primarily as a primitive eschatologist, in which "earth" is "then" and "heaven" is "now" (although for the dangers of an over-zealous elimination of the spatial dimension from *Auctor*'s argument in view of the *Christian* idea of overlapping of the two covenants, cf. my comments above and those of Minear in "Cosmology of the Apocalypse").

[155]Cf. F. Horton, (*The Melchizedek Tradition* [Cambridge, 1976] 164 n. 1), who observes that "in Heb. ix the earthly tent, the antitype, is also the 'first' tent (ix.2) whereas the true tent is the 'second' tent. . . ."

[156]H. Köster, "ὑπόστασις," *TDNT* 8. 586 n. 139 (italics mine).

[157]Cf. also Heb 12:25, where it is said that the old covenant was ratified on earth (ἐπὶ γῆς) and the other from heaven (ἀπ᾽ οὐρανῶ). In commenting on this passage G. Hughes (45) says that "we neither can, nor need dispute that throughout the epistle the qualities of earthly, fleshly, copied, temporal and mutable hang together as characteristics of the early form of revelation and that the heavenly, the eternal and the archetypal represents the perfection of these anticipatory forms. *But the point is:* They *are* earlier and later forms, they are a πρωτὴ and καινὴ διαθήκη; the one stands to the other as anticipation to achievement and therefore in horizontal or historical relationship." The last point is well taken, and it would be strengthened further by looking to Paul's juxtaposition in 1 Cor 15:47 (cp. especially ἐκ γῆς . . . ἐξ οὐρανοῦ with ἐπὶ γῆς . . . ἀπ᾽ οὐρανῶν in the two writings) of that which is "out of the earth" with that which is "out of heaven" in a horizontal, eschatological, non-"Hellenistic" framework. In the light of my findings regarding σκιά, ὑπόδειγμα and ἀντίτυπος, however (cf. *JTS* n.s. 34 [1983] 156ff.), it should be added that, against Hughes, one *should* and *need* dispute the premise that "throughout the epistle" promise and fulfillment

similarly conceived as "second" in time as compared with its prototypical "earthly" (9:1) counterpart, its ἀντίτυπος. [158]

If for *Auctor* the heavenly tent was the *second* tent rather than some eternally existing entity, it would explain why for him it needed its own inaugurative ceremony, its own purification with blood. The apocalyptic tradition would provide a cogent background for such a thought; Plato or Philo would not.

(c) *Heb 13:14.* "Here we have no lasting city, but we seek the city which is to be." We have already examined several of the apocalyptic and rabbinic texts which speak of a heavenly Jerusalem which is to come to earth. Barrett likewise suggests that the heavenly temple in Hebrews "is in heaven primarily that it may be manifested on earth," but he adds that *Auctor* "conceives its earthly manifestation *in a new way*." His explanation of this is that "the decisive act—the death and ascension of Christ—is already *past,* and the normal pattern of eschatological belief is thereby disturbed."[159] Yet this provides little, if any, basis for an "earthly" manifestation of the temple-city. What does the term μέλλουσαν in 13:14 indicate? Or, put another way, if the earthly manifestation is already "past," and if the city already "exists" (12:22), in what sense are these entities "to be"? The most Barrett will concede is that, according to the apocalyptic tradition (which, it should be remembered, he has claimed underlies Hebrews), "this heavenly city will *in some way* be manifested as the Jerusalem of the age to come."[160] His references to 4 Ezra (cf. 7:26, "then shall the city that now is invisible appear," and 13:36, "Sion shall come and shall be made manifest to all men, prepared and builded") seem relevant in this regard, containing as they do terms similar or identical to those found in Heb 11:1, 10, 16, and 22. But since Barrett views the idealist element in Hebrews as developed in quasi-Platonic and philosophical terms, he seems unwilling to go so far as to suggest that *Auctor,* in line with the rest of the apocalyptic tradition, feels that there is *yet to be* an "earthly" manifestation of the heavenly things, however "earthly" is defined. Yet, while there are no *explicit* statements of this kind in Hebrews, it should be borne in mind that the more *familiar* an idea is, the more allusively an author will treat it. Hofius[161] presents parallels between Hebrews and 4 Ezra, concluding that *Auctor* expected the heavenly city in terms similar to the author of that work, i.e., a

---

are work out in terms of "copied" and "the eternal and the archetypal."

[158]The viewpoint of 1 Enoch 90:28 (discussed above) could also help to explain the enigmatic argument of Heb 9:8: "The way into the holy place had not yet been made manifest while the first tent was standing." According to 1 Enoch 90:28f., "Before the new temple of the eschatological age is erected, the existing temple will have to be broken up and taken away" (McKelvey, 23). It is, of course, true that the old temple was still standing when *Jesus* entered the heavenly shrine, but (a) it was already "near to disappearing" (cf. Heb 8:13), and (b) the reference could be to the future entry by mankind in general at the consummation, at which point the earthly sanctuary would certainly have disappeard.

[159]"Eschatology of Hebrews," 389; cf. also 386 (italics mine).

[160]Ibid., 375f. (italics mine).

[161]O. Hofius, *Katapausis. Die Vorstellung vom endzeitlichen Ruheort im Hebräerbrief* (Tübingen, 1970) 92.

future earthly manifestation will occur;[162] and Michel[163] cites Rev 21:1f. as a parallel in his discussion of "the world to come" of Heb 2:5.

The manifestation of 13:14, of course, concerns the city. That it involves as well the eschatological temple cannot be proven, but that the heavenly city in 12:22 is called "Mount Zion" may point in this direction. McKelvey[164] asks with reference to 1 Enoch 25:3, "How could a Jew think of a descent of the heavenly Mount Zion without having in mind a descent of the heavenly temple?" The reference to Mount Zion in 12:22 may compel a similar question: How could a Jew think of the heavenly city *as* Mount Zion without thinking of a heavenly temple?[165]

(d) *Heb 12:18ff.* These suggestions will undoubtedly prove disturbing to those for whom *Auctor*'s "Platonism" allows no room for an apocalyptic city to come or a new heaven and earth such as is found in Rev 21:1ff. J. W. Thompson, in particular, has argued that the heavenly city of Hebrews is not the "physical" Zion of apocalyptic but the Platonic intelligible realm. This realm cannot be touched (ψηλαφώμενος, 12:18, 22) and is not made by hands (οὐ χειροποιήτος, 9:24). "The author's understanding of *polis* is comparable to Philo's interpretation of the *polis* in terms of the κόσμος νοητός."[166] Thompson argues in addition that the motif of the eschatological earthquake in 12:26f. precludes any apocalyptic interpretation of the heavenly Jerusalem. The key to *Auctor*'s logic, he claims, is the "stability motif," in which, after the climactic shaking, only the intelligible world remains (μένω, 12:27) as opposed to the sense-perceptible world. The latter, since it is "made" (ὡς πεποιημένων), is thus "removed" (μετάθεσις). πεποιημένα continues Thompson:

> is the equivalent of γένεσις, τὰ γενόμενα, which regularly appears in the Platonic literature for that which is made. Whereas Plato (Timaeus 37D) distinguishes that which abides from that which he describes as γένεσις, Hebrews distinguishes that which abides from that which is "made." The same distinction occurs in Philo (De Opif. Mund. 12; cf. also 16, 29, 31), who differentiates between the earthly sphere of change and the eternity of the world of forms.[167]

After the removal of the mutable/material world, says Thompson, "only the world which is presently unseen (11:1) and untouchable (12:18) remains."[168] This remaining is drawn

---

[162]G. W. Buchanan, (*"To the Hebrews"* [New York, 1972] 136) also admits that *Auctor* "may have expected the heavenly Jerusalem to be restored to earth. ..." (although this is hard to reconcile with his insistence elsewhere that "heavenly Jerusalem" is the earthly Zion of Palestine).

[163]Michel, *Hebräer*, 69.

[164]*New Temple*, 29.

[165]It could be said, of course, that Rev 21:22 proves that a Jew *could* think of a heavenly city without a temple; but Barrett is probably correct to emphasize the anomalous nature of this—it is the exception "which proves the rule" (383 n. 2). It should be added that John nowhere refers to the new Jerusalem as "Mount Zion" (14:1 indicates the earthly city which is the scene of the final battle).

[166]Thompson, *The Beginnings of Christian Philosophy*, 48.

[167]Ibid., 49.

[168]Ibid., 50.

directly from the Platonic distinction between the mutable and immutable.[169] Immutability comes only upon leaving the world of the created and material.[170] Unlike apocalyptic, which understood Hag 2:6 to mean that, after the climactic shaking, an abiding new heavens and earth would emerge (cf. 2 Bar 59:3, 4; Esdras 6:11ff., 10:25ff., Jub 1:29), *Auctor* views heaven and earth as "that which is made"; as such, it must be annihilated.[171]

There are numerous indications that Thompson has overstated his case and has read Hebrews through Platonic-colored metaphysical lenses.

(a) There is no certainty that the earthquake of Heb 12:26f. refers to "the end of the world" as that phrase is normally understood. While many[172] have taken the passage in this way, others have seen the "shaking" as in some sense *already* begun in the coming of the new covenant (with the resultant judgment upon all things which it brings). Westcott links the passage closely to the period beginning with the removal of the old covenant. This removal, symbolized by the destruction of the temple, was about to be accomplished in *Auctor*'s own day. "He makes no distinction between the beginning and the consummation of the age then to be inaugurated, between the catastrophe of the fall of Jerusalem and the final return of Christ . . . that which is essential to his view is the inauguration of a new order, answering to the 'new heavens and the new earth' (Isa 65:17, Apoc 21:1)."[173] Montefiore notes that elsewhere in the NT the apocalyptic shaking of the heavens and earth is "in some sense fulfilled in the death and resurrection of Jesus" (cf. Matt 27:45, 51) but denies that such is the case in Hebrews. As Westcott observes, however, Heb 12:27 bears some similarity to Acts 2:16-21, where Joel 2:28-32 is regarded as having been already fulfilled (note the effect upon "heaven above" and "earth beneath," Acts 2:19). "The difference between the shakable and the unshakable lies not in their natural status [i.e., "created" vs. "uncreated"], claims G. B. Caird, but in their relationship to God."[174] In this case the passage speaks of God's judgment within history (beginning with impending judgment upon Jerusalem) upon everything not in keeping with His purpose revealed in Christ. Such a view cannot be lightly dismissed. Thompson's assumption of a sudden extinction of the created, material realm needs more argumentation than he has provided.

(b) Contra Thompson, the fact that the realm cannot be "touched" (12:18, 22) is probably not on account of any noumenal concern of the philosopher, but results instead from the fact that it is essentially *future* (13:14). Christians have certainly "come" to it

---

[169]Ibid., 49.

[170]Ibid., 50f.

[171]Ibid., 49f.

[172]According to W. Robinson, *The Eschatology of the Epistle to the Hebrews* (Birmingham, 1950) 17, "This is one of the most apocalyptic passages in the book and certainly points to the end of the world." Cf. also Montefiore, *Hebrews*, 235f.; Héring, *Hebrews*, 118; Moffatt, *Hebrews*, 221f.; F. F. Bruce, *Hebrews*, 383f.; and Barrett, "Eschatology of Hebrews," among others.

[173]Westcott, *Hebrews*, 423. Cf. also Nairne, *The Epistle of Priesthood* (Edinburgh, 1913) 416f.; Milligan, *Theology of Hebrews*, 190; and Spicq, *Hébreux*, 411f. Cody, who seems elsewhere to view it as a climactic event at the end of history, speaks of "the transformation of movable, transitory things [which] is already accomplished in the new and eternal order established by Christ. . . ." (141).

[174]Caird, "The Christological Basis of Christian Hope," *The Christian Hope* (London, 1970) 23.

(12:22) and "received" it (12:28), but this is only through faith, a faith which treats the future as though it were the present (11:1). Just as faith sees those things yet "unseen" (2:8b, 11:3, 11:7), so it touches those things yet "untouched." Thompson's claim that οὖ χειροποίητος denotes a Platonic-type dualism ignores Mark 14:58 and Acts 7:48, 17:24 (cf. also ἀχειροποίητος in 2 Cor 5:1, Col 2:11—cf. Eph 2:11), texts which show this idea to be widespread in Jewish-Christian circles with no obvious contact with Platonism.

(c) Contra Thompson, there is no need to look beyond the LXX text of Haggai as understood by first century apocalyptic to discern *Auctor's* point. If Dodd is correct that, rather than being isolated proof-texts, many of these OT passages carried their contexts with them, the context of the passage in Haggai is important. There God will establish a new temple in the face of opposition and discouragement, and his message through the prophet is that both heaven and earth will be shaken in order to establish the new temple and kingdom. This shaking in Haggai is "the world cataclysm which is to be the prelude to the coming of the messianic age,"[175] a context which fits well with what *Auctor* wishes to say elsewhere, namely that the messianic age has already begun in Jesus. There is no need for the readers, like those in the day of Haggai, to be discouraged by the opposition (now Jewish?) to the establishment of the new (heavenly) city and temple. *Auctor* takes ἔτι ἅπαξ in Hag 2:7 not unreasonably to mean "*only* once more." Since, at the beginning of the first covenant, the mountain and surrounding earth were shaken but afterwards remained, he notes that in Haggai's promise the establishment of the new order, anticipated in Zerubbabel, would involve not only shaking but μετάθεσις. His logic is that, since this is God's *decisive* (one cannot but detect here an echo of Heb 7:27, 9:12, and 10:10) judgment on all things which he deems unworthy, it must be more than just a disturbance. What is the μετάθεσις of 12:27? Many have argued that it means either "change" (cp. Heb 7:12) or "removal" (cp. Heb 11:5).[176] The idea certainly *includes* removal. In this light it is interesting that in Haggai, immediately after the reiteration of the promise (2:21) of shaking, the result is defined in terms of "removal": of thrones, kings and the might of armies.[177] Nowhere in Haggai does this shaking denote an "end of history" cosmic catastrophe in which what follows has nothing to do with what precedes. What follows is the messianic age, during which the wealth of nations is brought into the new temple (2:8ff.). There is nothing in Hebrews which compels a different meaning. The coming of the new order means the inauguration of an earthquake-like judgment within the cosmos whereby all which occupies an improper relation to the new work will be shaken and removed. For Haggai this involved the contrast between contemporary authority and Zerubbabel's temple/kingdom; for *Auctor* it means all authority which is

---

[175]D. W. Thomas, "The Book of Haggai," *The Interpreter's Bible* (New York, 1953) 1045.

[176]For the view that it refers to the transformation of the universe leading to the new heavens and earth, cf. C. Mauer, "τίθημι, κτλ.," *TDNT* 8. 161; G. Bertram, "σαλεύω, σαλος," *TDNT* 7. 70; and A. Voegtle, "Das Neue Testament und die Zukunft des Kosmos: Heb. 12,26f. und das Endschichsal des Kosmos," *Bibel und Leben* 10 (1969) 242ff. For the view that it is the annihilation of the material universe, in addition to Thompson and Cody, see Käsemann, *Das wandernde Gottesvolk*, 29f.

[177]While the term μετάθεσις is not actually found in the LXX text of Haggai 2:23f., *Auctor* is fond of explaining OT texts with illustrative words not properly found in the text (cp. 8:13, where his explanation of Jeremiah's point employs terms such as παλαιόω, γηράσκω, and ἀφανισμός).

bound up with the old age (beginning with the old sanctuary) which is opposed to Christ's new sanctuary and kingdom. There is nothing "dualistic" or "metaphysical" in this; *Auctor*'s interpretation of Hag 2 in an apocalyptic setting explains all features of the text adequately.

(d) Thompson and others assert that *Auctor* has no use left over for the created, "material" cosmos after the shaking, but this results from a reading of Platonic-type metaphysics into the argument. *Auctor* nowhere uses a term such as ὕλη to denote a material-immaterial awareness.[178] What he does say is that the shakable things are removed "as that which has been made" (ὡς πεποιημένων). This is significant, but it cannot be pressed in the way Thompson attempts. The heavenly tent and city are "made" by God as well as the cosmos (8:12, 11:10).[179] What makes the heavenly tent superior to the earthly is not that it is uncreated (this would be Platonism), but that it is made by *God*, not man. As in Philo, for *Auctor* all things are created. The question taken up in Hebrews is to *which* creation a certain thing belongs: this, or another? Angels are thus "created" (1:7), but, as with the true tent, they are not of *this* creation.

(e) *Auctor*'s statement that shakable things are removed "as that which has been made" may be explained as an example of the curious absolutism which is characteristic of much biblical language. In Gen 6:8 God says "I will blot out man whom I have made (ἐποίησα) . . . for I am grieved that I have made (ἐποίησα) them," adding in 6:13 that "the end (lit. "time," καιρός) of all flesh has come before me (Heb בשר כל LXX παντὸς ἀνθρώπου) . . . and behold, I will destroy them and the earth"—a statement made in full knowledge that Noah, his family and numerous animals will be left to live, nor will the earth actually be destroyed. In other words, in one sense God destroys everything he has made, in another sense he does not (that *Auctor* knows Gen 6 and has adapted it to an eschatological setting is, incidentally, made clear by Heb 11:7). Similarly, in a passage redolent of the context of Hag 2:6, John of Patmos says that, after the old heaven and earth have passed away (21:1), "they shall bring into it (i.e., the new Jerusalem) the glory and the honour of the nations" (21:26; cp. v. 24). This statement is *prima facie* so jarring that Charles was induced, without textual evidence, to place the ingathering of the earthly riches *before* the destruction of the old heaven and earth.[180] Such surgery was unnecessary, for to the Hebrew mind there is no difficulty in postulating the annihilation of the old creation in absolute terms while at the same time assuming a continuity with what is old and familiar. In some sense God's new creation is always, even in the most apocalyptic and "annihilatory" texts, continuous with the old.

---

[178]Except for φαίνω (Heb 11:3), none of the specific terms which Philo uses to enforce a material-immaterial distinction (ὕλυ, αἰσθητά, σωματικός, τὰ νόητα) occur in Hebrews (cf. Williamson, *Philo and Hebrews*, 374-76). F. F. Bruce, "Hebrews," in *Peake's Commentary on the Bible* (Nelson, 1976) 1015, speaks of Christ's sacrifice as better than "*material* sacrifices" (italics mine) but since Christ's sacrifice is an offering of his *body* "once and for all" (10:10), it must be concluded that what distinguishes his sacrifice is not "immateriality," but its being offered out of a willing obedience (10:5ff.).

[179]Cf. Williamson ("The Eucharist of Hebrews," 305), who speaks of the true tent as "a sanctuary which, while a particular part of the 'created' realm, could properly be described as οὐ ταύτης τῆς κτίσεως."

[180]Cf. R. H. Charles, *A Critical and Exegetical Commentary on the Revelation of St. John* (Edinburgh, 1920) II, q.v.

The Hebrew language does not lend itself to the neat distinctions of the Greek philosophical tradition. It is precisely such Hebrew language which is closer to Heb 12:26ff. than any literature clearly or directly influenced by dualistic metaphysics. That "nothing unclean" shall enter the New Jerusalem (Rev 21:27) is John's counterpart of *Auctor*'s statement that "shakable things" will have no place in the messianic kingdom.

(f) Philo uses the terms ἀσάλευτος and μένω to describe the law of Moses.[181] This is something *Auctor* would never have done. Is he *correcting* Philo at this point? If so, it is strange that the correction would take the oblique form of an exegesis of Hag 2:6. It seems more likely that *Auctor* did not know Philo's teaching at this point, and that he is using terms drawn instead from the LXX of Hag 2.

(g) The claim that in Hebrews there is an annihilation of the created/material realm which allows for no new heaven and earth has occasionally been bolstered by a cross-reference of 12:26ff. with 1:11f. (Ps 102).[182] But the point of the catena of texts in chap. 1 is neither cosmology nor eschatology, but Christology. How far the language of the psalm may be used to illuminate concerns other than Christology is questionable.

(h) To say that μένω in 12:27 must indicate a Platonic concern with the continuation of the noumenal realm is tendentious. The LXX uses μένω often in translating עמד and קום both of which mean "to endure," "to be lasting." Isa 66:22LXX uses μένω for the new heaven and earth.[183] Is this "Platonic"? Hardly, particularly when it is noted that the term occurs in Zech 14:10LXX, a context concerning the New Jerusalem which is similar to Hag 2. In Zech 14, after a climactic *earthquake* which splits the Mount of Olives and displaces the surrounding mountains, it is said that "Rama shall remain (μενεῖ) in its place . . . and Jerusalem shall dwell securely" (v. 10f.). This context links the three motifs (earthquake, Jerusalem, and remaining) which figure prominently in Heb 12:22-28. The quotation of Hag 2:6 in chap. 12 may also bear some connection to Ps 16, a text not quoted by *Auctor*, but used by Luke (Acts 2:25-28). Luke, a writer with whom *Auctor* may have some affinity,[184] cites Ps 16:8 (Acts 2:25): "He is at my right hand so that I may not be *shaken*" (μὴ σαλευθῶ). Could this be the unstated link (via *gezerah shewah*) between *Auctor*'s argument elsewhere (cf. Ps 110:1) and Hag 2:6?[185] The thought in this case would be that those things which are in proper relation to God are "unshakable" precisely because they are aligned with Him who has Christ, the unshakable one (cf. Heb 13:8) at the right hand.

---

[181]Cf. De Vit. Mos. II.14: "But Moses is alone in this, that his laws, firm, unshaken, immovable, (βέβαι, ἀσάλευτα, ἀκράδαντα) . . . remain (μένει) secure . . . and we may hope that they will remain (διαμενεῖν) for all future ages as though immortal . . .").

[182]Cf. Cody, 85ff.

[183]The exegesis of Heb 12:25ff. may have been influenced by Isa 65:17, 66:22 and Dan 7 (for the "unshakable kingdom" of 12:28, cf. Dan 7:14; so Buchanan).

[184]Cf. C. P. M. Jones, "The Epistle to the Hebrews and the Lucan Writings," *Studies in the Gospels. Essays in Memory of R. H. Lightfoot,* ed. D. E. Nineham (Oxford, 1955) 113-43.

[185]For the use of Hag 2:6 in extra-canonical apocalyptic texts, see Jub 1:29; 4 Ezra 10:25-28; 2 Baruch 59:3; 1 Enoch 45:1, etc. For the use at Qumran of the motif of an eschatological earthquake, cf. 1QH 3:13ff. ("The fountains of the wall shall rock . . . the heavens shall roar . . . the world's foundations shall stagger and sway"). O. Betz ("The Eschatological Interpretation of the Sinai-Tradition in Qumran and in the NT," *RQ* 6 [1967] 89ff.) provides a useful discussion of the evidence.

VI
Conclusion

These indications suggest that there is little reason to turn aside from Jewish OT literature to literature directly influenced by Platonic-type metaphysical concerns in seeking to find the key to the writer's eschatology in these chapters. There is also little evidence to indicate that *Auctor* differs radically from the viewpoint of the mainstream apocalyptic tradition, for which there is a future heavenly Jerusalem and sanctuary to be manifested on earth. According to *Auctor*, Christ has already entered this shrine, but in some sense it is yet to appear in the course of human affairs.

Diachronic Development of Narrative and Exhortation Discourse Structures in Hebrew Epigraphical Sources

William J. Adams, Jr.

Middle East Center, University of Utah

This paper will attempt to describe how narrative and exhortation discourse structures changed and developed from the ninth century B.C. through the second century A.D. It is a semantic expansion of previous research done by the author and his co-workers (Adams et al., 1982).

Definitions

For this study we need to make the following definitions (Jones and Jones, 1979; and Longacre, 1983):

Discourse Structure is a concept which has come into modern linguistics only in the past decade or two. It is based on the fact that a speaker is attempting to communicate his ideas to a hearer. To do so they must be agreed on:

(a) the meaning of a set of sounds (morphophonology),
(b) how those sounds are to be organized into a meaningful sequence (syntax),
(c) how these meaningful sequences are to be ordered into a meaningful whole (discourse structure).

Thus, when a speaker says, "Let me tell you about our fishing trip," both speaker and hearer are going to be agreed on a procedure for putting the sentences together (discourse structure), so that there will be mutual understanding. With a statement like the above, the hearer knows that a narrative discourse will follow. He also knows that, if in English, the speaker will pay careful attention to the precise order in which the events occurred. The hearer will also expect information (such as when and where) as a background to the events. In each language specific genres (such as narrative and exhortation) are dealt with in specific ways in order to facilitate communication.

Levels of information has been referred to above. In a narrative the most important level of information is the chain of events. Lower levels of information deal with the general background of when and where the events occurred.

Foreground information in a narrative are the events which occurred. In exhortation it is the events which the speaker wishes will occur.

Backbone events are such statements as, "I caught a ten-pound bass.", "Buy a dress." They are unique to each narrative or exhortation context.

Ordinary events are events which one would normally expect to occur in a given context. In the context of the narrative of a fishing trip, an ordinary event would be a statement like, "I put a night crawler on the hook." In the exhortation of the purchase of a dress, an ordinary event would be a statement like, "And bring the sales slip home with you." Ordinarily a person is expected to do such, but in our example, the speaker was emphasizing that the ordinary be followed.

Background information in a narrative includes descriptions, thoughts, feelings, setting, participants, etc. In general, in both narrative and exhortation, they answer the questions, "When?", "Where?", "Why?", "Who?"

There are other levels of information, such as pivotal and peak events, which will not be addressed in this paper.

Methodology

As a method the author has found sentence outlining a useful tool. With this method the levels of information—backgrounding and foregrounding—assume positions. The sentences which are closest to margins (in the English) are generally backgrounding; the sentences which are in the middle of the outline are generally foregrounding. As we proceed, each example below will be outlined in English.

Control

The research in this paper will be controlled by considering what occurs in other world languages—either modern or ancient. By limiting ourselves to observed facts, we can be assured that our descriptions are within the realm of the possible.

NARRATIVE DISCOURSE STRUCTURE

From the ninth century came the Mesha stone (Anderson, 1966). Its discourse structure has been hinted at by Anderson, who first divided the stone into paragraphs (1966, 114-66). Following his suggestion we would outline his paragraphs as follows.

English

I.	I [am] Mesha, the son	אנכ.משע.בנ.
	of Kemosh, the king	כמש(ית).מלכ.
	of Moab, the Dibonite.	מאב.הדיהני.
	A. My father ruled	אבי.מלכ.
	over Moab [for]	על.מעב.
	thirty years.	שלשנ.שת.
	(And I ruled	ואנכ.מלכתי.
	after my father.)	אחר.אבי.
	1. And he built	ואעש.
	this high place	הבמת.זאת.

English	Moabite
for Kemosh	לכמש.
In Qarhoh . . . ,	בקרחה . . .
a. because	כי.
he saved me	השעני.
from all the kings,	מכל.המשלכן.
b. and because	וכי.
he made me triumph	הראני.
over all my enemies.	בכל.שנאי.
B. Omri ruled Israel.	עמרי.מלכ.ישראל.
1. And he humbled	ויענו.את.
Moab many years,	מעב.ימנ.רבנ.
a. because	כי.
Kemosh was angry	יאנפ.כמש.
with his land	בארצה.
2. And his son followed him.	ויחלפה.בנה.
3. And he also said:	ויאמר.גמ.הא.
4. "I will humble Moab."	אעמו.את.מעב.
C. In my time he spoke . . .	בימי.אמר.כמ.
1. But I triumphed	וארא.
over him and his house.	בה.ובבתה.
2. And Israel has indeed	וישראל.אבד
perished forever.	אבד.עלמ.
D. And Omri occupied	וירצ.עמרי.את.
all of the land of Medeba.	כל.ארצ.מהדבא.
1. And he dwelt there	וישב.בה.
his days and half of	ימה.וחצי.
the days of his son—	ימי.בנה.
forty years.	ארבענ.שת.
2. But Kemosh dwelt	וישב.בה.
there in my days.	כמש.בימי.
3. And I built Baal-meon.	ואבנ.את.בעלמענ.
4. And I made	ואעש.
the reservoir in it.	בה.האשוח.
5. And I built Qaryaten.	ואבנ.את.קריתנ.

This is half of the inscription and should give us sufficient data from which to draw conclusions. Since the left is background information we note that nearest this margin is the verbless sentence marked as (I.), which gives the background to the whole inscription. The configuration of the sentence is subject-complement (SC).

Next in rank, which gives a lesser degree of background, are the sentences marked with A, B, C, and D. Anderson refers to these sentences as "paragraph openers" (1966, 115). In modern English we might call these "topic sentences." Each of these sentences (except C) contains a subject, a verb, and an object (SVO). The verbs in each (except D) can be interpreted as perfects (*qatal*).

As we move further to the center towards foregrounding, we find the sentences marked with 1, 2, 3, etc. All of these (except C 2) begin with *waw* + imperfect (*wayyiqtol*). Each (except B 2, B 3, C 2, and D 2) does not contain a subject (VO).

Finally, the sentences marked a or b in A 1 and B 1 are relative clauses beginning with *ky*. The sentences in A 1 use *qatal* verbs and have no subject (*ky* VO); the sentence in B 2 mentions the subject and uses a *yiqtol* verb (*ky* VSO). Since background is defined as information not necessary for knowing the chain of events in a narrative, and since we would understand the chain of events narrated in this inscription without these three relative clauses, we may define them as background.

The following table will summarize our observations to this point.

Table 1

Levels of Information in Ninth-Century Narrative Discourse

Background Information	*Foreground Information*
SC nominal sentence	VO (wherein V = *wayyiqtol*)
SVO (wherein V = *qatal*)	VSO (wherein V = *wayyiqtol*)
OV (wherein V = *qatal*)	*waw* SV (wherein V = *qatal*) = C 2
Relative Clauses	

Notes: S = subject; C = complement; V = verb; O = object

In view of the general pattern here observed it may be wise to consider sentence C 2 as more on the background side of the outline. It also appears that the distinction between *qatal* and *wayyiqtol* and the presence or absence of a subject is a degree of background vs. foreground. This would give us a continuum as follows:

Table 2

Levels of Information Plotted on a Continuum

```
background - - - - - - - - - - - - - - - - - - - - - - - - - - -foreground
        SV                  V                 VS                V
   (V = qatal)         (V = qatal)       (V = wayyiqtol)   (V = wayyiqtol)

     SC  relative
         clauses
```

Another narrative discourse is the Siloam inscription from the seventh century B.C. (Vriezen, 1951: 28-30). Following is its outline:

English

I.	[This is] the tunnel.	(זה).הנקבה.
	And this was the	וזה.היה.
	story of the tunnel.	דבר.הנקבה.
	A. While [with] their axes	בעוד . . . . . הגרזנ.
	each man [was] facing another,	אש.אל.רעו.
	and while [there were]	ועוד.
	three cubits to the end,	שלש.אמת.להנ . . .
	1. And [there] was heard	וישמע.
	the voice of a man	קל.אש.
	calling to his co-worker	קרא.אל.רעו.

a. for [there] was	כי.הית.
an overlap	זרה.
in the rock	בצר.
on the left . . .	. . . מימנ
B. And at the time	ובימ.
the quarrymen	הנקבה.
drove through	הכו.
the tunnel	החצבימ.
each man facing	אש.לקרת.
his co-worker	רעו.
axes toward axes,	קרז . . . . רזנ.
1. and the waters	וילכו
flowed	המימ
from the source	מנ.המוצא
to the reservoir	אל.הברכה.
about two hundred	במאתימ.
and a thousand cubits.	ואלפ.אמה.
C. And a hundred cubits	ומ(א)ת. אמה.
was the height of the rock	היה.גבה.הצר.
above the heads of	
the quarry [men] .	. . . . על.ראש.החצב

We may surmise that the events being narrated are (1) the workmen could hear the voices of their co-workers digging from the other direction, and (2) the water was able to flow. The rest of the text then would be background to these two events.

Also from the seventh century is the letter of the servant's garment (Naveh, 1960). It can be outlined as follows:

English

I. May the official, my lord, hear the	
plea of his servant.	
A. Your servant was reaping	קצר היה עבדך
in Hasar-asam.	בחצר אשם
1. And your servant reaped	ויקצר עבדך
2. And he finished	ויכל
3. And I gathered	ואשמ
about a *ynm*	כינמ
before a rest	לפני שבת
B. As thy servant completed	כאשר כל עבדך
his reaping	את קצרו
he gathered in about a *ynm*.	אשמ כינמ
1. And Hashabiahu	ויבא חשביהו
ben Shobai came.	בנ שבי
2. And he took	ויקח את
the garment of your servant.	בגד עבדך
a. After I finished	כאשר כלת
my reaping	קצרי
(that [is] a *ynm*),	זה ינמ
he took	לקח את
the garment of	בגה עבהכ
your servant.	

Again we see the same patterns as encountered previously: backgrounding is achieved by relative clauses, and a nominal sentence; foreground information is conveyed by the use of VO (V = *wayyiqtol*) sentences. The salutation (I.) may also be considered as background since it is not necessary for understanding the chain of events. The seventh-century examples may be summarized as follows:

Table 3

Levels of Information in Seventh-Century Narrative Discourse

Background Information	Foreground Information
Nominal sentences	VS sentences (V = *wayyiqtol*)
SVO or OVS sentences	
(V = *qatal*)	
Ky clauses	
Kᵓšr clauses	

Moving on now to Qumran and the second century we find that most of the original writings of the community would be classified as a procedural genre (Longacre, 1983, 5). There are a number of recitals of history in the Zadokite Documents, but they are so overloaded with quotations from the Old Testament that they would not give us a clear picture of the narrative discourse structure of an original composition at the time of Qumran. However, the Habakkuk Commentary (Burrows, 1950, plates 55-61) contains narratives (without Old Testament quotations) as explanations of passages. For our purposes here we would like to sample the comments on Habakkuk 2:1-2, 2:5-6, and 2:15. These narratives can be outlined as follows:

Hab 2:1-2

I.	And God spoke	וידבר אל
	to Habakkuk	אל חבכוכ
	A. to write	לכתוב
	1. [that which]was to come	את הבאות
	upon the last	על הדור
	generation	האחרון
II.	But the moment of the end	ואת גמר הקץ
	He did not make known to him	לוא הודעו

Hab 2:5-6

I.	Its interpretation	פשרו
	[is] about the	על
	wicked priest	הכוהן הרשע
	A. who	אשר
	was called	נקרא
	by the name	על שם
	of truth	האמת

at the beginning	בתחלת
of his office	עומדו
but as	וכאשר
[he] ruled	משל
in Israel,	בישראל
his heart swelled	רם לבו
1. And he forsook God.	ויעזוב את אל
2. And he opposed	ו(י)בגוד
the statutes	בחוקים
for the sake of	בעבור
wealth.	הון
3. And he plundered.	ויגזול
4. And he sought	ויכבוץ
the wealth of the men of	הון אנשי
crime,	(ח)מס
a. who have	אשר
rebelled	מרדו
against God.	באל
5. And the wealth of the people	והון עמים
he took	לקח
to add upon himself	לוסיף עליו
the sin of guilt.	עון אשמה
6. And the ways of	ודרכי
abominations	ת(וע)בות
he did	פעל
in all the imputity of	בכול נדת
defilement	טמאה

Hab 2:15

I. Its interpretation [is]	פשרו
about the wicked priest	על הכוהן הרשע
A. who chased	אשר רדף
after the teacher of	אחר מורה
righteousness	הצדק
1. to swallow him	לבלעו
with the anger of	בכעס
his wrath,	חמתו
the fathers of exile.	אבות גלותו
B. And at the end of the	ובקץ
rest of the time of	מועד מנוחת
Yom Kippur	יום כפורים
he appeared	הופיע
to them	אליהם
1. to swallow them	לבלעם
2. and to trick them	ולכשולם
during the remainder	ביום צום
of their Sabbath fast.	שבת מנוחתם

The first item of interest which strikes us as we review the above is that the structure of previous ages is no longer functional. As we look at the comment on Hab 2:1-2, the first verb-form is a *wayyiqtol*; previously a *wayyiqtol* could only follow a *qatal*. Another striking observation is the occurrence of previously unencountered grammatical forms: the infinitive construct, the participles with *h-* to create a relative clause.

As we now seek the levels of information, we can note that the formula, "Its interpretation [is] concerning . . . ," sets the background. Also conveying background is the *h-* + participle construction. Finally, the *ᵓšr* clauses convey background information. But the *ᵓšr* clause in Hab 2:15, I A tends to answer the "what?" of the events conveyed. If for example we ask "What did the wicked priest do?", our first answer would be, "He chased the teacher." But this event is an *ᵓšr* clause. "What next did he do?" "He swallowed him with anger.", but this is an infinitive construct. In Hab 2:5-6 the foreground events (1-6) are conveyed by either VS (V = *wayyiqtol*) or a SV (V = *qatal*) sentences. Previously the latter had only been used for backgrounding.

With the following chart we may schematicize these observations:

Table 4

Levels of Information in Second-Century Narrative Discourse

Background Information	*Foreground Information*
Formula: "Its interpretation [is] about . . . ."	*wayyiqtol*
h- + participle	*qatal*
ᵓšr clauses (sometimes)	infinitive construct
	ᵓšr clauses (sometimes)

Unfortunately, no epigraphical sources with narratives have been found. Thus, we must stop here and proceed to an analysis of the structure of exhortation.

EXHORTATION DISCOURSE STRUCTURE

Among the eighth-century ostraca from Samaria is ostracon C1101 (Albright, 1936) which contains instructions to a person named Baruck. It may be outlined as follows:

I. Baruck: Peace.	ברכ שלמ
A. Baruck, pay attention.	ברכ הפעמ הקעב
1. And give Plny	ונתת לפלני
ben Ymn grain.	בנ ימנ סערמ

The address formula may be regarded as background information in which Baruck is prepared for the instruction which follows. The first instruction (pay attention) would ordinarily be expected. The second instruction would then be the backbone foreground information upon which Baruck is to act. The following table schematicizes the levels of information:

Table 5

Levels of Information in an Eighth-Century Exhortation Discourse

Background Information	Foreground Information	
	Ordinary	Backbone
Opening Formula	OV (V = imperative)	VO (V = wqatal)

This construction is seen frequently in Biblical Hebrew and has been the source of much debate over the functions of the Hebrew verb forms (Fall, 1982). The question has been: How can *qatal* be both past and present-future? Or: How can *qatal* be both perfect and imperfect? In this passage, the form *wntt* (for *w^{e}natatta*) is a *qatal* used imperfectly to convey a yet future action.

Perhaps the question should be asked: Why are there two ways (an imperative and a *wqatal*) for exhorting behavior? Earlier we could have asked: Why are there two ways (*qatal* and *wayyiqtol*) to convey the past tense in narrative? Our suggested answer then was to convey levels of information (*qatal* = background versus *wayyiqtol* = foreground). Our suggested answer here is the same: imperative = ordinary foreground versus *wqatal* = backbone foreground.

This raises a new question: Why does *qatal* convey background information in narrative but here in exhortation do a 180° turn and convey backbone foreground? As we turn to our controls we find the answer. Jones and Jones (1979: 24-25) have found in Mesoamerican and other native American languages a tendency for verb forms to switch functions as the type of discourse changes. Functionally, this helps the listener remember to which type of discourse he is listening. For the speaker, it reduces the number of forms which he must be able to generate in changing from one discourse to another.

As we now move forward in time to the sixth century we encounter the Arad letters (Aharoni, 1981) which are generally quite full of exhortation. Here is the outline of a few:

Arad #1

    I. To Eliashib: and now,   אל אלישב ועת

        A. give to the Kttym   נתנ לכתים

            3 baths of wine   ב 3 יינ 3

               1. and write the name   וכתב שמ

                  of the day.   הימ

        B. And from the rest of   ומעוד

           the first flour   הקמח ראשנ

           send a homer   תרכב חמר

           of flour   קמח

           to make for them bread.   לעשת להמ לחמ

        C. From the wine of   מיינ

           the *aganoth*-vessels   האגנת

           give.   תתנ

Arad #2

I. To Eliashib: and now,	אל אלישב ועת
A. Give to the Kttym	נתנ לכתתימ
2 baths of wine	ב 2 יינ
for four days	לארבעת היממ
and 300 [loaves of] bread	ו 003 לחמ
and a full homer of wine.	ומלא החמר יינ
1. And bring [all this] tomorrow,	והסבת מחר
2. don't be late.	אל תאחר
B. And if [there is] still vinegar,	ואמ עוה המצ
1. give [it] to them.	ונתת להמ

Arad #3

I. To Eliashib: and now,	אל אלישב ואת
A. Give from the wine	תנ מנ היינ
3 baths	3 ב
1. And Hananyahu will	וצוכ
command you	הנניהו
unto Beer Shiba	על באר שבע
with two loads	עמ משא צמד
of donkeys	חמרמ
2. And you will wrap up	וצררת
with them	אתמ
dough.	בצק
B. And count the wheat and bread	וספר החטמ והלחמ
and take	ולקחת . . .

Arad #17

I. To Nehum: and now,	אל נחמ ועת
A. Come to the house of	בא ביתה
Eliashib ben Eshiyahu.	אלישב בנ אשיהו
1. And take from there	ולקחת
one [jar of] oil.	1 שמנ
2. And send it	ושלח
to Zif quickly.	לזפ מחרה
3. And seal it	וחתמ
with tour seal.	בחתמכ

At the head of each letter is the formula "To . . . . : and now,". This formula sets the general background for each letter and would serve as an attention-getting device. In letter #1 there are three sets of instructions. The first one (A) is "give" (an infinitive absolute) followed by the incidental note to record the date (imperative). Instructions B and C are one sentence each with a *yiqtol* verb form.

In letter #2 there are two major concerns of the writer. In A the writer wants bread and wine delivered quickly. The "give" is the infinitive absolute (*ntn*); the "bring" is a *wqatal*; the "don't be late" is *ʾl + yiqtol*. In the second part (B) the concern is that vinegar be sent, if it is available.

Finally, in letter #17 the major concern of the writer is that oil be sent to Zif from the house of Eliashib. This major concern "take from there" is conveyed with *wlgḥt;* the other instructions are imperatives.

From these letters we may develop the following table:

Table 6

Levels of Information in Sixth-Century Exhortation Discourse

Background Information	*Foreground Information*	
	Ordinary	*Backbone*
The formula:	VO (V = imperative)	VO (V = inf. abs.)
"To . . . : and now,"	*ʾl* V (V = *yiqtol*)	OV (V = *yiqtol*)
VO (V = inf. const.)		VO (V = *wqatal*)
Nominal Clause (predicate N)		

The subdivision of foreground into ordinary and backbone levels is well attested in other languages. The ordinary events are what would be normally expected to occur, but are added by the author. For example in letter 1, part A, the instruction to "write the name of the day" would be expected to occur almost all of the time. But to give three baths of wine to the Kttym is not an ordinary event and is thus a backbone event. The same would be true of "don't be late." Ordinarily, deliveries in most cultures meet some type of a deadline.

We may now move on to the exhortation structure of the second century as exemplified by the writings of Qumran. The War Scroll (Yadin, 1962) column 12, lines 9b-15 contain a poem with direct instructions. It may be outlined as follows:

I.	Arise, O warrior.	קומה גבור
	A. Take the captive,	שבה שביכה
	O man of glory.	איש
	B. And take your booty,	ושול שללכ
	O doer of valiancy	עושי חיל
	C. Put your hand on the neck of	תנ ידכה בעורף
	your enemies	אויביכה
	and your foot on	ורגלכה על
	the dead of the slain.	במותי חלל
	D. Crush the nations,	מחצ גוים
	your adversary.	צריכה
	E. And your sword, let it devour	וחרבכה תואכל
	[the]flesh of [the] guilty.	בשר אשמה
	F. Fill your land [with] glory	מלא ארצכה כבוד
	and your inheritance	ונחלתכה

[with] blessings,	ברכה
a multitude of cattle	המון מקנה
in your inheritances	בחלקותיכה
and gold and precious	וזהב ואבני
stones	חפצ
in your places.	בהיכלותיכה

II. O Zion, rejoice exceedingly.   ציון שמחי מאדה
   A. Shine forth in praise,
      O Jerusalem   והופיעי ברנות ירושלים
   B. Be joyful, O all cities
      of Judah   והגלנה כול ערי יהודה
   C. Open your gates forever   פתחי שערכ תמיד
      to let into you the   להביא אליכ
      substance of nations   חיל גואימ
      and their kings will serve you.   ומלכיהמ יסרתוכ

The poem is in two parts: first, the warrior is called into action. Second, as a result of his efforts, Zion can rejoice. The entries I and II could be thought of as the backbone foreground events. Such events as "take the captive," "fill your land with glory" could be thought of as the ordinary events expected of a warrior. Also once Zion is able to rejoice, then the ordinary event expected would be "to give praise," "to include other cities in the festivities," "to leave the city gates open." Sentence I does have an imperative, *qwmh*, which has been lengthened by *-h*. But so does sentence I A. The rest of the imperatives appear normal. One interesting feature in part I, however, is the inclusion of the subject in sentences I, I A, and I B. The same occurs in II, II A, and II B. Of further interest in sentence II is the fact that the order is reversed by the occurrence of the subject first. Finally, we should note the order in which the listener would hear the information. In each part he would first hear the backbone information; this would then be followed by the ordinary, expected events.

Another exhortation passage we may analyze from Qumran is found in the Manual of Discipline (Burrows, 1950), column 9, lines 13-14. It can be outlined as follows:

I. To do the will of God	לעשות את רצונ אל
according to all	ככול
[which] has been revealed	הנגלה
from time to time.	לעת בעת
II. To study all	ולמוד
wisdom	השכל
[which] has been found	הנמצא
previously	לפי העתימ
and the law [for]	ואת חוק
different circumstances.	העת להבדיל

Here we find, for the first time in the epigraphical sources, an infinitive construct used for exhortation. (Another interesting first is the use of the definite participle as a relative clause). The use of this type of exhortation is quite common in the Manual of Discipline and elsewhere in Qumran. We are not able here to distinguish between backbone and ordinary events though seemingly each of the two above could be thought of as ordinary, since the hearers are to practice these prescriptions daily (Gaster, 58).

It may also be noted that in both of the above examples the background is set by the contents of the paragraphs which precede each of the above sets of exhortations. We may now summarize our discoveries in the following table:

Table 7
Levels of Information in Second-Century Exhortation Discourse

Background Information	Foreground Information	
	Ordinary	*Backbone*
The previous paragraph	Imperative	Imperative +
h + participle	without	Subject
	subject	
	Infinitive	Unusual Word
	construct	Order
	Second posi-	First Position
	tion in	in events
	events	listed
	listed	

Finally, a Bar-Kochba (Hestrin, 1973) letter can give us insights into the structure of second-century A.D. exhortation discourse. Here is a suggested outline for it:

I. From Shimon   משמעון
    to Yeshua ben Galgola,   לישוע בן גלגולה
    Peace!   שלום
    A. Send cereal,   תבו
        five *kors* of wheat   חמשת כורין חטין
        to my householders . . .   לביתי
        known by you.   אצלכ בדעת
    B. And prepare for them   ותתקן
        a suitable place.   מקום פנין
        1. They will be with you   יהו בו אצלכ
            this Sabbath,   תשבת הזה
        2. if they want to come.   אמ יהפצו לבו
    C. And take heart.   והתחזק
        1. And strengthen the others.   וחזק תמקום
        2. It [is]well.   הוי שלום
    D. And I have ordered someone,   ופקדת תמי
        1. that he will give you wheat. שיתנ לכ תהטינ

Paragraph D seems to be more explanation than exhortation and thus will not be considered here. We may plot the levels of information in this letter as follows:

Table 8

Levels of Information in Second-Century A.D. Exhortation Discourse

Background Information	Foreground Information	
	Ordinary	*Backbone*
Opening formula: "From . . . to Peace."	V (V = imperative) VO (V = imperative)	VO (V = yiqtol)
OV (V = inf. const.) ʾm VO (V = yiqtol) Nominal Sentence (N predicate)		

SUMMARY

Narrative Discourse Structure

As we now review the above we can discern groupings into which the various eras may be combined. For example, the pre-exilic narrative discourse structures appear to be quite similar; whereas the post-exilic examples are quite different. Also where the ʾšr clauses seem to be vacillating between background and foreground in the post-exilic era, we may surmise that the language (with respect to narrative discourse at the time of Bar-Kochba) was in a stage of flux and change, seeking a new balance. We may schematicize these observations in the following table:

Table 9

Diachronic Development of the Expression of
Levels of Information in Narratives in Hebrew Epigraphical Sources
(Ninth to Second Centuries B.C.)

Date	Background Information	Foreground Information
Pre-exilic	Nominal sentences SVO (V = qatal) OV (V = qatal) Ky clauses (k)ʾšr clauses Formulas	V(S)O (V = wayyiqtol)
Post-exilic	Nominal sentences Formulas h- + participle (k)ʾšr clauses (sometimes)	V(S)O (V = wayyiqtol) (sometimes without a preceding qatal) SVO (V = qatal) (k)ʾšr clauses (sometimes)

The shifts may be plotted as:

Table 10

Various Shifts and Innovations in Forms Used to Convey Various Levels of Information

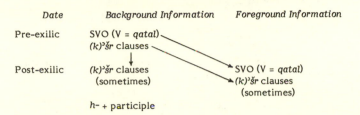

Date	Background Information	Foreground Information
Pre-exilic	SVO (V = *qatal*) *(k)ʾšr* clauses	
Post-exilic	*(k)ʾšr* clauses (sometimes) *h-* + participle	SVO (V = *qatal*) *(k)ʾšr* clauses (sometimes)

Exhortation Discourse Structure

As we consider, now, the structure of exhortation, we realize that it is useful to subdivide foregrounding into backbone events and ordinary events. In addition, there does not seem to be a sudden change as was observed in the narrative discourse. We may plot our findings as follows:

Table 11

Diachronic Development of the Expression of Levels of Information in Exhortation in Hebrew Epigraphical Sources (Eighth Century B.C. to Second Century A.D.)

Date (Century)	Background Information	Foreground Information	
		Ordinary	Backbone
8th B.C.	Formula	Imperative	*wqatal*
6th B.C.	Formula Infinitive construct (as object of a verb)	Imperative *ʾl* + *yiqtol*	Infinitive Absolute *wqatal* *yiqtol*
Exile 2nd B.C.	Previous context	Imperative Infinitive construct not as an object of a verb) Secondary position in list of events	Imperative with a a subject Unusual word order Primary position in list of events

2nd A.D.	Formula	Imperative	*yiqtol*
	Nominal		
	sentence		
	ʾm clause		
	Infinitive		
	construct		
	(as object		
	of a verb)		

As a matter of fact, we may say that the only real change over the millennium observed is the loss of *wqatal* with the exile.

CONCLUSIONS

In describing the language, the exile seems to have been the critical point for change in the discourse structure of narrative and the point for the loss of *wqatal* in the discourse structure of exhortation. In a future study the author will address the problem of "why" these changes occurred in this particular time.

There are other levels of information such as peak and pivotal events which need to be added to this description. Future research will include these plus new insights as they are discovered in general linguistics. Or even better still, insights from our research would aid general linguistics.

The author laments the fact that we have so little data with which to work. As new epigraphical sources are discovered they will be added to this description. But despite the small volume of sources available, this paper should alert us to the fact that what is available can reveal important insights.

It should be noted that the ultimate aim of the author's research is to develop a technique for dating passages in the Old Testament (Adams and Adams, 1977a; 1977b; Adams et al., 1982). As was mentioned early in the article, the author is concerned about the concept of control. He views the epigraphical sources as the major control for dating Old Testament passages. He does this on the basis that (1) archaeology has given us at least a relative chronology, if not an exact date for the various epigraphical sources and (2) the epigraphical sources are original autographs, which have not been passed through the hands of many copyists and recopyists. As more epigraphical sources are added to this research and as a fuller description is developed, the author will attempt to move from the control (the epigraphical sources) into the biblical text itself.

Finally, as was mentioned above in the discussion of Table 5, it appears that discourse grammar may yield the resolution to the age-old dilemma of what the function of the Old Testament Hebrew verb forms was. According to Fall (1982) and the author (Adams, 1972; 1975), the past resolutions have been tense (with *waw*-conversive) or aspect (with *waw*-consecutive). The author has been applying discourse grammar to a number of biblical passages (via the sentence outline method) with very productive results. But, alas, this also must be relegated to a future monograph.

BIBLIOGRAPHY

Adams, L. La Mar, William J. Adams, Jr., Wayne A. Larsen and Linden G. Sloan. 1982. In Press. "Computerized Dating of Biblical Texts by Use of Language Drift." In: *Computer Applications in Ancient Near Eastern Studies,* edited by James F. Strange.

Adams, Jr., William J. 1972. "The Functions of Biblical Hebrew Verb Forms as Determined by Statistical Sampling of Verbs." *Hebrew Abstracts* 13:69-72.

_____. 1975. "Determining the Functions of Biblical Hebrew Verb Forms by a Statistical Sampling of Verbs." *Hebrew Computational Linguistics* 9:E1-E21.

Adams, Jr., William J. and L. La Mar Adams. 1977a. "A Computer Generated Technique for Dating Biblical Passages." *Hebrew Computational Linguistics* 11:E1-E12.

_____. 1977b. "Language Drift and the Dating of Biblical Passages." *Hebrew Studies* 18:160-64.

Aharoni, Yohanan. 1981. *Arad Inscriptions.* Jerusalem: The Israel Exploration Society. Pp. 12-34.

Albright, William F. 1936. "Ostracon C 1101 of Samaria." *PEQ* 68:211-15.

Anderson, Francis I. 1966. "Moabite Syntax." *Orientalia* 35:81-120.

Burrows, Millar. 1950. *The Dead Sea Scrolls of St. Mark's Monastery.* New Haven: The American Schools of Oriental Research.

Fall, Leslie. 1982. *The Enigma of the Hebrew Verbal System: Solutions from Ewald to the Present Day.* Towbridge: The Almond Press.

Gaster, Theodore H. 1956. *The Dead Sea Scriptures in English Translation.* Garden City, NY: Doubleday.

Hestrin, Ruth. 1973. *Inscriptions Reveal.* Jerusalem: Israel Museum, Catalog No. 100. P. 188.

Jones, Larry B. and Linda K. Jones. 1979. "Multiple Levels of Information in Discourse." In: *Discourse Studies in Mesoamerican Languages,* edited by L. Jones. Arlington: The Summer Institute of Linguistics and the University of Texas at Arlington.

Longacre, Robert E. 1983. *The Grammar of Discourse.* New York: Plenum Press.

Naveh, J. 1960. "A Hebrew Letter from the Seventh Century B.C." *IEJ* 10:129-39.

Vriezen, T. C. and J. H. Hospers. 1951. *Palestine Inscriptions.* Leiden: Brill.

Yadin, Yigael. 1962. *The Scroll of the War of the Sons of Light against the Sons of Darkness.* Oxford: University Press.

A Rhetorical Typology for Classifying and Analyzing Pronouncement Stories

Vernon K. Robbins

Emory University

DEFINITION AND TYPOLOGY IN RECENT WORK

To inaugurate the initial period of research by the Pronouncement Story Group (1975-81), Robert C. Tannehill formulated a definition of a pronouncement story that guided the search through Mediterranean literature dated 250 B.C.E.—250 C.E. According to the definition:

> A pronouncement story is a brief narrative in which the climactic (and often final) element is a pronouncement which is presented as a particular person's response to something said or observed on a particular occasion of the past. There are two main parts of a pronouncement story: the pronouncement and its setting, i.e., the response and the situation provoking the response. The movement from the one to the other is the main development in these brief stories (1981:1).

This definition of a pronouncement story gave us a good start with a new approach. With this definition we have been able to go to various corpora of literature and find good examples of pronouncement stories.

Building on the definition, a typology of pronouncement stories was developed on the basis of the rhetorical feature essential for the movement from the situation to the response. From this perspective, the typology contained six basic types of pronouncement stories:

1. correction stories, where the story ends with the main character correcting one or more individuals;
2. commendation stories, where the story ends with the main character commending one or more individuals;
3. objection stories, where an objection calls forth the response from the main character;
4. quest stories, where a secondary person's success or failure in a quest of something important to human well-being had prominence alongside the main character's response;
5. inquiry stories, where the story ends with a response by the main character to an inquiry;
6. description stories, where the story ends with a description of the situation by the main character (Tannehill 1982:6-11).

The search through Mediterranean literature revealed that the largest percentage of pronouncement stories were correction stories, that the quest story appeared to be distinctive to New Testament literature, and that a surprisingly small number of pronouncement stories occur in Jewish literature before the Amoraic period, whether written in Greek, Hebrew or Aramaic.

On the basis of research in the χρεία and related forms in ancient rhetorical treatises,[1] I recommend three revisions of the definition. First the response of a particular person may be given either in speech or action or in a combination of speech and action. The ancient rhetoricians, observing this phenomenon in the χρεία, distinguished between the sayings χρεία   (ἡ λογική χρεία),   the action χρεία   (ἡ πρακτική χρεία), and the mixed χρεία containing both speech and action (ἡ μικτή χρεία) (Theon, *Progymnasmata* 202.18-20: Walz). Secondly, the main character in the story may be either the author or the recipient of the pronouncement.[2] The ancient rhetoricians, seeing this, distinguished between active χρεῖαι (performed by the main character) and passive χρεῖαι (performed on the main character) (Theon, *Progymnasmata* 205.19-21: Walz). Accordingly, pronouncement stories featuring either speech or action (or both) may be active or passive. Thirdly, both the setting and the response are vehicles for transmitting the ἦθος of the main character in the story. Here, the pronouncement story differs from the kind of χρεῖαι which contains a saying without a setting. A pronouncement story contains both a setting and a response. The major task of a rhetorical interpretation of a pronouncement story must be to discern and explain the goal toward which both the setting and the response move. I suggest, therefore, that the definition be revised as follows:

> A pronouncement story is a brief narrative in which the climactic (and often final) element is a pronouncement either in speech or action or a combination of speech and action. There are two main parts of a pronouncement story: the pronouncement and its setting, i.e., the response and the situation provoking the response. The pronouncement is closely associated with the main character who is the author or recipient of the poignant speech or action. Both the setting and the pronouncement are vehicles for transmitting the ἦθος of the main character and achieving the rhetorical goal of the story.

---

[1] I am indebted to Thomas M. Conley, who was my colleague at the University of Illinois at Urbana-Champaign, and to Burton L. Mack, Edward N. O'Neil, Ronald F. Hock, and James R. Butts—members of the Chreia Project at the Institute for Antiquity and Christianity at Claremont—for their guidance through ancient rhetorical literature. I must accept responsibility, however, for its application in this paper. I am also grateful to Peder Borgen, Dagfinn Rian, and others in the Religionsvitenskapelig Institutt, and Øivind Andersen, professor of Classics, at the University of Trondheim, Norway, where I produced the final version of this paper under the sponsorship of a Fulbright-Hays Research-Lecture Fellowship.

[2] Tannehill (1983:1) recommends that "the main character may, perhaps, be defined as other than the speaker of the pronouncement if (1) the recipient of the pronouncement is the main character in the context document or (2) the recipient is named and known while the speaker is not."

With this definition, both speech and action are given proper attention, both active and passive dimensions are accommodated, and both the setting and the response become the means for classifying the story.

Along with a revision of the definition should also come a revision of the typology. An admirable quality of the typology used during the initial period of research was its simple, direct observation of one basic rhetorical phenomenon in each pronouncement story. With this approach, however, certain problems began to appear. First of all, more than one rhetorical feature regularly plays a role in the movement from the setting to the response in a pronouncement story. Thus a system of classification needs to identify a basic type while allowing for a variety of features in the movement of the setting and the response toward its rhetorical goal. Second, both the definition and the typology should encourage detailed analysis of pronouncement stories. Detailed analysis is most natural when the basic types establish a framework for identifying sub-groups that share one or more features in common.

On the basis of 200 pronouncement stories I found in four of Plutarch's *Parallel Lives,* I revised Tannehill's typology to include more stories and distinguish more features than I thought I could include in the initial system (1981:29-52). Using insights from David E. Aune's study of Plutarch's *Banquet of the Seven Sages* (1979), I grouped the categories under three major headings—(1) aphoristic stories; (2) adversative stories; and (3) affirmative stories—and distinguished between first, second and third person address in the responses (see Crossan's diagram 1983:82). This procedure produced two new categories—the rebuff and the laudation—and differentiated self (first person), direct (second person) and indirect (third person) corrections and commendations (Robbins, 1981:29-52).

I am now convinced that my revision of the typology was not sufficient. Instead of using aphoristic, adversative and affirmative categories for distinguishing types of pronouncement stories, I should have used the standard rhetorical categories of deliberative, juridical (often called forensic) and epideictic. These three types of rhetoric were discussed at length by the ancient rhetoricians, and I propose that they offer a system for accurate classification and analysis of the stories.

When an interpreter organizes pronouncement stories under a system guided by deliberative, juridical and epideictic rhetoric, six basic types of stories emerge:

1. Display Stories
2. Thesis Stories
3. Exhortation Stories
4. Defense Stories
5. Praise Stories
6. Censure Stories

These types reflect the rhetoricians' basic use of the stories both in the literature which they wrote and in the settings where they taught. First and foremost, a pronouncement story displays the ἦθος of the person who is featured as the main character in the story. This means that the underlying framework of all pronouncement stories is epideictic rhetoric, the rhetoric of display (ἐπίδειξις). The display story reaches its rhetorical goal in a display in and of itself. Sometimes the display is clever and witty; sometimes it is simply an exhibition of the role and character of the person who is featured in the story. Every pronouncement story displays an attribute of the ἦθος of the main character, but a display story completes its rhetorical goal with that function. Second, the pronouncement in the story may function as a thesis about thought and action that is designed to engage the reader in reflection, interaction, and decision. When a pronouncement story reaches its goal in the presentation of a thesis, this kind of story can be called a thesis story. Third, the story may reach its goal in an exhortation by the main character. The exhortation invests either an attribute of ἦθος or a thesis held by the main character as a result of his ἦθος. A major sub-type of exhortation story regularly reaches its rhetorical goal in an exhibition of the response to the exhortation. Fourth, a particular investment of ἦθος or the statement of a thesis calls for a rationale. Placed in the epideictic setting of a pronouncement story, a rationale defends a particular form of action and thought. The defense story reaches its goal in the presentation of a rationale for a particular form of action and/or thought manifested in the story. Fifth, the exhibition of action and thought may bring forth evaluation either through praise or censure. Therefore, some pronouncement stories reach their goal in praise and others reach their goal in censure. These two categories bring the underlying epideictic nature of the pronouncement story full circle, since the most undeveloped type presents a sheer display of ἦθος and the praise and censure stories present an evaluation of display.

It is important to notice that this typology exhibits an essentially cumulative sphere of display in pronouncement stories. In other words, some rhetorical features may presuppose or build upon other rhetorical features. Regularly, then, rhetorical features which represent the goal in one type will contribute to a different goal in a different type of story. This means that the types of stories are determined by the final rhetorical goal attained by the story. Also, expansion of the story may either elaborate the original goal or introduce a new goal (and thus move the story into a new type).

Within any type of pronouncement story, a range of variation may exist. Often this variation results from the presence of rhetorical features the research group used to establish the typology during the initial period of research. For example, the declarative setting characteristic of the description story, the interrogative setting characteristic of the inquiry story, and the corrective setting characteristic of the correction story may be present in any of the basic types. These are rhetorical features subordinate to the overall goal of the story. They do not, therefore, determine the basic type of story but are present in various types. Also, a setting dominated by action or a response containing a comparison may be present. An interpreter may create sub-categories on the basis of the presence of one or more of the features that are regularly in other types. To illustrate how these features may be present, I have included five headings under each type, even when I have not furnished an example of the type with the feature in prominence:

1. Declarative Setting
2. Interrogative Setting
3. Corrective Setting
4. Action Setting
5. Comparative Response

Since various combinations of features may produce sub-types within a basic type, any number of groupings may be made under the basic types. Also, a single story may contain features which allow it to be placed under a number of sub-categories. Often these sub-categories are of little importance or are debatable, but sometimes a major sub-type appears. I have included one noticeable sub-type of the exhortation story—the call story (recently investigated by Arthur Droge)—to illustrate how a major sub-type may be found and investigated in terms of its own range of form and features. Virtually any category may feature declaration, inquiry, or correction. Also, the response may contain a comparison, and the object with which the thing is being compared may or may not be explicitly stated. Moreover, the main character may engage in direct action or speech, be the recipient of the action or speech, or be involved in a combination of initiation and receipt of action and speech. As a result, any category may be divided into sub-categories on the basis of this kind of variation in the story. I will include some sub-categories to illustrate how this works.

DISPLAY STORIES

Underlying every pronouncement story is epideictic rhetoric. Epideictic rhetoric concerns people. At its center is exhibition or display (ἐπίδειξις), and that which it exhibits or displays is the role, character and reputation (ἦθος) of a particular person. No matter what additional features may be present in a pronouncement story, every pronouncement story displays one or more attributes of a person's character. Some pronouncement stories are *simply* "display stories." The total rhetorical investment of the story is a display of an attribute of the character of a particular person, and this attribute is displayed by means of speech or action by themselves or in combination with one another. Examples of "display stories" are as follows:

A. *Declarative Setting*

1. Plutarch, Caesar 7.3:

    The day for the election came, and as Caesar's mother accompanied him to the door in tears, he kissed her and said "Mother, today thou shalt see thy son either pontifex maximus or an exile."

B. *Interrogative Setting*

2. Plutarch, Bellone an Pace Clariores Fuerint Athenienses 350D:[3]

    But Isocrates, although he had declared that those who had risked their lives at Marathon had fought as though their souls were not their own, and although he had hymned their daring and their contempt of life, himself (so they say), when he was already an old man, replied to someone who asked him how he was getting on, "Even as does a man over ninety years of age who considers death the greatest of evils."

3. Plutarch, Caesar 63.7:

    Moreover, on the day before, when Marcus Lepidus was entertaining him at supper, Caesar chanced to be signing letters, as his custom was, while reclining at table, and the discourse turned suddenly to the subject of

---

[3]The pronouncement stories from Plutarch's *Moralia* in this paper are quoted from Alsup.

what sort of death was best; before anyone else could answer Caesar
cried out: "That which is unexpected."

C. Corrective Setting

4. Plutarch, Demosthenes 8.3-5:

    Demosthenes was rarely heard to speak on the spur of the moment, but
    though the people often called upon him by name as he sat in the
    assembly, he would not come forward unless he had given thought to the
    question and was prepared to speak upon it. For this, many of the popu-
    lar leaders used to rail at him, and Pytheas, in particular, once told him
    scoffingly that his arguments smelt of lampwicks. To him, then, Demos-
    thenes made a sharp answer. "Indeed," said he, "thy lamp and mine, O
    Pytheas, are not privy to the same pursuits."

D. Action Setting

E. Comparative Response

In each of these stories, the rhetorical investment in the setting and the response has the
basic goal of displaying the ἦθος of the main character in the story. This dimension lies
at the base of every pronouncement story, but a story may display a particular thought or
action in a form that takes the reader into deliberative or juridical rhetoric. All three of
the basic kinds of rhetoric, therefore, may be present in a pronouncement story if the
story is more than a display story.

THESIS STORIES

While the display of one or more attributes of character underlies every pronouncement story, the action or speech may introduce a thesis. This thesis may be deliberative,
juridical or epideictic in nature.

I. Deliberative Thesis

A thesis story may be deliberative in nature, simply defining thought or action in a
reflective, deliberative mode. The purpose of deliberative rhetoric is to determine what
action is most expedient and what thoughts are most beneficial to accept. Therefore,
deliberative stories keep the rhetoric focused on a particular issue concerning action or
thought. A setting constituted by deliberative rhetoric usually concerns action not yet
performed and a way of thinking not yet revealed. In other words, the goal of the story is
to reveal an opinion concerning the expediency of alternative points of view and kinds of
action. Deliberative rhetoric does not entertain accusations or defenses of past action,
and it does not allow personal statements, positive or negative, to dominate. Deliberative
rhetoric concerns statement and counterstatement on ways of acting and thinking bene-
ficially. Examples of deliberative thesis stories are as follows:

A. *Declarative Setting*

1. Plutarch, Quomodo Quis Suos in Virtute Sentiat Profectus 79E:

   Aeschylus at the Isthmian games was watching a boxing-match, and when one of the men was hit and the crowd in the theatre burst into a roar, Aeschylus nudged Ion of Chios, and said, "You see what a thing training is; the man who is hit says nothing; it is the spectators who shout."

B. *Interrogative Setting*

2. Philostratus, Life of Apollonius of Tyana 1.37:

   When the king asked him (Apollonius) how he could rule with stability and security, he said, "Honoring many but trusting few."

3. Plutarch, Vitae Decem Oratorum 838F:

   When someone asked him (Isocrates) "What is oratory?" he said, "the art of making small things great and great things small."

4. Plutarch, Sayings of Spartans 215D:

   When asked what form of instruction was most in vogue in Sparta, he (Agis) said, "Knowledge of how to rule and be ruled."

5. Plutarch, Sayings of Spartans 224D:

   Being asked what freeborn boys had best learn, he (Leotychidas) said "Those things which may help them when they become men."

6. Diogenes Laertius, Lives 1.77:

   Once, when asked what is the best thing, he (Pittacus) replied, "To do well the work at hand."

7. 2 Clement 12.2 (Funk-Bihlmeyer: 76):[4]

   For when the Lord himself was asked by someone when his kingdom would come, he said, "When the two shall be one and the outside as the inside and the male with the female neither male nor female."

C. *Corrective Setting*

---

[4]The pronouncement stories from early Christian apocryphal literature in this paper are quoted from Stroker.

D. Action Setting

E. Comparative Response

II. Juridical Thesis (Definition of Law)

Instead of maintaining a strictly deliberative mode of interaction, the thesis story may invest itself in a juridical thesis. Juridical rhetoric concerns laws, accusations and the debating of guilt or innocence. The juridical thesis is the statement of a law. Once a law is stated or people think a certain law should be stated, juridical rhetoric ensues. Examples of juridical thesis stories are as follows:

A. Declarative Setting

1. Sifre Deut 80:[5]

    One time R. Judah b. Bathyra, R. Mattyah b. Harash, R. Hananyah b. Ahai, R. Joshua and R. Yonatan were leaving the Land (of Israel). When they reached Palton, they recalled the Land of Israel and they stood erect while their eyes shed tears. They rent their garments and recited this verse: "(*You shall indeed cross the Jordan to enter and to make the land your own that the Lord your God is giving you.) You shall possess it and shall live in it and you must keep and observe all the laws* . . ." (Deut 11:31). They said: "Living in the Land of Israel is equal to observing all of the (other) commandments (stated) in the Torah."

B. Interrogative Setting

C. Corrective Setting

2. M. Ber. 1.1:

    One time (R. Gamaliel)'s sons returned (after midnight) from a wedding feast. They said to him: "We have not yet recited the *Shema*." He said to them: "If the morning star has not yet risen, you (still) are obligated to recite (it)."

D. Action Setting

E. Comparative Response

III. Epideictic Thesis

The epideictic thesis story, in contrast to the deliberative or juridical thesis story,

---

[5]The pronouncement stories from rabbinic literature in this paper are quoted from Avery-Peck.

defines action or thought in a personal form. In other words, the epideictic thesis story introduces a thesis about personal character. Examples are as follows:

A. *Declarative Setting*

B. *Interrogative Setting*

    1. Tos. Shebu. 3.6:

        One time R. Reuben spent the Sabbath in Tiberias, and one philosopher found him. He said to him "Which is the one who is hated in the world?" (Reuben) said to him: "The one who denies his Creator." (The philosopher) said to him: "How (does he deny Him)?" (Reuben) said to him: *"Honor your father and your mother. Do not murder. Do not commit adultery. Do not steal. Do not bear false witness against your neighbor. Do not covet.* Behold, a man does not deny a thing until he denies (its) essential part. And a man commits a sin only after he has denied (the existence) of the one who commanded concerning it."

    2. Sifre Deut 13:

        Choose wise, understanding (and experienced) men (Deut 1:13). This is the question Arios asked R. Yose: (Arios) said to him: "Which is a wise man?" (Yose) said to him: "He who practices that which he teaches. Or perhaps (such a person) is (referred to) rather (as) an understanding man?" (Arios) said to him: *"Understanding men* is already said (in the above verse). What is the difference between a wise man and an understanding man?" (Yose said to him:) "A wise man is similar to a rich (gold) smith. When (others) bring him (gold) to examine (lit.: see) he examines (it). When (others) do not bring him (gold) to examine, he takes out his own (gold) and examines (it). An understanding man is similar to a poor (gold) smith. When (others) bring him (gold) to examine, he examines (it). When (others) do not bring him (gold) to examine, he must sit and be idle."

C. *Corrective Setting*

    3. Luke 9:57-58:

        As they were going along the road, a man said to him, "I will follow you wherever you go." And Jesus said to him, "Foxes have holes, and birds of the air have nests: but the Son of man has nowhere to lay his head."

D. *Action Setting*

E. *Comparative Response*

    4. Plutarch, Quomodo Quis Suos in Virtute Sentiat Profectus 79E:

        Brasidas caught a mouse among some dried figs, got bitten, and let it go:

thereupon he said to himself, "Heavens, there is nothing so small or so weak that it will not save its life if it has courage to defend itself."

EXHORTATION STORIES

Epideictic pronouncement stories may invest the character of the person in a thesis by having him adopt imperative mode of speech. The result is an exhortation story. In an exhortation story, the main character confronts another with a personal challenge. Examples of the exhortation story are:

A. *Declarative Setting*

1. Mark 1:14-15:

    Now after John was arrested, Jesus came into Galilee, preaching the gospel of God, and saying, "The time is fulfilled, and the kingdom is at hand; repent, and believe in the gospel."

B. *Interrogative Setting*

C. *Corrective Setting*

2. Gospel of the Egyptians, from Clement Alex., Strom. 3.9.66 (Stahlin-Fruchtel: 226):

    For when she said, "I have done well then in not having borne children," as if it were improper to engage in procreation, then the Lord answered and said, "Eat every plant, but do not eat the one which contains bitterness."

3. Plutarch, De Alexandri Magni Fortuna aut Virtute 331B-C:

    When the thigh of his father Philip had been pierced by a spear in battle with the Triballians, and Philip, although he escaped with his life, was vexed with his lameness, Alexander said, "Be of good cheer, father, and go on your way rejoicing, that at each step you may recall your valour."

4. Plutarch, De Alexandri Magni Fortuna aut Virtute 344F-345B:

    Finally, the Macedonians routed the barbarians, and, when they had fallen, pulled down their city on their heads. But this was of no help to Alexander: for he had been hurried from the field, arrow and all, and he had the shaft in his vitals: the arrow was as a bond or bolt holding his breastplate to his body. And when they tried forcibly to pull it out of the wound by the roots, as it were, the iron would not budge, since it was lodged in the bony part of the breast in front of the heart. They did not dare to saw off the protruding portion of the shaft, since they were afraid that the bone might be split by the jarring and cause excruciating pain, and that an internal haemorrhage might result. But when Alexander perceived their great perplexity and hesitation, he himself tried with his

dagger to cut off the arrow close to his breastplace: but his hand was
unsteady and affected by the torpid languor from the inflammation of
the wound. Accordingly with encouraging words he urged those that were
unwounded to take hold and not to be afraid: and he railed at some who
were weeping and could not control themselves, others he branded as
deserters, since they had not the courage to come to his assistance. And
he cried aloud to his Companions. "Let no one be fainthearted even for
my sake! For it will not be believed that I do not fear death, if you fear
death for me!"

D. *Action Setting*

E. *Comparative Response*

CALL STORIES

The call story is a special kind of exhortation story. This story contains both an
active and a passive dimension. The main character performs either the speech or action
that calls another person or persons to follow him. The person who is called then responds
positively or negatively to the main character.

A. *Declarative Setting*

1. Mark 1:16-18:

    And passing along by the Sea of Galilee, he saw Simon and Andrew the
    brother of Simon casting a net in the sea; for they were fishermen. And
    Jesus said to them, "Follow me and I will make you fishers of men." And
    immediately they left their nets and followed him.

2. Mark 1:18-20:

    And going on a little farther, he saw James the son of Zebedee and John
    his brother, who were in their boat mending the nets. And immediately
    he called them; and they left their father Zebedee in the boat with the
    hired servants and followed him.

3. Mark 2:13-14:

    He went out again beside the sea; and all the crowd gathered about him,
    and he taught them. And as he passed on, he saw Levi the son of
    Alphaeus sitting at the tax office, and he said to him, "Follow me." And
    he rose and followed him.

B. *Interrogative Setting*

4. Diogenes Laertius 2.48:

    They say that Socrates met him (Xenophon) in a narrow passage, and
    that he stretched out his stick to bar the way, while he inquired where

every kind of food was sold. Upon receiving a reply, he put another question, "And where do men become good and honourable?" Xenophon was fairly puzzled;

"Then follow me," said Socrates, "and learn." From that time onward he was a pupil of Socrates.

5. Diogenes Laertius 7.2-3:

Now the way he (Zeno) came across Crates was this. He was shipwrecked on a voyage from Phoenicia to Peiraeus with a cargo of purple. He went up into Athens and sat down in a bookseller's shop, being then a man of thirty. As he went on reading the second book of Xenophon's *Memorabilia*, he was so pleased that he inquired where men like Socrates were to be found. Crates passed by in the nick of time, so the bookseller pointed to him and said, "Follow yonder man." From that day he became Crates' pupil, showing in other respects a strong bent for philosophy, though with too much native modesty to assimilate Cynic shamelessness.

C. *Corrective Setting*

6. Mark 10:17-22:

And as he was setting out on his journey, a man ran up and knelt before him, and asked him, "Good Teacher, what must I do to inherit eternal life?" And Jesus said to him, "Why do you call me good? No one is good but God alone. You know the commandments: 'Do not kill. Do not commit adultery. Do not steal. Do not bear false witness. Do not defraud. Honor your father and mother.'" And he said to him, "Teacher, all these I have observed from my youth." And Jesus looking upon him loved him, and said to him, "You lack one thing: go, sell what you have, and give to the poor, and you will have treasure in heaven: and come, follow me." At that saying his countenance fell, and he went away sorrowful: for he had great possessions.

7. Luke 9:59-60:

To another he said, "Follow me." But he said, "Lord, let me first go and bury my father." But he said to him, "Leave the dead to bury their own dead; but as for you, go and proclaim the kingdom of God."

8. Diogenes Laertius, Lives 6.96-97:

She (Hipparchia) fell in love with the discourses and the life of Crates, and would not pay attention to any of her suitors, their wealth, their high birth or their beauty. But to her Crates was everything. She used even to threaten her parents she would make away with herself, unless she were given in marriage to him. Crates therefore was implored by her parents to dissuade the girl and did all he could, and at last, failing to persuade her, got up, took off his clothes before her face and said, "This is the bridegroom, here are his possessions; make your choice accordingly; for you will be no helpmeet of mine, unless you share my pursuits." The girl chose and, adopting the same dress, went about with her husband and lived with him in public and went out to dinners with him.

D. *Action Setting*

9. Cynic Epistles 163.12-30 (Malherbe):

And indeed, once when I went to the house of a lad, the son of extremely prosperous parents, I reclined in a banquet hall adorned all about with inscriptions and gold, so that there was no place where you could spit. Therefore, when something lodged in my throat, I coughed and glanced around me. Since I had no place to spit, I spit at the lad himself. When he rebuked me for this, I retorted, "Well then, So-and-So (speaking to him by name), do you blame me for what happened and not yourself? It was you who decorated the walls and pavement of the banquet hall, leaving only yourself unadorned, as a place fit to spit onto!" He answered, "You appear to be criticizing my lack of education, but you won't be able to say this anymore. I don't intend to fall one step behind you." From the next day, after he distributed his property to his relatives, he took up the wallet, doubled his coarse cloak, and followed me. These things happened to me in Olympia after you departed.

10. Mark 1:35-39:

And in the morning, a great while before day, he rose and went out to a lonely place, and there he prayed. And Simon and those who were with him pursued him, and they found him and said to him, "Every one is searching for you." And he said to them, "Let us go on to the next town, that I may preach there also; for that is why I came out." And he went throughout all Galilee, preaching in their synagogues and casting out demons.

E. *Comparative Response*

DEFENSE STORIES

The next major type of pronouncement story beyond the display, the thesis, and the exhortation is the story in which the main character produces a rationale. Since a rationale defends an action or thought, these stories are defense stories.

I. Deliberative Defense

First of all, a story may feature a deliberative defense. This kind of story simply presents a rationale for a particular thought or action without engaging in personal or juridical rhetoric. An example is as follows:

A. *Declarative Setting*

B. Interrogative Setting

    1.   Plutarch, Apophthegmata Laconica 230F:

> Pausanias, the son of Pleistonax, in answer to the question why it was not permitted to change any of the ancient laws in their country, said, "Because the laws ought to have authority over the men, and not the men over the laws."

C. Corrective Setting

D. Action Setting

E. Comparative Response

II. Juridical Defense

    Or a defense story may feature juridical rhetoric. These stories feature the defense of an action which has been performed or is being performed, and there is either a request to produce a legal rationale or there is an accusation that the action was illegal. The following are examples of juridical defense stories:

A. Declarative Accusation

    1.   Matthew 12:1-8:

> At that time Jesus went through the grainfields on the sabbath; his disciples were hungry, and they began to pluck heads of grain and to eat. But when the Pharisees saw it, they said to him, "Look, your disciples are doing what is not lawful to do on the sabbath." He said to them, "Have you not read what David did, when he was hungry, and those who were with him: how he entered the house of God and ate the bread of the Presence, which it was not lawful for him to eat nor for those who were with him, but only for the priests? Or have you not read in the law how on the sabbath the priests in the temple profane the sabbath, and are guiltless? I tell you, something greater than the temple is here. And if you had known what this means, 'I desire mercy, and not sacrifice,' you would not have condemned the guiltless. For the Son of man is lord of the sabbath."

B. Interrogative Setting

    2.   Mark 2:23-28:

> One sabbath he was going through the grainfields; and as they made their way his disciples began to pluck heads of grain. And the Pharisees said to him, "Look, why are they doing what is not lawful on the sabbath?" And he said to them, "Have you never read what David did, when he was in need and was hungry, he and those who were with him: how he entered the house of God, when Abiathar was high priest, and ate the bread of

the Presence, which it is not lawful for any but the priests to eat, and also gave it to those who were with him?" And he said to them, "The sabbath was made for man, not man for the sabbath; so the Son of man is lord even of the sabbath."

3. Sifre Deut 38:

One time R. Eliezer and R. Zadoq were reclining at a feast for the son of Rabban Gamaliel. Rabban Gamaliel mixed a glass (of wine) for R. Eliezer, but he did not wish to accept it. R. Joshua accepted it. R. Eliezer said to him: "What is this, Joshua? Is it right that we should recline and Gamaliel beRabbi should stand and serve us?" R. Joshua said to him: "Leave him alone that he might serve (us). Abraham, the greatest one of the world, served the ministering angels, even though he thought that they were Arab idolaters, for it is said, *And he lifted his eyes and looked, and behold, three men stood in front of him* (Gen 18:2). And is it not an *a fortiori* (argument)? Now if Abraham, the great one of the world, served the ministering angels, and he thought that they were Arab idolaters, should not Gamaliel beRabbi serve us?"

A. and B. Interrogation and Accusation

4. T. Pis. 4.13:

One time the 14th (of Nisan) fell on the Sabbath. They asked Hillel the Elder: "Does the Passover offering override the Sabbath?" He said to them: "And do we have only one Passover offering in the year which overrides the Sabbath? We have more than 300 Passover offerings in the year, and they (all) override the Sabbath." The whole courtyard collected against him. He said to them: "The continual offering is a community sacrifice. Just as the continual offering, which is a community sacrifice, overrides the Sabbath. Another matter: It is said concerning the continual offering 'its season' (Num 28:2), and 'its season' (Num 9:2) is said concerning the Passover offering. Just as the continual offering, concerning which 'its season' is said, overrides the Sabbath, so the Passover offering, concerning which 'its season' is said, overrides the Sabbath. And furthermore, (it is an) *a fortiori* (argument). Since the continual offering, which does not produce liability to (the punishment of) cutting off, overrides the Sabbath, the Passover offering, which does produce the liability to (the punishment of) cutting off, how much the more should it override the Sabbath. And further, I have received from my masters (the tradition) that the Passover offering overrides the Sabbath, and not (merely) the first Passover offering of the individual (overrides the Sabbath)." They said to him: "What will be the rule for the people who do not bring knives and Passover offerings to the Sanctuary (before the Sabbath, so as to prevent themselves from needing to do forbidden labor on the Sabbath itself)?" He said to them: "Leave them alone. The holy spirit is upon them. If they are not prophets, they are the disciples of prophets."

5. Oxyrhynchus Papyrus 840 (Grenfell and Hunt: 6-7):

And he took them and brought them into the place of purification itself
and walked about in the temple. And a certain Pharisee, a chief priest
named Levi, approached and spoke with them and said to the Savior:
"Who permitted you to walk in his place of purification and to view these
holy vessels, without having washed and without your disciples' having
washed even their feet? On the contrary, while still defiled, you have
walked in this temple which is a clean place, in which no one who has not
washed himself and changed his clothes walks or dares view these holy
vessels." Immediately the Savior stood still, along with the disciples, and
answered him: "Are you who are here in the temple therefore clean?" He
said: "I am clean, for I have washed in David's pool and have gone down
by one stair and come up by the other and have put on clean, white
clothes, and then I came and looked to these holy vessels." The Savior
answered and said to him: "Woe to you blind who do not see. You have
washed yourself in these poured-out waters in which dogs and swine have
wallowed night and day, and you have washed and wiped the outer skin
which harlots and flute girls also anoint, wash, wipe, and beautify for the
lust of men, whereas within they are full of scorpions and wickedness of
every kind. But I and my disciples, whom you say have not washed, have
been washed in waters of eternal life which come down from (heaven).
But woe to those who . . ."

C. *Corrective Setting*

D. *Action Setting*

E. *Comparative Response*

III. Epideictic Defense

Some stories invest themselves in epideictic defense. In these stories, the legal
nature of the action is not as clear as the question of the character and reputation of the
person who performed the action. The defense is therefore a matter of producing a rationale that exonerates the character and reputation of the person who performed it.
Examples of epideictic defense stories are as follows:

A. *Self-Defense*

(Declarative Setting)

1. Mark 3:19-35:

Then he went home; and the crowd came together again, so that they
could not even eat. And when his family heard it, they went out to seize
him, for people were saying, "He is beside himself." And the scribes who
came down from Jerusalem said, "He is possessed by Beelzebul, and by
the prince of demons he casts out the demons." And he called them to
him, and said to them in parables, "How can Satan cast out Satan?" If a

kingdom is divided against itself, that kingdom cannot stand. And if a house is divided against itself, that house will not be able to stand. And if Satan has risen up against himself and is divided, he cannot stand, but is coming to an end. But no one can enter a strong man's house and plunder his goods, unless he first binds the strong man; then indeed he may plunder his house. "Truly, I say to you, all sins will be forgiven the sons of men, and whatever blasphemies they utter; but whoever blasphemes against the Holy Spirit never has forgiveness, but is guilty of an eternal sin"—for they had said, "He has an unclean spirit." And his mother and his brothers came; and standing outside they sent to him and called to him. And a crowd was sitting about him; and they said to him, "Your mother and your brothers are outside, asking for you." And he replied, "Who are my mother and my brothers?" And looking around on those who sat about him, he said, "Here are my mother and my brothers! Whoever does the will of God is my brother and sister and mother."

2. Plutarch, De Recta Ratione Audiendi 41D-E:

He (Dionysius), as it appears, at some performance promised to a harp-player of great repute certain large gifts but afterwards gave him nothing, on the ground that he had already discharged his obligation. "For," said he, "all the time that you were giving pleasure to us with your singing, you were enjoying the pleasure of your hopes."

3. Plutarch, Sayings of Kings and Commanders 191A:

When he (Agesilaus) was about to break camp in haste by night to leave the enemy's country, and saw his favorite youth, owing to illness, being left behind all in tears, he said, "It is hard to be merciful and sensible at the same time."

(Interrogative Setting)

4. Plutarch, De Alexandri Magni Fortuna aut Virtute 331B:

Since he (Alexander) was the swiftest of foot of all the young men of his age, his comrades urged him to enter the Olympic games. He asked if the competitors were kings, and when his friends replied that they were not, he said that the context was unfair, for it was one in which a victory would be over commoners, but a defeat would be the defeat of a king.

5. Plutarch, Apophthegmata Laconica 230F:

When, in Tegea, after he (Pausanius) had been exiled, he commended the Spartans, someone said "Why did you not stay in Sparta instead of going into exile?" And he said, "Because physicians, too, are wont to spend their time, not among the healthy, but where the sick are."

(Corrective Setting)

6.   M. Ber. 2.5:

There was an incident concerning Rabban Gamaliel, who recited the
Shema on the night of his wedding. His students said to him: "Did you not
teach us, our Rabbi, that the groom is exempt from reciting the *Shema*
on the night of his marriage?" He said to them: "I will not listen to you
so that I would remove the Kingdom of Heaven from me for even one
hour!"

7.   M. Ber. 2.6:

(Gamaliel) washed on the first night after his wife had died. His students
said to him: "Did you not teach us, our Rabbi, that a mourner is
forbidden to wash?" He said to them: "I am not like other men, for I am
of feeble health."

8.   M. Ber. 2.7:

And when Tabi his slave died, (Gamaliel) received consolation because of
him. His students said to him: "Did you not teach us, our Rabbi, that one
does not receive consolation on account of slaves?" He said to them:
"Tabi was not like other slaves; he was ritually fit."

9.   Sifra 45:

It once happened that one of his students was rendering (legal) decisions
in (R. Eliezer)'s presence. (R. Eliezer) said to his wife, Imma Shalom:
"He will no longer live after the end of the Sabbath." And when he died
after the Sabbath, sages entered and said to (Eliezer): "Rabbi, you are a
prophet!" He said to them: "I am neither a prophet nor the son of a
prophet. However, thus I received from my teachers, that anyone who
renders legal decisions in the presence of his teacher deserves death."

10. Diogenes Laertius, Lives 6.63:

To one reproaching him (Diogenes) for entering unclean places he said,
"The sun, too, enters the privies but is not defiled."

11. Plutarch, Apophthegmata Laconica 234A-B:

In the case of another boy, when the time had arrived during which it
was the custom for the free boys to steal whatever they could, and it
was a disgrace not to escape being found out, when the boys with him
had stolen a young fox alive, and given it to him to keep, and those who
had lost the fox came in search for it, the boy happened to have slipped
the fox under his garment. The beast, however, became savage and ate
through his side to the vitals; but the boy did not move or cry out, so as
to avoid being exposed, and later, when they had departed, the boys saw

what had happened, and blamed him, saying that it would have been better to let the fox be seen than to hide it even unto death; but the boy said, "Not so, but better to die without yielding to the pain than through being detected because of weakness of spirit to gain a life to be lived in disgrace."

12. Mark 2:15-17:

And as he sat at table in his house, many tax collectors and sinners were sitting with Jesus and his disciples; for there were many who followed him. And the scribes of the Pharisees, when they saw that he was eating with sinners and tax collectors, said to his disciples. "Why does he eat with tax collectors and sinners?" And when Jesus heard it, he said to them, "Those who are well have no need of a physician, but those who are sick; I came not to call the righteous, but sinners."

(Action Setting)

(Comparative Response)

13. Plutarch, Sayings of Kings and Commanders 177A:

When Archelaus, at a convivial gathering, was asked for a golden cup by one of his acquaintances of a type not commendable for character, he bade the servant give it to Euripides; and in answer to the man's look of astonishment, he said, "It is true that you have a right to ask for it, but Euripides has a right to receive it even though he did not ask for it."

B. *Defense of Others*

1. Mekh. Ish. Vayassa 1:

Again it once happened that a student went (before the ark to lead the service) in the presence of R. Eliezer, and (the student) lengthened his prayers. (Eliezer)'s students said to him: "Our Rabbi, you saw that so-and-so lengthened his prayers." . . . (Eliezer) said to them: "He did not lengthen (them) more than Moses, for it is said: *So I fell down before the Lord forty days . . .*" (Deut 9:25). For R. Eliezer used to say: "there is a time to shorten (one's prayers) and a time to lengthen (them).

2. Mark 2:18-22:

Now John's disciples and the Pharisees were fasting; and people came and said to him, "Why do John's disciples and the disciples of the Pharisees fast, but your disciples do not fast?" And Jesus said to them. "Can the wedding guests fast while the bridegroom is with them? As long as they have the bridegroom with them, they cannot fast. The days will come, when the bridegroom is taken away from them, and then they will fast in that day. No one sews a piece of unshrunk cloth on an old garment; if he does, the patch tears away from it, the new from the old, and a worse tear is made. And no one puts new wine into old wineskins;

if he does, the wine will burst the skins, and the wine is lost, and so are the skins; but new wine is for fresh skins."

3. Sifre Deut 43:

And one time Rabban Gamaliel, R. Joshua, R. Eleazer b. Azzariah and R. Aqiba entered Rome. They heard a din from Petilon, 120 miles away. They began crying, but R. Aqiba laughed. They said to him: "Aqiba, why are we crying, but you are laughing?" (Aqiba) said to them: "And you, why are you crying?" They said to him: "Should we not cry, for the gentile idolators, who offer sacrifices to (false) gods and prostrate themselves before idols, sit in peace and ease. But the House which was the footstool of our God is burned with fire and has become a dwelling place for beasts of the field." (Aqiba) said to them: "It is even for that reason that I laugh. If (God) acted thus towards those who anger HIm, how much more (will He act in this way) towards those who do His will, (so that Israel eventually will also dwell in peace and ease)."

PRAISE STORIES

In addition to the display, thesis, exhortation and defense stories are the praise and censure stories. These stories bring the epideictic nature of pronouncement stories full circle, for in them the positive or negative evaluation of a person's role, character and reputation is expressed. Because the center of epideictic rhetoric is the role, character and reputation of a particular person, the specialty of epideictic rhetoric is the evaluation of persons through pronouncement of praise or censure. Instead of concerning itself with deliberative action or thought, or with juridical guilt or innocence, it concerns the character and reputation of people. By featuring personal support or attack on a person's character or reputation, it strengthens beliefs already held rather than challenging a person to reach a decision about expedient action or thought, or about guilt or innocence. Since the pronouncement story is at its center an epideictic form, there are many praise and censure stories:

A. *Self-Praise*

(Declarative Setting)

(Interrogative Setting)

1. Plutarch, De Garrulitate 504A:

And when a certain man at Athens was entertaining envoys from the king, at their earnest request he made every effort to gather the philosophers to meet them; and while the rest took part in the general conversation and made their contributions to it, but Zeno kept silent, the strangers, pledging him courteously, said, "And what are we to tell the king about you, Zeno?" "Nothing," said he, "except that there is an old man at Athens who can hold his tongue at a drinking-party."

(Corrective Setting)

(Action Setting)

(Comparative Response)

B. *Commendation (Active)*

(Declarative Setting)

(Interrogative Setting)

1.   Mark 12:28-34:

> And one of the scribes came up and heard them disputing with one
> another, and seeing that he answered them well, asked him, "Which
> commandment is the first of all?" Jesus answered, "The first is, 'Hear, O
> Israel: The Lord our God, the Lord is one; and you shall love the Lord
> your God with all your heart, and with all your soul, and with all your
> mind, and with all your strength.' The second is this, 'You shall love your
> neighbor as yourself.' There is no other commandment greater than
> these." And the scribe said to him, "You are right, Teacher; you have
> truly said that he is one, and there is no other but he; and to love him
> with all the heart, and with all the understanding, and with all the
> strength, and to love one's neighbor as oneself, is much more than all
> whole burnt offerings and sacrifices." And when Jesus saw that he
> answered wisely, he said to him, "You are not far from the kingdom of
> God." And after that no one dared to ask him any question.

(Corrective Setting)

2.   Sifre Num 75:

> *(And the sons of Aaron), the priests, (shall blow the trumpets)* (Num
> 10:3). "Whether blemished or unblemished"—the words of R. Tarfon. R.
> Aqiba says: "*Priests* is said here, and *priests* is said elsewhere" (Lev
> 1:11). "Just as *priests* which is said elsewhere (refers to) unblemished
> (priests) and not to blemished (priests), also here (*priests* refers to)
> unblemished priests and not to blemished (priests)." R. Tarfon said to
> him: "How long will you rake (words) together and bring them against us,
> Aqiba?" He was unable to bear up. "I swear by the life of my children
> that I saw Simon, my mother's brother, who girded his feet (for he was a
> cripple) standing and blowing the trumpets." (Aqiba) said to him: "Yes,
> (but) perhaps (he did this only) on Rosh HaShanah, Yom Kippur or the
> Jubilee year?" (Tarfon) said to him: "You are not refuted. Happy are you,
> Abraham, our father, for Aqiba has come out of your loins. Tarfon saw
> and forgot, (but) Aqiba explained (it) on his own and made (it) agree with
> the law. Behold, anyone who separates himself from you, (Aqiba), it is as
> if he separated himself from his own life."

3.   Tos. Ned. 5.15:

> It happened to Hananyah b. Hananyah that his father dedicated him to be

a Nazarite. He brought him before Rabban Gamaliel, (and) Rabban Gamaliel examined him to see if he were of age. (Hananyah) said to him: "Why are you worried? (Are you worried that) I am (not) under my father's authority, behold, I am a Nazarite. But if I am under my own authority, behold, I am a Nazarite from this moment (forward)." (Gamaliel) stood and kissed him on the head. He said: "I am certain that you will be an authoritative teacher in Israel before you die." And he did become an authoritative teacher in Israel before his death.

(Action Setting)

(Comparative Response)

C. *Laudation*

(Declarative Setting)

1. Mark 1:9-11:

In those days Jesus came from Nazareth of Galilee and was baptized by John in the Jordan. And when he came up out of the water, immediately he saw the heavens opened and the Spirit descending upon him like a dove; and a voice came from heaven, "Thou art my beloved Son; with thee I am well pleased."

2. Mark 3:7-12:

Jesus withdrew with his disciples to the sea, and a great multitude from Galilee followed; also from Judea and Jerusalem and Idumea and from beyond the Jordan and from about Tyre and Sidon a great multitude, hearing all that he did, came to him. And he told his disciples to have a boat ready for him because of the crowd, lest they should crush him; for he had healed many, so that all who had diseases pressed upon him to touch him. And whenever the unclean spirits beheld him, they fell down before him and cried out, "You are the Son of God." And he strictly ordered them not to make him known.

3. Mark 7:31-37:

Then he returned from the region of Tyre, and went through Sidon to the Sea of Galilee, through the region of the Decapolis. And they brought to him a man who was deaf and had an impediment in his speech; and they besought him to lay his hand upon him. And taking him aside from the multitude privately, he put his fingers into his ears, and he spat and touched his tongue; and looking up to heaven, he sighed, and said to him, "Ephphatha," that is "Be opened." And his ears were opened, his tongue was released, and he spoke plainly. And he charged them to tell no one; but the more he charged them, the more zealously they proclaimed it. And they were astonished beyond measure, saying, "He has done all things well; he even makes the deaf hear and the dumb speak."

(Interrogative Setting)

(Corrective Setting)

4. Mekh. Ish. Pisha 16:

> One time the students spent the Sabbath in Yavneh, but R. Joshua did not spend the Sabbath there. When his students came to him, he said to them: "What new thing did you (learn) in Yavneh?" They said to him: "After you, Rabbi." He said to them: "Who spent the Sabbath there?" They said to him: "R. Eleazar b. Azzariah." He said to them: "Is it possible that R. Eleazar b. Azzariah spent the Sabbath there and you did not (learn) anything new!" They said to him: "(He stated) this general statement (when) he explained (Deut 29:9-10): '*You are standing today all of you . . . your little ones and your wives.* Now did a little one actually know (enough) to understand (the difference) between good and evil? Rather, (they were mentioned in the verse) to give a reward for those who brought them (and) to increase the reward for those who do His will to establish what is said. *The Lord was pleased for his righteousness' sake*" (Is 42:21). He said to them: "This is a new teaching and more than that, (for) behold, I was like a person seventy years old, but I was not worthy (to understand) this thing until today. Happy are you, Abraham, our father, for Eleazar b. Azzariah came out of your loins. The generation is not an orphan generation, for Eleazar b. Azzariah dwells in it."

5. Sifre Num. 131:

> One time Sabta of Ulan hired his donkey to a gentile woman. When she reached the edge of the territory, she said to him: "Wait until I enter the temple of the territory's idol." When she came out, he said to her: "Wait for me until I enter and do as you have done." She said to him: "Is it possible that you, a Jew, (will enter and serve the idol)?" He entered (and uncovered himself) and wiped himself on the nose of Peor. Then all the gentiles laughed and said: "No man has served (Peor) like this before!"

6. Tos. Hag. 2.1:

> One time R. Yohanan b. Zakkai was riding on his donkey, and R. Eleazar b. Arak was close behind him. (Eleazar) said to him: "Rabbi, teach me one section of the Maaseh Merkavah." (Yohanan) said to him: "NO! Thus I have said to you previously, that they do not teach about the Merkavah to an individual unless he is a sage who understands his own knowledge." (Eleazar) said to him: "Now I wish to discuss with you." (Yohanan) said to him: "Speak." R. Eleazar b. Arak opened (his discourse) and expounded the Maaseh Merkavah. R. Yohanan b. Zakkai got down from his donkey and wrapped himself in his prayer shawl, and both of them sat on a stone under an olive tree, and he discussed before him. (Yohanan) stood and kissed him on his head and said: "Blessed is the Lord, the God of Israel, who gave a son to Abraham, our father, who knows (how) to understand to explain the glory of our Father in heaven. There are those who expound well but do not live well. But Eleazar b. Arak expounds well and

lives well. Happy are you, Abraham our father, for Eleazar b. Arak, who knows how to understand and to explain the glory of our Father in heaven, came out of your loins."

7. Tos. Kel. B.B. 1.2-3:

One time a certain woman who had woven a garment in cleanness came before R. Ishmael for (him) to examine her (concerning whether or not the garment indeed was to be deemed clean). She said to him: "Rabbi, I know that the garment was not rendered unclean; however, it was not in my heart to guard it (from uncleanness)." As a result of the examination of her which R. Ishmael conducted, she said to him: "Rabbi, I know that a menstruating woman entered and pulled the cord (so that she may have conveyed uncleanness to the garment by her shaking the web) with me." Said R. Ishmael: "How great are the words of sages, for they used to say, 'If one did not intend to guard it (from uncleanness), it is unclean.'"

8. Tos. Ber. 3.20:

They said about R. Haninah b. Dosa that he was praying when a lizard bit him; however, he did not stop praying. His students went and found it dead. They said: "Woe to the man whom a lizard bites; woe to the lizard that bites Ben Dosa."

9. Plutarch, Alexander 14:1-5:

And now a general assembly of the Greeks was held at the Isthmus, where a vote was passed to make an expedition against Persia with Alexander, and he was proclaimed their leader. Thereupon many statesmen and philosophers came to him with their congratulations, and he expected that Diogenes of Sinope also, who was tarrying in Corinth, would so likewise. But since that philosopher took not the slightest notice of Alexander, and continued to enjoy his leisure in the suburb Craneion, Alexander went in person to see him; and he found him lying in the sun. Diogenes raised himself up a little when he saw so many persons coming towards him and fixed his eyes upon Alexander. And when that monarch addressed him with greetings, and asked if he wanted anything, "Yes," said Diogenes, "stand a little out of my sun." It is said that Alexander was so struck by this, and admired so much the haughtiness and grandeur of the man who had nothing but scorn for him, that he said to his followers, who were laughing and jesting about the philosopher as they went away, "But verily, if I were not Alexander, I would be Diogenes."

(Action Setting)

(Comparative Response)

10. Plutarch, De Alexandri Magni Fortuna aut Virtute 331E-332A
     (cf. Plut., Ad principem ineruditum 782A):

     But when he (Alexander) came to talk with Diogenes in Corinth, he was
     so awed and astounded with the life and the worth of the man that often,
     when remembrance of the philosopher came to him, he would say, "If I
     were not Alexander, I should be Diogenes."

11. Plutarch, Sayings of Spartan Women 241A:

     Another woman, hearing that her son had fallen on the field of battle,
     said: "Let the poor cowards be mourned, but, with never a tear do I bury
     You, my son, who are mine, yea, and are Sparta's as well."

12. Mark 1:4-8:

     John the Baptizer appeared in the wilderness, preaching a baptism of
     repentance for the forgiveness of sins. And there went out to him all the
     country of Judea, and all the people of Jerusalem; and they were bap-
     tized by him in the river Jordan, confessing their sins. Now John was
     clothed with camel's hair, and had a leather girdle around his waist, and
     ate locusts and wild honey. And he preached, saying, "After me comes he
     who is mightier than I, the thong of whose sandals I am not worthy to
     stoop down and untie. I have baptized you with water; but he will baptize
     you with the Holy Spirit."

13. Plutarch, Sayings of Kings and Commanders 185D:

     Of his son, who was pert towards his mother, he (Themistocles) said that
     the boy wielded more power than anybody else in Greece; for the Athe-
     nians ruled the Greeks, he himself ruled the Athenians, the boy's mother
     ruled himself, and the boy ruled the mother.

14. Plutarch, Apophthegmata Laconica 235C-D:

     While the games were being held at Olympia, an old man was desirous of
     seeing them, but could find no seat. As he went to place after place, he
     met with insults and jeers, and nobody made room for him. But when he
     came opposite the Spartans, all the boys and many of the men arose and
     yielded their places. Whereupon the assembled multitude of Greeks
     expressed their approbation of the custom by applause, and commended
     the action beyond measure; but the old man, shaking "his head grey-
     haired and grey-bearded," and with tears in his eyes, said "Alas for the
     evil days! Because all the Greeks know what is right and fair, but the
     Spartans alone practice it."

CENSURE STORIES

A. *Self Censure*

1. Plutarch, Alexander 58.6:

   And at another time, when his Macedonians hesitated to advance upon
   the citadel called Nysa because there was a deep river in front of it,
   Alexander, halting on the bank, cried: "Most miserable man that I am,
   why, pray, have I not learned to swim?" and at once, carrying his shield,
   he would have tried to cross.

2. Plutarch, Caesar 45.7-8:

   When Pompey, on the other wing, saw his horsemen scattered in flight,
   he was no longer the same man, nor remembered that he was Pompey
   the Great, but more like one whom Heaven has robbed of his wits than
   anything else, he went off without a word to his tent, sat down there,
   and awaited what was to come, until his forces were all routed and the
   enemy was assailing his ramparts and fighting with their defenders. Then
   he came to his senses, as it were, and with this one ejaculation, as they
   say, "What, even to my quarters?" took off his fighting and general's
   dress, put on one suitable for fugitive, and stole away.

B. *Direct Censure*

   (Declarative Setting)

1. Luke 9:61-62:

   Another said, "I will follow you, Lord; but let me first say farewell to
   those at my home." Jesus said to him, "No one who puts his hand to the
   plow and looks back is fit for the Kingdom of God."

2. M. Avot. 2.6:

   Also (Hillel) saw one skull floating on the face of the water. He said to
   it: "Because you drowned (others) they drowned you, and in the end they
   that drowned you shall be drowned."

3. Sifra 58b-c:

   A certain student said before R. Aqiba: "I must say what I have learned:
   (*When a woman at childbirth bears a male) she shall be unclean seven
   days. . . . And on the eighth day (the flesh of his foreskin) shall be
   circumcised* (Lev 12:2-3). One might think (that he should be circumcised) fifteen days (after his birth; that is, the) eighth (day after her)
   seven days (of uncleanness; however) Scripture says, *on that day* (which
   proves that circumcision is on the eighth day after birth)." R. Aqiba said
   to him: "You sink in mighty waters and you bring clay up in your hands.

For is it not already said: *And a son eight days old you shall circumcise, all the males forever* (Gen 17:12)?"

4. M. Ber. 1.3:

R. Tarfon said: "I was going on the road and I reclined to recite the (evening) *Shema* according to the words of the House of Shammai, and (in doing so) I placed myself in danger from robbers." They said to him: "You deserved to lose your life, for you transgressed the words of the House of Hillel."

5. Lucian, Demonax 27:

When one of his friends said: "Demonax, let's go to the Aesculapium and pray for my son," he replied: "You must think Aesculapius very deaf, that he can't hear our prayers from where we are!"

6. Plutarch, De Liberis Educandis 4F-5A:

When a man asked him what fee he should require for teaching his child, Aristippus replied, "A thousand drachmas"; but when the other exclaimed, "Great Heavens! What an excessive demand! I can buy a slave for a thousand," Aristippus retorted, "Then you will have two slaves, your son and the one you buy."

7. Plutarch, De Liberis Educandis 2A:

Diogenes, observing an emotional and crackbrained youth, said "Young man, your father must have been drunk when he begot you!"

8. Plutarch, Quomodo Adulator ab Amico Internoscatur 71E:

Lysander, we are told, said to the man from Megara, who in the council of the allies was making bold to speak for Greece, that "his words needed a country to back them."

9. Plutarch, Cicero 25.4:

And when Crassus expressed his satisfaction with the Stoics because they represented the good man as rich, "Consider," said Cicero, "whether your satisfaction is not rather due to their declaration that all things belong to the wise."

10. Plutarch, Alexander 28.3:

When he had been hit by an arrow and was suffering great pain, he said: "This, my friends, that flows here, is blood, and not 'Ichor, such as flows from the veins of the blessed gods."

(Interrogative Setting)

(Corrective Setting)

11. Plutarch, Cicero 7.8:

And again, the orator Hortensius did not venture to plead the cause of
Verres directly, but was persuaded to appear for him at the assessment
of the fine, and received an ivory sphinx as his reward; and when Cicero
made some oblique reference to him and Hortensius declared that he had
no skill in solving riddles, "And yet," said Cicero, "thou hast the Sphinx
at thy house."

12. Codex Cambrai 254 (trans. from Hennecke-Schneemelcher 2:279;
Latin text in de Bruyne, 1908:153):

Peter, speaking to a (man) who bitterly complained at the death of his
daughter, said "So many assaults of the devil, so many struggles with the
body, so many disasters of the world she has escaped; and you shed tears,
as if you did know what you yourself have undergone (i.e., what you have
gained)."

13. Plutarch, Quomodo Adulator ab Amico Internoscatur 70C-D:

Excellent, too, was the retort of Diogenes on the occasion when he had
entered Philip's camp and was brought before Philip himself, at the time
when Philip was on his way to fight the Greeks. Not knowing who Diogenes was, Philip asked him if he were a spy. "Yes, indeed, Philip," he
replied, "I am here to spy upon your ill-advised folly, because of which
you, without any compelling reason, are on your way to hazard a kingdom and your life on the outcome of a single hour."

14. Augustine, Contra adv. legis et proph. 2.4.14 (Migne, PL, 42:647):

But, he said, when the apostles asked how the Jewish prophets were to
be regarded who were thought to have proclaimed in the past his coming,
our Lord, disturbed that they still held this conception, answered, "You
have forsaken the living one who is before you and speak about the
dead."

(Action Setting)

(Comparative Response)

15. Sifre Deut 322:

One time (when) Polmos was in Judea, a commander of horsemen ran
after an Israelite on a horse in order to kill him, but he did not reach
him. Before he reached him a snake bit (the commander) on the heel.
(The Israelite) said to him: "Because we were strong, you are delivered
into our hands. *Were it not that their rock had sold them*" (Deut 32:34).

C. *Defamation*

(Declarative Setting)

1. Plutarch, Cicero 26.3:

   Again, after hearing that Vatinius was dead, and then after a little learning for a surety that he was alive, "Wretchedly perish, then," said Cicero, "the wretch who lied!"

2. Plutarch, Caesar 62.9:

   Moreover, Caesar actually suspected him (Cassius) so that he once said to his friends; "What, think ye, doth Cassius want? I like him not over much, for he is much too pale."

3. Sifra 94a:

   One time an ulcer formed on the leg of Joseph b. Pakas, and he asked the doctor to operate. He said to him: "Let me know when (you) finish the operation and (the leg) remains (hanging) as if by a hair." The doctor (finished the operation and) left (the leg hanging) as if by a hair, and he made this known to him. (Joseph) called to his son, Nahunyah. He said to him: "Hunyah, my son, until now you have been obligated to care for me. From now on, go away, for one does not defile (himself) by the limb of a living person, even his father's." And when the matter came before the sages, they said that it was said (concerning him): "*There is a righteous man that perishes in his righteousness* (Qoh 7:15), (which means) the righteous one is lost, and his righteousness (is lost) with him."

(Interrogative Setting)

(Corrective Setting)

(Action Setting)

(Comparative Response)

CONCLUSION

Analysis of each basic type of pronouncement story should emerge naturally from the classification. As the interpreter explores the details of the display story, thesis story, exhortation story, defense story, praise story and censure story, the potential for sub-categories will always be available. Moreover, the manner in which a particular corpus interrelates deliberative, juridical and epideictic rhetoric in the setting of pronouncement stories will reveal important features of the approach to thought and action in that literature.

WORKS CONSULTED

Alsup, John E.
    1981   "Type, Place and Function of the Pronouncement Story in Plutarch's
                    Moralia." *Semeia* 20:15-27.

Aune, David E.
    1978   "Septem Sapientium Convivium (Moralia 146B-164D)." Pp. 51-105 in
                    Plutarch's Ethical Writings and Early Christian Literature. Ed. Hans
                    Dieter Betz. Studia ad Corpus Hellenisticum Novi Testamenti 4.
                    Leiden: E. J. Brill.

Avery-Peck, Alan J.
    1983   "Classifying Early Rabbinic Pronouncement Stories." *SBL Seminar
                    Papers* 22:221-44.

Crossan, John Dominic
    1983   "Kingdom and Children: A Study in the Aphoristic Tradition." *Semeia*
                    29:75-95.

Droge, Arthur J.
    1983   "Call Stories in Greek Biography and the Gospels." *SBL Seminar
                    Papers* 22:245-57.

Malherbe, Abraham J. (ed.)
    1977   *The Cynic Epistles: A Study Edition.* SBLSBS 12. Missoula, MT:
                    Scholars Press.

Robbins, Vernon K.
    1981   "Classifying Pronouncement Stories in Plutarch's *Parallel Lives.*"
                    Semeia 20:29-52.

    1983   "Pronouncement Stories and Jesus' Blessing of the Children: A
                    Rhetorical Approach." *Semeia* 29:43-74.

Stroker, William D.
    1981   "Examples of Pronouncement Stories in Early Christian Literature."
                    Semeia 20:133-41.

Tannehill, Robert C.
    1981   "Introduction: The Pronouncement Story and Its Types." *Semeia* 20:1-
                    13.

    1983   "Comments on Vernon Robbins' Paper, 'A Comprehensive System for
                    Classifying and Analyzing Pronouncement Stories'." Privately
                    produced.

Rhetorical Approaches to Greek History Writing in the Hellenistic Period

Kenneth S. Sacks

University of Wisconsin, Madison

In this paper, I intend to discuss how certain hellenistic writers viewed in theory the place of logoi within the historical narrative. The subject is not an easy one, for there is a decided lack of material, and we must at times draw on evidence from the classical and Roman periods to fill in the picture.

From what remains of hellenistic historiography, Polybius appears as the great crusader for authentic speeches. He seems to stand alone in demanding that speeches ought to contain only the actual words spoken, or at least a résumé of them,[1] and, quite convincingly, supports his principles in practice.[2] According to modern theorists, and indeed to Polybius himself,[3] nearly all other historians of the hellenistic period stand to the other side. Various fourth century schools of rhetoric and philosophy, headed by Isocrates, Aristotle, and their epigoni, urged a thoroughly creative approach to speeches in history writing. Historians under their influence believed that the inclusion of speeches was a license for rhetorical invention and indulgence.[4]

It is, of course, obvious to anyone who reads the extant historians of the hellenistic period—and here we must speak mainly of Diodorus Siculus, Dionysius of Halicarnassus and Polybius—that, with the exception of Polybius, they did engage in willful fantasy in the creation of logoi. Thus actual practice is not an issue here. Instead, what I hope to indicate is that those historians who came out of the so-called rhetorical schools may well have believed that their approach to logoi was perfectly consistent with an earlier and established historiographical tradition. Thucydides stands as a towering figure in the late hellenistic Greco-Roman civilization. Not just his history, but his pronouncements on historiography were taken to heart by these later writers. In this paper, I shall discuss the two authors known to me who directly concern themselves with Thucydides' pronouncements on logoi: Lucian and Dionysius of Halicarnassus. It will be shown that, while their understanding is certainly different from ours, they nevertheless employed Thucydides as a useful guide on the question of speeches in history writing.

We begin the investigation with Lucian and his essay, *How to Write History*. A somewhat tongue-in-cheek attack on contemporary historians, the work has been shown

---

[1] K. Sacks, *Polybius and the Writing of History* (1981) 79-95.

[2] F. Walbank, *Speeches in Greek Historians*: The Third J. L. Myres Memorial Lecture (1965) 11-18.

[3] Polybius attacks many of his colleagues for failing to write λογοὺς κατ' ἀλήθειαν: see Walbank, *Speeches*, 10.

[4] G. Avenarius, *Lukians Schrift zur Geschichtsschreibung*, (1956) 156-57; Paul Pédech, *La méthode historique de Polybe* (1964) 255 n. 12; contra Walbank, *Speeches*, 5.

to have a serious quality as well. In analyzing the various categories by which Lucian judges historians, Gert Avenarius has proven that Lucian reflects the general criteria for history writing expressed in the classical, hellenistic and Roman periods.[5]

When Lucian turns to the question of logoi, his discussion is quite brief: "If a person has to be introduced to make a speech, above all let his language suit his person and his subject, and next let these [words] also be as clear as possible. It is then, however, that you can play the orator and show your eloquence."[6] While Lucian clearly allows for rhetorical license in the last part of this passage, he does demand obedience to a certain standard: that the speech fit the speaker and the occasion (εἰοκότα τῷ προσώπῳ καὶ τῷ πράγματι οἰκεῖα). This demand for appropriateness to speaker and situation had become a commonplace by Lucian's day. We see the precise sentiment first expressed by Callisthenes, the grandnephew of Aristotle,[7] and the same phrase also occurs several times in the writings of Dionysius of Halicarnassus. Callisthenes and Dionysius, however, seem to be discussing the criteria for any type of oratory and not just for speeches recorded by historians. Thus, when Lucian, centuries later, echoes this sentiment and adds that the historian can also feel free to display his eloquence, it is easy to understand why his advice to historians is usually traced to a rhetorical tradition.

If such a tradition underlies Lucian's opinions on logoi, we would expect to find it elsewhere in the work as well. Instead, where an obvious influence is discernable, we invariably find Thucydides. He is cited, paraphrased, or directly quoted no fewer than thirteen times,[8] every reference reflecting Lucian's approval. The historian cited or quoted next most often is Herodotus: he is mentioned three times along with Thucydides (cc. 2, 18 and 54) and one time compared unfavorably to him as a writer of fiction (c. 42).[9] Thucydides is clearly Lucian's main inspiration.

Indeed, much of the material surrounding Lucian's discussion of logoi is drawn from Thucydides. The chapter preceding that on logoi discusses the appropriate length of descriptive passages,[10] and here Thucydides is given highest marks. Two chapters later,[11] Lucian sums up all his advice with the following: "do not write with your eye just on the present, to win praise and honor from your contemporaries; aim at eternity and

---

[5]Avenarius, passim.

[6]C. 58, Loeb trans.

[7]*FGH* 123 F 44; see Pédech, 255-56, for discussion and additional testimonia (cf. Walbank, *Speeches*, 5); to which add *Rh. Gr.* II, 115 Sp. (cf. Avenarius, 150). There is an excellent description of the fourth-century emphasis on characterization in R. B. Kembric's *In the Shadow of Macedon: Duris of Samos* (1977) 34-35.

[8]Cc. 2, 5, 15, 18, 19, 25, 38, 39, 42, 47, 53-54, 57, 61; see also Avenarius, 166-67, for other possible paraphrases. Cf. H. Homeyer, *Lukian: Wie man Geschichte schreiben soll* (1965) 29-34, 51ff.

[9]Xenophon is the third most cited author: twice with Thucydides (cc. 2, 39) and once alone (c. 23), in a neutral manner. Lucian's condemnation of Herodotus in c. 42 is especially significant because in another work (*Herodotus, or Aëtion*, c. 1) he praises his style highly. Cf. A. Momigliano, *Studies in Historiography* (1966) 134-35.

[10]C. 57: known as *exergesia* in Dionysius, *On Thucydides*, 15.

[11]C. 61. Cc. 59-60 are quite short: c. 59 could well describe methods employed by Thucydides (concerning praise/blame), while c. 60 discusses a manner of recording myths which could not pertain to Thucydides.

prefer to write for posterity . . .",[12] clearly a paraphrase of Thucydides' claim to writing κτῆμα ἐς αἰεί (I 22.4). Thus Lucian's discussion of logoi is found within a section of his work where Thucydides' presence figures heavily.

Moreover, it is clear that Lucian must have read Thucydides' statement on logoi. Thucydides discusses his own attitude towards speeches in that famous paragraph, I 22. But besides discussing logoi there, Thucydides also reveals his methods for collecting and judging pragmata and then proceeds to make his claim for a κτῆμα ἐς αἰεί. We have already noted that this latter statement is echoed by Lucian; but as well, Lucian also paraphrases Thucydides' statements on pragmata. Lucian writes:

> As for the facts themselves, [the historian] should not assemble them at random, but only after much laborious and painstaking investigation. He would for preference be an eyewitness, but, if not, listen to those who tell the most impartial story, those whom one would suppose least likely to subtract from the facts or add to them out of favour or malice . . ." (c. 47; Loeb trans.).

Lucian's main concerns here of putting forth an effort, being an eyewitness if possible, and severely testing the reports of others are, of course, precisely those voiced by Thucydides. Thus here Lucian has closely paraphrased Thucydides' sentiments on pragmata as well as his insistence on writing for posterity. As Thucydides himself introduces both of these issues within the same discussion as are found his statements on logoi, it is reasonable to suppose that Lucian may also have depended on Thucydides for his own ideas on logoi.

Thucydides' pronouncements on logoi have been endlessly interpreted.[13] For present purposes, suffice it to say that when Thucydides announces that he will record ta deonta ("what was required [by the circumstances]"), most modern scholars believe that he is allowing himself a certain license to make the speeches appropriate to the situation. However, it is also usually accepted that Thucydides has restricted his own freedom of invention with his subsequent clause that he will keep as near as possible to "the overall purport of what was actually said"[14] (I 22.1); that is, τῆς ξυμπάσης γνώμης τῶν ἀληθῶς λεχθέντων. It has been quite difficult for the modern mind to eliminate the inner tension between writing ta deonta, and yet keeping to "the overall purport of what was actually said." If, however, Lucian is paraphrasing all of Thucydides' pronouncement in stating only that the speeches should conform to the speaker and the situation, then he has, at least to his own satisfaction, resolved the problem. In order to understand how this may have come about, we turn to Dionysius of Halicarnassus.

Living at the very end of the hellenistic period, Dionysius wrote both a history of Rome from its founding to the outbreak of the First Punic War and a number of rhetorical treatises. His *Roman Antiquities* has, in fact, little on the question of logoi, and for present purposes more can be learned from his rhetorical writings, in particular the

---

[12]Loeb trans.; cf. cc. 5, 42, 63.

[13]The bibliography and discussion are in *RE Supp.* XII: 1169-83 (Luschnat).

[14]The bibliography on τῆς ξυμπάσης γνώμης is immense; I employ the translation of W. K. Pritchett, *Dionysius of Halicarnassus: On Thucydides* (1975), on 20,356.

lengthy essay, *On Thucydides*. This work analyzes Thucydides' history so that the reader[15] might emulate the better aspects of the work.

As we should expect, much of Dionysius' analysis is devoted to Thucydides' speeches. In one of his longest discussions (cc. 37-41), Dionysius harshly criticizes the Melian Dialogue. Thucydides is brought to task mainly because what the Athenian envoy is made to say is inappropriate (*ou prepon*) to the glorious tradition of Athens.[16] Towards the end of his attack, Dionysius claims that, since he was exiled to Thrace, Thucydides could not have been present at Melos, nor could he have heard from those Athenians and Melians who actually delivered the speeches. And so, Dionysius continues, ". . .it remains to be examined whether [Thucydides] has made the dialogue appropriate to the circumstances and befitting the persons who came together at the conference . . ."[17] Now this criterion of appropriateness to person and circumstance is the same employed by Lucian and Callisthenes, and, indeed, Dionysius appeals to it frequently throughout his works.[18] There is, moreover, nothing in this standard which is inconsistent with Thucydides' own phrase, *ta deonta*. But Dionysius immediately thereafter adds to his criterion for judging the Melian Dialogue by quoting Thucydides himself: "'adhering as closely as possible to the overall purport of what was actually said,' as [Thucydides] himself has stated." This is a remarkable passage. Dionysius has already argued that Thucydides has no access to first-hand information as to what was actually said at Melos; nevertheless, Dionysius would judge him by Thucydides' declared standard, which modern scholars interpret to mean a general fidelity to the actual words spoken. What is the nature of Dionysius' subsequent judgment? It is that Thucydides composed speeches which are inappropriate to speaker and circumstance: or, *ou prepon*.[19] It is clear that, despite quoting Thucydides' claim to keeping as closely as possible to "the overall purport of what was actually said," Dionysius does not expect Thucydides to record the *ipsissima verba*, or anything close to

---

[15]Intended for the reader, as a writer of *political logoi* in the creation of *pragmateia*, on which see K. Sacks, "Historiography in the Rhetorical Writings of Dionysius of Halicarnassus," *Athenaeum* 61 (1983) 65-87; aimed also at the historian as a guide to *lexis*: cc. 42 and 50.

[16]40,394. Also 39,391 (ἥρμοττε, προσήκοντα), 40,393 (προσήκοντα) and throughout 41,395-396.

[17]41,395; Pritchett trans. On what Thucydides may have actually found out concerning the events at Melos, see Pritchett, 126 n. 9.

[18]*On Thucydides* 18, 34, 36, and 45; *Lysias* 9 and 13 (cf. 4); *Dem.* 13; *Mimesis* 425 = *Letter to Pompeius* 776/7; *Mim.* 426 = *Let. to Pomp.* 779; *Arrangement* XX (198, 22-23, Roberts). On appropriateness in general, see the bibliography and excellent discussion in Pritchett, xxvi-xxx. *To prepon* need not involve rhetorical invention, for real-life speakers are at their most effective when they deliver *to prepon*: see C. Wooten, "The Speeches of Polybius: An Insight into the Nature of Hellenistic Historiography," *AJP* vc (1974) 235-251, where the key concept for Polybian oratory is *to sympheron*—close enough to *to prepon*.

The idea of *to prepon*, when considering logoi, frequently involves appropriateness, not just to the speaker and circumstances, but to the audience as well: see M. Pohlenz, "Τὸ πρεπόν. Ein Beitrag zur Geschichte des griechischen Geistes," *Nachrichten von der kgl. Gesellsch. d. Wissenschaften z. Gottingen. Phil.-Hist. Klasse* (1933) 61-62. Note that some of his references do not support his argument: Dionysius, *On Thucydides* 36, 41 and 45; *Arrangement* 20. The instances where the connection remains do not pertain to historiography but rather to forensic and deliberative oratory.

[19]Cf. Luschnat, 1167-68.

it; rather, Dionysius expects only *to prepon* (i.e., what is appropriate), or in Thucydidean terms, *ta deonta*. This, then, is how Dionysius read Thucydides' entire statement on logoi at I 22.1. Indeed, though time does not permit further elaboration of this point, Dionysius elsewhere as well expresses unequivocally his assumption that Thucydides is inventing his speeches only in accordance with appropriateness to speaker and circumstance.[20]

Dionysius' discussion marks a progression from Lucian in our understanding of the present question. It seems likely that Lucian was echoing something of Thucydides on logoi, but determining precisely what proved elusive. Though Lucian is given to paraphrasing Thucydides' sentiments in their entirety, his criterion of appropriateness to speaker and circumstance could reflect just the *ta deonta* aspect alone, and not at all pay heed to Thucydides' second (and to modern understanding limiting) phrase of "keeping as closely as possible to the overall purport of what was actually said." Dionysius, however, has emphatically included this latter statement as part of his interpretation of Thucydides, which is, simply, *to prepon*. Thus, as Lucian has accurately paraphrased the rest of Thucydides I 22, there is now reason to believe that he, too, was presenting this reading of Thucydides' entire argument on logoi.

To appreciate how Dionysius and Lucian could have understood Thucydides' second phrase as having a force similar to his first, *ta deonta*, we must examine hellenistic theories of oratory and, in particular, a phrase found frequently in Dionysius, *alethinoi agones*. Dionysius employs the term *alethinoi agones* as an important criterion for judging whether speeches created by historians and orators are worthy of imitation, and he especially applies that standard to the speeches of Thucydides.[21] In his translation and commentary of the *On Thucydides*, Pritchett renders *alethinoi agones* as "actual pleadings" or more literally, "real contests."[22]

---

[20]Dionysius simply expects that Thucydides will invent speeches when he castigates the Athenian for not attempting τοὺς ἐνόντας εὑρεῖν τε καὶ ἐξειπεῖν λόγους of an Athenian embassy to Sparta in 430 (15,347). Τοὺς ἐνόντας λόγους is used here for the only time in the extant Dionysian writings. In Polybius, it refers to the actually-spoken arguments (Sacks, *Polybius*, 79-89). That meaning is unlikely here because of the presence of εὑρεῖν, which probably refers to the process of *heuresis*, or the Latin *inventio*. *Heuresis* is "the discovery of what is required to be said in a given situation (τὰ δέοντα εὑρεῖν), the implied theory being that this is somehow already 'there' though latent, and does not have to be made up as a mere figment of imagination" (Russell, quoted by Pritchett, 115 n. 3). But it should also be noted that not *heuresis*, but *chresis* seems to be associated with appropriateness at *On Thucydides* 34,381 (on *heuresis*, see also 45,401 and *Dem.* 51). In any case, Thucydides could certainly have got the details from the participants, but this is not what Dionysius demands of him. Another example is at 18,350-353, where Dionysius accuses Thucydides of creating the *Epitaphios* and of putting it at an insignificant moment in order to grace Pericles. To Dionysius, a more appropriate place for such a eulogy would have been after the victory at Pylos or the Sicilian disaster. Here, Dionysius claims that the speech is appropriate to the person (Pericles), but not the occasion.

[21]*Let. to Pomp.* 782 = *Mim.* 427; *On Thucydides* 42,398 and 53,413; see also cc. 49-50 in general.

[22]Pritchett, 127, n. 7; cf. W. R. Roberts, *Dionysius of Halicarnassus: the Three Literary Letters* (1901) 184, s.v. ἀγών Though the meaning of *agon* seems clear enough in Dionysius, it is less so in Aristotle's *Rhetoric*, where it appears at least partially influenced by the *type* of audience (1414a; cf. 1358a-b and discussion by D. A. G. Hinks, "Tria Genera Causarum," *CQ* 30 [1936] 172, who defines agonistic oratory as "controversy

Because Dionysius uses the phrase throughout his rhetorical writings, we are able to get a better sense of its meaning.[23] With many rhetoricians of his day, Dionysius believes that there are three types of oratory. Only two of these types, however, are appropriate for "oral contests": namely, speeches delivered in law courts and those delivered in public assembly.[24] The one type of oratory that is not suitable for "real contests" is the epideictic form.[25]

Isocrates, of course, wrote essentially *epideixeis,* for most of his writings are not intended to be read aloud in courts or public assembly, before a jury or deliberative body.[26] Indeed, Dionysius judges his work precisely by this standard:

> [Isocrates'] speeches will bear recitation on ceremonial occasions and pri-
> vate study, but cannot stand up to the stress of the assembly or the law
> courts . . . Hieronymous the philosopher says that one could read his dis-
> courses effectively, but to disclaim them in public . . . with the appropriate
> techniques of delivery that are used in live oratory would be quite impos-
> sible.[27]

In other respects Dionysius is quite favorable to the writings of Isocrates,[28] yet he has clearly marked them out as a separate genre of oratory. Isocrates, however, is not alone: various writings of Plato and Antiphon are also considered epideictic and hence inappro-priate for *alethinoi agones,* for "real contests."[29]

This concern for the *agon,* or contest, takes on special significance for our pur-poses when Dionysius mentions in the opening prooemium of his historical work, the *Roman Antiquities* (I 8.3), that he will include *enagonioi logoi,* that is "speeches suitable for debate."[30] In the *Roman Antiquities* Dionysius does not go on to explain *enagonioi*

---

with a defined issue" [p. 174]; cf. also G. Kennedy, *The Art of Persuasion in Greece* [1963] 153).

[23]I *Amm.* 3 (56, 12 Roberts); *Dem.* 32; *Isoc.* 2 and 11.

[24]I *Amm.* 3 (56, 12 Roberts); *Lysias* 6; *Isoc.* 2; *Isaeus* 6 and 20; *Dem.* 4; cf. *Arrangement* 25.

[25]Epideictic material is distinctly set apart from the other two types of speeches as not suitable to the *agon,* at *Dem.* 44-45, *Lysias* 3, and *Isaeus* 2. So too, Aristotle: see n. 35. On epideictic generally, see Kennedy, 152-202.

[26]*Isoc.* 15, 18 and 20, and *Dem.* 22 and 45 indicate that Dionysius considered some of Isocrates' writings forensic and deliberative, as they were intended for the law court or public assembly. Six forensic orations by Isocrates survive, and apparently in antiquity more could be pointed to (Kennedy, 140, 176-77), but Isocrates and his son seem to deny their authenticity (Kennedy, 176-77).

[27]*Isoc.* cc. 2 and 13; Loeb trans. Note the presence of *agon.* See also: *Dem.* 4 and 18; *Isoc.* 11; cf. *Lysias* 6. Isocrates himself admits his works are not suitable for the *agon* (*Panegyricus* 11) and denies that he even wrote forensic speeches: see n. 26.

[28]*Isoc.* cc. 4-9.

[29]*LSJ,* s.v. *Dem.* 32 (Plato), *Isaeus* 20 (Antiphon). Dionysius also employs it as an arete of *lexis: Mimesis,* 427.

[30]Dionysius includes two other types of material in his work: the narrative (διηγηματική) and the speculative (θεωρητική). The *enagonios* aspect is quite distinct from historical narrative, as Dionysius indicates elsewhere: *Dem.* 18; *Arrangement* IV (90, 6 Roberts). *Enagonioi logoi* are meant specifically for *politikoi logoi.* The latter term, for Dionysius, includes forensic, political and epideictic material (Roberts, *Three*

logoi further, but he uses the term frequently in his rhetorical writings. We have seen that Dionysius distinguishes epideictic material from forensic and political oratory, for only the latter are intended for "real contests." Dionysius maintains this distinction with *enagonioi logoi* as well, using the term only with deliberative and forensic oratory,[31] and stating further that it is not applicable to the essays of Plato and to the set pieces of Isocrates.[32] It is clear, then, that Dionysius' use of *enagonioi logoi* in the prooemium of the *Roman Antiquities* indicates that he will include in his historical work examples of deliberative and forensic speeches.

Dionysius' discussions of *enagonioi logoi* and *alethinoi agones* reveal his interest in the types of speeches applicable to political and forensic situations—that is, arguments delivered before and judged by actual audiences. This is a natural concern for Dionysius in his rhetorical works, where he instructs the reader on the types of speeches which are worthy of imitation. But it is an equally important consideration historiographically, when Dionysius must decide the types of materials he will include in his *Roman Antiquities*. *Enagonioi logoi* are speeches which involve decisions of state and thus are of central importance to the historical narrative.

Dionysius was not the first to make this distinction between agonistic and epideictic speeches. It has its roots at least as far back as Gorgias and Plato,[33] but it is Aristotle, the main influence on Dionysius' rhetorical formulation, who writes most on the

---

Letters, 203; see especially *Let. to Pomp.* I [92, 8-9 and 21, Roberts]), but as n. 26 indicates, the *enagonios* aspect does not appear to include epideictic material. In earlier rhetorical theory, as in Plato and in the *Rhetorica ad Alexandrum, politikoi logoi* pertains just to forensic and deliberative oratory, to the exclusion of epideictic (Hinks, 170-71; cf. Kennedy, 114-15; see also Isocrates XIII 9). It appears to be Dionysius who first argues for the inclusion of epideictic material in *politikoi logoi* (Roberts, op. cit.). The first certain classification of all three types of oratory is set out in Aristotle's *Rhetoric* 1358b; and 1414a ff.; cf. the discussion of Pritchett, 82, n. 36 and the article by Hinks cited therein.

[31] W. R. Roberts (*Dionysius of Halicarnassus: on Literary Composition* [1910] 298, s.v.), Pritchett (82 n. 36) and *LSJ*, s.v., associate the *enagonios* aspect with forensic speeches only and ignore the possible association with deliberative speeches. This may be the meaning, e.g., of *Isoc.* 12 and *On Thuc.* 23 (though in the latter it could refer to agonistic dialogues, such as the Theban and Melian analyzed by Dionysius, and so distinguished from *demegoria*) and perhaps (but not likely) of *On Thuc.* 13. On the other hand, *Dem.* 53 suggests that it can also be used for *politikoi logoi* generally, and the context of the entire chapter of *On Dem.* 45 and *On Thuc.* 48 definitely indicates that *enagonion* includes both deliberative and forensic speeches there. Of course, the use of *enagonios* in the orators reflects its forensic application. Moreover, forensic oratory was the more important branch of oratory in the hellenistic states, as the Roman conquest limited opportunities for deliberative addresses (Hinks, 176). Thus, it is likely that Dionysius in his *SR* assumed that the reader would be more interested in forensic application. However, in Aristotle's formulation, before the Roman conquest, deliberative oratory is considered more suitable for the *agon* than forensic (*Rhet.* 1414a); cf. the discussion in Plato's *Phaedrus* 261b (n. 34). In fact, when Dionysius uses the term in the opening prooemium of his *Roman Antiquities*—that is, within a historiographical context—it would seem to make sense only if he is stressing deliberative orations. See also note 30.

[32] *Dem.* 30 (Plato), *Dem.* 45 (Isocrates), *Isaeus* 20 (Isocrates—whose work is, in the same breath, contrasted with those written with *akribeia*).

[33] Hinks, 170.

question. He states clearly that there are two styles (*lexis*) of oratory: *graphike* and *agoniste*: that is, the written style and that intended for public address. Deliberative oratory, aimed at political assemblies, is the most agonistic, that is, the most given to public presentation; the epideictic type is *graphike* and so usually confined to written compositions; and, depending on circumstances, the style of forensic oratory falls somewhere in the middle.[34] To Aristotle, the *agon*-type of oratory suggests the actual deliverance of political and, to a lesser extent, forensic speeches before an audience designed to judge the merits of the presentation. Political and forensic oratory, in turn, are distinguished from rhetorical essays, panegyrics, and all other forms of epideictic literature, what are termed *graphike*. These are frequently written, set pieces, but even those examples of *epideixeis* which are delivered publicly are presented at ceremonial occasions, such as panegyrics at funerals, when no specific question is at issue.[35]

We return now to Thucydides I 22.1. There is no trouble in understanding how Dionysius and Lucian could interpret Thucydides' statement concerning *ta deonta*, as being similar to their own demand for *to prepon*, or "appropriateness." But as well, Dionysius specifically includes within his criterion of *to prepon* Thucydides' promise to adhere "as closely as possible to the overall purport of what was actually said." To understand Dionysius' approach, the usually controversial phrase "overall purport" (τῆς ξυμπάσης γνώμης) is not nearly so important as that for which the translation is casually accepted: τῶν ἀληθῶς λεχθέντων, that is, "what was actually said."

We have seen the concern of Dionysius, Aristotle, and others to define the various types of oratory. Within this hellenistic tradition, Thucydides' phrase, τῶν ἀληθῶς λεχθέντων, may assume a special rhetorical significance. Indeed, Dionysius employs a phrase quite similar to τῶν ἀληθῶς λεχθέντων that is, *alethinoi logoi*, as a synonym for his important concept of *alethinoi agones*.[36] Thus, if *alethinoi agones* means "real con-

---

[34]Aristotle, *Rhetoric* 1413b-1414a. Reflected elsewhere: *Rhetorica ad Alexandrum* 1440b 13-14; Cicero, *Brutus* 316; cf. Roberts, *Three Letters*, 184, s.v. ἀγών. Other references in *LSJ*, s.v. ὑπόκρισις II, 2. Plato, *Phaedrus* 261b, may well be making the same slight distinction, that deliberative speeches are, even more than forensic speeches, reflective of the pure agonistic style. For the question of whether Thucydides distinguished among the three types, see Luschnat, 1152.

[35]So also by Polybius: ix 32.4; xii 27.8; xxix 24.11 (cf. A. Mauersberger, *Polybios-Lexikon* [1968], Band 1, s.v., 2b) and by Diodorus Siculus, xx 1.2. See also the discussion of Aristotle in n. 22.

[36]*Isaeus* 20, on Polycrates, with *logoi* understood from the discussion of Antiphon. Moreover, it should be pointed out that, for Dionysius, *to prepon* seems to be the most important *arete* for *alethinoi agones* (e.g., *On Thuc.* 42, *Let. to Pomp.* 782 = *Mim.* 427). As *to prepon* and *ta deonta* are readily synonymous, it is then easy to see how Dionysius could understand τῶν ἀληθῶς λεχθέντων as equivalent to his *alethinoi agones*. Further, Thucydides' famous claim to writing κτῆμά τε καὶ ἐς αἰεὶ μᾶλλον ἢ ἀγώνισμα ἐς τὸ παραχρῆμα may have influenced Dionysius into making the association of ἀγώνισμα with *agones*. The concept of ἀγώνισμα at Thuc. I 22.4 may be interpreted in an oratorical context, as Pliny (*Letters* V 8) did. There is, of course, no logical connection between Thucydides' claim at I 22.4 and his statement on logoi at I 22.1. But, as part of the same discussion, the mention of *agonisma* might have helped establish the meaning of λεχθέντων for Dionysius. I 22.4 was employed as a common sentiment in antiquity: see also Polybius III 31.12-13 and Philo, *de Somn.* II 90 (cf. Luschnat, 1295-96) and, of course, Lucian, as cited in this paper. Thucydides was not without his detractors: not just Dionysius, but possibly Praxiphanes also. See F. Wehrli's commentary to Praxiphanes F18 in

tests," then Thucydides' τῶν ἀληθῶς λεχτέντων could be understood by Dionysius as "real speeches." This translation, completely within the bounds of Greek grammar,[37] does not refer to speeches that were in fact actually delivered. Instead, it indicates the *genres* of speeches intended for actual delivery: the deliberative and forensic types. And thus, the second part of Thucydides' statement no longer contains a claim to recording actual speeches with accuracy; rather, it is a simple declaration of the general types of speeches his history will include: the agonistic types, delivered publicly in hopes of carrying an issue.

This understanding of Thucydides would be a natural one for Dionysius: it is completely consistent with his own terminology and immediately eliminates the inner tension of the passage. Whereas the modern interpretation creates a troublesome dichotomy between the allowance for *ta deonta* and yet a concern for faithfulness to actual speeches, there are now two promises for appropriateness: first, that the speeches will fit the characters and circumstances (that is, *ta deonta*); and second, that they will reflect the agonistic style.[38] It is, after all, the agonistic style which is the true stuff of decision-making situations and hence of history writing; a consideration which Dionysius himself expresses in the prooemium to his own historical work.

There is, moreover, corroborating evidence that Dionysius understood Thucydides in such a manner. The two other extant historians of the hellenistic period both display an awareness of the types of oratory appropriate to history writing. Polybius, on two occasions, strongly condemns the inclusion of *epideixeis*, asserting that it has no place at all in historical works. Diodorus Siculus, on the other hand, in his one clear discussion of

---

Die Schule des Aristoteles (1957) IX, 112.

[37] The change from "what was actually said" to "real speeches" involves two considerations. First, the participle is now translated as a pure substantive, "speeches." This, of course, is a natural rendering, and λεχθέντων has been understood as such by translators of authors from Herodotus (de Selincourt on III 46.1) to Josephus (Thackeray on *Life* 279). More to the point, Thucydides frequently intends his participles as substantives, as, for example, τὸ λεγόμενον meaning "proverb" (Crawley translation of VII 68.1 and 87.6). When Thucydides forms such participial substantives, he employs the neuter form (H. Smyth, *Greek Grammar* 1153b N. 2). To modern understanding, τῶν λεχθέντων has frequently been rendered as if it has the masculine οἱ λόγοι as its understood antecedent: "the actual words spoken." It could, however, just as easily have an indefinite neuter antecedent, in which case it would accord perfectly with the abstract *ta deonta*, which Thucydides has obviously intended it to parallel. The second consideration in this new translation concerns the adverb, ἀληθῶς: there are more than ample examples of the adverb in the attributive position being understood as an adjective (Smyth, s.v. "Adverbs, in attrib. position as adjs . . .").

[38] It is worth noting that Thucydides has only one example of epideictic material in his work, Pericles' *Epitaphios*, and Dionysius assumes the historical circumstances, as well as the speech, were thoroughly contrived by Thucydides (*On Thuc.* 18). According to Marcellinus (*Life of Thucydides*, 41), there is only one example also of a forensic-style speech in Thucydides: the Plataean/Theban speeches at III 53-59 (cf. Luschnat, 1151). The question of how moderns have classified the Thucydidean speeches is discussed by Luschnat, 1151-66. See also Pritchett, 82, n. 36. By the interpretation presented here, it is not necessary to assume that Thucydides is declaring that *all* his speeches will be agonistic. The agonistic part of his discussion may well have been subordinated to his insistence on *ta deonta*: what is most important is appropriateness, of course all the while maintaining a general fidelity to the agonistic form.

logoi, allows for epideictic material in the form of praise/blame judgments, but unquestionably subordinates it in importance to agonistic oratory. The statements by Polybius and Diodorus indicate that the *types* of oratory suitable to history writing were an important consideration in the hellenistic period. Thus Dionysius would only have been consistent with his contemporaries in reading this concern into Thucydides' pronouncement.[39]

Of course, Dionysius' understanding of Thucydides is certainly not consistent with our own, and we need not feel bound by it. As Adam Parry remarked: ". . . what [Dionysius] is least capable of understanding is likely to be most characteristically Thucydidean."[40]

Nevertheless, we can say that Dionysius quite clearly, and Lucian more than likely, understood all of Thucydides I 22.1 as a call for appropriateness. While that much appears certain, I have tried to indicate how this interpretation may have come about: rhetorical writers seem to have read Thucydides' statement on logoi in the most rhetorical way possible. Whether such an interpretation was an overt attempt to justify the rhetorical excesses current in historiography or was just an honest application of contemporary intellectual values, we cannot tell from what has been preserved.[41]

Besides Dionysius and Lucian, only Diodorus and Polybius have left us their thoughts on speeches. I have merely touched on Diodorus, because his statement on logoi presents some methodological problems and is, in any case, not completely pertinent to the present question (see n. 39). Polybius, however, is an important source for speeches in history writing. In fact, what is preserved in Polybius' *Histories* are far and away the most extensive and developed discussions on logoi that we have from antiquity. Yet, Polybius, who consistently demands the *ipsissima verba* or the closest thing to it, appears intellectually isolated. Dionysius asserts that Polybius was largely unread by later generations[42] and thus must have had little influence. Certainly, we know of no other writer who insisted on such a vigorous approach to speeches. Thucydides' pronouncements, however, became common *sententiae* and were often invoked. Here I refer not just to his statements on logoi, for his discussions of *aitia* ("causality") and *opheleia* ("benefit/

---

[39]Polybius, whose historiography influenced Dionysius to some extent (Sacks, *Athenaeum* 1983, passim), is distinctly opposed to *epideixeis* in history writing: xii 28.8ff and xvi 18.2. Diodorus Siculus discusses logoi at xx 1-2. It has recently been argued anew that this passage derives from Duris of Samos and signals a substantial change in the way that ancients viewed logoi: C. W. Fornara, *The Nature of History in Ancient Greece and Rome* (1983) 143-51. There is no opportunity here to discuss this thesis in detail, except to point out that Duris's authorship is highly unlikely. In general see K. Sacks, "The Lesser Prooemia of Diodorus Siculus," *Hermes* 110 (1982) 434-43. Diodorus does allow for the inclusion of epideictic material (in the form of praise/blame: xx 1.2), but clearly subordinates its importance (ἐπὶ δέ) to δημηγορίαί, the genre which is continuously mentioned (1.1, 1.3, 2.1). Diodorus' other discussion of logoi, at i 2.5-8, is obtuse.

[40]*Yale French Studies* 45 (1970) 5, quoted by Pritchett, xxiii. Perhaps the most damning judgment of Dionysius is by Eduard Norden, *Die Antike Kunstprosa* (5th ed.), 79-80: "Dionys ein aüsserst bonierter Kopf zu sein scheint."

[41]It is interesting to note that some ancients considered history a part of the science of rhetoric; thus it would have been natural to interpret historiographical principles by rhetorical categories. The evidence is in Fornara, 2, n. 6. Polybius, and possibly the Peripatetics, however, asserted that history was an independent genos: Homeyer, 58-59.

[42]*On Lit. Comp.* IV (94, 5 Roberts).

utility"), as well as his claim to writing κτῆμα ἐς αἰεί ("a possession for all time") were also frequently cited and received various interpretations in antiquity.[43] Thucydides' methodological statements, then, were likely the best-known in the Greek literary world. The reason for their popularity, perhaps, was not only their power of expression, but as well their ambiguities, which allowed them to be interpreted and applied according to the current historical fashions.[44]

---

[43]See note 36. Also note Lucian, c. 42, which interprets Thucydides I 22.4, on *ophelima*.

[44]It is interesting to note that Polybius clearly draws on Thucydides for his understanding of *aitiai* (Walbank, *Speeches*, 8-11) and perhaps *opheleia* (ibid., but contrary, Adam Parry, *Logos and Ergon in Thucydides* [1957, 1981] 105). Yet while Polybius paraphrases Thucydides I 22.4 (at III 31.12-13), which indicates that he probably knew Thucydides I 22.1 as well, it is clear that he never builds his extensive system of thought concerning logoi on Thucydides's pronouncement of I 22.1. Perhaps the interpretation of Thucydides I 22.1, discussed in this paper as giving unbridled license to creativity, discouraged Polybius from using it himself.

Polybius is the only historian of the period who unambiguously connects logoi with utility (Sacks, *Polybius*, 91-95). This might help explain his singular insistence on the *ipsissima verba*. Diodorus (xx 1.2) and Dionysius (*Mim.* 427) offer a tenuous connection between logoi and utility, but both also allow for free invention (Diodorus: κατ' ἰδίαν at xx 1.2; Dionysius in the text of this paper and n. 20). Thucydides' claim to *opheleia* at I 22.4 is quite ambiguous and may not indicate the reified *opheleia* that Polybius speaks of (see the excellent discussions by Pritchett, 72-73, n. 9, and Parry, *Logos*, 103ff). On the other hand, the statements of Dionysius (*On Thuc.* 7, 334) and Lucian (c. 42) indicate that *they* understood Thucydides' *opheleia* in that manner. But even so, Thucydides' association of knowledge of τῶν γενομένων and τῶν μελλόντων with *opheleia* seems to refer to *pragmata* only (and not logoi): I 22.4 begins with a rejection of τὸ μυθῶδες which is obviously juxtaposed to τῶν πραχθέντων.

The Interpretation of the History of Culture in Hellenistic-Jewish Historiography

Arthur J. Droge

University of Chicago

In the *Jewish Antiquities,* a universal history with a biblical center, Flavius Josephus attempts to point out the ways in which Jewish "archaeology" was distinguished and, indeed, superior to Greek history and tradition. Both in the *Antiquities* and its apology, the *Contra Apionem,* Josephus boasts that the Jews enjoyed a history going back five millennia, making them an older people than the Greeks, and that they possessed accurate records of the earliest period of their history.[1] These claims did not go unnoticed. To be sure, some readers disputed them; but they do not seem to have found anything illogical in Josephus' notion of evidence, namely, archaic history. For all his criticism of Jewish religion, the Roman historian Tacitus nevertheless granted it legitimacy on the basis of its extreme antiquity.[2]

This advantage over the Greeks was something which many eastern peoples shared, or claimed to share, with the Jews. The *Babylonian History* of Berossus, the *Egyptian History* of Manetho, and the *Phoenician History* of Philo of Byblus all make essentially the same claims as Josephus' *Jewish Antiquities.* Interestingly enough, support for their claims could even be found in the testimony of the Greeks themselves. Herodotus (2.143), for example, had described the encounter between Hecataeus of Miletus and the Egyptian priests of Thebes as a contest between two civilizations of different antiquity: Hecataeus' sixteen generations of ancestors cut a rather poor figure against the Egyptian priest who could trace his ancesters back through 345 generations. In the *Timaeus* (22AC) Plato related a similar meeting between the Athenian lawgiver Solon and the Egyptian priests of Sais. Having engaged them in a discussion of archaic history (περὶ τῶν ἀρχαίων), Solon "discovered that neither he himself nor any other Greek knew anything at all about such matters." Indeed, as one priest pointed out to him, "Solon, there is no such thing as an old Greek, for you possess not a single belief that is ancient and derived from old tradition, nor yet one science that is hoary with age." In the Hellenistic period the same point was made again and again by eastern peoples who had learned to write history in the Greek way.

I

One of the results of the encounter between Hellenism and the civilizations of the ancient near east was the development on the part of non-Greeks of elaborate historical

---

[1] On this, cf. T. Rajak, "Josephus and the 'Archaeology' of the Jews," *JJS* [*Essays in Honor of Y. Yadin*] 33 (1982) 465-77.

[2] *Hist.* 5.4-5.

theories concerning the *barbarian* origin of Greek culture. It was common phenomenon for eastern writers to dispute (in Greek!) the claim that the Greeks with their gods and heroes had been the civilizers of mankind. Diodorus Siculus describes it thus:

> With respect to the antiquity of the human race, not only do the Greeks put forth their claims but many of the barbarians as well, all holding that it is they who are autochthonous and the first of all men to discover the things which are of use in life, and that it was the events of their own history which were the earliest to be held worthy of record.[3]

This kind of argument became a distinguishing characteristic of the native historical works of the Hellenistic period. These works, which have been called nationalistic or apologetic histories, describe the rise of civilization as an evolutionary process, with various figures (divine and human) responsible for introducing the technology of civilization. But in addition to this, and hence the designation nationalistic history, each historian claims these cultural benefactors as his own nation's ancestors. Moses and the patriarchs are turned into culture-bringers by Jewish writers like Artapanus in the second century B.C.; and in the first century A.D. the Phoenician Philo of Byblos boasts of having found Phoenician writers older than the Trojan War who described in great detail how Phoenician gods and heroes had been the civilizers of mankind.[4]

Real impetus was given this kind of historiography by Hecataeus of Abdera, a philosopher, historian, and grammarian, whom Ptolemy I Soter commissioned to write a history of Egypt in the last decades of the fourth century B.C. Hecataeus has been aptly referred to as "the first orientalist," because in his work we see the first full-scale application of the theory which traced Greek culture and religion back to the east, in this case to Egypt.[5] Although no longer extant, a substantial part of Hecataeus' work survives in the first book of Diodorus' *Bibliotheca* (1.10-98).[6] The text of Diodorus appears to

---

[3] *Bibliotheca Historica* 1.9.3. For a general treatment of this phenomenon, cf. T. Hopfner, *Orient und griechische Philosophie* (Beihefte zum Alten Orient, 4; Leipzig: Hinrichs, 1925) esp. 20-26.

[4] Cf. the excellent analysis of R. A. Oden, "Philo of Byblos and Hellenistic Historiography," *PEQ* 110 (1978) 115-26.

[5] At a minimum it can be said that Hecataeus' theory is a more extensive application of tendencies already apparent in fifth- and fourth-century descriptions of Egypt by historical and philosophical writers. How much Hecataeus owes to his predecessors is discussed by O. Murray, "Hecataeus of Abdera and Pharaonic Kingship," *JEA* 56 (1970) 164-66.

[6] This was first established by E. Schwartz ("Hekataios von Teos," *Rh. Mus.* 40 [1885] 223-62) and subsequently worked out in detail by F. Jacoby (*Die Fragmente der griechischen Historiker* [Leiden: Brill, 1943] IIIa: Kommentar zu Nr. 264 F 25, pp. 75-87). This hypothesis has been challenged, though not refuted in my opinion, by A. Burton, *Diodorus Siculus, Book I: A Commentary* (EPRO, 29; Leiden: Brill, 1972) 1-34. She contends that "it is safer to conclude that in Book I Diodorus drew upon Agatharchides or Artemidorus for chs. 37-41 and possibly for part of chs. 30-36; while for the rest of the book he undoubtedly made some use of Hecataeus of Abdera, at the same time incorporating material from other widely different authors into the framework of his own construction" (p. 34). For a fresh appraisal, cf. F. H. Diamond, "Hecataeus of Abdera: A New Historical Approach" (Diss., UCLA, 1974).

retain the sequence of the original work, though parts of it have no doubt been excerpted and interpolated with occasional remarks of Diodorus himself. Nevertheless, we can see from Diodorus that Hecataeus was concerned above all to demonstrate both the antiquity and superiority of Egyptian culture, and the derivation of Greek culture from it.[7]

Hecataeus' history of Egypt (the exact title is unknown, perhaps Περὶ Αἰγυπτίων) is much more than a collection of casual observations of a world-traveler. It is perhaps the best example of a complete ethnographic and historical description of a particular people, and served as a model for many later writers. Purporting to be based not only on personal observation but also on the sacred archives of the priests of Egypt, Hecataeus' work falls into four main sections: 1) on the native cosmogony and theology; 2) on the geography of Egypt; 3) on the native rulers; and 4) on Egyptian customs. The first section (Diod. 1.10-29) begins at the beginning, with a cosmogony and theology, or "theologoumena." The first men looked up to heaven and worshipped the sun (Osiris) and moon (Isis), together with the five elements: spirit (Zeus), earth (Demeter), air (Athena), fire (Hephaestus), and water (Oceane). These are the heavenly gods who have existed from the beginning. Then there is a second rank of gods who were once mortal kings but were later deified for their wisdom and cultural benefactions. These are the Olympian deities. (In some cases their names are the same as the heavenly gods [cf. Diod. 1.13.21].) This part of the work is very confused, but it is clear that Hecataeus is concerned to demonstrate the identity of the Greek and Egyptian gods, which in turn facilitates the introduction of the theory that the Greeks owed their advances in civilization to these deities. Thus, Osiris, who is called Dionysus by the Greeks, goes on a triumphant civilizing mission to India and other remote countries, and Thoth, the priestly scribe of Osiris, teaches the Greeks the science of interpretation (περὶ τὴν ἑρμηνείαν), for which he is given the name Hermes. "In general," Hecataeus claims, "the Greeks appropriate to themselves the most renowned heroes and gods of the Egyptians, and also the colonies sent out by them" (Diod. 1.23.8). Indeed, this was the age of Egyptian colonization, and Hecataeus' account of the spread of civilization from Egypt throughout the entire world brings this first section to a close (Diod. 1.28.1-29.6).

Next comes a geographical history of Egypt (Diod. 1.30-41), beginning with a description of the natural boundaries which defend and isolate the country, followed by a note on the great population of Egypt both in the early period and under Ptolemy. At this point, however, Hecataeus' account appears to break off, for Diodorus inserts a long digression on the Nile, its animal life and the causes of its rising, which can be shown to come from Agatharchides of Cnidos (*FGrHist* 86 F 19; cf. Diod. 1.41.4).

After the mythical period there follows a full-scale history of the country covering five millennia of mortal rule from Menas (Mneves) to Amasis (Diod. 1.43-68). In this section Hecataeus owes much to Herodotus (especially in the accounts of Sesostris and Psammetichus), but there is also some evidence of personal observation (e.g. in the description of the mortuary temple of Rameses II and the Pyramids), as well as of direct reference to priestly records.

Perhaps the most interesting section is the final one, on the customs (νόμιμα) of Egypt, which were eagerly admired and appropriated by the Greeks, and the excellence

---

[7]The continuous narrative of Diodorus 1.10-98, minus the few passages due to Diodorus himself, is printed by Jacoby in *FGrHist* IIIA: 264 F 25 (pp. 22-64). For convenience, I give the references to the text of Diodorus.

of which is shown by the political stability and prosperity of the country for more than
4,700 years (Diod. 1.69-95). This section reveals clearly that one purpose of Hecataeus'
work was to contrast the two cultures of Greece and Egypt to the advantage of the latter
(cf. Diod. 1.73.5; 74.7; 77.5-6; 79.4).

The work then seems to have concluded with a description of the debt of Greece
to Egypt, telling how famous Greeks, both mythical and historical, visited Egypt and
owed their ideas to what they learned there (Diod. 1.96-98): of mythical figures, Orpheus,
Musaeus, Melampus, and Daedalus; Homer and Lycurgus, on the borders of history; and
then Solon, Plato, Pythagoras, Democritus, and others. Thus, according to Hecataeus, the
Orphic and Dionysiac mysteries derive from those of Osiris and Isis and from Egyptian
notions of the afterlife, as also Homer's description of the abode of the dead. In addition,
he claims a close connection between Greece and Egypt in *myth* (e.g. Aphrodite is called
"golden" in Homer, as also by the native Egyptians), *architecture* (e.g. Daedalus copied
the labyrinth and built the propylon of the temple of Ptah at Memphis), *law* (Lycurgus,
Solon, and Plato incorporated many Egyptian ideas in their legislation), *mathematics*
(Pythagoras), and *sculpture* (Telecles and Theodorus). In this way, Greek civilization is
shown to be heavily dependent on Egypt.

The propagandistic nature of Hecataeus' history is evident throughout the work
but especially in the section on the spread of culture from Egypt to the rest of the world.
According to Hecataeus,

> a great number of colonies were spread from Egypt over all the inhabited
> world. To Babylon, for example, colonists were led by Belus, who . . . estab-
> lished himself on the Euphrates and appointed priests, called Chaldeans by
> the Babylonians . . . , and they make observations of the stars, following the
> example of the Egyptian priests, physicists, and astrologers. Those who set
> forth with Danaus, likewise from Egypt, settled what is practically the old-
> est city of Greece, Argos, and that the nation of the Cholci in Pontus and
> that of the Jews, which lies between Arabia and Syria, were founded by cer-
> tain emigrants from their country; and that is the reason why it is a long-
> established institution among these two peoples to circumcise their children,
> the custom having been brought over from Egypt. Even the Athenians are
> colonists from Sais in Egypt . . . ; moreover, certain rulers of Athens were
> originally Egyptians. In general, the ancestors of the Egyptians sent forth
> numerous colonies to many parts of the inhabited world by reason of the pre-
> eminence of their former kings and their great population.[8]

A variant form of this account occurs in Diodorus 40.3.1-8,[9] and contains the additional
claim that

> a man called Moses, highly distinguished in both practical wisdom and cour-
> age, went out from Egypt into what is now called Judaea. He took possession
> of the region and founded a number of cities, among them the one named

---

[8]Diod. 1.28.1-29.5.

[9]*FGrHist* 264 F 6 (= Photius *Bibliotheca* 244). The section on the spread of culture
from Egypt has suffered at the editorial hand of Diodorus. See e.g. Diod. 1.29.6; and cf.
J. G. Gager, *Moses in Greco-Roman Paganism* (SBLMS 16; Nashville: Abingdon, 1972) 28-
31.

Jerusalem which is now the most famous. He also dedicated a temple most honored by them, introduced the ritual and worship of the deity, and legislated and regulated political affairs (40.3.3).

This is the earliest reference to Moses in pagan Greek literature.[10]

This section of Hecataeus' work, which describes in detail how every other civilization was derived from Egypt, served as an effective claim for the attention of the civilized world on behalf of the nascent Ptolemaic state. Certainly Ptolemy obtained what he wanted: a propagandistic history portraying Egypt in a light which would appeal to Greek, and perhaps even Egyptian, educated opinion.[11] Moreover, Hecataeus' history appears to have provoked responses from other Hellenistic historians under different patronage. Berossus and Megasthenes replied for Babylonia and India, for the Seleucids were just as interested in promoting the belief in the great antiquity and cultural superiority of their own kingdom. Indeed, as O. Murray aptly describes it, the publication of Hecataeus' history of Egypt began a "war of books" among the Hellenistic monarchies; and this phenomenon continued long after the kingdoms of Alexander's successors had dissolved under Roman hegemony.[12]

The extent of Hecataeus' literary influence has not been fully appreciated. His history, so complete and well documented, immediately became and remained the standard work on Egypt and a model for the new Hellenistic historiography of native cultures.[13] His popularity among Jews, for example, is due not only to the fact that he was the first to mention them; it also attests his general literary importance. Apart from the forgeries attached to his name, the Jewish historians Eupolemus, Pseudo-Eupolemus, and Artapanus appear to have used Hecataeus' Egyptian *Kulturgeschichte* as a model for their own attempts to (re)present biblical history in Greek form. At the same time, however, these writers also reverse the picture of Hecataeus, claiming that, so far from the Jews

---

[10]So W. Jaeger, "Greeks and Jews: The First Greek Records of Jewish Religion and Civilization," *JR* 18 (1938) 127-43; and Gager, *Moses,* 26-37. Whether Hecataeus or, in fact, Theophrastus was the first Greek writer to mention the *Jews* is much debated. For the arguments *pro* and *contra,* cf. M. Stern and O. Murray, "Hecataeus of Abdera and Theophrastus on Jews and Egyptians," *JEA* 59 (1973) 159-68.

[11]Cf. C. B. Welles ("The Ptolemaic Administration in Egypt," *JJP* 3 [1949] 39-44), who aruges that "the history of Hecataeus was a 'command performance,' an interpretation of Pharaonic Egypt in the terms of Greek political philosophy," prompted by the notion of Egypt as the ideal state of the philosophers. So also F. Jacoby, "Hekataios aus Abdera," *RE* 7 (1912) 2762-65. P. M. Fraser (*Ptolemaic Alexandria* Oxford: Clarendon Press, [1972] 1. 497) admits that Hecataeus "was anxious to demonstrate both the antiquity and superiority of Egyptian culture, and the derivation of Greek culture from it," but prefers to leave open the question "whether in so doing he was simply following the Greek tradition regarding the priority of Egypt, which was already fully developed in Herodotus, and of which Plato is the main and devoted exponent, or acting merely as the mouthpiece of the Egyptian priests, whose records he quotes so often, or whether again, as seems very likely, he intended these various elements to serve a further purpose, the glorification of Ptolemy and his kingdom."

[12]O. Murray, "Hecataeus of Abdera" 166; and idem, "Herodotus and Hellenistic Culture," *CQ* 22 (1972) 207-10. Cf. also M. Braun, *History and Romance in Graeco-Oriental Literature* (ET Oxford: Blackwell, 1938) 1-5.

[13]On traces of the use of Hecataeus in general, cf. Jacoby, *FGrHist* IIIa, pp. 37-38; and Jaeger, "Greeks and Jews," 134-39.

having received their culture from Egypt, it was Moses and the patriarchs who were responsible for Egyptian civilization. It is to these historians that we now turn.

II

Our knowledge of Jewish historiography during the Hellenistic period depends almost entirely on the work of the first-century B.C. Greek historian Alexander, surnamed "Polyhistor" because of his vast literary output.[14] Born at Miletus c. 105 B.C., Alexander was brought to Rome as a prisoner of war during Sulla's campaign against Mithradates, and was sold as a slave to Gnaeus Cornelius Lentulus, who made him the paedagogue of his children. He later obtained his freedom and Roman citizenship (c. 80 B.C.), and took the name L. Cornelius Alexander. Toward the end of his life he became the teacher of Hyginus, whom Augustus later placed in charge of his Palatine library. Since Hyginus himself was brought to Rome from Alexandria by Julius Caesar in 47 B.C., Alexander must have been active in the 40s, and perhaps even the 30s B.C. A tireless researcher, Alexander wrote "more books than can be counted," among them a history of the various schools of Greek philosophy and an interpretation of the Pythagorean *symbola*.[15] His greatest contribution, however, was a series of historical and geographical monographs on nearly all the countries of the known world. Included among these was a book *On the Jews* (Περὶ 'Ιουδαίων) for which Alexander excerpted a large number of Hellenistic-Jewish writings. None of these has survived, and were it not for Alexander's collection our knowledge of Hellenistic-Jewish literature before Philo and Josephus would be greatly diminished. Indeed, much of this literature must have been obscure in Alexander's own time, for even Josephus retained but a vague and faulty memory of writers such as Theophilus, Theodotus, Philo the Elder, Demetrius, and Eupolemus.[16] Unfortunately, only fragments of Alexander's writing survive, preserved for the most part by Eusebius of Caesarea in the *Praeparatio Evangelica*. Nearly two-thirds of the ninth book consists of excerpts taken from Alexander's monograph *On the Jews*. Although he excerpted parts of it, Eusebius seems to have kept intact the sequence of the original, and thus evidently has preserved the basic structure of Alexander's work.[17] With some

---

[14]For the details of Alexander's life and writings, cf. Jacoby, *FGrHist* IIIa: Kommentar zu 273 (pp. 248-62). The fact that he is cited as an authority that Moses was a woman (!) suggests that he was not Jewish (*FGrHist* 273 F 70).

[15]*FGrHist* 273 T 1, FF 85-94. No less than twenty-five titles of his works have been preserved. Jacoby gives the years 80-35 B.C. as the period of Alexander's literary productivity.

[16]*Contra Apionem* 1.215-18 confuses these Hellenistic-Jewish writers with pagan authors (e.g. Demetrius with Demetrius of Phalerum!). The fact that a Greek writing in Rome in the first century B.C. was familiar with such an extensive corpus of Jewish literature is itself significant. According to Jacoby (*FGrHist* IIIa, pp. 256-57 and 269), Alexander's specialized monographs on various barbarian peoples were inspired by Pompey's conquest of the east. Indeed, he suggests that Pompey actually patronized Alexander, and that the latter's monographs were not merely antiquarian tracts, but handbooks that served as background for the Roman occupational forces. It may be argued with equal cogency, however, that Alexander's works were the result of a general curiosity about the cultural and religious history of the east.

[17]From this we can infer that Alexander's work *On the Jews* probably began with an account of the giants, followed by a history of the patriarchs and Moses, and continued

degree of certainty therefore we can say that Alexander quoted at least thirteen Hellenistic-Jewish authors, including the three historians to be discussed here: Eupolemus, Pseudo-Eupolemus, and Artapanus. As we will see, these authors take up the Hellenistic interest in the history of culture and respond to it by presenting the patriarchs and Moses as the bringers of culture not only to the Jews, but to the entire world. Thus, they represent some of the earliest attempts to interpret biblical history in light of contemporary trends in Hellenistic historiography.[18]

Among the excerpts of Hellenistic-Jewish writers preserved by Alexander Polyhistor are those of the historian Eupolemus, whom Freudenthal identified as a Greek-educated Jew of Palestine.[19] In view of the point at which his history concludes (158/57 B.C.),[20] this writer may be identical with the Eupolemus mentioned in 1 Macc 8:17 as the leader of the Jewish delegation to Rome in 161 B.C.[21] If this is the case, then the author was a member of one of the leading priestly families in Jerusalem. This is significant not only for the light it sheds on a public figure in Jerusalem at a crucial period in Jewish history, but also because it offers us a glimpse into the social world of Hellenistic-Jewish writers during the second century B.C. We will return to this point at the conclusion of the present study.

The surviving fragments of Eupolemus' history,[22] which deal with Israelite history from Moses to Solomon, the construction of the temple, the eventual fall of Jerusalem, and universal chronology, suggest that the original work must have been a reinterpretation of biblical history along the lines of Hellenistic historiography. Of special interest is F 1 which comes from that part of Eupolemus' history dealing with Moses and his

---

down to the destruction of the temple in 586. Whether or not Alexander brought the history of the Jews down to his own time remains an open question. The fact that Eusebius' quotations cease with the destruction of Solomon's temple is not conclusive proof that Alexander also ended his work here. As an apologist, Eusebius was interested in Alexander primarily as a witness to the *antiquity* of Judaism and, by implication, Christianity. Jacoby (*FGrHist* IIIa, p. 269) assumes that Alexander's history concluded with Pompey's annexation of Syria.

[18]The best treatment of this material remains J. Freudenthal, *Alexander Polyhistor und die von ihm erhaltenen Reste jüdischer und samaritanischer Geschichtswerke* (Hellenistische Studien, I-II; Breslau: Skutsch, 1875). There are several collections of the fragments. To be consulted in the first place is C. R. Holladay, *Fragments from Hellenistic Jewish Authors, Volume I: Historians* (SBLTT 20; Pseudepigrapha Series, 10; Chico, CA: Scholars, 1983). Holladay reprints K. Mras' text of Eusebius' *P.E.*, along with his *apparatus criticus*, supplemented from other editions, especially Jacoby's. In addition, Holladay includes an English translation for each historian (which we follow), together with introduction, notes, and extensive bibliography.

[19]Cf. *Alexander Polyhistor* 105-30 and 208-15. See now B. Z. Wacholder, *Eupolemus: A Study of Judaeo-Greek Literature* (Monographs of the Hebrew Union College, 3; Cincinnati: Hebrew Union College, 1974) 1-26; and Holladay, *Fragments*, 93-156 (with additional bibliography).

[20]This follows from the chronological calculations in F 5 (Holladay, *Fragments*, 134-35 = Jacoby, *FGrHist* 723 F 4): Eupolemus reckoned 5,149 years from Adam to the fifth year of Demetrius I Soter.

[21]So Freudenthal, *Alexander Polyhistor*, 127. His thesis has found general acceptance, cf. Wacholder, *Eupolemus*, 1-4; and Holladay, *Fragments*, 93.

[22]Apparently entitled: *On the Kings of Judaea*; however, only Clement of Alexandria (*Strom.* 1.153.4) gives this as the title of Eupolemus' work.

contributions to the advance of civilization. Moses is called the *first wise man* (πρῶτος σοφός), and is credited with the invention of the alphabet and written laws. The Phoenicians are then said to have taken their alphabet from the Jews, and the Greeks from the Phoenicians. Thus, Eupolemus presents Moses not simply as the transmitter of god's law to Israel, as in biblical tradition, but as the author of wisdom and a great cultural benefactor.

In calling Moses the first wise man Eupolemus indicates his familiarity with contemporary Greek ideas about the history of philosophy, and in particular with the notion that philosophy originated among the barbarians. This view, which was widespread in the Hellenistic and Roman periods,[23] can be traced to the young Aristotle's dialogue Περὶ φιλοσοφίας, which appears to be the first attempt to sketch the history of σοφία.[24] Not confining himself to Greek philosophy after Thales, Aristotle went back to the east and mentioned its ancient and wonderful inventions with interest and respect. Penetrating to the earliest times, he discussed the Magi and their teaching. Then came the venerable representatives of the oldest Greek wisdom, "the theologians"; then the doctrines of the Orphics; and finally the proverbial wisdom traditionally ascribed to the Seven Sages. A similar schema is presented much later by the influential polymath Posidonius of Apamea. Like Aristotle, Posidonius endeavored to trace the history of philosophy back beyond Thales, indeed, back to mythical times. After extensive research he discovered that the first philosophers were "Mochus the Phoenician, Atlas the Libyan, and Zalmoxis the Thracian," each corresponding to the three parts of the world. According to Posidonius, Greek philosophy ultimately derived from these barbarian *Urphilosophen*.[25] A similar theory underlies the presentation of Egyptian history by Hecataeus of Abdera. According to him, philosophy, along with the other arts and sciences, originated in Egypt and only later came to Greece.

> But now . . . we must enumerate what Greeks, who have won fame for their wisdom and learning, visited Egypt in ancient times, in order to become acquainted with its customs and learning. For the priests of Egypt recount from their sacred records that they were visited in early times by Orpheus, Musaeus, Melampus and Daedalus, also by the poet Homer and Lycurgus of Sparta, later by Solon of Athens and the philosopher Plato, and that there also came Pythagoras of Samos and the mathematician Eudoxus as well as Democritus of Abdera and Oenopides of Chios. As evidence for the visits of all these men they . . . offer proofs from the branch of learning which each

---

[23]Cf. O. Gigon, "Die Erneuerung der Philosophie in der Zeit Ciceros," in *Recherches sur la tradition platonicienne* (Entretiens sur l'antiquité classique, 3; Geneva: Fondation Hardt, 1955) 23-61; and the material collected by A. J. Festugière, *La révélation d'Hermès Trismégiste, I: L'astrologie et les sciences occultes* (Paris: Gabalda, 1950) 19-44.

[24]Cf. W. D. Ross (ed.), *Aristotelis Fragmenta Selecta* (Oxford: Clarendon, 1955) 73-96; and W. Jaeger, *Aristotle: Fundamentals of the History of his Development* (2nd ed.; ET Oxford: Clarendon, 1948) 128-38.

[25]Gigon, "Die Erneuerung der Philosophie" 30, drawing on Diogenes Laertius 1.1 and Sextus Empiricus *Adv. Phys.* 1.363. The other side of this debate is defended by Diogenes Laertius, who argues that philosophy is a Greek invention, barbarian claims notwithstanding (1.1-21). Indeed, Pythagoras was the first to use the term, and the first to call himself a philosopher (1.12).

one of these men pursued, arguing that all the things for which they were admired among the Greeks were transferred from Egypt.[26]

It is in this context that Eupolemus' depiction of Moses should be interpreted. By claiming Moses as the first wise man Eupolemus contends that wisdom originated among the Jews, and, by implication, that Greek philosophy is ultimately dependent on Moses. His next two statements, that Moses invented the alphabet and written laws, remove any doubt as to what Eupolemus meant by portraying Moses in this fashion.

The question of the origin and transmission of the alphabet was widely discussed throughout antiquity, with a variety of nations claiming it, or being credited with it, as their own contribution to civilization. As early as Hecataeus of Miletus (c. 500 B.C.) it was supposed that the alphabet originated in Egypt, from where Danaus brought it to Greece before the time of Cadmus.[27] Other writers ascribed its invention to the indigenous Pelasgians of Arcadia, the Cretans, Assyrians, and Babylonians, as well as to Linus and Herakles.[28] However, the fact that φοινικήϊα γράμματα was the Greek term for the ancient Ionic script led many historians, beginning with Herodotus (5.58), to trace the origin of the alphabet to Phoenicia, from where Cadmus introduced it into Greece. But whether this script was actually indigenous to Phoenicia or was a modification of Egyptian hieroglyphs remained a disputed question.[29]

In the face of such claims many Hellenistic historians could not resist the temptation to ascribe the invention of writing to the heroes and gods of their own tradition. The Egyptian theory was defended by Hecataeus of Abdera, who maintained that the alphabet was invented by Thoth(-Hermes), the scribe of Osiris. Although he granted Herodotus' contention that Cadmus brought the alphabet to Greece, Hecataeus claimed that Cadmus was a native of Egyptian Thebes.[30] Berossus, on the other hand, author of the *Babyloniaca*, asserted that the divine messenger Oannes "gave to men the knowledge of letters and sciences and crafts of all types."[31] In the same fashion, Philo of Byblos, author of a history of Phoenicia, attributed the invention of writing to the Phoenician hero Taaut, called by the Egyptians Thouth and by the Greeks Hermes.[32] The Phoenician origin of the alphabet was denied altogether by Zeno of Rhodes (early second century B.C.). In his "archaeology" of Rhodes, a universal history from the beginnings to his own day, Zeno argued that the alphabet, like astrology and the other sciences, was discovered by the Heliadae ("children of the sun"), the indigenous inhabitants of Rhodes. Eventually these discoveries spread out to the rest of the world; but when the native Heliadae perished in a flood, the Egyptians unfairly claimed the invention of writing as their own, while the Greeks, ignorant of the alphabet's true origin, ascribed it to the foreigner Cadmus.[33]

---

[26]Diod. 1.96.1-3. Cf. D.L. 1.10-11 (= *FGrHist* 264 F 1).

[27]*FGrHist* 1 F 20; cf. Jacoby's commentary, *FGrHist* Ia, pp. 323-24.

[28]Cf. Pliny *N.H.* 7.192-93; Tacitus *Ann.* 11.14.

[29]For the debate, cf. *Suidae Lexicon* s.v. φοινικήϊα γράμματα (ed. Adler 4.769).

[30]Diod. 1.16.1 (Hermes is credited with ἡ εὕρεσις τῶν γραμμάτων). On Cadmus, cf. Diod. 1.23.2-8; 40.3.

[31]*FGrHist* 680 F 1. Berossus, a priest of Bel, composed his history c. 281 B.C. and dedicated it to Antiochus I.

[32]*FGrHist* 790 F 1.

[33]*FGrHist* 523 F 1. Note that Polybius (16.14), though he used Zeno's history, criticized its patriotic exaggerations.

The frequency of these claims (and counter-claims) demonstrates how historical arguments of this sort could be used to "prove" the cultural priority of an individual nation or people. It seems fairly clear that Eupolemus also was a participant in this debate, and that his image of Moses as the inventor of writing was developed in this literary context. Although he knows the tradition which credited the Phoenicians with the discovery of the alphabet, he does not hesitate to advance his own theory, identifying Moses as the πρῶτος εὑρετής.[34] In so doing, he seeks to prove the antiquity, and hence superiority, of Judaism, and the cultural dependency of other nations, above all the Greeks.

The third discovery attributed to Moses is the creation of written laws: "Moses was the first to write down laws, and he did so for the Jews." There were of course many candidates for the title of first lawgiver. According to Dicaearchus, what distinguished the Seven Sages was not so much their wisdom as their skillful legislation: "They were neither sages (σοφοί) nor philosophers (φιλόσοφοι), but shrewd men with a turn for legislation (νομοθετικοί)."[35] Eupolemus' claim that Moses was the first lawgiver should therefore not be taken as an independent assertion; but is best interpreted as part of a single thought: Moses, as the first wise man, was the author of Greek philosophy, the alphabet, and written laws. All three inventions were indispensable for the development of civilization, and, according to Eupolemus, were Moses' legacy to mankind.

Eupolemus' depiction of Moses as a culture-hero is such a radical reinterpretation of the biblical account that it therefore demands explanation. Naturally consideration must be given to the possibility that Eupolemus was responding to the disparaging legends about Moses which Josephus attributes to the Egyptian priest Manetho, and which were often repeated. Yet this alone does not explain why Eupolemus turned Moses into a great cultural benefactor. Here it is important to note that this glorified image of Moses occurs both in Jewish and pagan texts, suggesting that both may be based on the same model. Interestingly enough, the source of this positive image of Moses appears to be Greek, not Jewish.

The earliest reference to Moses in Greek literature occurs in the *Aegyptiaca* of Hecataeus of Abdera. All that remains of his description of Moses are two references in Diodorus (1.94.2; 40.3.3-8). That latter passage, part of which was cited above, describes Moses as a wise and courageous leader who left Egypt and colonized Judaea. Among his many accomplishments, he founded cities, established a temple and religious cult, and issued laws. In the former passage Moses' name occurs in a list of the most famous lawgivers known to mankind. According to Hecataeus, who advocated a pan-Egyptian theory of the history of culture, the foremost of these lawgivers was the Egyptian king Mneves.

> After the establishment of settled life in Egypt in early times, which took place, according to the mythical account, in the period of the gods and heroes, the first . . . to persuade the multitudes to use written laws was

---

[34]Indeed, as Holladay rightly observes (*Fragments*, 137 n. 5), F 1 reads like a miniature catalogue of inventions. For an excellent treatment of this *topos* on which Eupolemus draws, cf. K. Thraede, "Erfinder II," *RAC* 5 (1962) 1191-1278. A more elaborate catalogue of Moses' inventions occurs in Artapanus (F 3).
[35] *Apud* D.L. 1.40; cf. Plutarch *Solon* 3.4-5.

Mneves, a man not only great of soul but also in his life the most public-spirited of all lawgivers whose names are recorded.[36]

Hecataeus' statement that Mneves was "the first to persuade the multitudes to use written laws" (πεῖσαι πρῶτον ἐγγράπτοις νόμοις χρήσασθαι τὰ πλήθη) sounds strikingly similar to Eupolemus' claim that Moses was the first to give written laws to the Jews (νόμους τε πρῶτον γράψαι Μωσῆν τοῖς 'Ιουδαίοις). Although conclusive proof is lacking, it is possible that Eupolemus' attribution of written laws to Moses was modeled on Hecataeus' account of Mneves, and intended to supersede it.[37] There is of course a certain orthographical resemblance between the names Μωσῆς (or Μωυσῆς) and Μνεύης, so that Eupolemus could have argued that the latter was an Egyptian corruption of the former. As we will see, the Jewish historian Artapanus identified Moses with the legendary poet-prophet Musaeus by using the same technique.[38] Furthermore, an anonymous Christian apologist of the third century, in an attempt to prove the antiquity of Moses, cited Diodorus 1.94.1 and substituted the name Moses for Mneves.

> And your most renowned historian Diodorus . . . in the first book, having said that Moses was an ancient lawgiver, and, indeed, the first, wrote of him in these very words: "After the establishment of settled life in Egypt . . . the first to persuade the multitudes to use written laws was *Moses*."[39]

It is therefore possible that Eupolemus modelled his portrayal of Moses on Hecataeus, as Pseudo-Justin did his on Diodorus.

The fact that Hecataeus himself linked Moses with Mneves renders Eupolemus' dependence on him even more likely. Describing Mneves as "a man not only of great soul but also in his life the most public-spirited of all lawgivers," Hecataeus goes on to compare him with Greek and barbarian lawgivers of similar stature.

> According to the tradition he [sc. Mneves] claimed that Hermes had given the laws to him, with the assurance that they would be the cause of great blessings, just as among the Greeks, they say, Minos did in Crete and Lycurgus among the Lacedaemonians, the former saying that he received his laws from Zeus and the latter his from Apollo. Also among several other peoples tradition says that this kind of device was used and was the cause of much good to such as believed it. Thus it is recorded that among the Arians Zathraustes claimed that the Agathos Daimon gave him his laws, among the people known as the Getae, who represent themselves to be immortal, Zalmoxis asserted the same of their common goddess Hestia, and among the Jews Moyses referred his laws to the god who is invoked as Iao. They all did this either because they believed that a conception which would help humanity was marvelous and wholly divine, or because they held that the common crowd would be more likely to obey the laws if their gaze were directed towards the majesty and power of those to whom their laws were ascribed.[40]

---

[36]Diod. 1.94.1. For proof that this section derives from Hecataeus, cf. Gager, *Moses*, 30-31.

[37]On this, cf. Wacholder, *Eupolemus*, 86.

[38]Cf. Holladay, *Fragments*, 208-9 (F 3.3); and our discussion, *infra*.

[39]Ps.-Justin, *Cohortatio ad gentiles* 9 (ed. Otto 3.2:40-42).

[40]Diod. 1.94.1-2.

This euhemeristic, pro-Egyptian account, however, was unacceptable to Eupolemus. Doubtless he would have agreed with Hecataeus that the pagan gods were merely human inventions, devices to keep the common crowd in line; but not so the god of Moses. Thus, as Wacholder suggests, "by ignoring the other names mentioned in the source and by paraphrasing the passage in such a way that places Moses far above Mneves, Eupolemus altered the Euhemeristic spirit of the original."[41] Unlike Artapanus, who as we will see, identified Moses with Hermes, the deity to whom Mneves attributed his laws, Eupolemus avoided mentioning the deity altogether, thus crediting Moses alone with the invention of laws. Furthermore, by identifying Moses with Mneves, Eupolemus in effect overturned Hecataeus' pan-Egyptian theory of the origin of civilization, and replaced it with his own account centered on the figure of Moses, the great *Kulturbringer*. This adaptation of Hecataeus by Eupolemus is a significant example of how the biblical text could be interpreted in light of contemporary trends in Hellenistic historiography.

III

Included among the Hellenistic-Jewish fragments preserved by Alexander Polyhistor are two excerpts from the work of an anonymous historiographer who attempted to reinterpret the early history of Genesis (and in particular the Abraham-narratives) in light of Greek and Babylonian mythology. The author's intention is not merely to confirm the truth of Genesis, which he treats very freely, but more importantly to glorify the figure of Abraham as the father of civilization.[42]

Although Alexander attributes F 1 to Eupolemus, it seems preferable, for a number of reasons, to regard it as the work of an anonymous historian. The fragments that truly belong to Eupolemus suggest that he did not depict Abraham as the great cultural benefactor, since it is Moses whom he casts in this role.[43] Furthermore, F 2, containing only several lines of text and merely summarizing the contents of F 1, is ascribed by Alexander to "some anonymous writings" (ἐν δὲ τοῖς ἀδεσπότοις εὑρομεν). In light of these considerations Jacoby labeled the two fragments "Anonymous (Pseudo-Eupolemus)."[44] Freudenthal, moreover, was convinced that the author of these two fragments was not a Jew, but a Samaritan. The mention of the Samaritan temple, the translation of "Argarizin" as "Mountain of the Most High," and the assertion that Abraham met Melchisedek there all seem to point in the direction of Samaritan authorship.[45] If this is the case, as seems probable, then it is hard to believe that a Samaritan would have entitled a work dealing with Abraham, *On the Jews*. Freudenthal suggested that

---

[41] Wacholder, *Eupolemus*, 87.
[42] On what follows, cf. especially Freudenthal, *Alexander Polyhistor*, 82-103; B. Z. Wacholder, "Pseudo-Eupolemus' Two Greek Fragments on the Life of Abraham," *HUCA* 34 (1963) 83-113; and Holladay, *Fragments*, 157-87, with additional bibliography.
[43] According to Eupolemus (F 1a, b), Moses was the first wise man and the inventor of writing. The anonymous writer, on the other hand, credits Abraham (and Enoch) with the invention of the sciences. The differences can be easily exaggerated, however, since their respective discoveries do not specifically overlap. Cf. Holladay, *Fragments*, 158-59 and 162 n. 11.
[44] *FGrHist* 724 F 1.
[45] Freudenthal, *Alexander Polyhistor*, 85-86, 91-92, and 96. This has emerged as the scholarly consensus, cf. Holladay, *Fragments*, 163 n. 18.

perhaps the original title was Περὶ 'Εβραίων; but no such title has come down to us from the Hellenistic period.[46] It must then be assumed that Alexander was mistaken both in attributing the fragment to Eupolemus and crediting him with a work *On the Jews*. A possible solution is that the title Περὶ 'Ιουδαίων, used very frequently in Hellenistic literature, refers to the *contents* of the work. Unaware of the differences between Jews and Samaritans, Alexander assumed that a work dealing with Abraham must have had the Jews as its subject.[47]

The date of the anonymous Samaritan is unknown, except that he wrote after c. 281 B.C., the date of Berossus' *Babyloniaca* (which he uses), and before the composition of Alexander's monograph on the Jews (mid-first century B.C.). Since the real Eupolemus lived in the middle of the second century, the anonymous Samaritan is frequently assigned a similar date, though this is by no means necessary. Jacoby cautiously dates him to this time, but adds a question mark. Since the author's implicit hostility toward Egypt and defense of Babylon seem to reflect a period when the Ptolemies and Seleucids competed for control of Palestine, we may not be too far wrong in assuming that the anonymous Samaritan wrote in the first half of the second century, or perhaps a little earlier.[48] In any case, his history contains one of the earliest treatments of the Abraham-narratives written originally in Greek.

The author begins his story of Abraham with an account of the patriarch's ancestry and the founding of the first city. In so doing, he presents an astonishing interpretation of the legends of Genesis 6-11:

> The city of Babylon was the first city founded by those who were saved from the flood. They were the giants and built the well-known tower. When it fell as a result of the action of god, the giants were scattered throughout the whole earth (F 1.2-3).

Here the author follows the Genesis stories of the flood and the tower of Babel, except for the striking addition that Noah and his descendants are considered *giants*. This is explicitly stated in F 2:

> Abraham traced his family to the giants. While these giants were living in Babylonia, they were destroyed by the gods because of their wickedness. One of them, Belus, escaped death and came to dwell in Babylon. There he built a tower and lived in it. It was named Belus, after Belus who built it.[49]

The story in Gen. 6 of the *nephilim*, which the LXX renders γίγαντες, seems to be the basis of the anonymous author's account. No doubt also in the background is the story of Nimrod, referred to as the first *gibbor* (translated by the LXX, γίγας), who ruled in Babylon (Gen. 10:8-10). But while the Genesis account of the tower and the foundation of Babylon contains no reference to any name (Gen. 11:1-9), the anonymous writer identifies Belus as the leader of the giants and architect of the tower. The reason for this identification is not hard to discern. It appears to be based on the *Babyloniaca* of Berossus, a

---

[46]Freudenthal, *Alexander Polyhistor*, 207.

[47]So Wacholder, "Pseudo-Eupolemus," 85.

[48]According to Wacholder ("Pseudo-Eupolemus," 112): "in Samaria *circa* 200 B.C.E."

[49] I.e. Βήλου Βῆλον = Babylon.

priest of Bel in Babylon, who dedicated his history to Antiochus I.[50] Berossus credited
Belus with the creation of the world, as well as with the foundation of Babylon and the
construction of its walls.[51] Thus, the anonymous Samaritan's statement that Belus was
the builder of the tower of Babylon represents a synthesis of biblical and Babylonian
traditions. There is, however, a basic difference between the anonymous author's treatment of Belus and that of his source. Whereas Berossus regarded Belus as the deity who
created the world, according to the anonymous Samaritan, Belus is merely the pagan
name for one of Abraham's ancestors. In euhemeristic fashion, our author asserts that the
chief Babylonian deity was originally a mere mortal.

This "demythologizing euhemerism," as Hengel calls it,[52] is made explicit in the
discussion of Noah's descendants at the end of the first fragment:

> The Babylonians say that first there was Belus (who is Kronos), and that from
> him was born Belus and Canaan. This Belus fathered Canaan, the father of
> the Phoenicians. To him was born a son, Cush, who is called by the Greeks
> Asbolus, the father of the Ethiopians, the brother of Mizraim, the father of
> the Egyptians (F 1.9).[53]

That the anonymous Samaritan should equate Belus with Noah, and these two with
Kronos, is curious, but in light of his euhemeristic tendency not surprising. By identifying
the biblical hero of the flood with Kronos, who, according to Hesiod, was the father of
Zeus, and with Belus, whom Berossus described as the creator of the world, the anony-
mous Samaritan in effect overturns the theology of both the Greeks and Babylonians.
Furthermore, he makes both the Greeks and Babylonians, as well as the Phoenicians,
Ethiopians, and Egyptians, dependent on the biblical Noah for their culture.[54]

Having discussed the descendants of Noah, the anonymous Samaritan digresses to
deal with one of his favorite themes: the discovery and dissemination of astrology.

---

[50]So P. Schnabel (*Berossos und die babylonisch-hellenistische Literatur* [Leipzig
und Berlin: Teubner, 1923] 67-93), who assumed that the anonymous Samaritan's entire
account of the tower and the foundation of Babylon was dependent on Berossus. However,
in a postscript (ibid., 246), Schnabel came to believe that the anonymous author made no
use of Berossus, but that an *oral* tradition current among the Samaritans coincided with
that of the Babylonian priest. Schnabel's first position appears to be more likely. The
formulas in F 1.9, "the Babylonians say" and "the Greeks say," point to the use of literary
sources. Moreover, several passages in F 1 show a coincidence of phrasing which can only
be explained if direct dependence on Berossus is assumed.
[51]*FGrHist* 680 F 1.7-9. Cf. S. M. Burstein, *The Babyloniaca of Berossus* (Sources
from the Ancient Near East, 1.5; Malibu: Undena, 1978) 15, 17.
[52]M. Hengel, *Judaism and Hellenism: Studies in their Encounter in Palestine in the
Early Hellenistic Period* (ET Philadephia: Fortress, 1974) 1. 89.
[53]The Greek text is quite confused. I have followed Holladay's version (*Fragments*,
174-75; cf. 186 nn. 32, 33, and 35).
[54]Not that the anonymous author claims that Cush and Mizraim were the *sons* of
Canaan, whereas in Gen 10:6 they are his *brothers*. The author has intentionally altered
the biblical genealogy in favor of Canaan, thereby asserting the precedence of Palestine
over Egypt and Ethiopia.

> The Greeks say that Atlas discovered astrology. (Atlas and Enoch are the same.) To Enoch was born a son, Methuselah, who learned all things through the help of the angels of god, and thus we gained our knowledge (F 1.9).

Here it should be pointed out that our author had already mentioned the invention of astrology.

> While Abraham was living in Heliopolis with the Egyptian priests, he taught them many new things. He introduced them to astrology and other such things, saying that he and the Babylonians had discovered these things. But the original discovery he traced back to Enoch, saying that this man Enoch, not the Egyptians, had discovered astrology first (F 1.8).

It seems fairly clear that the author's repeated digressions on the origin of the astral sciences are primarily intended to deflate Egyptian claims for pre-eminence in fields of endeavor then regarded as the most significant achievements of man. According to him, Abraham and the Babylonians were the first civilized people, followed by the Phoenicians. The Egyptians, on the contrary, were rather latecomers.[55]

Against this background our author proceeds to embellish the figure of Abraham as a universal culture-hero. Born in the tenth generation after the flood,[56] Abraham is described as one who

> excelled all men in nobility of birth and wisdom. In fact, he discovered both astrology and Chaldean science. Because he was eager in his pursuit of piety, he was well-pleasing to god (F 1.3).

While Abraham's piety is not overlooked, the emphasis in both fragments is on his discovery and dissemination of astrology:

> In response to the commandments given by god he came into Phoenicia and dwelt there. By teaching the Phoenicians the movements of the sun and moon and everything else as well, he found favor with their king (F 1.4).

Here we have essentially the same *Erfindertopos* as we encountered in Eupolemus, except that Abraham is the discoverer, not Moses, and astrology is the focus of attention, not the alphabet or laws. That Abraham was a great astrologer is a common theme in Jewish literature of the period, no doubt inferred from the statement in Gen 15:5 that Abraham was told by god "to number the stars of heaven." According to Josephus, the patriarch derived the idea of monotheism from observing the celestial bodies (*Ant.* 1.156). Josephus

---

[55]The Greek claim that Atlas discovered astrology, a favorite theme of Hellenistic mythographers (e.g., Herodotus, *FGrHist* 31 F 13 [with Jacoby's commentary, *FGrHist* Ia, p. 504]; Dionysius Scytobrachion, 32 F 7; and Xenagoras, 240 F 32), is refuted by the simple device of identifying Atlas with Enoch. Freudenthal's view (*Alexander Polyhistor*, 82f.) that this identification represents a "Samaritan concession" to polytheism stands in need of correction. To the anonymous author, these identifications served to overturn pagan mythology, and to make Greece and Babylon dependent on biblical tradition.

[56]The stress on the tenth generation after the flood also occurs in Berossus, *FGrHist* 680 F 6.

further states that Abraham introduced arithmetic and astronomy to the Egyptians (*Ant.* 1.167-68), a view, as we will see, also shared by Artapanus. As there is no reason to suppose that either Artapanus or Josephus was dependent on the anonymous Samaritan, it should be assumed that Abraham's mastery of the "Chaldean science" was widely held at this time.[57] Nevertheless, not all Jews shared the anonymous author's positive endorsement of Abraham's discovery. The book of Jubilees, for example, actually polemicizes against such a view. According to Jub. 12:16-18, Abraham is rebuked for star-gazing.

> Abram sat up throughout the night . . . to observe the stars . . . in order to see what would be the character of the year with regard to the rains, and he was alone as he sat and observed. And a word came into his heart and he said: "All the signs of the stars, and the signs of the moon and of the sun are all in the hand of the Lord. Why do I search them out? If he desires he causes it to rain; and if he desires, he withholds it, and all things are in his hand."[58]

This perspective is shared by 1 Enoch 6-11 in which astrology is included among the secrets betrayed by the fallen angels (8:3). Mankind, the apocalyptic writer implies, was not meant to possess this *techne*. The anonymous Samaritan, on the other hand, does not share the cultural pessimism of the apocalyptic tradition. Rather, he maintains that the knowledge of the *science* of astrology is an indication of civilized life. Indeed, he makes astrology the main theme of Abraham's accomplishment.

Following an account of Abraham's defeat of the Armenians (F 1.4) and his encounter with the priest-king Melchisedek (F 1.5), the anonymous Samaritan reports that Abraham journeyed to Egypt with Sarah (F 1.6-7). This sequence of events is a reversal of the Genesis account, in which the story of Abraham's journey to Egypt *precedes* the war against the four kings and his encounter with Melchisedek (Gen 12:10-20; 14:1-20). However, to have adopted the sequence of events reported in Genesis would have weakened the author's thesis that Abraham brought culture *first* to Phoenicia and only thereafter to Egypt. In order to support his contention that the Phoenicians mastered astrology and the other sciences before the Egyptians, our author lengthened Abraham's stay in Phoenicia before describing his departure for Egypt. To be sure, the precedence of the Phoenicians over the Egyptians was only a matter of years, but evidently for the Samaritan author it was a priority nevertheless.[59]

Another departure from the Genesis account is the author's claim that

> while Abraham was living in Heliopolis with the Egyptian priests, he taught them many new things. He introduced them to astrology and other such things, saying that he and the Babylonians had discovered these things. But the original discovery he traced back to Enoch, saying that this man Enoch, not the Egyptians, had discovered astrology first (F 1.8).

Since Gen 12:10-20 does not mention the place of Abraham's residence in Egypt, the reference to Heliopolis deserves special attention. It suggests that the author is familiar

---

[57] On this, cf. W. L. Knox, "Abraham and the Quest for God," *HTR* 28 (1935) 55-60; and Holladay, *Fragments,* 180-81 n. 12.

[58] Trans. by R. H. Charles, *APOT* 2. 31. Cf. Philo, *Abr.* 68-72: Abraham's departure from Chaldea symbolizes, among other things, his abandonment of astrology.

[59] Cf. Wacholder, "Pseudo-Eupolemus," 108.

with the tradition found in Herodotus which described the inhabitants of Heliopolis as "the most learned (λογιώτατοι) of the Egyptians," and the Egyptians as "the wisest (σοφώτατοι) of all men."[60] The fact, then, that Abraham is portrayed as the *teacher* of the Egyptians, and in particular of the priests of Heliopolis, makes their great and venerable civilization ultimately dependent on the Hebrews. Furthermore, the anonymous author's specific reference to the Egyptian priests indicates that he also has in view the pan-Egyptian theory of Hecataeus which asserted that "all things for which the Greeks are admired were taken over from the priests of Egypt."[61] Thus, while our author admits Hecataeus' claim that the Greeks derived their culture from Egypt, he qualifies it by insisting that it was Abraham who established Egyptian civilization.

As M. Hengel has pointed out, the fragments of the anonymous Samaritan display an explicit interest in the history of culture, expressed above all in the sequence of Abraham's journeys: first Babylonia, then Phoenicia, and only finally Egypt.[62] In this way Abraham becomes the *Kulturbringer* of the entire ancient near east and, indirectly, of the Greeks, since according to Hecataeus and others they derived their wisdom and learning from the Egyptians.

IV

The Egyptian *Kulturgeschichte* of Hecataeus plays an even greater role in the work of the second-century B.C. Jewish historian Artapanus.[63] In the three fragments of his work, *On the Jews*, which survive, Artapanus challenges the hypothesis of Hecataeus, which made Egypt the source of civilization, by demonstrating that the apparent Egyptian discoveries were actually taught to them by the Jewish heroes Abraham, Joseph, and especially Moses. Thus, F 1 relates how Abraham instructed the pharaoh in astrology; F 2 narrates how Joseph, after becoming chief administrator of Egypt, first divided up the land, introduced agriculture, and invented metrics; and F 3, the longest, describes how Moses discovered "many useful things," including philosophy and even Egyptian religion.

A number of scholars have drawn attention to Artapanus' interest in aetiological explanations of various names and religio-political customs.[64] For example, in F 1 Artapanus offers the following etymology for the name *Hebrews*: "They were called Hebrews from Abraham" ('Εβραίους ἀπὸ 'Αβραάμου). In the same passage we also learn that "the Jews were named Hermiouth ('Ερμιούθ), which means Jews when translated into the

[60]Herodotus 2.3 and 160.
[61]Diod. 1.96.1-3; cf. 1.69.5.
[62]Hengel, *Judaism and Hellenism*, 1. 90.
[63]Cf. Freudenthal, *Alexander Polyhistor*, 143-74, 215-18; and Holladay, *Fragments*, 189-243. In addition to the literature cited by Holladay (199-201), see G. Mussies, "The Interpretatio Judaica of Thot-Hermes," in *Studies in Egyptian Religion Presented to Jan Zandee* (SHR, 43; Leiden: Brill, 1982) 89-120. With regard to date, it can only be said that Artapanus was a predecessor of Alexander Polyhistor. He is usually assigned a date in the early or mid-second century B.C.; however, J. J. Collins (*Between Athens and Jerusalem: Jewish Identity in the Hellenistic Diaspora* [New York: Crossroad, 1983] 32-33) prefers a date toward the end of the third century. Artapanus' reliance on Egyptian traditions strongly suggests that his work was composed in Egypt.
[64]Cf. especially O. Weinreich, "Gebet und Wunder: Zwei Abhandlungen zur Religions- und Literaturgeschichte," in *Genethliakon Wilhelm Schmid* (TBA 5; Stuttgart: Kohlhammer, 1929) 301-2.

Greek language." Since Moses is later referred to as Hermes (F 3.6), the strange designation "Hermiouth" probably derives from this identification.[65] The same etymological interest can be seen in Artapanus' euhemeristic identification of Moses with several figures from Greek mythology. In F 3.3-4 he claims that Musaeus, the pre-Homeric poet-prophet, is merely the Greek name for Moses, whom Artapanus makes even more important by appointing him the *teacher* of Orpheus (a clear reversal of the Orpheus-Musaeus tradition). Since Orpheus was reputed to be one of the pillars of Greek civilization, and, according to Hecataeus, acquired his wisdom and learning in Egypt,[66] the implication of Artapanus' claim is that Moses is the ultimate source of Greek wisdom and religion.[67]

The obvious reason for identifying Moses with Musaeus, and not, for instance, with Orpheus, is of course the similarity between the two names. The second-century A.D. Platonist Numenius of Apamea, for example, does know the name "Moses," but in general refers to "Musaeus" as the leader of the Jews (F 9 des Places). However, another reason why Moses could be considered the same as Musaeus, who in Greek mythology invented singing and poetry, is that Moses is the first person in the OT to have composed songs: one on the miraculous crossing of the Red Sea (Exod 15:1-18; "Moses' song," as it is called in Rev 15:3), and another which he recited before he gave his final blessing to the tribes (Deut 32:1-43). That Moses was considered to be a poet on a par with the Greek epic poets appears also in Josephus' comment on these two passages: Moses composed his songs in hexameters (*Ant.* 2.346; 4.303).

In the same fragment Moses is also credited with the invention of hieroglyphics (F 3.4). Indeed, the Egyptian priests called him Hermes, "because of his interpretation of the sacred writings" (F 3.6: διὰ τὴν τῶν ἱερῶν γραμμάτων ἑρμηνείαν). This identification of Moses with Hermes is not incongruous with the simultaneous identification with Musaeus, since Hermes was also considered to be an inventor of hymns and music. However, Artapanus' claim is best understood in light of what Hecataeus has to say about Hermes as a *Kulturbringer*:

> The one most highly honored by him [sc. Osiris-Dionysus] was Hermes, who was endowed with unusual ingenuity for devising things capable of improving the social life of man. For it was by Hermes that the common language of mankind was first articulated, and that many objects which were still name-less received a name, that the alphabet was invented, and that ordinances regarding the honors and offerings due to the gods were duly established. He was also the first to observe the orderly arrangement of the stars and the harmony of musical sounds and their nature, to establish a wrestling school, and to give thought to the rhythmical movement of the body and its proper development. He also made a lyre and gave it three strings, imitating the seasons of the year. . . . And he also taught the Greeks the science of

---

[65]Cf. Holladay, *Fragments,* 226 n. 4.

[66]Diod. 1.96.1-6.

[67]Orpheus was an important figure about whom priority claims were made. For example, Ephorus (*FGrHist* 70 F 104) tried to establish the superiority of Crete over Greece by asserting that the Idaean Dactyls taught Orpheus his mysteries. By inverting the traditional relation between Orpheus (the teacher) and Musaeus (the pupil), Artapanus may also be suggesting that Orphic religion and literature derived ultimately from Moses. A similar claim was made by the Jewish philosopher Aristobulus (*apud* Eusebius *P.E.* 13.12.2-5).

interpretation [τὰ περὶ τὴν ἑρμηνείαν], and it was for this reason that he was given the name Hermes. In short, Osiris, taking him for his priestly scribe, communicated with him on every matter and used his counsel above that of all others.[68]

By identifying Moses with the Egyptian Hermes in this way, Artapanus betrays that his source is the *Aegyptiaca* of Hecataeus. As far as we know, only Hecataeus and the writers dependent on him made Egypt the source of all culture and technology, emphasizing Hermes as the versatile deity who contributed many useful things to the social life of mankind. However, in contrast to Hecataeus, Artapanus argues in euhemeristic fashion that Hermes was a mere mortal, Moses, and that it was this Jewish hero who was responsible for Egyptian civilization and, by implication, universal culture.[69]

Artapanus goes on to portray Moses as the great benefactor of Egypt. He founds cities (e.g. Hermopolis and Meroë, F 3.8-9, 16), divides Egypt into thirty-six nomes and assigns the priests special tracts of land (F 3.4), and in general keeps the monarchy secure for the Egyptian king (F 3.5). For these and other benefactions he is greatly loved by the people and "honored like a god" (ἰσοθέου τιμῆς) by the priests (F 3.6). Above all, it is Moses who establishes the entire Egyptian religious organization. He not only carries out the division of Egypt into thirty-six nomes, he also assigns a god to be worshiped in each, thereby accomplishing a task usually credited to the gods Osiris, Isis, and Hermes, and to the hero Sesostris. Indeed, the foundation of the much-derided animal cults is claimed for Moses: cats, dogs, ibises, and the Apis bull are specifically mentioned (F 3.4). While many Jewish (and pagan) writers polemicized against these cults,[70] Artapanus credits Moses with the benefits associated with them: they are part of Moses' practical efforts in ordering Egyptian society. This is consistent with the sociological explanation of the origin of these cults in Hecataeus. According to him, the αἰτία of the worship of animals is directly attributable to "the service which each one of these animals renders for the benefit of community life and of mankind."[71] In similar fashion, Artapanus explains that Moses consecrated the ibis and the ox because of the usefulness of these animals to man (εὔχρηστον τοῖς ἀνθρώποις, F 3.9, 12). It seems fairly clear therefore that Artapanus' portrayal of Moses has been shaped by the Egyptian *Kulturgeschichte* of Hecataeus.[72]

Nevertheless, Artapanus does not seem to be completely approving of these cults. This much is implied by his statement that the Egyptian animal gods were eventually destroyed by fire and flood (F 3.35, 37). Furthermore, it should also be noted that,

---

[68]Diod. 1.15.9-16.2.

[69]Cf. the similar claim of Philo of Byblos (*FGrHist* 790 F 1) that the Phoenician hero Taaut was the inventor of writing, called by the Egyptians Thouth, and by the Greeks Hermes.

[70]References in Holladay, *Fragments*, 234 n. 51.

[71]Diod. 1.87.1; cf. 1.83.1-90.4.

[72]In particular, cf. Artapanus' statement that Moses "consecrated the ibis because this bird kills animals that are harmful to man" (F 3.9) with Hecataeus' remark that "the ibis is useful as a protector against snakes, locusts, and caterpillars . . . which cause the greatest destruction to man" (Diod. 1.87.6). Similarly, Artapanus' statement that Moses singled out the ox "because of its usefulness in tilling the land" (F 3.12) recalls Hecataeus' claim that the bull was venerated by the Egyptians because of its usefulness in agriculture (Diod. 1.21.10).

according to Artapanus, the ibis is not consecrated by Moses, but by his associates (F 3.9). Nor is Moses responsible for the Apis *cult*. He is only credited with the brilliant suggestion as to why the ox is useful to mankind. Chenephres, not Moses, is explicitly mentioned as the one who named the bull Apis and directed the masses to consecrate a temple to it (F 3.12). Still, Moses plays an instrumental role in both cases. Artapanus seems to be implying therefore that Moses did not introduce animal cults in the strict sense; rather, these were a later perversion of Moses' original benefaction.

Perhaps the most interesting section of Artapanus' work, from the standpoint of cultural history, is his discussion of the inventions of Moses in F 3.4 (cf. F 3.12: τὰ τοῦ Μωύσου ἐπινοήματα). Here the author has incorporated a more elaborate version of the same *Erfindertopos* we encountered in Eupolemus and the anonymous Samaritan. To be sure, the number of inventions attributed to Moses is rather meagre when compared to the all-embracing list of inventions attributed to a figure like Prometheus, for whom πᾶσαι τέχναι are claimed.[73] Nevertheless, Moses is said to have transmitted "many useful things to mankind." Moreover, his discoveries are singularly beneficial to Egypt. "Ships" and "hydraulic machinery" immediately call to mind the Nile, while "instruments for quarrying" would be especially useful to the builders of the pyramids. "Egyptian weapons" and "devices for fighting" foreshadow the military role which Moses later assumes. Of special importance, however, is Artapanus' claim that Moses invented "philosophy," a statement that recalls the view of Eupolemus.[74] As already noted, the idea that Greek philosophy ultimately derived from the wisdom of the barbarians had thoroughly penetrated the Hellenistic world by the time Artapanus wrote. Aristotle and Posidonius were chiefly responsible for promoting this view; but it was Herodotus, Plato, and above all Hecataeus of Abdera who identified Egypt as the source of Greek philosophy. Indeed, Hecataeus concluded his history of Egypt with an account of famous Greek poets, sages, and philosophers who had visited Egypt and owed their ideas to what they learned there. It seems fairly clear that Artapanus is familiar with this tradition; however, he also seeks to qualify it by maintaining that philosophy was taught to the Egyptians by the Jewish sage Moses. In so doing, Moses becomes the source of Greek philosophy. It is significant that Artapanus' claim did not go entirely unnoticed. The second-century A.D. philosopher Numenius of Apamea affirmed this theory of dependence without qualification: "What is Plato," he asked, "but Moses in Attic Greek?" (F 8 des Places).

There are some rather conspicuous omissions from Artapanus' list of inventions. Considering the important role which *law* played in catalogues of inventions, it is quite surprising that Artapanus, unlike Eupolemus, makes no reference to the law(s) of Moses. Perhaps it is to be seen behind the ἱερὰ γράμματα which Moses gave to the Egyptian priests. Or it may be that Artapanus simply did not value the law of Moses very highly at all. We know, for example, from Strabo's excursus on Judaism that some Jews regarded the law as a later corruption of the originally pure religion established by Moses: the work of "superstitious and tyrannical men," who introduced circumcision and dietary

---

[73]Aeschylus *Prometheus Vinctus* 500-06.
[74]In his otherwise excellent treatment of Artapanus, D. L. Tiede (*The Charismatic Figure as Miracle Worker* [SBLDS 1; Missoula: Scholars Press, 1972] 152) attaches no significance to the inclusion of φιλοσοφία in the list of Moses' inventions. He refers to it as "the bland inclusion of philosophy."

regulations.[75] Artapanus' omission of laws suggests therefore that he too is to be identified with a form of Judaism that viewed the Mosaic legislation as an unfortunate development. Also absent from the list of Moses' inventions is agriculture, a very common
item in such catalogues; but Artapanus had already attributed this *techne* to Joseph (F
2.2).

It becomes apparent that Artapanus' list has been compiled to fit his portrait of
Moses as a cultural benefactor and loyal political leader:

> He did all these things for the sake of keeping the monarchy stable for
> Chenephres, for prior to this time the masses were disorganized [ἀδιά-
> ταϰτοι] and they would sometimes depose, sometimes install rulers, often the
> same persons, but sometimes others (F 3.5).

The adjective ἄταϰτος (and its cognates) was a *terminus technicus* in Greek discussions of
the history of culture, used to describe the state of man before civilization. The *Sisyphus*
fragment of the poet-politician Critias, for example, states that "there was a time when
the life of man was *unordered*, bestial, and the slave of force" (88 B 25 Diels-Kranz). This
is also the way Hecataeus describes the state of early man: "the first men to be born led
an *unordered* and bestial life" (Diod. 1.8.1). By claiming that Moses' inventions brought an
end to disorganized life Artapanus emphasizes Moses' stature as the founder of Egyptian
civilization (and also indicates his awareness of Greek discussions of the history of culture). Moreover, in F 2.2 Artapanus makes a similar claim for Joseph: his inventions
brought to an end the disordered (ἀτάϰτως) life of the Egyptians.

This account of Moses' social, political, and religious contributions bears a striking
resemblance to Hecataeus' description of the accomplishments of the Egyptian hero
Sesostris.[76] Like Artapanus' Moses, Sesostris is portrayed as a military genius (Diod.
1.54.1-55.12), who successfully campaigned against the Ethiopians (1.55.1). He is specifically credited with being the first to build (war)ships (1.55.2). His role in providing for
the building of stone temples and irrigation canals (1.57.1-8) recalls Moses' invention of
devices for laying stones and drawing water. Both Sesostris (1.54.3) and Moses are
credited with dividing Egypt into thirty-six nomes. Sesostris' care in observing local
religious customs by building "in each city of Egypt a temple to the god who is held in
special reverence by its inhabitants" (1.56.2) corresponds to Moses' designation of a god
to be worshiped in each nome. Artapanus' report of the Egyptians' great love for Moses is
perhaps too general a motif to provide compelling evidence for the connection between
Artapanus and Hecataeus. Nevertheless, the picture of Sesostris as a great ruler who is
the beloved benefactor of the masses and inaugurates a period of secure peace and
prosperity is a prominent theme in Hecataeus' account (1.54.2; 55.12; 56.1-2; 57.2). Even
Artapanus' claim that the Egyptian priests regarded Moses as worthy of being honored
like a god is similar to the reverence accorded Sesostris by the priests of Egypt (1.58.3-

---

[75]Strabo *Geogr.* 16.2.35-39. Cf. A. D. Nock ("Posidonius," *JRS* 49 [1959] 8), who
traces this passage to the work of a hellenized Jew familiar with the ideas of Posidonius
on the history of religion. See further, Gager, *Moses*, 38-47. A similar view is expressed
by Paul in Gal 3:10, 19-25.

[76]As well as to the gods Osiris (Diod. 1.14.1; 15.8; 17.4; 27.5), Isis (1.14.1; 25.2, 6;
27.4), and Hermes (1.16.1-2). On what follows, cf. the excellent discussion of Tiede, *The
Charismatic Figure*, 153-55.

4). In view of these similarities it seems fairly clear that Artapanus has modeled his presentation of Moses on the native Egyptian figures described in Hecataeus' *Aegyptiaca*. In the fragments of Artapanus, Moses combines in himself the political, military, religious, philosophical, and technological achievements which in Hecataeus' account were shared by the deities Osiris, Isis, and Hermes, and by the hero Sesostris. Not only does Moses surpass each one individually, but also all of them combined. Thus, we conclude with O. Murray that "Artapanus used Hecataeus in his portrayal of Moses, reversing the picture of Hecataeus, and claiming that, so far from the Jews having taken their instructions from Egypt, it was Moses who established Egyptian civilization."[77]

This panegyric on Moses also functions as a counterblast to the anti-Jewish account of the career of Moses. Freudenthal already recognized that Artapanus' portrayal is directed against the views of certain Egyptians and Greeks.[78] More specifically, P. M. Fraser has shown that it is primarily aimed at the hostile picture of Moses attributed to the Egyptian priest Manetho.[79] The account of Jewish history set forth by Manetho focused on three aspects of the Jews' relationship to Egypt: 1) their anti-Egyptian activities, especially the destruction of the sacred animals and temples; 2) their leader Moses, an Egyptian priest; and 3) their expulsion from Egypt.[80] According to this account the Jews were originally Egyptians who suffered from leprosy (and other diseases), and because of this were compelled to labor in the stone-quarries, segregated from the other Egyptians. It is further stated that these lepers rose up in revolt against the Egyptian king Amenophis, and chose Moses as their leader, a priest of Heliopolis named Osarsiph, who was also afflicted with leprosy. This Moses gave them a law not to worship any gods and not to spare any of the animals revered in Egypt; but, on the contrary, to slaughter all and eat them. The "polluted people" then terrorized Egypt in the most horrible manner. Not only did they burn down cities and villages, they also looted temples, destroyed the statues of the gods, and even forced the priests and prophets to slaughter the sacred animals. Only after fleeing to Ethiopia for help was Amenophis able to return and drive the polluted people out of Egypt, "killing many of them and pursuing the remainder to the frontiers of Syria."

Artapanus' story of Moses develops along lines which are in sharp contrast to the account of Manetho. In Artapanus, Moses is not the traitor and rebel leader before whom the king must flee to Ethiopia, but the untiring and unselfish protector of the throne, who is especially concerned with keeping the monarchy secure. Furthermore, Artapanus portrays Moses as the great benefactor of Egypt: the organizer of its life in every respect. Moses does not destroy cities; he founds them. He does not oppress the Egyptians and their priests; rather, he wins the admiration of the people and the religious reverence of the priests, who address him as Hermes. It is Moses, moreover, who endows the priests with special tracts of land, although Manetho had charged that he drove them out naked. Above all, Moses is neither a plunderer of temples nor a slaughterer of the

---

[77] "Hecataeus of Abdera," 167.

[78] *Alexander Polyhistor,* 161.

[79] *Ptolemaic Alexandria,* 1. 704-6.

[80] *Apud* Josephus, *C. Ap.* 2.227-53. I leave aside for now the question how far Manetho actually bears responsibility for this description of the Jews. It may well be that Manetho only provided the material and his authority which were later (mis)used to form the anti-Jewish Moses legend (pseudo-Manetho). On this, cf. Gager, *Moses,* 113-18, and the literature there cited.

sacred animals. On the contrary, he establishes the entire Egyptian religious organiza-tion. These claims of Artapanus contain the strongest possible protest against the allega-tions that Moses forbade his followers to worship the gods, or that he made the slaughter of the animals a religious duty.

In attempting to identify the genre of Artapanus' work scholars generally err by treating the Moses-fragment in isolation from the Abraham- and Joseph-fragments. Thus, F 3 has been described as a "Moses-romance," or even an aretalogy of a θεῖος ἀνήρ. However, when F 3 is isolated from the other two, the features common to all three are thereby obscured. As Holladay has shown, there is far more justification for classifying Artapanus' work as a whole as a nationalistic or apologetic history in the same genre as Hecataeus' *Aegyptiaca* and Berossus' *Babyloniaca*.[81] Like these authors, Artapanus writes a propagandistic history intended to glorify his national heritage, and he employs the same argumentative strategy by calling attention to its great antiquity and cultural contributions. It is equally incorrect to equate Artapanus' work with the sub-literary, popular national romances of various figures like Ninus, Semiramis, and Sesostris.[82] In the first place, unlike these popular romances, Artapanus' work is not written anony-mously; and, however deficient his literary style, it is certainly no worse than that of Berossus, Manetho, or Philo of Byblos. In fact, Weinreich has shown that Artapanus was not unaware of literary conventions.[83] He points, for example, to the two versions of the crossing of the Red Sea (F 3.35), where in the first account the inhabitants of Memphis report that Moses was familiar with the region and waited for the water to ebb, while in the second the people of Heliopolis give the more miraculous version. By offering an alternative, rationalistic explanation and separating the two accounts with a μέν/δέ construction, Artapanus indicates at least some awareness of the literary conventions of Hellenistic historiography.

CONCLUSION

Our study of the fragmentary remains of the historians Eupolemus, the anonymous Samaritan, and Artapanus has revealed a number of common tendencies or motifs. While the highly individual character of each historian should not be overlooked, we have observed that in their interpretation of the history of culture they show a remarkable similarity. These works describe the rise of civilization as an evolutionary process, with various OT figures responsible for the technological discoveries which advance culture. Eupolemus portrays Moses as "the first wise man," whose inventions include (Greek) philosophy, the alphabet, and written laws. In this way, Egyptian and Phoenician claims are challenged, and especially those of the Greeks, who were acknowledged to have received their culture from either Phoenicia or Egypt. Similarly, the anonymous Samari-tan makes Abraham the founder of civilization and, more specifically, the one from whom the Babylonians, Phoenicians, and later the Egyptians learned astrology. Artapanus'

---

[81]C. R. Holladay, *THEIOS ANER in Hellenistic-Judaism* (SBLDS 40; Missoula: Scholars Press, 1977) 215-18. However, in *Fragments*, 190-91, he classifies Artapanus as "popular romance literature" (cf. 196-97 n. 16). Note that in F 1 the title of Artapanus' work is given as ᾿Ιουδαϊκά; that is, the same form as the titles of the historical works of Berossus, Manetho, Philo of Byblos, and others.

[82]As does M. Braun, *History and Romance*, 1-6 and 26-31.

[83]"Gebet und Wunder," 306.

history describes *both* the patriarchs and Moses as great inventors who introduced the technology of civilization. Indeed, Moses is identified both with Hermes and with Musaeus, and thus becomes the founder of both Egyptian and Greek culture.[84]

A second tendency exhibited by these historians is their international, or universal, orientation.[85] While the focus of each of these writers is eventually his own nation and customs, this is achieved in the context of an account of other lands and peoples. Our three historians are proud of the history and antiquity of their own tradition, but at the same time they are interested in and tolerant of general Hellenistic culture. Thus, they attempt to build a bridge between Hellenistic culture and their own on the basis of the biblical text. Indeed, they are among the first to present biblical history in Greek form. Their radical departures from the biblical text therefore should not be attributed to carelessness or ignorance, but to the authors' attempts to represent these traditions in light of contemporary trends in Hellenistic historiography. To that end, they refer back to writers such as Hesiod and Berossus, but above all to Hecataeus of Abdera. Here is evidence that these texts were read in Jewish and Samaritan circles in the second century B.C.

Another feature which all three historians have in common is their tendency toward euhemerism: the gods of the Babylonians, Egyptians, and Greeks are shown to be none other than the biblical patriarchs and Moses, who so aided the advance of culture that they were elevated to divine rank.[86]

Here it should be pointed out that these tendencies not only typify the works of our three historians, but are characteristic of Hellenistic historiography in general. In his study of Philo of Byblos, R. A. Oden isolated five tendencies "which shaped the writing of history, particularly history as written by historians from among the subject nations of the eastern Mediterranean, in the Hellenistic and Roman eras."[87] They are: 1) euhemerism, 2) the impulse to write history on a universal scale, 3) the tendency to interpret the history of culture from a nationalistic perspective, 4) a defensive stance with respect to Greek civilization, and 5) the claim to historical records which were superior to those of the Greeks both in age and reliability. Admittedly, this five-fold division is somewhat artificial and overlapping. Many passages in the fragments of the Hellenistic historians exhibit several or all the tendencies at once. Nevertheless, the isolation of these five tendencies serves to demonstrate how thoroughly typical of Hellenistic historiography are the writings of Eupolemus, the anonymous Samaritan, and Artapanus. Indeed, their histories compete admirably with those written on behalf of the Egyptians, Babylonians, and Phoenicians. Like these works, they attempt to account for the rise of civilization, and leave no doubt as to whom credit for the progress is to be given. Thus, they show

---

[84]In this regard, note the use of the *Erfindertopos* by all three historians: the decisive first inventions (e.g., astrology, writing, laws, philosophy, and so on) come from the patriarchs and Moses.

[85]I.e., both geographically and chronologically. Despite the apparent title of his work, *On the Kings of Judaea,* Eupolemus begins long before this, with Adam.

[86]Whether "euhemerism" originated with Euhemerus or, in fact, with Hecataeus of Abdera is much debated. Cf. Murray, "Hecataeus of Abdera," 151, who argues that "it was Hecataeus, not Euhemerus (whose debt to Hecataeus in this and other particulars is clear), who first systematically worked out the theory that the gods are divinized kings."

[87]R. A. Oden, "Philo of Byblos" 118-24.

themselves to be participants in the "war of books" that began with the publication of Hecataeus' Egyptian *Kulturgeschichte*.

Finally, something should be said about the social context of these historians. In his famous study of "Graeco-Oriental literature," M. Braun distinguished two levels at which this literature flourished: 1) the literary level, maintained by priests or educated writers, and directed to audiences of comparable social status within the dominant culture (e.g., the historical works of Berossus, Manetho, and Josephus); and 2) the non-literary level, expressing itself in popular romances developed around national heroes (e.g., Ninus, Semiramis, Sesostris, and so on).[88] While there are certain problems with Braun's application of this analysis to specific texts, his comments on the literary level appear to me to be useful in understanding the three historians discussed in this paper.

> On the whole there are two distinct strata within "national" literature. The one emerges from the better educated and socially superior class of the subjected people, whose spokesmen, mostly priests or their descendants, display to the foreign ruling class the great antiquity, virtues, and achievements of their own nation. At the same time, they fight for "truth" against current rumors and lies. They are personalities of repute and social dignity who, while defending their own people, also enter into the service of the Greek or Roman rulers.[89]

It is our contention that the three historians we have considered should be situated in this "better educated and socially superior class." Indeed, one of them, Eupolemus, seems to have been a member of one of the priestly families of Jerusalem and a leader of the Jewish delegation to Rome in 161 B.C. Furthermore, all three argue for "the antiquity, virtues, and achievements of their own nation" and against "current rumors and lies." Finally, all three adopt an accommodating stance toward Hellenism, properly understood as being dependent on Jewish culture.

---

[88]Braun, *History and Romance,* 1-6.

[89]Ibid., 3. It should be pointed out that Braun relegates Artapanus to the non-literary level (incorrectly, in my opinion).

Manifestations of Hellenistic Historiography in Select Judaic Literature

Phillip Sigal

University of Michigan

I. Introduction

Hellenistic historiography is manifest in a variety of ways in Judaic literature from the earliest intertestamental writings to those of Josephus.[1] In this paper I am able only to cursorily consider elements of biography, aretalogy, and *chriae*.[2] Hellenistic historiography usually is characterized by standard hellenistic rhetorical devices, but not always, and I can refer only to these in passing.[3] This essay can do no more than briefly examine Fourth Maccabees and examples from Philo, the New Testament and rabbinic literature in order to determine which hellenistic ingredients inform these Judaic religious writings.

We are beyond the point of having to resolve whether Judaic writings were influenced by hellenistic civilization.[4] This paper will suggest that while absorbing hellenistic

---

[1] The earliest intertestamental or apocryphal book might be Tobit which cannot be dated with certainty. The latest actual historical event alluded to in the book is that of the rebuilding of the Temple (ca. 515 B.C.). There is no allusion to the persecution by Antiochus or of the Hasmonean developments. In the light of these facts it is likely that the book was written 500-200 B.C. See on Tobit, George W. E. Nickelsburg, *Jewish Literature Between the Bible and the Mishnah* (Philadelphia: Fortress, 1981) 30-35; see J. Lebram, "Die Weltreiche in der jüdischen Apokalyptik," *ZAW* 76 (1964) 328-31, who argues for a date after Alexander the Great's conquest of the Persian Empire, which would place it around 300 B.C. D. C. Simpson, "Tobit," *The Apocrypha and Pseudepigrapha of the Old Testament* (ed. R. H. Charles; 2 vols.; Oxford: Clarendon Press, 1913) 183-85, concludes that it was written between 350 B.C. and 170 B.C. C. C. Torrey (*The Apocryphal Literature* [New Haven: Yale, 1945] 85) dates the work to the period between 200-250 B.C.

[2] By "aretalogy" is meant a biographical narrative relating to a divine figure which tells of his *aretas*, his virtues and miraculous deeds, and which is usually used in a liturgical context. *Chriae* are brief anecdotes about a sage usually concluding with a terse aphorism or moral teaching. See further on aretalogy and *chriae* sections II-V below.

[3] Thus, for example, Polybius opposed the inclusion of horror stories that aroused pity. He wrote, "A historical author should not try to thrill his readers . . . but simply record what really happened and what really was said. . . ." See Polybius, *The Histories* (trans. W. R. Paton; 6 vols.; Loeb Classical Library; Cambridge-London: Harvard University Press, 1960) II, 56 (10).

[4] See Saul Lieberman, *Greek in Jewish Palestine* (New York: Jewish Theological Seminary, 1942); *Hellenism in Jewish Palestine* (New York: Jewish Theological Seminary,

rhetoric and style and undergoing the corollary process of emulating hellenistic themes, Judaic literature frequently transformed the genres of the literature to which it was acculturating. This was true both in the writings of history directly and in the genres of biography and its handmaidens, anecdotes and episodes related to singular personalities.

At the outset it must be borne in mind that a great deal more literature than we have was written and circulated in its time. This is true of many a historian known to us. But it also suggests that there were others not now known to us. An analogy quite evident in our time might be drawn from the relatively recent discoveries of the massive Qumran and Nag Hammadi libraries. Thus, there was much antecedent literature to the gospels, and undoubtedly Paul wrote and taught more than has been preserved in his few letters found in the New Testament collection. This caveat must also be applied to rabbinic literature. What we have in the extant corpuses of talmudim and midrashim is the ultimate product of selection, sifting and abridging. We have what certain disciples or others chose to preserve, and what the process of memorization for oral presentation allowed to be preserved.[5]

We must confront the reality of a haphazard preservation of materials. This was determined by personal ideological preferences, the ravages of war, the deficiencies of copyists, population transportation and even indirect or direct censorship such as the omission of Sadducean materials from the oral rabbinic corpus and later the minimization of Shammaitic materials by the dominant Hillelite forces from the written rabbinic corpus. The consequence of these factors was that our judgments must be based upon fragmentary evidence. This is a pattern quite obvious in the compilation of the Talmuds which were merely collected and never really edited. In another manner it follows logically from what we know, for example, about the abridgment of the five volume work of Jason of Cyrene which we know as 2 Maccabees. This is true as well of the abridgment of the Gospel of John.[6]

Although certain other matters will be noted, discussion in this essay will center first on whether the account of Eleazar in Fourth Maccabees and the Philonic and Gospel accounts of Moses and Jesus respectively were aretalogies. And second, it will examine the use of *chriae* in rabbinic literature, understanding this literature in very broad terms

---

1950); Martin Hengel, *Judaism and Hellenism* (trans. John Bowden; 2 vols.; Philadelphia: Fortress, 1974).

[5]Martin Hengel, *Acts and The History of Earliest Christianity* (trans. John Bowden; Philadelphia: Fortress, 1980) 7-9, 11. On the subject of transmission of the ancient sources in general, see Birger Gerhardsson, *Memory and Manuscript* (Uppsala: C. W. K. Gleerup, 1961).

[6]On the Talmud see Phillip Sigal, *The Emergence of Contemporary Judaism*, Volume One, *The Foundations of Judaism*, Part One, *From Biblical Origins to the Separation of Christianity*, Part Two, *Rabbinic Judaism* (Pittsburgh: Pickwick Press, 1980); see Part 2, pp. 233f.; see 2 Macc 2:23 where the author clearly calls himself an epitomist, indicating that *di henos syntagmatos epitimein*, he will attempt ". . . to epitomize into one treatise" the five books of Jason of Cyrene. For comprehensive discussion see Jonathan Goldstein, *II Maccabees* (AB; Garden City, NY: Doubleday, 1983). On John see John 20:30 which indicates that the core upon which the gospel as we have it was based was originally a much longer miracle-story work. See on this George W. Buchanan, "The Samaritan Origin of the Gospel of John," *Religions in Antiquity* (ed. J. Neusner; Leiden: E. J. Brill, 1968) 149-175, 172.

as an integral part of Judaic hellenistic historiography. This is so since from this literature we garner much of our knowledge for the Graeco-Roman era.

II. Fourth Maccabees[7]

Josephus, like Polybius, summed up the major purpose of history to be to teach
people what to avoid and what to embrace in life. Josephus wrote, ". . . the main lesson
to be learned . . . is that men who conform to the will of God . . . prosper . . . as they
depart from the strict observance of these laws . . ." they end in disaster.[8] It is, therefore, not surprising if scholars expect that aretalogies played a role in Judaic historiography. An aretalogy told of the *aretas* (virtue) and of the miraculous deeds of a singular
personality.[9] This became a distinct form of biography. One element of an aretalogy
often included the recounting of a miraculous birth and death, the latter frequently the
result of martyrdom. The life-span between birth and death usually included the hero's
ability to work wonders and a propensity to aggravate rulers.[10]

The story of the martyrdom of the ninety-year-old *grammateus* (scribe), Eleazar,
is told briefly in 2 Maccabees.[11] This version is expanded in 4 Maccabees where Eleazar
is termed a priest and even a *nomikos*, an expert in the *nomos*, a proto-rabbi.[12] The
amplification is such that it is considered to be an aretalogy.[13] In any event the martyrdom of Eleazar as told in 4 Maccabees became a basic staple of patristic writers. This
work played no less a role than the celebrated account of the martyrdom of Polycarp who
was also a ninety-year-old priest. The paradigm of Eleazar was part of a glorification of

---

[7] *The Third and Fourth Book of Maccabees* (ed. and trans. Moses Hadas; New York:
KTAV, 1953). The text and translation of Hadas was the only one consulted for this essay.
[8] Josephus, *Jewish Antiquities* (10 vols.; Loeb Classical Library; Vol. IV, trans. H.
St. J. Thackeray; Vol. V, trans. H. St. J. Thackeray and Ralph Marcus; Vols. VI-VII, trans.
Ralph Marcus; Vol. VIII, trans. Ralph Marcus, Allen Wikgren; Vols. IX-X, trans. L. H.
Feldman; Cambridge, MA/London: Harvard University Press/William Heinemann, 1978-
1981). See *Ant.* I, 3 (14); 4 (20). Polybius had written "the surest and indeed the only
method of learning how to bear bravely the vicissitudes of fortune (*tyche*) is to recall the
calamities of others." See, *Histories*, I, 1 (2); I, 35 (9). See further on Polybius, Michael
Grant, *Ancient Historians* (London: Weidenfeld and Nicolson, 1970) 144-64. There were
many affinities between Josephus and Polybius, as well as some differences. But the
scope of this paper does not allow for further discussion of these interesting facets of the
two historians.
[9] *Aretas legein* "to speak the wonders [virtues]" is often used in LXX. Therefore a
composition reciting the virtues and wondrous deeds of a hero or god or hero-become-god
was called an *aretalogia*. See Moses Hadas and Morton Smith, *Heroes and Gods* (New
York: Harper and Row, 1965) 61.
[10] Hadas-Smith, 3f.
[11] 2 Macc 6:18-31. The text and translation consulted for this paper was *The
Second Book of Maccabees* (trans. Sidney Tedesche; ed. Solomon Zeitlin; New York:
Harper and Brothers—Dropsie, 1954). See also Jonathan Goldstein, *II Maccabees* (n. 6
above).
[12] 4 Macc 5:4-7:15. The term *nomikos* is at 5:4. On the term "proto-rabbi" see
Phillip Sigal, *The Emergence of Contemporary Judaism*, Vol., Part 2, Chapter One.
[13] Hadas-Smith, 88ff.

the Maccabees who were highly venerated by the early fathers of the church. They saw in Hasmonean martyrdom a type and inspiration for Christians.[14]

But while it has aretalogical features Fourth Maccabees is in itself not an aretalogy. The book is actually a complex of various elements, its central burden being a philosophical approach to Judaism, emphasizing that it is a religion of reason that teaches the believer to transcend passion.[15] At its base is an adaptation of Platonic and Stoic philosophy which emphasized prudence, temperance, justice and courage as the four major virtues that stand over against emotion. But its direction is turned by the assertion that these virtues are best inculcated by the *nomos*, either the Torah of Moses, or extended torah, the precepts exegeted out of a midrashic endeavor, the interpretive torah.[16] In a very real sense 4 Maccabees should be seen as a didactic sermon or discourse. It contains various evidences of hellenistic historiography but it cannot be said to have been intended either as a history or as an aretalogy for Eleazar and the seven brothers who committed martyrdom. Certainly it contains the aretalogical flavor in the story of Eleazar. And it clearly exhibits the hellenistic rhetorician's proclivity for sensationalism and hyperbole in the detailed description of the torture first of Eleazar and later of the seven brothers. Their tortures and their farewell speeches are given in great detail, typical of one school of hellenistic historiography even if in contradiction to another school.[17] Similarly, the speech of the mother given to each of her seven sons is

---

[14]Hadas (*Fourth Maccabees*, 94) mentions in this connection Origen, Cyprian, Ambrose, Augustine, and John Chrysostom. Martyrs were believed to have supernatural powers. There was a tomb of Maccabee martyrs in Antioch which was venerated by early Christians because of a belief that the martyrs were capable of curing the sick. The church was perturbed that Christians turned to Jewish saints for succor and consequently transformed the place into a Christian shrine where the Maccabees were henceforth glorified as Christian saints. In the days of John Chrysostom a vigil and a feast were held annually at this shrine. John preached sermons in which he urged Christians to be willing to suffer martyrdom as the Maccabee prototypes were and drew parallels between the aged Eleazar and the apostle Peter. See *Saint John Chrysostom, Discourses Against Judaizing Christians* (trans. Paul W. Harkins; *The Fathers of the Church*, Vol. 68; Washington, DC: Catholic University of America Press, 1977) xliv-xlvii; Discourse VIII, 6.8 and p. 228 n. 43; see also Robert Wilken, *John Chrysostom and the Jews* (Berkeley: University of California, 1983). See also my forthcoming review of Wilken's book in *Judaism*, likely Winter 1985.

For Polycarp see *The Martyrdom of Polycarp* (trans. William R. Schoedel; *The Apostolic Fathers*, Vol. 5; London: Thomas Nelson & Sons, 1967) 47-85.

[15]For 4 Maccabees see Nickelsburg, 223-27; *The Third and Fourth Books of the Maccabees*, ed. Hadas, 86-248.

[16]4 Macc 1:3f.; 13-30; at 1:17 *nomos* is named. This term cannot be confined to the five books of Moses and should certainly not be translated as "The Law" in some kind of definitive reference to the Pentateuch. See on this especially in reference to 4 Maccabees, Paul Redditt, "The Concept of *Nomos* in Fourth Maccabees," *CBQ* 45 (1983) 249-270. See also my paper, "A Brief Inquiry Into the Term *Nomos*," delivered before the Eastern Great Lakes Biblical Society annual meeting at Duquesne University in Pittsburgh in April 1977, and now being readied for publication in the *Calvin Theological Journal*, scheduled for April 1985.

[17]4 Macc 6:1-11; 24-26; the martyrdom of the seven brothers is at chapters 8-12. The description of the martyrdoms violates the canons of historiography as stressed by the antipathetic school exemplified by Polybius but is in keeping with the style of Josephus.

given in detail.[18] All of this is obviously material to which the writer, not having been an eyewitness, had no access. But this is no different from the creative approach to speeches of figures in histories from Thucydides to Josephus. Nevertheless, although containing these historiographical elements, 4 Maccabees is something other than either a history or an aretalogy.

Fourth Maccabees is a didactic tract that aims at teaching two still-indecisive doctrines, the doctrine of expiatory suffering and the doctrine of immortality. It might even be suggested that the author of 4 Maccabees was struggling with how to articulate the doctrine of resurrection as over against, or in tandem with, the doctrine of spiritual immortality. But more significant is the doctrine of expiatory suffering using Isaac as the prototype which then becomes a staple of early Christianity. At 2 Maccabees the sixth of the seven martyred brothers is reported to have said, "We suffer these things because of ourselves, because we sinned against our own God." This has no hint of vicarious expiation. On the other hand vicarious atonement looms large in 4 Maccabees.[19]

There is a plausible view that Fourth Maccabees was a discourse recited at a special commemoration of martyrs in Antioch.[20] Moses Hadas suggests that this view might be rejected on the grounds that "contact with the dead is prohibited in the Law."[21] But this is rather gratuitous. Commemoration or a eulogistic assembly is not "contact with the dead." First, two source references given by Hadas prohibiting contact with the dead apply only to a priest and to a *nazir*, one who has taken a vow of abstinence.[22] Although in post-biblical times the prohibition was extended to disallow a priest's visiting a cemetery as well, it is difficult to know when this was done, and in any case it would be irrelevant to a commemorative, eulogistic assembly from which even a pious priest need not absent himself, being able to stand beyond the boundary of the cemetery. Second, although one reference appears to declare impure any lay person who comes into contact with the dead, this is a very particular and explicit context in which the person has been a *nogea^c bemet*, where one has actually touched a dead corpse.[23] Third, the concern

---

[18]4 Macc 16:16-23.

[19]On the doctrine of resurrection see 2 Macc 7:9, 14; 12:44; 14:46; for the sixth brother, 2 Macc 7:18. See below for the theme of expiatory death. On the ^cakedah of Isaac as expiatory death see Geza Vermes, *Scripture and Tradition in Judaism* (Leiden: E. J. Brill, 1961) 192-227; J. Danielou, "La typologie d'Isaac dans le christianisme primitif," *Biblica* 28 (1947) 363-93; Shalom Spiegel, *The Last Trial* (Philadelphia: JPS, 1967); Robert J. Daly, "The Soteriological Significance of the Sacrifice of Isaac," *CBQ* 39 (1977) 45-75; Phillip Sigal, "Aspects of Paul's Judaic Thought: The Akedah," to appear in *Proceedings*, Eastern Great Lakes-Midwest Biblical Societies, Vol. 4, November 1984. The literature is massive, and further bibliographical citation here is not germane to the focus of this paper. See for resurrection George W. E. Nickelsburg, Jr., *Resurrection, Immortality and Eternal Life in Intertestamental Judaism* (HTS 26; Cambridge: Harvard University Press, 1972) 109-11.

[20]Rampolla de Tindaro, "Martyre et Sepulture des Machabées," *Revue de l'Art Chrétien* (1899) 295ff.; See Hadas, *IV Maccabees*, 104-9.

[21]Hadas, op. cit., 104f. n. 28.

[22]Lev 21:1-5; 10f.; Num 6:6-9. A third source offered by Hadas, the prohibition against divining and calling up the dead for advice, Deut 18:9-12, is entirely irrelevant, as are Deut 26:14 and Isa 65:4.

[23]Num 19:1-19; vv. 11, 13.

there is lest he who touched a corpse would defile God's sanctuary. Fourth, the entire passage under consideration is specifically addressed to a situation in which one is in the room in which a person has just died or one touches a corpse, a bone, or a grave.[24]

Furthermore, Hadas refers to the disclaimer of the rabbis of any association between "a place of worship and a tomb."[25] First, this runs the risk of anachronism, and second, the source references do not warrant this as an objection to a eulogistic assembly or a martyrdom commemoration. The talmudic passage merely refers to a room onto which a synagogue opened, or as one might more accurately phrase it, in a synagogue building with several rooms the chapel or room used for worship opened into a room in which there was a dead person. The rabbis raised the question of whether if a corpse were there this would spread defilement to the chapel and whether, in that event, priests can go there to worship while the corpse was still in that adjoining room. The question was not related to whether there can be worship at a tomb, and the discussion there in no way prohibits such worship.[26]

Hadas suggests that the widespread usage of a cult of heroes in the hellenistic world might have been adapted to Jewish usage, that is, that such memorialization might be seen as a "hellenization."[27] But this appears to me an unnecessary construction. There is no evidence that Jews could not have observed their own graveside liturgical forms independently of the cult of heroes. This is not to deny that acculturation to the usages of the broader society was not prevalent in all periods of Judaic history, and certainly in the hellenistic. It is only to suggest that memorialization of martyrs was not "un-Jewish" to begin with, and that there appears to be no prohibition upon such activity in classical Judaism.[28]

Fourth Maccabees was a didactic treatise used as a sermonic discourse, possibly but not necessarily at a commemoration of the Maccabean martyrs at a tomb in Antioch.[29] This possibility is heightened by the references in the book to "this season," denoting the time when the martyrdom took place. This, however, would not necessarily be at Hanukah time because Hanukah was not the occasion of the martyrdom. The martyrdoms took place several years before the event that Hanukah celebrates.[30] But while

---

[24]Num 19:13f.; 16, 18.

[25]Hadas, *IV Maccabees*, 105.

[26]*B. Meg.* 26b; the other reference given by Hadas, *B. Ber.* 17b, is irrelevant. It and its parallels deal with personal mourning at the time of the death of a next of kin and have no relevance for later memorialization at a tomb.

[27]Hadas, *IV Maccabees*, 105.

[28]On acculturation in all periods of history see Phillip Sigal, *The Emergence of Contemporary Judaism*, Vol. I, passim; Vol. II, *From the Seventh to the Seventeenth Century* (Pittsburgh: Pickwick Press, 1977) passim. *The Emergence of Contemporary Judaism*, Vol. III, *Renaissance, Reformation and the Dawn of Contemporary Judaism*, is now at the publisher, Pickwick Publications, and is to appear in early 1985. This volume continues the survey of Judaism during the era of the Italian and Dutch Renaissance and the Protestant and Catholic Reformations, again pointing to the tendency of acculturation. This is not to minimize the historical reality of tension between the acculturationists and the traditionalists, a theme also examined for Italy and Holland in *Emergence*.

[29]See n. 14 above.

[30]Clearly the martyrdoms as recorded at 2 Macc 6-7 occurred before the Maccabee struggle which eventuated in the liberation of Jerusalem (2 Macc 10), the event commemorated by the Judaic festival of Hanukah. This struggle lasted some three years. For

it is highly probable that it was a didactic commemorative panegyric-sermon, this need not have been at a shrine. It equally could have been in a school or synagogue. There is no apparent liturgical material in the book other than the doxology at the end which was a normal way to close a sermon. There is also no allusion to a liturgical framework. Furthermore, its length and level of content hardly seem appropriate for an audience at a tomb, although it can be argued that the emotionalism aroused by the spectacular descriptions of torture would be appropriate to the masses. Yet, commemorative discourses of this type need not have been presented at a shrine or a tomb but could be used to mark an occasion in the classroom or pulpit, or even as part of a regular synagogue order of worship.

Further, it appears to me that if 4 Maccabees was not written before 40 A.D. it was at least in part a response to the burgeoning Christian community in Antioch.[31] The essence of the Christian message was the expiatory death of Jesus. The author of 4 Maccabees sought to trace the concept of expiatory death to Isaac and to attribute this function to every martyr who died for *kidush hashem,* "the sanctification of the Name [of God]," the technical term for martyrdom.[32] The description of horrible suffering recorded in the book did not discourage the spread of Christianity, and in time the book was even endeared to the Christian community because it spoke to their great devotion to martyrdom. The Christian could accept Isaac as a type of Jesus in good conscience and could eulogize all martyrs as doing what is proper: emulating Jesus. Jesus had warned his disciples that they would be persecuted and even expelled from communities and 4 Maccabees would serve to strengthen their resolve. It was its adoption by Christians which motivated Jews to abandon the book. In its place arose rabbinic martyrologies. Possibly fragments of such martyrologies of R. Akiba and others are embedded in talmudic accounts of their deaths.[33]

That 4 Maccabees was originally known in rabbinic circles is clear from the parallel story of the martyrdom of the mother and her seven sons found in the Babylonian

---

historical background see Victor Tcherikover, *Hellenistic Civilization and the Jews* (trans. S. Applebaum; Philadelphia: Jewish Publication Society, 1959); *I Maccabees* (trans. Jonathan Goldstein; AB; Garden City, NY: Doubleday, 1976), "Introduction," *II Maccabees,* trans. Goldstein, "Introduction."

[31] On the dating of the book see Hadas, *IV Maccabees,* 95-99.

[32] That the martyr dies an expiatory death is found at 1:11; 6:29; 9:24; 17:20-22; 18:4. On the ʿakedah of Isaac, its typology for Jesus and its pre-Christian Judaic venue see further my paper referred to earlier, "Aspects of Paul's Judaic Thought," (n. 19 above).

[33] Matt 10:23; *B. Ber.* 61b. There is a midrash called *Asara Haruge Malkhut* (The Ten Put to Death by the State) which is epitomized in the Yom Kippur liturgy in the prayer called *Elah Ezkerah* (These Do I Remember). See Rashi's (R. Solomon of Troyes) commentary to a passage at *B. Yeb.* 122a which used the term *rigli,* "festivals" or "pilgrimages" (from *regel,* "a foot"), beginning *talata rigli.* Rashi wrote that he found in *Teshuḇot Hagaonim* that where ʾamoraic *rigli* are referred to the term signifies an annual commemorative day observed in honor of a great scholar, when scholars and ordinary people gather at his grave for remembrance and halakhic discussion in his honor. See also *B.A.Z.* 17b where anecdotes are told of two other martyrs of the Hadrianic persecution: R. Eleazar ben Perata and R. Ḥanina ben Teradyon. These anecdotes might also have been extracted from a more formal martyrology. See also *B. San.* 14a; *Lam. R.* II, 4 to Lam 2:2.

Talmud and other rabbinic sources, where it begins basically as a midrash to Ps 44:23.[34]
There are of course variations in the accounts, and the talmudic account is much briefer
than that of 4 Maccabees. This rabbinic version does not relate the story to the Hasmoneans but rather to the Herodian era. This is to be expected for various reasons. First,
considering rabbinic dissatisfaction with the entire Hasmonean enterprise, there would be
a tendency to shift the stories. Second, the genre was functional without reference to
chronology or accuracy of factual details. Another variation was that while in the
accounts of both 2 Maccabees and 4 Maccabees the king is demanding that the victims
violate the double sin of eating of swine's flesh and of idolatrous offerings, in the Talmudic account, the *kaisar* (Caesar) demands idolatrous worship. The king orders each in turn
pelaḥ laʿaḅodat ʾelilim (worship the gods), each in turn cites a different scriptural verse
prohibiting idolatry and polytheism and each in turn is executed.[35] Finally in desperation
Caesar suggests to the last brother that he will simply throw his royal seal before him
that he may stoop to pick it up and thereby appear to be paying worshipful homage. But
this too is rejected. As they lead him away to be executed, the mother speaks. She tells
all seven sons to tell Abraham that while he bound one altar she bound seven. Then she
committed suicide by throwing herself down from a roof. The story is concluded by a
heavenly voice declaring, "A joyful mother of children" (Ps 113:9). Presumably her joy is
derived from the knowledge that her seven martyr-sons enjoy eternal bliss, and the
expectation that her own martyrdom to avoid being violated by the soldiers will also gain
for her eternal life.[36]

In this rabbinic version there is no explicit reference to the expiatory element
unless one assumes that the mother's "speech" referring to Abraham alludes to that. The
allusion might be eloquent in its obscurity, in that it came from a time when the ʿakedah
story itself was being suppressed.[37] Many rabbis of the Hadrianic period in which the
talmudic story is set were not entirely gratified by the proliferation of martyrdom and
sought to bring the tendency under control. Furthermore the expiatory elements of
4 Maccabees were omitted in order to minimize analogy being drawn to the death of
Jesus. For this was also the time when the Isaacology was suppressed. The historical era
was also revised, for far from connecting the story with the Hasmoneans in which they
had minimal interest, they connected it with the ninth of ʾAb, the date of fasting for the
destruction of the Temple.[38]

An interesting statement that recalls a New Testament discussion of resurrection
between Jesus and Sadducees is made by Eleazar in the story of his martyrdom in

---

[34] *B. Git. 57b; Lam. R.* I:50 to Lam 1:16; *Seder Eliyahu Rabbah* 30; see the more
accessible *Tanna Debe Eliyahu* (trans. William G. Braude, Israel J. Kapstein; Philadelphia:
JPS, 1981) (30) 28, pp. 371-73; *Pesikta Rabbati* 43.

[35] They cite Exod 20:2; 20:3; 22:19; 20:5; Deut 6:4; 4:39; 26:17f. In different rabbinic accounts, however, there are also variations in the verses cited. Similarly, some
versions give the mother's name as Miriam, others omit it.

[36] In some versions the mother "fell" from the roof (*Lam. R.* I:50), in others she
"threw herself down." It is not germane to our purpose to analyze these texts and to
appraise the more authentic.

[37] See also 4 Macc 14:20; 15:28; 17:6.

[38] See *Lam. R.* I:50; *Seder Eliyahu R.* 30. In the latter version the reference to
expiatory death is more discernible when the mother is reported to have told her sons,
"you were in the world only in order that His [God's] great name be hallowed. . . ." It is to
be recalled that "to sanctify the name" is the standard term for martyrdom.

4 Maccabees. He declared that those who are fully committed to religion to the point of dying for it believe that they do not die to God, as neither did Abraham, Isaac, and Jacob, but live to God.[39] In this connection it has yet to be settled whether the author of 4 Maccabees taught a doctrine of bodily resurrection or only of immortality of the soul, or alternatively whether for at least one school of thought resurrection and immortality were identical at that time. That is, it must be determined whether the belief that the soul survives the body and is revivified in a spiritual, celestial form might in effect have served for some as the doctrine we call resurrection.[40] The passage under consideration (4 Maccabees 7:18f.) might also be seen as a midrash to Deut 30:20. At Deut 30:19 the two ways of life and death, blessing and curse, were presented to the Israelite, and he was urged to choose life in order that he and his progeny live. Life, we are told in Deuteronomy, is attained "By loving the Lord your God, listening to His voice and cleaving to Him; for He is your life and the length of your days to dwell upon the land which the Lord swore to give to your ancestors, Abraham, Isaac and Jacob" (v. 20). The author or midrashist is taking the phrase *kee hu ḥayekha*, "He is your life" (or even "*this* is your life," that is, your source of life is this love of God), in a spiritual sense, as referring to life in the hereafter. He is taking *ʾadamah* (the land) in the same way as *ʾereṣ* of Isa 60:21 was taken by a contemporary midrashist and as is reflected in both the New Testament and rabbinic literature.[41]

---

[39] 4 Macc 7:18f.; 16:25; cf. Matt 22:32; Mark 12:26; Luke 20:37f.; Rom 6:10; 14:8; Gal 2:19; B. Ber. 19ab.

[40] Resurrection is clearly stated as a doctrine at 2 Macc 7:9, 23; 14:46. But in 4 Maccabees some verses are ambiguous, e.g., 13:17; 16:25; yet, cf. 18:17ff. Ezek 37:2-4 on the dry bones living refers to bodily resurrection as is evident from vv. 5-10, and hence pre-Christian midrash saw personal revivification and not only national rejuvenation as a possibility. Dan 12:2 certainly implies bodily resurrection, as does Isa 26:19. See *Third and Fourth Maccabees*, ed. Hadas, 118. The contemporary of the author of 4 Maccabees, Philo of Alexandria, believed in immortality of the soul. See Philo, *Questions and Answers in Genesis* (trans. Ralph Marcus; Loeb Classical Library; Cambridge, MA/London: Harvard/Heinemann, 1979) III, 11. See also Nickelsburg, *Resurrection*, 110.

[41] M. San. 10:1. It is my view that Matt 5:3, 5 are not antithetical but rather are parallel. Both refer to the Kingdom of Heaven, that is, to *ʿolam habaʾ*, the world to come. Matthew has Jesus using *tēn gēn*, "the earth," at v. 5 in the same sense as the *ʾagadist* takes *ʾereṣ* "the land" of Isa 60:21, as metaphorical for the future existence. Although most people point to Ps 37:11 as the source for Matt 5:5, Isa 60:21 should not be overlooked. Bruce Metzger (*A Textual Commentary on the Greek New Testament* [United Bible Societies, 1971] 12) suggests that if Matt 5:3 and 5 would ever have followed one another, no scribe would have thrust v. 4 between them, and yet manuscripts dating from the second century indicate that copyists did reverse the order of vv. 4-5 to place v. 5 next to v. 3 as its antithesis. I am suggesting that the order originally might have been 3, 5, 4, and that these verses as spoken by Jesus were correctly understood as parallelism. Copyists later separated them when they did not grasp that Jesus meant to refer to *ʿolam habaʾ*, overlooking that the motif in these verses is eschatological, that they allude to Isa 61:1-3 with its mention of the poor in spirit, the meek and the sorrowing (Matt 5:3, 5). They were oblivious to the idea that Jesus might have spoken these beatitudes as part of a sermon on the *haftarah* (prophetic lection reading) he is reported to have recited at Luke 4:16-19. It should also be noted that in the context of attaining eternal life at 4 Macc 18:19 the Alexandrinus text reads *makariotēs*, "blessedness," in citing Deut 30:39 *ʾorekh yamekha*, "length of your days," where Sinaiticus reads *makrotēs*, "length." The

That the author of 4 Maccabees was likely engaging in this midrash is brought out more fully at 18:18f. where he conflated Deut 30:20 with 32:39, citing the latter first, "I cause death and I revivify," and adding from Deut 30:20, "for this is your life and the length of your days." The "this" is intended to refer to living God's word as is clear from his previous verses.[42] Finally, when we see 4 Macc 18:20-24 as a typical doxology and consider the close, in reference to God, "to whom be glory forever and ever," it is clear that the treatise must have served as a didactic sermon delivered at a religious commemoration or in the regular weekly sequence of worship.[43]

In sum, then, I would adjudge Fourth Maccabees not to be an aretalogy but a specimen of an expanded martyrology. It was designed to be theologically didactic and religiously inspirational and to be used as a sermon-lecture or lection reading in Antioch during a commemoration of martyrs, possibly at the Hanukah season. It was designed to teach the doctrines of immortality and/or resurrection and expiatory death. Like its later imitator, *The Martyrdom of Polycarp*, it was copied and sent for use in other communities, and because of its origin in the area contiguous to that of the Babylonian *ꜣamoraim*, its tradition is found albeit tendentiously rabbinically revised in the Babylonian Talmud.[44]

III. Philo's Moses

Philo's account of Moses is considered an aretalogy.[45] Morton Smith described an aretalogical pattern for the Philonic account of Moses in the following manner: Moses was a Chaldean by birth who arose to become an Egyptian prince, was taught Egyptian, Greek and Chaldean science, astrology, philosophy, and practical Stoic asceticism, came under suspicion of plotting a revolution, and fled Egypt.[46] It is necessary at this juncture to make certain strictures regarding Smith's understanding of Philo. Smith asserted that where Philo referred to Moses as a Chaldean by birth, he alluded to his early acquisition

---

significance to this might only be that the thought reflected in 4 Maccabees was very much afloat in first-century Palestine. It is probable that a much more in-depth study of 4 Maccabees and the New Testament would be a useful exercise.

[42]4 Macc 18:1-2; 15-17; indeed, this idea is stressed throughout the chapter.

[43]3 Macc 7:23 closes with "Praised be the deliverer of Israel forever." Cf. Tobit 14:15; Ben Sira 51:30, for closing doxologies which were probably used when these writings or parts of them were used as lection readings. A similar doxology also follows *The Martyrdom of Polycarp* (see n. 14 above). It is highly probable that the account of Polycarp's martyrdom was sent to various churches for further distribution ("Salutation," ibid.), to be read in the churches on the anniversary of Polycarp's "birthday," or rather, his day of re-birth to eternal life, as would occur upon martyrdom. See ibid., 18:3. The half-kaddish still recited after the Torah reading is an expanded doxology in the tradition of closing a lectionary reading with a doxology.

[44]"Salutation," ibid., p. 51; *B. Git.* 57b.

[45]Hadas-Smith, *Heroes,* 129-60 (Part II of this work which includes the lives of several ancients is the work of Morton Smith and will be so identified in following notes). Philo, *Moses* (trans. F. H. Colson; Loeb Classical Library 6; Cambridge, MA/ London: Harvard University Press/William Heinemann, 1966) 276-594 (even-numbered pages, Greek text), 277-595 (odd-numbered pages, English translation). See also Erwin R. Goodenough, *By Light, Light* (New Haven: Yale University Press, 1935) 180-234.

[46]Philo, *Moses* I, 2 (5); 3 (8); 5 (19); 5 (21-24); 9 (46f.). See Hadas-Smith, 130f.

of the art and knowledge of the astrologer or magi. Smith further commented of the elements listed here, "All this is quite unknown to the Bible, while on the other hand characteristic biblical traits are discreetly omitted: the Bible says Moses fled Egypt because he had committed a murder and was afraid it would become known."[47]

A telling argument against considering the Philonic account of Moses as aretalogy is Hadas's notion that Socrates was the paradigm for aretalogy.[48] The significant culmination of Socrates' life was his martyrdom for truth, while such martyrdom is in no way associated with Moses. Furthermore, other matters cast doubt upon the idea that Philo was creating an aretalogy. For example, when Philo began his account of Moses he said he hoped to bring the life of "the greatest and most perfect of all men" to all who sought to know of him. But Philo did not allude to or use in this connection the term *aretas*, "virtue," in order to lead us to infer that he was writing an aretalogy. He was writing a biography, using the term *bios*, "life." And he clearly indicated that Moses was "by *genos*," that is, by ethnic or ancestral stock a Chaldean, alluding not to his being a child-prodigy astrologer, but to the origins of Abraham. Smith also overstated the case concerning Moses' flight from Egypt. True Philo's reason for Moses' flight was somewhat amplified over that given in Exodus, but the Exodus account is rather laconic.[49] It should be recalled that Moses chastised a violent Israelite and was challenged by the perpetrator with the words, "who has made you into prince or judge among us?" Then "Moses was afraid and thought, 'if this be so, the matter is known,'" that is, the matter of his having killed an Egyptian guard on a previous occasion. We then read that Pharaoh heard about the matter and sought to kill Moses. The entire account begs for midrash. What did the Israelite perpetrator really mean in his challenge to Moses? Could he not have implied that Moses has not been recognized as the leader of an Israelite liberation movement? Of what was Moses afraid if it merely be known to Pharaoh that he killed an Egyptian? He was, after all, Pharaoh's grandson and possibly crown prince. Would Pharaoh destroy him merely because he killed an Egyptian? What did Pharaoh really hear that set him to seek to kill Moses? These and other questions arise from the obviously truncated account in Exodus. Philo supplied current midrash in order to provide a coherent flowing account. This is in accord with his own statement that he will provide information from both the sacred books of Moses himself and that which he has garnered from the elders, the *presbyterōn*. Philo wrote "for I always interwove what I was told with what I read. . . ." In other words while Philo was not engaged in gathering oral history, he spent his Sabbaths in the synagogue and heard from elders midrashic expansions of the Torah's account of the early life of Moses.[50]

The same type of midrashizing was true of Josephus who amplified his account of Moses with much non-biblical material. Such Philonic or Josephian midrash sometimes does and sometimes does not coincide with rabbinic midrash, but this is not germane to our present concerns and need not delay us.[51] Thus, for example, Josephus had Amram's wife already pregnant when he introduced the story of Moses.[52] Josephus also exhibited

---

[47]Hadas-Smith, 130.

[48]Hadas-Smith, *Heroes*, 49.

[49]*Moses* I, 1 (1); 2 (5); *On Abraham* XIV, 67, found in the same volume of the Loeb Classical Library, pp. 38-39. See also *Moses* I, 8 (45) - 9 (46); Exod 2:13ff.

[50]*Moses* I, 1 (4).

[51]Josephus, *Ant.* II, 9, 1 (201) - II, 2 (258).

[52]*Ant.* II, 9, 3 (210).

certain features in agreement with Jubilees, for example, in naming Pharaoh's daughter Thermuthis.[53] This points up the fact that non-biblical traditions were afloat that surfaced in both Philo and Josephus. They used these materials in their own way, sometimes agreeing with one another and sometimes diverging. But they did not invent their material in order to write an aretalogy. In fact, the account of Moses cannot at all be considered an aretalogy because in the account of neither Philo nor Josephus was Moses martyred.[54]

Smith finds some problem with Philo having a mediating angel speak to Moses from the burning bush. But again Philo merely midrashized scripture which states "And there appeared a *mal³akh* of the Lord to him within a flaming fire in the midst of the thornbush . . . and God called to him from the thornbush. . . ."[55] Thus scripture has a *mal³akh* of Yhwh appearing to Moses, and later *³elohim* speaks. For midrashic fancy there is no reason why Philo could not see *³elohim* as speaking through the *mal³akh*. But in any event while there is certainly scriptural warrant for Philo's introduction of an angelic participant, contrary to Smith Philo did not really "insert a mediating angel." He said that Moses saw a radiant form unlike any visible object, while Philo understood to be *eikona tou ontos einai,* "an image of Him who is," that is, an image of God. For lack of a better way to express the ineffable Philo said, "but let us rather call it an angel." He then proceeded with an allegory of the burning bush including not that the angel was a mediator but was a symbol of God's providence.[56] As a matter of fact the angel is not a mediator in Philo at all. Philo merely said that the total image Moses saw, including the extraordinary phenomenon of the unconsumed bush, the unusual radiance caused by the miraculous celestial fire and that ineffable image within the flames testifying to God's presence, can be "thought of" as a voice, but not that it spoke. On the contrary, after recording what we can imagine the celestial image might have said, Philo informed us that "*God* begins in oracular speech" (italics mine). Finally we should not overlook the fact that at times the *logos* and son of God were also called God by Philo.[57]

Smith finds another flaw in Philo's view that Moses disdained sexual intercourse. Again, however, this was also a midrashic view and is paralleled in rabbinic literature.[58] But no further purpose can be served by an in-depth analysis of Smith's misreading of Philo's account of Moses. Smith has overlooked an entire dimension of exegesis in order to affirm the presupposition that Philo's "changes" were based on the aretalogical pattern. Philo's amplifications of scripture, however, should be viewed as based upon traditions he received from the sages of his time. The omissions, such as Exodus 4:24 in which

---

[53]Jub 47:5; *Ant.* II, 9, 5 (224).

[54]See on this the critique of the aretalogy theory by Howard C. Kee, "Aretalogy and Gospel," *JBL* 92 (1973) 402-22; see p. 405. Kee rejected the Hadas-Smith views of aretalogy and specifically concerning the gospel Jesus-account. See, e.g., pp. 404f. I will return to Kee's arguments in the next section on Jesus.

[55]Hadas-Smith, 130; Exod 3:2ff.; Philo, *Moses* I, 12 (66).

[56]*Moses* I, 12 (67).

[57]Ibid., 13 (68f.); 14 (71ff.). As a matter of fact Philo refers to Moses and God being "alone" together at 14 (80). See also *On Dreams* I (228-230); *QG.* II (62). Philo might have had in mind that the *mal³akh* represented the *logos* and can therefore be identical with *³elohim, theos.*

[58]*Moses* II, 14 (69); *B. Shab.* 87a. The reason given for Moses' celibacy was that he was always at call of the shekhinah. This could very well have been the motivating force in Paul's view of celibacy.

God sought to kill Moses, must be understood from a hellenistic apologetic perspective. Philo would avoid attributing so crass a possibility to the perfect philosophical deity he labored to portray to his gentile readers. Certainly Philo's Moses underwent a transfiguration at Sinai. Later he underwent a transformation from mortal humanity to immortality, in which his two-fold nature of soul and body, as Philo put it, was resolved into a single unity. In this state, Philo informed us, Moses entered into a state of exaltation to make an upward flight to heaven, his former physical body was entombed by immortal powers and honored with a monument of special dignity which no person has ever seen. Philo did not bother to explain how the entombment and monument of Moses can have such superior significance if nobody has ever beheld it. The only explanation must be that in the absence of such physical evidence, as in the case of Jesus' empty tomb, resides the faith that he was transfigured and exalted to heaven. Philo already recorded a proleptic notion along these lines concerning Moses when he wrote that the human-divine composite in Moses was already discernible in his early years even before the episode at the burning bush. Philo exalted Moses in other ways. He described him as a co-possessor with God of all of nature, a partner of the Father and Creator and one who was honored to be named "god" and allowed into the incorporeal archetypal essence of existing things.[59]

Hellenistic patterns influenced Philo's account of Moses, including such elements as philosophical and mystical flights of rhetoric, imaginary speeches, aspects of the hellenistic romance, and the status of the philosopher as model for Moses. And while coincidentally certain aspects of the aretalogy are present, especially in the acclamation of Moses' virtues and superior features, two essential elements are missing: martyrdom and the liturgical recital of the account. It was not even used liturgically at the Pesaḥ seder when it would have been natural to do so. As a matter of fact, Philo's *Moses* is too long to be an aretalogy and to serve a liturgical function. But it is certainly an excellent example of biography in the hellenistic mode.[60]

Josephus's account of Moses had elements in it that were akin to Philo's and also different. This again was not aretalogical but might be said to have affinities with birth and infancy stories told of other heroes.[61] Thus Josephus has a section in which Moses' adoptive mother saves him from a plot to kill him, a scene which is also found in rabbinic tradition.[62] When Josephus reached the episode of the burning bush he left out the angel entirely.[63] On the other hand Philo omitted the entire pre-exodus paschal episode, while Josephus included it briefly.[64] Yet again at the death of Moses Josephus spoke of a cloud that descended upon Moses into which he "disappeared." And Josephus, seeking to

---

[59] *Moses* II, 51 (288, 291); *Moses* I, 6 (27). See also I, 10 (57); 28 (157-158); for the transfiguration see *Moses* II, 14 (68-70). See also Tan. *vezoʾt haberakhah* 1 to Deut 33:1. See also Tan. *behaʿalotekha* 9.

[60]Philo creates speeches for God as well as Moses, as, e.g., his imaginative approach to Num 9:1-14 at *Moses* II, 41 (222-232) where God allows a make-up Passover for those who missed the paschal rite of Nisan 14.

[61]See Otto Rank, *The Myth and the Birth of the Hero* (ed. Philip Freund; New York: Random House, n.d.); for Moses see pp. 15-18; Jesus, pp. 50-56; for interpretation of the birth stories see Chapter III.

[62] *Ant.* II, 9, 7 (233-237).

[63]Ibid., 12, 1 (264-269).

[64] *Ant.* II, 14, 6 (312f).

minimize the divinity-orientation in Moses lore then explained that Moses wrote that he died lest people say that he had returned to the Deity.[65]

In sum it might be said that while the accounts of Moses in Judaic hellenistic literature exemplified by Philo and Josephus contain elements in common with aretalogies it is by no means a foregone conclusion that these accounts were designed as aretalogies. The aretalogical elements contained in them are easily explainable as normative hellenistic style: philosophical discourse, rhetorical amplifications, and imaginary speeches. The miraculous deeds recorded of Moses need not be associated with aretalogy, but rather with their Old Testament sources, just as Jesus' miracles described in the Gospel of John are closely related to the miracle pattern of Elijah and Elisha in 1 and 2 Kings.[66]

IV. Jesus

What has been said concerning the distancing of the accounts of Moses in Philo and Josephus from aretalogy might also be said of the gospel accounts of Jesus.[67] For one thing, such elements as Smith presents for Moses as his training in all wisdom are not present in the narratives of Jesus at all.[68] While Smith argued that Philo made of Moses an ascetic philosopher, Jesus informed his disciples that he was looked upon as a glutton.[69] Smith argued that what appealed to Philo in the aretalogical tradition was the portrayal of the hero as philosopher, prophet, and wonder-worker.[70] But actually Philo's emphasis is upon Moses' characteristics of king, lawgiver, priest, and prophet. This delineation can only be remotely related to the aretalogy patterns Smith advanced and more correctly connected with Old Testament traditions flavored by the model of hellenistic kingship and the Platonic ideal. Philo had stated that Moses embodied the Platonic ideal of philosopher-king and was unique in that he also possessed the function of lawgiver, high priest and prophet.[71] Similarly Jesus is presented as king, law-giver (teacher), prophet and priest, if not so comprehensively in the gospel accounts, by combining those accounts with other New Testament writings, most especially Hebrews.[72]

---

[65]Ibid., IV, 7, 48 (326).

[66]See next section.

[67]Hadas-Smith, 161-95. For Jesus see also Charles H. Talbert, *What is a Gospel?* (Philadelphia: Fortress, 1977). See also J. Z. Smith, "Good News is No News: Aretalogy and Gospel," *Christianity, Judaism and Other Greco-Roman Cults: Part One—New Testament* (ed. J. Neusner; Leiden: E. J. Brill, 1975) 21-38; Morton Smith, "Prolegomena to a Discussion of Aretalogies, Divine Men, the Gospels and Jesus," *JBL* 90 (1971).

[68]Ibid., 130.

[69]Matt 11:19.

[70]Hadas-Smith, 131.

[71]*Moses* II, 1 (2-3); see also 51 (292); *Moses* II, 35 (187).

[72]The kingship of Jesus underlies his role as Christ, but he is also directly referred to as *basileus* (king) of the Jews at Matt 2:1; Matt 27:11 is indecisive, as are Mark 15:2 and Luke 23:3. He is the law-giver in his role as eschatological teacher, *didaskalos* (Matt 12:38; 19:16; 22:24; 22:36; and Jesus so refers to himself at 26:18); and rabbi (Matt 26:25); his role of prophet pervades the gospels but is certainly clearly perceived in the Elijah-Elisha-like miracles he performed, and at Matt 24; his priesthood is emphasized at the eucharist as he transforms the cultic rite and administers a new atonement rite but is most especially pronounced in Hebrews, as are other aspects of this four-fold identifica-

It can be argued that the story of Jesus matches aretalogy in the martyrdom of Jesus and in that the narratives of the gospels were used liturgically. Yet it is highly questionable whether the presence of these two elements, liturgical-usage and martyrdom, necessarily decisively determine that an account was designed to be an aretalogy. It is also true that one might argue that aretalogies were not only recitals of the great events of the life and the deeds of a human hero but were recitals of the acts of a divinity in a cultic context, and that this too would apply to Jesus.[73] Thus one can plausibly argue that at least on the surface the gospels fit the paradigm of the aretalogy developed by Moses Hadas.[74] Yet this begs the question whether when the original traditions were ultimately combined into the genre we call "gospel" the model was a martyrology or aretalogy, or some other indigenous Judaic model, especially the model of Moses. As one might point out in reference to Moses one might also say in reference to Jesus that if Socrates is a paradigm for aretalogies, the accounts of neither Moses nor Jesus follow the pattern. Socrates performed no miracles nor was he regarded under the aspect of kingship as were Moses and Jesus.[75] At best, therefore, one can say that the gospels incorporate elements common to aretalogy but in themselves were not aretalogies.

There has been much debate over the gospel genre. Some have maintained that there is no prototype for it.[76] Others have shown that two components of the gospels, miracle stories and sayings, have many parallels in ancient cultures and are found frequently in hellenistic literature.[77] On the other hand these components can be identified with rabbinic parallels where similar motifs are found.[78] Among such motifs are

---

tion. Thus, Heb 3:1 has Jesus as both "apostle" (that is, a messenger of God, and hence one who is "sent" as are the canonical preachers of the Old Testament), and high priest; high priest at 4:14 and passim; the analogue is the high priesthood of Melkiẓedek which is also a kingship (Hebrews 7); and in this role too his law-giving function is embedded at 8:6.

[73]Kee, "Aretalogy," 404.

[74]See Hadas-Smith, 87-97.

[75]For Jesus see n. 72. For Moses see Wayne A. Meeks, "Moses as God and King," *Religions in Antiquity*, 354-71. Moses ". . . was named of the whole people *theos kai basileus* (God and King). . . ." See Philo, *Moses* I, 28 (158). The Philonic "kingship" of Moses is attested to at *Num. R.* 15:13 and paralleled at Tan. *beha^calotekha* 9 where the midrashist draws upon Deut 33:5 (in some texts this is incorrectly annotated as Deut 32) "he became king in Yeshurun," and says "The Holy One, blessed is He, said to Moses, 'I have made you king. . . .'" This is also in the context of Moses as lawgiver (Deut 33:4), the whole chapter being a function of his role as prophet.

[76]Kee, 408. See Eduard Norden, *Die antike Kunstprosa* (Leipzig: Teubner, 1898); K. L. Schmidt, "Die Stellung der Evangelien in der allegemeinen Literaturgeschichte," *Eucharisterion . . . für Hermann Gunkel* (Göttingen: Vandenhoeck & Ruprecht, 1923) 50-134; S. J. Rose, "Herakles and the Gospels," *HTR* 31 (1938) 141. See also references at n. 67.

[77]W. A. Jayne, *The Healing Gods of Ancient Civilizations* (New Haven: Yale University Press, 1924) 285-91; Rudolf Bultmann, *History of the Synoptic Tradition* (2d ed.; New York: Scribner, 1935).

[78]Paul Fiebig, *Judische Wundergeschichten im Zeitalter Jesu* (Tübingen: Mohr, 1911); see Kee, 414; Henry Fischel, "Story and History: Observations on Graeco-Roman Rhetoric and Pharisaism," *American Oriental Society, Middle West Branch Semi-Centennial Volume* (ed. Denis Sinor; Asian Studies Research Institute, Oriental Series, 3; Bloomington, IN: Indiana University, 1969) 59-88; also found in *Essays in Greco-Roman*

heavenly voices, miraculous feedings, healings, raising the dead, encounters with demons, signs of impending disaster, and exorcism. Although specific healing of the lame and blind in their own milieu was not specified by rabbis, some pointed to this precise miracle in reference to the birth of Isaac.[79]

In general the gospel narratives of Jesus include anecdotes, aphoristic narratives, and wonder stories.[80] Such narratives as the birth and infancy stories, with the elements of the star, virgin conception, precocious childhood, divine protection and the manifestation of the *logos* in Jesus, were influenced by the hellenistic tendency to glorify exceptional personages.[81] But this does not make an aretalogy of the narratives. The miraculous powers attributed to Jesus and the divine intervention in his birth and safety need not have been either imitations of the hellenistic divine-man model or of the aretalogy. For Judaic models were clearly a more likely antecedent in the context in which the gospels were born, namely, the Judaic milieu of the first century.[82] Such Judaic antecedents were evident in the model of Moses, the canonical charismatic figures such as Elijah and Elisha, the eschatological redeemer-figure in the apocalyptic literature, sayings-traditions such as are found in Proverbs, Ecclesiastes, and Ben Sira, shorter oracles found in the writings of such canonical preachers as Isaiah, Jeremiah, and Amos among others, as well as among the *logia* or axioms of rabbinic figures.[83]

Furthermore, strong considerations must be given to the probability that the gospels were in part modeled on Deuteronomy which includes history, biography, a lack of exact chronology, anecdotes, teachings, vicissitudes of the hero (Moses) and his mysterious departure. In the case of Moses both his death and its aftermath were enveloped in mystery, and in the case of Jesus it was the aftermath of his death which was so enveloped. Other Old Testament models can also be found to stand behind various segments of the gospel narratives, especially the Elijah-Elisha cycle of stories.[84] This is not to say that elements common to hellenistic romances and aretalogical narratives played no role at all in influencing the gospel of Jesus, But it does emphasize that the influence was stylistic, derived from hellenistic history and biography, but the account was not designed as aretalogy.

It is important to bear in mind that within Christian tradition there was a wholly different concept of the gospels. These contained fragments of liturgy but were not seen as liturgies, such as aretalogies were designed to be, but rather as teaching media. Like the Old Testament, the gospels were included in worship celebrations as lection readings but were not in themselves considered "liturgies." They were considered "reminiscences"

---

and Related Talmudic Literature (ed. Henry A. Fischel; New York: KTAV, 1977) 443-72.

[79]On Isaac see Louis Ginzberg, *The Legends of the Jews* (Philadelphia: JPS, 1961) I, 261f., Tan. *toledot* 2. Regarding exorcism, Kee (p. 414) incorrectly wrote that the motif of exorcism is not found in rabbinic literature; see *B. Shab.* 67a; *Lev. R.* 24:3; exorcism, or power over the potency of demons is also alluded to at *B. Pes.* 112ab; *Ex. R.* 30:16; Josephus, *Ant.* VIII, 2, 5 (45f.). Written amulets, spoken incantations, and recital of scriptural texts, were all regarded as important devices with which to overcome demons.

[80]Howard C. Kee, *Jesus in History* (New York: Harcourt, Brace, 1970) 271-75.

[81]Kee, "Aretalogy," 420.

[82]Kee, 422. The births of Isaac and Samson were both heralded by celestial visits to the parents and proclamations of the coming birth as was that of Jesus. And Johannine elements can be Philonic adaptations.

[83]Ibid.; Kee does not include shorter oracles and proto-rabbinic *logia*.

[84]See Hengel, *Acts,* 30f.; Buchanan, "Samaritan Origin," 166-173.

or a genre that made for biographical and historical recall. They were called *apomnēmo-neumati*, "memoirs" or "reminiscences," by both Justin and Papias. The latter averred that he received the idea from an earlier presbyter who taught that Mark served as Peter's interpreter and wrote down the words and deeds of Jesus as he "remembered them" (*emnēmoneusen*).[85]

In view of the likelihood that the gospels were designed to be biographical and theological reminiscences and were patterned after Old Testament models, it is highly questionable that aretalogy played a role in their composition. Two qualifications, however, should be made. First, this judgment is not to rule out their relationship to hellenistic historiography. With Polybius there began a major emphasis upon biographical sketches as part of historiography, and these were written not only of rulers but of significant founders of religions and schools of philosophy.[86] Second, aretalogies were primarily the product of cultic rites requiring recitations and hymns depicting the wonderful acts of a deity or a divinized human. These were used for religious propaganda and were recited in public.[87] Thus far one might compare the function at least of the gospel birth and passion narratives to aretalogies. But further, the gentiles easily made the transfer of powers from divine figures to humans and deified human kings. They were, therefore, easily able to praise a human as a god, and hence when the church became predominantly gentile biography and aretalogy merged.[88] Aretalogies included the miraculous, and as a result we find that hellenistic biographies of great philosophers and founders of religious movements began to include miracles and other extraordinary elements.[89] In this sense it can be understood why some scholars felt justified in claiming that the gospels are of the genre aretalogy. But such consideration would be limited to the function of the birth and passion narratives from the second century in the gentile church.

Even at that, however, there must be expressed great skepticism. It is axiomatic that the birth and passion narratives are at the root of the attribution of divinity to Jesus. In this respect the *logos* pericope of the first chapter of the Gospel of John is a

---

[85]Justin Martyr, *St. Justin, Opera. Apology*, ed. J. C. T. Otto (Jenna: 1876) 33:8; 66:4-5; in the latter source Justin refers to the "memoirs which are called gospels"; 67:4. See also *St. Justin, Opera, Dialogue With Trypho*, ed. J. C. T. Otto (Jenna: 1848) Vol. I, Part 2, 100:11; 101:9; 102:13; 103:19, and elsewhere; in these passages of the *Dialogue*, Justin's Greek describing the gospels with the term *apomnēmoneumati* is rendered by Otto in Latin as *commentariis*, both terms to be translated as "memoirs." Eusebius, *The Ecclesiastical History* (Loeb Classical Library; 2 vols.; trans. Kirsopp Lake; London/ Cambridge MA: William Heinemann/Harvard University Press, 1959) III, 39 (15), indicates by his terminology that Mark was Peter's *hermēneutēs* (interpreter) who wrote what *emnēmoneusen* (he remembered), that the gospel account of Jesus was primarily a teaching document, for Mark gathered the gleanings of Peter "who used to give teaching as necessity demanded," and as Mark *apemnēmoneusen* (remembered). See Hengel, *Acts,* 27f. For easier access to Justin's chapters in *Apology* and *Dialogue* see *Writings of St. Justin Martyr* (trans. Thomas B. Falls; *The Fathers of the Church*, Vol. 6; Washington, DC: Catholic University Press, 1965).

[86]Helmut Koester, *History, Culture and Religion of the Hellenistic Age* (2 vols.; Philadelphia: Fortress, 1982) 1. 134.

[87]Ibid.

[88]Ibid., pp. 134f.

[89]Ibid., p. 135.

midrash on the birth narrative.[90] But this attribution of divinity to Jesus is neither antithetical to the Judaism of the day, nor is it sufficient reason to argue that the gospel genre was an aretalogy cultically celebrating a divine person. For we have similar attribution of divinity to Moses, and it might therefore be argued that the Jesus pattern is modeled after Moses.[91] As a matter of interest, although John ranks Jesus above Moses, the very fact that Moses is the point of reference indicates that the model for some elements of the gospel treatment of Jesus was Moses and not hellenistic aretalogies.[92] As for the divinity of Moses, a subject referred to earlier and requiring separate in-depth treatment, post-biblical tradition centered on various verses.[93] Clearly, syntax requires that *mosheh 'ish ha'elohim* (Deut 33:1) be translated "Moses the man of God," that is, the godly man, or the man being used by God for His purposes. Nevertheless the midrashist saw fit to interpret it as "Moses, man and God," thus attesting to the tradition that ascribed divinity to Moses, a divinity that he had to acquire before he ascended into heaven, for Exod 7:1 certainly represents the earliest part of his ministry, and there already God appoints him "god" to Pharaoh.[94]

Finally, in rejecting aretalogy as the paradigm for the Moses and Jesus "biographies" in Philo and the New Testament and in seeking the model from within the Judaic matrix, it is not meant to reject hellenistic influences. As indicated, stylistic influences certainly played a role. Furthermore, cognizance must also be taken of another

---

[90]John 1:1-18. V. 18 is a very difficult one, and the focus of this paper does not allow for a thorough exegesis. Let it suffice to say that if Jesus is here referred to as "god" this would be in keeping with Philo's usage of *logos* as "son of God" and "second God"; see *On Husbandry* 12 (51); *QG* II, 62. Nevertheless, it should be kept in mind that throughout the New Testament a distinction is made between the Father and the Son, God and Jesus, and the two are not merged.

[91]On Jesus as a second Moses see W. D. Davies, *The Setting of the Sermon on the Mount* (Cambridge: University Press, 1964) 25-93. Davies does not discuss the question of the divinity of Jesus or Moses and is cautious in the extent to which he sees Jesus as a new Moses. The subject is indeed complex. But germane to this paper is simply the idea that the Moses model was there, and on the subject at hand, the divinity of the redeemer figure, we have antecedents relating to Moses.

[92]John 1:17 ranks Jesus above Moses. Paul does the same at 2 Cor 3:7-18, a midrash on Exod 34:29-35.

[93]See above on Moses; Meeks, "Moses as God" (n. 75 above). The relevant verses are Exod 7:1; Deut 33:1. See *Pesikta de R. Kahana,* supplement 1, 3 accessible in *Pesikta de Rab Kahana* (trans. William G. Braude, Israel J. Kapstein; Philadelphia: JPS, 1975) 446f.; *Deut. R.* 11:4; *Mid. Pss.* 90:5. See also Erwin Goodenough, *By Light, Light,* 224-29; cf. *Sif. Deut.* 342 (*Sifre,* [ed. Louis Finkelstein; New York: Jewish Theological Seminary, 1969]). The text at *Mid. Pss.* inquires: "If human, how God? If God, how human?" The midrash provides several expository comments, the most germane for our purposes being (a) that after Moses made his ascent into heaven and his descent back to earth he was God; (b) that he was composed of two substances, from his middle and above was God, and from his middle and below he was human. See also Tan. *vez'ot haberakhah* 1; *beha'alotekha* 9.

[94]Midrashic references at n. 93 above. See also Morton Smith, "The Image of God" *BJRL* 40 (1958) 478ff.

hellenistic genre, *chriae,* and the plausibility that the form of the *chria* rather than the aretalogy played a role in the composition of the gospels.[95]

V. *Chriae*[96]

The *chriae* consisted of relatively brief anecdotes about a sage and normally concluded with a spiritual or moral value expressed in the form of an apophthegm, a wise saying or a terse aphorism. According to some current research the *chriae* genre was employed in the celebration and idolization of founders of the Cynic school.[97] Similarly it has been argued that Judaic *chriae* served the same function and are evident, for example, in reference to Hillel, of whom there might be as many as twenty-five tannaitic stories that fit this category.[98] In one of these *chriae* told of Hillel, he commended his wife with a paraphrase of an ancient aphorism. He told her "all that you have done you have only done for the sake of heaven." This is clearly a repetition of the aphorism, "let all of your deeds be for the sake of heaven."[99] Although the aphorism is given in the name of R. Yosi hakohen, (the priest) a disciple of Yoḥanan ben Zakkai, it is clear from its citation in the name of Hillel that it was an older, popular aphorism that circulated in rabbinic circles and was attributed to more than one authority. In such cases one must date it earlier than the earliest named authority. In this case the aphorism is to be dated to or earlier than Hillel and offers an interesting example of how rabbinic materials should be dated earlier than the corpus in which they are found.[100]

One modern scholar has argued that the chriic character of the saying makes it transferable to other authors.[101] But actually since it is reported in the name of Hillel, and since *chriae* are known to have been an older Graeco-Roman genre widely disseminated in the spread of rhetoric during the first century B.C., its attribution to R. Yosi hakohen is not merely a product of its transferability. In Yosi's case it is not part of a *chria* but of a distilled series of teachings. Thus R. Yosi offers three maxims. This was

---

[95]The Greek term *chriae* was defined by Liddell-Scott (*Lexicon*) in the fourth item under that entry, as used in rhetoric, "a pregnant sentence, maxim, remark, borrowed from some other author. ..." In its gospel application it should be seen as episodic maxims, or precepts taught within the context of a biographical anecdote. The Romans used the term *chria*. Talbert (*What is a Gospel?*) did not take into consideration the genre *chreia,* nor did J. Z. Smith and Morton Smith (see n. 67 above).

[96]Henry A. Fischel, "Studies in Cynicism and the Ancient Near East: the Transformation of a *Chria*," *Religions in Antiquity,* 372-411.

[97]Fischel, "Studies," 374.

[98]Ibid., 375. See *Derekh Ereẓ Rabbah* 6; *Ab. de R. N.* A., 12-15, passim; B, 24-27, passim; *B. Ket.* 67b; *Ber.* 60a; *Shab.* 30b, 31a; *Bez.* 16a; 20a-b; *Pes.* 66a; *Yom* 35b; *Lev. R.* 34:3. (The edition of *Ab. de R. N.* is that of Solomon Schechter [New York: Feldheim, 1945].) Cf. Elijah *chriae,* e.g., *B. Ber.* 3a.

[99]*Derekh Ereẓ Rabbah* 6; *M. Ab.* 2:17. (The edition of *Ab.* is *The Ethics of the Talmud* [trans. R. Travers Herford; New York: Schocken, 1962].)

[100]This is one of many examples that ought to serve as corrective to the current tendency to date rabbinic materials late. See on this also my paper referred to earlier, "Aspects of Paul's Judaic Thought: the Akedah," *Emergence,* I, Part 2, p. 249 n. 44. See further below regarding the teaching of R. Yosi hakohen.

[101]Fischel, "Studies," 400.

the pattern of that particular chapter of Mishnah Abot.[102] There is no evidence that he originated any of these three since they sum up what were already basic values of pre-first century proto-rabbinic Judaism. Thus, for example, the second maxim on the importance of study was already preceded by Shammai a century earlier, and even averred in other forms two centuries earlier by the "men of the great assembly," by Simon the Righteous, soon thereafter by Yosi b. Yoezer (ca. 170 B.C.), later Hillel and finally Yohanan b. Zakkai. Similarly his third maxim has an antecedent with Hillel, and one can only guess how much earlier than Hillel and with whom it originated. So too with the teaching that one's actions be for the sake of heaven. A story, as noted, was already told of Hillel that all of his actions were for the sake of heaven.[103] This being the case it is highly probable that the phrase was a stereotypical idiom current in pre-first-century society.

It has been shown that motifs found in Hillel *chriae* are the same as those in *chriae* related to Cleanthes, Thales, and Diogenes. These include such themes as the sudden catapulting of the hero to leadership, the hero forgetting his learning, the hero learning anew what he had forgotten by observing what simple, unlearned people do, and the device of using sheep as media by which to solve problems; in the case of Hillel, for transporting a knife in their wool on the Sabbath.[104] In the Hillel *chriae* under consideration it is not Hillel who forgets his learning but the Bene Batyra, and his erudition

---

[102] *M. Ab.* 2. This pattern also predominated in Chapter 1. It will be noticed that each paragraph with rare exception in Chapter 2 records three teachings of a sage, and in some cases two sets of three precepts. In such cases perhaps the paragraph was originally subdivided. Paragraphs 3 and 4 together constitute three teachings and might at one time have been joined. Paragraph 5 appears superficially to be a rare exception, citing five maxims in the name of Hillel. Actually this pericope should be understood as having originally had six, with one probably having dropped out. Alternatively the sixth is found at Paragraph 7 which has only one maxim, and follows better upon his reflections at Paragraph 5 rather than after his strictures at Paragraph 6. Again, the pattern is broken at Paragraph 8 with eleven sayings, one probably having dropped out; and at Paragraph 9 with only one saying cited from Yohanan b. Zakkai. Alternatively, Paragraph 9 might have been attributed to Yohanan but was the twelfth teaching of Hillel in Paragraph 8. It certainly fits naturally at the end of Paragraph 8. The pattern is suspended from 10-12 but resumed when teachings are resumed at 13-14. The next section, 15-19, is in fact prefaced at Paragraph 15 with the remark, "They each said three things." R. Eliezer, however, is reported to have said nine (three triads). At 16-21 the triadic pattern is resumed. Superficially this does not appear to be the case at Paragraph 20, but this should be read: (1) The day is short and the work great; (2) the workers are lazy but the reward much; (3) the master urges on. Paragraph 21 should be read in the light of 20 and as an expository amplification of it. The triad: (a) you need not complete the labor but must not desist from it; (b) if you study you receive commensurate reward from a faithful employer; (c) reward of the righteous is in the future world. The triadic pattern emphasized here was also recognized in part by Benedict Thomas Viviano, *Study as Worship* (Leiden: E. J. Brill, 1978) 3.

[103] *M. Ab.* 1:1 "set up many disciples"; 1:2 "Torah" is one of the three pillars of the world's endurance; 1:4, that one's house be a gathering place for the *hakhamim*, that is, the proto-rabbinic scholars, and to drink their words with thirst; 2:8, the increase of Torah increases life, and the acquisition of Torah is the acquisition of life in the world to come; 2:9, one was created to study Torah. Cf. *B. Bez.* 16a.

[104] Fischel, "Studies," 402f. n. 1.

catapults him to leadership. Yet, soon he too forgot a halakhah and rescued himself by being attentive to popular practice. The purpose and function of the Judaic *chriae* appear to be the setting of halakhic precedent. Where the halakhah was in doubt, a *chria* is told in order to infer from the reported episode what the traditional halakhah had been with a view to applying it now. That is, a *ma⁽aseh*, an episode, a halakhic *chria*, is cited in order to establish out of a one-time general event or an episode in the life of the sage how the halakhah was reflected in the ordinary events of his daily life. This is then interpreted to be normative practice.[105]

This particular talmudic source is important for another lead it provides for the hellenistic influence upon rabbinic method and teaching although not in historiography in which they appear to have had no interest. Hillel's discussion with the Bene Batyra who forgot their learning and could not decide whether one may slaughter the paschal lamb on the Sabbath indicates that he interpreted halakhah with the help of certain hermeneutical principles.[106] These have frequently been attributed erroneously to Hillel, for they were really of prior hellenistic usage.[107] It is important to us in the present discussion that in the unit of *chriae* represented in the text cited here we are led to the highlighting of another aspect of hellenistic influence on Palestinian Judaism. Lieberman examined the halakhic and ⁾agadic hermeneutical rules and indicated the extensive affinity between this rabbinic methodology and hellenistic rhetoric. He discussed what the two hermeneutical processes had in common. Of especial interest are two basic devices upon which much halakhah is grounded. One is *kal vehomer*, deducing from the major to the minor or from the minor to the major. The other is the *gezerah shavah*, or analogy.[108] The *gezerah shavah* is a little-understood term signifying the establishment of a conclusion based upon terminology which is similar in two separate cases. The term might perhaps be best translated literally as "equalizing the decision," but in actuality it means that one is reading the decision through the hermeneutical process of analogy. Thus, where two words are used in different contexts, by analogy the rabbi would apply the halakhah of the one to the other.[109]

There are also *chriae* that were not designed to establish halakhah. Rather, they were intended to legitimate certain practices that prevailed in Graeco-Roman society.

---

[105]Ibid., 409. See *B. Pes.* 66a. Ofter the *chria* begins with the word *ma⁽aseh*, "a story." In usage, as in the source cited here, the *chria* is sometimes supplemented by a scriptural verse or a hermeneutical device to support the conclusion inferred from the episode. See also Saul Lieberman, *Hellenism in Jewish Palestine* (New York: 1950), Appendix I, 194-199; Gerhardsson, *Memory*, 181-89.

[106]These are given as seven at *T. San.* 7:11; see also *Sifra debe Rab* (ed. I. H. Weiss; Vienna: 1861) p. 3a; *Ab. de R. N.* A., 37.

[107]Lieberman, *Hellenism*, 54. The chapter of which this discussion is a part is also found in *Essays in Greco-Roman and Related Talmudic Literature*, 289-324.

[108]Ibid., 54ff. and nn. 64, 78.

[109]Lieberman (p. 59) connected the Hebrew term *gazar* with the Greek *krinein*, "to decide," citing the LXX use of *sygkrisis* for Hebrew *mishpat*, in which the meaning is "decision" in third-century B.C.E. papyri. This term was used by Greek rhetors to define a comparison of two things juxtaposed, whether two equal things, or a lesser and a greater; and thus with the term *shavah*, meaning "equal," this hermeneutical device refers to the comparison of two similar terms in order to equalize the halakhah in both cases. See also David Daube, "Rabbinic Methods of Interpretation and Hellenic Rhetoric," *HUCA* 22 (1949) 239-64.

Among these were such practices as might have been considered questionable in Judaism, such as those bordering on forbidden divination. For example, two rabbis were making a sick call upon a third and decided to take their cue from a *bat kol,* the celestial voice, a term synonymous with that of *ruaḥ hakodesh,* the holy spirit.[110] That is to say, they sought the advice of the *bat kol.* Upon so doing they heard a woman asking a friend whether the lamp had gone out, and the friend replied that it had not. The rabbis concluded that the sick rabbi whom they planned to visit was still alive and proceeded on their sick call.[111]

It is *chriae* of both halakhic and ᵓagadic nature that might have played a role in gospel traditions just as they did in rabbinic traditions. Such episodic narratives as "The Faith of the Centurion," and certain healing stories are reminiscent of the genre.[112] In "The Faith of the Canaanite Woman" Jesus learns from her to universalize his teaching as Hillel learns from the common people that one can offer the paschal lamb on the Sabbath.[113] The motifs are not always the same, but there are elements that point to an adaptation of *chriae.* These elements are the presence of a brief episodic-biographical reminiscence, often a surprise twist, and when the unexpected occurs Jesus concludes with a teaching. This *chriic* characteristic of the gospel traditions still requires intensive analysis.

When one attempts to categorize the *chriae* precisely as having to contain X, Y, and Z features, it might not be possible to define certain New Testament episodes as *chriae.* But the urge for precise classification is western Aristotelianism and should not be imposed upon anecdotes with a teaching that originated in the Near East. The New Testament gospels contain a considerable number of *logia,* teachings, attributed to Jesus of Nazareth. Some of these teachings are embedded in parables. Some are ascribed to sermons or lectures delivered at particular times. And some are part of biographical episodes or anecdotes. All the latter can be seen as *chriae* even if they do not all contain the same specific elements delineated by some modern scholars.[114] That is to say, the venerable hellenistic genre, used prolifically during the Graeco-Roman era, was

---

[110]See *P. Shab.* 8c; Lieberman (*Hellenism,* 195 n. 11) explains that to "use" a *bat kol* or *ruaḥ hakodesh* means to consult it. See *B. Meg.* 32a; *Hul.* 95b, where the method of consultation is by listening for hints in their environment, especially to verses recited by children in the synagogue school, as Egyptians and Greeks did with children in heathen temples. See Lieberman, ibid., 196f.

[111]For rhetorical affinities with rabbinic ᵓagadic interpretation see Lieberman, *Hellenism,* 68-82.

[112]Matt 8:5-13.

[113]Matt 15:21-28. It should be noted here that after completing this paper and researching the transmission of gospel tradition I noted that Birger Gerhardsson (*Memory and Manuscript,* 195 n. 8) refers to J. Kurzinger's translation of Papias's words given by Eusebius in a manner pointing to the chriic model. Eusebius, (*The Ecclesiastical History* [2 vols.; trans. Kirsopp Lake; Loeb Classical Library; London: William Heinemann, 1926] Book III, 39 [15]) cited Papias as saying *hos pros tas chreias epoieito tas didaskalias.* Lake translated "who used to give teaching as necessity demanded," a reasonable translation for *chreias.* Kurzinger, however, translated in German as "Dieser machte seiner Unterweisungen nach Art der chreiai."

[114]See Fischel, "Studies"; "Story and History," *Essays in Greco-Roman and Related Talmudic Literature,* 443-72; see 451, 452f. for chriic motifs in an anecdote about Hillel.

transformed in response to their particular needs and style by proto-rabbinic and early Christian usage. Thus, it is quite conceivable that there circulated a variety of biographical writings about Jesus in the form of the usual *bioi* ("lives") or *apomnēmoneumata* ("reminiscences") that were frequently found for philosophers of the time. Just as the latter were consulted by the rhetor so the former were consulted by the missionary or preacher.[115]

It is just this aforementioned urge to categorize the *chria* that leads some scholars to reject the historicity of anecdotes.[116] It should be considered, however, that *chriae* are to be seen within wider, flexible parameters as biographical anecdotes containing aphorisms or teachings. Thus, for example, instead of seeking the classification of a separate so-called *sophos* genre, legends concerning a sage in which difficult questions are raised, the response to which required a definition of the ultimate ethical value, it is convenient to see these as *chriae*.[117] For example, of both Hillel and Jesus an anecdote is told in which each declared what is the basic principle of Torah. In the case of Hillel the setting is a proselyte story. The prospective proselyte indicated his desire for Hillel to admit him to Judaism on condition that he will teach him the entire Torah while he stood on one foot. Hillel told him: "whatever is hateful to yourself, do it not to your fellowperson; this is the entire Torah, and anything else is its interpretation. . . ."[118] Of Jesus it is said that he was asked which is the greatest commandment in the Torah, and Jesus responded with the injunctions to love God and one's fellowhuman.[119] The

---

[115]On this feature in Greco-Roman society see Fischel, "Story and History," 444f. It is necessary here to say that while Fischel recognizes that there was a "considerable difference between Pharisees and Tannaim" (p. 447 n. 16) he discusses the material as "Pharisaic-Rabbinic," and refers to "Pharisaic parallels." In my view we are simply dealing with proto-rabbinic materials. These scholars were contemporary with Pharisaism but are not to be identified with that large and amorphous movement which included Essenes, Therapeutae, the Qumran people, and other pietistic and separatistic groups. See Sigal, *Emergence* I, Part 2, Chapter One. Thus, while Fischel calls Hillel a "great Pharisaic leader" (p. 451 n. 40), I maintain that Hillel was anti-pharisaic as is evidenced by his saying "do not separate (*al tifrosh*) yourself . . ." (*M. Ab.* 2:5), the verb *parash* being the term from which the *perushim-pharisaioi* took their identity as separatists as well as pietists.

[116]Fischel, "Story and History," 453.

[117]Ibid., 455f.

[118]*B. Shab.* 31a.

[119]Matt 22:34-40; Mark 12:28-34; Luke 10:25-28. The Lukan version is not in the same context as that of Matthew and Mark but is rather more in the "proselyte" context of the story of Hillel. In Luke the person wants to know how to attain salvation. For this reason, and because Matthew blurs the *pharisaioi* (Pharisees) with a *nomikos* (an expert of the *nomos*, that is, a proto-rabbi) as the questioner, Mark refers to *grammateōn* and Luke has only *nomikos*, it appears to me Luke has the best version. The critical apparatus of *The Greek New Testament*, ed. Aland et al. (Stuttgart: United Bible Societies, 1968) suggests that *nomikos* does not belong in the Matthean text. Nevertheless, Bruce M. Metzger (*A Textual Commentary on the Greek New Testament* [N.P.: United Bible Societies, 1971] 59) concedes that there is "an overwhelming preponderance of evidence" supporting the reading although he uses other arguments for maintaining that it is a questionable reading. Among these arguments is that Matthew nowhere else uses *nomikos*. Possibly copyists took it from Luke and added it to Matthew. But either way, whether Matthew originally said that a pharisaic *nomikos* asked the question or only that a pharisee did so,

anecdotes do not share all details, but the basic motif is the same: teaching the ultimate spiritual value. The process of adoption is also partly a process of transformation, and one need not look for a mirror image. Just because the same anecdote is told of Shammai, Hillel, and Jesus, furthermore, does not mean it is unhistorical. Similar happenings in the lives of sages are not necessarily to be precluded as an *a priori* impossibility. Thus I would not rule out historicity on the basis of its having affinity with other *chriae*. In this case in which Shammai did not respond to the candidate with a teaching but drove him away with a contractor's measuring rod, it is apparent that disciples of Hillel told a tendentious unhistorical anecdote to contrast Hillel's gentleness with Shammai's sternness. We know that Shammai too was esteemed for his kindness and affability. It is therefore questionable whether stories told to contrast him unfavorably with Hillel are historical, but this is not because they are *chriae*.[120]

Similarly it is beyond literary or textual requirement to deny historicity to an anecdote or *chria* simply because the same similes are used in anecdotes about different people, for example, Hillel and Seneca.[121] Of Hillel it was said that he was walking along with his disciples and taught them that bathing one's body is a *mizvah*. Using a *kal vehomer*, he argued: if the person who cares for the statues of kings is exalted for his work, how much more so the human who maintains with care the image of God.[122] There is no reason why many sages in addition to Hillel and Seneca could not have drawn upon the common hellenistic feature of the statue as a simile in their teaching. In other words, to acknowledge the influence of hellenistic rhetoric and philosophical modes upon proto-rabbinic and rabbinic *logia* does not require that one reject the historicity of an anecdote. The same argument would hold true for anecdotes concerning Jesus.

Hellenistic categories were common to pagans and Jews, and many hellenistic features went back to older Greek tradition. Thus an old saying attributed by some to Socrates and by others to Thales told of how the philosopher thanked *tyche* that he was not created a beast, a woman, or a barbarian.[123] This was part of the stock of hellenistic culture. It helps understand why some rabbis adopted this three-fold gratitude to be recited in morning prayers with variation, substituting either the uncultivated person or

---

it is possible that Luke either dropped the Pharisee connection he found in Matthew because he was frequently more accurate than Matthew in his Judaic material or worked from an independent source. Mark, as usual, the latest of the synoptic writers, is least precise and uses "scribes" loosely. See regarding Matthean priority from the perspective of the Judaic or proto-rabbinic material in Matthew and Mark, my article, "Matthean Priority in the Light of Mark 7," *Proceedings,* Eastern Great Lakes Biblical Society, Vol. 2 (1982) 76-95; "Further Thoughts on Matthean Priority," ibid., Vol. 3 (1983) 122-35; "Aspects of Mark Pointing to Matthean Priority," *New Synoptic Studies* (ed. William R. Farmer; Macon, GA: Mercer University Press, 1983) 185-208.

[120] *B. Shab.* 31a; on Shammai's general nature, *M. Ab.* 1:15. That scholars have been adversely influenced by Hillelite anti-Shammai stories is evident in R. Travers Herford's comment to this saying, "One would expect this to have been said by Hillel rather than by Shammai." See Fischel's comments on adoption, adaptation, and transformation ("Story," 469f.).

[121] Fischel, ibid., 458 n. 80.

[122] *Lev. R.* 34:3.

[123] Diogenes Laertius, *Lives of Eminent Philosophers* (2 vols.; ed. R. D. Hicks; Loeb Classical Library; London/New York: Heinemann/G. P. Putnam's Sons, 1925) 1. 33.

the slave for a beast.[124] But that some rabbis found this narrow pagan approach to humanity satisfying only reinforces what we all now know, that rabbinism was considerably influenced by the milieu in which it arose. It does not of itself serve as a reason to disqualify *chriae* in which teachings are embedded as legitimate historiography. That various sages are reported to have taught similar values does not discredit the historicity of the occasion when they taught these values.[125] It only highlights the interdependence of religions and cultures and contradicts the conceit of uniqueness. Thus, for example, the ubiquitous Greek emphasis upon the athlete and the games became a common metaphor in both Judaism and Christianity throughout the Roman period. It is used by Philo and Paul in the first centuries B.C. and A.D. and by John Chrysostom at the end of the fourth.[126]

VI. Conclusion

This cursory adumbration has ranged over a wide area of hellenistically-related materials including diverse literary works. Josephus wrote history, Philo wrote philosophy of religion, theology, and ethics in addition to biography. Fourth Maccabees was for use at liturgical functions. The Gospels were designed as lection readings at the gatherings of a new religious movement. Philo's account of Moses was virtual biography in the grand style. The gospel account of Jesus was undoubtedly collected from biographical notes ("reminiscences") treasured by disciples, such as the birth and passion narratives, and from a wide range of *chriae*. In this manner it would also be possible to compose a gospel of Moses, Elijah, Elisha, or Hillel. The proto-rabbinic materials were never systematically collected or edited, and so *chriae* are embedded within large amorphous masses of unrelated material.

Josephus was a hellenistic historian even when he ignored the sage counsel of Polybius as, for example, by including miracles as part of serious history. Philo recorded traditions that were clearly Judaic in origin and went back to Hebraic sources. Fourth Maccabees, like Philo, was hellenistic and philosophical in style even as it taught specifically Judaic doctrine. The gospels adapted Judaic modalities to the hellenistic-style *chriae*, and in the case of John drew upon the Judaic hellenism exemplified by Philo. None of the biographical accounts in Philo, Josephus, Fourth Maccabees, the gospels, and the rabbinic corpus, however, were found to be aretalogies. But they were found to incorporate hellenistic rhetorical style, historical theory and the literary genre *chriae*.

---

[124]See any standard prayerbook, e.g., *The Authorized Daily Prayerbook* (ed. J. H. Hertz; New York: Bloch, 1948) 18-20 (Hebrew) 19-21 (English). *T. Ber.* 7:18 substitutes the *bor*, the uncultivated or ignorant person for the slave; cf. *P. Ber.* 13b which has the same three as Tosefta although in a different order; at *B. Men.* 43b gratitude for not having been made a barbarian or *goy* is replaced with the positive for having been made an Israelite, and in the current version of the traditional prayerbook, the slave is introduced.

[125]Contra Fischel, 460f.

[126]See, e.g., Philo, *Moses* II, 32 (171) where the Levites who executed the sinners in the story of the golden calf (Exodus 32) are described as coming to their work as "racers from the starting point." Paul uses the athlete image, e.g., at 1 Cor 24-27; Gal 2:2; 5:7. For Chrysostom see, e.g., throughout his discourses on judaizers: Saint John Chrysostom, *Discourses Against Judaizing Christians* (trans. Paul W. Harkins; *The Fathers of the Church*, Vol. 68, ed. Hermigild Dressler et al.; Washington, DC: Catholic University Press, 1979).

Interpreting Jesus since Bultmann: Selected Paradigms and Their Hermeneutic Matrix

Irvin W. Batdorf

United Theological Seminary, Dayton, OH

PRECIS

A review of selected paradigms since Bultmann's *Jesus and the Word* (German ed., 1926, ET 1934) explores his suspension of the quest, the new quest, a highly modified resumption of the old quest, and four more recent options neither new nor old. It focuses on Jesus as authentic person, as prophet, as Jew, as Messiah, as liberator, as story-teller, and as magician. It speaks of the storied Jesus, the existential-historical Jesus, and Jesus as interpreted by the social sciences. An analysis of the hermeneutic matrix underlying this segment of the quest suggests (1) that the present pursuit of Jesus by a variety of methods is healthy, (2) that detailed work on limited texts should be balanced by persistent attention to the connection established by the canon between the life of Jesus, his death, and his resurrection and (3) that interpreters of Jesus need to abandon the myth of objectivity by identifying their personal bias, the particular image of Jesus they prefer, and the relation of both to the "big picture" sketched by the canon.

*   *   *   *   *

Accepting Bultmann's rejection of both old and new quests as an arbitrary benchmark, we shall attempt to describe certain lives of Jesus written since then, and then to analyze their hermeneutic presuppositions. We make no attempt at completeness or consensus. Undoubtedly many important contributions to the ongoing quest will be made between the writing of this paper and its printing and still others between its printing and our discussion at the annual meeting. We can only hope that the paradigms here chosen will be sufficiently illuminating to suggest major trends in Jesus research since Bultmann.

DESCRIPTION

I. The Suspension of the Quest by Bultmann, Both Old and New

Bultmann's *Jesus and the Word,* which appeared in 1926, proposed a non-biographical approach to Jesus by turning the temporal progress of Schweitzer's Jesus toward the cross into three concentric circles of eschatological, ethical, and existential concern (Bultmann, 1934). His famous essay of 1941, "New Testament and Mythology" (Bultmann, 1953) sounded the theme spelled out in his *Theology of the New Testament*, first published in 1948 (Bultmann, 1951), and reiterated in his rebuke to the practitioners of the new quest in his lecture of 1961, "The Primitive Christian Kerygma and the Historical Jesus" (Bultmann, 1964). While we can be certain, for example, that Jesus was anti-Sabbath, non-ascetic, opposed to legalism, gathered outcasts at table, performed exorcisms, and preached the Kingdom authoritatively with an implied Christology (Bultmann, 1964, 22-24, 28), he is still not known to us in the same sense as he was known to the first Christian generation (1951, pp. 1-25, 1964). Most basic of all, we can not know whether he went to the cross willingly nor how Jesus' authority carries over to our time, nor how what happened once can be described as a once-for-all occurrence. The "thatness" of Jesus is clear but the what and the how remain undetermined, the logical presupposition of New Testament theology but not its beginning. That beginning is to be found in the indispensable apostolic kerygma, that once-for-all revelation of God's love in the cross, by confrontation with which alone one moves from unfaith to faith.

II. The New Quest

A. Jesus as authentic person:
G. Bornkamm, *Jesus of Nazareth*, ET 1960

Bultmann's rejection of the old quest called forth a strong reaction from his own students. Sparked first by E. Käsemann (1964), it found expression in the works of G. Ebeling (1961), E. Fuchs (1964), James Robinson (1959), and G. Bornkamm, as well as H. Conzelmann (1973), Willi Marxsen (1979), and Herbert Braun (1979). To separate the kerygma so completely from Jesus, they said, might lead to docetism. On the other hand, if one could show that the understanding of existence in Jesus was similar to that found in the kerygma the latter could find its concrete grounding in him. While Ebeling emphasized in particular the continuity established by faith and Fuchs appealed to linguistic event, Bornkamm stressed the immediacy of God's presence in Jesus' ministry.

This theme is developed chiefly in Bornkamm's third chapter entitled "Jesus of Nazareth." He claims to find beneath the surface "undistorted and primary" data "prior to any pious interpretation" (53). All who come to Jesus experience the "unmediated presence" of God (62). In Jesus' presence each person appears as he or she actually is, stands in an absolutely "new present" (63), and enters into a new world. Jesus himself acts with such sovereignty, perception, thorough involvement and great consistency that the authority he exercises raises messianic expectations. As *the* supremely authentic person he begets authenticity in others.

Since this perception of Jesus does not depend on any chronological arrangement of his deeds, Bornkamm gives no weight at all to any of (what are for him) the incidental facts he is able to discover about Jesus' actual ministry. Bornkamm knows that Jesus was baptized by John, praised him as the greatest of the prophets, proclaimed the coming of God's kingdom, and appears himself as prophet and rabbi although transcending each. He calls twelve disciples, journeys to Jerusalem, makes a ceremonial entry, cleanses the temple, celebrates a final eschatological meal, is betrayed, tried and executed as "King of the Jews" (165). None of these deeds, however, carries any weight in assessing who Jesus is and what he intends. They are simply subordinated to the fact that Jesus brings to an end the world each hearer knows (76) and opens up the present as a time of decision for the future. In spite of the authority he wields and the Messianic hopes he arouses, Jesus makes no Messianic claims for himself, and his story ends abruptly in death.

The same preference for existential history that characterizes Bornkamm's treatment of Jesus' life also appears in his treatment of its aftermath. Somehow the church experienced Jesus' risen presence and on that basis bore witness to him in faith, but just how or why a very sober Bornkamm is careful not to say. Somehow, after Jesus' death, the church gave to him the titles and the dignity he himself had refused, ostensibly by reason of his pre-Passion ministry in their midst; but once again Bornkamm does not say how or why. His final result hardly moves the quest beyond Bultmann's *Jesus and the Word,* as Schubert Ogden and Van Harvey are quick to point out (1964). For both Bultmann and Bornkamm existential history is the final court of appeal, whether in Jesus' own ministry as the supremely authentic person or (in the case of Bultmann) in the apostolic proclamation concerning him that followed.

III. The Continuation of a Highly Modified Version of the Old Quest

A. Jesus as prophet:
M. Enslin, *The Prophet from Nazareth,* 1968

Morton Enslin (1968) writes in response to Schweitzer, Bultmann, and the new quest, but what he says is a highly modified version of the liberal Jesus, so vehemently attacked by Schweitzer and so sharply exemplified in the earlier seminal presentation of S. J. Case (1927). Enslin agrees with Bornkamm that no biography is possible but that Jesus *can* be known by juxtaposing later interpretations with those few authentic insights that emerge here and there in their midst. What he looks for is not existential history but a "flesh and blood" Jesus, whose "personality" swept all before him (xiii, 6, 126-129). Unlike Bornkamm Enslin does not ignore Jesus' first century Palestinian environment but makes it his touchstone, testing it at every point to undergird his truly remarkable portrait of Jesus (87-88, 108-109).

Jesus believed that a new age was about to dawn when God himself would establish his long-promised rule on earth, and that right soon (37, 45-56, 70-74, 84-89). He thought of himself as God's herald, destined to proclaim that kingdom. "The prophet like unto Moses, long expected, had finally appeared. As the mouthpiece of God he uttered his call, confident that God through him was calling the nation to repentance and to ready itself for the final chapter" (68). Seized by God's Spirit Jesus was so confident of his vocation and message that he often appeared to others to be insane (57-69).

He was not a disciple of the Baptist nor baptized by him (42-45). Why he began his ministry we can't be sure (84). He called for repentance (76-77) and used the word "Gospel" (83). Above all, contrary to Mark's later reinterpretation, Jesus was clearly understood both by his enemies and his friends (90-97). Those on the bottom of the heap followed him with boistrous enthusiasm. Those Jews responsible for the religious and social arrangements that kept Judaism afloat in troubled Roman waters, considered him a rabble-rouser, an ignorant upstart and when he came to Jerusalem, a threat to national existence (111-120). With unerring insight Jesus made the poor his friends and excoriated the rich (98-110). This fact is the key to his fate. As a good Jew he taught nothing new either about the Scripture or about God. His miracles are made believable by the enthusiasm the common people had for him (149-158). He did not favor Gentiles nor inaugurate a Gentile mission (159-166). He thought of himself as a herald of a cosmic judgment soon to come at the hands of a supernatural judge, the Son of Man, although his disciples later called *him* by that name and made John the Baptist *his* forerunner (137-148).

Given all these factors, when he finally did take his proclamation to Jerusalem at Passover time—for what reason we cannot say—his fate was sealed (167-208). The people continued to support him with noisy and jubilant demonstrations. It did not help that with such support he directed his sharpest denunciations toward the sacred Temple nor that he accompanied these with an acted parable in its overcrowded market precincts, all the while announcing the end of the old order and the coming of the new. The orthodox authorities considered these the "insolent and outrageous mouthings of an ignorant and untrained peasant" (176). His brash attack on tradition as unauthorized prophet and upstart layman together with his unlawful "hobnobbing" (176) with publicans and sinners was just too much! Though most of the details surrounding his arrest, trial, and death are lost to us, he was probably seized by night by a Jewish posse as an insurrectionist against public order and handed over to Pilate for a routine execution. He died knowing he had failed since the kingdom he had heralded as prophet had not come.

The miracle that followed this debacle was resurrection indeed but not his resurrection. It was the resurrection of his followers. "There is little need of wandering into the strange arcana, contrary to all we think we know of an orderly universe, and postulating magical changes on a tired and broken body. The real Easter miracle was not a changed Jesus but changed disciples" (129). So much had his flaming personality become a part of theirs that they felt he simply could not die. By this token they then "saw" him alive among them, gave him the honors he had not claimed for himself and took up his task as their own (209-217). "Had not Jesus built himself, unbeknownst to them and perhaps to him, into them so completely that he was even then living in them?" (213).

Although he explains the resurrection far differently, and with far less reticence, Enslin turns just as fervently as Bornkamm to the life of Jesus as the sole source of Christian faith. It is the Jesus of history not the Christ of faith by whom we are saved (xiii). Personality, the sum total of what we are, can not be lost. The sum total of Jesus' person continues to live in us as it did in his earliest disciples. "There is such a thing as the immortality of influence" (9). In this light the quest for this Jesus must be assigned the highest priority. It is "the quest for the flesh-and-blood man who scratched a match long years ago which started a mighty conflagration still blazing today" (xiii).

B. Jesus as Jew:
David Flusser, *Jesus,* 1969

It is somewhat anomalous to include Jewish lives of Jesus as part of a modified form of the "old" quest, since the reasons for Jewish questing are quite different. Sometimes they wish to reclaim Jesus as long-lost brother. Sometimes they want to clarify the contribution Jesus made to first century Judaism in order to deal more successfully with church/synagogue relationships. In all cases they bring special skills to the analysis of Jewish source materials and from their particular point of viewing often open up old questions in fresh and provocative ways. In any event they tend to approach Jesus in a biographical way as they would Hillel, so that their quest, if classifiable at all in our terms, is more "old" than "new."

It is dangerous even to hint, as the title of this section may suggest, that there is only *one* Jewish view of Jesus. Of the five most recent interpreters in the English speaking world Klausner (1925) is openly hostile to Jesus, Sandmel (1965) thought the records too skimpy and too biased to let us know who Jesus was, Schonfield (1966) makes Jesus an imposter, and Geza Vermes in his *Jesus The Jew* (1981) has only begun a study he hopes someday to complete. His new book, *Jesus and the World of Judaism* (1983) is a step in that direction. The fifth such scholar is David Flusser. As an ecumenically minded professor at the Hebrew University of Jerusalem he wants to celebrate Jesus as an outstanding Jew of the first century and a prophet, as he says, "the enormity of whose life . . . speaks to us today" (12).

Drawing on an "old account" (69) of Jesus' life plus a collection of Hebrew/ Aramaic sayings preserved only by Jewish disciples, Flusser traces the course of Jesus' ministry along somewhat traditional lines. Jesus had a superior Jewish education as a boy (as Luke 2 shows). His trade as a joiner at Nazareth was typical of contemporary Jewish teachers so that the title "Rabbi" was not inappropriate. He early left his home at Nazareth out of alienation from his family and this put a deep psychological mark upon him. He most certainly accepted baptism at the hands of John and at that time was anointed by the Spirit and knew what his vocation as a prophet was to be. He labored mostly in Galilee, gathered traveling disciples, preached the Gospel, and thought of himself as herald of a new age without at that time "declaring that he was the coming Messiah" (36). He regarded John as Elijah the one in whom "the end-time begins" (40). He "is the only Jew of ancient times known to us who preached not only that men were on the threshold of the end of time, but that the new age of salvation had already begun" (90). Jesus expected the coming of the Son of Man in the future as exalted eschatological judge (Daniel, 1 Enoch, Ps 110, Matthew 25:31-36) but finally came to believe that he himself would be that judge and so declared before his persecutors at his trial. After a ministry lasting at the most two years or perhaps only a year, Jesus went to Jerusalem either to die as a prophet or perhaps in the hope that his cause will succeed. He does not go as atoning sacrifice or suffering Messiah, although as a result of Caesarea Philippi and the transfiguration he knows he must die. He predicts the fall of the Temple, and cleanses its outer court, and thus arouses once more the hatred of its protectors, the Sadducees. He used his last Passover to prepare the disciples for his death, but before the High Priest confessed his messiahship, perhaps in the hope of experiencing a resurrection like that of Elijah (122). Condemned by a rump session of Sadducean priests, not by the Pharisees, he died without a real trial, the victim of "the grisly interplay of naked spheres of interest" (129). He died asking mercy for his executioners and perhaps crying to God as one forsaken by him.

While this recital interprets Jesus as a prophet set in an eschatological frame and except at points does not depart too far from conventional analyses, what Flusser proposes *otherwise* is quite startling. Jesus was a *bona fide* Jew who knew the Law better than Paul and obeyed it completely. His reported conflict with the Law and the Pharisees is a figment of later interpretation. He sent his disciples only to the Jews but rejected the Zealots in their strong animus against Rome.

Much more important, the basic thrust of his ministry was to emphasize love of enemies and to include in the kingdom first of all "the poor, the hungry, the meek, the mourners and the persecuted" (91). This was a real revolution that threatened the established order long before he got to Jerusalem. What is more, this emphasis has its roots in the Essene community, *not* in its *major* program but in what Flusser calls the "Essene fringe" (as seen partly in Ecclesiasticus or the Testament of the Twelve Patriarchs). On top of all this we are to think of Jesus as a special Son of God in the light of a genuine

Jewish tradition that gave such a title to those Jewish sages able to perform miracles (like Hanina bar Dossa). Matthew 11:25-27 is a genuine prayer of Jesus celebrating in ecstasy his relation to God as Father much in the spirit of the Essene book of hymns. It is this prophetic ecstatic figure, obedient to the law, so close to the most sensitive Essene ideals, who sees the Kingdom spreading by love and exalting the poor, that enables Flusser to herald Jesus' moral contribution to our own age.

C. Jesus as Messiah:
Ben F. Meyer, *The Aims of Jesus,* 1979

With Meyer we find an interpreter for whom the question of hermeneutical options is paramount. His brief survey of the quest from Reimarus to Bornkamm highlights three intertwining hermeneutical concerns: the order (i.e. the date) of the sources, the nature of the sources, and the presuppositions by which the sources have been interpreted. Responding to all three he builds a hermeneutical foundation on which he is able to carry on his own investigations.

Hermeneutical Foundations

(1) He points out how often the quest has depended on isolating a body of material that by appropriate tests seems earlier than the rest. Thus Mark and "Q" as earlier than Matthew, Luke, and John have been the basis for many lives of Jesus, and more recently various parables and sayings have been isolated to form an authentic core of Jesus' teachings around which one's impressions of Jesus are formed. Over against this tendency Meyer points out that even the earliest strata of the tradition are nevertheless inter- preted tradition. Nothing has escaped the bias of post resurrection days. By the same token what is cast in later form may also contain genuine insights about Jesus. What is needed is to resist the reductionism of appealing solely to what is allegedly early, as though these interpreters should have the last word. The historian, says Meyer, must not relinquish his/her task to the earliest source on the theory that such a source reflects pure eyewitness reporting. Rather the historian must weigh sources and propose what hypotheses in this case may reveal to us the aims of Jesus, given the tradition he pro- duced. Aims can be ascertained from *de facto* outcomes, in this case a church, regarding itself as the remnant of Israel, bearing witness to the resurrection of Jesus as Lord and Christ, and breaking with the synagogue.

(2) Meyer goes to some lengths to show that the tradition concerning Jesus (as used by Paul and seen, for example, in Acts) actually intends history. It really gives us data on Jesus and can be trusted not to misinterpret him intentionally. In other words the nature of the sources beyond the Gospels demands that the church live by what she can say concretely and honestly about Jesus. Thus she speaks of resurrection and death together since resurrection is the vindication of one who, though just, died a shameful death. In this way a life of righteousness, shameful death, and resurrection as vindication stand at the center of the proclamation. Consequently the history of Jesus as eschatological drama is of prior and crucial importance, an indispensable necessity to the preaching of the Gospel and the experiencing of the risen Lord now. It follows that to create the life of Jesus *out of whole cloth* in an oral culture whose religion depended on history would have been impossible, if the church expected the Gospel to be believed at all.

(3) Finally Meyer has a further word on hermeneutical presuppositions. We have just mentioned four of these. (a) That aims are to be discovered by outcomes, moving from what is known to what is unknown. (b) That the aims of an historical personage can be deduced from the tradition that such a person has produced. In this case Meyer is not interested simply in what Jesus taught or did but in "the Jesus of ancient Palestine" himself (19), what he aimed to do, and what the consequences were. (c) That history is not a matter of reading the bare facts off the surface of alleged early reports. History requires reconstruction, the proposing of hypotheses, starting with the known and moving to the unknown and then the verifying and confirming what one has learned. (d) That in dealing with any tradition one must be guided either by methodical credulity or methodical skepticism. There is no possibility of effectively interpreting any past tradition until the interpreter has really entered into the historical consciousness that created that tradition in the first place.

Two further presuppositions apply to the whole quest. (e) All depends on what questions the interpreter is permitted to ask, in this case about Jesus, and what range of possible answers are available by way of response. Meyer believes that the quest has been stifled by supposing that the universe is a closed system and that on this account no penetration of the human sphere by the divine is possible. It is this, for example, that has ruled the exegesis of Bultmann. (f) Meyer also believes that a similar obstruction has been set up by following the principle of analogy to the effect that what is human and what is reasonable is determined *a priori* by what has been generally thought of as human and reasonable in all times and places. Such a presupposition rules out even the possibility of conceiving Jesus as the tradition presents him and of course leads to the choice between faith and intellectual honesty so sharply put by such an interpreter as Van A. Harvey. Both these presuppositions, says Meyer, have now been set aside by the work of Lonergan and need not trammel our efforts further.

Hermeneutical Practice

(1) History is now defined as knowledge gained by inference, whose technique is hypothesis and verification. History is not simply reporting what the earliest sources say and responding to the impact of the events they record.

(2) The whole operation by which history turns unknowns into knowns must be much more carefully monitored. We start with the data the texts supply by recognitive exegesis, seeking the intention each text proposes. Then we proceed by historical interpretation and explanation to find out what the historical actors in question intended and why. On the basis of the text as known we ask questions, propose hypotheses, and seek verification with unceasing care. When we ask whether any NT text gives us data on Jesus we must be prepared to arrange our results in three columns, yes, no, and do not know. Verification may be *direct*, considering the witnesses' intention, knowledge, and veracity or it may be *indirect*, considering the indices of discontinuity, originality, personal idiom, resistive form, multiple attestation, multiform attestation, and Aramaic substratum.

(3) We can no longer pretend that the use to which the interpreter puts history or the value assigned it is unimportant. It will certainly affect the kind of history uncovered. We must openly confront the fact that history can not be written without pre-

understandings or presuppositions. Where faith is one of those presuppositions, particular care must be taken to define the relation between faith and historical research and to sensitize ourselves to the different kinds of history that are mandated when these two are differently related. As the second part of Meyer's book shows, faith opens up rich possibilities for understanding by taking the text more seriously on its own terms. In this way, while faith can never produce absolute certainty and does not depend on that, it *can* be instructed and corrected by historical research, since by its very nature it intends history and is rooted in history.

Jesus as Messiah

John baptized in the wilderness and in the manner of Elijah called all Israel to repentance in view of the coming judgment. Jesus accepted John's mission fully as the eschatological restoration of Israel, already under way in Jesus' ministry. Jesus' public proclamation went beyond John's to say that God's rule comes now as a pure gift of God's unbounded love, meant specifically for restored Israel in-the-process-of formation, the poor, the hungry, the mourners, the lame, and the blind. The Kingdom comes by God's initiative and repentance is redefined as accepting the gift of the kingdom. What is in store is marriage banquet, new Temple, and new wine. Jesus' public teaching has the same eschatological emphasis as ethics for a restored Israel, prescriptive, revelational, and personal. When all this is seen to converge on Jesus' public actions, his eschatological vocation as the one who seeks the restoration of Israel becomes clear. It is in the light of such an aim that we are to understand Jesus' call of the twelve disciples coming from four quite disparate groups in Israel, his healing miracles as signs of the dawning kingdom, his table fellowship with sinners, the public debate about his mission, and his final entry into Jerusalem to cleanse the Temple. Commenting on the parable of the mustard seed, Meyer writes "Jesus not only understood himself as the revealer of God's final saving act but as the author of its nascent realization in time" (164).

But the story does not end here. One further question may be raised. What do we learn about Jesus' aims from his esoteric teaching—that given only to his disciples to illuminate his mission as Messianic (as in the account Mark 8 gives of Peter's confession at Caesarea Philippi)? Meyer does not wish to find the messianic consciousness of Jesus (an old "liberal" ploy) nor debate (with the more traditional interpreters of Jesus) what it means theologically to identify Jesus as Messiah. He wants quite directly to put the question in an historical way: "Did Jesus identify himself as Messiah? Did the disciples of the pre-paschal period identify him as Messiah?" (175-176). We do not know enough of the post-paschal Easter experience to argue on this basis what may have been possible before Easter nor does the *titulus* on the cross identifying Jesus as King of the Jews help us to know beyond public expectation what he himself thought or what his disciples understood about his messianic role.

Meyer finds his starting point for the answering of such questions in Jesus' word about the destruction of the Temple and the building of a new Temple. This is an esoteric word on eschatological tribulation to be followed by triumph, illuminated by texts from both the Old Testament and the New, from Qumran, and from rabbinic tradition, notably Nathan's oracle on 2 Samuel 7 and Jesus' word to Peter in Matthew 16 (185-197). Along with this word is Jesus' cleansing of the Temple seen as "prophetic critique, fulfillment event and a sign of the future" (197). This cryptic word and this parabolic event bring all we have learned about Jesus' public proclamation, teaching and action to resolution.

According to Meyer, Jesus "was the builder of the house of God" (201) and this identifies him prior to the Passion as Messiah.

When we ask further how this was to be accomplished Meyer turns to those texts that speak of tribulation and vindication. By the acceptance and rejection of Jesus Israel would be divided and a new Messianic remnant emerge. Jesus himself would suffer death through this expiation but be vindicated as the Saviour of Israel and triumphant Son of Man (as in Mark 8-10). By taking such esoteric traditions seriously the whole public ministry of Jesus from his baptism onward converge on an intelligible pattern. Jesus' aim was the eschatological restoration of Israel (221).

It should be added that a wide variety of studies move in the direction exemplified by Meyer, where further analysis would surely yield a rich harvest. I mention only a few by way of illustration: A. E. Harvey (1982), T. W. Manson (1977), Leonard Goppelt (1981), E. Schillebeeckx (1979, 1980), J. Jeremias (1971), and G. W. Buchanan (1984).

IV. Four Further Options of More Recent Vintage, Not Strictly "Old" or "New"

What is proposed here in its methodology and picture of Jesus is newer than some of the more traditional images with which we have been dealing, Jesus as Jew, as prophet, and as Messiah. Here we have images of Jesus as well as treatments of the tradition that in very pronounced ways strongly reflect contemporary culture. They rise not so much out of a desire to interpret current culture as to find what we can of our culture in the ancient record.

A. A Continuing Rejection of the Quest

1. The Storied Jesus:
Hans Frei, *The Eclipse of Biblical Narrative*, 1974

Hans Frei's book rests on the assumption that the story of Jesus, like some modern novels, is salvific simply by reason of its being told. He thinks we misread the story of Jesus, submit it to tests it was never meant to undergo, when we seek in it any reference to the concrete particulars of the life of Jesus as lived out in first century Palestine, whether ostensive or real. In his follow-up volume, *The Identity of Jesus Christ*, 1975, he sketches the pattern established by this storied Jesus. According to Frei Jesus asserted the power of God in weakness in such fashion that he identifies himself as the "unsubstitutable" person revealing God to us. By this pattern we ourselves may live.

2. The Existential-historical Jesus:
Schubert Ogden, *The Point of Christology*, 1982

It is somewhat of an anomaly to speak of Schubert Ogden in the same breath with Hans Frei. I do so here because they do agree in rejecting both the "old" and "new" quests, and they do appeal in the final analysis to a salvific pattern discoverable in the Jesus material. Otherwise, of course, as with the whole of the modern quest, the differences between them are complex and worthy of a much more detailed study.

In this 1982 volume, Ogden is attracted by the work of modern scholars in isolating the earliest corpus of traditions about Jesus in the Gospels. In analyzing what they find there, he makes a distinction between the "empirical-historical Jesus" and the "existential-historical Jesus." The empirical-historical Jesus is Jesus "as he actually was" (55). This represents what the Evangelists *assumed* about Jesus. The existential-historical Jesus is "Jesus in his meaning for us," not Jesus "as he actually was" or "Jesus in his being in himself" (56). This represents what the earliest church *asserted* about Jesus.

To separate these two kinds of Jesus is "historically impossible and theologically unnecessary" (122). That is, such are the difficulties of Synoptic analysis that we can never be certain whether we are talking about Jesus as he was or Jesus as he is. The picture in the Gospels is fairly clear. Jesus did exist. He does authorize Christian existence. He has a certain understanding of himself that implicitly made him the revealer of God's will. He ran afoul of the authorities, was tried, condemned, and executed. But, says Ogden, "We have to allow for the possibility that even what clearly seem to be assumptions about Jesus as he actually was are really assumptions about Jesus as he truly is" (58). The upshot however is not disastrous because the empirical-historical Jesus is not necessary for theology and the existential-historical Jesus is a quite suitable norm for all Christology. The pattern we discover in *this* Jesus is clear. It is both true and appropriate to the needs of our culture since the demand of our culture is for freedom and the Christology it demands must be liberationist. The existential-historical Jesus brings to us both the gift and demand of God's unbounded love. If we respond to this norm we can experience both unbounded love and radical freedom.

All of this reconstruction involves what Ogden had demanded of Bultmann in his earlier book *Christ Without Myth*, 1962, namely that Jesus be stripped of all mythology. It should be noted, however, that Ogden now substitutes for Bultmann's Christ-kerygma, the Christ who rises first of all in the preaching of the early church, his scholars' version of the Jesus-kerygma, the existential-historical Jesus. The latter carries for Ogden the same authority that the Christ-kerygma carried for Bultmann and in sum produces the same result, since the existential-historical Jesus is "the decisive representation of ultimate reality, and hence the explicit primal source authorizing the authentic understanding of one's existence in relation to this ultimate reality" (129). In the final analysis this norm brings us all the assurance we need for our salvation. That is, by paying attention to the existential-historical Jesus we can gain authentic self-understanding. Ogden here is as thoroughly existentialist as Bultmann. With either one our salvation lies in gnosis: to wit, what the earliest church proclaimed about Jesus, whether his pre-Passion or his post-Passion history. In neither case can we really know who Jesus was or what he did or what he intended!

B. Jesus as Story-teller:
James Breech, *The Silence of Jesus:*
The Authentic Voice of the Historical Man, 1983

Much attention in recent days has been focused on Jesus as a fashioner of language. Since language is the house of being, rhetorical and structuralist studies of Jesus are carried out with great vigor in the hope of penetrating his mind and ministry. Countless issues of the magazine *Semeia* have been devoted to this subject with such luminaries as Robert Funk, (1975, 1982), Robert Tannehill (1975), Dominic Crossan (1973, 1976, 1979, 1980), and Daniel Patte contributing to them and writing in addition a continuous stream of articles and books about the linguisticality of Jesus. Crossan says at one point that the historical Jesus is for him simply a name conveniently applied to such Jesus material as scholarly consensus has stamped with approval (1973, p.33). Such authentic material is the arena where Jesus is to be encountered if anywhere at all.

James Breech works with eight sayings representing such an authentic core, plus seven photodramatic parables and five phonodramatic parables, equally identified by scholarly consensus as pure Jesus material. At the outset then we learn that Breech's methodology is reductionist from the ground up. If we are to hear, as Breech says, "the authentic voice of the historical man" we must listen *only* to what Jesus says in this previously designated authentic core of pure material.

Whatever occurs here by way of action or concrete historical reference may be accepted but all the rest of the Synoptic interpretation of Jesus must be rigorously excluded from our consideration. Jesus' words, not his actions, are primary and the historical setting in which both happened to occur is of no moment whatsoever in attempting to understand who Jesus was.

In addition we are free to roam far and wide over the centuries to glean from the wise of all times and cultures whatever wisdom they may contribute to the issues raised in this core material. This means, of course, together with the restriction of our concern to Jesus' words and the exclusion of anything pertaining to his action or the cultural setting in which he ministered, that Jesus is effectively transported by one fell swoop out of ancient Palestine. This Jesus, truly pictured "in vacuo," is to be seen in the company of such worthies as Nietzsche, T. S. Eliot, and J. D. Salinger's *Franny and Zooey.*

What then does Breech conclude is the "authentic voice of the historical man?" John the Baptist and Jesus are viewed together as possessing what Breech calls "a mode of being as free persons" (30) that their tribalized contemporaries deeply resent. Jesus tells his stories to celebrate this free mode of being. The shepherd, the woman searching for a coin, the good Samaritan, the master of the unjust steward, the man who gives a banquet, the owner of the vineyard who hires laborers at all hours of the day, all these people do what they do as free beings. It is they who are pictured at the outset and it is their words we hear at the end. They are not forced to love simply because people are in distress and do not exist as living beings because other people have experienced misfortune. They love because they choose to do so in independent and transcendent fashion. The Good Samaritan (whose name Breech insists should be simply person number three alongside persons one and two, the priest and the Levite) does indeed impart life to the man who fell among thieves. He does indeed give the opportunity for life to the innkeeper. But we never hear whether the good Samaritan returns as he promised at the end. He goes his way serenely and independently having involved himself on the Jericho road only to demonstrate what a free mode of being really is like. This is what Jesus himself did and this is what his disciples learned to do after his death.

Since this alone is what the core material teaches us, the silence of Jesus is deafening. He says nothing about apocalyptic, nor Jewish sectarian life, nor social class, nor religious institutions, practices or beliefs (219), nor the Jewish people as a nation. He does not indulge in exhortation. He does not teach or illustrate ideas, nor point to history as the locus of his stories. Within the stories themselves Jesus does not describe the characters who appear there nor elucidate their motives nor tell his hearers what to think about them. Like Jesus they do not re-act against anyone nor are they egocentric. Each acts in a concerned but transcendent way to model his own inner mode of being. These persons "live" (134-139, 210-212) in Jesus' stories in the same way that Jesus himself "lived" and this is their challenge now to us.

C. **Jesus as Interpreted by the Social Sciences**

1. John Riches, *Jesus and the Transformation of Judaism*, 1982

With John Riches, Paul Hollenbach, and Morton Smith we come upon a wide-spread modern attempt to use the social sciences to understand Jesus as he really was, an attempt far more technical and precise than S. J. Case's appeal to social experience in the twenties. As we all know from Paul Hollenbach's paper (1983) prepared for last year's annual meeting, the work of these three represents a massive attempt on the part of many scholars to interpret Biblical literature by drawing on the scholarly insights generated in this arena.

Against a broad background sketching the history of Jesus research, Riches opts for a revival of the "history of religions" approach. In the spirit of Troeltsch, and over against the idealist Jesus of C. H. Dodd and the existentialist Jesus of Bultmann, Riches asks how Jesus reworked Jewish language and what effect such a change in religious language might have on the political situation of Jesus' day. His thesis is that what one says depends upon both the core meaning of the sentences employed and the context within which one speaks, whether external or internal. "The originality of the religious innovator," he writes, "thus lies not least in his ability to forge new terms, retaining their core-meaning, deleting some associations and creating new ones" (37). Riches tests this proposal by discussing in turn Kingdom, purity, God language, and Jesus' own role in the transformation of Judaism.

With the Zealots, Pharisees, and Essenes kingship meant power, judgment and justice while for Jesus it meant God's forgiveness and mercy and the love of one's enemies. To communicate in his immediate environment Jesus must retain the core meaning conveyed by the rule of God but new horizons emerge when the poor, the oppressed, and even children enter the kingdom and when the kingdom is felt to be present now in Jesus' own healing and reconciling ministry.

What Jesus inherited by way of purity was the conviction of Leviticus 20:20-26 that to be a true Israelite one must not do as the Gentiles do and that only by practicing the law in all its purity could one draw close to God. This urgency was particularly strong at Qumran where the community sought by withdrawal and meticulous observance to prepare for the final battle of the Sons of Light. Whereas both Pharisee and Essene used the law to separate Jew from Gentile and Jew from Jew, Jesus was critical of the law and sought by its radicalization to open its blessings to all and sundry. Riches is convinced that Mark 7:15 rejecting cultic purity is a genuine word of Jesus and that he cleansed the Temple "to initiate a *national* renewal of prayer and dedication" (142).

According to Riches, the problem of theism for Jesus is whether God can be seen as blessing all people and at the same time be the judge of those who oppress the poor. "How can God be said to rule while his people are oppressed?" (154). While Jesus did not tie up the loose ends of this question of theodicy, he expected the end soon, thought of final judgment by some sort of heavenly Son of Man and envisaged some sort of vindication of the poor afterwards. At the same time he shifted the emphasis from the end time to his own immediate ministry of healing and forgiveness where Holy War of a new kind was already proving victorious over Satan.

Drawing on his knowledge of first century culture in Palestine Riches says that Jesus can be compared to those leaders in Israel who were set for its renewal. He was a teacher who at the same time called for sacrificial discipleship and expected public confession of his way as preparation for the final judgment by a heavenly Son of Man. He was identified as a prophet in many ways, not least by his declarations saying "I am come" to do this and that. As an alternate way of meeting the challenge of Hellenism and foreign domination Jesus sought to reorder "fundamental apprehensions about God, man and the world" and to translate these "into social terms" (185). In this he not only initiated change but by identifying himself with the poor and the persecuted and carrying out spiritual warfare through healings and exorcism, he symbolized the transformation he intended.

2. Paul Hollenbach, "Jesus, Demoniacs, and Public Authorities: A Socio-Historical Study," *JAAR* 49 (1981) 567-88

Hollenbach objects that Riches has fallen into the trap of the idealistic approach he sought at the outset to avoid. According to Hollenbach, Riches thinks of Jesus as seeking to change perceptions about God, man, and the world, he thinks of this change as only the beginning of what will come later on, and he symbolizes this preparationist program rather than initiating here and now concrete social strategies. For Hollenbach all this is not enough. In a private review of Riches' book he writes, "I tend to think that Jesus' identification with the Galilean poor was not only symbolic, but initiated actual social, economic, legal and political moves." Jesus' whole ministry would then be evaluated not by whether he had prepared Israel for social change but by whether he had taken steps to effect that change concretely prior to his death. In this vein Hollenbach's article on exorcism listed above proposes that Jesus used exorcism not simply to signal the advent of God's rule but also to release those oppressed by Roman rule from the deadening effect of that rule upon them and thus with purpose aforethought to disrupt the political status quo.

3. Morton Smith, *Jesus the Magician*, 1978

Method

This truly remarkable book needs the most careful reading.

(a) Smith says that the attempt to separate the Christ of faith from the Jesus of History has failed inasmuch as the whole of the first century was mythological. "Both general probability and specific evidence require us to recognize the possibility that the 'Christ of faith' originated in the life-time, if not in the mind of 'the Jesus of history' and that one of the first to believe in 'Jesus the Christ' was Jesus himself. Consequently we cannot suppose that all Gospel elements reflecting the 'Christ of faith' must be unhistorical" (5).

(b) The basic question then is to ask what we *can* find from analyzing the Gospels as the end products of the career Jesus had, whatever that may have been. Smith puts it this way: "What sort of man and what sort of career, in the society of first century Palestine, would have occasioned the beliefs, called into being the communities and given rise to the practices, stories and sayings that then appeared, of which selected reports and collections have come down to us" (6).

(c) Once our task has been so focused Smith has no difficulty showing how integral to the Gospel tradition are the miracles of Jesus. In the ancient world one who healed free of charge was sure to collect a mob so that we can be sure that "Such cures made Jesus famous" (9). When one analyzes each separate source, Mark, "Q", the special material of Matthew and Luke and the Gospel of John, one must admit that Jesus is either praised or defended throughout as a worker of miracles. "The comments are consistent, plausible, fit the historical situation and (except for their naive exaggeration) present no excuse for doubt" (14). The burden of proof is on those who deny that Jesus attracted followers by working miracles and that because he worked miracles "he was believed to be the Messiah and the son of a god. Anyone who wants to deny the truth of these reports must try to prove that within forty to sixty years of Jesus' death all the preserved strands of Christian tradition had forgotten or deliberately misinterpreted, the most conspicuous characteristic of the public career of the founder of the movement" (15).

(d) Beginning at this point it is possible to show how Jesus was also regarded as a prophet or teacher of the law but the current is not likely to move in the opposite direction. Moreover it is quite easy to move from the miracles to the crucifixion. As a miracle worker Jesus attracted great crowds and was thought to be Messiah. When, with such support and such pretensions, he finally came to Jerusalem and attacked the Temple, the priests were rightly concerned for public order and the Romans as well. The Passion story is basically sound in its motivation and the suggestion in particular of John 11:47 rings true (16-17).

(e) All such analysis as this requires a radically different approach to the quest for Jesus. The wide differences of interpretation among scholars are due not simply to the uncertainty of the sources and the conflicting theological views of the interpreters but to wrong methods. We must abandon "uncontrolled structural analysis of selected New Testament passages, to discover their components, and equally uncontrolled conjecture as to the social matrices from which these components might have come" (17). What can be determined are "the social types" current in Jesus' world (18). These provide "parameters of the possible" (18), within which to discover Jesus' identity. We have some indication what that might be from Luke's account in Acts 5:34ff., where Jesus is described in terms of Judas and Theudas, who between them illustrate such types as teacher, magician, Messianic claimant, and revolutionary (20).

(f) Smith proposes to explore this question by probing what was being said about Jesus the magician both by outsiders and by insiders. He does not think that any previous scholar has tried to do this. He thinks that where these two traditions agree or intersect in their concerns we must find ourselves that much closer to an accurate picture of the one who is being either so praised or so vilified.

Jesus as Magician

(a) Smith analyzes what the Gospels say about enemy attacks on Jesus as magician and locates their origin in the scribes of Jesus' own day. By teaching with authority Jesus upset their apple cart and they explained his invasion of their territory by branding him in rough terms as a magician, one who gained power from Beelzebub (31-32). The Gospel writers would not have invented such charges but only answer them because they were forced to do so by the facts! At the same time, by analyzing a broad range of materials outside the Gospels from Josephus to the magical papyri to Celsus and Lucian (and much more), Smith points to a substantial, independent tradition criticizing Jesus in a similar vein. The picture these outsiders had of Jesus Smith sums up as follows:

> The son of a soldier named Panthera and a peasant woman married to a carpenter, Jesus was brought up in Nazareth as a carpenter, but left his home town and, after unknown adventures, arrived in Egypt where he became expert in magic and was tatooed with magical symbols or spells. Returning to Galilee he made himself famous by his magical feats, miracles he did by his control of demons. He thereby persuaded the masses that he was the Jewish Messiah and/or the son of a god. Although he pretended to follow Jewish customs, he formed a small circle of intimate disciples whom he taught to despise the Jewish Law and to practice magic. These he bound together and to himself by ties of 'love,' meaning sexual promiscuity, and by participation in the most awful rites, including cannibalism—they had some sort of ritual meal in which they ate human flesh and drank blood. Surrounded by this circle he travelled from town to town deceiving many and leading them into sin. But he was not always successful. The members of his own family did not believe him; when he went back to Nazareth his townspeople rejected him and he could do no miracle there. Stories of his libertine teaching and practice leaked out and began to circulate. The scribes everywhere opposed him and challenged his claims. Finally, when he went to Jerusalem the high priests had him arrested and turned him over to Pilate, charging him with the practice of magic and with sedition. Pilate had him crucified, but this did not put an end to the evil. His followers stole his body from the grave, claimed he had risen from the dead and, as a secret society, perpetuated his practices (67).

(b) What the outsiders meant by branding Jesus as magician is that he exercised divine power over a whole host of invisible supernatural beings, either on a lower level as a spurious *goes* or on a higher plane as a *magus* or divine man like Apollonius of Tyana. The latter was a contemporary of Paul who studied magic in India and Egypt, taught itinerating disciples, worked cures, was eventually brought to trial for sedition and magic, escaped miraculously and later was worshipped as a son of God, a being of supernatural power (68-94).

(c) When we turn back to the Gospels we find evidence there all the way through that the Evangelists responded to this picture constructed by outsiders (94-139). They then tried to moralize Jesus the magician and make him a teacher of the law or a prophet but all this is an edited account of definitely later origin. When this evidence is tabulated it can be seen that what they say in this vein about Jesus as prophet is demonstrably secondary (158-164). What Jesus actually did can not be explained on that basis, but can only be interpreted by taking seriously the much earlier magical tradition Smith has sketched. Thus Jesus had a supernatural birth (97). He received a spirit at baptism, perhaps eventually the spirit of the dead Baptist (102-104) that enabled him to work magic. Like a shaman he went into the wilderness (105-106). His whole career of itineration, with disciples following and cures performed, matches what one would expect of a *magus* like Apollonius, even to the forgiveness of sins and the prediction of the future (and much else) (111-129). His teaching is either relevant to magic or has parallels in magical texts. The Lord's prayer pictures Jesus' followers as the poor in need of bread. He performs miracles, gaining in this way both authority and bread and then earning for himself the right to instruct his benefactors in the mysteries of the kingdom, which are part and parcel of his magic power (133-137). The Eucharist in particular is "a familiar type of magical ceremony in which the magician identifies himself with a deity and identifies wine and/or food with the blood or body of this deity and himself. The wine and/or food is then given to a recipient who by consuming it is united with him and filled with love for him" (138).

(d) The upshot of this rereading of the Gospel tradition in the light of the outsiders' magical tradition is crystal clear for Smith. He writes, "We have merely read the Gospels with some knowledge of ancient magical material and noticed what, in the light of that material, the Gospel stories and sayings really say. The resultant picture obviously accords with the one given by the outsiders' tradition which it commonly supplements rather than contradicts. That these two agree so often as to the facts reported and differ chiefly in their evaluation of these facts, is a strong argument for supposing the facts correct" (139). What all this means is that the range of social types for the classification of Jesus within the parameters of possibility is considerably reduced. Jesus was a magician of a special type characterized by compulsive behavior, neglect of the law and enlarged supernatural claims. (143-147) All attempts to make him a teacher of the law, an opponent of the (later!) Pharisees or the initiator of a special kind of Passover meal are later attempts to modify a much earlier tradition picturing Jesus as a divine being who possessed spirits to do his bidding. In the end, we have three legitimate models from which to proceed; the official portrait of Jesus as Son of God, the outsiders' portrait of 'Jesus the god'" lying behind the present Gospel portrait (149). When these pictures intersect they give us a consistent, coherent, credible, and early account of Jesus as a person possessed of magical powers.

D. Jesus as Liberator:
Jon Sobrino, *Christology at the Crossroads:*
A Latin American Approach, 1978

Liberation theology as developed by Catholic theologians in Latin America demonstrates with crystal clarity how hermeneutic theory may be shaped by the life situations addressed (Sobrino, xxvi, 1-2, 12-14, 17-22, 33-37, 273-307). Speaking on behalf of the oppressed and the poor these theologians reject all dogmatic religious formulations that prop up oppressive political and economic regimes. They put orthopraxis above orthodoxy, concrete history above sublime abstraction, relationality above essence, and conflict above idealization (xv-xxvi, 1-14, 17-22).

Thus to know Jesus the interpreter must be a follower of Jesus (xxi, xxiv-xxv, 29). The total image of Jesus can only be worked out as one follows the historical process by which he becomes the Son of God (xxi-xxii, 2-3). Moreover, it is necessary to follow this historical process consistently from Jesus' life through his death and resurrection (xxiii-xxiv). In this way the study of Jesus becomes historical, trinitarian, and ecclesial (xx-xxvi). From this basic hermeneutic formulation the words of Jesus can not be separated from his deeds (xxii). By the same token later ecclesial tradition can be as trustworthy a guide as an alleged authentic core standing at the beginning of the process. Thus the Epistle to the Hebrews gives us invaluable insights into the historicity of Jesus (89-91).

From such a hermeneutic matrix we are asked by these interpreters to behold Jesus' own faith, his prayers, and his service to the Kingdom. We are asked to trace the relation of such a life to his death and to see its ultimate outcome in the various canonical theologies of resurrection and to use the clues such theologies provide as a critique of all later theological dogma (2-9). It is a breath-taking, thoroughly revolutionary proposal.

Jesus must then be seen as one who points beyond himself to God's kingdom (41-74). Rooted in the activism of the Old Testament God's rule is proclaimed as "authentic liberation at every level of human existence" (44). It means concrete action to achieve brotherhood in response to the initiative of God's grace that appears in the midst of "oppressive situations" (47). This is Jesus' prophetic mission to the poor, the sick, the sinners and the demon possessed. Sin is structurally both personal and social and must not simply be forgiven but "eradicated" (51). Those who have faith are those who are willing to participate in this effort, both here and now and in full anticipation of the Kingdom's future coming. Those who sin will not give themselves into God's hands but will build up collective power to protect themselves against God and to oppress others (53). "The personal dimension of sin can be tangibly verified in the oppression to which it gives rise" (54). Sin is power wrongly exercised against God and others.

At first Jesus proclaimed the kingdom so understood and called disciples to do the same. But when he was rejected (as in Mark 8-16) Jesus had to open up new ways into the kingdom by presenting himself as the suffering servant of Yahweh. It was the same with his disciples. "Instead of being sent out with power, his followers would now have to follow the suffering-laden pathway of Christ himself, with all the perilous social, personal and political implications involved" (58). This sets them against their own Jewish heritage and requires their following a new and painful way solely pioneered by Jesus. This means that orthodoxy is replaced by orthopraxis, that the latter is defined solely in terms of Jesus' own action and that we as interpreters may now approach his divinity in relational rather than absolute terms. The kingdom is eschatological because it creates a genuine crisis here and now. Only by focusing on praxis not theory can we receive the kingdom as a gift to be brought by God alone in the future and to act on its behalf here and now (61-67). It is by his own praxis (which alone controls entrance to the kingdom) that Jesus reveals *indirectly* his relation to the Father (67-74).

Turning his back on more traditional Catholic attempts to explain Christology in formal terms, Sobrino follows the concrete faith of Jesus historically in a total and holistic way, as a series of conflicts in "a sinful world which must be transformed" (77). He chooses faith for this focus since Jesus interpreted himself in these terms from the Old Testament and since Sobrino sees a "real parallel" (87) at this point between Jesus and Latin America. Jesus "learned obedience from what he suffered" (90). "Faith is the very mode of Jesus' existence and . . . . it has a history" (90). Such faith relates itself to the kingdom and is expressed by Jesus' prayer (146-177) and his mission. It takes sides "with human beings in a concrete situation where the existing politico-religious structure has dehumanized people" (92).

Seen in this light Jesus' public career exhibits two stages. In the first stage Jesus lives such inherited faith in pure form and is accepted. In the second stage, Jesus realizes that he has failed in his mission as heretofore conceived and must alter his praxis. Now he trusts God as before but expects only his own death and hence not the coming of the kingdom. He no longer exercises miraculous power but surrenders his very self, in order to "shoulder the very burden" (95) of the sin he had denounced. His faith is seen in human terms both in his being put to the test and in his ignorance. These are the ways in which his faith is concretely brought to perfection (95-98) as he decides what kind of power will really bring God's kingdom into being. Thus, "if we view Jesus in terms of his concrete history, we can say that what Jesus reveals to us is the way of the Son, the way one becomes Son of God" (105). All this means once again that the only way we can know Jesus as the Son of God is to follow "the path of his faith." (108) We become children of God by building creative justice among our sisters and brothers (109-139). As Jesus takes a "class outlook" (123) and positions himself with the poor and enters into the conflict this entails, so must we. As he suffered the loss of power and life so must we.

It is in this light that we must relate Jesus' life to his death. Jesus put his faith in God completely and yet was abandoned to death on the cross. "Jesus dies as the Son, as the one who proclaimed the nearness of his heavenly Father and then died completely abandoned by that Father" (188). Despite the efforts of much subsequent theology to escape this real life scandal of the cross its concrete location in Jesus' own history must be kept (179-209). Jesus' death must not be construed as the result of misunderstanding. He knowingly and boldly attacked the use of political power to oppress people in the name of God. God is not power but love. But when precisely this God abandons Jesus, he must die in "total discontinuity with his life and cause" (218). In the cross God abandons the Son but in this not only criticizes the world but shows "his ultimate solidarity with it" (225).

It is here that the history of Jesus becomes trinitarian. Because his death involves God the Father and he as the Son is abandoned, the question is whether the Spirit will continue their common work. This is what actually happens. "The Spirit makes us children of God, but it does not do so in any idealistic way. It does so through the structure of the Son. It introduces us into God's own attitude toward the world, which is an attitude of love. But since the world is dominated by sin and hence riddled with conflict, it makes us co-actors with God in history" (226). This in turn is our clue to the meaning of resurrection. Since it is not just any one but rather Jesus who is resurrected, the hope this engenders is that the oppressed will finally be vindicated and oppression finally overcome. There is still the struggle and disappointment that characterized his own historical life but ultimate triumph is assured (236-256, 258-271). At the same time, since the resurrection is an eschatological event—i.e. related to the purpose of God—it carries with it the command to engage in mission. Such mission in the pattern of Jesus puts us into the only position from which he can be known.

ANALYZING THE HERMENEUTIC MATRIX

Where we find such varied results in the short compass of some sixty years of the quest it is inevitable we should ask why such sharp differences emerge. When historical reason is applied to a tradition filled with the miraculous and rising out of a very particular faith in the resurrection of its founder, it is as obvious now as it has always been in the quest that the limits of historical reason are being tested. This was the burden of R. R. Niebuhr's excellent study of a previous generation (1957). It receives particular attention from Ben Meyer (1979) and Jon Sobrino (1976). Beyond the few paradigms we have discussed it is also the concern of A. E. Harvey (1982), E. Schillebeeckx (1979, 1980, 1981) and George W. Buchanan (1984). We confine ourselves to three suggestions.

I. Choosing a Method

Some of the differences we have observed do appear because the methods chosen differ. Since Hans Frei makes no attempt to enter the historical arena at all his storied Jesus by definition would be quite different from Jesus the magician of Morton Smith. In the first case a literary pattern gives us access to Jesus. In the second case we are asked to understand Jesus on the basis of the sociological types appearing in the first century Palestine and above all to immerse ourselves in the realities of popular magic as experienced then. Whereas Morton Enslin (whose methodology is mainly literary and historical) explains Jesus' miracles in terms of the authority he generated as *the* prophet of God (149-158), Morton Smith (who is pursuing sociological typology) subordinates Jesus the prophet to Jesus the magician. In each case the method adopted creates the historical judgment made.

On the other hand, in by far a larger number of cases the method of analysis adopted does *not* give us the clues we might expect to the ultimate image of Jesus that emerges.

This would be the case, for example, with those who work from the viewpoint of the social sciences. In John Riches' book Jesus appears as a radical prophet whose exorcism is part of the Holy War that will establish the kingdom on earth. For Morton Smith all talk of Jesus as prophet and teacher is secondary and his exorcisms make him no more than a magician like Apollonius of Tyana. Paul Hollenbach objects that the Jesus of John Riches does not expect concrete social change now as he should. Once again, although both work from a basic existentialist understanding of Jesus, Bornkamm knows much more about Jesus the authentic person than Schubert Ogden.

That there is no necessary connection between method and result would also seem to be demonstrated by the similarity that emerges in the image of Jesus as portrayed by scholars using different approaches. Although Morton Enslin has a far different orientation toward tradition than Jon Sobrino, particularly where the resurrection is concerned, Jesus emerges from the work of each as a prophet of doom whose critique of the establishment leads to his death. Substantially the same judgment is made by Ben F. Meyer (1979, p. 170) and D. Flusser (106-114).

II. Reading between the Lines

When the limitations of method are probed as above it soon becomes clear that the particular modern tools adopted to understand Jesus in his own environment are not sufficient in themselves to account for the differences that do appear in the resulting portraits of Jesus. It is still necessary for scholars to read between the lines and this appears to lie solely within the province of each interpreter. For the most part our only recourse is to record and understand what gives each such interpreter the authority to root scientific study in a very personal orientation to reality. What we are observing are the preconceptions that fuel all hermeneutic theory, wherever practiced. What we are observing in the case of the quest for Jesus is an unacknowledged tension between a preconceived personal image of Jesus and consciously adopted method. This tension is perhaps most vividly exhibited in Ben Meyer's analysis of hermeneutic presuppositions and practice. He surely recognizes the tension that does in fact exist and tries to turn it into meaningful dialogue (1979, 13-113). The one other interpreter who goes out of his way to make clear his own (Latin American) preunderstandings is Jon Sobrino (xi-xxvi, 1-40).

A. Total orientation

This observation can be documented, first of all, by calling attention in the broadest possible way to the total orientation underlying the work of various scholars.

Bornkamm, Enslin, Flusser, Meyer, and Breech, for example, all use the current methods of historical and literary analysis. All of them recognize the necessity of isolating the earliest stratum of Jesus' teaching as a possible control over the use of other materials which can not be so neatly identified. We think here of Breech's reliance on an authentic core of Jesus' sayings and his treatment of what he calls the phonodramatic and photodramatic parables (Appendices, 225-240). One thinks also of the meticulous way by which Ben Meyer sifts the pre-resurrection from the post-resurrection materials by the criteria of discontinuity, originality, personal idiom, resistive form, multiple attestation, multiform attestation, and Aramaic substratum (1979, 76-94, 111-113). Bornkamm and Enslin are of the same mind, each refusing to allow what they regard as later formulations to influence basic tradition from the Jesus level. Bornkamm claims to find in Jesus' authority "undistorted and primary" data (53). Enslin believes that in spite of much later interpretation (139-149) Jesus *can* be known as a flesh and blood person through the quality of his life (xi-xiv, 6, 126-129) and specifically through his vocation as prophet (57-69). We remember in this vein that Flusser writes specifically to show how much can be known of Jesus as an ancient Jew and how he sifts the available material using his special skills as a student of ancient Judaism (7-24).

But with all this agreement on basic methodology what amazingly different portraits of Jesus emerge! Bornkamm has no eyes for anything but Jesus' authenticity. He knows much of what Enslin knows about Jesus' mission but none of it is important for understanding Jesus and above all for relating him to Israel. With Enslin Jesus' first century environment is all important, as is his relation to Israel. It is precisely by analyzing contemporary Jewish concern for the Kingdom (15-56) that we know that Jesus was *the* prophet promised by Deuteronomy and that we can make sense of the immense authority he wielded. Neither Enslin (130-148) nor Bornkamm (167-193) will affirm that Jesus thought of himself as Messiah whereas Meyer by meticulous analysis finally reaches that conclusion (172-202) and describes him basically as the builder of the house of God (201). Flusser proposes that Jesus did not think of himself as Messiah during his ministry as herald of the kingdom (36) and only confessed it under duress before the High Priest (122). Over against all these scholars James Breech sets his view of Jesus as a story teller, neither Messiah nor prophet nor in any other way related to the destiny of Israel. Much like Bornkamm he sees Jesus as the conveyor of a kind of existentialist authenticity but unlike Bornkamm does not acknowledge its presence except in Jesus' teaching. Flusser meanwhile is explicitly attracted to Jesus because in his teaching about love of enemies and care for the oppressed (69-94), he stands in a kind of sectarian way with the "Essene fringe" (77, 80, 81). Each scholar as a scientific historian is sifting ancient material but each scholar is also, in the most personal way, reading between the lines.

B. Specific Texts

In still more specific cases, it is possible to show how special bias emerges when various interpreters read between the lines to claim for Jesus texts whose assignment to him is otherwise vigorously disputed.

Thus Enslin has a special interest in showing that Jesus thought of himself as the prophet like Moses whose rise is predicted in Deuteronomy. To do this he is not able to quote any word of Jesus himself but must rely solely on Acts 3:22 and 7:37. He deduces that the prophecies quoted here by Peter and Stephen would not have appeared had not Jesus made such a claim for himself. But what he alleges in this specific instance is pure guesswork! He makes a similar deduction from the cry of derision in the Passion story at Mark 14:65.

Likewise Riches assigns to Jesus himself the revolutionary words of Mark 7:15 on the basis of his concurrent study of purity, although this assignment is widely disputed (112-144).

Flusser is much impressed with Jesus' kinship to the Essenes and believes that Jesus could legitimately be called Son of God on the basis of his healing miracles. On this score he assigns to Jesus the Johannine-like words from Q in Matthew 11:25-27 (95-96), although they exhibit a distinctly un-Synoptic flavor. Ben Meyer claims that these verses also belong to Jesus but for quite different reasons (1979, 309, note 119). For him they stand at the center of the whole esoteric teaching of Jesus characterized by riddling words and symbolic deeds, around which Meyer's basic interpretation of Jesus is organized. For much the same reason he assigns to Jesus Matthew 15:24, words that appear only in Matthew (167). In similar vein he puts Luke 19:9 at the center of Jesus' major intention to restore eschatological Israel, a theme central to Meyer's reading between the lines, even though 19:9 occurs only in this one Lukan story (161). Flusser does the same for Luke's sole word of forgiveness from the cross because it has what he calls "an authentic ring" (131, 149). In his finding such authenticity we remember that it is around Jesus' whole ministry of love that Flusser builds his particular portrait of Jesus (65-74). Flusser also assigns to Jesus three eschatological texts rarely claimed directly for him: Matthew 25:31-36, Matthew 19:28, and Mark 12:35-37 (100-104). He is undoubtedly prompted to do this because he sees Jesus drawing on apocalyptic perceptions that also appear in the Essene literature, around the exalted Son of Man and an exalted Melchizedek.

III. Testing the Canon

Beyond using new methods and reading between the lines all the proposals made test the limits set by the canon. The canonical story establishes such an unshakable connection between Jesus' life, death, and resurrection that his life becomes inexplicable when it stands alone. The various ways in which this expectation is addressed needs further probing. Can a believable image of Jesus be constructed apart from his death and resurrection? What presuppositions about his life are operative when this connection is broken? How far are we really able to establish as historians what the canon calls for? Is there an unresolved conflict between reason and faith? We move now from one end of this particular spectrum to the other to identify how each interpreter addresses the issues at hand.

A. Hollenbach, Frei, Ogden

In his 1981 article Paul Hollenbach reads Jesus' intent in exorcising as political, as an act of insurrection calculated to upset the aura of authority assumed by the ruling class. In his 1982 article Hollenbach sees Jesus' exorcisms as a personal experience of God's rule among the poor, sufficient in its impact to make him abandon the Baptist's sole demand that the powerful repent of their oppressive ways. In the first case Hollenbach puts to one side the canonical suggestion that the meaning of Jesus' healing was Holy Warfare on behalf of establishing God's rule now. In the second case Hollenbach is strangely silent about the canonical juxtaposition of baptism and temptation and its obvious defining of Jesus' temptation not as the burden of an anguished personal conscience but in corporate and Messianic terms as a call to a new vocation.

In the several passages Hollenbach uses to explain Jesus' alleged conversion from being a disciple and colleague of John's to inaugurating a different sort of ministry, he consistently overlooks the assumed Messianic dignity of Jesus underlying each. The tradition assumes that Jesus changes scribal custom (prayer, fasting) because the kingdom is here and he is the bridegroom. His healing is a fulfillment of Isaiah's prophecy. His gathering of the poor makes way for the joyful restoration of Israel. He gives dignity to the Baptist not as a former buddy and fellow baptizer but because he sees so much better than John sees the different ministries they each have in the brand new economy of God.

With all these possibilities supplied by the tradition and no positive evidence to lead us in another direction, for some undeclared reason Hollenbach imagines that in rejecting canonical assumptions he remains more faithfully in the first century, more historical (!) and less theological. Where this well defined suspicion of the canon will lead in his total reading of the Jesus story we have yet to find out as his work progresses.

While Frei and Ogden are not committed to the quest at all we must take note that the particular form of the Jesus story each embraces does allow them to take it seriously in its totality. In this respect each interpreter does honor some sort of canonical pattern. What we know of Jesus establishes for each of them the possibility of salvation.

B. Breech and Smith

For James Breech Jesus is not a man of his own time. To be sure he does point out that Jesus "came from Nazareth, that he was associated with John the Baptist, that he probably borrowed John's Kingdom language . . . that he ate with men and women who were excluded by observant Jews and that his mode of being human evoked a violent response, even death on the cross" (216-17). At the same time, according to Breech, on all the relationships to Israel which the canon assigns to him Jesus was silent, and on all that the canon indicates he said about himself Jesus is silent. In this sense, by confining itself to Jesus' sayings and parables and to what can be gleaned of his environment from them, Breech's book is a violent attack on the canon (216-222). We are not surprised then that Breech says nothing about the outcome of Jesus' life with respect to the canonical version of death and resurrection. He does intimate that Jesus goes on living in the personal mode of transcendence exhibited by his stories, that he expects his disciples to do the same, and that this is what Jesus may mean for us today (213-214).

Morton Smith is equally violent in his treatment of the canon. As we have seen he compares magical traditions, favorable and unfavorable to Jesus, and deduces from this comparison the substratum of Jesus' actual ministry (93-95). All else in the canonical account is a layered re-reading of this magical core, a kind of re-Judaizing of it under the influence of Paul and James (148). The most obvious example of this is their revision of the canonical version of the Lord's Supper. Smith comments, "In all the sources we see it variously interpreted, moralized and adjusted to Old Testament legend, by additions to the wording, by commentary or by location in a secondary theologically motivated framework. When such window dressing is stripped away, what remains is an absolutely primitive figure: a magician God who unites his followers to himself by giving them his body and blood to eat and drink. Can there be any doubt as to which element is original or where it came from?" (146).

On this basis Smith conjectures that Jesus' death was the result of the great public following his magic engendered and the challenge this posed to the status quo as defended by both Galilean scribes and the Jerusalem authorities (36-43). On this basis Smith feels that the acceptance of Jesus' resurrection by his disciples is understandable but otherwise makes no attempt to analyze the history of the post-paschal church (149-152), nor to extend Jesus' story beyond the first century.

C. Bornkamm and Enslin

Bornkamm is immeasurably more respectful of the canon than either Smith or Breech. This respect may be seen in the care with which he traces the journey of Jesus toward Jerusalem and the events of the last week (chapters VI-VIII). Jesus' authority is given a Messianic designation only after his death by his disciples but the movement of broken Messianic hopes we can still detect by reading between the lines is authored by him (172). This history binds together all we need to know to give substance to his trial and death. We are free to speak of a final journey to Jerusalem with his disciples to "seek the final decision" (155) about Jesus' work, as also of this being a "turning point" for him (154). When history is separated from legend we can also speak in truth of a special entry into Jerusalem, a cleansing of the temple, of a *bona fide* conflict between Jesus and the authorities, and of a last supper with his disciples pointing to a kingdom yet to come. Gethsemane and the word at the trial about building and destroying the temple are genuine insights into Jesus' history. The role of Pilate and the denial of Peter and the bearing of the cross by Alexander and Rufus all have eye-witness quality (151-168). Such events of the last week express a basic continuity with his total ministry. "In Jesus' attitude to the law, and in his efforts to put God's will into action we meet again and again the claim and secret of his mission. . . . The calling of the disciples, the choosing of the Twelve and the movement which he originates, can only be thought of in connection with this claim. His entry into the Holy City, the conflict which he there initiates, the cleansing of the Temple all express it" (170).

In view of this faithful and sympathetic reading of Jesus' history it is all the more remarkable that Bornkamm does not comment further about the salvific impact of Jesus' death. Likewise, in view of his meticulous and studied reading of Jesus' post-paschal history in Chapter IX it is also remarkable that he makes no attempt to relate Jesus' death to his resurrection.

He will not succumb, as he says, to the oft-used ploy of explaining how the post-paschal experience of the disciples led to their belief in the resurrection. He soberly insists that their account is genuine. They had the experience which took them by surprise and their faith grew subsequently out of that experience. It was not their faith that created the experience of Jesus' presence but their experience of Jesus' presence that created their subsequent faith. Perhaps the reason for this meticulous care is twofold. On the one hand Bornkamm wants to maintain a rigorous distinction between the believer and the historian (100) on the theory that faith tends to create legends that cloud the outlines of concrete history. As with Breech and Smith but in a more restrained way the tradition is held to be suspect and requires the most vigorous sifting. On the other hand, as we have seen, Bornkamm's overriding interest is in the existential history he had sketched in Chapter III. As with Robinson, Crossan, and Breech the link between Jesus and us lies precisely here, in the authenticity Jesus once generated among his contemporaries and can still generate in us. There is no basic need to insist on or to explain the continued presence of the risen Jesus around which, as Bornkamm himself insists, the whole of the New Testament revolves.

With much the same critical understanding Enslin prunes the tradition as thoroughly as Bornkamm (36-44; 137-148). He finds a flesh-and-blood person who thought himself sent by God as the prophet like Moses prophesied in Scripture (57-70). Contrary to Mark's theory of secrecy, Jesus *was* understood by the people (90-97). The enthusiastic following he thus generated, coupled with his fanatic proclamation of a New Age soon to blossom in Jerusalem itself, made him an enemy of the status quo. Both Jews and Romans conspired to bring about his death as an insurrectionist. He died thinking himself forsaken by God and his mission a failure (36-37, 107, 111-129, 167-208). But the tradition is in error to put so much emphasis on Jesus' death. The contribution Jesus made was his life. By the authority he exercised he so impressed his personality on his disciples that they thought he had been raised from the dead. What really happened was not the resurrection of Jesus but the resurrection of his disciples. It is this that gives him meaning for us today (xiii, 16-17, 91, 128-129, 209-217).

The upshot then is the same for both Bornkamm and Enslin. While they have more respect for the tradition than either Breech or Smith they all four agree in bypassing the salvific nature of Jesus' death. They all four separate his death from his resurrection. Jesus' life, so far as it can be reconstructed, is made to stand alone, i.e. the basic connections that give meaning to Jesus' whole career in the canon are cut. In each case *three* hermeneutic considerations are dominant. *All four scholars believe that the tradition misinterprets Jesus in fundamental ways. All four agree that the historian must replace the believer in pruning tradition for modern consumption. All four agree that a fragmented life of Jesus, torn out of its canonical context, is all that can make sense today for post-Enlightenment man.* As a footnote it should be observed that only Bornkamm and Enslin bother to investigate the post-paschal situation of the church. Enslin declares outright that resurrection as the canon proposes it is simply unthinkable in the modern world (129). Morton Smith seems content to let Jesus the magician remain an inhabitant of the ancient world alone.

D. Flusser and Riches

Flusser deserves special consideration since he writes as a Jew and can not be expected to take seriously the canon's insistence on continuity between life, death, and resurrection. At the same time it must be said that he does take the tradition very seriously indeed and with astonishing receptivity follows up the clues it supplies. From his vantage point Jesus is not only deeply involved in Jewish eschatology but is an innovator in ethical practice. Jesus' revolution on behalf of the poor began long before his death. He went to Jerusalem with intention, defied the authorities there, and dared to think of his eventual resurrection in the spirit of Elijah (122). He died with full knowledge that his mission had failed and perhaps with forgiveness on his lips for his enemies (131-132). Thus Jesus was a celebrated Jew fully engaged in the affairs of his nation. He lives today for Flusser not in the strict canonical sense but by reason of his moral impact. Aside from the reflections on Jesus from ancient to modern times which Flusser appends to his account (133-137), his own words about Jesus' influence today are remarkable indeed. "The enormity of his life, too, speaks to us today, the call of his baptism, the severing of ties with his estranged family and his discovery of a new sublime sonship, the pandemonium of the sick and possessed, and his death on the cross. Therefore the words which Matthew (28:20) puts into the mouth of the risen Lord take on for us, a new, non-ecclesiastical meaning: 'Lo, I am with you always, to the close of the age'" (12).

John Riches also deserves separate mention since he is not proposing to write a full fledged life of Jesus. However, his careful probing of the tradition reveals his sympathy with its basic aims. With charismatic creativity Jesus was a prophet set for the renewal of Israel, a renewal he both initiated and symbolized by his actions (180-189). Toward that transformation he identified with the poor, conducted Holy War on behalf of God's kingdom now, and in so doing created a "subtle dialectic" between this grappling with power assumptions and the vindication of the poor at the final judgment (167).

E. Meyer and Sobrino

It should now be obvious that in the work of Meyer and Sobrino we have reached the other end of the spectrum from Bornkamm and Enslin, not to mention Smith and Breech. Both Meyer and Sobrino trust the clues laid down by the tradition and they do not think it amiss to read the story of Jesus from within the household of faith (Meyer, 1981). They find that the rhythm of that story carries on through life to death and resurrection and far beyond to our own day.

Meyer believes that the tradition intends history. He boldly works on the hypothesis that the aims of Jesus can be deduced from the movement he created. He knows what we have documented thus far; that each interpreter reads between the lines according to the questions he feels able to ask and the answers he thinks are legitimate. He refuses to accept the tyranny of the so-called earliest sources, although this is the point at which he always begins using the most thoroughgoing criteria to establish them.

He sees the intentionality of Jesus' working with the kingdom message of the Baptist but going beyond that in his healing, his message of grace, his choice of disciples from all sections of Israel, and his mission to the Gentiles. He defines Jesus' aim as the joyous eschatological restoration of Israel and relates to this his gathering of the poor and his prescriptive, personal, and revelational ethics. He dares to believe that Jesus' public teaching and actions converge on his esoteric teaching, his riddled words, and his symbolic actions. Action and word interpret each other. He concludes that Jesus "was the builder of the house of God" (201), and as such cleansed the Temple, confident that tribulation would be followed by his own vindication and the emergence of a new Messianic remnant. On this basis his last supper with his disciples was a remnant-forming act. He did all this knowing that he was Messiah prior to his passion and giving himself in love to God on behalf of Israel. He knew that by giving his life he would bring salvation both to Israel and the world (221).

Although Meyer does not move beyond Jesus' intentionality in life, death, and looked-for-vindication, Jon Sobrino boldly declares at the outset that Jesus' ministry is historical, ecclesial, and trinitarian. He sees Jesus' faith tested and triumphant in his ministry, his death as God's Son a vindication of precisely that ministry, and the coming of the Spirit a final validation of God's revelation to us. What God does in his Son and by the sending of the Spirit sets the pattern for our own struggle against sin as agents of his liberating grace.

IV. Conclusions

A. The testing of various methodologies should certainly proceed, as it is now, full steam ahead. It is only by pushing each method to its limits as skillfully as possible and seeing its results that we can judge what is adequate and what is not. Likewise our present happy opportunity in this seminar to share what we are doing with each other should be enlarged and strengthened. I rather suspect that methodological eclecticism will produce more fruitful results than sole reliance on one method alone to the exclusion of others.

B. We need to work *both* on exegetical units of limited scope *and* on the big picture set forth by the canon. We need to ask what makes sense as we interpret Jesus living, dead, and risen. And if the word "risen" raises too many obstacles to understanding we need at the very least to see Jesus as the one in whom the resurrection tradition and the formation and mission of the whole church have their origin. Whatever we finally conclude, we can not be satisfied to explain the life, death, and subsequent influence of Jesus in piecemeal fashion. Was Jesus disappointed and his mission a failure? In that case we must follow this with some explanation of how the church arose and prospered. Was Jesus fulfilled and his mission a success? In that case we must explain why the church put so much weight on his death and resurrection. Given canonical insistence on telling the *whole* story of Jesus, this emphasis on the big picture is an obligation for any and all interpreters, whatever our attitude toward church and canon happens to be. An ancient document can scarcely make any contribution to our understanding unless taken seriously first of all on its own terms.

C. We ought to acknowledge that none of us can be scientifically "objective." Tradition, even in a so-called authentic core of Jesus' teaching, nonetheless is itself the product of interpretation. Each of us carries into the task of interpretation a peculiar bias, whether we decide to read the story of Jesus from outside or from within. It is now incumbent on us to clarify where we stand as interpreters. In sum, we need as participants in the quest (1) to abandon the myth of objectivity, (2) to formulate for public inspection what our personal hermeneutic prejudices are, (3) to formulate for public inspection the total image of Jesus on the basis of which our investigations proceed, and (4) to make explicit how personal bias and total Jesus image are related to each other and to the canon's insistence on reading the story of Jesus in its totality.

BIBLIOGRAPHY

Bornkamm, G.
    1960   *Jesus of Nazareth* (3rd ed., trans. L. and E. McLuskey with James M. Robinson). Harper.

Braun, Herbert
    1979   *Jesus of Nazareth. The Man and His Time* (trans. E. R. Kalin). Fortress.

Breech, James
    1983   *The Silence of Jesus. The Authentic Voice of the Historical Man.* Fortress.

Buchanan, G. W.
    1984   *Jesus, the King and His Kingdom.* Mercer.

Bultmann, R.
    1934   *Jesus and the Word* (1st ed., 1926, trans. from the German by L. P. Smith and E. Huntress). Scribner's.

    1951   *Theology of the New Testament* (trans. K. Grobel). Scribner's.

    1953   "New Testament and Mythology." Pp. 1–44 in H. E. Bartsch (ed.), *Kerygma and Myth: A Theological Debate.* S.P.C.K.

    1964   "The Primitive Christian Kerygma and the Historical Jesus." Pp. 15–42 in C. E. Braaten and R. A. Harrisville (eds. and trans.), *The Historical Jesus and the Kerygmatic Christ.* Abingdon.

Case, S. J.
    1927   *Jesus. A New Biography.* University of Chicago.

Conzelmann, H.
    1973   *Jesus* (trans. J. R. Lord, ed. J. Reumann). Fortress.

Crossan, J. D.
    1973   *In Parables. The Challenge of the Historical Jesus.* Harper.

    1976   *Raid on the Articulate. Comic Eschatology in Jesus and Borges.* Harper.

    1979   *Finding Is the First Act.* Fortress.

    1980   *Cliffs of Fall.* Seabury.

Ebeling, G.
    1961   *The Nature of Faith* (trans. R. G. Smith). Muhlenberg.

Enslin, M.
    1968   *The Prophet from Nazareth* (1st ed., 1961). Schocken.

Flusser, D.
    1969   *Jesus* (1st German ed., 1968,. trans. R. Walls). Herder and Herder.

Frei, Hans W.
    1974   *The Eclipse of Biblical Narrative. A Study in Eighteenth and Nineteenth Century Hermeneutics.* Yale University Press.

Frei, Hans W.
1975   *The Identity of Jesus Christ. The Hermeneutical Bases of Dogmatic Theology.* Fortress.

Fuchs, E.
1964   *Studies of the Historical Jesus* (trans. A. Scobie). SCM. (Studies in Biblical Theology, No. 42).

Funk, R.
1975   *Jesus as Precursor.* Fortress.

1982   *Parables and Presence.* Fortress.

Goppelt, L.
1981   *Theology of the New Testament* (German ed., 1975, Vol. I, trans. J. E. Alsup, ed. J. Roloff). Eerdmans.

Harvey, A. E.
1982   *Jesus and the Constraints of History.* Westminster.

Hollenbach, Paul
1981   "Jesus, Demoniacs, and Public Authorities: A Socio-Historical Study." *JAAR* 49: 567-88.

1982   "The Conversion of Jesus: From Jesus the Baptizer to Jesus the Healer." Pp. 196-219 in *Aufstieg und Niedergang der Römischen Welt,* II. 25, 1 (ed. Wolfgang Haase). de Gruyter.

1983   "Recent Historical Jesus Studies and the Social Sciences." Pp. 61-78 in *Society of Biblical Literature 1983 Seminar Papers* (ed. Kent H. Richards). Scholars Press.

Jeremias, J.
1971   *New Testament Theology.* Scribner.

Käsemann, E.
1964   "The Problem of the Historical Jesus." Pp. 15-47 in W. J. Montague (trans.), *Essays on New Testament Themes.* SCM. (Studies in Biblical Theology, No. 41).

Klausner, J.
1925   *Jesus of Nazareth, His Life, Times and Teaching* (1st ed. 1922, trans. H. Danby). Macmillan.

Manson, T. W.
1977   *The Servant-Messiah* (1st ed., 1953). Baker Book House.

Marxsen, W.
1979   *The Beginnings of Christology* (trans. P. J. Achtemeier and L. Nieting). Fortress.

Meyer, Ben F.
1979   *The Aims of Jesus.* SCM.

1981   "The 'Inside' of the Jesus Event." Pp. 197-210 in *Creativity and Method: Essays in Honor of B. Lonergan, S.J.* (ed. M. Lamb). Marquette University Press.

Niebuhr, Richard R.
    1957   *Resurrection and Historical Reason: A Study in Theological Method.*
                Scribner's.

Ogden, S. M.
    1961   *Christ without Myth.* Harper.

    1982   *The Point of Christology.* Harper.

Ogden, S. M., and Harvey, V. A.
    1964   "How New is the 'New Quest of the Historical Jesus.'" Pp. 197-242 in
                The Historical Jesus and the Kerygmatic Christ (ed. C. E. Braaten and
                R. A. Harrisville). Abingdon.

Riches, John
    1982   *Jesus and the Transformation of Judaism.* Seabury.

Robinson, James
    1959   *A New Quest of the Historical Jesus.* SCM. (Studies in Biblical Theol-
                ogy, No. 25).

Sandmel, S.
    1965   *We Jews and Jesus.* Oxford.

Schillebeeckx, E.
    1979   *Jesus. An Experiment in Christology* (1st ed., 1974, trans. U. H.
                Nelissen). Seabury.

    1980   *Christ. The Experience of Jesus as Lord.* Seabury.

    1981   *Interim Report on the Books Jesus and Christ.* Crossroad.

Schonfield, H.
    1966   *The Passover Plot.* Bantam.

Smith, Morton
    1978   *Jesus the Magician.* Harper and Row.

Sobrino, Jon
    1978   *Christology at the Crossroads: A Latin American Approach* (1st ed.,
                trans. John Drury, 1976). Orbis.

Tannehill, R. C.
    1975   *The Sword of His Mouth.* Fortress.

Vermes, G.
    1981   *Jesus the Jew* (1st ed., 1974). Fortress.

    1983   *Jesus and the World of Judaism.* Fortress.

The Composition of Acts 3-5:
Narrative Development and Echo Effect

Robert C. Tannehill

Methodist Theological School in Ohio

This paper is a piece of a larger work on Luke-Acts, which might be called a commentary but not of the traditional kind, for it will focus on features of Luke-Acts ignored or treated lightly in traditional commentaries. It will study Luke-Acts as a unitary narrative. This requires attention to continuous plot lines which unify the story. But, as we will see below, linear plot development is overlaid with patterns of recurrence which enrich the context in which individual events can be viewed, helping to give them imaginative resonance. I am trying to keep the two volume work continually in view as the interpretive context for understanding each part of it. The significance of particular features of an episode may only appear when we note connections with other sections of Luke-Acts. The work as a whole is the best guide to the special perspectives and values of the implied author. Apart from an understanding of Luke-Acts as a unitary narrative, judgments about these perspectives and values are hazardous, for in narrative it is always possible to qualify or undermine the supposed implications of earlier scenes through later developments.

I am not just searching for theological themes, if by that is meant a set of static statements about God, Jesus, and humanity which are supposedly the essence of the author's message. The implied author does have theological perspectives which limit and control the intended meanings of the story, and these must be understood in order to interpret it. But the author's methods also give the story imaginative impact, stimulating an imaginative response from readers which cannot be entirely controlled. A "narrative world" is being created[1] which is an imaginative world, both in the sense that it is the product of a human imagination and also in the sense that it engages others imaginatively. This is both power and risk, for basic perceptions of readers may be changed through this imaginative engagement, but no author can completely control what readers will make of the work once the imagination is let loose.

Furthermore, we must always be sensitive to how repeated themes function within a narrative as a developing whole. Themes which, isolated from their narrative context, appear to be constant may actually shift significantly in meaning through some new development in the plot. Thematic expectations at the beginning may be recalled to highlight their disappointment or their fulfillment in some unexpected way. Thus we must keep in mind where we are in a story that may be full of twists and turns, rather than reducing Luke-Acts to a set of static theological themes.

---

[1] See Norman Petersen, *Literary Criticism for New Testament Critics* (Philadelphia: Fortress, 1978) 40.

Although we will focus primarily on Acts 3-5, we must recognize that Acts 1:1-8:3 is carefully composed as a unified narrative of the mission in Jerusalem. Continuity is maintained as events develop from one scene to the next, finally reaching a climax with Stephen's speech and death. In the course of this development, the crucial decision faced by the people of Jerusalem and their leaders is revealed with clarity, and the opposition to the apostles' message gradually develops to the point of drastic action. Along with this major plot development there is a minor theme of the unity of the church expressed through sharing of possessions (2:44-45, 4:32-37), a unity of heart and soul which is threatened but, through prompt action, restored (5:1-11, 6:1-6).[2] The scenes at the beginning of chapters 3 and 6 may seem to introduce new material which causes a major break in the narrative, but when we read on, we discover that these scenes will contribute to the continuous plot which unites Acts 1:1-8:3. The healing of the lame man causes a series of important events, and the choice of the seven in 6:1-6 introduces Stephen, the key figure in the next stage of the conflict which dominates Acts 4-7.

I. NARRATIVE DEVELOPMENT IN ACTS 3-5

1. Healing and Speech to the People

The healing of the lame man instigates a series of encounters among the apostles, the "people," and the Sanhedrin in 3:11-5:42. The healing causes "all the people" to gather (3:11), which becomes the occasion for Peter's speech in 3:12-26. This speech in turn provokes the temple authorities to arrest Peter and John (4:1-3). The whole sequence of events in 3:1-4:22 takes place on an afternoon and the next day and is directly caused by the healing of the lame man and by Peter's speech to the crowd attracted by this event. There are repeated references to the healing of the lame man in this section as Peter and John explain what it reveals about the "name" of Jesus Christ and the Sanhedrin struggles with the question of how to respond to what has happened (3:12, 16; 4:7-12, 14, 16). The section ends as it began with a reference to the healing of the lame man and its effect on the people (4:21-22). Thus the sequence of events in 3:1-4:22 is unified causally, one event provoking the next. It is unifed temporally by the short span of time. It is also unified by the persistent presence of the healed man with Peter and John. Remarkably, the lame man is physically present even at the hearing before the Sanhedrin after the apostles' arrest (4:14). He is a persistent reminder of the power of Jesus' name.

The causal chain does not end at 4:22. The hearing of Peter and John before the Sanhedrin concludes with the threats of the Sanhedrin, who are trying to force the apostles to stop speaking in the name of Jesus. The prayer of the church which follows in 4:23-31 is a response to this threat, and, following a second arrest and hearing, the complaint of the Sanhedrin is that the apostles have disobeyed the command not to teach in Jesus' name (5:28). They attempt again to enforce their order, but their efforts are ineffectual. So 5:17-42 is tied to 4:5-31 because it is the continuation of the story of the church's response to the threats of the Sanhedrin. The one section also reduplicates the

---

[2]See Joseph Tyson, "The Problem of Food in Acts: A Study of Literary Patterns with Particular Reference to Acts 6:1-7," *Society of Biblical Literature 1979 Seminar Papers* (Missoula: Scholars Press, 1979) 1. 69-76.

other, each moving from arrest to hearing to release, thereby emphasizing the courage of the apostles and the inability of the Sanhedrin to respond effectively.

Acts 2-5 is also united by the frequent references to the "name" of the Lord or of Jesus Christ, references which are especially characteristic of this section of Acts. This begins with the reference to the "name of the Lord" at the end of the Joel quotation in 2:21, followed by the reference to being baptized "in the name of Jesus Christ" in 2:38. Then the name of Jesus Christ is presented as the effective power behind the healing of the lame man (3:6, 16; 4:7, 10, 12), and there are repeated references to Jesus' name as the apostles encounter the rulers' threats (4:17, 18, 30; 5:28, 40, 41). In following chapters the "name" of Jesus is also important. Indeed, Christians are described as those who "call upon the name" (9:14, 21; 22:16), a reminder of the Joel quotation in Acts 2:21 with which the theme is introduced. Following Acts 2-5 references to the name of Jesus are first associated with the mission of Philip in Samaria (8:12, 16) and then with Paul's call and early preaching (9:14, 15, 16, 21, 27, 28), perhaps as a deliberate means of emphasizing the continuity of the preaching of Philip and Paul with the preaching of the apostles. After Acts 9, however, references to Jesus' name become less frequent and concentrated, occurring at 10:43, 48; 15:26; 16:18; 19:5, 13, 17; 21:13; 22:16; 26:9. The comparative infrequency of references to Jesus name in Acts 10-28 suggests that the frequent references in Acts 2-5 and 8-9 are not merely the result of habits of expression but show deliberate emphasis in a section of Acts where this theme contributes to narrative continuity. The lame man becomes a paradigm of salvation through the name of the Lord, in fulfillment of the Scriptural promise quoted in 2:21, and the promised salvation then passes to others through the missions of the apostles, Philip, and Paul.

The narrator places some emphasis on the lame man's "leaping" immediately following the healing, using the rare word ἅλλομαι and its compound form ἐξάλλομαι together in 3:8.[3] This not only demonstrates the healing vividly but, for those as familiar with the prophecies of Isaiah as our author is, recalls Isa 35:6, part of a passage which probably influenced the summary description of Jesus' mighty acts in Luke 7:22. In the context of Acts 3, this allusion to Isaiah would support Peter's claim that "all the prophets . . . proclaimed these days" (3:24).

Peter's second speech is given in response to the amazed crowd which gathers after the healing of the lame man. Peter begins by correcting a possible false impression, that the apostles had "made him walk by our own power or piety" (3:12). In Acts, Peter and Paul do mighty works similar in kind to those of Jesus in the Gospel. Therefore, it is important to make clear that these mighty works are performed not by the disciple's own power but by the power of Jesus' name, as Peter will explain in 3:16. The same sort of correction is made more dramatically when Paul heals a lame man, for Paul and Barnabas must stop the people of Lystra from sacrificing to them as gods (14:14-15). Peter, too, must correct a gentile who treats him as more than human (10:25-26). The care with which Peter and Paul distinguish between themselves and the power which is at work through them contrasts with the claims of religious charlatans like Theudas and Simon Magus who claim that they themselves are "somebody" or "somebody great" (5:36, 8:9). The sensitivity which Peter and Paul show on this issue is also an indication of the change

---

[3] ἐξάλλομαι occurs only here in the NT. ἅλλομαι is used in Acts 14:10 in a scene which parallels the healing of the lame man in Acts 3. Elsewhere in the NT it is found only at John 4:14.

that has taken place in Jesus' followers through the appearance of the risen Christ and the gift of the Spirit. While in Luke the disciples engaged in disputes over who was the greatest, even at the Last Supper (Luke 22:24, cf. 9:46), Jesus' warning that "everyone who exalts himself will be humbled, and the one who humbles himself will be exalted" (Luke 14:11, 18:14; cf. 9:48, 22:26) has now taken hold in the lives of Jesus' witnesses.

Even more clearly than the Pentecost speech, the speech in Solomon's portico aims to awaken repentance. It must be understood in its narrative context, for it addresses a specific audience, the Jerusalem Jews who lived at the time of Jesus' death and (in the eyes of Peter and the implied author) were responsible for it. The special involvement of the audience in what has happened and is happening is stressed. They are involved in two ways: (1) They "delivered up and denied" him, asked for a murderer in his stead, and "killed" him (3:13-15). The accusation is made vivid by the repeated verbs and by descriptive details from Luke's passion story (Pilate's decision to "release ἀπολύειν]" Jesus— cf. Luke 23:16; the crowd asking for Barabbas, the "murderer"—cf. Luke 23:18-19), and the involvement of the audience receives further stress through the double use of the emphatic nominative pronoun "you (ὑμεῖς)." (2) Emphatic second person plural pronouns return at the end of the speech, now in order to emphasize the audience's involvement in the promised blessing (3:25—emphatic nominative pronoun; 3:26—dative pronoun in emphatic position at the being of the sentence). This emphasis may suggest that the rather frequent use of the second person plural pronoun throughout 3:19-26 is also significant.[4] The reference in 3:20 to Jesus as "the Messiah chosen for you" is also a significant indication of the concern to make clear that it is precisely their Messiah and their promises concerning which they must now make a decision. Thus the application of the message to this audience is especially emphasized, and this is particularly clear at the beginning and end of the speech. The audience is involved in God's work through Jesus both negatively and positively. They bear responsibility for rejecting and killing Jesus. Nevertheless, God is working through Jesus and his witnesses to fulfill the covenantal promise to them. To be sure, there is a hint at the end of the speech that the promised blessing is not for them alone, but it is for them *first*, for they are "the sons of the prophets and of the covenant" (3:25-26). Peter makes clear that the promised blessing is still available to them, if they repent.

The stress on the audience's involvement, negatively and positively, in God' work through Jesus heightens both danger and opportunity. It discloses a situation of high tension, a tension which can only be released through turning away from past rejection and accepting the promised blessing through Jesus. The speech is shaped to fit its narrative setting and to move its audience in the narrative to action. It is meant to call the people of Jerusalem to repentance. Thus Dibelius was mistaken when he concluded that the author of Acts is presenting the type of Christian sermon customary in his own day, with the implication: "This is how the gospel is preached and ought to be preached!"[5] The author has composed a speech which, in his opinion, was appropriate to the speaker and the audience. This is not surprising, for appropriateness was an important criterion of good speech in Greco-Roman rhetoric, and in Greco-Roman education students were

---

[4]The three occurrences in the following sentence are especially striking: "The Lord *your* God will raise up a prophet for *you* from *your* brethren, a prophet like me" (3:22) (my emphasis). The first *your* is textually uncertain. The LXX of Deut 18:15 has singular rather than plural pronouns in all three cases.

[5]Martin Dibelius, *Studies in the Acts of the Apostles* (London: SCM, 1956) 165.

trained in the art of "impersonation (προσωποποι ία)."[6] Thus the speech has narrative significance. It is meant to move characters in the story to action. It directs the readers' attention forward to indications of how the people of Jerusalem will respond to Peter, for fateful decisions are being made.

Peter still hopes, and encourages the people of Jerusalem to hope, that they will share in the "times of the restoration of all that God spoke" through the prophets. This will include the sending of their Messiah to them, provided they repent (3:19-21). Since the birth stories in Luke, readers have been led to expect that Jesus would establish a Messianic kingdom for Israel. Gabriel told Mary that her son "will reign over the house of Jacob for ever" on the throne of David (Luke 1:32-33), and Zechariah blessed God for the "horn of salvation . . . in the house of David" whom God has "raised up" (Luke 1:69). This fulfills what God "spoke through the mouth of his holy prophets from of old" (1:70), a statement which is repeated almost verbatim by Peter in Acts 3:21. Peter's statement includes the same hope of the Messianic kingdom promised in Scripture, a kingdom which, according to Zechariah, will bring political freedom for the Jewish people (Luke 1:71, 74). Acts 1:6-7 also supports the view that the hope which Peter holds out to the Jews of Jerusalem in 3:20-21 includes the Messianic kingdom for Israel. The disciples ask the risen Jesus, "Are you at this time restoring the kingdom to Israel?" Peter's statement in 3:21 is not only linked to the disciples' question about the kingdom for Israel by the unusual words "restore" and "restoration (ἀποκαθιστάνω, ἀποκατάστασις)"[7] but also by the references to "times" and "seasons (χρόνοι, καιροί)" in both passages (1:7, 3:20-21). While Jesus in 1:7 indicates that his followers cannot know the times and seasons, he does not reject the hope for Israel's restored kingdom. So authoritative speakers at the beginning of Luke (Gabriel and Zechariah) declare that the Messianic kingdom for Israel is part of God's promises in Scripture which are being realized through Jesus, and this hope remains alive at least through Peter's speech in Acts 3. If this hope is not fulfilled, the story has taken a tragic turn, and the high hopes and expectations for Israel's redemption encouraged in the story itself will emphasize the tragedy.[8]

The Jews of Jerusalem must repent in order to share in the promised times of relief and restoration (3:19-21). Even though there is no indication yet of the reaction of Peter's hearers, his speech contains some hints of what will happen. The statement with which Peter closes, "To you first . . . God sent his servant," indicates that the offer of salvation to the Jerusalem Jews is only the first stage of a longer process. This should be no threat to Peter's audience, for those who know the prophecies of Isaiah should know that God intends to bring salvation to gentiles as well as Jews. Nevertheless, the inclusion of gentiles will, in fact, become a cause of Jewish rejection in later scenes (13:44-

---

[6]See Donald L. Clark, *Rhetoric in Greco-Roman Education* (New York: Columbia University, 1957) 100: "Language should be appropriate to the speaker, to the audience, and to the subject." Training in "impersonation" was one of the prescribed "elementary exercises" in Greco-Roman education. Students were asked to "compose an imaginary monolog which might appropriately be spoken or written by a historical, legendary, or fictitious person under given circumstances" (ibid., 199). See also William S. Kurz, "Hellenistic Rhetoric in the Christological Proof of Luke-Acts," CBQ 42 (1980) 186.

[7]ἀποκαθιστάνω or ἀποκαθίστημι is used once more in Luke-Acts, of the restoration of a hand (Luke 6:10), and occurs six times in the rest of the NT. Acts 3:21 is the only occurrence of the noun in the NT.

[8]See Robert C. Tannehill, "Israel in Luke-Acts: A Tragic Story," *JBL* (forthcoming).

48, 22:21-22). This cannot be a cause of rejection in Acts 3-5, for the reference to the gentile mission in 3:25-26 can only be understood in the context of Luke-Acts as a whole.[9] Here we have a subtle hint of a future development that will involve Jewish resistance. In 3:23 the harsh warning about the possibility of being "destroyed from the people" may also anticipate a downward turn of the plot for some of Peter's audience. Immediately following Peter's speech the temple officials will demonstrate their refusal to hear the prophet like Moses and Peter, his witness (4:1-3). Such anticipation of rejection in the speech of a major character prior to its actual appearance is typical of Luke-Acts (see Luke 4:23-30, Acts 13:40-47).

In 3:17 Peter says, "Brothers, I know that you acted in ignorance, just as also your rulers did." This failure to recognize and accept God's servant requires repentance, as Peter goes on to say, but it is something which can be forgiven. Paul, too, will refer to the ignorance of the inhabitants of Jerusalem and their rulers, as well as the gentiles' ignorance—ignorance of the true God—which requires repentance from them (13:27; 17:23, 30). The mission speeches in Acts are efforts to overcome this ignorance, which amounts to an ideologically caused blindness leading to the denial that God and God's Messiah can be what Luke-Acts proclaims them to be. Faced with this ignorance and blindness, the preachers repeatedly cry, "Let this be known to you" (2:14; see 2:36, 4:10, 13:38, 28:28). For the inhabitants of Jerusalem, both the people and their rulers, enlightenment involves recognition of their own responsibility for Jesus' death. When this happens (as in 2:37), we have a recognition scene similar to the recognition scenes in tragic drama, in which characters, acting in ignorance, recognize a tragic event after it has happened.[10] However, Peter makes clear that it is still possible to correct their error. The denouement need not be tragic.

The new possibility is dramatized by the story of Jesus' followers in Luke, for until they encountered the risen Christ, the disciples shared the ignorance of the people of Jerusalem. They did not understand (ἠγνόουν) Jesus' statements that he must be rejected and killed (Luke 9:45; see 18:34). The ignorance of both the disciples and the people of Jerusalem includes a failure to understand what was written by the prophets (Luke 18:31; 24:25-27, 32, 44-46; Acts 13:27; cf. 3:17-18). Thus Peter, in speaking to the people of Jerusalem, is trying to convey the new and revolutionary understanding which removed his own blind ignorance when he was instructed by the risen Christ.[11] The issue is whether his hearers will recognize what they have done and repent or whether their blindness will continue and harden.

The narrator emphasizes strongly that the "people," indeed, "all the people," saw the healed man and heard Peter's speech, the term λαός appearing no less than five times just before and just after the speech in Acts 3. This term is especially frequent in Acts 2:47-6:12 and plays a role in a significant development. In 2:47 we are told that the

---

[9]In 3:25 the use of πατριαί ("families") instead of ἔθνη ("nations," "gentiles")—the reading of Gen 18:18 LXX—introduces ambiguity, permitting an application to the Jewish "families of the land."

[10]On the role of "ignorance (ἄγνοια)" in the tragic plot see Aristotle, *Poetics* 1453b-1454a. On "recognition (ἀναγνώρισις)" see ibid., 1450.

[11]This point is noted by M. Dennis Hamm, "This Sign of Healing, Acts 3:1-10: A Study in Lucan Theology" (diss., Saint Louis University, 1975) 156. Hamm also notes that Peter, who accuses the Jerusalem Jews of having "denied" Jesus (3:13-14), is himself "a denier only recently reformed" (p. 119).

Jerusalem Christians were viewed favorably by "all the people." This favor continues. The temple authorities, who in 4:1-3 begin to oppose the apostles, are unable to act effectively because the apostles enjoy the people's support (4:21; 5:13, 26). The rulers are annoyed because the apostles are teaching the people (4:2), usurping their own authority. They try to stop this by threats but fail. The situation mirrors the passion story, where the people support Jesus as he teaches in the temple, preventing the authorities from taking action against him (Luke 19:47-48; 20:19, 26; 21:38; 22:2). In Acts the people are a fertile field for the Christian mission (see 2:41, 47: 4:4; 5:14), yet, just as in the passion story, they are fickle and easily swayed by false charges. The opposition turns deadly when opponents are finally able to arouse the people by false charges against Stephen (6:11-13). In Jesus' trial before Pilate the people, despite their previous support, suddenly shift their attitude and join in calling for Jesus' death (Luke 23:13-25).[12] Readers will be reminded of this in Acts 4:25-28. The role of the people in Stephen's death is not as clear as in the passion story, but, following this event, the Jewish people appear frequently as an opposing and threatening group, which represents a significant shift from the way in which the people was presented in Acts 2-5. The converted Saul must escape a conspiracy by "the Jews" of Damascus (9:23) and then encounters in Jerusalem the same opposition that Stephen faced (9:29). In 12:3-4, 11 "the people of the Jews" is a threatening group, from which Peter must be rescued. In this passage Herod and the Jewish people stand together as persecutors, just as another Herod and the people of Israel joined together against Jesus, according to Acts 4:25-28. As the mission of Paul develops, the Jews of Antioch turn against him (13:45, 50), and in Acts 14 we begin to hear of Jews who are persistent persecutors, even following Paul from city to city (14:19). Such opposition by Jews appears repeatedly. It is significant that in the scene of Paul's arrest in Jerusalem, references to the "people (λαός)" reappear with sudden frequency (21:28, 30, 36, 39, 40). Here we find reminders of the passion story in Luke, including the cry "Away with him!" (21:36, 22:22; cf. Luke 23:18, which differs from Matthew and Mark). It is the "people" who shout for Paul's death, just as they supported Herod's persecution of the church according to Acts 12:3-4, 11. The charge that the Christian mission endangers the Jewish people and its way of life is false, as Paul will reiterate as late as 28:17. Nevertheless, the Jewish "people," who are presented as supporters of the Christian mission in Acts 2-5, will act primarily as opponents following the death of Stephen. This shift in attitude has a major effect on the course of the narrative.

2. First Arrest and Interrogation

Conflict first arises with the temple authorities. This involves a split between the people and their religious leaders. The leaders feel threatened by the apostles and their message; the people regard them favorably. The conflict between the early church and nonbelieving Judaism evolves by careful stages and only after there are strong indications of the powerful impact of the works and words of the apostles on the people of Jerusalem.

This arrest and the following release is the first of a series of arrests and releases of the preachers of the Word in Acts. The extensive development of the theme of rescue

---

[12]On the role of the people in Luke's passion story, see David L. Tiede, *Prophecy and History in Luke-Acts* (Philadelphia: Fortress, 1980) 103-18.

in Acts suggests that the implied author believes in the possibility of rescue of the missionary by divine intervention, either miraculously or through a human instrument, but also knows that the missionary does not always escape. The basic belief is in the power of God's purpose to fulfill itself in the world in spite of, or even by means of, the suffering caused by human opposition.

It is only as the apostles stand before the Sanhedrin, facing the first powerful opposition, that the full significance of the Joel quotation in 2:21 and of the healing of the lame man is made clear. The promise from Scripture quoted in 2:21, "Everyone who calls on the name of the Lord will be saved," is reflected in the exhortation of Peter to "be saved" in 2:40 and in the reference to "those being saved" in 2:47. But these general references are not enough. In Acts 3-4 the healed lame man, who in his leaping demonstrates the fulfillment of the prophecies (see Isa 35:6), becomes a paradigm of salvation through Jesus' name. The healed man takes on this significance through the speeches which follow the healing. Peter's statement in 3:12 that he and John had not healed the man "by our own power" raises the question of whose power is behind this wonder. A first answer is given in 3:16. Acts 3:16 is an overloaded and awkward sentence, but close inspection suggests reasons for its awkwardness. It places great emphasis on faith and on Jesus' name as the keys to the healing of the lame man. First a prepositional phrase linking the two key concepts is placed at the beginning of the sentence as a heading: "On the basis of faith in his name." This is followed by two linked sentences with "his name" and "faith" as subjects, arranged chiastically so that these two key terms are brought together ("this one . . . his name, and the faith which is through him . . ."). The result is emphasis on "faith" and "his name," and on their close connection with each other, through repetition, through making them active causes of the healing, and through word order.[13] The emphasis on faith does not fit the healing story itself. The lame man did not show faith prior to being healed; indeed, he was expecting alms, not healing (3:5-6). The emphasis on faith is the belated addition of an element which is necessary if the healing of the lame man is to be understood as a paradigm of salvation through Jesus, for "those being saved" (2:47) are "the believers" (2:44).

The first hearing before the Sanhedrin continues the development of the paradigmatic significance of the healed lame man. The question of the Sanhedrin in 4:7 borrows the language previously used by Peter in connection with the healing ("by what power"— cf. 3:12; "by what name"—cf. 3:6, 16), thereby connecting this scene to the preceding narrative and providing a perfect setup for Peter's disclosure of the full meaning of the healing.[14] In answer to the question by whom this man "has been saved (σέσωται)," Peter proclaims that it was "by the name of Jesus Christ." The verb σῴζω can, of course, be applied to healing, but the choice of this word here is an important indication that the healing is being transformed into a symbol of something greater. The combination of salvation and the name of the Lord first appeared in 2:21, and in 2:38-40 salvation was related to the release of sins, the gift of the Spirit, and the fulfillment of the promise. While the reference to the lame man being saved (or healed) in 4:9 may be calculated ambiguity, Peter's climactic statement in 4:12 makes clear that the healing is a symbol of a multidimensional salvation which includes all the benefits previously promised to

---

[13]On 3:16 see Gerhard Schneider, *Die Apostelgeschichte* (Freiburg: Herder, 1980) 1. 320-21.
[14]Admittedly, this is a bit too neat for modern ideas of verisimilitude in narrative.

those who repent and call on Jesus' name. Peter tells the Sanhedrin that the name of Jesus is the means "by which we must be saved." The salvation which the lame man received represents a greater salvation which is offered to all: the apostles, the Sanhedrin, and "all the people of Israel" (4:10). Indeed, Jesus' name is the inescapable decision point concerning salvation for Peter's hearers, because "there is no other name under heaven" given to people for salvation.[15] For Peter's audience this salvation does not mean healing of lameness but the gifts of repentance, release of sins, and the blessings of the Messianic kingdom. The healed lame man is the continuing symbol of the salvation for all offered in Jesus' name.

According to 4:13, Peter's words in 4:8-12 are a demonstration of παρρησία (boldness, especially boldness of speech in circumstances that might inhibit frank speech). Peter demonstrates boldness both in his proclamation of the name of Jesus and in his blunt accusation of the rulers for their rejection of Jesus. The short speeches in 4:8-12 and 5:29-32 are important because, in the former, the theme of salvation in Jesus' name is developed, and, in the latter, readers are reminded of themes from the Pentecost speech, thus rounding off the series of speeches by the apostles in Jerusalem. But these short speeches are also important because they dramatically demonstrate the *persistent* speaking of the Word in the face of opposition. It is dramatically important that the apostles repeat what they have said in spite of threats from the powerful. The importance of boldness in the face of opposition is made clear by the church's prayer for such παρρησία and by the answer to that prayer (4:29, 31), as well as by the repeated declarations of allegiance to God's command, rather than the Sanhedrin's, in 4:19-20, 5:29.

The authorities command the apostles to stop teaching in the name of Jesus and back this command with threats (4:17-18). This threatening command heightens the tension in the situation and provides a further test of Peter and John, a test which they immediately pass, defiantly announcing that they will not stop preaching (4:19-20). Their defiant words are a reaffirmation of the commission which they received when the risen Christ charged them to be his witnesses (Luke 24:48, Acts 1:8). The statements in 4:19-20 epitomize the apostles' stance in a dramatic situation, which helps to give the declaration impact. This declaration will be repeated in 5:29, again drawing the contrast between God and human authorities, and even Gamaliel will warn the Sanhedrin that it must respect the difference between what is "from God" and what is "from humans," lest they become foolish "fighters against God (θεομάχοι)" (5:38-39). The repetition of this contrast between divine and human authority in several dramatic scenes and from the mouths of both the apostles and Gamaliel indicates emphasis, suggesting that we are encountering narrative rhetoric which is meant to convey a message not only between characters in the story but also from the implied author to the reader. This message indicates approval of those who, in proclaiming the name of Jesus, obey God rather than humans and suggests their boldness as a model for others. It is also a message about how the story is to be interpreted. This is a story about what happens when a purpose which is "from God" is recognized by persons willing to obey God in spite of human hostility.

The defiance of Peter and John in 4:19-20 reveals the impotence of the Sanhedrin, for it can only make additional threats and release the apostles. Nevertheless, the narra-

---

[15]The δεῖ in 4:12 probably refers, as elsewhere, to a necessity which derives from God's purpose, in this case God's saving purpose through Jesus Christ which aims at salvation for "all flesh" in accordance with the promise of Isa 40:5 (cf. Luke 3:6).

tive leaves open the question of what the Sanhedrin will do if the apostles not only state their defiance but also disobey the Sanhedrin's command to stop preaching. This uncertainty enables the conflict to develop, moving to a new stage in 5:17ff.

The prayer scene in 4:23-31, in which the church prays for boldness in preaching in the face of threats, makes clear the source of the boldness already demonstrated by Peter and John. This scene also places the developing conflict in the context of sacred paradigms provided by Scripture and the passion story of Jesus, a matter that I will discuss in Part II, 2. The church appeals to God both for the power to speak the Word boldly and for the continuation of the signs and wonders through Jesus' name (4:29-30). The importance attributed to the healed lame man as a sign of Jesus' saving power, a sign recognizable even by outsiders and opponents, suggests why signs and wonders have an important role in strengthening a mission under pressure, in the author's eyes. Both aspects of the church's appeal are answered. Bold and powerful speaking is recorded in 4:31, 33. "Many signs and wonders" are reported in 5:12-16, along with the addition of new believers to the church. Individual healings are not reported, but some details emphasize the eagerness of the multitude, who come even from surrounding cities, bringing their sick, all of whom were being healed. This leads into the next stage of the conflict with the Sanhedrin. Just as the healing of the lame man and Peter's preaching to the crowd led to the first arrest, so now the continued preaching and healing which is attracting multitudes leads to a second arrest and the attempt of the high priest's party to enforce the previous prohibition of preaching in Jesus' name.

3. Second Arrest and Interrogation

The importance of the conflict with the temple authorities is made clear by the space devoted to it in Acts 4-7. The conflict develops in three stages (the third focusing on Stephen), and each stage is dramatized through a face to face confrontation between the temple authorities and Jesus' witnesses, with speeches in direct discourse.[16] The narrative makes the similarity between the confrontations in Acts 4 and 5 especially clear. Similar wording is used in 4:1-3 and 5:17-18 to introduce the two episodes. In both cases we have a sequence of arrest, imprisonment, hearing before the Sanhedrin with a short speech by an apostle, deliberation by the Sanhedrin while the apostles are outside, and release of the apostles, even though they continue to defy the ban placed on their preaching.

The narrator makes use of these similar sequences to present an evolving conflict which moves toward a crisis. The repetitive sequences contribute to the development, for the situation in Acts 5 is not exactly the same as in Acts 4. Both parties must deal with the fact that the apostles have defied the command not to teach in Jesus' name (see 5:28). The previous threats by the high priestly party would seem to require them to take punitive action or else acquiesce in the loss of their own authority. The stakes have increased since the first encounter. Certain differences in detail between Acts 4 and 5 show this increase in tension. In Acts 5 the apostles in general, not just Peter and John, are arrested. There is imminent danger of death (5:33), and the apostles do not escape without physical suffering through flogging (5:40). Furthermore, the high priest and his

---

[16]A narrator can highlight material by presenting it in a dramatic scene or subordinate it in a brief summary. This material is highlighted in dramatic scenes.

party are reacting not only to the apostles' refusal to keep silent but also to the accusation that the Sanhedrin is responsible for Jesus' death and must repent (5:28). The teaching which they are trying to suppress is not only a word about Jesus but also a stinging word about themselves. The apostles repeat their charge and their offer of repentance and forgiveness (5:30-31), bringing the narrative to the brink of crisis, for the hearers are infuriated and want to do away with them (5:33). But then the tension relaxes as Gamaliel intervenes.

This, however, is not the end of the conflict. After a brief narrative which introduces Stephen, we find a third scene in which a witness of Jesus[17] is brought before the Sanhedrin (6:11-8:1). To be sure, a new protagonist has been introduced, the accusation against his hearers at great length. Nevertheless, this is a new phase of the same conflict, with the Sanhedrin still trying to suppress the witness to Jesus. This time the conflict comes to the brink of crisis and spills over. The action contemplated in 5:33 is carried out against this new witness: Stephen is killed. The continuity is made clear to the reader by the use of the same verb of strong emotion, the verb διεπρίοντο (literally, "they were being sawn through," Acts 5:33, 7:54, and only there in the New Testament). In the one case this leads to the desire to "do away with" the apostles (5:33). In the other case it leads to the actual "doing away with" Stephen (8:1). Thus in Acts 4-7 we have a continuous narrative which depicts a series of similar confrontations, each representing a surge toward the crisis marked by Stephen's death and the great persecution which accompanied it.

The arrest and hearing in Acts 5 also exceeds the similar sequence of events in Acts 4 in that the apostles are rescued from prison by an angel of the Lord. This is narrated briefly and without dramatic emphasis. As much attention is given to the angel's command to continue speaking in the temple as to the opening of the prison. Furthermore, the rescue from prison does not affect the course of the plot, for the apostles are still in danger and must still appear before the Sanhedrin. The rescue from prison does, however, provide the basis for the following scene (5:21b-26), which is developed with direct discourse and dramatic detail despite the fact that the apostles are not present. This scene is an ironic description of the embarrassment and confusion of the high priest and his party when they discover that the imprisoned apostles have vanished. The scene is introduced with a solemn formality which contributes to its burlesque quality ("the Sanhedrin and all the senate of the sons of Israel," 5:21). The scene focuses on the reports of messengers who tell the Sanhedrin what the reader already knows, provoking smiles at their surprise and confusion. In 5:23, part of the first messenger's report, we find some of the descriptive detail that we might have expected in the earlier narrative of the rescue from prison. The messenger makes clear that the expected security measures were carried out, yet the apostles are gone. The narrator's focus on the report to the Sanhedrin, rather than on the rescue itself, shows that the primary interest here is not in miraculous rescues as such but in the impotence of human authorities to control the course of events. Although the apostles end up just where they would have been apart from the prison release—standing before the Sanhedrin accused of disobedience—the threat from the Sanhedrin has been undermined by irony and burlesque. The point which Gamaliel will later make ("If it is from God, you will not be able to destroy them"; 5:39) has already been made by the narrator through the rescue from prison and the ensuing

---

[17]Stephen, like the apostles and Paul, is called Jesus' "witness" in 22:20.

scene of discovery. Here we have an instance of reinforcement through reiteration. A message is first suggested by an event and then clearly stated in the interpretive commentary of a story character.[18]

The rescue from prison by an angel in 5:19-20 is accompanied by the command to continue speaking to the people in the temple, an activity and place which directly challenge the authority of the high priest. So, in spite of their release, the apostles are brought before the high priest and must answer his charges. The release of the apostles in 5:40 shows that there are two rescues in Acts 5, one by the intervention of an angel, one by the intervention of a human being, Gamaliel. Gamaliel, a person of insight and reason, intervenes as the plot moves toward crisis and corrects those carried away by their murderous passions (5:33). The speech of Gamaliel shows that there are still cool heads within the Sanhedrin. He is persuasive; he is able to convince the Sanhedrin that the apostles should not be put to death. There are several indications that Gamaliel, although he does not speak as a Christian, serves as spokesman for the implied author. As I have indicated, the point made by Gamaliel in 5:39a has already been supported by the narrator, who chose to highlight the impotence of the temple authorities in 5:21-26. Furthermore, in speaking of the two possibilities of "this purpose or this work" being "from humans" or "from God," Gamaliel shifts from the conditional sentence with ἐάν and subjunctive to εἰ and indicative. The latter construction often, as here, comes close to the causal meaning "since."[19] The shift in construction suggests that "this purpose" really is from God, showing that the implied author is placing his own view in the mouth of Gamaliel.[20] Also, the contrast between what is "from humans" and what is "from God" in 5:38-39 continues a theme which has already appeared in the responses of the apostles before the Sanhedrin, who have demonstrated which side they stand on by declaring, "It is necessary to obey God rather than humans" (5:29, cf. 4:19). Gamaliel also seems to recognize that Jesus and his followers are different from the followers of Theudas and Judas the Galilean, who disappeared with the death of their leader. Gamaliel's warning to "take care . . . what you are about to do" and to beware of becoming "fighters against God" emphasizes the significance of the decision about to be made by the Sanhedrin. Gamaliel's argument is persuasive on this occasion, but the danger of which he warns will reappear in the trial of Stephen.

Again the bold persistence of the apostles is expressed in a brief speech in which they repeat the proclamation concerning Jesus (5:30-32). This, the last speech by the apostles to the people of Jerusalem or their leaders, briefly summarizes themes from previous speeches, including some which have not been mentioned since Acts 2 ("God exalted him at his right hand," cf. 2:33; "the Holy Spirit which God gave," cf. 2:33, 38).

---

[18]Susan Rubin Suleiman presents an elaborate classification of types of narrative "redundancy" in her article "Redundancy and the 'Readable' Text," *Poetics Today* 1 (1980) 119-42. Among the types are cases in which "an event is redundant with the interpretive commentary made by a C character . . . concerning it" (p. 128). Gamaliel may not be interpreting the prison rescue directly, but it is at least an illustration of his point.

[19]See F. Blass and A. Debrunner, *A Greek Grammar of the New Testament and Other Early Christian Literature,* translated and revised by Robert W. Funk (Chicago: University of Chicago, 1961) no. 372, 1.

[20]This is the opinion of Hans Conzelmann, *Die Apostelgeschichte* (Tübingen: J. C. B Mohr, 1963) 42; and Ernst Haenchen, *The Acts of the Apostles* (Philadelphia: Westminster, 1971) 253.

The authorities are again accused of killing Jesus, but this is still followed by the proclamation of repentance and release of sins, a gift of God through the exalted Messiah
which is still valid for Israel.[21] The sermons with their persistent themes demonstrate
the persistence of the apostles, who neither crumble before powerful opponents nor
despair of the possibility of repentance.

II. ECHO EFFECT IN ACTS 3-5

To this point I have followed a consecutive reading of Acts, noting how the story is
building up to a point of crisis and decision, although there have been references to
related material in other parts of Luke-Acts which help us understand the narrative lines
developing in Acts 3-5. The story is comprehensible through such a consecutive reading.
However, our experience of the story is greatly enriched when we note that Acts 2-5 (as
well as other material) can produce a complex echo effect. Characters and events in this
section of Acts echo characters and events already presented in the Gospel, and recall of
these earlier characters and events suggests a complex set of similarities, differences,
and fulfillments which contribute to the significance of the story. Therefore, the text
takes on resonance. The previous story resonates with the new events, so that meanings
are both amplified and enriched. We can also say that the previous story provides commentary on the current story. At some points this commentary seems clear and specific,
so that the echo effect serves to control interpretation. The echo adds emphasis, helping
to specify and ensure communication of central meanings. But the echoes multiply,
producing tantalizing hints of meaning which are difficult to control. Echo added to echo
produces a resonance which surrounds the central meanings with overtones which the
writer cannot fully control and the reader cannot easily exhaust.

We are discussing what is often called "parallels" within Acts and between Acts and
Luke's Gospel.[22] In discussing such parallels, we should remember that they serve to
enrich narrative lines which keep moving into the future. Absolute sameness would bring
movement to a halt. The "parallels" always suggest *similarity* in events that are not the
same, each event retaining the uniqueness which contributes to a sense of verisimilitude.
Furthermore, the discovery of similarity may also accent important differences, and
exploring these differences may also contribute to the significance of the story. We
become aware of similarities and differences together as comparisons come to mind.

---

[21]Luke T. Johnson believes that the offer of repentance and release of sins no
longer applies to the leaders, who have already rejected Jesus a second time. See *The
Literary Function of Possessions in Luke-Acts* (Missoula: Scholars Press, 1977) 69. However, no distinction is made between the leaders and the rest of Israel in 5:30-32.
Whether the leaders' rejection of Jesus is final and irrevocable, bringing upon them the
curse of 3:23, is unclear at this point in the narrative. The apostles speak to them as if
there were still hope of repentance.

[22]For a recent discussion of such parallels see Charles H. Talbert, *Literary
Patterns, Theological Themes and the Genre of Luke-Acts* (Missoula: Scholars Press,
1974). The study of G. W. Trompf on *The Idea of Historical Recurrence in Western
Thought* (Berkeley: University of California, 1979) provides further evidence that patterns of recurrence are widespread in writings of the ancient Mediterranean world and
that ancient readers would not be surprised by them. Trompf discusses Luke-Acts at
length and believes that it reflects notions of recurrence from both Hebraic and Greco-
Roman tradition.

Significant comparisons may multiply. The discovery of similarities between two events does not preclude connections with other events as well. Nor do the events which resonate together all occur between the birth of Jesus and Paul's preaching in Rome. The story also awakens echoes of Old Testament figures. Here, however, I will confine myself to echoes within Luke-Acts, discussing features of composition and wording which suggest that conscious or unconscious choices were made by the author, enabling one scene or statement to echo another within this literary work.

1. Echoes of the Beginning of Jesus' Mission

A first set of similarities appears when we compare the beginning of the mission of the apostles with the beginning of the mission of Jesus.[23] In each case we must consider not single scenes but a development through several chapters, encompassing a group of scenes which have thematic connections. Both the mission of Jesus and the mission of the apostles begins with prayer and the coming of the Spirit, followed by an inaugural speech which relates the coming of the Spirit to the new mission through a Scripture quotation. The inaugural speech also proclaims "release (ἄφεσις)." Soon afterwards we are told of the healing of a paralytic or lame man, which becomes the occasion for a fundamental disclosure concerning Jesus' saving significance. The disclosure also involves the interpretation of something from the Scripture quotation in the inaugural sermon. This same healing is the occasion for the appearance of the first opposition to the new mission from Jewish leaders.

To explain this series of similarities in greater detail: In Luke 3-4 we are told that Jesus, praying, received the Holy Spirit (3:21-22) and later delivered an inaugural speech which, through a Scripture quotation, related his mission both to the coming of the Spirit and to the proclamation of "release" (4:18-19). In Acts 1-2 the apostles, having been told by Jesus of the coming of the Spirit, pray (1:14) and on Pentecost receive the Spirit, which leads to Peter's inaugural speech containing a Scripture quotation which relates the apostles' mission to the coming of the Spirit (2:17-21). In his speech Peter also offers "release of sins" to his hearers (2:38).

The first opposition from Pharisees and teachers of the law appears when Jesus offers release of sins to a paralytic (Luke 5:17-26), an important fulfillment of Jesus' commission to proclaim release, announced in 4:18. This scene is both the beginning of a continuing conflict with the scribes and Pharisees and an occasion for highlighting Jesus' authority to release sins (5:24), an authority basic to his ongoing ministry, as is made clear by the narrator's tendency to link later scenes with Luke 5:17-32.[24] The narrative in Acts 3-4 is linked to Peter's inaugural sermon by the theme of the saving power of Jesus' name (2:21; 3:6, 16; 4:7-12). The development of this theme begins with the healing of a lame man. While there are some similarities of expression between the story of Jesus' healing of the paralytic and the story of the healing of the lame man at the temple gate, these similarities might simply reflect the fact that both stories report the healing

---

[23]See C. Talbert, *Literary Patterns,* 16.

[24]In material which is still unpublished, I point out how the narrator uses the stories of the healing of the paralytic and the meal in the tax collector's house to interpret Jesus' ongoing ministry through a series of reminiscences of these stories in later episodes of the Gospel.

of a man who could not walk.[25] The connection between the two stories becomes striking, however, when we consider the function of the stories in the larger narrative. Both
stories, placed early in the missions of Jesus and the apostles, are associated with a basic
proclamation of Jesus' saving significance which has continuing importance for the
mission, and both provoke opposition from Jewish leaders, which will continue into following chapters. We have seen how the healing of the lame man in Jesus' name leads up
to the general proclamation about salvation in Jesus' name in 4:7-12, thereby explaining
the offer of salvation to those who call upon the name of the Lord in the Scripture quotation in 2:21. The healing of the paralytic in Luke 5:17-26 is also linked to the preceding
inaugural sermon (through the theme of "release") and develops the understanding of
Jesus' salvific work found there by presenting a general claim about Jesus' authority to
do what he has done for the paralytic (5:24). This general claim is made in the face of
opposition already expressed by Jewish leaders, just as Peter speaks to the temple
authorities about Jesus after he and John have already been arrested and must defend
themselves. In both cases the opposition from Jewish leaders has just appeared but will
continue in scenes which follow closely.

Thus the similarity between Jesus' healing of the paralytic and Peter's healing of
the lame man lies less in the healing itself than in the function of these scenes in the
larger narrative. In both cases the healing becomes the occasion for a fundamental claim
about Jesus' saving power, emphasizing its importance and general scope ("on earth"—
Luke 5:24; "under heaven"—Acts 4:12). In both cases it is the occasion for speaking of a
salvation which encompasses more than physical healing. In both cases the claim is made
in the face of new opposition and develops the significance of the mission announced in
the Scripture quotation in the inaugural sermon.

One feature of Acts 3 resembles the scene in which Jesus is rejected in Nazareth
more closely than it resembles Luke 5:17-26. Before Jesus is rejected in Nazareth, he
announces that he is a prophet who will not be accepted in his homeland and hints that
God's saving work will extend to the gentiles (4:24-27). His statement that he will not be
accepted is immediately confirmed by the response of the people. Before the opposition
from the temple authorities appears, Peter warns of the consequences of failing to hear
the prophet like Moses and hints that God's servant will be sent elsewhere, having been
sent to the people of Jerusalem "first" (Acts 3:23, 26). Immediately afterwards, the
authorities show that they are not willing to accept the prophet like Moses proclaimed by
Peter.[26]

Conviction that these similarities are not accidental increases when we note that
the sequence appears a third time at the beginning of the section of Acts which is
devoted to Paul.[27] After prayer and fasting, Paul and Barnabas are set aside for their
mission, according to the command of the Holy Spirit, the divine power behind this
mission (13:2-4). Shortly thereafter we find a major scene in which Paul gives a speech
which resembles Jesus' speech at Nazareth in its setting and resembles Peter's speech at
Pentecost in significant points of content. The speech contains Scripture quotations, but

---

[25]The similarities in wording are clearer between Acts 3:1-10 and 14:8-11 (Paul's
healing of a lame man) than between Acts 3:1-10 and Luke 5:17-26.

[26]Opposition to Jesus, from different parties, appears in both Luke 4:28-30 and
5:21. Acts 2-4 refers to only one group of opponents, and parts of these chapters
resemble both Luke 4:16-30 and 5:17-26.

[27]See C. Talbert, *Literary Patterns*, 23.

the quotation which corresponds most closely with those at the beginning of Jesus' and Peter's inaugural speeches, because it discloses the nature of the speaker's mission, is found in 13:47. There Paul, a week later but still speaking to the same group, says, "Thus the Lord has commanded us, 'I have placed you for a light of gentiles, so that you may be for salvation to the end of the earth.'" Paul discloses this commission in the face of Jewish opposition, opposition about which he warned in advance at the end of his synagogue speech (13:41). In light of the other similarities to the narratives of the beginning of Jesus' and the apostles' missions, it is not surprising that a healing of a lame man by Paul occurs shortly after the speech in Antioch of Pisidia. The connection between Peter's and Paul's healings of lame men is emphasized by the narrator through repetition of words and phrases (compare 3:2 with 14:8, 3:4 with 14:9, 3:8 with 14:10, 3:12 with 14:15).

Although the narrator in 14:8ff. recalls the earlier healing of a lame man by Peter through use of similar wording, the scenes are only partially similar in function. They agree in referring to the healed man's leaping, recalling the prophecies of Isaiah, and in the negative point that the power to heal does not reside in the healer himself. The positive side of this, the saving power of Jesus' name, is not repeated in 14:8-18, and the opposition which appears following Peter's healing and preaching has already been encountered by Paul before 14:8. Nevertheless, we have found a bundle of similarities which stretch across a sequence of scenes near the beginning of the sections which focus on Jesus, Peter, and Paul. It is hard to believe that these similar combinations in analogous locations in the narrative are accidental.

The similarities between Luke 6:17-19 and Acts 5:12-16, which include summary description of the coming of multitudes and of works of healing and exorcism, even through touch or shadow, suggest that another element from Luke's narrative of Jesus' early ministry has been repeated in Acts. There is similar material in the story of Paul, but it is divided between 14:3 (which also recalls Acts 4:29-30) and 19:11-12.

2. Echoes of Luke's Passion Story

We have noted similarities between Acts 1-5 and a series of important events reported near the beginning of Jesus' ministry in Luke. There are also a number of similarities between the Jerusalem section of Acts and the Jerusalem section of Luke. Thus there is a second set of echoes of the Jesus story. Reading Acts 3-7 against the background of both the beginning and ending of Jesus' ministry in Luke adds greatly to the resonance of the Acts account.

There is explicit recall of the rejection and death of Jesus in the four speeches of Peter in Acts 2-5, and we have already noted the close connection between Acts 3:13-15 and the trial scene before Pilate, especially Luke 23:16-19.[28] Furthermore, there is continuity of characters between the passion story in Luke and the Jerusalem section of Acts. Peter in his speeches is addressing people who were directly involved in Jesus' death, and he emphasizes their guilt. The high priest and the Jerusalem Sanhedrin play key roles in both the confrontation with Jesus and with the apostles. This provides an opportunity for the narrator to suggest that similar situations are reoccurring, and the narrator takes advantage of this opportunity. After Peter has recalled the circumstances

---

[28]See Part I,1 above.

of Jesus' death in his first two speeches, a sequence of events takes place which partially reduplicates the passion story. Like Jesus, Jesus' witnesses are arrested, they are called to account before the Sanhedrin, and the third sequence of arrest and trial in Acts leads to a death. The report of Stephen's death both recalls and parallels the narrative of Jesus' death in Luke. Stephen's speech ends by recalling Jesus' death (7:52). Stephen's next words recall Jesus' words to his accusers about the exalted Son of Man (Luke 22:69, Acts 7:56). His final words parallel Jesus' words from the cross (Luke 23:34, 46; Acts 7:59-60). Thus the sequence of arrests, trials, and death in Acts 4-7 reaches its climax in a scene in which the connections with Luke's passion story are quite clear.

Details of description indicate a desire to suggest such connections not only at Stephen's death but also in the series of events leading up to it. Note the following similarities between the description of the arrest and examination of the apostles in Acts 4 and the arrest and examination of Jesus in Luke: Acts 4:1 refers to "the captain (στρατηγός) of the temple"; Luke 22:52 also refers to "captains of the temple" (differs from Matthew, Mark). The temple officials "laid hands on (ἐπέβαλον τὰς χεῖρας)" the apostles (4:3, 5:18); the same phrase is used in reporting the frustrated attempt of scribes and high priests to arrest Jesus in Luke 20:19 (differs from Matthew, Mark). Acts 4:5 places the examination on the morning after the arrest, as with Jesus (Luke 22:66, differs from Matthew, Mark), and Acts 4:5-6 agrees further with Luke 22:66 in referring to the groups constituting the Sanhedrin having been "gathered together" (aorist passive of συνάγω). The reference to "rulers (ἄρχοντας)" in Acts 4:5 corresponds to Luke 23:13, 35; 24:20 (differs from Matthew, Mark).

Most of Jesus' speaking in Jerusalem is done prior to his arrest, and the primary location of his teaching is the temple. The narrative in Acts recalls some of this material in shaping the dialogues between the rulers and the apostles, who also teach in the temple. In Luke 20:2 Jesus was asked, "By what authority are you doing these things?"; in Acts 4:7 Peter and John are asked, "By what power or what name did you do this?" The same group poses the question in the two instances. Peter, in responding to the question, refers to the stone scorned by the builders which has become head of the corner (Acts 4:11), repeating (with some variation in wording) a scripture quotation used by Jesus in Luke 20:17 in a scene which ends with the attempt of the scribes and high priests to arrest Jesus. In this scene Jesus has just accused the rulers of killing God's greatest messenger, using the indirect form of a parable. This accusation will become explicit in the Acts speeches. So the Scripture reference to the stone in Acts 4:11 recalls the rejection and vindication of Jesus in imagery already used by Jesus. In both Luke and Acts the "people (λαός)" support Jesus or the apostles, preventing the rulers from taking action against them (Luke 19:47-48, 20:19, 22:2; Acts 4:21, 5:26). This will delay, but not prevent, the death toward which the narrative is moving.

The similarities between Acts 4-5 and the Jerusalem narrative in Luke help to make clear that the conflict in Jerusalem over Jerusalem's Messiah has not been resolved. It simply enters a new phase, with the apostles as Jesus' witnesses. The apostles now assume the risky role of proclaiming Jesus and of calling the people of Jerusalem and their rulers to repent of their blind error. Their new role shows that the apostles have changed in important ways. The similarity of the situation (arrest and trial) and the continuity of the opposition (from the high priests and others associated with the temple or Sanhedrin) highlight the difference in the behavior of the apostles before and after the resurrection and sending of the Spirit. Luke alone reports Peter's declaration that he was ready both to die and to go "to prison" with Jesus (Luke 22:33). He failed to keep this promise when he denied Jesus. In Acts Peter no longer denies Jesus, though threatened by powerful people, and he does go to prison. His boldness before the rulers is the opposite of his previous denial. The boldness of the apostles helps the rulers to recognize that Peter and John "were with Jesus" (Acts 4:13). This is what Peter denied, according to Luke 22:56, 59.

Having been transformed by the risen Jesus and the Spirit, the apostles are now able to follow the instructions about facing opposition which Jesus gave during the journey to Jerusalem. In following his instructions, they also experience the fulfillment of his promises. A number of descriptive details in the narrative of the apostles' arrests recall Jesus' teaching about persecution in Luke 12:11-12 and 21:12-15. Jesus prophesied in Luke 21:12 that "they will lay their hands on you" (see Acts 4:3, 5:18), "handing you over . . . to prisons . . . because of my name" (see the emphasis on Jesus' name in Acts 3-4). Jesus promised, "It will lead to witnessing" (Luke 21:13; see Peter's witness before the rulers in Acts 4:8-12 and 5:29-32). The promise that the opponents will not be able to "contradict (ἀντειπεῖν)" them (Luke 21:15) is fulfilled in Acts 4:14, and the related promise that they will be taught by the Holy Spirit what they should say (Luke 12:12) is fulfilled in Acts 4:8.[29] The inability of the opponents to reply to or contradict the apostles also fits an emphasis within stories of Jesus, for Jesus had silenced his opponents both during his temple teaching (Luke 20:26, 40) and earlier (Luke 13:17, 14:6). The points that we have noted show that the similarities between the situation of Jesus in the passion story and the situation of the apostles in Acts 3-5 serve in part to highlight the transformation of the apostles, who were unable to face danger courageously but now are able. This, in turn, makes possible the fulfillment of some specific promises of Jesus to his witnesses.

The theme of persecution because of Jesus' "name," developed as a prophetic preview in Luke 21:12-19, reappears at the end of the narrative of the apostles' arrests and releases (Acts 5:40-41), and there may be additional points of contact between these verses in Acts and Jesus' teaching about persecution in Luke. The apostles leave "rejoicing (χαίροντες) . . . because they were counted worthy to be dishonored on behalf of the name: (Acts 5:41). In Luke 6:22-23 Jesus instructed his disciples to "rejoice (χάρητε)" at persecution, a strikingly odd response shared by these two passages in Luke-Acts. The verb "dishonor (ἀτιμάζω)" is found not only in Acts 5:41 but also in the parable of the wicked vineyard tenants (Luke 20:11). Since it is a rare word in Luke-Acts, occurring only twice and on both occasions associated with beatings, this link suggests that Jesus' parable of the wicked tenants may still be working in the imagination of the author,[30] who sees the beaten and dishonored servants of the vineyard owner as an apt image for the apostles. These points of contact reveal particular aspects of the story of Jesus which had sufficient appeal to the author's imagination to shape the vision of the early church in Acts.

The connections which we have noted between Acts 4-5 and the passion story become explicit when the church responds to its first crisis by turning to God in prayer (4:23-31). The church prefaces its petition with a reference to the passion story, inter-

---

[29]It is possible that the rulers' judgment that the apostles are uneducated and untrained (Acts 4:13) in part reflects the fact that they did not plan a polished oration in advance, in accordance with Jesus' instructions in Luke 12:11, 21:14.

[30]We have already noted reminiscences of Luke 20:17, 19, which conclude this scene.

preted as fulfillment of Scripture. This recall of Jesus' passion is relevant because Jesus' situation, threatened by rulers and peoples, is viewed as essentially the same as the church's situation, faced with the threats of the Sanhedrin. The prayer moves directly from a reference to "Herod and Pontius Pilate with the gentiles and peoples of Israel," those who gathered against Jesus the Messiah, to a petition concerning "their threats," meaning the threats of the Sanhedrin which the apostles have just encountered. Ernst Haenchen speaks of a "rift between verses 27 and 29," since "their threats" does not refer to threats by Herod and Pilate, as vss. 27-28 would seem to suggest.[31] However, the distinction which is important to Haenchen is not important in the prayer; indeed, it is deliberately eliminated. The opponents of Jesus and of the church are viewed as one continuous group, a simplification which is facilitated by the fact that the Sanhedrin had a leading role in both situations.[32] Although the connection drawn in 4:27-29 may seem strange to some modern interpreters, these verses disclose a mode of thought presupposed throughout Acts 3-7, as is shown by the repeated parallels drawn between the passion story in Luke and the experience of the early church. The prayer of the church (and later the speech and death of Stephen) reveals that there are actually two levels of echoes which may be heard in the story. The conflict of the mission with the Sanhedrin is echoed by the passion story in Luke, and both are echoed by Scripture.

The explicit parallel between Jesus' passion and the church's situation which is basic to the structure of the prayer provides important evidence that the similarities with the passion story which we have already noted are not accidental. It should also stimulate us to ask whether the church's prayer has a more specific connection with material in the passion story. In Luke 22:39-46, just before Jesus' arrest and just after Peter's assertion that he is ready to go with Jesus to prison and death, Jesus urged the disciples to pray in order that they might not enter into temptation. Instead, the disciples fell asleep and were unprepared for the crisis which immediately followed. In Acts 4:23-31 Jesus' followers are again confronted with the dangerous opposition of the Sanhedrin. Now they pray as they had been told to do when Jesus and his followers first faced this threat. As a result they receive power from God to continue the mission despite the opposition. We have already noted that Peter's boldness before the Sanhedrin in Acts contrasts with his denial of Jesus in Luke. The church in Acts which finds power for bold witness in prayer also contrasts with the disciples who sleep when they should pray in Luke. These contrasts support the narrator's picture of the dramatic transformation which has taken place in Jesus' followers.

The Acts speeches repeatedly affirm God's active presence in the story of Jesus. It is clear that the implied author believes that God continues to be active in the life of the church, and the narrative has various ways of signaling this active presence of God: angels, visions, messages from the Spirit, etc. One further way of bringing God into the narrative is to report a prayer and answer to prayer. This is an opportunity to show how God responds to the characters and events of the narrative.

This is also an opportunity to characterize God more fully, so that readers have a

---

[31]See E. Haenchen, *Acts,* 228.

[32]Rather than Herod representing the "kings" and Pilate the "rulers" of 4:26 (so Haenchen, *Acts,* 227), there is some evidence that the "kings" are political authorities and the "rulers" religious authorities, i.e., the Sanhedrin, which is otherwise not mentioned in 4:26-27. Compare 4:26 with 4:5, where "rulers" appears in a reference to the Sanhedrin. Both verses use the aorist passive of συνάγω.

clearer impression of the God who is acting through the human events of the story. The church's petition in 4:29-30 is preceded by a five verse preface which is basically characterization of God. God is creator of all things and therefore sovereign (δεσπότης) over all. This sovereignty is revealed as God announces in Scripture a preordained purpose and brings this to fulfillment. God's sovereignty is even more clearly revealed when opponents of God's purpose become instruments of its realization. The chief instance of this is celebrated in 4:25-28: Jew and gentile gathered in opposition to God and God's Messiah but ironically fulfilled God's purpose.[33] This is a theological vision of a God who works by irony. Human actors do not see truly what is happening, for reality is in conflict with appearance. Blind human actors commit themselves to a course of action, only to discover that its meaning and results are quite different than they thought. The implied author traces the work of God in a series of such ironies. The irony of the realization of God's purpose through the blind rejection of God's Messiah provides the interpretive key. The church at prayer recalls this event, which enables it to trust in the sovereign God when it must face human opponents. It prays for the power to continue the mission of preaching and healing in the face of the Sanhedrin's threats, and its prayer is answered. Remaining faithful to its mission, it will discover again that the sovereign God can twist the human purposes of opponents to fulfill the divine will, as the "great persecution" in Jerusalem (8:1) leads to the spread of the Word to new areas and Saul, the most devoted persecutor of the church, becomes a witness of Jesus to all people.

The first opposition to the mission comes from the Jewish rulers in Jerusalem. But the Psalm quotation in 4:25-26 refers also to gentiles, and gentiles are included among the opponents of God's Messiah when the Psalm is applied to Jesus' death in 4:27. The church has not yet experienced opposition from gentiles, but it will. Paul's arrest and imprisonment in Philippi (16:16-24) and the riot in Ephesus (19:23-40) are dramatic accounts of such opposition. I am suggesting that the church's prayer in 4:23-31 relates not only to the specific situation of the apostles' arrest by the Sanhedrin and the previous situation of Jesus' rejection and death. It also anticipates the recurrent opposition from Jews and gentiles which the mission will encounter from this point on. Furthermore, the church's prayer for power to speak the word with "boldness (παρρησία)" and for signs and wonders is not answered solely by the outpouring of the Spirit in 4:31. These characteristics of bold and powerful speech, accompanied by signs and wonders, are passed on from the apostles to Stephen (6:8-10), Philip (8:4-7), and Paul (9:27-28, 14:3) as the narrative progresses. Indeed, Acts ends with the picture of the imprisoned Paul faithfully preaching "with all boldness" (28:31). The powerful and hardy witness which the Spirit inspired in response to the church's prayer persists to the very end of Acts and appears in the narrator's last statement. It is in 4:23-31 that we learn that the Spirit not only inspired the mission in the beginning (2:1-21) but also inspires the bold speaking which maintains the witness despite all opposition and danger.

3. Echoes within Acts 1-5

We have discussed similarities between the early chapters of Acts and (1) the beginning of Jesus' ministry in Luke, (2) Jesus' temple teaching and the passion story in

---

[33]Note that 4:28 repeats and reemphasizes the assertion in 2:23 that God's preordained purpose was realized in the death of Jesus.

Luke. We have noted that themes associated with the beginning of Jesus' and the apostles' mission also appear in the story of Paul's mission.[34] Paul's final journey to Jerusalem, arrest, and trials will also be told in ways that echo Jesus' journey to Jerusalem and final days there,[35] so that the Pauline section of Acts echoes two sections of the Jesus story, just as Acts 1-7 does.

In Acts 1-5 the similarities with the Gospel which we have discussed are overlaid with a third pattern of similarities, for there is reduplication within Acts 1-5 itself. This is clearest when we compare 4:1-22 with 5:17-42, the two narratives of the arrest of the apostles, their appearance before the Sanhedrin (including short speeches which both reaffirm the apostles' message about Jesus 4:10-12, 5:30-32 and declare that the apostles will obey God rather than the Sanhedrin 4:19-20, 5:29), deliberation by the Sanhedrin without the apostles being present (4:15-17, 5:34-39), resulting in the release of the apostles, although the Sanhedrin prohibits speaking in Jesus' name. Although the sequence of events is so similar, it is clear that the second arrest and hearing builds upon the first, for the second interrogation by the Sanhedrin begins with the accusation that the apostles have disobeyed the rulers' command in the first hearing (5:28), and the second response of the apostles to the Sanhedrin puts them in danger of death (5:33).

Charles Talbert believes that the pattern of correspondences is more extensive. He compares 1:12-4:23 with 4:24-5:42.[36] It does seem significant that in both of these sections of Acts we hear of the church gathered at prayer (1:14, 4:24-30), then filled with the Holy Spirit and speaking by the Spirit's power (2:4, 4:31). The two descriptions of the communal life of the church which follow the Pentecost scene and the renewed outpouring of the Spirit are also closely related (2:42-47, 4:32-35), and the signs and wonders of the apostles are noted before each of the arrests (2:43, 3:1-10, 5:12-16). This pattern of reduplication contributes to the story of the developing conflict between the church and the Sanhedrin. It helps to build suspense as the resolve of both parties to the conflict is tested under increasing pressure. It shows the apostles and the church holding firm under this pressure. That the apostles and church continue or repeat what they have already done makes the point of their firmness in the face of the threats. But tension also increases, for the rulers, frustrated in their attempts to silence the apostles, must either give up their authority or take more drastic action. That the narrative is building to a climax through these patterns of reduplication becomes clear when we have a third sequence of arrest and trial before the Sanhedrin (6:8-7:60), this time resulting in the death of Jesus' witness and the scattering of the church (8:1).

4. The Significance of Repetitive Patterns in Luke-Acts

Various types of repetition in narrative have been discussed by some recent theorists under the heading of "redundancy." Redundancy, far from being strange and unusual, is a necessary aspect of effective communication. In narrative it may take many forms. Susan Rubin Suleiman has proposed an elaborate "classification of the types of

---

[34]See above, Part II, 1.

[35]On this see Walter Radl, *Paulus und Jesus im lukanischen Doppelwerk* (Bern: Herbert Lang & Frankfurt/M.: Peter Lang, 1975).

[36]See *Literary Patterns*, 35-39.

redundancy possible in realistic fiction."[37] Many of her types of redundancy occur in Luke-Acts. In our discussion we have noted as especially important the repetition of the same type of event or sequence of events happening to different characters (Jesus, Peter, and Paul are filled with the Spirit and deliver inaugural sermons which comment on the missions which they are beginning), similar events or sequences of events happening to the same characters (apostles are twice arrested and appear before the Sanhedrin), and similarity between an event as presented and interpreted by the narrator and an interpretation offered by a character. Examples of the last type of redundancy are the narrator's declaration in 2:4 that the church was "filled with the Holy Spirit," an interpretation which is repeated in Peter's speech (2:15-17), despite brief reference to an alternative view (2:13, 15), and the ironic portrayal of the Sanhedrin's impotence in 5:17-26, followed by Gamaliel's statement, "If it is from God, you will not be able to destroy them" (5:39).

What is the function of the rather elaborate patterns of repetition or "redundancy" which we have noted? Why would one compose a story in this way? The answer must be complex, embracing at least the following points:

1. Information theorists note that every channel of communication is subject to "noise," i.e., "disturbances . . . which interfere with the faithful transmission of signals," and "a certain degree of redundancy is essential . . . in any communication system in order to counteract the disturbing effects of noise."[38] In Luke-Acts one major source of "noise" is the length of the narrative, offering the reader a large opportunity to forget what has already happened. Redundancy combats the tendency to forget.

2. Repetition is a means of emphasis. Selective emphasis enables authors to convey the views which they regard as most important for arriving at the correct interpretation of the events being narrated. Thus emphasis serves the "education of the reader"[39] in what is central to understanding the story. Since a particular interpretation is being suggested, other options are being rejected, reducing the amount of indeterminacy in the text. However, the closing of options may guide the reader to an interpretation which the author regards as particularly rich, with its own broad field of meanings, a field not likely to be explored if the reader is not led to it. Since repetition conveys interpretation through emphasis, it is important for the reader to take careful note of *what* is repeated. Interpretation takes place through *selective* repetition.

3. Repetition has a persuasive effect. The events, characters, or assertions seem "right" because they fit what is already known. Or, as Susan Wittig says,

The creation . . . of a multi-level set of expectancies not only allows the audience to predict the occurrence of successive items, but also provides for

---

[37]"Redundancy and the 'Readable Text,'" *Poetics Today* 1 (1980) 126-32.

[38]John Lyons, *Semantics* (2 vols.; Cambridge: Cambridge University, 1978) 1. 44. Quoted by Fred W. Burnett, "Prolegomenon to Reading Matthew's Eschatological Discourse: Redundancy and the Education of the Reader in Matthew" (Unpublished paper presented at the annual meeting of the Society of Biblical Literature 1983) 3 and nn. 18-19.

[39]A phrase used by Fred W. Burnett. See the preceding note.

that audience's *assent* to the sequence, for if the listener can predict the next item (perhaps he may even repeat it silently before it occurs) he will be more likely to accept it and agree to it.[40]

4. Characters in Acts who show qualities and patterns of behavior similar to Jesus and to Scriptural models take on some of the authority of these authoritative figures. This is true of Peter, Stephen, and Paul, whose missions and sufferings resemble those of Jesus, while Jesus' mission and rejection reflect the experience of Moses with the rebellious Israelites (see Acts 3:22, 7:22-39).[41]

5. Reading is a constant process of forming and revising expectations, both focal expectations, relating to the immediate context, and global expectations, stretching over large sections of the work.[42] The need to continually revise expectations involves the reader actively in the work and can be a major means of holding the reader's interest. To be most effective, the reader must have some basis for anticipating events, perhaps through suggestive patterns of repetition, but must lack certainty. The lack of certainty pertains not only to what will happen but also to how, when, and why it will happen. Furthermore, the process of building and revising expectations in reading can be used effectively to guide readers toward a climax in the narrative. Confirmation of expectations through a growing repetitive pattern allows the reader to anticipate a climactic instance of the pattern, which will fulfill expectations in the highest degree, as in the triple pattern of arrests and confrontations with the Sanhedrin which lead up to Stephen's death.[43]

6. The same or related characters may be presented in similar situations in order to highlight an important change. The similarities make the differences stand out sharply, suggesting an important development in the narrative. In Acts 4-5 Peter and the other apostles face situations similar to those in Luke's passion story. The contrast in behavior highlights their transformation. Now Peter faces the threat of the Sanhedrin by boldly confessing Jesus, while this threat causes the church to turn in prayer to God, the source of power to withstand opposition.

7. The use of repetitive patterns preserves a sense of unity of purpose and action in

---

[40]Susan Wittig, "Formulaic Style and the Problem of Redundancy," *Centrum* 1 (1973) 131. Quoted by Janice Capel Anderson, "The Implied Reader in Matthew," (Unpublished paper presented at the annual meeting of the Society of Biblical Literature, 1983) 26. Emphasis by Wittig.

[41]Luke T. Johnson (*Possessions*, 38-78) discusses similarities among Moses, Jesus, and Jesus' witnesses, who are portrayed according to a common model which Johnson labels "men of the Spirit." Furthermore, Charles Talbert understands the parallels between Jesus and his witnesses in Luke-Acts as a way of indicating who are the authentic successors of Jesus. See *Literary Patterns*, 125-36.

[42]See Frank Smith, *Understanding Reading: A Psycholinguistic Analysis of Reading and Learning to Read* (2nd ed.; Holt, Rinehart and Winston, 1978) 168-72. Smith's work is discussed by Janice Capel Anderson. See n. 40 above.

[43]See the discussion of "building" (along with emphasizing, echoing, and complicating) in chap. 2 of Bruce F. Kawin, *Telling It Again and Again: Repetition in Literature and Film* (Ithaca: Cornell University, 1972).

spite of significant developments. Very important changes take place as the mission moves from Nazareth to Jerusalem to the gentile world, but the author succeeds in presenting all this as the manifestation of a single purpose of God, in part through the recurrence of unifying patterns in different sections of the narrative. The author seems to be especially careful not to allow innovations to disrupt the continuity of the narrative.

8. Repetitive patterns in narrative encourage interaction among characters and events in the reader's experience. The character or event is experienced not in isolation but against a background which gives it "resonance." That is, we are able to detect overtones and echoes of other characters and events which add suggestive richness to the narrative episode now being read. Such resonance is not entirely controllable by an author. Once some parallels have been suggested in the narrative, other related ones may occur to the reader, whether intended by the author or not. This is especially true when possible interconnections are multiple, with several systems of echoes working at once, as in Acts 1-7. The thick layers of background which produce resonance appeal to the reader's imagination. The reader is sent actively exploring the rich associations, involving both similarity and contrast, which may exist among characters and events. In reading, resonance is a cumulative experience. Connections among narrative materials build up, so that more and more is available as background for exploring those nodal points of narrative where many lines of connection cross. When an author emphasizes certain images and patterns through repeated use, much will depend on the capacity of the selected material to grow in significance through the creative work of the author. Repetition without growth soon becomes monotonous. On the other hand, an author may convince us of the value of central images and patterns if we discover that they expand in meaning. This may happen as we find that they encompass more and more of human experience, including, perhaps, the reader's experience. It may also happen as we are led to a deeper grasp of their implications. The discovery of an expanding symbol is a powerful enticement to explore a new perspective on life. Repetition may lead us to deepening discovery of such symbols, as familiar material returns in new contexts and with new significance. Having experienced the power of the symbol to expand in the story, the reader is more likely to believe that it hides residues of meaning which call for further exploration.[44]

In Acts 3-5, it seems to me, the repetitive patterns help to give resonance to a vision of the God who works by irony, subverting and overruling the human powers who appear to be in control. Because of this God, there can be a mission in which courageous people speak boldly of realities denied and rejected by these human powers.

---

[44]The remarks concerning the expanding symbol were suggested by E. K. Brown, *Rhythm in the Novel* (Toronto: University of Toronto, 1950) 33-59. According to Brown, "the expanding symbol is repetition balanced by variation, and that variation is in progressively deepening disclosure" (p. 57). "By the use of an expanding symbol, the novelist persuades and impels his readers towards two beliefs. First, that beyond the verge of what he can express, there is an area which can be glimpsed, never surveyed. Second, that this area has an order of its own which we should greatly care to know" (p. 59).

Asceticism, Apocalypticism and Alternatives—Hypotheses for Spectra of Occurrences: Studies and Summaries of Three Times in Early Church History

Anitra Bingham Kolenkow

Berkeley, California

Asceticism often has been associated with apocalypticism. Asceticism is said to be a common way persons may feel called upon to act in the face of the end time. Sabbatai Sevi's communities are cited as examples of the giving up of normal lifestyles because of apocalyptic expectation. However, asceticism is not only related to apocalypticism (and the lack of need to store up goods or progeny for the future); it is also related to socially recognized and regulated approaches to divinity. To understand what is happening in early Christianity one must look at some spectra of the occurrences of asceticism and apocalypticism separately—and one must see where apocalypticism and asceticism interact. Further one must look at the spectra of possibilities between organized peacetime asceticism and apocalyptic asceticism. Also one must realize that, for ancient society, asceticism is both proof of power and yet related to madness.

I. Asceticism has a spectrum of empowerment and legitimation*
    A. Prerequisite for vision and miracle (Philo *Moses* 2:68, 1:155-7)
    B. If a person is ascetic, it is believed he can do miracles.
    C. The societal requirement for miracle doer or prophet
        1. Classification of "religious" vs. "goes"
        2. Proof of prophet vs. status quo; revolutionary (heretic)
        3. Requirement for apostle ("Q" blessings and Pauline lists) —as societal protection (made eunuch, fasting so that leader does not take advantage of a worshipping society)
        4. Asceticism substituted for martyrdom
    D. Requirement for Church membership; proof of repentance
        Asceticism proves one is not seeking power after persecution ceases.
    E. Punishment → reintegration raising sinner to religious status
    F. Preparation for martyrdom; riches (Hermas *Vis* 3:6:6) and comfort will prevent readiness for martyrdom.
II. Apocalypticism has a spectrum of relation to absence or presence
    A. A feeling of forcibility (man can bring Ass Mos 9:6; rabbis: if all of Israel keeps the law for one day, if all of Israel repents (note repentance means fasting, etc.)

---

*Note problem: God's will beyond asceticism, power without asceticism (John came, Son of Man comes); people can be ascetic and evil (give up one's body to be burned and have not love).

B. A feeling of the presence of absolute evil (worst of all possible times); best or intermediate "best time" (cf. 2 Macc 14:4-15); realized eschatology?

C. A feeling of absence: will it occur (as Paul's letters), what puts it off

III. Asceticism has a spectrum in relation to apocalypticism.

A. What one does now (asceticism or not) is related to judgment (rich man and Lazarus, Mark 10:29-30)

B. Bringer, forcer of the end time (cf. I:A, II:A above). Asceticism (fasting and obedience) as what God wants and what causes God's concern and pity (cf. John Climacus 5:4, 18)

C. Proper response to endtime—be like angels; do not eat, marry (vs. do not change or become ascetic; stay as called)

D. What one does (martyrdom, punishment of persecutors) prevented the endtime or keeps doing so; asceticism does so when martyrdom not possible.

I. Paul's 1 Corinthian community—appealing to what people believe but moving beyond and back to what "had been"

A. Marriage

1. "It is good for a man not to touch a woman" (7:1)

2. In apocalyptic situation—Do not change (7:17, 26) but live as though you had no wife—appointed time short (7:29); cf. "be as I am" (7:7-8); note that the early church thought he was married (Origen, Methodius, etc.)

3. Marry

   a. Due to immorality (7:2)

   b. Fasting and continence only for a time (7:5)

B. Apostleship

1. Normal (Jewish) leaders—right to travel with wife (7:5); right to be supported (9:6-12)

2. Apostleship as spectacle for world in endtime (1 Cor 4:9); hunger and thirst (4:11, cf. "Q" beatitudes addressed to disciples who are apostles); travel without wife (chastity) (9:4)

3. Freedom to act as communities needed—i.e., eat kosher food and not cause difficulty for oneself or others (not test God—10:9)

II. Montanism

Montanism would seem to be a reflection of the type of ascetic ethics found in apocalyptically oriented societies (such as that of the later Sabbatai Sevi).

Maximilla is said to say she is the last of the prophetesses: after her is the consummation (Epiphanius *Haer* 48:2). Apollonius (Eusebius *Hist* 5:18:2ff.) talks of Montanus as one who annuls marriages, enacts fasts and receives money. All these would be recognized characteristics of an endtime (and monastic) community especially since, according to Didache, one is supposed to give to a prophet or to the "poor."

Indeed, one may see traces of Jewish Christianity (as has often been claimed for the Montanists).

In Asia Minor, Jews and Christians are said to be closely related with Jews allowing Christians to be buried in Jewish tombs. One of the charges against the Montanists is that the Montanists are not persecuted by the Jews. One also notes that they say the disciples are to stay in Jerusalem for twelve years (cf. Luke-Acts). They used the apocalyptic-Jewish oriented book of Revelation.

In Apollonius, one also sees the church's societal use of the tests of a "goes": in terms of "change of appearance" and taking money (as well as gambling and lending, 5:18:11).

Those of the "true" faith (as the opponents of Montanus called themselves) generally have problems with "heresies" for heretics may be more ascetic and become martyrs (cf. Eusebius *Hist* 5:16:21; this was also a problem for the Montanists as an alternative to the claims to the Gnostics and particularly saw asceticism as practice for martyrdom.

III. Monasticism

What then does one say about asceticism and apocalypticism in the archetypal example of asceticism, monasticism. Melania's call for monastic flight and poverty is made in the face of the barbarian Antichrist of 409-10 (Palladius *Lausiac History* 54:5, 7; cf. Jerome *Letters* 118-25). The church also used asceticism as an alternative to martyrdom and to prevent individual judgment as well as corporate destruction.

A. Asceticism and Anachoresis as Alternatives to Martyrdom

Asceticism had long been recognized as an alternative to martyrdom (Origen) or even better than (the Gnostics, for example). This belief found support both in the world of the pagan empire and in the Christian empire.

From the stories of alternatives to martyrdom, a Coptic Oxyrhynchus papyruis tells of virgins who fled artyrdom to become a part of an ascetic community away from the city[1] (cf. the Meletian houses?) and one has the stories of Jerome's Paul the Ascetic, Eusebius *Hist* 6:42:2) and Basil's grandparents.

Part of the acceptance of asceticism and anachoresis was due, in the pagan empire, to the fact that asceticism was recognized as the "philosophic life" (and later monasticism was also known thus: Eusebius *Hist* 6:10, Sozomen *Hist* 6:28, 33)— especially from the lives of the Pythagoreans. At the same time, the ascetic life lived outside society was a tenable alternative for opponents of the society; one could oppose the society if one separated oneself from the society and did not take benefit from it (cf. S. C. Humphreys on philosophers,[2] in the Christian world cf. Irenaeus *Haer* 4:30:3, Narcissus in Eusebius *Hist* 6:10). Going out to become an ascetic outside society was also recognized as following the Gospel (Frontonius of Nitria and companions, Antony).

---

[1] Cited by E. Reymond and J. Barns in *Four Martyrdoms from the Pierpont Morgan Codices* (Oxford: 1973) 16.

[2] *Anthropology and the Greeks* (London: 1980), 236. For the more complete analysis of the theories presented in the present author's argument cf. the forthcoming study "Monasticism in an Age of Anxiety," to be published in connection with the Claremont Institute's *Roots of Egyptian Christianity* project.

B. Monasticism as an alternative to lengthy ascesis in the world (with fear of death
   and judgment before completion)

Even before Constantine, joining the church had also meant a purifying process.
Asceticism (fasting, chastity, humble bearing) became the entry way into the church—
especially for those who had worshiped other Gods. For Gentiles, asceticism was related
to exorcism (demons ate meat, fostered lust, etc.). For the lapsed, the lengthy time spans
allotted (and the severity of the ascesis equivalent to monasticism but requiring up to ten
years before one could rejoin the church) left one in fear of death and judgment.

As testified in the lives of Antony, Pachomius, Sheneute and Martin (cf. John
Climacus' shepherd, 4:11), monasticism became a way of quick forgiveness (either at the
becoming of a monk or the Easter afterwards) and one may argue that a great growth of
monasticism was the result. One's spiritual father became the guarantor of one's fate,
while the society was guaranteed a continual asceticism until one's death. Thus one has
not only the Melanian response to the apocalyptic endtime, but also communities (fathers
and individuals) response to the thought of an individual's own endtime.

C. Martyrdom and Asceticism as Explanations for Lack of an Endtime

From 250-400 and later (as testified to by Cyprian, Eusebius, Suplitius Severus' Life
of Martin, etc.), apocalypticism had been in the air. From time to time, those like
Melania (see above) had suggested monastic poverty and flight to avoid the Antichrist's
coming to Rome. What to do when the endtime did not come? One explanation used by
Eusebius and others is that the endtime did not come because of the martyrdom of the
saints, the punishment of the persecutors—and then, after the time of martyrdom was
over, prayers and lives of the monks (cf. *Hist Mon* Preface 9, "through them the world is
kept in being," and the saying about Apa Jeremias of Egypt, "he bowed until he removed
the sins of the whole world"). These ascetic lives became vehicles for changing God's
mind (cf. Jonah).

One then has the familiar phenomenon that the one outside society or punished by
society is the one who suffers and becomes one upon whom the society depends for
salvation. One may suggest that the asceticism of the lapsed or "sinner become monk"
became joined with that of the philosopher into a whole which made the monk understood
as a "vehicle for social salvation" in a way philosophers were not.[3]

---

[3]Oedipus might be the closest equivalent in the Greek world.

The Social Setting of Mark:
An Apocalyptic Community

Howard Clark Kee

Boston University

Under the impact of German Protestant scholarship, Mark is widely described as a document originating in the Pauline wing of early Christianity. "A passion story with an extended introduction"—that is the way Martin Kähler characterized Mark's gospel in a footnote more than seventy years ago.[1] The form-critics, Bultmann and Dibelius, accepted that dictum as self-evident, assuming that the passion section alone had been preserved in pre-Markan tradition, from which it was expanded into the gospel as we now have it. Another way to phrase this assumption is to say that Mark as a whole is primarily an elaborated form of the Pauline kerygma. The second generation Bultmannians have accepted this view, and through their students, this opinion has become widely accepted as self-evident in North America.

More recently an outgrowth of these theories about the origins of Mark has been the notion that Mark includes his picture of Jesus as a miracle-worker only to disabuse the reader of the notion that this is what is significant about Jesus. The positive aim of Mark, it is claimed, is to counter the picture of Jesus as a wonder-working *theios aner,* or divine man, by stressing the centrality of his suffering and death.[2] An alternative hypothesis is the idea that Jesus' choice of suffering and death in Mark is a sign that he is a divine man,[3] which is to say, a divine being who has assumed the appearance of a human.

Actually none of these theories provides a satisfactory or adequate basis for dealing with the evidence from Mark. The links with the specifically Pauline kerygma are tenuous, since the resurrection appearance of Christ, which was central for Paul's own conversion and apostolic call, as well as for his kerygma, is only anticipated and never actually portrayed in Mark. In the Markan text we have only the *predictions* that Jesus will be raised from the dead. In spite of many foreshadowings of the cruel death of Jesus in Mark, much of that gospel has no link with the passion, and the passion account itself takes up only one fifth of the book as a whole. As for the theory of combatting or modifying basically a divine man christology, the term itself is too indefinite and so completely subject to change with changing cultural setting that it is useless as a christological category for which Mark is allegedly providing a corrective.

Rather, we must ask ourselves, What are the conceptual, literary, and sociological

---

[1] Martin Kähler, *The So-called Historical Jesus and the Historic, Biblical Christ* (Philadelphia, 1964) 80 n. 11.
[2] T. Weeden, *Mark—Traditions in Conflict* (Philadelphia, 1971).
[3] Hans-Dieter Betz, "Gottmensch," in *Reallexikon für Antike und Christentum,* col. 301-2.

models which enable us to identify the purpose and readership for which Mark was produced? After the opening verse, which serves as a title for the book as a whole, the opening stress falls on twin features: (1) the claim of the fulfillment of scripture in the events already taking place, and (2) the sense of eschatological urgency. The latter theme pervades the message of John the Baptist, as well as the words and works of one of his notable candidates for baptism: Jesus (1:2-4, 15). Even the syntax and the vocabulary of Mark with the mix of parataxis and stylized phrases—especially the 40 occurrences of *euthys* in Mark!—convey a sense of urgency in the whole of the gospel. That urgency is clearly linked in Mark with the expectation of a new and eschatologically imminent consummating act of God.

A third prominent feature of Mark is the alternation between public statement or act by Jesus and private disclosure or explanation to the inner core of his followers. The term, *kat'idian,* occurs in connection with Jesus' explanation to his disciples of the meaning of the parables; the retreat with the disciples to a desert place prior to the feeding of the 5000, which for Mark is a re-enactment on significantly new terms of the feeding of the covenant people in the desert of Sinai; Jesus' withdrawal with the disciples in connection with the healing of the deaf and dumb man in the Decapolis (7:33); the retreat in preparation for the transfiguration (9:2); the private explanation of the failure of the disciples to heal the child with the dumb spirit (9:28); the elaboration to the inner core of his followers following Jesus' prediction of the destruction of the temple (13:3). In every case the open testimony is followed by private clarification or amplification.

Closely akin to these phenomena of esoteric instruction are the series of predictions in which it is announced to the disciples that Jesus is going to Jerusalem to suffer, to die, and to rise from the dead (8:31; 9:31; 10:33). Of great importance in each of these instances is the link between the announcement of impending suffering and the promise of divine vindication that will follow the martyrdom. Mark makes clear that there was in Jewish thought of the time no self-evident paradigm, no standard messianic job-description for this predicted experience of suffering, death, and resurrection. The disciples remonstrate with Jesus following each of these predictions, and in Mark 9:10 the evangelist tells us that the disciples were "questioning what the rising from the dead meant" (9:10). Jesus' expectations are not portrayed as following an established pattern in detail, though as we shall see, the basic notions of the suffering of the obedient faithful, and of the consequent vindication of them by God are characteristic features of one type of Jewish literature.

Often neglected in analysis of Mark is the pervasive interest of this gospel in defining the people of God. This takes place in Mark through details which stand in explicit contrast to the prevailing options in Judaism of the first century. What the prevailing alternatives were in Judaism of the period of the Second Temple are easily sketched when one considers the sects mentioned by Josephus: the Sadducees, the Pharisees, and the Essenes—though one must consider them in terms of Jewish conventional identity rather than in the form of philosophical schools, as Josephus seeks to depict them. For the Sadducees, the essence of Judaism was the maintenance of and participation in the cultus prescribed in Torah. Their lack of interest in the Prophets and the Hagiographa was not so much a sign of theological conservatism as a reminder that for them the center of their existence was the temple, as the visible, operative locus and instrument of their link with the God of Israel.

As Jacob Neusner's monumental investigations of the development of rabbinic Judaism have shown,[4] the Pharisaic disillusionment with the Hasmoneans, and therefore with their definition of Israel as fundamentally a politically autonomous state, led them to appropriate the cultic code of scripture for the informal assembling of the faithful in the home or gathered small group. Thereby they transferred the code from the sanctuary to the setting of table fellowship. When the revolt of the Jewish nationalists was crushed in 66-70, and both they and the members of the priestly bureaucracy were scattered or destroyed, the Romans turned to the Pharisees as the group to reorganize the Jewish people, and to do so along the lines of passive, voluntary, apolitical gatherings devoted to personal piety.

The Essenes had—apparently in the second century B.C.—chosen yet another alternative to the definition of covenant people: under the leadership of the One who Teaches Rightly they had withdrawn from a society dominated, in their view, by a coalition of pagan political power: Jewish collaborationists, the priestly bureaucracy, and a largely indifferent local populace. In the Judean desert, at the very spot where the River of Life that Ezekiel promised would flow down from the Temple, renewing the desert and changing the Dead Sea into a fresh-water lake, they established their refuge of purity. There they could maintain separate identity—separate from both Gentiles and the rest of Judaism, which they regarded as apostate—as they awaited the divine acts of deliverance that would vindicate them, and would establish them as the leaders of the purified and proper cultus of the Temple.

In all three of these developments within post-exilic Judaism we may see operative the factors to which Mary Douglas's anthropological analyses have drawn attention: the definition of boundaries by a group in order to maintain identity and to demarcate between insiders and outsiders. The various options chosen by Jews in the Graeco-Roman period exemplify what Professor Douglas has called "the central concern for holiness," which she describes as not only a mode of setting apart the faithful, but of promoting a system of order in which human affairs may prosper as a consequence of the keeping of covenant with the deity by the observance of his precepts and ceremonies.[5] A symbolic universe is created: by conforming to holiness, human beings may prosper, and by deviating from it they invite destruction. Holiness is unity, integrity, and perfection of the individual or kind, so that those types of animals are unclean which are imperfect members of a class. The injunctions to inscribe the law on the heart, on the frontlets between the eyes, and on the doorposts are symbolic ways of declaring that these laws and precepts are the ground of ordered life in the divinely ordered cosmos.[6] Although Prof. Douglas's observations are based at this point on the Levitical Code of scripture, the same basic principles are operative in the three Jewish sects we have sketched above. The details, of course, vary significantly with respect to the specific precepts, but the basic pattern of holiness defined as boundary and divinely established order prevails in each example.

It is against precisely this range of options that we must inquire about the social setting of Mark. In a variety of ways, Mark differentiates the role of Jesus and the definition of his community of followers from each of these contemporary Jewish options

---

[4]Jacob Neusner, *The Rabbinic Traditions about the Pharisees before 70* (Leiden: Brill, 1971) Part One: The Masters; Part Two: The Houses; Part Three: Conclusions.
[5]Mary Douglas, *Purity and Danger* (London: Routledge & Kegan Paul, 1966, 1976) 5.
[6]M. Douglas, *Purity*, 50-57.

for covenant fulfillment. On the matter of the nationalistic form of expectation, Jesus uses the rhetoric of God's rule from the beginning to the end of his ministry (1:14; 15:2), but he makes no effort to start an insurrectionist movement. He enjoins his questioners to pay taxes to Caesar (12:17), and refuses to encourage the nationalistic urges of either his followers (10:35-45) or of the populace at large (11:1-11). It is only in mockery that he is identified as King of Israel—while he is hanging on the cross! For many in Judaism, the title Messiah would be understood as equivalent to king, but it is a serious historical and methodological error simply to equate kingship and messianic role. At Qumran, for example, the more prestigious of the two messianic figures awaited at the End of the Age was the Anointed Priest (1QS 2:12-22). Historically, as well as for Mark, messiah and kingship over a nation are not interchangeable terms.

The priestly definition of the covenant people—shared by Sadducees and Essenes, though with basic differences between the two groups—is also set aside by Jesus in Mark. He visits the temple twice, according to Mark: once as a sightseer (11:11), and once to denounce the activities carried on there in connection with the official cult (11:15-18). His last reported teaching is a prophecy of the temple's destruction, as part of the calamities predicted to occur prior to the End of the Age (Mark 13:1-2). Clearly, there is no positive place for the temple in the Markan scheme of divine redemption, either now (as among the Sadducees) or in the future (as claimed by the Essenes).

It is with the Pharisees that the conflict is most extended and most explicit. Whereas the Sadducees are mentioned only once in Mark (12:18), the Pharisees are referred to 12 times. In all but one of these texts, the issue is a challenge to Jesus for having set aside or allowed his disciples to set aside the laws or traditions which served to maintain the separate identity of Jews: Table-fellowship for persons of like persuasion only (2:16); fasting (2:18); sabbath observance (2:24; 3:6); ceremonial washing before eating (7:1, 3); observance of traditions (7:5). His attitude on such subjects as divorce and stance toward the Roman state is challenged as well (10:2; 12:13), and he is requested to have God perform a confirmatory sign (8:11), just as rabbinic teachers are reported in their traditions to have had their interpretations confirmed by signs from God.[7] The remaining reference to the Pharisees in Mark (8:15) is an enigmatic statement about the "leaven of the Pharisees and Herod(ians)," which in its present context seems to refer symbolically—under the symbolism of the two miraculous feedings reported in Mark 6 and 8—to the access by both Jews and Gentiles to participation in the covenant community.[8] The picture is consistent therefore: Mark represents the Pharisees as the major group whose understanding of the covenant relationship and its maintenance stands in sharp contrast with the way Jesus defines participation in the people of God. To refer back to Mary Douglas's proposals, the issue of holiness as a mode of definition of the community is as important for Mark as it is for the Essenes or the Pharisees, or for their forebears who compiled Leviticus. What is different are the ground rules which Jesus is portrayed as laying down for sharing in the New Covenant community. What are those qualifications for participation?

For Mark, participation in the covenant community has neither hereditary or ethnic dimensions. Instead, it is a voluntary matter, based on one's response to the message of

---

[7] Paul Fiebig, *Jüdische Wundergeschichten im Zeitalter Jesu* (Tübingen, 1911).

[8] H. C. Kee, *Community of the New Age* (Macon, GA: Mercer University Press, 1977, 1983) 111-12.

Jesus, the gospel of the nearness of God's Rule, which the hearers are called to believe (1:15). Those who do respond in trust are assigned the role of calling others, under the image of "fishers of men" (1:17). They are later directly commissioned to preach and to perform exorcisms, which are the pre-eminent sign in Mark of the inbreaking of God's kingdom. What is called for is trust in the one who controls the demons, stills the storm, and pronounces forgiveness of sins. The primary principle that is to characterize their common life is love of God and neighbor (12:28-34), which expresses itself in compassion for the poor (12:41-44). It is evident as well in the marital relationship, in that—contrary to the precept laid down in Torah (Deut 24:1-4)—Jesus is reported as appealing to the basic principle of the unity of male and female in the creative act of God, in Gen 2:24, as the ground for insisting on full mutuality of responsibility between man and woman with regard to fidelity and stability in marriage. This contrasts sharply with the rabbinic traditions on this subject, wherein the issue was debated as to how one was to understand the legally sanctioned condition for males to effect divorce: "If *he* has found some indecency in *her* . . ." (Deut 24:1). For Mark, by contrast, the fundamental principle is one of reciprocal responsibility.

A pervasive emphasis in Mark is that the follower must be prepared to accept persecution and the prospect of martyrdom. The private interpretation of the Parable of the Sower, for example (4:18), is a warning about the need to persevere in resistance to persecution and worldly enticements. The familiar phrase of Jesus' call is "Take up the cross" (8:34). The disciples are forewarned that they will be called upon to "drink the cup" and to undergo the "baptism" which Jesus himself experienced in death on the cross. The demands are severe for discipleship, but they are not defined in terms of ritual or even of ethical principles. They involve, rather, commitment to Jesus and his gospel, to the point of suffering and death.

Running throughout Mark is another dimension of the purity-and-boundary issue, to use Mary Douglas's terms. In Mark all the major definitions of covenantal purity, as drawn up by the Pharisaic movement, are repudiated, either by direct statement or by unmistakable implication. The explicit laws of sabbath observance and culinary and dietary purity are set aside in favor of the higher priority: basic human need (Mark 7, especially 7:19, where all foods are declared clean). Jesus seems to go out of his way in the Markan narratives to make contact with precisely those items which render one unclean by Jewish standards of community boundaries: tombs, corpses, spittle, body fluids, and above all, table fellowship with Gentiles and marginal people. When pressed to seek a divine sign to confirm the heavenly sanction for his radical reinterpretation of the Law of God, as seems to have been a familiar phenomenon in the rabbinic tradition, he flatly refuses (8:11; 11:27-33). Understandably, therefore, he is depicted in the Parable of the Vineyard (Mark 12:1-12) as facing certain rejection by the leaders of the Jewish people. The choice of the subject of the parable, deriving as it does from Isaiah's powerful and classic judgment on the infidelity of the covenant community, underscores the point in Mark: the vineyard is to be given to others, and the leaders are fully aware of this implication of the parable, as 12:12 makes explicit: "They perceived that he had told the parable against them." The quotation from Psalm 118 about the new structure that God is erecting through the very person that the leaders have rejected makes the point powerfully that what is at stake for Mark is not only the fate of Jesus but the reconstitution of the covenant people as well.

That impression is confirmed in two symbolic accounts included in Mark: the two stories of miraculous feeding, in Mark 6 and 8. The analogies with the experience of

Israel in Sinai are obvious, and are of course made explicit in John's version of this miracle (John 6). It is no accident, incidentally, that this is the single miracle story found in all four of the canonical gospels. The repetition of the story in Mark—one in Jewish territory and the other in a Gentile district—combines with the use of the symbolic numbers, 7 and 12, to indicate that what is being represented symbolically here is the assembling of the new people of God from both Jewish and Gentile peoples (cf. 8:14-21). The covenantal significance of these stories is evident from the direct correspondence of language between them on the one hand and the eucharistic scene in 14:22-28 on the other—"took, blessed, broke, gave"—in that the latter incident is explicitly declared to be the sacrifice that ratifies the new[9] covenant, as shown by its link with the coming of God's Rule.

We raise once more the question as to the background—in Judaism or in the wider hellenistic world—against which such a notion of community might have arisen. Clearly there are some links with Paul: the motif of perseverance in light of eschatological vindication; the promise of the establishment of God's Rule, grounded in the resurrection experience; the factor of secret disclosure of the divine plan to Paul and the faithful, as in the eschatological mystery mentioned in 1 Cor 15:51; in his private vision, in the tradition of Jewish-Chariot-throne mysticism, in 2 Cor 12:1-10. But the distinctive Pauline elements are missing from Mark: Stoic virtues, conscience, justification by faith, a developed doctrine of the cross, the centrality of the resurrection appearances. Unlike Paul, whose letters evince no interest in the career of Jesus, Mark concentrates on the narrative of Jesus' public activity, culminating in his death and the promise of his resurrection. Absent from Mark are the characteristic Pauline formulas of redemption. Clearly, therefore, Mark is not an expansion of the Pauline kerygma.

Where, then *do* we find precedent or approximation for the work we know as the Gospel of Mark? What is the social context out of which Mark has been produced? Or to put the issue yet another way, what is the social purpose for which Mark was written? The clues to answers for all three of these questions come to us from Jewish apocalypticism, especially when we approach that phenomenon as a social mode with literary and conceptual dimensions, rather than as merely a representation of a conceptual point of view. The most important evidence comes from Daniel and from some of the Qumran documents. For both these sources, apocalyptic involves a world-view shared by a community, not merely a theological construct. Central to both sources are the narratives about the experiences of the central figures: Daniel and his friends in the first instance, and the Teacher of Righteousness in the other. There are narratives of the difficulties and threats through which they passed as they sought to fulfill the divine destiny that unfolded before them. In Daniel that path included determination to remain obedient to God in the face of threats of martyrdom by the hostile political power. In the Scrolls, the Teacher experienced hostility from the religious leaders until he withdrew in order to live the life of purity in the wilderness, from which God would lead him and the faithful back to Jerusalem and vindication. The guidelines for the life of the elect community are implied in Daniel, and carefully, elaborately traced out in the Scroll of the Rule and the Damascus Document. In both cases, there is conviction that the hopes laid down in

---

[9]The textual variant in 14:14 raises the question of whether *kaine* is part of the original text. The newness is implied even though that word were to be omitted, since the direct connection is made immediately with the eschatological fulfillment which Jesus' death makes possible (in 14:25).

scripture are to be fulfilled for and through the elect. As a consequence of their fidelity to the divine will, God will establish the divine order through them and for their benefit. Beyond obedience and suffering is the triumph of God, in which they will be the chief beneficiaries. The clues as to what God is doing have not been conveyed in univocal language, but through visions and especially through divinely granted insight into the plan of God as set forth in scripture. For both groups, the essential requirement for participation in the eschatological fulfillment is the maintenance of purity. It is no accident that the frequency in Mark of quotations from and allusions to Daniel as compared with references to the rest of the Old Testament, is utterly out of proportion to the size of that book. The apocalypse in Mark 13 is in many ways a kind of midrash on Daniel.[10] And of course Mark's favorite designation for Jesus, Son of Man, is a phrase which derives from Daniel.[11] Yet what Mark depicts Jesus as doing with this apocalyptic tradition is by no means a slavish conformity to it. Quite the contrary, Jesus is represented as transforming that tradition, even while highlighting most of the issues which it raises concerning the nature of God's people, the agent of divine deliverance, and the consummation of the divine purpose.

Although commentators and theologians inquiring after the term, "son of man" in Daniel and Mark have discussed at length the linking of this phrase with "the saints of the Most High" in Dan 7:18, 22, 25, 27, very little attention has been paid to the characteristics and membership qualifications of this group.

Careful analysis of Daniel as a whole discloses a group with a clearly definable symbolic universe, and with precisely drawn boundaries. Fundamental is the conviction that "the Most High" is in control of human destiny, including that of both his friends and those who oppose Him and His people. Even the pagan rulers must acknowledge his sovereign power, as Belshazzar, Nebuchadnezzar, and Darius do (Dan 5:22; 6:25-27). Insight into the divine purpose is granted to Daniel, as the representative leader of the faithful community. To him—borrowing phrases from Mark 4—has been given the mystery of the Kingdom of God, while to those outside everything is in riddles. He and his friends are declared by the writer to have wisdom and understanding ten times better than that of the magicians and enchanters in all the rest of the kingdom (1:20). He alone can interpret the mysterious image which represents successive world empires, all of which are doomed to destruction (2:31). He alone can recall and interpret the king's dream (Dan 4) and can explain the handwriting on the wall (5:12). Confirmation of his insight into the divine purpose is given in the form of signs and wonders (Dan 4:3; 5:11).

The essential quality which enables Daniel and his friends to be included among the "saints of the Most High" is their strict, courageous maintenance of purity. The threats to that sanctified status include the command to eat the king's rich, but impure food (1:8), the demand that all subjects honor his image (3:6, 15), and the prohibition against offering petitions to anyone but the king (6:7). In each case, the firm stand in defiance of the imperial decree carries with it the threat of suffering and death. This is made explicit in Dan 3:28, where we read that these faithful ones "yielded up their bodies

---

[10]H. C. Kee, "The Function of Scriptural Quotations and Allusions in Mark 11-16," in *Jesus und Paulus*, Festschrift for W. G. Kümmel (ed. E. E. Ellis and E. Grasser; Göttingen, 1975). Also Lars Hartmann, *Prophecy Interpreted: The Formation of Some Jewish Apocalyptic Texts and of the Eschatological Discourse Mark 13 par* (Lund, 1966).

[11]Joseph Fitzmyer, "The New Testament Title 'Son of Man' Philologically Considered," in *A Wandering Aramean* (Chico, CA: Scholars Press, 1979) 143-60.

rather than worship any god except their own God." When one moves from the narrative parts of Daniel to the visions, the theme of the maintenance of purity under threat of death is amplified, as may be seen in the prediction that the little horn will make war on the saints (7:21), or that the great king in the hellenistic tradition shall seek to destroy "mighty men and the people of the saints" (8:24). Those who remain true to their status as the holy ones of God are forewarned that they "shall fall by sword and flame, by captivity and plunder" (11:33). The suffering of the righteous remnant of the people of God is a fundamental axiom of the apocalyptic world-view, whether in Daniel or in Mark, however participation in the elect community may be defined.

In contrast to the perseverance of the saints, as Daniel depicts it, is the infidelity of the mainstream of Israel, as it is described in the extended confession of sin in behalf of historic Israel, in Daniel 3:19. After noting Israel's rebellion against the divine ordinances, her failure to listen to the prophets, her treachery against God, her rebellion, her failure to obey the laws and her transgression of them (9:5-11), Daniel recalls the act constitutive of Israel as God's covenant people—the deliverance from Egypt—and pleads for the restoration of the sanctuary and city of Jerusalem (9:15-17). In spite of the petition for renewal, however, the prophet announces the destruction of the city and its temple (9:25-26). Here Daniel's outlook is akin to that of the Qumran community, which looks beyond the judgment that will fall on the corrupt majority to the vindication and restoration that God will effect in behalf of the faithful minority. It is no surprise, therefore, that the apocalyptic vision in Mark 13 is concerned precisely with this judgmental event: the destruction of the temple by pagan powers. Even the language used to describe the ultimate desecration—the abominable sacrilege, in Mark 13:14—derives directly from Daniel (9:27; 11:31; 12:11).

Closely akin to the theme of the suffering of the faithful is the motif of divine vindication. This is described directly, though probably intended symbolically, in Dan 1:8, where the faithful Israelites who refuse the royal food are after ten days trial period "better in appearance and fatter in flesh than all the youths who ate at the king's table" (1:8). Fidelity to God brings deliverance from the fiery furnace and from the mouth of the lions, as well as from the other threats of the rulers in the visions. But the suffering of those who falter will refine and cleanse the visions. And the ultimate deliverance will come at the End of the Age, when "Your people shall be delivered, everyone whose name shall be found written in the book" (12:1). The holy people, though suffering and even if martyred, will be raised and redeemed: "Many shall purify themselves, and make themselves white and be refined" (12:7-10). Daniel himself, lest he falter in the face of powerful opposition, is granted a mystical vision, whereby he is visibly transformed (Dan 10:8), even though his companions are unaware of what is happening. The kinship of this experience is clear, not only with Merkavah mysticism, as Ithamar Gruenwald's study *Apocalyptic and Merkavah Mysticism*,[12] rightly suggests, but also with the transfiguration of Jesus in Mark 9. In Daniel as in Mark, the mystical vision is granted on the eve of unprecedented suffering, in order to provide a basis for confidence in divine vindication that is to occur in the near future.

The timing of the End of the Age as presented in Daniel is also significant as a characteristic feature of the apocalyptic world-view. The scheme set forth in Daniel 9, with its seventy weeks, or heptads of years, builds on Jeremiah's prediction of the 70

---

[12]Ithmar Gruenwald, *Apocalyptic and Merkavah Mysticism* (Leiden: Brill, 1980).

years until the restoration of Israel (Jer 25:12). The prophet sees himself as living in the last half of the final week before the "decreed end" takes place (Dan 9:24-27). Similarly, Jesus tells his disciples to expect the End within the then living generation (Mark 9:1; 13:30).

Against the background of apocalyptic, how does Mark represent Jesus as summoning the community of the New Covenant? Unlike the Essenes, the Pharisees, or John the Baptist, the rallying point for Jesus' call is not amendment of life or the striving for purity along ritual or even ethical lines, but acknowledgment of one's need and expectant participation in the proclamation of the coming of God's Rule. The invitation goes out to those who are on the fringes of Judaism, including tax collectors and sinners, as well as to those outside the pale completely. To those who respond to the gospel with trust, there is granted insight into the meaning of Jesus' exercise of authority over the powers of Satan as well as over the basic laws by which Judaism defined its separate existence: sabbath, fasting, ritual purity. To them is also given insight into the meaning of Jesus' esoteric teaching in the form of parables, as well as an understanding of the significance of both Jesus' suffering and death and their own, which will follow his example. They are forewarned about the fall of Jerusalem, but they are enjoined to submit to the demands of Caesar, rather than to engage in political insurrection. They are also informed of Jesus' and their own future vindication, beyond the immediate prospect of persecution and martyrdom. Meanwhile, however, there are some basic rules of mutual love and responsibility that are to guide their common life until the end of the age comes.

What we see in Mark is that all the issues which are to the fore in Jewish apocalyptic are present in Mark and operate in the same general pattern of meaning, but the answer to those individual issues is radically different, especially at the point of who the prospective members of the "saints of the Most High" are, and what the qualifications are for maintaining good standing among the elect community. As we noted in our consideration of the Parable of the Vineyard in Mark 12, the vineyard has been "given to others," whose criteria for membership are dramatically at variance with the other Jewish options of the period.

Thus far, we have had little to say about messianic roles or titles. This deferral has been intentional, because one cannot—as so much New Testament theological writing does—detach the significance of a messianic title from the community affirming that messiahship. Indeed, if we were to limit our inquiry to titles as such, we should miss out on the range of redemptive, eschatological roles that are operative in Judaism in this period, as well as in early Christianity. Clearly, the phrase "son of man" in Daniel is a simile for the humanity of the agents of divine rule ("the saints of the Most High") in contrast to fearsome beasts who symbolize the cruel pagan powers which God's Rule replaces. As I have sought to show elsewhere, both the author of 4 Ezra toward the end of the first century, and the author of the Similitudes of Enoch earlier in that century are reworking older prophetic and apocalyptic tradition in order to bring to bear the hope of divine deliverance in their own immediate presence. 4 Ezra, for example, is quite explicit: in 2 Esdras 12:10-12 the seer is told that "The eagle which you saw coming up out of the sea is the fourth kingdom which appeared in a vision to your brother Daniel," but the revealer asserts that "It was not explained to him as I now explain it to you." Just as Daniel reworks in midrashic fashion the prophecy of Jeremiah, so 4 Ezra is adapting not only Daniel, but also such themes as Ezekiel's valley of Dry bones, the reconstitution of the covenant people, the restoration of the sanctuary, the ascent to power of David's heir, and Gentile acknowledgment of the Rule of Israel's God.[13] Similarly, the Similitudes of Enoch includes a midrash on Isa 24:17-23.[14] This process of apocalyptic adaptation of older tradition to the new situation—which is what can be seen occurring in Mark as well as in these strictly Jewish apocalypses of the first century and earlier—has been shown by O. Plöger[15] to be the effort to revive the eschatological dimension of the prophetic tradition so as to express "the future hope of a community which was conscious of being a religious body absolutely separate from the national and religious life of the rest of mankind and which, being unique, could only express a future hope in terms of its own distinctive existence, while living at the same time in the belief that 'the manner of this world is passing away.'"[16] That is a precise formal description of the community in Mark. But the uniqueness of the Markan community lies in the dual claims this gospel makes with regard to (1) admission to the community and (2) the role of the redemptive figure, Jesus.

There does not seem to have been in existence prior to the first century a messianic or redemptive title Son of Man, though it surfaces in that century, not only in the New Testament but in such Jewish writings as Enoch and 4 Ezra as well. In Mark, Son of Man is used paradoxically of the authority roles of Jesus, both in the present (forgiving sin, lordship over the sabbath) as well as in the Future (coming as judge, and in triumph). The imagery, the issues, the depiction of cosmic conflict, the definition of the faithful remnant, the esoteric information and the visions of fulfillment of the divine plan, are all part of the common currency of apocalyptic. But the distinctive way in which these items are perceived is the contribution of the Markan Jesus. Instead of rising up in opposition to the pagan power, the redemptive figure fulfills his mission by submitting to death on the cross.

Most strikingly different from Daniel, Qumran, 4 Ezra and Enoch, however, is the Markan definition of the eschatological community. Instead of remaining content with its esoteric information, Mark's community is also called to be aggressively evangelistic. Instead of concentrating on the maintenance of ritual purity, it defies those cultic boundaries in the interests of human need and inclusiveness. Rather than condemn fellow Israelites for failure to maintain separation, it calls—both symbolically and explicitly -- for potentially universal participation in the New Covenant people. Yet it builds on Israelite tradition, in its claim to be the fulfillment of scripture, in its reworking of the prophetic and apocalyptic tradition, and in its symbolic equivalent of the Sinai experience; the miraculous feeding which is understood in terms of the eucharist.

Mark is, therefore, to be seen as the foundation document for an apocalyptic group of early Christians. The story of Jesus is their story. He is the paradigm for their suffering, for their mission, and for the effectiveness of their struggle with the powers of

---

[13]H. C. Kee, "The Man in IV Ezra: Growth of a Tradition," *SBL 1981 Seminar Papers*, 199-208, which builds on Ferdinand Dexinger's study of the Enoch Apocalypse of Ten Weeks.

[14]David Suter, *Tradition and Composition in the Parables of Enoch* (SBLDS 1979) 38-72.

[15]Otto Plöger, *Theocracy and Eschatology* (trans. S. Rudman; Oxford: Blackwell, 1968) 30-42.

[16]Plöger, *Theocracy*, 50.

Satan, as well as for their perseverance to the End of the Age. Their knowledge of this is perceived in terms of private revelation, "To you has been given the mystery of the Kingdom of God." Only hints are available about the specific geographical provenance of this group. As I suggested in my *Community of the New Age*, Mark's special interest in Syria and the Decapolis may mean that it was written in that region, perhaps in Damascus, where violation of covenantal purity aroused the vindictive wrath of a Pharisee named Paul.[17] The fact that Mark quotes the scriptures in Greek indicates that his community was not basically a semitic-speaking group. The fact that the Jewish nationalists in this region were violent in their attack on fellow-members of their tradition who did not join in the revolt against the Romans, as Josephus reports, fits well with the Markan Jesus' injunction to give one's just dues to Caesar, as well as his refusal to make a pitch for seizing power. Of course, such a passive reaction to the issue of Jewish nationalism need not have been limited to that area.[18] Details of Syro-Palestine culture, such as mention of the mud-roofs of village houses—which Luke changes to tiles!—may also support a Syro-Palestinian origin.

But far more important than the geographical origin is the sociology-of-knowledge question: What was the life-world in which Mark was produced? Here the answer is clear and unambiguous. It was an apocalyptic world view, which built on the traditional materials from Jewish apocalyptic in its portrait of Jesus. But in light of the figure of Jesus, building on the Jesus tradition, it radically transformed both the definition of the group and its leader, as well as its vision of what the Rule of God would be in its consummation. It is these factors which enable us to discern the characteristics of leadership and group identity, and thereby to determine what in fact was the social setting of Mark's gospel.

---

[17]Sean Freyne, *Galilee from Alexander the Great to Hadrian* (Wilmington and Notre Dame, 1980) 357-80.
[18]Kee, *Community*, 100-105.

Power and the Man of Power in the Context of Hellenistic Popular Belief

Gail Paterson Corrington

Penn State University

After eight decades of research, it might seem as though inquiry into the vexed question of whether or not there ever existed in antiquity the concept of a "divine man" (*theios anēr*), charismatic and wonder-worker, ought to have been settled once and for all. Instead, scholarship continues to be occupied with the idea of such a semi-divine figure and with his supposed background in Hellenistic Judaism and Christianity. What has been largely neglected by this research is how the audiences of antiquity understood the messages presented to them and how their own pre-suppositions affected in what way these messages were framed by contemporary missionaries. I am speaking here about the Hellenistic popular audience, not the sophisticated audience of the "Hellenizing" Jewish apologists and *litterateurs*.

In attempting to describe this audience, most previous scholarship has focused on its description by the satirists of the time (e.g., Lucian of Samosata and Juvenal) or has assumed that we can understand its point of view from the apologetics of Philo or Josephus. In the first case, the satirists' evidence shows only that we must deal with an unsophisticated audience, whose attention could be most readily won by displays of thaumaturgy and promises of transcendent power. Thus, we may not accept the witness of satire unless we do so in a "negative" way. Further, the audience so derided by satirists and philosophers would not be the same one at which the complex arguments of a Philo would be aimed. If we suppose that the history of divine man research has been an attempt to place "popular" documents like the canonical (and extra-canonical) Gospels and Acts into a context, then that context must be one of "popular" perceptions of the world and one's place in it, perceptions which of necessity include popular philosophy, thaumaturgy, magic, and other forms of *Volksglaube*.

This popular belief must moreover be located within the larger Hellenistic world-view and its pre-occupation on all levels with power. It is within this horizon that the concept of the "embodied power" of the *theios anēr* may be found. This notion of "embodied power" produced the saviors of the Hellenistic world: gods, heroes, powerful rulers, and then philosophers, thaumaturges, magicians, and other religious figures. These saviors and their attributes may be known from inscriptions, philosophical writings, both "popular" and those critical of the popular; and from more "personalized" views of power found in such documents as the *Hermetica* and the *Greek Magical Papyri*. Thus, given these ways of seeing power and its working within the world, we may see how these concepts were manipulated by the missionaries of the Hellenistic world to produce conversion.

The tremendous political changes which occurred in the Mediterranean area, beginning in the fourth century B.C.E., both coincided with and helped to shape philosophical and religious changes, especially in relation to their views of power. The rise of the superman Alexander and his powerful Diadochi seemed to indicate their control over the destinies of lesser people, not unlike that of gods on earth. When the influence of skeptical philosophy and Euhemerism turned "gods" back into powerful humans, when both religion and philosophy dissolved deity into potency,[1] the control over or display of power seemed so much more to be evidence of the divine. In the Hellenistic world, concern for the safety and security of the person and the city (*sōtēria*) resulted first in reverence for those capable, through their power, of securing that *sōtēria*. At first, these "saviors" (*sōtēres*) were the patron deities of the city or deme, but the term was later transferred to the heroes, who were also procurers of local *sōtēria*, and thence to the conquering generals and emperors who were responsible for continuing that sense of security. On earth, this *sōtēria* paralleled the sense of personal assurance of safety in relation to the governing powers of the universe. From this point, belief developed in an earthly power corresponding to that of the patron deity, which was embodied in a powerful general or ruler, whose control over one's personal destiny seemed scarcely less cosmic than a god's.

The philosophical movements of the Hellenistic period fostered this type of belief in an earthly power or powers corresponding to those in heaven. In describing popular philosophies of these era, historians have tended to see them as part of a "decline" into credulity, mysticism, and theosophy.[2] This view may result from the fact that many of the beliefs of developing Stoicism and Cynicism come remarkably close to what Nilsson calls "lower" beliefs, one of the most striking correspondences being in their views of power. For the Stoic Poseidonius, whose influence upon Graeco-Roman Stoicism was pervasive, *dynamis*, or, in his phrase, *dynamis zōtikē*, was not a physical or "natural" power: it was a life-giving force, the "absolute cosmic principle,"[3] later referred to by Cicero as *vis divina*, the divine power analogous to the older *Logos* (*De Divinatione* 1.52.118). Like this better-known *Logos*, *dynamis* was not only the guiding principle of the world, but was manifested in the earthly and human sphere by *dynameis*, acts of power. Thus, one's own *dynamis* needed to be in tune with this cosmic power. On the more popular level, Bolos of Mendes, a Graeco-Egyptian writer of the third century B.C.E., claimed that these powers were resident in all parts of the natural realm, not merely in humans. Philosophical thinking has here come very close to the sphere of magical belief, in that one may "awaken" the power of these elements of nature through knowing the correct formulae, thus transforming the *sophia* of philosophical explanation into the occult wisdom so characteristic of later antiquity.

Philosophy had itself taken to the street-corners, beginning in the third century, with Bion of Borysthenes. The Cynic preachers, in the name of *autarkeia*, had renounced ties of family and city, and of the methods and rhetoric of philosophical "schools" (e.g., Epictetus *Dissertationes* 3.23.30). Even these schools, however, in their idealization of their founders, had shown the growing influence of the popular interest in the bizarre and foreign, wonder-tales and adventure-stories, in their development of philosophical *bioi*, which were less biographies than simply collections of *paradoxa* surrounding famous philosophers.

Pythagoras is a case in point. In the Pythagorean revival of the first century, the

---

[1]Martin P. Nilsson, *Greek Piety* (Oxford: Clarendon, 1948) 108-9.
[2]Ibid., 105-6.
[3]Walther Grundmann, "*Dynamis*," *TDNT* 2. 287.

oral traditions concerning Pythagoras, "purged" of their legendary and miraculous elements by Aristotle,[4] made their way back, through the writings of Apollonius the Paradoxographer, who recounts four miracles of the great mathematician in his *Historiae Thaumasiae:* a golden thigh, a divine voice, miraculous appearances in two places at once, a sea-miracle, and survival from snake-bite. These "wonderful tales" even find their way into Iamblichus' eulogistic biography of Pythagoras (*Vita Pyth.* 61). This model of the "divine" Pythagoras, rather than that of the heroic Socrates, is the more characteristic paradigm of the Hellenistic *sophos*.[5] Pythagoras represents the older *theios* of folk-belief in his transformation, as the *theios philosophos*, the increasingly idealized philosopher, "internalizes" the *theios* of *Volksglaube*.[6] Thus, as philosophy grew closer to the universal Hellenistic concern for salvation and power, the "lives" of its philosophical heroes also changed.

This transformation is also seen in Philostratus' *Vita* of Apollonius of Tyana, who, not surprisingly, was a Pythagorean. Although Philostratus' account is rather late (second century C.E.), it is based upon an earlier, more "popular" account, the "awkward and barbaric" one of the Assyrian Damis, who worshipped Apollonius "as if he were a *daimon*" (*Vita Apoll.* 1.19.22). Yet Philostratus does not "purge" his own account of the philosopher's wonder-working deeds. Philostratus also claims that Apollonius has "something divine" (*theion ti, Vita* 3.43.8-9) in him, and his miracles are proof of that "god-like nature" (*theia physis, Vita* 7.38.16). This philosophical understanding of "virtue" (*aretē*) as "something divine" finds its place in Stoic-Cynic philosophy, such as that of Epictetus (*Diss.* 3.22.69-70), Cicero (*De Divin.*, *De Natura Deorum*), Plutarch (*De Iside et Osiride*), and Cornutus, who uses the term in reference to the demi-god, Asclepius (*Theologiae Graecae Compendium, 33*). By the time of Philostratus, we see this notion of *aretē* as quality ("virtue") being translated into *aretē* as visible *dynamis*.

The satiricists also provide us with a picture of popular piety. In his *Demonax*, Lucian of Samosata derides Apollonius and presents the "true" philosopher, the older model of virtue, as "the epiphany of a god" (*Demon.* 63.11) because he refuses to prey upon the naïveté of the vulgar. Lucian's bitterest attacks are reserved for those who take advantage of the *polloi* by offering them false wares for the true life of philosophy (e.g., *Biōn Prasis* 2.11-12). The greatest pretenders to philosophy as quasi-religious power are Peregrinus Proteus, whose name indicates both his itinerant life and his quick-change nature; and Alexander of Abonuteichos, whom Lucian calls a "false prophet." Both are believed by the *idiōtai*, the "unlearned" (*Peregrinus* 11.10-12; *Alexander* 12.7), to be divine, when they are actually charlatans and sorcerers (*goēs kai technitēs, Peregrinus* 13.22).

What these two examples, taken from a satirist who is also a Cynic philosopher, show is that there is really no distinction, either in the critic Lucian's mind or in the minds of those he satirizes, between the beliefs commonly "for sale" by street-corner preachers and magical belief. Charges of charlatanry (*goēteia*), sorcery (*mageia*), or

---

[4]J. A. Philip, *Pythagoras and Early Pythagoreanism* (Toronto and Buffalo: University of Toronto Press, 1966) 159ff.

[5]Cf. David L. Tiede, *The Charismatic Figure as Miracle-Worker* (SBLDS 1; Missoula: Scholars Press, 1972) 16ff.

[6]Cf. Ludwig Bieler, *THEIOS ANĒR* (Darmstadt: Wissenschaftliches Buchgesellschaft, 1967) 5 n. 10, citing Hans Windisch, *Paulus u. Christus* (Leipzig: J. C. Hinrichs, 1934) 60-62.

"wonder-working" (*terateia*), common in the Hellenistic period against the preachers of new philosophies or religions, indicates not only the success they had in winning the unsophisticated *polloi* but the similarity (or apparent similarity) of the methods they used. Clearly, these methods were such as opened themselves up to charges like "magic" and "sorcery": namely, the performance of wonders. This type of performance demonstrated the preacher's own possession of power (like Paul's "signs of the apostle"?) or the power granted by his particular belief. In addition, stories were told about the *thaumasta* of the founders of philosophical and religious movements so as to impress the audiences with their divine power. The very success of this method shows how firmly ingrained in the minds of the audience addressed was this attitude towards power. To Lucian, appealing to such a concept seemed to be taking a cheap, sophisticated advantage of ignorance and the desire for a "simple and secure way of life (*bios*)" (*Menippus* 3.3, 4) felt to be the necessary *sōtēria* in an insecure world.

That such displays of power appeared not only miraculous but magical to the popular mind, we have the evidence of the *Corpus Hermeticum*, itself a blend of popular philosophy, popular religion, and magical power; and the record of more personal attempts to control power, the *Greek Magical Papyri* (*PGM*), both of which appear also to be influenced by Hellenistic Judaism of a definitely non-Philonic strain. There is of course some difficulty with using these materials, since their dating is rather late, as evidence for a world-view of earlier times. However, although the final form of *CH* is attested in the 2nd-3rd centuries C.E. and later, A. D. Nock claims that it contains material which may actually date from the 2nd century B.C.E.[7] Collections of *materia magica* similar to the *PGM* are known to have existed much earlier than its dating in the 4th century C.E. In Acts 19:19, Luke refers to a burning of such "books of magic," while Juvenal in *Satire VI* criticizes the sale of magical *carmina* in Domitian's Rome. Like the *Hermetica*, the magical papyri contain a mixture of Greek cosmological speculation, Egyptian occult "wisdom," and a strong, at times dominant, admixture of Judaism, particularly in the "names of power" (Iao, Sabaoth, Adonai, Michael, Gabriel, Uriel, Raphael) it uses amongst the "names of power" of Greek and Egyptian deities.

What this type of evidence tells us about the popular mind of the Graeco-Roman period is exactly what we have found from the evidence of satire: that, under the dominating desire for access to divine power, there was little if any distinction made between the philosophical (which often appears as occult *sophia*), the magical, and the religious. Hence, the *magos* could be seen as a type of philosopher (*sophos*), or even as *theios*, because he could address, awaken, and control the powers which were, for the Hellenistic world, the essence of divinity. Similarly, the *sophos*, especially when obliged by his concept of "mission" to preach philosophy on the street corners, opened himself up to charges of *mageia* when he performed or recited "wonders" which were required to gain the attention of the public. As Nock has also observed, philosophy and religion, religion and magic, were becoming more alike in the Hellenistic world:

> The religious practised magic, and it could hardly be said that in their belief they were free from magical conceptions. . . . At the same time, magicians

---

[7] A.D. Nock, Introduction to A. M. J. Festugière, *La révélation d'Hermès Trismégiste* (Paris: J. Gabalda, 1944-54) vol. I, p. i.

accumulated religious formulae in their endeavor to secure the greatest possible amount of divine power for their purposes. . . .[8]

The unifying element of all three—magic, religion, and philosophy—was an attitude towards power: desire for understanding its control over the world, to know who possessed it, how to address it, and eventually how to channel it to oneself or through oneself. The *Paris Magical Papyrus* (*PGM* I.IV.1275) expresses it thus: "I call upon thee, greatest power (*dynamin*) in heaven, marshalled by the Lord God." *CH* I (*Poimandres*) mentions the "powers" of the universe (7-8; 26), which are also referred to in *CH* XIII (The "Mountain-Top" Discourse) as the seven planets and three higher powers, "goodness, light, and life"; the first group being cosmological or astrological, the second being more abstract, like Poseidonius' *theia dynamis*. Humans can themselves become "one of the powers" (*CH* I.26).

In the magical papyri, not only are the epithets of the Jewish God (Iao/Adonai), Jesus with the holy spirit, and the archangels "names of power," but also the names of the patriarchs, Solomon, and Moses, the latter being especially efficacious. Solomon, as might be expected from his reputation for occult wisdom (cf. Josephus, *Ant.* 8.45-49), is the author of several charms (*PGM* I.IV.354-55; 850). Moses, true to his standing in the ancient world as a "magician,"[9] is author of two "books" of magic, the "Diadem of Moses" (*PGM* II.VII.620ff.) and "The Holy Book of the Monad" (*PGM* II.XIII).

In the magical papyri, the most "popular" of all documents examined here, the heroes of Judaism are light-years removed from their portrayal as exemplars of virtue (*aretē*) by the Stoic Philo. Here, their *aretai* can truly be said to represent powerful acts (also called *aretai*), even magical acts. Here we are much closer to the notion of a truly "divine" man: that is, a person with the power of a god. As Gager has noted, the Moses of the papyri is "an inspired prophet, endowed with wisdom and power, whose very name guaranteed the efficacy of magical claims and provided protection against the hostile forces of the cosmos."[10] Here indeed could be said to be a *sōtēr* of the popular mind.

Let us conclude, too briefly, with the reflection that it is to such an audience, with its conception of power and the operation of power, that Jesus, the one "attested to you by signs and wonders" (Acts 2:22), is preached by those who also perform similar *sēmeia kai terata*, in keeping with their idea of mission. The confusion in the popular mind between philosophy, religious claims, and magic as evidences of divine *dynamis* working in the human realm could open up such "apostles," like the itinerant Jewish exorcists and philosophers of Apollonius' type, to charges of charlatanry and sorcery. Yet, these methods had to be used, because, as we have seen in several cases, they were the most attractive. We have only to keep in mind as example the futility of Paul's insisting to the Corinthians, attracted by the "signs of the apostle," that God's strength was "perfected in weakness" (2 Cor 12:9).

---

[8]Nock, "Studies in the Graeco-Roman Beliefs of the Empire," *JHS* 45 (1925) 84.
[9]Cf. John Gager, *Moses in Graeco-Roman Paganism* (Cambridge: Harvard University Press, 1968) 137-38, 159-60.
[10]Gager, *Moses*, 159-60.

Those Elusive Eleusinian Mystery Shows

Luther H. Martin

The University of Vermont

Modern treatments of the Mysteries can be dated from G. F. Creuzer's comprehensive *Symbolik und Mythologie der alter Völker, besonders der Griechen* (1810-1923),[1] and C. A. Lobeck's critical rejoinder, *Aglaophamus sive de Theologiae Mysticae Graecorum Causis* (1829).[2]

Creuzer, together with Friederich Schelling, exemplified the nineteenth century "Symbolists" who argued that all mythology gave symbolic expression to underlying primordial truths or archetypal patterns.[3] This romantic essentialism was taken up by J. J. Bachofen,[4] directly influenced the developing thought of the psychologist C. G. Jung,[5] and informed C. Kerényi's study of the Eleusinian Mysteries.[6]

The classicist, Lobeck, on the other hand, challenged the "fanciful speculations" of the Symbolists.[7] Anticipating Leopold von Ranke's positivistic dictum that the task of the historian was "simply to show how it really was" (*wie es eigentlich gewesen*),[8] Lobeck set out to establish "everything that is really known about Greek mysteries."[9] He concluded that since the Mysteries were open to all Greeks without distinction, including slaves, and later even foreigners, they did not involve the revelations of profound religious secrets.[10] Creuzer's student, Erwin Rohde, who J. E. Sandys judged to have written

---

[1](Leipzig and Darmstadt: Carl Wilheim Leske).

[2](Rpt. Darmstadt: Wissenschaftliche Buchgesellschaft, 1968).

[3]See J. E. Sandys, *A History of Classical Scholarship* (Cambridge: University Press, 1908) vol. III, pp. 66f.; and "Religionsgeschichte," in *Die Religion in Geschichte und Gegenwart* [*RGG*] (3rd ed.; Tübingen: J. C. B. Mohr Paul Siebeck , 1957-1965) vol. V, col. 990.

[4]*RGG*, 2nd ed., 1927-1931, vol. 1, col. 723; and *RGG*, 3rd ed., vol. 1, col. 830f.

[5]*Memories, Dreams, Reflections*, recorded and ed. Aniela Jaffé (trans. Richard and Clara Winston; New York: Vintage Books, 1961) 162.

[6]*Eleusis, Archetypal Images of Mother and Daughter* (trans. Ralph Manheim; New York: Pantheon Books, 1967), despite his protestations otherwise in *Asklepios, Archetypal Image of the Physician's Existence* 1947; rpt. Darmstadt: Wissenschaftliche Buchgesellschaft, 1956; trans. Ralph Manheim (New York: Pantheon Books, 1959) xxif.

[7]Sandys, op. cit., 104; W. Brede Kristensen, *The Meaning of Religion* (The Hague: Martinus Nijhoff, 1960) 401-4.

[8]E. H. Carr, *What Is History?* (New York: Vintage Books, 1961) 5f.

[9]Sandys, op. cit., vol. III, p. 104.

[10]"Mysterion" in H. G. Liddell and R. S. Scott, *A Greek-English Lexicon* (3rd ed.; Oxford: University Press, 1849) p. 908.

"the most important work on the Eleusinian Mysteries since Lobeck,"[11] concluded that "it was difficult to let out the 'secret,' for there was essentially no secret to let out."[12] Rohde referred, by example, to the profaning actions of Alcibiades which provide us with one of the few accounts of anyone actually charged with a breach of silence concerning the Mysteries.

Alcibiades, according to Plutarch, was indicted for committing crime against the goddesses of Eleusis, Demeter and Core, by "mimicking the mysteries and showing them forth to his companions in his own house . . ." (*vit. Alc.* xxii).[13] However, the force of this charge against Alcibiades, for which he was subsequently convicted, was less the "showing forth" of the Mysteries than it was the "mimicking" of the Mysteries. And, indeed, Plutarch's own interpretation of the charge was that Alcibiades had parodied the Mysteries of Eleusis in a drunken revel, that is, he had profaned the Eleusinian goddess" (*vit. Alc.* xix). According to Plutarch, then, the conundrum of the Mysteries had less to do with kept secrets or occult knowledge than with hierophany which was not to be profaned. This interpretation would account for the reverence and respect generally shown the Mysteries by initiate, uninitiate, and apostate alike.

At the beginning of this century, J. B. Jevons argued similarly that:

> if participation in and knowledge of the mysteries were withheld from all who were not duly initiated, the object of such exclusion was not a desire to keep the mysteries a secret, but fear of the danger which contact between the holy and unclean would bring upon both.[14]

Nevertheless, the romantic secrecy theory became an accepted view of scholarship. George E. Mylonas, for example, concludes his authoritative study of the Eleusinian Mysteries with the lines:

> We cannot know, at least we still do not know, what was the full content and meaning of the Mysteries of Demeter held at Eleusis. . . . The ancients kept their secret well. And Eleusis still lies under its heavy mantle of mystery."[15]

And Kerényi is convinced that his archetypal analysis has penetrated the secret of the Eleusinian Mysteries.[16]

Lobeck's critique of the Symbolist's romantic view of the Mysteries first introduced a historical challenge to describe the contents of the Eleusinian Mysteries. This positivistic emphasis on content led to L. R. Farnell's comprehensive study of *The Cults of the*

---

[11] Ibid., 186.

[12] *Psyche, Seelenkult und Unsterblichkeitsglaube der Griechen* (Tübingen: J. C. B. Mohr [Paul Siebeck], 1890-1894, trans. of 8th ed. W. B. Hillis, 1923; rpt. London: Routledge and Kegan Paul, 1950) 222.

[13] Trans. B. Perrin, *The Parallel Lives*, vol. IV (Loeb Classical Library; Cambridge, MA: Harvard University Press, 1916).

[14] *An Introduction to the History of Religion* (London: Methuen; New York: Macmillan, 1912) 268-362.

[15] *Eleusis and the Eleusinian Mysteries* (Princeton: Princeton University Press, 1961) 316.

[16] Op. cit., 26.

Greek States at the beginning of this century.[17] In this study, Farnell described the contents of the Eleusinian Mysteries in terms of five characteristics recorded by the second century Platonist, Theon of Smyrna:[18] *katharmos*, or initial purification; *teletes paradosis*, or mystic communication; an *epopteia*, or sacred vision; *anadesis* or *stemmon epidesis*, or an honorary crowning with garlands; and finally, the *eudaimonia*, or happiness that arises from friendship and communion with the deity.[19] Farnell went on to describe the essence of the Eleusinian initiation in terms of a "*drama mystikon*," a drama that likely would involve "some kind of *hieros logos* . . . explaining the sacred things that might be shown to the eyes of the privileged."[20] This non-technical attempt to describe the essential contents of the Eleusinian initiation appeared seven years later in Paul Foucart's *Les Mystères d'Éleusis* now formalized as the well-known tripartite Mystery formula: the *dromena*, the *deiknymena*, and the *legomena*.[21]

Foucart's formulaic configuration, however, occurs nowhere in ancient literature, as he and later interpreters claimed.[22] Despite this lack of evidence, the Mystery formula became firmly ensconced in academic convention by the second decade of the century.[23] And modern scholars continue to assert this formula as central to their understanding of the Mysteries.[24]

Creuzer, Bachofen, Jung, and Kerényi had emphasized the mystic and symbolic dimension of religious expressions. In terms of the Mystery formula, their concern was with the *legomena*, the mythic dimension of the Mysteries (e.g., Creuzer), or with the *deiknymena*, with the symbolic or expressive dimension of the Mysteries (e.g., Kerényi). As W. Brede Kristensen has noted, however, "the whole concept of a religious symbol was unknown to the Ancients."[25]

On the other hand, Farnell's revaluation of the importance of the *dromena* or ritual over other aspects of the initiation[26] allied him with the comparative concerns of the so-called "Cambridge School,"[27] and anticipated the priority of cult to myth argued by the

---

[17](Oxford: Clarendon Press, 1896-1909) 5 vols.

[18]*De utilit. math.*, Eduard Hiller, ed., *Theonis Smyrnaei* (Leipzig: B. G. Teubner, 1878; trans. in S. Angus, *The Mystery-Religions*, 2nd ed. (1928; rpt. New York: Dover Publications, 1975) 76f.

[19]Farnell, op. cit., III (1907) p. 131; see also Farnell's article on "Mystery" in *The Encyclopaedia Britannica*, 11th ed., 1910-1911, vol. XIX, p. 117.

[20]Op. cit., vol. III, (1907) pp. 130f.

[21]*Les Mystères d'Éleusis* (1914, rpt. New York: Arno Press, 1975) 356f.

[22]Ibid.

[23]E.g., Axel W. Persson, "Der Ursprung der eleusinischen Mysterien," *Archiv für Religionswissenschaft*, 21 (1922) 305, cited by G. Bornkamm, "*Mysterion*" in Gerhard Kittel, ed., *Theologisches Wörterbuch zum Neuen Testament* (Stuttgart: W. Kohlhammer, 1942) 4. 814 n. 45. In the authoritative encyclopedia, *Die Religion in Geschichte und Gegenwart*, op. cit., this formula first appears in the second edition, (vol. 4, [1930] col. 327) as a confident description of the mystery celebrations.

[24]In addition to those cited above, see Mylonas, op. cit., 261; and Kerényi, op. cit., 52, 96.

[25]Op. cit., 401.

[26]*The Cults of the Greek States*, op. cit., vol. III, p. 192; see also Farnell's article on "Mystery," op. cit., 121.

[27]The Cambridge School consisted of Jane Harrison, A. B. Cook, and F. M. Cornford at Cambridge University, and Gilbert Murray, Farnell's colleague at Oxford.

English "Myth and Ritual School" of the 1930s.[28] What all of these researchers acknowledged in common was the influence of anthropology upon their study of religion.[29] This influence of the anthropological school reinforced nineteenth century evolutionary concerns with discovering the essence of the Mysteries, (e.g., the tradition of Creuzer) or their origins (e.g., Foucart's Egyptian theory, or Persson's Cretan theory). Under these comparative and evolutionary emphases, earlier concerns with primordial revelation and geographical origin were largely replaced with concerns about nature or vegetative backgrounds,[30] and speculation about the secret essence of the Mysteries shifted from vegetative insights comparable to other "primitive rites" to later "higher" analogues.[31] With the popularity of the anthropological school at the early part of this century, the academic conventions characterizing the Eleusinian Mysteries as certainly consisting of the *dromena, deiknymena,* and *legomena,* but as secret and thus finally unknowable, became conflated and continue to inform contemporary research.

Contrary to nineteenth century evolutionary theories, soteriology was always linked to agriculture in Eleusinian discourse.[32] In a recent analysis of the Homeric Hymn to Demeter, Larry Alderink has shown that agriculture and the mysteries are linked systematically at Eleusis in a common network of relations, the nature of which is mytho-cosmological.[33] Alderink argues that Demeter's actions following the abduction of her daughter transformed the relationship between the four major deities of the Eleusinian myth: Demeter, Persephone, Plouton, and Zeus[34] and transformed agriculture as well, "from a natural process to a human activity surrounded by divine guarantees. . . ."[35] In this way, Gods and humans not only became linked through Demeter's identification with Eleusinian agrarian life, but the agrarian life itself becomes valued. Eleusinian discourse is the discourse of the land.

In what is perhaps its most oft-cited and well-known passage, the Homeric Hymn to Demeter proclaims the initiate as "happy" (*olbios*), a designation which became formulaic

---

See G. S. Kirk, *Myth, Its Meaning and Functions in Ancient and Other Cultures* (Cambridge: University Press; Berkeley and Los Angeles: University of California Press, 1970) 3-5. In the Preface to Volume 1 of *The Cults of the Greek States* (1896), Farnell refers to the new interest in Greek ritual and myth, especially at Cambridge (p. vii).

[28]On the Myth and Ritual School, see S. G. F. Brandon, "The Myth and Ritual Position Critically Considered" in S. H. Hooke, ed., *Myth, Ritual, and Kingship* (Oxford: Clarendon Press, 1958) 261-91.

[29]Farnell acknowledged especially the work of Robertson Smith, James Frazer, and Andrew Lang, as, indeed, did most everyone else at the time. See *The Cults of the Greek States,* Preface, op. cit., viif. At the time he published Volume III of his work in 1907, however, he acknowledged this debt much more circumspectively (p. iv). On the anthropological influence on the Cambridge School, see Kirk, op. cit.; on the Myth and Ritual School, see Brandon, op. cit.

[30]N. J. Richardson, ed., *The Homeric Hymn to Demeter* (Oxford: Clarendon Press, 1974) 13.

[31]E.g., Farnell, op. cit., vol. III, p. 143.

[32]Richardson, op. cit., 14.

[33]"Mythic and Cosmological Structures in the Homeric Hymn to Demeter," *Numen* 29 (1982) fasc. 1, pp. 1-16.

[34]Ibid., 5.

[35]Ibid., 8.

in the ancient world.[36] Alderink follows most interpreters of this passage by referring this happiness primarily to the afterlife.[37] In Homer, however, *olbios* always refers to worldly goods.[38] And as Farnell has argued, Demeter's gift is more than simply corn; she is the giver of all good things which the earth nourishes.[39] Therefore, it would seem the Eleusinian initiate's happiness embraces the entire agrarian mode of life.

The word *olbios* implies more than mere outward prosperity.[40] Thus, the Homeric Hymn distinguishes the initiate from the uninitiate in another important way. Initiatory happiness also is the valuation by the Eleusinian goddess of the agrarian life through participation in her share of divine honor, (*time*).

Time is a major theme of the hymn. It is first and foremost a cosmic characteristic of the immortals. Plouton's *time* is that he rules a third share of the cosmos (*H. Hymn Dem.* 85-87). It is Plouton's prerogative to distribute *time* from his share (*H. Hymn Dem.* 364-66) as it is that of his brother Zeus (*H. Hymn Dem.* 441-47) and, indeed, that of "all the blessed and eternal gods" (*H. Hymn Dem.* 325f.). As "the greatest help and cause of joy" for both the immortals and the mortals, Demeter claims her own share of *time* (*H. Hymn Dem.* 268f.). Her withdrawal from the company of gods and the famine she subsequently brings upon earth (*H. Hymn Dem.* 301-13) effectively robbed the Olympians of their rightful *time* (*H. Hymn Dem.* 311-13, 351-54). In response, Zeus promised both Demeter and Persephone whatever *time* they might choose among the immortals (*H. Hymn Dem.* 441-47, 459-62).[41]

Demophoön is the only mortal in the Homeric Hymn who shares *time*. Accepting the hospitality of the Eleusinians during the quest for Persephone, Demeter attempted to show her gratitude, and at the same time adopt a substitute for her abducted daughter, by investing her charge, Demophoön, with the quality of the company she had fled, immortality. However, as the realms of the immortal gods (*athanatoi theoi*) and the mortals (*thnetoi anthropoi*) are "two disparate and incommensurate levels of existence,"[42] this gift of the goddess was fated to fail (*H. Hymn Dem.* 260-64). While it was not possible in the Greek order of things for even a goddess to bestow immortality upon a mortal, she could bestow upon him—and upon all of the children of Eleusis—honor (*time*).

It would seem, therefore, that Demophoön, who has laid upon Demeter's knees and

---

[36] *H. Hymn Dem.* 480f. See Martin P. Nilsson, *Greek Folk Religion* (1940; rpt. New York: Harper & Brothers, 1961) 58-59.

[37] Alderink suggests a relationship between agriculture and ante-mortem happiness, and the mystery and post-mortem happiness (op. cit., 8, 11, 12). However, he also suggests a more existential (and more interesting!) interpretation in which initiates "received a new option as they faced [!] death: neither resignation nor fear, but the happiness afforded by participation in Demeter's mysteries" (ibid., 3).

[38] Liddell-Scott, op. cit., New (ninth) edition, (1940); in the Homeric Hymn to Demeter *olbios* is opposed to *makaros*, the characteristic of the immortals (*H. Hymn Dem.* 303, 325, 345).

[39] Farnell, op. cit., III, pp. 32, 37f.; see also G. Zuntz, *Persephone, Three Essays on Religion and Thought in Magna Graecia* (Oxford: Clarendon Press, 1971) 100f.

[40] Liddell-Scott, op. cit.

[41] Persephone received *time* only during the four months she was in the underworld, i.e., a third of her husband's third share of *time*.

[42] Ibid., 10. While "disparate and incommensurate," these two realms are nevertheless cosmically bound into a systemic whole. See *H. Hymn Dem.* 11, 22, 43, 55, 62, 73.

slept in her arms, is the first of Demeter's initiates at Eleusis, before her epiphany to the Eleusinians (*H. Hymn Dem.* 268-83), and before she revealed her mysteries to their leaders. The *time* that was bestowed by Demeter upon Demophoön was "unfailing" (*aphthitos*) (*H. Hymn Dem.* 263) whereas the uninitiate is described as perishing, *phthimenos* (*H. Hymn Dem.* 482).

The Eleusinian Mysteries, then, established a we/they distinction between initiate and uninitiate.[43] The initiated "we," as the "children" of Demeter, participate in her honor, her rule over the gifts of the earth, and are happy in this agrarian way of life.

In his provocative work, *The Class Struggle in the Ancient Greek World,* G. E. M. de Ste. Croix has summarized the importance of the land to the economy of the ancient world:

> Wealth in the Greek world, in the Archaic, Classical and Hellenistic periods, as in the Roman empire throughout its history, was essentially wealth in land, upon which was conducted the cultivation of cereals (providing the main source of food) and of other agricultural products. . . .[44]

And he has emphasized the distinction made between the land (*chora*) and the city *polis*:[45] "Greco-Roman civilisation was essentially urban, a civilisation of cities."[46] Citing the estimate of the medievalist, Lynn White, Ste. Croix notes that ten people were needed in the land to enable one to live in the polis,[47] as "a Greek city normally expected to feed itself from corn grown in its own *chora,* or at any rate grown nearby."[48]

We might conclude, therefore, that the Eleusinian discourse of the *chora* established the agrarian life as a value in itself through in the honor of the Eleusinian goddess, and established happiness in the face of political and economic domination by Athens, and by the later Roman empire.[49] In the face of Hellenistic cosmopolitan civilization; in the face of the Ptolemaic cosmological expansion; in the face of religions in late antiquity which sought escape from this cosmic view altogether, the Eleusinians never relinquished their grasp upon the land and the values of the rural life. It was this persistence of the "locative" over against an encroaching and exploitative urban civilization which marked Eleusis as a religious center for so many throughout antiquity.[50]

---

[43]Alderink, op. cit., 15f. n. 15.

[44](London: Duckworth; Ithaca: Cornell University Press, 1981) 120.

[45]Ibid., 9-19.

[46]Ibid., 10.

[47]Ibid., 10f.

[48]Ibid., 11.

[49]F. R. Walton has argued that the Homeric Hymn was in fact an Eleusinian polemic against the Athenian dominance. "Athens, Eleusis, and the Homeric Hymn to Demeter," *Harvard Theological Review* 45 (1952) 105-14.

[50]The important distinction between "locative" to signify religious structures bound to particular space, and "utopian" to signify religious structure bound to "no space" is Jonathan Z. Smith's in *Map is Not Territory* (Leiden: E. J. Brill, 1978) 100-103.

Taking Things Apart
to See How They Work

Jacob Neusner

Third Annual Plenary Address,
"How My Mind Has Changed,"
Society of Biblical Literature, December 1984, Chicago

With thanks to the Program Committee for the honor of the invitation to talk about myself, I shall not pretend to be coy or uncharacteristically retiring. No one would believe me anyway. I am asked to explain myself, so let me try. A long time ago, when I was a boy in West Hartford, I framed two fundamental traits that have never changed for me. First, I had to see for myself. Second, I liked to take things apart and to try to put them together again to see how they work. Whether it is a toy car or a system of Judaism, it would always be the same: on that my mind has never changed. As a boy I loved learning things, finding nearly everything interesting, nearly everybody with a story to tell. That is why I chose as my life trying to see for myself how Judaism worked, learning things about nearly everything in the interest in that one thing: on that my mind has never changed. I want to see how diverse groups of Jews worked out that way of life and that world view that framed their world. I want to know what it is about us as human beings that we learn from them, I mean, how, in the mirror of their world, we see some slight detail of ourselves, of us as humanity, as we are in God's likeness, in God's image. On that my mind will never change: we are in the likeness, we are in the image.

But on most other things, in the nature of things, my mind changes every day, and why not? For to reflect and reconsider is a mark of learning and growth, a measure of curiosity and intellectual capacity. For us who spend our lives as teachers and learners in the realm of religion in the here and now, to reach a firm and final "position" means to die, to stop our quest. If, both in books and in the faces of the day, we search for the record of God's image and God's likeness, then we can never master all the data or reach a firm conviction, short of knowing everything about everything and understanding it all.

I will be forgiven, therefore, if in the small and remote corner of the world in which I conduct my quest for what it means to be a human being, I seek, and find, new things from day to day. To say how my mind has changed is to catalogue all the things I have learned, specifying what is worth remembering, what forgetting, as well. My career, that is to say, my education in the study of Judaism, goes back to 1954, when I became a beginning student at the Jewish Theological Seminary of America. Happily for oratorical purposes, it divides into three periods, each a decade, the historical, the literary, and the cultural. I work on the Talmud and related literature. In my historical period, in the 1960s, I wanted to know what happened in the *time* of the Talmud. In my literary period, in the 1970s, I wanted to know what happened in the *pages* of the Talmud. In my cultural period, in the 1980s, I wanted to know what happened because of what is *said* in the Talmud.

So for a decade I worked on the Talmud and related writings as a historical source, for another decade I worked on the Talmud as a literary problem, and in the present period I work on the Talmud as a statement of culture, as an artifact of human expression, as a solution to someone's problem. For thirty years my mind remained constant that in hand we have, first, the record of a remarkable experiment in being human, hence a historical record, second, a complex and subtle experiment in recording, through *how* things are said as much as through what is said, the things people have learned from their experiment, hence, a literary monument. But, third and most important, there is something still more immediate. For what makes the Talmud and related literature not only interesting but also important for contemporary discourse on the human situation is not its historical facts or literary presence. If only Jews searching for their own heritage studied the Talmud as a work of law and theology, history and literature, or as a labor of faith and devotion to God's word, as Jews do study the Talmud in these dimensions, the rest of humanity would lose out on a small but valued part of the treasury of humanity. It is the testimony of the Talmud and related literature on a common human problem that we then should press.

Let me explain. When we consider the human situation of those Jews whose history and literature, whose law and theology, we have at hand, we understand the critical importance of that third dimension, that third decade—the 1980s—of my own life as a scholar, the dimension of the Talmud as a social construct, as a statement, beyond itself and its details, of a transcendent, a larger whole. But who can hear it all, and all at once? The genius of a composer is to draw together many voices and enable them not only to speak all at once, which is mere cacophony, but to speak simultaneously and yet intelligibly and harmoniously, which is music, opera for instance. What composer can draw together so vast a literature, so diverse a set of themes and motifs, and form the whole into a whole? That, phrased in the language of music we all share, is the problem of my labor. Is it any wonder that, as I said at the outset, my mind should change and change and change? But if I am to be judged, as we all must be judged if we propose to do things with our lives, then let me be condemned if I waste my opportunities, or let me be exonerated if I have freely exercised my powers of imagination and used my strength to grasp the whole and hold it all in balance and proportion, if I have shown imagination and capacity.

Let me then spell out what is wrong with reading the Talmud and related literature as only a historical record, as only a literary monument, and what is right about listening for its statement of culture and seeing it as an artifact of humanity faced with a particular problem. To do so I want to ask you to think not about ancient Israel, in the aftermath of a catastrophe of defeat, ancient Israel no longer in control of its land and of its life, ancient Israel facing a world less hospitable than any it had ever known. Rather I want to speak of Wales after Edward, Scotland after 1745, and of Ireland after Cromwell, after England. I swim every day with a sculptor of Canadian-Scottish origin. He explained to me why the Scots in Canada—at least, his family—will not plant Sweet William in their gardens and why they wear a black arm-band on the 16th of April. After nearly two and a half centuries and two nations later, the Scots remain defeated, beleaguered, out of kilter. Some people here may have followed the Masterpiece Theater performance of "To serve them all our days," and may recall that the Welsh hero, in an English public school, tells the headmaster that he cannot make it in England because he is "of the wrong nationality," and tells his girl-friend that the castles on the English-Welsh border are there to keep out "his" ancestors. The Welsh have not had their own nation for nearly seven centuries. But in mind they are Israel beyond catastrophe. And who needs to be reminded of the suffering of the Irish, whose history rivals that of us Jews for its pathos

—and also, its resentment and its sense of long-nursed righteous grievance. I could not watch the end of the TV history of Ireland, any more than I could watch TV portrayals of the murder of the Jews of Europe. I cannot distinguish among those events that fall into the classification of "holocaust," to use the prevailing language-symbol. This digression carries us far from a meeting to talk about biblical and related studies, but it is important in explaining why I see the Talmud and related literature as a worthy object of today's imagination. It is worth trying to grasp the whole and hold it all in balance, because, only in that way shall we be able to see the humanity in the circumstance preserved in those difficult and contentious writings, and only in that way shall we gain access to that distinctive version of a human experience common to us all. I mean defeat, disappointment, resentment, but also of renewal and sanctification.

That is why, to state matters briefly, I changed my mind about the value of historical inquiry by itself, and rejected the self-evidence of the worth of literary inquiry by itself. But I affirm them both in a larger search for meaning, for insight resting upon learning. We have to know what really happened, what came first and what took place next. The sources at hand, however, will stand in judgment on our work and find it insufficient, if that is all we want to ask them. For they have *more* to tell us. But, I think most of us now realize, they also have much *less* to tell us. The Talmud and related literature do not come to us from the hand of trained reporters, with tape recorders and video-cameras, and people have to read these sources in the same critical spirit that guides their reading of the Hebrew Scripture and the New Testament and much else. The first ten years of my life, marked by the *Life of Yohanan ben Zakkai* and the *History of the Jews in Babylonia*, marked off a long struggle to emerge from fundamentalist reading of rabbinic tales and stories, on the one side, and fundamentalist description of the life and culture of the Jews of that age, on the other.

I thought that if we could show *how* the sources work, we could gain accurate access at their historical records. That is why, in the next ten years, I took up problems of literary criticism, involving, in particular, the familiar and routine methods of form-analysis, redaction-criticism, dissection and reconstruction, and, in all, of an acerbic and cool mode of encounter. The decade at hand—the 1970s—marked the transition that is critical to the future. I began with an interest in problems of a historical character, which I proposed to investigate through a critical reading of the diverse sources generally alleged to give information about those problems. To take my three studies, they involved a first-century rabbi—Yohanan ben Zakkai revisited, then the Pharisees before 70, and finally, a critical figure in the age of reconstruction after the destruction of the Temple in A.D. 70, Eliezer ben Hyrcanus. In all three cases I wanted to read the sources critically, as they had not been read, essentially so as to produce answers to historical questions, such as had been answered many times before. The method was new to its field (but only to that field). But the program was very old and familiar indeed. That was the first half of the decade, from the late 1960s to the middle 1970s. But, alas, minds change.

Throughout the work at hand—now under way for fifteen years—I faced the growing sense that everything I was doing was beside the point of the sources. By the mid-1970s, I realized that the questions were mine, but *not* theirs. Now my Orthodox Jewish friends always had told me so, since they thought history irrelevant (they called it, the story of what a rabbi had for lunch, not the story of what he stood for). They thought critical literary methods either heretical or old-hat (I never could tell which). But the questions of my Orthodox Jewish friends were those *of* the text. They asked nothing of interest in our own day. What I needed to find would be questions that were my questions, but questions also congruent to the answers that the *texts* provided in their ancient day. To move forward, in the same decade, in the late 1970s, I shifted my program. I wanted still to read the sources critically, and I wanted still to come up with historical answers, I mean, a picture of how things were, not merely how the text portrays them. But what questions, what answers? I determined to ask the texts to tell me what *they* wanted to discuss, rather than what interested me. That meant to ask the Mishnah to be the Mishnah, the Tosefta, its supplement, to speak in *its* terms and along its own lines, so too the two Talmuds and the more important collections of exegeses of Scripture ("midrashim").

The present decade, the 1980s, for me is the age in which I am trying to describe the documents one by one *but each one whole.* I have thus far addressed the Mishnah as a whole and in its components, in my *Judaism: The Evidence of the Mishnah,* in that same exercise dealing also with the Tosefta. I have completed my first soundings in the Talmud of the Land of Israel, with the results in the paired works, *the Talmud of the Land of Israel.* Vol. *35. Introduction. Taxonomy,* and *Judaism in Society: The Evidence of the Yerushalmi,* and I have dealt at some length with one collection of scriptural exegeses and asked how the framers of that collection appear to have thought they made a cogent and intelligible statement. This work is in *Judaism and Scripture: The Evidence of Leviticus Rabbah.* My present work takes up the same issues for the Babylonian Talmud. Essentially, therefore, I have reached that point that, in my childhood, I would reach when I had taken the toy car apart and laid out all its bits and pieces.

No one will be surprised to know that it is harder to put things together than it is to take them apart. In three works I have tried to follow the familiar path of working on a particular problem, this time along a route dictated by the character of the documents at hand. Exploiting the earlier results of the description of documents one by one, and each one whole, I asked about the three fundamental questions of description of any religious system: revelation and canon, teleology and eschatology, and generative symbol. The works that have come out are *Midrash in Context. Exegesis in Formative Judaism, Messiah in Context. Israel's History and Destiny in Formative Judaism,* and *Torah: From Scroll to Symbol in Formative Judaism.* Clearly the third decade is nearly over.

What lies before is that ultimate question of childhood: *how does it really work?* Once, as I said, we have taken the car apart and seen how it is made up, can we put it together again? Just where and why and how did the system work, I mean, that system of Judaism created by the ancient rabbis and attested in their writings? To state matters somewhat differently, we know that the documents at hand fall into a single context, namely, that of the ancient rabbis. We also know that they come in a single classification, namely (for ancient times) (A) Jewish, and (B) rabbinical, writings. We know, more important, that the ancient documents are represented in various ways as being connected to one another. They not only fit together in one classification, but they also join together in one or another *within* that classification. The real question before us is not one of classification or connectedness, therefore, but rather, one of continuity. Are these texts continuous, and if so, *what moves from one to the next and how does the movement take place?* How do the diverse documents constitute one "Judaism"? In the eye of faith all of the documents at hand form a single statement, one of "Judaism," or, in the language of the faith, "Torah." But that conviction forms a datum of the contemporary faith, not an analytical or categorical postulate. No one present thinks otherwise, unless you also regard the deepest conviction that there is one holy Catholic church, a single Christianity, a "church that is one in Christ"—unless you regard those profound Christian affirmations as serviceable descriptions of the this-worldly history and character of Christian churches. So too with "Judaism" or "Torah,"—let the work of reconstruction begin.

Since I have tried to spell out the things I have learned in thirty years of work and in twenty-five years of scholarly writing, let me conclude with an appeal that the Society of Biblical Literature learn two things from this occasion.

First, I ask that you demand from scholars who work on Judaism exactly the same critical and collegial standards that you yourselves accept in work on the Old Testament and the New Testament.

You would not print an article of a historical or descriptive character that ignores the entire critical program of the nineteenth and twentieth centuries in biblical studies. Stop printing Jewish fundamentalism in the guise of scholarship.

You would not print an article in the JBL in which authors carefully do not cite scholars of whose work they do not approve, or whose work is proscribed in certain circles. You would not be party to a boycott of a given approach or position in a study of a New Testament problem. Stop printing articles that pretend my work has not been done, or that simply do not cite my books and articles on the topics on which the scholars claim to work.

Second, the SBL should not take part in boycotts. It should not treat as pariahs and lepers the proponents of serious approaches to learning. Let there be argument, not boycott. If you think I exaggerate, as to unabashed, naive fundamentalism, reread Steven Katz's use of evidence in his article on the separation of Judaism and Christianity. If you think I exaggerate, as to a boycott, try to find my name or the names of my students in Albert Baumgarten's article on the Pharisees. It follows that the JBL should stop printing vulgar Jewish apologetics, since you will not print vulgar Christian apologetics, stop printing the same for Judaism. If you will reread Katz's article, you will see what I mean. Impose the same enlightened standards of scholarly discourse on both Judaism and Christianity.

Clearly the problems to be solved by the JBL and the SBL give testimony to tensions in the field at hand. No one will accuse me of boasting, if I claim responsibility for those tensions. But while my mind has changed many times and will, God willing, change still more, my path remains the same. All I have done, on the sources on which I work, is what you do every day in your studies of the sources on which you work. I ask questions of the age in which I live, and I make use of the methods of today. That is not for a motive more elevated than the one that led me as a boy to insist on two things: first, to see for myself, and, second, to take things apart so as to put them back together to see how they work.

Hybrists Not Gnostics in Corinth

Peter Marshall

Zadok Centre, Canberra, Australia

I

Since W. Schmithals initiated Paul's churches into the full mysteries of second-century Gnosticism,[1] they have returned to a more amorphous state. Now we hear of "proto-Gnostics,"[2] a "gnostic party" or a "quasi-gnostic context,"[3] and "incipient Gnosticism."[4] Commentators are well aware of the historical fallacies in earlier discussions, but gnostic terminology[5] and an antignostic Paul still control many of the discussions, especially in 1 Corinthians.

The pneumatic seed, it seems, has been planted again. This time it is in Paul, the gnostic apostle of second-century gnostic exegesis.[6] Pagels's analysis comes as a most welcome correction to previous discussions and also as a warning that we "may learn from the debate to approach Pauline exegesis with renewed openness to the texts."[7] Wilson had earlier alerted us to the problems of method and procedure in the gnostic debate. He asks:

> If a passage can be understood without recourse to Gnosticism—or Gnosis—but takes on a new meaning in the light of later gnostic thought, which interpretation is to be preferred? Where does the burden of proof lie, with those who assert a gnostic influence or with those who deny it? If some concept occurs in second-century Gnosticism, and in the New Testament, and also in Jewish apocalyptic Platonism or elsewhere, is it to be described as gnostic without much ado, and added to the list of gnostic motifs in the New Testament? Or should we identify it precisely as apocalyptic, Platonic or Stoic,

---

[1] *Gnosticism in Corinth* (ET Nashville, 1971); *Paul and the Gnostics* (ET Nashville, 1972).

[2] H. Conzelmann, *1 Corinthians* (ET Philadelphia, 1975) 15-16.

[3] C. K. Barrett, *The First Epistle to the Corinthians* (London, 1971) 144-45.

[4] F. F. Bruce, *Apostle of the Free Spirit* (Exeter, 1977) 261. See also G. Bornkamm, *Paul* (ET London, 1971) 71.

[5] Terms such as maturity, wisdom, knowledge, spirit, freedom and word. Ideas such as mysticism and dualism. Conduct such as sexual looseness, acting excessively and as if superior.

[6] E. H. Pagels, *The Gnostic Paul* (Philadelphia, 1975).

[7] Ibid., 164.

recognize that it does become gnostic later, but suspend judgment as to its gnostic character at the New Testament stage."[8]

The full scope of the gnostic exegesis of 1 Corinthians is not possible, but I have chosen two passages, one from each of 1 and 2 Corinthians (1 Cor 4:6-13; 2 Cor 10-12) where Paul contrasts himself directly with his opponents. The language and ideas expressed in them must reflect directly upon the nature of the conflict in Corinth. The former passage is interpreted as evidence of Corinthian spiritual elitism. In v. 8 in particular (*kekoremenoi este, eploutēsate, ebasileusate*) scholars see them as religious enthusiasts, proponents of a realized eschatology.[9] As an alternative explanation, I will argue that the controlling ideas in this passage and Paul's innuendo of the immoderate fool in 2 Cor 10-12 are drawn from the *hybris* and *sōphrosynē* traditions.[10] I will:

a. outline the ideas of *hybris* and *sōphrosynē* in Greek literature;
b. indicate how in 1 Cor 4:6-13 Paul uses ideas of excess to rebuke the Corinthians and notions of social shame to contrast himself with them;
c. show how he castigates his enemies as hybrists by innuendo while presenting himself as a man of restraint;
d. point to the implications for Corinthian studies;
e. suggest how this study might be extended to other areas of the Corinthians correspondence.

II

Hybris in Greek Tradition

Hybris is one of the most common Greek ethical notions.[11] Though usually translated as "pride" or "arrogance," it includes among its uses a wide range of excessive social behavior, a state of mind of the agent, the effect of shame and dishonor upon the victim and his feelings of outrage. It appears as early as Homer where it denotes excessive eating and drinking, arrogance and dishonor.[12] It represents the self-indulgent arrogant behavior of the rich and powerful and privileged youth which disregards and oversteps the set limits of human and divine authority. MacDowell describes it this way:

---

[8]R. McL. Wilson, "How Gnostic were the Corinthians?," *NTS* 19 (1973) 68-69.
[9]E.g., C. K. Barrett, *1 Corinthians* 108-9; H. Conzelmann, *1 Corinthians* 87-88; N. A. Dahl, "Paul and the Church of Corinth according to 1 Cor 1:10-4:21," in *Christian History and Interpretation*, ed. W. R. Farmer, C. F. D. Moule and R. R. Neibuhr (Cambridge, 1967) 332.
[10]This study of *hybris-sōphrosynē* and its application to 1 and 2 Corinthians is developed in much greater detail in P. Marshall, *Enmity and Other Social Conventions in Paul's Relations with the Corinthians* (Ph.D. diss., Macquarie University, 1980; Wissenschaftliche Untersuchungen zum Neuen Testament, forthcoming).
[11]For a detailed study of *hybris* see P. Marshall, *Enmity*, 283-302; D. M. MacDowell, "Hybris in Athens," *G&R* 23 (1976) 14-31; N. R. E. Fisher, "Hybris and Dishonor: I," *G&R* 23 (1976) 177-93.
[12]E.g., *Od.* 1.224-229; 3.207. See also D. M. MacDowell, "Hybris in Athens," 16; N. R. E. Fisher, "Hybris and Dishonor," 186.

a. *Hybris* is always bad;
b. it is always voluntary;
c. it is most frequently the result of such things as youth, wealth, excess of food and drink;
d. it is not as a rule religious;
e. it often involves a victim, and is more serious when it does.[13]

Hybris has a rich and extensive vocabulary of synonyms, associated words, and concepts.[14] Many will appear in this brief account together with its traditional antithesis, *sōphrosynē* and its related terminology. In particular, it is almost equivalent with *koros* ("fullness, surfeit, satiety, having too much") or *korenymmi* ("to be sated or glutted with a thing"). Both notions are often associated with *ploutos* ("wealth") with *hybris* said to either produce *koros* and *ploutos* or to be produced by them. They are interchanged frequently in the regular appearance of this saying.[15] Hybristic behavior is implicit in many instances where these associated terms are used, singly or as a complex, to portray excessive social conduct, though the term *hybris* is not used explicitly. This is important to notice, for Paul uses *hybrizō* only once in the two passages under study, though many of the terms are found in the *hybris-sōphrosynē* vocabularies and are used in the same way.

There are a number of familiar forms of conduct or figures in the hybristic tradition. Three of them are central to our study—wealth or the rich; power or the ruler; sexual looseness. First, wealthy people were considered especially susceptible to *hybris*.[16] Wealth became their standard of measurement and made them hybrists.[17] This caused them to be overconfident and to consider themselves superior to others.[18] Unrestrained by virtue as in the truly great, they delight in insulting and ridiculing even the disadvantaged, bringing them shame and dishonor.[19] But the display of superiority of the wealthy hybrist is not limited towards social inferiors; it is also directed against his social equals leading to resentment and division in private social relations.[20]

Second, *hybris,* kingship and power, especially in the form of the tyrant, formed

---

[13]"Hybris in Athens," 21-23 and 15-23 generally.

[14]See H. G. Robertson, "The Hybristes in Aeschylus," *TAPA* 98 (1967) 373-74 for an extensive list in Aeschylus; P. Marshall, *Enmity,* 336-37 n. 1 for both *hybris* and *sōphrosynē.*

[15]E.g., *koros-hybris:* Solon (West, IEG) 6, Theognis 153; Pindar, *O.* 13.10; Herodotus 8.77; Stobaeus 4.7.65; Philo, *de Virt.* 30.162; *Flacc* 11.91; *de Prov.* 2.12; *ploutos-hybris-koros:* "Euripides Fr. 438; Pindar, *I.* 3.2; *Aeschylus Ag.* 382 (ibid., 374-80); Aristophanes, *Wealth* 563f.; Theognis 751; Dio Chrysostom, *Disc.* 65.7. See further R. R. Doyle, "OLBAS, KOROS, HYBRIS and ATH from Hesiod to Aeschylus," *Traditio* 26 (1970) 293-303; D. M. MacDowell, "Hybris in Athens," 16.

[16]E.g., Aristotle, *EN* 4.3.21-22; *Pol* 4.9.4-6; Philo, *de Virt.* 30.161. See also N. R. E. Fisher, "Hybris and Dishonor," 182.

[17]Aristotle, *Rhet.* 2.16.1-4.

[18]Id., *EN* 4.3.21.

[19]Id., *Rhet.* 2.8.2-3, 6; 16.1-4; Xenophon, *Cyr.* 7.2.18; Plutarch, *Mor.* 631CDF; 634DEF.

[20]So N. R. E. Fisher, "Hybris and Dishonor," 183.

common themes in Greek authors.[21] As with *koros* and *ploutos*, *hybris* formed a cause and effect relationship with *tyrannos*.[22] For example Herodotos was concerned with a ruler's abuse of unbridled power and privilege. The king, sated with power, can do as he will, acting hybristically towards his subjects.[23] On the same theme, Dio Chrysostom urges restraint (*sōphrosynē*); for rulers have the power to do anything (*exesti panta poiein*). Thus he asks, "who needs more *sōphrosynēs* than he *hǭ panta exesti?*" The phrase *panta exestin* not only characterizes rulers obsessed with their power and rights but is a familar catchcry of people of rank and status asserting their independence from those who would impinge upon their freedom.[24] *Hybris* in these contexts is very close in meaning to *panta exestin*.[25] The clusters of terms in Herodotos and Dio are significant for our discussion. In the former *hybris* is associated with *korenymmi* and kingship and the maxim of unrestrained freedom *poiein ta bouletai*. In Dio, *sōphrosynē* is linked with *panta exestin*, *basileia*, and *tyrannis*.

Third, *hybris* is used of excessive sexual activity. The verb *hybrizō* refers to adultery,[26] and to a man treating a free woman as he pleased.[27] Aeschylus uses both noun and verb frequently of excessive male desire for women and *hybris* can be translated as "lust."[28] It covers a wide range of sexual outrages which shame and dishonor the victims.[29]

The *hybrist* insults or injures others for his own pleasure and with the specific intention of shaming and dishonoring his victim. It is these intentions to exult over and to disgrace which makes abuse and assault an act of *hybris*.[30] His victim not only desires revenge and recovery of honor but can do so by a legal action called the *graphē hybreōs*.[31] This conduct is disruptive of social relations and one of the more common characteristics of *hybris* is *stasis* and similar notions of discord.[32] From the foregoing, it can be seen that *hybris* is a moral or social term rather than religious. Seldom does this motif appear in other contexts.[33]

Finally, *hybris* is behavior which oversteps the bounds or limits or which exceeds the mean. *Sōphrosynē*, its traditional antithesis, is translated variously as "moderation,"

---

[21]Cf. K. H. Waters, "Herodotos and Politics," *G&R* 19 (1972) 136-50; P. A. L. Greenhalgh, "Aristocracy and Its Advocate in Archaic Greece," *G&R* 19 (1972) 190-207.

[22]Sophocles, *OT* 873.

[23]3.80.

[24]*Disc.* 62.2.4; cf. *Disc.* 3.10.

[25]See M. Pohlenz, *Freedom in Greek Life and Thought* (ET Dordecht, 1966) 52-56. H. F. North, "A Period of Opposition to Sophrosyne in Greek Thought," *TAPA* 78 (1947) 1-17; P. Marshall, *Enmity*, 438-43.

[26]*El.* 947; cf. *Hipp.* 1073; *Hec.* 785.

[27]19.309.

[28]See D. M. MacDowell, "Hybris in Athens," 17. Cf. Plato, *Leg.*, 835D; Dio Chrysostom, *Disc.* 77/78.29; Plutarch, *Mor.* 555C.

[29]See N. R. E. Fisher, "Hybris and Dishonor," 187-88.

[30]Cf. Aristotle, *Rhet.* 1.13.10; 2.2.5-6; *EN* 7.6.4; N. R. E. Fisher, "Hybris and Dishonor," 180.

[31]Cf. Aristotle, *Rhet.* 2.2.12; Isocrates 396A; Demosthenes 11.976; Athenaeus, *Deipn.* 6.266F-267A.

[32]See Aristotle, *Pol.* 5.2.3-4; 5.3.3; 5.6.4-5; Theognis 1081-2.

[33]Cf. D. M. MacDowell, "Hybris in Athens," 22-23; N. R. E. Fisher, "Hybris and Dishonor," 178; R. Lattimore, *Story Patterns in Greek Tragedy* (Ann Arbor, 1969) 24-25.

"self-control," "restraint," "sanity," or "prudence."[34] Like *hybris*, it has a considerable complex of ideas linked with it. Two of the most common *topoi* of this motif are the familiar maxims *mēden agan*, "nothing too much," and *gnōthi sauton*, "know yourself."[35] *Mēden agan* is a proverb of restraint or moderation commonly linked with the doctrine of the mean, the rule of right conduct or of no excess. It represents the limits or measure set by the gods or society upon human conduct.[36] Together these notions embody the traditional Greek inclination for moderation, restraint, and measure in all things.[37] What commends a person is acting *kata metron*.[38] Conversely, conduct which is judged to be *ametra* or *hyper metron* is censured as immoderate or exceeding the limits.[39]

Gnōthi sauton as self-knowledge is an important element of *sōphrosynē*.[40] Heraclitus shows the relationship between the ideas: "It is possible for all men to know themselves and *sōphrosynein*"; and further *"sōphrosynein* is the greatest virtue and wisdom (*sophia*) consists in speaking the truth and acting in accordance with nature."[41] Such knowledge understands the laws which govern man and the cosmos. The association of *sōphrosynē* with self-knowledge and *sophia* contrasts clearly with *hybris* as ignorance of one's true self and thus foolishness.[42] This behavior is at times called *mania*, "madness," irrational conduct resulting from an error of common knowledge.[43]

III

The *Hybris* Tradition in 1 Cor 4:6-13

Paul tells the Corinthians in v. 6 that he has focused the discussion on himself and Apollos *hina en hēmin mathēte to mē hyper ha gegraptai*. The elliptical phrase *to mē hyper ha gegraptai* remains an enigma to scholars. Those who accept its integrity are

---

[34]See the major study by H. North, *Sophrosyne: Self-Knowledge and Self-Restraint in Greek Literature* (Ithaca, New York, 1966).

[35]See H. W. Parke and D. E. W. Wormell, *The Delphic Oracle* (Oxford, 1956) 386-392.

[36]Cf. Diodorus Siculus, 9.10.1-3. And see equivalent sayings in Solon, *mēte lian* (5.8); *en metroisi* (4.7); *metron gnōmosynēs* (16.1-2). Refer also H. North, *Sophrosyne*, 33-50; H. Polenz, *Freedom*, 55-59.

[37]E.g., Pindar, *Pyth.* 2.34; *Is.* 6.71; Hesiod, *Op.* 629, 718. For the doctrine of the mean (*to meson, to metrion*) see Aristotle, *EN* 2.2.6-7; 2.9.9; 4.3.8, 18; 4.5.1.

[38]E.g., Hesiod, *WD* 720; Panyassis, Fr. 14.1.5-6 (Kinkel) where *kata metron* is opposed directly to *hyper metron* and *hybris*; Pindar, *Is.* 6.71; Solon 4:7. Hesiod, *WD* 694; Cleobulus, *DK* 10.1.

[39]E.g., Panyassis, Fr. 14.1.5-6 (Kinkel); Plato, *Lg.* 690E; *Rep.* 621A; Xenophon, *Cyr.* 1.6.34; Theognis 498. Pindar, *Pyth.* 2.27-34.

[40]See H. North, *Sophrosyne*, 4-5, 150-58.

[41]Fr. 116DK; 112DK. Cf. H. North, *Sophrosyne*, 27.

[42]Cf. Aristotle, *EN* 4.3.3, 13, 20-21, 36; Xenophon, *Mem.* 3.9.4-6; 1.1.16 where *sōphrosynē* and *sophia* are near equivalents and can be used interchangeably. Both are opposed to *hybris* and *mania* without distinction.

[43]Cf. Xenophon, *Mem.* 1.1.16, 3.9.6; H. F. North, "The Concept of Sophrosyne in Greek Literary Criticism," *CP* 43 (1948) 1-17; id., *Sophrosyne*, 124, 128.

uncertain of its meaning and suggest it is unintelligible.[44] Others believe the text is corrupt[45] or that the phrase is a marginal gloss.[46] Far from being incomprehensible, I suggest it is equivalent to the maxim *mēden agan* and is a warning against excessive behavior (instances of which occur in the surrounding chapters) and commences a theme of *hybris* throughout this passage.

The term *hyper*, either as a preposition or adverb or as a compound word, is used frequently to express hybristic behavior.[47] It is so characteristic of excess that it has wrongly been held that *hybris* is cognate to *hyper*.[48] It has been suggested that *hyper* functions in v. 6 as an adverb as in the phrase *hyper egō* in 2 Cor 11:23, a phrase which has hybristic connotations in our second passage.[49] But it is difficult to see the connection between *ha gegraptai* and an adverbial *hyper*. As it stands it would make sense to see it as introducing a prepositional phrase which functions as an adverb or adjective. But this elliptical construction is common enough in Greek literature. The negative *mē* with a substantive adjective or adverb is used either generically or without the article, either with or without a verb. For instance, the phrase *hē mē 'impeirian* is translated as inexperience and is equivalent to the phrase *to mē echein empeirian*.[50] There are many instances like this and they provide a form to reconstruct our phrase.[51]

An almost synonymous phrase occurs in Rom 12:3, in a passage which the classical scholar, H. North, describes as almost Hellenistic in its use of the doctrine of *sōphrosynē*.[52] Paul warns the Romans not to think beyond what is proper (*mē hyperphronein par' ho dei to sōphronein*) because of the gifts given by God. Rather they must limit themselves to the measure of faith (*metron pisteōs*) assigned them by God (*ho theos emerisen*). This set of ideas is also present in 1 Cor 4:6-7 and in 2 Cor 10-12.

I suggest that implicit in *ha gegraptai* are limits or boundaries, ones which Paul and Apollos have kept by their exemplary conduct. These boundaries are set by God in scripture. More specifically, the Jewish scripture from which Paul has quoted on five occasions in the previous chapters.[53] On four of these occasions he introduces the quote with *gegraptai*. In all of them God is depicted as true wisdom, knowledge, and power compared with limited and fallible man. The *gegraptai* quoted seem to remind the Corinthians that they are only human; that is, that there are boundaries which they are in danger of

---

[44]E.g., H. Conzelmann, 1 Cor, 85-86; C. K. Barrett, *1 Cor*, 106.

[45]E.g., J. Moffatt, *The First Epistle of Paul to the Corinthians* (London, 1938) 46.

[46]E.g., W. G. Howard, "1 Corinthians 4:6 Exegesis or Commendation," *ET* 32 (1922) 479-80; A. Legault, "Beyond the Things That are Written (1 Cor IV.6)," *NTS* 18 (1972) 227-31.

[47]Among others: *hyperkompos, hyperbasia, hyperbolē, hyperechein, hyperphialos, hyperephania*.

[48]See W. C. Greene, *Moira: Fate, Good, Evil* (Cambridge, MA, 1944) 18 n. 45, 22. But for a more likely origin, see O. Szemerenyi, "The Origins of the Greek Lexicon: EX ORIENTE LUX," *JHS* 94 (1974) 157.

[49]So P. Wallis, "Ein neuer Auslegungsversuch der Stelle 1 Kor 4.6," *ThLZ* 75 (1950) 506-8.

[50]Aristophanes, *Ec.* 115.

[51]E.g., Demosthenes, 18.296; Sophocles, *OT* 682; *Ant.* 370.

[52]*Sophrosyne*, 317.

[53]M. D. Hooker, "Beyond the Things Which are Written: an Examination of 1 Cor iv.6," *NTS* 10 (1964) 128-30 is correct on this point.

overstepping.[54] Paul then is saying that the Corinthians may learn from his example "not to be unscriptural," "not to think unscripturally," or "not to go beyond the bounds of scripture"; while the variant is poorly represented, it is not at all surprising that a few Greek texts insert *phronein* after *mē*.[55] It is not needed at all. The entire clause parallels closely the idea of gaining true self-knowledge in Euripides: "that he may triumph not over my woes, and taking of my pain, may learn sound wisdom's temperance (*sōphronein mathēsetai*)."[56]

The excessive conduct implied in our phrase is made more explicit in vv. 6b-8. First, the Corinthians immoderation is characterized by arrogance. Some of them are puffed up (*physioun*), favoring one person over another (Paul, Apollos, Cephas) (v. 6b). Paul is referring to the social schisms or disorders (*schismata, erides*) earlier mentioned in 1:10-13 and 3:13.[57] Arrogance or pride (*physioun*) is characteristic of Corinthian conduct in a variety of social matters. It not only creates division, but epitomises the attitude of some of the Corinthians towards him (4:18-19). It underlies a case of extreme sexual depravity (5:2), an overemphasis on knowledge and lack of consideration for those who are socially inferior (8:1ff.), and excessive evaluation of a spiritual gift (13:4).

Second, the notion of superiority and assigned limits are contained in three questions. Paul asks, "Who concedes you any superiority (*diakrinō*)?[58] What do you possess that you did not receive (*elabes*)? If in fact you have received (*elabes*) it, why do you boast (*kauchasai*) as if you have not received (*labōn*) it?" Behind the second and third questions is the idea of God as the benefactor who gives all things to humankind. In return, a man must recognize the gifts with due gratitude. Acceptance of gifts, implicit in the three uses of *lambanō*, required reciprocity and obligation. This is a basic framework for *hybris* and *sōphrosynē*; reverencing the gods; honoring the limits set by them; knowing one's true self and limitations; using possessions, and respect for others.[59] Paul thus far has argued that the Corinthians have acted as if the benefactions were inherently theirs and not a gift. Instead of showing gratitude and humility they were arrogant and boastful, acting as if superior to others. They had thus overstepped the boundaries.

What follows in v. 8 is a very Greek conclusion to this theme of excess; *ēdē kekoresmenoi este· ēdē eploutesate· choris hemōn ebasileusate.* The ideas of satiety (*koros*), wealth (*ploutos*) and power (in the form of *basileus* or *tyrannis*) form a hybristic triad, offering convincing evidence indeed that the doctrine of *hybris* underlies this passage.

A passage in Philo's *On the Virtues* 30.16:1-32.176 is remarkable for its similarity of terminology and ideas with 1 Cor 4:6-13. It not only reinforces my argument but will introduce the kind of contrast which follows in vv. 9-13. In it Philo makes only one explicit reference to *hybris* in the form of the proverb "satiety begets violence" (*ti ktei koros hybrin*) (162) but the passage is rich in the *hybris* tradition.

Pride and arrogance (*hyperophia kai alazoneia*) are often the vices of those upon whom riches, honors, and high offices (*ploutos, doxai, hēnemoniai*) are bestowed and they lead to violence against slave and free alike. Being elated and puffed up (*diairomenoi kai*

---

[54]1 Cor 1:19, 31; 2:9, 16; 3:19-20.

[55]E.g., D[3], L, P, Syrr., Copt., Arm—a practice followed by most translations.

[56]*Hipp.* 730-731.

[57]The ideas of excess and arrogance are connected in consecutive purpose clauses. Paul's example is of moderation and humility.

[58]"diakrinō" Arndt and Gingrich, *A Greek English Lexicon,* 183, i.b.

[59]Cf. Seneca, *de Ben.* 2.30.1-2, for a Roman example.

physōmenoi) they forget that their strength (*ischys*) is a gift received from God (*hoi dōron eilēphe para theou*). Having become rich and received glory and honor (*doxa, timē*) they make others poor and bring them ingloriousness and dishonor (*adoxia, atimia*). Philo argues that as they have received (*lambanō*) their gifts from God they should use them as God intended, for the universal benefit of others, making them rich and honored and so on. Rather the *alazōn* considers himself to be more than human and "wholly divine" (*holon daimona*) and claims "to overstep the limits of human nature" (*hyper tous horous tēs anyrōpines physeōs*). In conclusion, the hybrist "considers himself superior to all in riches, estimation, beauty, strength, wisdom, temperance, justice, eloquence, knowledge; while everyone else he regards as poor, disesteemed, unhonored, foolish, unjust, ignorant, outcast, in fact good for nothing."

A comparison of the terms in this last paragraph and 1 Cor 4:10-12 and their use indicates the close proximity of ideas in Philo and Paul.

entimotatos	*endoxi*
ischyrotatos	*ischyroi*
phronimōtatos	*phronimoi*
atimoi	*atimoi*
aphrones	*mōroi*
katharmata	*perikatharmata*

Philo's clear reference to *hybris* leads me to suggest this tradition is the basis for under-standing both passages.[60]

In preparation for the similar contrast Paul makes in vv. 10-12 between himself and his opponents, he says with heavy irony: "And would that you did reign, so that we might share the rule with you" (v. 8b). But somewhat invidiously in comparison, he depicts himself as a humiliated captive, exposed to death in the arena, a spectacle to all (v. 9). Three traditional antitheses follow in which he presents himself in terms of social shame as inferior in status. He is *mōros, asthenēs, atimos*. They are *phronimoi, ischyroi, endoxi*. The first and second pairs reflect the important motifs in ch. 1-3—foolishness and wisdom, strength and weakness. Here they are clearly social terms, as I suggest they are, fully or in part, in other contexts in 1 and 2 Corinthians.[61] The three antithesis are also in keeping with Paul's rather direct disavowal of the Greek social system in 1:26-28: God has chosen *ta mōra, ta asthenē, ta agenē*, i.e., *ta mē onta*, rather than the expected *sophoi, dynatoi, engeneis*, to remove all grounds for boasting other than in the divine. Paul assumes the position of someone who is socially disadvantaged and inferior in status. Or, to put it another way, he may reflect on his own keenly felt humiliation and shame as he stepped down the status ladder.[62] He may be insinuating, with himself as the example, that the hybrists in Corinth have dishonored and shamed others and himself in particular. Certainly Philo contrasts these ideas in this way, but they are regularly opposed like this in the *hybris* tradition.[63]

---

[60]See ibid., 6.3.1-2; 2.13.1-3; 4:5.1-6.5 for a similar treatment.

[61]Cf. C. Forbes, "'Strength' and 'Weakness' as Terminology of Status in St. Paul" (BA Hons thesis, Macquarie University, 1978).

[62]For Paul's loss of status see P. Marshall, *Enmity*, 613-21; E. A. Judge, "Cultural Conformity and Innovation in Paul," *TB* 35 (1984) 3-24.

[63]E.g., Aristotle, *Pol.* 4.9.1-5; 4.10.1-2; *Rhet.* 2.17.6; *Lysias* 24.15.

Paul's description of himself as a socially and economically disadvantaged person is singularly developed in vv. 11-13. He depicts himself as a maltreated stranger, a manual worker, and the object of ridicule, abuse, and violence. While these are not necessarily the effects of *hybris*, the violation of the itinerant's rights to hospitality and protection is a theme of *hybris*, and ridicule (*loidorein*) can be an hybristic act.[64] The emphasis throughout is on shame and dishonor which is the explicit intention of the *hybrist*. Paul concludes this parade of shame portraying himself as a worthless man, as "offscouring" (*perikatharmata*) and "scum" (*peripsema*) (v. 13). Is it with further irony that he tells the Corinthians that he has not said this to shame (*entrepein*) them (v. 14)?

IV

Hybris as Innuendo in 2 Cor 10-12

Paul uses the conventional language of moderation and excess to commend his own conduct and to discredit his enemies in 2 Cor 10-12.[65] First, he uses rhetorical devices of restraint to present himself as a moderate person. The controlling form in these chapters is the rhetorical technique of comparison (*synkrisis*)[66] but it is accompanied by innuendo and irony throughout. Innuendo and irony are very similar, the former having some of the characteristics of the latter.[67] It can be an ambiguous and satirical form of censure. E. W. Bower describes one of its approaches as denying "that we intend to discuss opponents and then subtly to introduce the topic while seeming not to do so."[68] The aim is to discredit indirectly or even discreetly especially when faced with a hostile audience.

Paul commences his comparison and innuendo with the ironical disclaimer that he would not dare (*tolman*) compare himself with the self-recommenders in Corinth (10:1). At 11:21 he adds: "But whatever anyone dares (*tolman*) to boast of—I am speaking *en aprosynē*—I also dare (*tolman*) to boast of that." The terms *tolman* and *tolma* can be used pejoratively to denote hybristic behavior,[69] and in this context of excess Paul is insinuating that it is his enemies who have boasted immoderately. He concludes the comparison by claiming he was forced (*hymeis me ēnagkasate*) into retaliatory comparison (12:11). It was one of the techniques of rhetoric that an orator should seem to be reluctant and under compulsion with something he is most concerned to prove.[70] On two occasions, he states it was necessary for him to boast (*kauchasthai dei*) (11:30; 12:1) and that is an acceptable ground for defense according to the conventions of self-praise.[71] Given that, he would only boast of his failings. Even on matters he could legitimately praise himself

---

[64]E.g., Xenophon, *Cyr.* 7.2.18; Aristotle, *Rhet.* 2.17.6; Plutarch, *Mor.* 631CDF; 634D-F.

[65]For a fuller discussion, P. Marshall, *Enmity*, 563-88.

[66]For comparison, ibid., 87-91, 538-46; and especially the excellent study by C. Forbes, "Comparison, Self-Praise and Irony," *NTS* (forthcoming), who prefers the allied notion of the boastful fool to *hybris*.

[67]Demetrius, *On Style* 291.

[68]"Ephodos and Insinuatio in Greek and Latin Rhetoric," *CQ* 52 (1958) 224; Cf. Demetrius, *On Style* 290-295.

[69]E.g., Sophocles, *OC* 1029-1030; Plato, *Apol.* 38D.

[70]So Cicero, *de Or.* 2.43.182; cf. Plutarch, *Mor.* 542E.

[71]For self-praise, P. Marshall, *Enmity*, 546-53; C. Forbes, "Comparison."

he would not do so (10:16; 11:23; 12:6). And he repeatedly asserts that it is only by adopting the guise of a fool that he can enter into retaliatory comparison (11:1, 16, 17, 21; 12:11). Throughout these chapters, then, Paul conducts his invective with restraint and moderation. He does not attack his enemies directly and seems to make a conscious effort to abide by the rules.[72] On the one occasion his denunciation of them is grossly abusive, it is done anonymously, an act which itself commends the speaker as a man of dignity.[73] By doing so Paul implies that his enemies have indulged in excessive self-praise in their invective against him.

Second, Paul intimates that his enemies have gone beyond the limits of acceptable conduct (10:12-18). He accuses them of "measuring themselves by one another and comparing themselves with one another" (*en heautois heautous metrountes kai synkrinontes heautous heautois*) and as such "they are without understanding" (*ou syniasin*) (10:12). They have made the comparison according to their own standards and by these consider themselves superior to Paul. The encomium Paul and his rivals use in the comparison indicates the standards are those of a cultured Greek.[74] Almost without exception, when Paul competes with them on these terms he depicts himself in terms of *psogos*, and then only as a fool.[75]

By comparison Paul will not boast *eis ta ametra*, a phrase which tells us what *en heautois heautois metrountes* involves. Rather he will keep to the limits of his appointment (*kata to metron tou kanonos*) which God has assigned him (*hou emerisen hēmin ho theos metrou*) (10:13).[76] The rivals' hybristic behavior is implied by *eis ta ametra* and includes their excessive boasting, abuse and ridicule of Paul, and the attempt to displace him as apostle in Corinth. *Kata to metron* implies Paul's moderation and *kanōn* represents his appointment by God as the parent-apostle of Corinth. Very pertinently, he draws attention to their *hybris* with the hybristic notion *hyperekteinō* ("overreaching," "overstepping the limits"): "I don't stretch beyond the measure assigned me when I claim this, for I was the first to reach you with the gospel" (10:14). The innuendo continues in vv. 15-18, but the emphasis is more clearly upon his rivals as violators of his apportioned lot. He repeats that he will not boast *eis ta ametra* in another man's work (as they have done) (10:15). By keeping to his appointed limits he will never claim someone else's achievements as his own (10:16) (as they had to) (cf. 11:12). Throughout this section the measure of apostleship which Paul avows and exemplifies is *ho theos metrou*. It is akin to *to mē hyper ha gegraptai* but quite distinct from the standard or measure which he accuses his enemies of adopting. He seems to be suggesting they offend even by that

---

[72]So C. Forbes, "Comparison." Enmity allows a breach of the rules of invective, but Paul is restrained. Cf. Cicero, *de Or.* 2.56.229; *Or.* 89.

[73]For the invective of non-naming, P. Marshall, *Enmity*, 528-38.

[74]Ibid., 503, 506; C. Forbes, "Comparison."

[75]2 Cor 11:23-33.

[76]*kanōn*, like *metron*, can denote the limits of appropriate conduct and be translated as "standard" or "measure"; e.g., Epictetus 3.4.4-6; Euripides, *Hec.* 602; *El* 52; Aristotle, *EN* 3.4.4-5; Demosthenes 18.296. See 1 Cor 7:17 where *kanōn* is associated with the calling of God and one's lot in life. More recently, and importantly for despairing commentators, see G. H. R. Horsley, *New Documents Illustrating Early Christianity 1* (North Ryde, 1981) 44-45, where it means "official schedule," a term which Horsley suggests Paul "took over" to express "their understanding of the way God had measured out their territorial commitments."

standard, but in the eyes of the Corinthians their behavior seems to be laudable and acceptable (e.g., 2 Cor 3:1-3; 11:4, 19).

The superiority his enemies assert is twice alluded to in Paul's comparison. In the first instance the topoi are eloquence and knowledge. In the second they are the signs or deeds of an apostle. He claims that he is not *hysterēkenai tōn hyperlian apostolōn* (11:5), a claim he restates at the conclusion of his comparison (12:11). The term *hyperlian* is mostly translated as "super" or "superlative" in these passages, but I suggest a better sense would be "beyond measure" or "excessive." As with *hyper, lian* used pejoratively denotes excess and, in various constructions, is a term of *hybris*.[77] Paul here is more directly disparaging his enemies. These are the apostles who have gone beyond the bounds, who have invidiously compared their rhetoric, knowledge, achievements, and other cultural qualities with his own. They are shameful hybrists. I suggest that *hoi hyperlian apostoloi* be rendered "the hybristic apostles."

Third, Paul has claimed that he would boast only according to the set limits which he explicitly states as *en kuriō* (10:17). But he enters into boastful comparison with them, in the guise of the fool (*alazōn*) to ridicule the self-praise and comparison of his enemies. The *alazōn* in Greek tradition is the person who has lost the awareness of his own limitations.[78]

Paul has previously accused them of lacking understanding (*ou syniasin*) (10:12) and commences his parody with "bear with me in a little foolishness" (*aphrosynēs*) (11:1). He concludes his comparison with "I have been *aphrōn*" (12:11), but only under compulsion. The use of innuendo is clear in 11:16-23. He warns the Corinthians not to think him a fool, but wishes to be accepted as one so that he too can indulge in a little boasting himself (11:16). The standard is not his own, which is *kata kyrion* but that of his enemies who boast *kata sarka* (11:17-18). It is an accusation he himself has faced over his inconstancy (10:2). As they gladly put up with fools (his enemies), they should accept him also (11:19). What in fact they put up with, suggests Paul, is misuse of power and privilege, exploitation, arrogance, abuse, and violence, all types of hybristic conduct typical of superior social status. With savage irony Paul asserts "To my shame (*kata atimian*), I must say, we were too weak for that"; that is, too weak for *hybris* and *alazoneia* (11:20-21).

His point for point comparison picks up the arrogance of the hybrist. He "dares to boast" of "whatever anyone dares to boast of," but, he concedes, as a fool. His birth and racial status are the equal of theirs. And where it really matters: "Are they servants of Christ? I am a better one (*hyper egō*)—I am talking like a madman" (11:21-23). But he proceeds to state his apostolic superiority by listing all the worse things, those things which are socially and culturally opposites of the standards of his enemies (11:23-33).[79]

Fourth, the deliberate stance of shame is developed at length in one particular point at the end of his comparison (12:1-10). Paul argues that if anyone has grounds for boasting, it is himself. He admits that the extraordinary visions and revelations he received would justify boasting (by the hybrist standards). Even then, he discusses it in the third person as if "to avoid any hint that he saw it as something that he himself

---

[77]E.g., Euripides. *Phoen* 584; *Andr* 866; *Hipp* 264; Lysias 24.15, 25; Aristotle, *EN* 4.7.15; 7.4.5; 10.6.6; Solon 5.8: *mēte lian*.

[78]See especially C. Forbes, "Comparison."

[79]See P. Marshall, *Enmity*, 553-63; C. Forbes, "Comparison."

possessed, of which he could boast."[80] "On behalf of this man I will boast," he says, but of himself, only his social humiliations, his weaknesses. But then he asserts on his own behalf that if he wished to boast, he would not be *aphrōn* but would speak *alētheian*. That is to say, he would not transgress the limits of self-knowledge, as his enemies had done (12:6). The association of *kauchasthai, aphrōn* and *alētheia* is typical of *hybris*.[81]

Paul claims that his restraint is to prevent anyone from thinking of him above (*hyper*) what "he sees in me or hears from me." This is somewhat ironical, for his speech and physical appearance had been savagely ridiculed (10:10, 11:6). He concedes that he might have succumbed to *hybris* himself, but God humiliated him, imposing on him a thorn in his side. It prevented him from being too elated (*hyperairōmai*) by the excess (*hyperbolē*) of revelation (12:7). Betz correctly translates *hyperaiōmai* as "presumption" or "arrogance" and notes the nuances of *hybris* in the passage.[82] The "thorn in the flesh" imposed a humiliating social disability on Paul, a lesson which taught him to boast only of his weaknesses (12:8-9).[83]

Throughout these chapters Paul resorts to the doctrines of *hybris* and *sōphrosynē* as innuendo to disparage his opponents and to commend himself as a moderate man. It provides a popular and social context into which we can place his boasting and foolishness. It almost provides us with two distinct standards of apostleship. If Paul's arrivals are to be accused of *hybris*, of excess and immoderation, he by contrast consciously depicts himself as deficient of the mean, by a remarkable display of self-derision. This standard of humiliation and shame is for him the mark of a true apostle of Christ (11:30; 12:9; 13:3-4). Thus he concludes his invective of *hybris*: "For the sake of Christ, then, I am content with weaknesses, insults (*en hybresin*), hardships, persecutions, and calamities; for when I am weak, then I am strong" (12:10).

V

Some Implications and Directions for Corinthian Studies

It is puzzling indeed that the purportedly rampant *gnosis* of 1 Corinthians is decorous in the extreme in 2 Corinthians. And such moderation must have happened in the short space of the twelve months which elapsed between 1 and 2 Corinthians. Even Pagels's gnostics found less to enthuse over in the second letter, if her analysis is to be a reliable guide in this matter.[84] Arising from this the consensus was that 2 Corinthians represents a dissimilar situation to the first.[85] I suggest that opinion is changing and that a new consensus is emerging which sees a firm connection between events and issues in both letters.[86] The enmity between Paul and his opponents had worsened by the second

---

[80]So C. Forbes, "Comparison."

[81]E.g., Aristotle, *EE* 2.3.4.

[82]H. D. Betz, *Die Apostel Paulus und die sokratische Tradition* (Tübingen, 1972) 95.

[83]I suggest it is a physical debility which detracts from his public speaking, see my *Enmity*, 240-42, 515-16, 586.

[84]"The Gnostic Paul," 95-100.

[85]So C. K. Barrett, "Paul's Opponents in II Corinthians," *NTS* 17 (1971) 236.

[86]Recent work by N.T. social historians and sociologists has demonstrated these links (e.g., Theissen, Hock, Malherbe).

letter which represents almost exclusively his attempt to reestablish his position as the apostle of Corinth. The situation had not changed; rather it had become intensified and individually focused.

My analysis of *hybris* in 1 Cor 4:6-13 and 2 Cor 10-12 indicates that Paul's enemies in both letters exhibit a common pattern of behavior. It is feasible to suggest that the two groups are related. The opponents of 1 Corinthians have formed an alliance with people of similar status and values to their own. These rivals continue the enmity and invective against Paul, but now in direct comparison and rivalry.[87] As I have indicated, *hybris* is a social and moral term, and it provides us with a new social context to understand the conflict in Corinth. Unlike a gnostic tradition, it represents a familiar and contemporary tradition of long standing in Greek life and thought, something which cannot be claimed confidently about first century Gnosticism. It offers a recognizable and comprehensive context in which to explain the complex of nuances (status, excess, measurement, moderation, superiority, arrogance, shame, knowledge, freedom, wisdom) and a range of related social conduct which appear in 1 and 2 Corinthians.

Hybris also adds to our understanding of the social status of the Corinthians and Paul's enemies in particular. Hybristic conduct is about wealth and power, and the way Paul utilizes the doctrines of *hybris* and *sōphrosynē* in Corinthians indicates that his opponents are of privilege and high status in their own environment. It also explains in part why Paul adopts in both passages the position of the humiliated person and of the fool. I suggest that we should call Paul's enemies hybrists rather than gnostics.

In conclusion, I have analyzed two key passages in 1 and 2 Corinthians and hinted how they might explain other passages, particularly those dealing with wisdom and freedom. I have also pointed to the hybristic character of certain arrogant social conduct in 1 Corinthians. There are also many other passages which can profitably be assessed in the light of the doctrines of *hybris* and *sōphrosynē*.[88] We may find in the end that we need look no further to posit the vocabulary and outlook of these people than that of educated Hellenists who were conversant with popular ideas which circulated at their status level and who were well entrenched in social convention.

---

[87]See my discussion, *Enmity*, 503-26.
[88]Ibid., 336-37 n. 1.

Did the Romans Have a Religion?

Charles Robert Phillips, III

Lehigh University

> Roman religion was made up of traditional practice and animated by patriotic spirit; it was not a matter of belief.
>
> Arthur Darby Nock

Although Nock wrote those words some fifty years ago, like conceptualizations appear in the works of such distinguished later scholars as Latte, Liebeschuetz, Syme, and Weinstock.[1] And, lest they all be taken as an elder generation's dated notions, consider Andrew Wallace-Hadrill's words: "For the Roman, worship was indeed a matter of ritual practice: it made no demands on the intellect or the emotions."[2] Today, few scholars of either religion studies or social sciences would accept the patently absurd, self-contradictory idea that a religious system without belief can exist. How, then, did it happen that classicists, who once had close working relations with both religion studies and the social sciences, should still cling to a discarded idea? This paper seeks to answer that question through sketching a preliminary hermeneutic of the definitions of Roman religion. It will first examine how ancient Roman material seemed to imply the notion of a "religion of mere cult acts" and then trace how the aforementioned divergence has arisen in scholarship since the medieval period. Put briefly, classical studies, religion studies, and the social sciences shared theoretical presuppositions until early in this century, Then classical studies diverged: as the other disciplines modified their erstwhile formulations, classicists almost eagerly chose to fossilize themselves.

The very abundance of classical literary texts ensures that any treatment of Roman religion will rely heavily on those texts. But cautious use of those texts is in order, given their premier position, since a misformulation (i.e., "religion of cult acts") will appear to

---

[1] *CAH* 10.469. Cf. Kurt Latte, *Römische Religionsgeschichte* (Munich, 1960) 61; J. H. W. G. Liebeschuetz, *Continuity and Change in Roman Religion* (Oxford, 1979) 3; Ronald Syme, *Tacitus* (Oxford, 1958) 2.523; S. Weinstock, rev. Latte, *JRS* 51 (1961) 210. The following paper comprises the second part of a threefold elaboration. The first part appears in my "The Sociology of Religious Knowledge in the Roman Empire to A.D. 284," *ANRW* 2.16.3, section III.A with nn. 75-81, in galley proof at the time of this writing; I refer to it below as *SRK*. This material will ultimately receive considerable expansion in my book, *Roman Religious Knowledge Against Its Traditions* (Princeton University Press). I am grateful to Professor William M. Calder, III (Department of Classics, University of Colorado) for a stimulating exchange of letters, ideas, and bibliography on the interpretative traditions.

[2] Andrew Wallace-Hadrill, *Suetonius* (New Haven, 1983) 190.

have the imprimatur of an entire literary tradition, in consequence becoming very difficult to modify. This paper suggests that just such a misformulation has dominated the
study of Roman religion; although it may well have arisen for legitimate reasons, equally
compelling reasons now exist for discarding it. The nature of the misformulation will
appear in the following consideration of the three main sources of information on Roman
religion that an ancient author possessed: *Annales Maximi,* family histories, and antiquarian traditions.

The *Annales Maximi,* traditional Roman priestly records, received considerable
attention in antiquity.[3] Cato's content statement is famous: *quotiens annona cara, quotiens lunae aut solis lumine caligo aut quid obstiterit;* likewise Cicero's observation *quibus
nihil potest esse ieiunius.*[4] These complaints about aridity do not lack basis, for the
Annales, as a record of events Roman religious specialists deemed important for their
ongoing work, inevitably emphasized publicly observable phenomena such as prodigies,
expiation rituals, and festivals. Thus the very genre militated against both detailed
reports and, especially, the insertion of any "belief" statements. Moreover, when the
priests transcribed the whitened boards, on which the notices were first recorded, to
more permanent records, condensation eliminated not only details but also stray editori-
alizing.[5] The resultant transcription thus appeared as a series of brief anecdotes in
chronological order; scholars are only now beginning to appreciate how importantly
anecdotes influenced Roman knowledge systems both sacred and secular.[6] Although much
controversy rages over the ways in which the transcribed texts reached authors late in
the second century B.C., it does appear clear that, in some way, the information did
become widely available.[7] The tables' venerable antiquity virtually ensured their canonic
status for the ancient author researching Roman religion, while their anecdotal contents
ensured that the information on Roman religion which got into a given literary work
would be equally anecdotal.

As for family histories, many *nobiles* traced their connections back to a putative
divine ancestor or, at least, claimed long-standing association with a particular cult.[8]
Sometimes inscriptions and funeral laudations preserved the material, while sometimes it
appears in written family histories.[9] Here again the mode of preserving information
favored anecdotes of the publicly observable phenomena of cult acts; there existed no

---

[3]The fullest modern study is Bruce Frier, *Libri Annales Pontificum Maximorum:
The Origins of the Annalistic Tradition* (Rome, 1979) which should be read with Robert
Ogilvie's review, *JRS* 71 (1981) 199-201. Much valuable discussion appears in H. Peter,
Historicorum Romanorum Relliquiae, 2nd ed. (Leipzig, 1914) 1.iii-xxix.

[4]Cato ap. Gel. 2.28.6; Cic. *Leg.* 1.6.

[5]P. Fraccaro, "The History of Rome in the Regal Period," *JRS* 47 (1957) 61.

[6]Richard Saller, "Anecdotes as Historical Evidence for the Principate," *G&R* 2d.
Ser. 27 (1980) 69-83; this theme appears repeatedly in my *SRK.*

[7]Frier (above, n. 3) chap. 8.

[8]S. Weinstock, *Divus Julius* (Oxford, 1971) 4-5; T. P. Wiseman, "Legendary Geneal-
ogies in Late-Republican Rome," *G&R* 2d Ser. 21 (1974) 153-64.

[9]For example, the epitaphs of the Scipios: *CIL* I^2 6, 7; 8, 9 (*Dedet Tempestatebus
aide*); 10; 11; 12; 15. Funeral laudations: Schanz-Hosius 1.22-24 with A. Momigliano,
"Perizonius, Niebuhr and the Character of Early Roman Tradition," *JRS* 47 (1957) 104-14.
Family history: Weinstock (above, n. 8), 4 with nn. 4-6; cf. L. Julius Caesar's activities
(Serv. *Aen.* 1.267).

possibility in genre, or information source either, for that matter, to transmit an ancestor's deep feelings for a given cult.

The antiquarian tradition contained encyclopedic compendia of curiosities which authors such as Plutarch, Pliny the Elder, Posidonius, Valerius Maximus, and Varro produced. They had diverse sources: free-floating oral traditions, oral traditions attached to various monuments and, of course, the two aforementioned sources.[10] Indeed, Vergil unintentionally gives an accurate account of oral religious traditions when he depicts Evander acting the cicerone to Aeneas (*Aen* 8.355-358): *haec duo praeterea disiectis oppida muris,/reliquias ueterumque uides monimenta uirorum./hanc Ianus pater, hanc Saturnus condidit arcem;/Ianiculum huic, illi fuerat Saturnia nomen.*

Consequently it should not occasion surprise when a Livy or Tacitus dwells solely on the cultic aspects of Roman religion, since their information sources contained nothing else. Moreover, even if information on religious feeling were to hand, it would have been unusable, since the generic rules for historiography forbade psychologizing except in set speeches, compositions whose religious "belief" statements derive from rhetorical tags rather than reliable historical information.[11] Thus the anecdotal, ritualistic nature of the source material occasioned anecdotal, ritualistic accounts of Roman religion. Classicists, especially for reasons this paper will shortly elaborate, imbibed those literary descriptions of a religion of cult acts and considered the case closed, since the evidence seemed to speak clearly. Another kind of ancient literature further bolstered their confidence, namely the Roman philosophical writings. Cicero and Seneca not only offered predictably ritualistic accounts of traditional Roman religion, but seemed to express considerable adherence to philosophical systems such as Stoicism or Epicureanism. All seemed clear: the Roman intellectuals has wisely jettisoned their traditional impoverished religious system of cult acts in favor of philosophical parameters, all the while making obeisance to traditional rituals. This picture seemed all the more credible since ancient philosophy, especially as mediated through first Roman philosophy and then Neoplatonism, had strongly influenced the development of Christian theology; investigators of the Christian persuasion, as most were, recognized glimmerings of his faith in Roman philosophy, thus confidently concluding that any religious strivings the Romans had found fulfillment in philosophy.[12] What of the non-intellectual Romans, the lower orders? Traditionally conceived in ancient sources as an ignorant rabble, a veritable *plebs sordida*, they were deemed to continue to practice traditional religion in their alleged spiritual torpor, along with various unsavory magical activities.

The scholars who thought they had produced an adequate explanation of traditional Roman religion, namely an empty series of cult acts for which intellectuals wisely substituted philosophy, should have thought further. Cicero's philosophical works, it is true, do seem to suggest that. But what of his letters which were not intended for publication?

---

[10]E. Gabba, "True History and False History in Classical Antiquity," *JRS* 71 (1981) 60-62. See my observations in *SRK* III.C., D.; Professor William Harris advises me of his preparation of a book dealing with the role of oral traditions and literacy in classical antiquity; cf. the suggestive study of the medieval period: Brian Stock, *The Implications of Literacy* (Princeton, 1983).

[11]Evidence collected in *SRK* n. 42, e.g., Sen. *Con.* 1.1.16, 1.8.15-16, 2.1.27.

[12]*SRK*, n. 86 gives some preliminary indications to the vast secondary material; see especially H. Chadwick, *Early Christian Thought and the Classical Tradition* (New York, 1966) 111-19.

They contain emotional statements about traditional Roman religion. But not only do we lack other such personal sources, but scholars have usually not cared to read the philosophical works in context of the letters. In short, classical antiquity lacked a literary genre of religious confessional literature, a lack Christianity was soon to remedy with works like Saint Augustine's *Confessions*. Now the Judaeo-Christian system had long represented the system to which most scholars had owed at least nominal adherence; since they found no parallels to their own religion's confessional dimensions in Roman materials, they concluded that the Romans had nothing to confess, blaming religion rather than genre. Imagine the strange emphases if two thousand years hence a scholar offered a description of Christianity based solely on a *Liber Usualis*, without benefit of Cardinal Newman.

This paper now turns to its second concern, namely the tracing of what the scholarly tradition has done with, or to, the Roman materials, and the reasons for that treatment. Medieval and Renaissance thinkers eagerly conned the ancient philosophical texts as a means to develop their own systems, taking the various comments on traditional Roman religion as curiosities, enlightening anecdotes when taken in context of some newly unearthed monument or literary text.[13] The dominance of Christian theology did not encourage investigators to attempt to conceptualize a religious system on different terms: that which was not Christian was not religion. The Enlightenment shows the first significant appearance of alternate models of religions. Experimental work in the natural sciences, along with missionary reports of non-European folk, made the philosophes consider the possibility of other explanations for the order of things than the hitherto-dominant theologically based ones. Many, already revolted by what they deemed clerical excess, found the true *homo religiosus* in the non-Christian systems. Many too, regardless of their evaluation of other religions, found them convenient weapons with which to belabor Christianity.[14] But those weapons remained unexamined, and mainly consisted of anecdotes of Roman religion deriving from earlier encyclopedic compilations, themselves dependent on Roman anecdotal traditions. Thus Gibbon observed how Christianity had ruined the Roman Empire, but did not dwell on the belief system allegedly ruined in that process.

The nineteenth century, incidentally the beginning of "modern" classical studies, produced several intellectual currents which caused the further establishment of the hitherto-dominant "mere cult acts" view of Roman religion. Science, building on the Enlightenment's experiments and theorizing, seemed able, especially after Darwin, to explain everything in the world in terms of observable natural facts; it could thus continue the previous era's concern to combat the allegedly mendacious theological explanations.[15] Indeed, "scientific" notions greatly influenced studies of religion at this time, Roman religion among them. The combination of ethnographic reports and armchair

---

[13]Gabba (above, n. 10) and Eric Sharpe, *Comparative Religion* (New York, 1975) 10-15.

[14]The best introduction to this complex period remains Peter Gay, *The Enlightenment: An Interpretation. The Rise of Modern Paganism* (New York, 1977); cf. *SRK*, III.A., B.

[15]Sharpe, (above, n. 13) 47-71; his citations of primary texts are often very unreliable and should be checked, where possible, against the convenient collection in Tess Cosslett, *Science and Religion in the Nineteenth Century* (Cambridge, 1984), which also has valuable introductory materials.

theorizing by adepts of the new discipline of anthropology seemed to confirm the "cult acts" idea, since the non-European societies seemed exact parallels. Of course, the Enlightenment had observed the same thing, but the new observations, based on supposedly rigid "scientific" parameters, seemed correct by definition, since science was already enjoying considerable prestige, both as an explanatory system and as a driving force in the century's rapid industrialization. In actuality, of course, the ethnographic material was tainted, since the observers carried with them ideas of what religion "was," based on their particular versions of Christianity; native systems which did not measure up according to the standards of the colonial empires which ruled them were considered primitive at best, magical and lacking even in souls at worst. While probably the majority of the ethnographic reports arose as a result of the British Empire, making the United Kingdom the natural center for such comparative studies, the Germans were taking a somewhat different route. A relentless application of the "scientific" principles to the materials of scholarship was beginning to produce immense collections of data, data which should be able to speak for itself, without the bane of human prejudices. The empirically-derived classical religious data, which this paper has just described, obviously contained little but information on cult acts; in light of the empiricist parameters, the "facts" had spoken, and matters were closed.

Anthropology represented one important influence on studies of Roman religion in the United Kingdom; theology provided the second. Virtually all work in classical studies took place at Oxford and Cambridge where, overwhelmingly, the dons were in Holy Orders.[16] This ensured that the ethnographic materials and Roman materials alike would seem wanting in the light of Anglicanism. Nevertheless, British scholarly productions bulked few in number and of generally indifferent quality when compared with the fruits of the Germans' "scientific" scholarship. The Germans lacked the British clerical dominance in universities and thus turned their interpretative attentions almost entirely to collections of data, producing such monuments as Muller's *Handbuch*, *Pauly-Wissowa*, *Roscher's Lexikon*, and the Teubner series of classical texts.[17] Interestingly, the British concatenation anthropology/classics/theology and the German classics/empiricist facts produced like results: Roman religion was now provably comprised of mere cult acts.[18] William Warde Fowler of Lincoln College, Oxford, represents an important exception. Fowler seems actually to have felt that the Romans had a religious experience, devoting considerable energy to making the point.[19] But Fowler only began his serious scholarly work early in the present century, when the Germans' empiricism had swept everything else aside; no epigonoi took up his view as even his student H. J. Rose subscribed to the "cult acts" position as "proven" by German empiricism. Moreover, the very bulk and value of the Germans' production ensured that their views would have a prominent place in classical studies.

----

[16]A. J. Engel, *From Clergyman to Don. The Rise of the Academic Profession in Nineteenth-Century Oxford* (Oxford, 1983) 2-5, 177, 286; my remarks on the state of research rely on this work, as well as E. J. Kenney, *The Classical Text* (Berkeley, 1974) 116-17, 144.

[17]E. Menge and Herbert Max, trans. C. Garton, "The Firm of B. G. Teubner and its Connection with Classical Learning," *Arethusa* 2 (1969) 203-11.

[18]Thus W. Warde Fowler, *CR* 16 (1902) 117, complains of Wissowa's hostility to anthropology.

[19]E.g., his *Religious Experience of the Roman People* (London, 1911).

Curiously, studies of ancient Greek religion fared differently. Some, like Farnell, did specialize in the cultic, but many others, such as Jane Harrison and Gilbert Murray, stressed the validity of the Greek religious experience.[20] Several reasons for this obtain. First, the Hellenic tradition had preserved, as the Roman had not, some very personal statements which put flesh on the bones of cultic anecdotes: Homer, Sappho, Sophocles, Euripides. Second, the nineteenth century had appropriated the Greeks and Romans differently; it saw kindred spirits in the Greeks, witless trolls of empire-builders in the Romans. In consequence, many practiced a kind of double-think, accepting the thinking Greeks as models for mental life, the mindless Romans as models for modern empires.[21] Third, and perhaps somewhat perversely, I would point to the existence of A. E. Housman as an inhibiting factor on studies of Roman religion; compare Bowra's observation "Moreover, the study of Latin was hampered by a barely visible but by no means inaudible presence operating from Cambridge."[22] Housman felt the classicist's proper work lay in the editing of texts; since he worked with Latin authors for most of his career, his emphasis naturally dominated there.[23] A whole generation of scholars thus was discouraged from doing other than textual work, literary scholars as well as historians, since Housman's emphases for this latter group fit contemporary theorizing about the practice of historiography in general. Students of Roman religion, perhaps a bit guilty that they did not have a vast quantity of texts to edit, tried at least to toe the scholarly line through compilations of data and explications of various cultic minutiae. But by the twenties of this century, most classicists, whether Latinists or Hellenists, had simply stopped listening to other disciplines at all, thus losing step with considerable modifications in theoretical positions. They stopped, and fossilized, as it were, with either their empiricism or their theories of cult acts, regardless of derivation; some have clung to old controversies, as Latte fulminated against animism, many sneered at the theoretical concerns of an "interloper" like Dumézil.[24] But changes have appeared. Some classicists have utilized theoretical guidelines from the social sciences to assist their studies of Roman religion (Beard, Gordon, Hopkins, Price), while scholars of religion studies have trained their wider methodological training on ancient religion, most often Greek (Alderink, Hlegeland, McGinty, both Smiths; the dominance of the University of Chicago merits more consideration). The renewed signs of dialogue are encouraging, as each group learns from others. Dare one hope that from this detente Roman religion may finally receive its due?

---

[20]Park McGinty, *Interpretation and Dionysos* (The Hague, 1978) chap. 3; Professor Calder (above, n. 1) usefully reminds me that scholars may have trained their theories on Greek religion because it seemed amenable to such theories.

[21]R. Jenkyns, *The Victorians and Ancient Greece* (Cambridge, Mass., 1980).

[22]C. M. Bowra, *Memories* (Cambridge, Mass., 1967) 253.

[23]In general, N. Page, *A. E. Housman. A Critical Biography* (New York, 1983) 162-178; cf. J. P. Sullivan, *Arion* 1.2 (1962) 105 ff.

[24]Latte (above, n. 1) 94 n. 1, 100 n. 2; on classicists' criticisms of Dumézil, C. Scott Littleton, *The New Comparative Mythology,* 3rd ed. (Berkeley, 1982) 193-97.

Firstborn of Many Brothers:
A Pauline Notion of Apotheosis

James Tabor

University of Notre Dame

Over the past one hundred years specialists in New Testament and historians of religions of the Hellenistic period have put forth an enormous effort in investigating the origin and development of what is usually termed the "Christology" of earliest Christianity. How is it that the historical figure of Jesus of Nazareth, executed by the Romans around 30 C.E., within two or three decades is viewed by adherents of the new cult as a pre-existent divine figure who becomes a human being, dies, is raised from the dead and exalted to the level of the highest heavenly glory as Christ, Lord, and Son of God.[1] Are there analogies in the ancient world which might serve as parallels or even sources for such an evaluation of Jesus? The possibility of a pre-Christian gnostic redeemer myth, the notion of the *theios anēr*, Hellenistic Jewish Wisdom speculations and the dying and rising gods of the mystery religions have all been proposed and extensively debated as possible keys to solving this problem. In this paper I would like to focus on what might be called the other side of this "Christology" question, namely, Paul's notion of *many* "sons of God," who expect a similar transformation from mortal to immortal life and an exaltation to heavenly glory, to that of Jesus. In this regard I will stress two points: (1) the close link between a select group of "sons of God" with the status of Jesus as Son of God; (2) the cosmic role and function of such a group as God's agents in the culmination of history. In this portion of my paper I have limited my investigation to six letters which are recognized by most scholars as undoubtedly from Paul's hand: 1 Thess, Gal, 1-2 Cor, Rom and Phil. I then turn to ask how such a notion of what I would call "mass apotheosis" might be set in the context of various Hellenistic ways of understanding divinity.

SON OF GOD—SONS OF GOD

In the letters mentioned above Paul refers to Jesus as Son of God (υἱός) 15 times.[2] On the other hand, he speaks of believers in the cult as sons of God (using the plural υἱοί) 10 times.[3] Two of the clearest descriptive passages are Rom 8:14 and Gal 3:26:

For all who are led by the Spirit of God are *sons of God*.

---

[1]Of the many works one might cite I would mention here Martin Hengel's recent collection of essays, *Between Jesus and Paul* (Philadelphia: Fortress Press, 1983) which is up to date and contains extensive notes and bibliography.

[2]Rom 1:3, 4, 9; 5:10; 8:3, 29, 32; 1 Cor 1:9; 15:28; 2 Cor 1:19; Gal 1:16; 2:20; 4:4, 6; 1 Thess 1:10.

[3]Rom 8:14, 19; 9:26; 2 Cor 6:18; Gal 1:26; 4:6, 7; 1 Thess 5:5.

. . . for in Christ Jesus you are all *sons of God* through faith.[4]

I am interested here in the connection between the one and the many, particularly in terms of cosmic destiny. Paul's most programmatic statement is in Rom 8:29-30. Here we have a sequential outline of what he calls the plan or purpose (πρόθεσιν—v 28) of God:

> For those whom he foreknew he also predestined (προώρισεν) to share the image (συμμόρφους τῆς εἰκόνος) of his Son, that he might be the first-born (πρωτότοκον) of many brothers, and the ones he predestined he also called, and the ones he called he also justified, and the ones he justified he also glorified (ἐδόξασεν).

I want to take some of the key vocabulary from this text and trace it through other texts which appear to be closely related in general theme.

Προορίζω also occurs in 1 Cor 2:7:

> But we impart a secret (μυστηρίῳ) and hidden wisdom of God, which God *determined* (προώρισεν) before the ages *for our glorification* (εἰς δόξαν ἡμῶν).

What is particularly striking about this passage is that προορίζω is directly connected to the idea of δόξα/δοξάζω here, as well as in Rom 8:30, even though the vocabulary and context of this section of 1 Cor are quite different.[5] In both texts Paul speaks of God's predetermined plan which involves the heavenly *glorification* of a select group. Further, this plan is hidden from the ἀρχόντων τοῦ αἰῶνος (1 Cor 2:8), which I take as a reference to hostile spirits who rule the cosmos.[6] I would also note that Paul's use of μυστήριον here should be compared with 1 Cor 15:51 (which I will take up below) where he speaks directly of the transformation (i.e., glorification) of the group of believers as a "secret."[7]

Σύμμορφος occurs elsewhere only in Phil 3:21 which seems to directly parallel the thought of Rom 8:29-30:

---

[4]Unless otherwise indicated the translations of N.T. texts and emphases therein are my own.

[5]On the special vocabulary and complexities of 1 Cor 1:18-2:16 see Ulrich Wilckens, *Weisheit und Torheit: eine exegetisch-religionsgeschichtliche Untersuchung zu 1 Kor 1 und 2* (BHT 26; Tübingen: J. C. B. Mohr, 1959) and Birger A. Pearson, *The Pneumatikos-Psychikos Terminology* (SBLDS 12; Missoula: Scholars Press, 1973).

[6]See Martin Dibelius, *Die Geisterwelt im Glauben des Paulus* (Göttingen: Vandenhoeck & Ruprecht, 1909) 90-96. On the position that the reference is to human rulers see André Feuillet, "Les 'Chefs de ce siècle' et la Sagesse divine d'après 1 Co. II, 6-8," *Le Christ Sagesse de Dieu d'après les épîtres pauliniennes* (Paris: Gabalda, 1966) 25-36.

[7]He also uses μυστήριον for the historical purpose of God in initiating his Gentile mission and its function for the salvation of Israel (Rom 11:25-56; 16:25-26). Cf. also 1 Cor 4:1; 13:2; 14:2 and the deutero-Pauline materials (Eph 1:19; 3:3-9; 6:19; Col 1:26-27; 2:2; 4:3).

For our commonwealth exists *in the heavens* from which we expectantly await a Savior, the Lord Jesus Christ, who will *transform* (μετασχηματίσει) our lowly body *into the same form* (σύμμορφον) as his *glorious* body (τῆς δόξης αὐτοῦ), by the power with which he is able to *subject everything* to himself.[8]

Here we have a more descriptive commentary on this central Pauline notion of glorification. It is something which is to occur at the *parousia* of Jesus from heaven (cf. 1 Thess 1:9-10; 1 Cor 15:51). The identification of the exalted heavenly state of Jesus with that expected by believers is exact. It involves a transformation (μετασχηματίζω) from ταπείνωσις to δόξα Also involved is Jesus' power to subject "all things" (τὰ πάντα) to himself, a concept Paul elaborates in 1 Cor 15 when he deals with this identical notion of heavenly glorification.

The transformation, taking the entire phrase of Rom 8:29, is a "sharing of the *image* of his Son" (συμμόρφους τῆς εἰκόνος τοῦ υἱοῦ αὐτοῦ). This use of εἰκών seems parallel to that of 2 Cor 3:18:

But we all, with unveiled face, beholding the *glory of the Lord,* are being *transformed* (μεταμορφούμεθα) *into his image* (εἰκόνα) from one degree of glory to another; for this comes from the Lord who is the Spirit.

The precise meaning of this verse and its context is extremely difficult,[9] however, I do not think one finds here, nor in the following section of 5:1-10, any shift from Paul's idea that full or final transformation/glorification is at the *parousia.* The thought is essentially the same as that of Rom 8:29 and Phil 3:21, indeed the verb μετασχηματίζω in the latter text is parallel to μεταμορφόομαι here in 2 Cor 3:18. The connection of εἰκών and δόξα occurs further on in 2 Cor 4:4. There Paul speaks of the "god of this age" (i.e., Satan) blinding the minds of unbelievers that they may not see the light τοῦ εὐαγγελίου τῆς δόξης τοῦ Χριστοῦ ὅς ἐστιν εἰκὼν τοῦ θεοῦ. Then in verse 6 he says that God's illumination of the hearts of believers brings about the φωτισμὸν τῆς γνώσεως τῆς δόξης τοῦ θεοῦ ἐν προσώπῳ Χριστοῦ. Paul's gospel message is a gospel *of* the glory of Christ, i.e., a γνῶσις of the glory of God seen in the exalted figure of Christ who is the εἰκών of God. My point here is that all which is included in the idea of "Christ as the image of God" is applied in the most *direct* way to the anticipated future of those who "believe" the message.

Paul further clarifies what he has in mind with the phrase εἰς τὸ εἶναι αὐτὸν πρωτότοκον ἐν πολλοῖς ἀδελφοῖς (Rom 8:29), which stands as an explanation of συμμόρφους τῆς εἰκόνος τοῦ υἱοῦ αὐτοῦ. Πρωτότοκος occurs only here in Paul.[10] Again, the

---

[8]I cannot agree with Erhardt Güttgemanns (*Der leidende Apostel und sein Herr: Studien zur paulinischen Christologie* [FRLANT 90; Göttingen: Vandenhoeck & Ruprecht, 1966] 240-47) that Phil 3:20-21 is pre-Pauline. See the discussion and critique of this position by Robert H. Gundry, *Soma in Biblical Theology with Emphasis on Pauline Anthropology* (SNTSMS 29; Cambridge: University Press, 1976) 177-83.

[9]See Dieter Georgi, *Die Gegner des Paulus im 2 Korintherbrief: Studien zur religiösen Propaganda in der Spatantike* (WMANT 11; Neukirchen-Vluyn: Neukirchener Verlag, 1964) 258-89.

[10]Since the language and thought of Rom 8:29 are so closely linked to 1 Cor 15:20-28; 42-58, where the phrase ἀπαρχὴ τῶν κεκοιμημένων is used in v 20 as a basis for argu-

identification of Jesus the Son of God with the *many* glorified sons of God which follow is direct. The idea is that God is bringing into existence a *family* (i.e., "many brothers") of beings, the Sons of God, who share his heavenly δόξα. Jesus, then, stands at the head of a new *genus* of cosmic "brothers" who now await their own exaltation at his *parousia.*

The verb δοξάζω in Rom 8:30 stands for both of these phrases in verse 29, i.e., "to share the image of his Son" and "the firstborn of many brothers." Thus, in these two verses, 29 and 30, Paul summarizes the important notion of the ἐλπίδος τῆς δόξης τοῦ θεοῦ which he introduced in Rom 5:1 and develops in 8:17-25. To be a υἱὸς θεοῦ according to 8:17 is to be a co-heir (συγκληρονόμος) with Jesus. Such a relationship involves a suffering with him, which in turn leads to a "co-glorification" (συνδοξάζω). Paul frequently uses the various forms of the word κληρονόμος.[11] There is a close connection between the terms κληρονόμος and δόξα and his idea of participating in the "Kingdom of God" (cf. 1 Cor 6:9-10; 15:50-53; Gal 5:21; 1 Thess 2:2). A summary of his thought in this regard might run like this: *what* one inherits is the Kingdom of God; *when* it is inherited is at the *parousia* of Jesus; *how* one enters this Kingdom is through a transformation to immortal heavenly glory.

In Rom 8:18-25, the section which precedes vv 29-30, Paul expands upon his vision of the future, Without trying to deal with this complex passage as a whole I would note here the following verses:

> For I think that the sufferings of this present time are not worth comparing with the *glory* that is about to be *revealed in us!* (v. 18)

> For the creation expectantly longs for the *revealing* (ἀποκάλυψιν) *of the sons of God.* . . . (v 19)

> . . . we ourselves . . . groan inside waiting for our *sonship* (υἱοθεσίαν), that is, the *redemption of our bodies.* (v. 23)

The use of υἱοθεσία in 8:23 to refer to the *parousia* expectation is significant. Several manuscripts (chiefly Western) omit the word, probably because it appears to contradict 8:15:[12]

> For you did not receive the spirit of bondage to fall back into fear, but you have received the spirit of sonship (πνεῦμα υἱοθεσίας) in which we cry out "Abba! Father!"

---

ing that Jesus' resurrection and glorification will be followed by the transformation of those "in Christ" at the *parousia,* the central idea of πρωτότοκος in Paul seems to be anticipatory, pointing toward recapitulation. Thus "firstborn" implies more than preeminence, it points to those "later born." In Heb 2:10 the phrase ἀρχηγὸν τῆς σωτηρίας is juxtaposed with πολλοὺς υἱοὺς εἰς δόξαν ἀγαγόντα (an expression which is certainly "Pauline" in meaning). The point appears to be the same, i.e., Jesus as the preliminary figure of God's plan is representative of the many to follow.

[11] κληρονομέω occurs in 1 Cor 6:9, 10; 15:50; Gal 4:30; 5:21; κληρονομία once in Gal 3:18. κληρονόμος occurs in Rom 4:13, 14; 8:17; Gal 3:29; 4:1, 7. Cf. Eph 1:11, 14, 18; Col 3:24.

[12] See Bruce M. Metzger, *A Textual Commentary on the Greek New Testament* (New York: United Bible Societies, 1971) 517.

In Gal 4:4-7 Paul expresses the identical thought:

> But when the fullness of time arrived, God sent forth his Son, born of woman, born under the law, to redeem those who were under the law, so that we might *receive sonship* (υἱοθεσίαν). And because *you are sons,* God has sent the Spirit of his Son into your hearts crying, "Abba! Father!" So through God you are no longer a slave but a son, and if a son then an *heir* (κληρονόμος).

There is a certain tension here between present realization and future consummation, something common in Paul.[13] The believers *now* receive the *spirit of sonship* (Rom 8:15) and *are* sons and heirs of God. Gal 4:4-7 parallels this thought: the reason for the "sending of the Son was that they might receive υἱοθεσία. But this "sonship" is precisely defined in Rom 8:23 as τὴν ἀπολύτρωσιν τοῦ σώματος ἡμῶν. This is what Paul meant by the "revealing" of the sons of God, their transformation, glorification and exaltation at the *parousia* of Jesus. This is his "hope" which he says is not *yet* seen (8:24-25).

Beginning with Rom 8:29-30 I have strung together this rather complicated web of passages (1 Cor 2:7; Phil 3:20-21; 2 Cor 3:18; 4:4-6; Rom 8:17-25) to demonstrate that Paul is very single-minded about this central idea, even in disparate contexts. The key terms (δόξα/δοξάζω; σύμμορφος; μετασχηματίζω; μεταμορφόομαι; εἰκών; κληρονόμος; υἱοθεσία) show a strikingly consistent interconnection.

I now turn to a brief consideration of portions of 1 Cor 15 where Paul defends his notion of "resurrection of the dead" (plural) on the basis of faith in Jesus' resurrection. What I would emphasize here is that while the occasion of Paul's discussion was some type of denial of the resurrection of the *dead* (v 12), the chapter as a whole deals not so much with resurrection per se (which for the community would apply only to the minority who had died) as with *transformation* to immortality of both living and dead at Jesus' *parousia*. In other words, the lines of his discussion in vv 20-28 and 35-58 apply to those alive at this expected *parousia* as much as to those who have died. Thus he writes:

> Lo! I reveal to you a secret! We shall not all sleep, but we shall *all be changed* (ἀλλαγησόμεθα), in a moment, in the twinkling of an eye, at the final trumpet. For the trumpet will sound and the dead will be raised *imperishable* and we shall be changed. (vv 51-52)

In this context, then, affirming the resurrection of the dead is Paul's way of affirming the *participation* of those who had died in the events of the *parousia* (the same point is made in 1 Thess 4:13-18; 5:9-10). "All shall be made alive" (πάντες ζωοποιηθήσονται) he declares (v 22), but clearly ζωοποιέω does not refer merely to the *dead* being raised but is equivalent to ἀλλάσσω in vv 51-52 (compare ζάω in 1 Thess 5:10). The crux of his argument involves his idea of the two Adams. He declares in verse 21:

> For as by a *man* came death, by a *man* has come also the resurrection of the dead.

---

[13]See the recent study of A. T. Lincoln, *Paradise Now and Not Yet: Studies in the Role of the Heavenly Dimension in Paul's Thought with Special Reference to his Eschatology* (SNTSMS 43; Cambridge: University Press, 1981).

Then further in verse 45:

> Thus it is written, "The first man Adam *became* a living being" (ψυχὴν ζῶσαν),
> the last Adam *became* a life-giving spirit (πωεῦμα ζῳοποιοῦν).

Paul uses the phrase "resurrection of the dead" to refer to a new phenomenon in the cosmos—the transformation of a mortal human being to immortal, glorified, heavenly life. That Jesus is *human* is crucial to Paul's argument since his transformation is representative for all those "brothers" to follow. In this chapter he lists seven contrasts which specify his understanding of this move from a mortal human state to that of glorified Son of God:

First Adam	Last Adam
1. ψυχὴν ζῶσαν	1. πνεῦμα ζῳοποιοῦν
2. φθορά	2. ἀφθαρσία
3. ἀτιμία	3. δόξα
4. ἀσθένεια	4. δύναμις
5. σῶμα ψυχικόν	5. σῶμα πνευματικόν
6. ἐκ γῆς χοϊκός	6. ἐξ οὐρανοῦ
7. εἰκόνα τοῦ χοϊκοῦ	7. εἰκόνα τοῦ ἐπουρανίου

Transformation involves a change from the existence characterized under "First Adam" to that under "Last Adam." The point I would emphasize here is that the terms under "First Adam" apply *equally* to the man Jesus and to all humankind, while those under "Last Adam" apply *equally* to Jesus as exalted Son of God and to the heavenly destiny of the many "sons of God." One is reminded here of the pattern expressed by Paul in Rom 1:3-4:[14]

> The gospel concerning his Son, who was descended from David according to the flesh and *appointed Son of God in power* according to the Spirit of holiness by his resurrection from the dead, Jesus Christ our Lord.

The text stands as a short statement of the content of Paul's "gospel," i.e., Jesus as human being/Jesus as exalted Son of God.

COSMIC RULE OF THE SONS OF GOD

The notion of Jesus being appointed "Son of God in power" (ἐν δυνάμει) implies a cosmic rule and subjugation of the hostile powers of the heavenly world. I have already noted Phil 3:21 which speaks of the "*power* with which he is able to subject all things to himself" (ἐνέργειαν τοῦ δύνασθαι αὐτὸν . . . ὑποτάξαι). This idea of "subjecting all things" is an important one to Paul. He deals with it in some detail in the complicated

---

[14]Most scholars have concluded that this text contains an early, pre-Pauline confession. See the massive list of studies in Ernst Käsemann, *An die Römer*, (HNT 8a; Tübingen: J. C. B. Mohr, 1974) 2 and the special study of Klaus Wengst, *Christologische Formeln und Lieder des Urchristentums* (SNT 7; Gütersloh: Gütersloher Verlagshaus, 1972).

pericope 1 Cor 15:22-28. Here Paul offers an extended midrash on Ps 8:6 which is in turn related to Gen 1:26.[15] God has placed "all things under his feet" (v 27). His role is to destroy "every rule (ἀρχὴν) and authority (ἐξουσίαν) and power (δύναμιν) (v 24). The use of τάγμα (v 23), followed by ἔπειτα and εἶτα (v 24) seems to imply an interval between the *parousia* and what he calls the "τέλος" in which the sons of God share in this role of rule and subjugation.[16] In 1 Cor 3:21-23 and Rom 8:32 he assures the believers that "all things" (τὰ πάντα) belong to them. He chides the Corinthians for going to law courts to settle their internal disputes and reminds them of their cosmic destiny:

> Don't you know that the saints are going to judge the world (τὸν κόσμον)? If the world is to be judged by you, are you incompetent to handle petty cases? Don't you know that we will judge angels? How much more things pertaining to this life! (6:2-3)

Earlier in the letter he sarcastically taunts those who viewed themselves as *already* exalted:

> Already you are filled! Already you have become rich! Without us you are reigning as kings! I wish that you were ruling so we could share the rule with you! (4:8)

The very notion of "inheriting the Kingdom of God" (especially see 1 Cor 15:50) has to do with participating in a role of cosmic rule and judgment. In summary, Jesus heads a group of transformed, glorified, exalted Sons of God who have been given power over "all things" to bring about the final goal of history (1 Cor 15:28).

HELLENISTIC CONTEXTS

I now want to ask what analogies to this idea of many sons of God one might find in the Hellenistic period. I would propose first a broad, then a narrower context for Paul's thinking in this regard.

Broadly I would relate the Pauline concept to what Nilsson calls a "new cosmology" which emerges in the Hellenistic period.[17] This cosmology involves a fundamental shift

---

[15]Heb 2:5-18, also based on Ps 8, offers a fascinating parallel to 1 Cor 15:20-28 as well as Rom 8:29-30. The emphasis there is that the future "world" (οἰκουμένην) belongs not to angels but to humankind, and that Jesus is the "pioneer" (ἀρχηγὸν—v 10) man who has inherited "all things" and offers the same to the "many sons" that God is bringing to glory.

[16]This interpretation hinges on the use of ἔπειτα/εἶτα (vv 23-24) and whether the verbs of v 24 with the double use of ὅταν refer to what is to be accomplished in a time period *between* the *parousia* and what he calls τὸ τέλος. I am inclined to translate ὅταν καταργήσῃ as "after destroying" (see RSV and NEB).

[17]A convenient summary of Nilsson's thesis in this regard is found in *Greek Piety* (trans. H. J. Rose; New York: W. W. Norton, 1969) 92-185, which is based on his *Geschichte der griechischen Religion* (Handbuch der Altertumswissenschaft, 5.2; 2 vols.; Munich: Beck, 1967). Also see his masterly survey article, "History of Greek Religion in the Hellenistic and Roman Age," *HTR* 36 (1943) 251-75 and "The New Conception of the Universe in Late Greek Paganism," *Eranos* 44 (1946) 20-27. Also see the important article

in the perception of human place. In such a cosmology the earth is the center and lowest
level of a vast and expanded universe. It is surrounded by planetary spheres or "heavens,"
usually seven in number, each dominated by its respective powers.[18] Above the highest
sphere is the pure dwelling of God. God and humankind are thus separated by an inter-
minable distance filled with intermediate, often hostile, powers. Humans, dwelling at the
lowest level of this vast cosmos, are no longer at home. They are out of place. Human
destiny is to dwell with God in the highest heaven, free from the bonds of death and the
mortality of the body. One often encounters the language of exile—humans are strangers
and pilgrims in this sensible world. Salvation comes to mean "getting out" or "going
home," i.e., to be released from the earthly condition and obtain immortality in heaven.
Whether one is dealing with a dualistic notion of humans as intrinsically immortal but
somehow imprisoned in a mortal condition, or the idea that mortal humans have the
potential to obtain immortality through some kind of transformation, the fundamental
perception is the same—the *proper* destiny of mortal humanity is immortal heavenly life.
Guthrie's rubric of Greek religion—gods are immortal; humans are mortal—remains, but
the great gulf is increasingly transcended by a more general idea of *apotheosis* as potential not only for heroes, emperors and rulers, but for anyone and everyone.[19]

   More specifically I would relate Paul's concept of many sons of God to a host of
Jewish texts in and around the Second Temple period which speak of the destiny of both
individuals and select groups in terms of heavenly transformation, glorification, or even
enthronement.[20] I have in mind texts like Dan 12:3 which speak of those resurrected to
eternal life as shining "like the brightness of the firmament" and "like the stars forever
and ever." This theme of an immortal, celestial, or astral glory is common (2 Esdr 7:97;
2 Enoch 66:7; 2 Baruch 51:10; 1 Enoch 104:2; 4 Macc 17:5). Many texts speak of mortals
being transformed like "angels," (i.e., "sons of God"; "hosts of heaven," et al.). 2 Baruch
51:13 promises that the glory of the righteous "will surpass that of the angels" (cf.
2 Enoch 23:10; 1QS XI 7b-8; 1 Enoch 104:7). The idea of enthronement is often included
in such heavenly exaltation. Enoch (1 Enoch 71), Abel (T. Abraham 12), Job (T. Job 33:2-
9), most of the Patriarchs (T. Benj. 10:6-7), and the righteous in general (1 Enoch 108:13)

---

by Jonathan Z. Smith, "Birth Upside Down or Rightside Up?" *Map is Not Territory*, SJLA
23 (Leiden: E. J. Brill, 1978) 160-66.
   [18]The usual order was Saturn, Jupiter, Mars, Sun, Venus, Mercury, Moon. See Cicero,
Republic 6.17 and *Poimandres* 26. In Jewish materials as in Paul these spheres are controlled by various angels, cf. *b. Hagigah* 12b. For a full study see Hans Bietenhard, *Die
himmlische Welt im Urchristentum und Spätjudentum* (WUNT 2; Tübingen: J. C. B. Mohr,
1951).
   [19]See W. K. C. Guthrie, *The Greeks and their Gods* (Boston: Beacon Press, 1950).
Also the classic studies: Lewis Farnell, *Greek Hero Cults and Ideas of Immortality*
(Oxford: Clarendon Press, 1921); Franz Cumont, *Afterlife in Roman Paganism* (New
Haven: Yale University Press, 1923); Erwin Rohde, *Psyche: The Cult of Souls and Belief
in Immortality Among the Greeks* (trans. W. B. Hillis; 8th ed.; New York: Harcourt, Brace
& Co., 1925).
   [20]On this material see the studies of George W. E. Nickelsburg, Jr., *Resurrection,
Immortality and Eternal Life in Intertestamental Judaism* (HTS 26; Cambridge, MA: Har-
vard University, 1972) and H. C. C. Cavallin, *Life After Death: Paul's Argument for the
Resurrection of the Dead in 1 Cor. 15: Part I: An Enquiry into the Jewish Background*
(CBNT 7:1; Lund: C.W.K Gleerup, 1974).

are seated on thrones, usually at the right hand of God, performing functions of judgment. Even in the Markan-Synoptic tradition the resurrected are spoken of as immortal, angelic-like "sons of God" (Luke 20:36). This specific kind of language, set against the general background of a Hellenistic understanding of *apotheosis* sheds the best light on the Pauline concept I have briefly set forth in this paper.

Finally, it seems to me that the more specific aspects of Paul's expectations stem from two sources. First, there is his own visionary experience. Twice he declares that he has "seen" Jesus (1 Cor 9:1; 15:8). Whatever the nature of this experience he becomes convinced that the glorified Son of God, enthroned in heaven (Rom 8:34), is indeed the crucified Jesus.[21] He further relates that he has been raptured up to the "third heaven" and entered "Paradise" (2 Cor 12:1-4). This language reminds one of a whole host of ascent texts in which the visionary sees or even experiences the "glory" of the heavenly world. In the same context he reports having received messages from Jesus (2 Cor 12:9). These kinds of experiences, of both epiphany and ascent, are characteristic of religions of the period.[22] I think there is a necessary relationship between Paul's message and his perceived experience of the heavenly world. Second, Paul seems to develop his ideas from texts in the Hebrew Bible. We know that such key texts were fundamental to earliest Christian interpretations of Jesus.[23] I suggest that the same holds true for Paul's notion of many glorified sons of God. The major ones appear to be Gen 1:26; 2:7; Psa 8:3-8 which is particularly crucial, Psa 2:7 and Psa 110:1.

---

[21]See the recent study of Seyoon Kim, *The Origin of Paul's Gospel* (WUNT 2nd Series, 4; Tübingen: J. C. B. Mohr, 1981).

[22]See the fine article by Jonathan Z. Smith, "Hellenistic Religions," *New Encyclopedia Britannica*, 15th ed., Macropedia, vol. 8, pp. 749-51.

[23]On the *pesher* and *midrashic* techniques in early N.T. texts see especially Norman Perrin, *A Modern Pilgrimage in New Testament Christology* (Philadelphia: Fortress Press, 1974) especially chap. 2, pp. 10-22.

The Preaching of John:
Work Sheets for the Reconstruction of Q

James M. Robinson

Claremont Graduate School

The following work sheets are considerably more developed than those published in the book of *1983 Seminar Papers* ("The Sermon on the Mount/Plain: Work Sheets for the Reconstruction of Q," pp. 451-454). For the removal of material not shared by Luke and Matt produces in some instances such a tattered result as to be difficult to follow. For this reason it is prefaced by the texts of Luke and Matt with the sigla superimposed on their complete text, so that once the non-shared material is removed the place in the hypothetical Q document can be identified. The fragmented text itself is here designated "Pap Q," which is intended not to be taken as an illegitimate claim but as a bit of humor amid the pedantry, and to distinguish this minimal Q text, from which the reconstruction begins, from the various stages of reconstruction that will progressively emerge (which is then simply designated "Q").

The footnote numeration is envisaged in terms of variants, which may involve more than one word. This should facilitate the discussion of a single issue in the footnote and the non-repetition of the same discussion (or a cross reference) in more than one note. Of course in the actual filling out of these notes refinements on the preliminary definition of variant units will no doubt emerge. Each note is also organized schematically to focus attention on each of the logical alternatives. When the Marcan text needs to be considered, a decision has to be made whether the text can be explained as derived from Q. In the latter case, a choice has to be made between Luke and Matt, unless they agree. In each of these decisions it is proposed that the discussion be carried on pro and con for each option, at least hypothetically. For a decision e.g. that Luke has altered the Q text does not necessarily mean that Matt preserves the Q text. The inclusion of reasons for each option pro and con also collects the whole discussion on a given issue, so that a consultation of the notes can provide nuances of probability that the sigla do not fully measure, and makes possible the assessment of new reasons in the context of the whole discussion. Thus a reason that may tip the scales to produce a different decision in the text is in the note still imbedded in the whole spectrum of discussion. The nuanced alternatives in the notes may be more permanent and hence more valuable than the resultant text at any given juncture of the reconstruction.

The book of 1984 Seminar Papers contains, in addition to these work sheets for Q 3, work sheets for Q 4 that have been prepared and filled in with a reconstruction of the Q text by Leif Vaage, Research Associate at the Institute for Antiquity and Christianity. The reconstruction of Q 3-4 by Ulrich Luz and of Q 3:16-17 by Harry Fleddermann are also included here. Attention should also be drawn to previously published editions of the Q text (in addition to the classic by Adolf von Harnack). Athanasius Polag, *Fragmenta Q:*

Textheft zur Logienquelle (Neukirchen: Neukirchener Verlag, 1979; 2nd ed. 1982), translated without the apparatus by Ivan Havener, O.S.B., St. John's University, Collegeville,
MN 56321, who has circulated the unpublished translation privately, *The Fragments of Q:
Text for the Study of the Sayings Source*. Wolfgang Schenk, *Synopse zur Redenquelle der
Evangelisten: Q-Synopse und Rekonstruktion in deutscher Übersetzung mit kurzen Erläuterungen* (Düsseldorf: Patmos, 1981), in German translation without the Greek text. Siegfried Schulz, *Q: Die Spruchequelle der Evangelisten* (Zürich: Theologischer Verlag, 1972),
provides much of the raw material for a reconstruction without actually presenting the
reconstruction itself. Members of the Consultation are invited to prepare in advance
their own reconstruction in time enough to be circulated to the mailing list prior to the
meeting.

Regarding sigla, one should refer to the Leiden convention adopted by the Papyro-
logical Section of the 18th International Congress of Orientalists in Leiden, 10 IX 32.
Sterling Dow, *Conventions in Editing: A Suggested Reformulation of the Leiden System*
(Greek Roman and Byzantine Scholarly Aids 2; Durham, NC: Duke University, 1969), has
provided a convenient updating and clarification, though with epigraphy primarily in
view. Since Q is (unfortunately) attested neither on papyrus nor stone, much of this
system of sigla will not be applicable. And the situation of Q calls for special sigla. A
further cause of special considerations is due to the fact that we are working with word
processors and hope to convert what is now on floppy discs to computer tape. The Institute for Antiquity and Christianity currently uses a Vectorgraphic with Memorite III as
the program; the printer is a NEC 5515 Spinwriter, using the Courier type font. Dow's
judicious presentation is useful when such special considerations are not involved. The
following extensive adaptations are proposed for the editing of Q:

[ ]   Square brackets are used to indicate that what is contained in square
           brackets is in Luke but not in Matthew.

( )   Parentheses are used to indicate that what is contained in parentheses is
           in Matthew but not in Luke.

[( )]   Both are used to indicate that at this position there is something in both
           Luke and Matthew, but something different in each case.

{ }   Braces are used to indicate that what is contained in braces, though
           there is some reason at least to consider whether it might be in Q, is also
           in Mark.

/ /   Slashes are used to indicate that what is contained between slashes is in
           the other Gospel in a different position. That diverging position is
           indicated by double slashes // at the position where the material occurs
           in the other Gospel. When the Marcan text is also involved, the slashes
           may be surrounded by brackets, parentheses or braces to indicate which
           Gospels present the sequence indicated by the slashes.

Greek is transliterated in capital letters ABGDEZHQIKLMNCOPRSTUFXYW. This is the transliteration system used with the IBYCUS computer. It may become possible to transfer what
the word processor has put on floppy disk onto computer tape, in which case the IBYCUS

transliteration system could be used to print in Greek characters. This use of capital letters for the transliteration means that capital letters cannot be used to indicate letters that are legible but whose interpretation is unclear (see Dow, pp. 9-10).

Luke 3:1   EN [ETEI][1] DE [PENTEKAIDEKATW THS HGEMONIAS TIBERIOU KAISAROS,...]][1]

Matt 3:1a   EN DE (TAIS HMERAIS EKEINAIS)[1]

Pap Q 3:1   EN [   ][1] DE [(   )][1]

Q 3:1

[1]

    Luke = EN [ETEI] DE [PENTEKAIDEKATW THS HGEMONIAS TIBERIOU KAISAROS...]
    Matt = EN DE (TAIS HMERAIS EKEINAIS)
    Pap Q = EN [   ] DE [(   )]
    Q =

Text = 'minor agreement' EN DE
Pro:
Con:

Text = Q EN DE and time reference.
Pro:
Con:

Q = Luke EN [ETEI] DE [PENTEKAIDEKATW THW HGEMONIAS TIBERIOU KAISAROS...]
Pro:
Con:

Q = Matt EN DE (TAIS HMERAIS EKEINAIS)
Pro:
Con:

Luke 3:2b-3   {[E]G[E]NET[O]}[1] [RHMA QEOU EPI][2] {IWANNH}[3][N
T][2]{O}[3][N][2] [ZAXARIOU UIO][4][{N}][2] //[5] {EN TH ERHMW}[6] (   )[7]. **3:3**
{KAI}[5] [HLQEN EIS][8] [9]/ PASA[N T][8]H[N][8] PERIXWRO[N][8] TOU IORDANOU /[9] [5]/
{KHRUSSWN} /[5] {[BAPTISMA] METANO[IAS EIS AFESIN AMARTIWN]}[10], (//[9] Matt 3:5
between Luke 3:6 and 7)

Matt 3:1b.2.5
(PARA)[1]{G}[1](I)[1]{NET}[1](AI)[1] {IWANNH}[3](S)[2] [   ][2]O[3][   ][2] (BAPTI}[4]STH)[4](S)[2] [5]/
{KHRUSSWN} /[5] {EN TH ERHMW}[6] (THS IOUDAIAS)[7] **3:2**
{KAI //[9] //[5] (LEGWN)}[5]: {METANO(EITE}[10]: {HGGIKEN}[10] GAR {H BASILEIA T}[10]WN
OURANWN)[10]. ... **3:5** (TOTE {ECEPOREUETO PROS AUTON} {//[8] {IEROSOLUM}A {KAI}
[8]{/} PASA H IOUDAIA KAI {/}[8])[9]/ PASA H PERIXWRO(S)[8] TOU IORDANOU /[9],

Mark 1:4-5, 14b-15[E(G)E(NET)O][1] [(IWANNH][3]S[2] [O][3] BAPTI)[4]ZW[N][2] [(EN TH
ERHMW)][6] [(KAI)][5] [(KHRUSSWN)][5] [BAPTISMA (METANO)IAS EIS AFESIN AMARTIWN][10].
1:5 KAI (ECEPOREUETO PROS AUTON) //[8] (PASA H IOUDAIA) XWRA (KAI) [8]/ OI
(IEROSOLUM)ITAI PANTES /[8], (KAI EBAPTIZONTO / UP' AUTOU / EN TW IORDANH POTAMW
// ECOMOLOGOUMENOI TAS AMARTIAS AUTWN)[10]. ... **1:14b** (KHRUSSWN)[5] TO
EUAGGELION TOU QEOU **1:15**(KAI LEGWN)[5] OTI PEPLHRWTAI O KAIROS KAI HGGIKEN
H BASILEIA T)[10]OU QEOU: (METANOIETE)[10] KAI PISTEUETE EN TW EUAGGELIW.

Pap Q 3:2b-3   [(   )][1]{G}[1][(   )][1]{NET}[1][(   )][1]
[   ][2] {IWANNH}[3][(   )][2]{O}[3][   ][2] [(   )][4][(   )][2] //[5] {EN TH ERHMW}[6] (   )[7]
3:3 {KAI}[5] [(   )][8] [9]/ PASA[   ][8]H[   ][8] PERIXWRO[(   )][8] TOU IORDANOU /[9] [5]/
{KHRUSSWN} /[5] (   )[5] [   ][10] {METANO}[10][(   )][10] (//[9] Matt 3:5 between Luke
3:6 and 7)

Q 3:2b-3

1

    Luke = {[E]G[E]NET[O]} RHMA is the subject.
    Matt = (PARA){G}(I){NET}(AI) IWANNHS is the subject.
    Mark = [E(G)E(NET)O] IWANNHS is the subject.
    Pap Q = [(   )]{G}[(   )]{NET}[(   )]
    Q =

Text = Mark   [E(G)E(NET)O] IWANNHS is the subject.
Pro:
Con:

Text = Q
Pro:
Con:

Q = Luke   {[E]G[E]NET[O]} RHMA is the subject.
Pro:
Con:

Q = Matt   (PARA){G}(I){NET}(AI) IWANNHS is the subject.
Pro:
Con:

2

    Luke = [RHMA QEOU EPI] {IWANNH}[3][N T]{O}[3][N] [ZAXARIOU UIO][4][{N}]
    Matt = {IWANNH[3](S) [   ]O[3][   ] (BAPTI}[4]STH)[4](S)
    Mark = [(IWANNH][3]S [O][3] BAPTI)[4]ZW[N]
    Pap Q = [   ] {IWANNH}[3][(   )]{O}[3][   ] [(   )][4][(   )]
    Q =

Text = Mark $[(\text{IWANNH}]^3\text{S}\ [\text{O}]^3\ \text{BAPTI})^4\text{ZW}[\text{N}]$
Pro:
Con:

Text = Q
Pro:
Con:

Q = Luke $[\text{RHMA QEOU EPI}]\ \{\text{IWANNH}\}^3[\text{N T}]\{\text{O}\}^3[\text{N}]\ [\text{ZAXARIOU UIO}]^4\ [\{\text{N}\}]$
Pro:
Con:

Q = Matt $\{\text{IWANNH}^3(\text{S})\ \text{O}^3\ (\text{BAPTI}\}^4\text{STH})^4(\text{S})$
Pro:
Con:

3

    Luke = $\{\text{IWANNH}\}[\text{N T}]^2\{\text{O}\}[\text{N}]^2$
    Matt = $\{\text{IWANNH}(\text{S})^2\ [\quad]^2\text{O}[\quad]^2$
    Mark = $[(\text{IWANNH}]\text{S}^2\ [\text{O}]$
    Pap Q = $\{\text{IWANNH}\}[(\quad)]^2\{\text{O}\}[\quad]^2$
    Q =

Text = Mark $[(\text{IWANNH}]\text{S}^2\ [\text{O}]$
Pro:

Text = Q
Pro:
Con:

Q = Luke $\{\text{IWANNH}\}[\text{N T}]^2\{\text{O}\}[\text{N}]^2$
Pro:
Con:

Q = Matt $\{\text{IWANNH}(\text{S})^2\ [\quad]^2\text{O}[\quad]^2$
Pro:
Con:

4

    Luke = $[\text{ZAXARIOU UIO}][\{\text{N}\}]^2$
    Matt = $(\{\text{BAPTI}\}\text{STH})(\text{S})^2$
    Mark = $(\text{BAPTI})\text{ZW}[\text{N}]^2$
    Pap Q = $[(\quad)][(\quad)]^2$
    Q =

Text = Mark $(\text{BAPTI})\text{ZW}[\text{N}]^2$
Pro:
Con:

Text = Q
Pro:
Con:

Q = Luke [ZAXARIOU UIO][{N}]^2
Pro:
Con:

Q = Matt ({BAPTI}STH)(S)^2
Pro:
Con:

5

    Luke 3:2b = // {EN TH ERHMW}^{6} (   )^7. **3:3** {KAI} [HLQEN EIS]^8 ^{9}/
PASA[N T]^{8}H[N]^8 PERIXWRO[N]^8 TOU IORDANOU /^{9} / {KHRUSSWN} /
    Matt 3:1b = / {KHRUSSWN} / {EN TH ERHMW}^{6} (THS IOUDAIAS)^7 **3:2**
{KAI //^{9} // (LEGWN)}
    Mark 1:4 = BAPTI)^{4}ZW[N]^2 [(EN TH ERHMW)]^6 [(KAI)] [(KHRUSSWN)]... **1:14b**
(KHRUSSWN) TO EUAGGELION TOU QEOU **1:15** (KAI LEGWN)
    Pap Q 3:2b = // {EN TH ERHMW}^{6} (   )^7 **3:3** {KAI} [(   )]^8 ^{9}/
PASA[   ]^{8}H[   ]^8 PERIXWRO[(   )]^8 TOU IORDANOU /^{9} / {KHRUSSWN} / (   )
    Q =

Text = Mark 1:4 BAPTI)^{4}ZW[N]^2 [(EN TH ERHMW)]^6 [(KAI)] [(KHRUSSWN)]...
1:14b (KHRUSSWN) TO EUAGGELION TOU QEOU **1:15** (KAI LEGWN)
Pro:
Con:

Text = Q
Pro:
Con:

Q = Luke 3:2b // {EN TH ERHMW}^{6} (   )^7. **3:3** {KAI} [HLQEN EIS]^8 ^{9}/
PASA[N T]^{8}H[N]^8 PERIXWRO[N]^8 TOU IORDANOU /^{9} / {KHRUSSWN} /
Pro:
Con:

Q = Matt 3:1b / {KHRUSSWN} / {EN TH ERHMW}^{6} (THS IOUDAIAS)^7 **3:2**
{KAI //^{9} // (LEGWN)}
Pro:
Con:

6

    Luke = {EN TH ERHMW}
    Matt = {EN TH ERHMW}
    Mark = [(EN TH ERHMW)]
    Pap Q = {EN TH ERHMW}
    Q =

Text = **Mark** [(EN TH ERHMW)]
Pro:
Con:

Text = **Q** Luke and Matt agree {EN TH ERHMW}.
Pro:
Con:

7

    Luke = {EN TH ERHMW}[6] (   )
    Matt = {EN TH ERHMW}[6] (THS IOUDAIAS)
    Pap Q = {EN TH ERHMW}[6] (   )
    Q =

Q = **Luke** {EN TH ERHMW}[6] (   )
Pro:
Con:

Q = **Matt** {EN TH ERHMW}[6] (THS IOUDAIAS)
Pro:
Con:

8

    Luke 3:3 = [HLQEN EIS] [9]/ PASA[N T]H[N] PERIXWRO[N]
    Matt 3:5 = (TOTE {ECEPOREUETO PROS AUTON} {//} {IEROSOLUM}A {KAI} {/}
PASA H IOUDAIA KAI {/}) [9]/ PASA H PERIXWRO(S) TOU IORDANOU /[9] ,
    Pap Q 3:3 = [(   )] [9]/ PASA[   ]H[   ] PERIXWRO[(   )] TOU IORDANOU /[9]
    Q =

Q = **Luke 3:3** [HLQEN EIS] [9]/ PASA[N T]H[N] PERIXWRO[N]
Pro:
Con:

Q = **Matt 3:5** (TOTE {ECEPOREUETO PROS AUTON} {//} {IEROSOLUM}A {KAI} {/}
PASA H IOUDAIA KAI {/}) [9]/ PASA H PERIXWRO(S) TOU IORDANOU /[9] ,
Pro:
Con:

9

Luke 3:3 = / PASA[N T]^{8}H[N]^8 PERIXWRO[N]^8 TOU IORDANOU / ^{5}/ {KHRUSSWN}
/^{5} {[BAPTISMA] METANO[IAS EIS AFESIN AMARTIWN]}^{10}, (// Matt 3:5 between Luke 3:6 and 7)
Matt 3:2,5 = // //^{5} (LEGWN)}^{5}: {METANO(EITE}^{10}: {HGGIKEN}^{10} GAR {H BASILEIA T}^{10}WN OURANWN)^{10}. ... **3:5** (TOTE {ECEPOREUETO PROS AUTON} {//}^{8} {IEROSOLUM}A {KAI} ^{8}{/} PASA H IOUDAIA KAI {/}^{8})^8 / PASA H PERIXWRO(S)^8 TOU IORDANOU /,
Pap Q 3:3 = / PASA[   ]^{8}H[   ]^8 PERIXWRO[(   )]^8 TOU IORDANOU / ^{5}/ {KHRUSSWN} /^{5} (   )^5 [   ]^{10} {METANO}^{10}[(   )]^{10} (// Matt 3:5 between Luke 3:6 and 7)
Q =

Q = Luke 3:3 / PASA[N T]^{8}H[N]^8 PERIXWRO[N]^8 TOU IORDANOU / ^{5}/ {KHRUSSWN}
/^{5} {[BAPTISMA] METANO[IAS EIS AFESIN AMARTIWN]}^{10}, (// Matt 3:5 between Luke 3:6 and 7)
Pro:
Con:

Q = Matt 3:2 // //^{5} (LEGWN)}^{5}: {METANO(EITE}^{10}: {HGGIKEN}^{10} GAR {H BASILEIA T}^{10}WN OURANWN)^{10}. ... **3:5** (TOTE {ECEPOREUETO PROS AUTON} {//}^{8} {IEROSOLUM}A {KAI} ^{8}{/} PASA H IOUDAIA KAI {/}^{8})^8 / PASA H PERIXWRO(S)^8 TOU IORDANOU /,
Pro:
Con:

10

Luke = {[BAPTISMA] METANO[IAS EIS AFESIN AMARTIWN]}
Matt = {METANO(EITE}: {HGGIKEN} GAR {H BASILEIA T}WN OURANWN)
Mark 1:4 = [BAPTISMA (METANO)IAS EIS AFESIN AMARTIWN]... **1:15** ...
PEPLHRWTAI O KAIROS KAI (HGGIKEN H BASILEIA T)OU QEOU: (METANOEITE) KAI PISTEUETE EN TW EUAGGELIW.
Pap Q = [   ] {ומבפוס}[(   )]
Q =

Text = Mark 1:4 [BAPTISMA (METANO)IAS EIS AFESIN AMARTIWN]... **1:15** ...
PEPLHRWTAI O KAIROS KAI (HGGIKEN H BASILEIA T)OU QEOU: (METANOEITE) KAI PISTEUETE EN TW EUAGGELIW.
Pro:
Con:

Text = Q
Pro:
Con:

Q = Luke {[BAPTISMA] METANO[IAS EIS AFESIN AMARTIWN]}
Pro:
Con:

Q = Matt {METANO(EITE}: {HGGIKEN} GAR {H BASILEIA T}WN OURANWN)
Pro:
Con:

Luke 3:4 = [1]{/} [{WS GEGRAPTAI EN} BIBL{W} LOGWN][2] {HSAI}[3]OU {T}[3]OU
{PROFHT}[3]OU (   )[4]: {FWNH BOWNTOS EN TH ERHMW: ETOIMASATE THN ODON KURIOU,
EUQEIAS POIEITE TAS TRIBOUS AUTOU:}[5] {/}[1] ({//}[1] Mark 1:2a,3, which is prior to
Luke 3:1)

Matt 3:3 = [1]{/} (OUTOS GAR ESTIN O RHQEIS DIA)[2] {HSAI}[3]OU {T}[3]OU {PROFHT}[3]OU
(LEGONTES)[4] : {FWNH BOWNTOS EN TH ERHMW: ETOIMASATE THN ODON KURIOU, EUQEIAS
POIEITE TAS TRIBOUS AUTOU.}[5] {/}[1] ({//}[1] Mark 1:2a,3, which is prior to Matt 3:1)

Mark 1:2a,3 = [1]/ KAQ[WS GEGRAPTAI EN][2] T[W][2] [(HSAI)][3]A [(T)][3]W [(PROFHT)][3]H:
... [(FWNH BOWNTOS EN TH ERHMW: ETOIMASATE THN ODON KURIOU, EUQEIAS POIEITE
TAS TRIBOUS AUTOU,)][5] /[1] (//[1] Luke 3:4 = Matt 3:3, which is after Mark 1:4)

Pap Q 3:4 = [1]{/} [(   )][2] {HSAI}[3]OU {T}[3]OU {PROFHT}[3]OU (   )[4] {FWNH BOWNTOS EN
TH ERHMW ETOIMASATE THN ODON KURIOU EUQEIAS POIEITE TAS TRIBOUS AUTOU}[5]
{/}[1] ({//}[1] Mark 1:2a,3, which is prior to Luke 3:1 and Matt 3:1)

Q 3:4 =

1
   Luke 3:4 = {/} [{WS GEGRAPTAI EN} BIBL{W} LOGWN][2] {HSAI}[3]OU {T}[3]OU
{PROFHT}[3]OU (   )[4]: {FWNH BOWNTOS EN TH ERHMW: ETOIMASATE THN ODON KURIOU,
EUQEIAS POIEITE TAS TRIBOUS AUTOU:}[5] {/} ({//} Mark 1:2a,3, which is prior to Luke
3:1)
   Matt = {/} (OUTOS GAR ESTIN O RHQEIS DIA)[2] {HSAI}[3]OU {T}[3]OU {PROFHT}[3]OU
(LEGONTES)[4] : {FWNH BOWNTOS EN TH ERHMW: ETOIMASATE THN ODON KURIOU, EUQEIAS
POIEITE TAS TRIBOUS AUTOU.}[5] {/} ({//} Mark 1:2a,3, which is prior to Matt 3:1)
   Mark = / KAQ[WS GEGRAPTAI EN][2] T[W][2] [(HSAI)][3]A [(T)][3]W [(PROFHT)][3]H:
... [(FWNH BOWNTOS EN TH ERHMW: ETOIMASATE THN ODON KURIOU, EUQEIAS POIEITE
TAS TRIBOUS AUTOU,)][5] / (// Luke 3:4 = Matt 3:3, which is after Mark 1:4)
   Pap Q = {/} [(   )][2] {HSAI}[3]OU {T}[3]OU {PROFHT}[3]OU (   )[4] {FWNH BOWNTOS EN
TH ERHMW ETOIMASATE THN ODON KURIOU EUQEIAS POIEITE TAS TRIBOUS AUTOU}[5]
{/} ({//} Mark 1:2a,3, which is prior to Luke 3:1 and Matt 3:1)
   Q =

Text = Mark + 'minor agreement' / KAQ[WS GEGRAPTAI
EN]² T[W]² [(HSAI)]³A [(T)]³W [(PROFHT)]³H: ... [(FWNH BOWNTOS EN TH ERHMW:
ETOIMASATE THN ODON KURIOU, EUQEIAS POIEITE TAS TRIBOUS AUTOU,)]⁵ / (// Luke
3:4 = Matt 3:3, which is after Mark 1:4)
Pro:
Con:

Text = Q The order in Luke and Matt agrees; the Lucan wording: {/} [{WS
GEGRAPTAI EN} BIBL{W} LOGWN]² {HSAI}³OU {T}³OU {PROFHT}³OU (   )⁴: {FWNH
BOWNTOS EN TH ERHMW: ETOIMASATE THN ODON KURIOU, EUQEIAS POIEITE TAS TRIBOUS
AUTOU:}⁵ {/}¹ ({//} Mark 1:2a,3, which is prior to Luke 3:1 and Matt 3:1)
Pro:
Con:

2

    Luke = [{WS GEGRAPTAI EN} BIBL{W} LOGWN]
    Matt = (OUTOS GAR ESTIN O RHQEIS DIA)
    Mark = KAQ[WS GEGRAPTAI EN] T[W]
    Pap Q = [(   )]
    Q =

Text = Mark KAQ[WS GEGRAPTAI EN] T[W]
Pro:
Con:

Text = Q
Pro:
Con:

Q = Luke [{WS GEGRAPTAI EN} BIBL{W} LOGWN]
Pro:
Con:

Q = Matt (OUTOS GAR ESTIN O RHQEIS DIA)
Pro:
Con:

3

    Luke = {HSAI}OU {T}OU {PROFHT}OU
    Matt = {HSAI}OU {T}OU {PROFHT}OU
    Mark = [(HSAI)]A [(T)]W [(PROFHT)H
    Pap Q = {HSAI}OU {T}OU {PROFHT}OU
    Q =

Text = Mark + 'minor agreement' [(HSAI)]A [(T)]W [(PROFHT)H
Pro:
Con:

Text = Q Luke and Matt agree: {HSAI}OU {T}OU {PROFHT}OU
Pro:
Con:

4

    Luke = (   )
    Matt = (LEGONTES)
    Pap Q = (   )
    Q =

Q = Luke (   )
Pro:
Con:

Q = Matt (LEGONTES)
Pro:
Con:

5

    Luke = {FWNH BOWNTOS EN TH ERHMW: ETOIMASATE THN ODON KURIOU, EUQEIAS
POIEITE TAS TRIBOUS AUTOU:}
    Matt = {FWNH BOWNTOS EN TH ERHMW: ETOIMASATE THN ODON KURIOU, EUQEIAS
POIEITE TAS TRIBOUS AUTOU.}
    Mark = [{FWNH BOWNTOS EN TH ERHMW: ETOIMASATE THN ODON KURIOU, EUQEIAS
POIEITE TAS TRIBOUS AUTOU,)]
    Pap Q = {FWNH BOWNTOS EN TH ERHMW: ETOIMASATE THN ODON KURIOU, EUQEIAS
POIEITE TAS TRIBOUS AUTOU}
    Q =

Text = Mark [(FWNH BOWNTOS EN THI ERHMWI: ETOIMASATE THN ODON KURIOU, EUQEIAS
POIEITE TAS TRIBOUS AUTOU,)]
Pro:
Con:

Text = Q Luke and Matt agree: {FWNH BOWNTOS EN TH ERHMW: ETOIMASATE THN ODON
KURIOU, EUQEIAS POIEITE TAS TRIBOUS AUTOU:}
Pro:
Con:

Matt 3:5, between Luke 3:6 and 7, = Q 3:3.9

Luke 3:7 ¹/ [ELEG]²EN /¹ [OUN]³ ⁴/ (   )⁵TOIS /⁴ //⁶ E[KPOREU]⁷OMENO[I]⁸S ⁶/
[OXLOIS]⁹ /⁶ (   )¹⁰ BAPTIS[QHNAI UP']¹⁰ AUTOU //¹ //⁴: GENNHMATA EXIDNWN, TIS
UPEDEICEN UMIN FUGEIN APO THS MELLOUSHS ORGHS;

Matt 3:7 //¹ (IDWN DE)³ //⁴ ⁶/ (POLLOUS TWN FARISAIWN KAI SADDOUKAIWN)⁹ /⁶
E(RX)⁷OMENO(U)⁸S //⁶ (EPI TO)¹⁰ BAPTIS(MA)¹⁰ AUTOU ¹/ (EIP)²EN /¹ ⁴
(AU)⁵TOIS /⁴: GENNHMATA EXIDNWN, TIS UPEDEICEN UMIN FUGEIN APO THS MELLOUSHS
ORGHS;

Pap Q 3:7 ¹/ [(   )]²EN /¹ [(   )]³ ⁴/ (   )⁵TOIS /⁴ //⁶
E[(   )]⁷OMENO[(   )]⁸S ⁶/ [(   )]⁹ /⁶ (   )¹⁰ BAPTIS[(   )]¹⁰ AUTOU
//¹ //⁴ GENNHMATA EXIDNWN TIS UPEDEICEN UMIN FUGEIN APO THS MELLOUSHS ORGHS

Q 3:7

1
    Luke = / [ELEG]²EN / [OUN]³ ⁴/ (   )⁵TOIS /⁴ //⁶ E[KPOREU]⁷OMENO[I]⁸S ⁶/
[OXLOIS]⁹ /⁶ (   )¹⁰ BAPTIS[QHNAI UP']¹⁰ AUTOU //
    Matt = // (IDWN DE)³ //⁴ ⁶/ (POLLOUS TWN FARISAIWN KAI SADDOUKAIWN)⁹ /⁶
E(RX)⁷OMENO(U)⁸S //⁶ (EPI TO)¹⁰ BAPTIS(MA)¹⁰ AUTOU / (EIP)²EN /
    Pap Q = / [(   )]²EN / [(   )]³ ⁴/ (   )⁵TOIS /⁴//⁶
E[(   )]⁷OMENO[(   )]⁸S ⁶/ [(   )]⁹ /⁶ (   )¹⁰ BAPTIS[(   )]¹⁰ AUTOU //
    Q =

Q = **Luke** / [ELEG]²EN / [OUN]³ ⁴/ (   )⁵TOIS /⁴ //⁶ E[KPOREU]⁷OMENO[I]⁸S ⁶/
[OXLOIS]⁹ /⁶ (   )¹⁰ BAPTIS[QHNAI UP']¹⁰ AUTOU //
Pro:
Con:

Q = **Matt** // (IDWN DE)³ //⁴ ⁶/ (POLLOUS TWN FARISAIWN KAI SADDOUKAIWN)⁹ /⁶
E(RX)⁷OMENO(U)⁸S //⁶ (EPI TO)¹⁰
BAPTIS(MA)¹⁰ AUTOU / (EIP)²EN /
Pro:
Con:

2
    Luke = [ELEG]EN
    Matt = (EIP)EN
    Pap Q = [(   )] EN
    Q =

Q = **Luke** [ELEG]EN
Pro:
Con:

Q = **Matt** (EIP)EN
Pro:
Con

3
    Luke = [OUN]
    Matt = (IDWN DE)
    PAP Q = [(   )]
    Q =

Q = **Luke** [OUN]
Pro:
Con:

Q = **Matt** (IDWN DE)
Pro:
Con:

4
    Luke = / (   )^{5}TOIS / //^{6} E[KPOREU]^{7}OMENO[I]^{8}S ^{6}/
[OXLOIS]^9 /^{6} (   )^{10} BAPTIS[QHNAI UP']^{10} AUTOU //^{1} //
    Matt = // ^{6}/ (POLLOUS TWN FARISAIWN KAI SADDOUKAIWN)^9 /^{6}
E(RX)^{7}OMENO(U)^{8}S //^{6} (EPI TO)^{10} BAPTIS(MA)^{10} AUTOU ^{1}/ (EIP)^{2}EN /^{1} /
(AU)^{5}TOIS /
    Pap Q = / (   )^{5}TOIS / //^{6} E[(   )]^{7}OMENO[(   )]^{8}S ^{6}/
[(   )]^9 /^{6} (   )^{10} BAPTIS[(   )]^{10} AUTOU //^{1} //
    Q =

Q = **Luke** / (   )^{5}TOIS / //^{6} E[KPOREU]^{7}OMENO[I]^{8}S ^{6}/
[OXLOIS]^9 /^{6} (   )^{10} BAPTIS[QHNAI UP']^{10} AUTOU //^{1} //
Pro:
Con:

Q = **Matt** // ^{6}/ (POLLOUS TWN FARISAIWN KAI SADDOUKAIWN)^9 /^{6}
E(RX)^{7}OMENO(U)^{8}S //^{6} (EPI TO)^{10} BAPTIS(MA)^{10} AUTOU ^{1}/ (EIP)^{2}EN /^{1} /
(AU)^{5}TOIS /
Pro:
Con:

5
    Luke = (   )TOIS
    Matt = (AU)TOIS
    Pap Q = (   )TOIS
    Q =

Q = **Luke** (   )TOIS
Pro:
Con:

Q = **Matt** (AU)TOIS
Pro:
Con:

6

    Luke = // E[KPOREU]^{7}OMENO[I]^{8}S / [OXLOIS]^9 /
    Matt = / (POLLOUS TWN FARISAIWN KAI SADDOUKAIWN)^9 /
E(RX)^{7}OMENO(U)^{8}S //
    Pap Q = //^{6} E[(   )]^{7}OMENO[(   )]^{8}S / [(   )]^9 /
    Q =

Q = **Luke** // E[KPOREU]^{7}OMENO[I]^{8}S / [OXLOIS]^9 /
Pro:
Con:

Q = **Matt** / (POLLOUS TWN FARISAIWN KAI SADDOUKAIWN)^9 / E(RX)^{7}OMENO(U)^{8}S //
Pro:
Con:

7

    Luke = E[KPOREU]OMENO[I]^{8}S
    Matt = E(RX)OMENO(U)^{8}S
    Pap Q = E[(   )]OMENO[(   )]^{8}S
    Q =

Q = **Luke** E[KPOREU]OMENO[I]^{8}S
Pro:
Con:

Q = **Matt** E(RX)OMENO(U)^{8}S
Pro:
Con:

8

    Luke = E[KPOREU]^{7}OMENO[I]S
    Matt = E(RX)^{7}OMENO(U)S
    Pap Q = E[[(   )]^{7}OMENO[(   )]
    Q =

Q = **Luke** E[KPOREU]⁷OMENO[I]S
Pro:
Con:

Q = **Matt** E(RX)⁷OMENO(U)S
Pro:
Con:

9
    Luke = [OXLOIS]
    Matt = (POLLOUS TWN FARISAIWN KAI SADDOUKAIWN)
    Pap Q = [(   )]
    Q =

Q = **Luke** [OXLOIS]
    Matt = (POLLOUS TWN FARISAIWN KAI SADDOUKAIWN)
    Pap Q = [(   )]
    Q =

Q = **Luke** [OXLOIS]
Pro:
Con:

Q = **Matt** (POLLOUS TWN FARISAIWN KAI SADDOUKAIWN)
Pro:
Con:

10
    Luke = (   ) BAPTIS[QHNAI UP']
    Matt = (EPI TO) BAPTIS(MA)
    Pap Q = (   ) Bבנפי⁷[(   )]
    Q =

Q = **Luke** (   ) BAPTIS[QHNAI UP']
Pro:
Con:

Q = **Matt** (EPI TO) BAPTIS(MA)
Pro:
Con:

Luke 3:8 POIHSATE OUN KARPO[US]¹ ACIO[US]¹ THS METANOIAS, KAI MH
[AR]²CH[SQ]²E LEGEIN EN EAUTOIS: PATERA EXOMEN TON ABRAAM: LEGW GAR UMIN OTI
DUNATI O QEOS EK TWN LIQWN TOUTWN EGEIRAI TEKNA TW ABRAAM.

Matt 3:8-9   POIHSATE OUN KARPO(N)[1] ACIO(N)[1] THS METANOIAS,   **3:9**   KAI MH
(DO)[2]CH(T)[2]E LEGEIN EN EAUTOIS: PATERA EXOMEN TON ABRAAM: LEGW GAR UMIN OTI
DUNATAI O QEOS EK TWN LIQWN TOUTWN EGEIRAI TEKNA TW ABRAAM.

Pap Q 3:8 POIHSATE OUN KARPO[(   )][1] ACIO[(   )][1] THS METANOIAS KAI MH
[(   )][2]CH[(   )][2]E LEGEIN EN EAUTOIS PATERA EXOMEN TON ABRAAM LEGW GAR UMIN
OTI DUNATAI O QEOS EK TWN LIQWN TOUTWN EGEIRAI TEKNA TW ABRAAM

Q 3:8

1

    Luke = KARPO[US]
    Matt = KARPO(N)
    Pap Q = KARPO[(   )]
    Q =

Q = Luke KARPO[US]
Pro:
Con:

Q = Matt KARPO(N)
Pro:
Con:

2

    Luke = [AR]CH[SQ]E
    Matt = (DO)CH(T)E
    Pap Q = [(   )]CH[(   )]E
    Q =

Q = Luke [AR]CH[SQ]E
Pro:
Con:

Q = Matt (DO)CH(T)E
Pro:
Con:

Luke 3:9 HDH DE [KAI][1] H ACINH PROS THN RIZAN TWN DENDRWN KEITAI: PAN OUN
DENDRON MH POIOUN KARPON KALON EKKOPTETAI KAI EIS PUR BALLETAI.

Matt 3:10 HDH DE [   ][1] H ACINH PROS THN RIZAN TWN DENDRWN KEITAI: PAN OUN
DENDRON MH POIOUN KARPON KALON EKKOPTETAI KAI EIS PUR BALLETAI.

Pap Q 3:9 HDH DE [   ]^1 H ACINH PROS THN RIZAN TWN DENDRWN KEITAI PAN OUN
DENDRON MH POIOUN KARPON KALON EKKOPTETAI KAI EIS PUR BALLETAI

Q 3:9

1
   Luke = [KAI]
   Matt = [   ]
   Pap Q = [   ]
   Q =

Q = Luke [KAI]
Pro:
Con:

Q = Matt [   ]
Pro:
Con:

Luke 3:16 [APEKRINATO {LEGWN} PASIN O IWANNHS]^1: ^{2}{/} {EGW}^{3} MEN //^{4} ^{5}/
(   )^6 {UDATI}^{3} /^{5} {BAPTI}^{3}ZW ^{4}/ {UMAS}^{3} /^{4} //^{5} (   )^7 {/}^{2} : ^{8}(/) ({
})^9 {ERX[ETAI]} (/)^8 ^{10}{/} {DE} {/}^{10} {O} (//)^8 {ISXUROTEROS MOU}^{11} (   )^{12},
{OU OUK EIMI IKANOS}^{13} ^{14}(/) {[LU]SAI (/)^{14} T[ON IMANTA TWN]^{15} UPODHMAT[WN]^{15}
[AUTOU]}^{15} (//)^{14}: {//}^{2} {AUTOS {//}^{10} ^{17}{/} UMAS {/}^{17} BAPTISEI {//}^{17} EN
PNEUMATI AGIW}^{16} KAI PURI:

Matt 3:11 [   ]^1 ^{2}{/} {EGW}^{3} MEN ^{4}/ {UMAS}^{3} /^{4} //^{5} {BAPTI}^{3}ZW //^{4} ^{5}/ (EN)^6
{UDATI}^{3} /^{5} (EIS METANOIAN)^7 {/}^{2}, //^{8} {O} ^{10}{/} {DE} {/}^{10} ({OPISW
MOU})^9 /^{1} ^{8}/ {ERX}(OMENOS) /^{8} {ISXUROTEROS MOU}^{11} (ESTIN)^{12}, {OU OUK EIMI
IKANOS}^{13} //^{14} {T}^{15}(A)^{15} {UPODHMAT}^{15}(A)^{15} [   ]^{15} ^{14}/ (BASTA)^{15}{SAI}^{15} /^{14}:
{//}^{2} {AUTOS {//}^{10} ^{17}{/} UMAS {/}^{17} / BAPTISEI {//}^{17} EN PNEUMATI
AGIW}^{16} KAI PURI:

Mark 1:7-8 KAI EKHRUSSEN [LEGWN]^1: //^{2} ^{8}(/) (//)^9 [(ERX)ETAI] (/)^8 //^{10} [(O)]
(//)^8[(ISXUROTEROS MOU)]^{11} (OPISW MOU)^9, [(OU OUK EIMI IKANOS)]^{13} ^{14}{/} KUYAS
^{18}/ [LU(SAI) (/)^{14} (T)ON IMANTA TWN (UPODHMAT)WN AUTOU]^{15} (//)^{14}. **1:8** ^{2}/
[(EGW)]^3 (//)^4 [//]^5 E[(BAPTI)]^{3}SA ^{4}(/) [(UMAS)]^3 (/)^4 ^{5}[/] [(UDATI)]^3 [/]^5
/^{2}, [(AUTOS ^{10}/ DE /^{10} //^{17} BAPTISEI ^{17}/ UMAS /^{17} EN PNEUMATI AGIW)]^{16}.

Pap Q 3:16 [   ]^1 ^{2}{/} {EGW}^{3} MEN //^{4} ^{2}/ ^{5}[/] (   )^6 {UDATI}^{3} [/]^5
{BAPTI}^{3}ZW ^{4}/ {UMAS}^{3} /^{4}[//]^5 (   )^7 {/}^{2} ^{8}/ ({   })^9 {ERX}[(   )] /^{8} ^{10}{/}
{DE} {/}^{10} {O} //^{8} {ISXUROTEROS MOU}^{11} (   )^{12} {OU OUK EIMI IKANOS}^{13} ^{14}/
[(   )]^{15}{SAI}^{15}/^{14} {T}^{15}[(   )]^{15} {UPODHMAT}^{15}[(   )]^{15}[   ]^{15} //^{14} {//}^{2} {AU
TOS {//}^{10} ^{17}{/} UMAS {/}^{17} BAPTISEI {//}^{17} EN PNEUMATI AGIW}^{16} KAI PURI.

Q 3:16

1

    Luke = [APEKRINATO {LEGWN} PASIN O IWANNHS]
    Matt = [   ]
    Mark = KAI EKHRUSSEN [LEGWN]
    Pap Q = [   ]
    Q =

Text = **Mark** KAI EKHRUSSEN [LEGWN]
Pro:
Con:

Text = Q
Pro:
Con:

Q = **Luke** [APEKRINATO {LEGWN} PASIN O IWANNHS]
Pro:
Con:

Q = **Matt** [   ]
Pro:
Con:

2

    Luke = {/} {EGW}^{3} MEN //^{4} ^{5}/ (   )^6 {UDATI}^{3} /^{5} {BAPTI}^{3}ZW
^{4}/ {UMAS}^{3} /^{4} //^{5} (   )^7 {/}:
^{8}/ ({   })^9 {ERX[ETAI]} /^{8} ^{10}{/} {DE} {/}^{10} {O} //^{8} {ISXUROTEROS MOU}^{11}
(   )^{12}, {OU OUK EIMI IKANOS}^{13} ^{14}(/) {[LU]SAI (/)^{14} T[ON IMANTA
TWN]^{15} UPODHMAT[WN]^{15} [AUTOU]}^{15} (//)^{14}: {//}

    Matt = {/} {EGW}^{3} MEN ^{4}/ {UMAS}^{3} /^{4} //^{5} {BAPTI}^{3}ZW
//^{4} ^{5}/ (EN)^6 {UDATI}^{3} /^{5} (EIS METANOIAN)^7 {/}, //^{8}{O} ^{10} {DE} ^{10} ({OPISW
MOU})^9 /^{1} ^{8}/ {ERX}(OMENOS) /^{8} {ISXUROTEROS MOU}^{11} (ESTIN)^{12}, {OU OUK EIMI
IKANOS}^{13} //^{14} {T}^{15}(A)^{15} {UPODHMAT}^{15}(A)^{15} [   ]^{15} ^{14}/ (BASTA)^{15}{SAI}^{15} /^{14}:
{//}

    Mark = //^{2} ^{8}/ [(ERX)ETAI] /^{8} //^{10} [(O)] //^{8}Matt[(ISXUROTEROS
MOU)]^{11} (OPISW MOU)^9, [(OU OUK EIMI IKANOS)]^{13} ^{14}/ KUYAS ^{18}/ [LU(SAI) /^{14}
(T)ON IMANTA TWN (UPODHMAT)WN AUTOU]^{15} //^{14}. **1:8** / [(EGW)]^3
//^{4}Matt //^{5}Luke E[(BAPTI)]^{3}SA ^{4}/ [(UMAS)]^3 /^{4} ^{5}/ [(UDATI)]^3 /^{5} /

    Pap Q = {/} {EGW}^{3} MEN //^{4} ^{2}/ ^{5}/ (   )^6 {UDATI} /^{5} {BAPTI}ZW ^{4}/ {UMAS}^{3}
/^{4}//^{5} (   )^7 {/}^{2} ^{8}/ ({   })^9 {ERX}[(   )] /^{8}{DE}^{10}{O} //^{8} {ISXUROTEROS MOU}^{11}
(   )^{12} {OU OUK EIMI IKANOS}^{13} ^{14}/ [(   )]^{15}{SAI}^{15}/^{14} {T}^{15}[(   )]^{15}
{UPODHMAT}^{15}[(   )]^{15}[   ]^{15} //^{14} {//}

Text = Mark + 'minor agreement'
Pro:
Con:

Text = Q The order in Luke and Matt agrees; the Lucan wording: {/} {EGW}[3] MEN
//[4] [5]/ (   )[6] {UDATI}[3] /[5] {BAPTI}[3]ZW [4]/ {UMAS}[3] /[4] //[5] (   )[7] {/}: [8]/ ({
})[9] {ERX[ETAI]} /[8] [10]{/} {DE} {/}[10] {O} //[8] {ISXUROTEROS MOU}[11] (   )[12],
{OU OUK EIMI IKANOS}[13] [14]/ {[LU]SAI /[14] T[ON IMANTA
TWN][15] UPODHMAT[WN][15] [AUTOU]}[15] //[14]: {//}
Pro:
Con:

3

    Luke = {EGW} MEN //[4] [5]/ (   )[6] {UDATI} /[5] {BAPTI}ZW [4]/ {UMAS}
    Matt = {EGW} MEN [4]/ {UMAS} /[4] //[5] {BAPTI}ZW //[4] [5]/ (EN)[6] {UDATI}
    Mark = [(EGW)] (//)[4] [//][5] E[(BAPTI)]SA [4](/) [(UMAS)] (/)[4] [5]/ [(UDATI)]
    Pap Q = {EGW} MEN //[4] [2]/ [5]/ (   )[6] {UDATI} /[5] {BAPTI}ZW [4]/ {UMAS}
    Q =

Text = Mark [(EGW)] (//)[4] [//][5] E[(BAPTI)]SA [4](/) [(UMAS)] (/)[4] [5]/ [(UDATI)]
Pro:
Con:

Text = Q The order in Luke and Matt agrees; the Lucan wording: {/} {EGW} MEN
//[4] [5]/ (   )[6] {UDATI} /[5] {BAPTI}ZW [4]/ {UMAS}
Pro:
Con:

4

    Luke = // [5]/ (   )[6] {UDATI}[3] /[5] {BAPTI}[3]ZW / {UMAS}[3]
    Matt = / {UMAS}[3] / //[5] {BAPTI}[3]ZW //
    Mark = (//) [//][5] E[(BAPTI)][3]SA (/) [(UMAS)][3] (/)
    Pap Q = // [2]/ [5]/ (   )[6] {UDATI}[3] /[5] {BAPTI}[3]ZW / {UMAS}[3]
    Q =

Text = Mark (//) [//][5] E[(BAPTI)][3]SA (/) [(UMAS)][3] (/)
Pro:
Con:

Text = Q // [2]/ [5]/ (   )[6] {UDATI}[3] /[5] {BAPTI}[3]ZW / {UMAS}[3] /
Pro:
Con:

Q = Luke // [5]/ (   )[6] {UDATI}[3] /[5] {BAPTI}[3]ZW //[5] / {UMAS}[3] /
Pro:
Con:

Q = **Matt** / {UMAS}^{3} / //^{5} {BAPTI}^{3}ZW //
Pro:
Con:

5

   Luke = / (   )^6 {UDATI}^{3} / {BAPTI}^{3}ZW ^{4}/ {UMAS}^{3} /^{4} //
   Matt = // {BAPTI}^{3}ZW //^{4} / (EN)^6 {UDATI}^{3}
   Mark = [//] E[(BAPTI)]^{3}SA ^{4}/ [(UMAS)]^3 (/)^4 [/] [(UDATI)]^3 [/]
   Pap Q = / (   )^6 {UDATI}^{3} / {BAPTI}^{3}ZW ^{4}/ {UMAS}^{3} /^{4} //
   Q =

Text = **Mark** [//] E[(BAPTI)]^{3}SA ^{4}(/) [(UMAS)]^3 (/)^4 [/] [(UDATI)]^3 [/]
Pro:
Con:

Text = **Q**
Pro:
Con:

Q = **Luke** / (   )^6 {UDATI}^{3} / {BAPTI}^{3}ZW ^{4}/ {UMAS}^{3} /^{4} //
Pro:
Con:

Q = **Matt** // {BAPTI}^{3}ZW //^{4} / (EN)^6 {UDATI}^{3} /
Pro:
Con:

6

   Luke = ( )
   Matt = (EN)
   Pap Q = ( )
   Q =

Q = **Luke** ( )
Pro:
Con:

Q = **Matt** (EN)
Pro:
Con:

7

   Luke = ( )
   Matt = (EIS METANOIAN)
   Pap Q = ( )
   Q =

Q = **Luke** (   )
Pro:
Con:

Q = **Matt** (EIS METANOIAN)
Pro:
Con:

8

    Luke = (/) ({   })^9 {ERX[ETAI]} (/) ^{10}{/} {DE} {/}^{10} {O} (//)
    Matt = // {O} ^{10}{/} {DE} {/}^{10} ({OPISW MOU})^9 /^{1} / {ERX}(OMENOS) /
    Mark = (/) (//)^9 [(ERX)ETAI] (/) //^{10} [(O)] (//)
    Pap Q = (/) ({   })^9 {ERX}[(   )] (/) ^{10}{/} {DE} {/}^{10} {O} (//)
    Q =

Text = **Mark** (/) (//)^9 [(ERX)ETAI] (/) //^{10} [(O)] (//)
Pro:
Con:

Text = Q
Pro:
Con:

Q = **Luke** (/) {/} ({   })^9 {ERX[ETAI]} (/) ^{10}{/} {DE} {/}^{10}{O} (//)
Pro:
Con:

Q = **Matt** //^{8} {O} ^{10}{/} {DE} {/}^{10} ({OPISW MOU})^9 /^{1} / {ERX}(OMENOS) /
Pro:
Con:

9

    Luke = ({   })
    Matt = ({OPISW MOU})
    Mark = (OPISW MOU)
    Pap Q = (   )
    Q =

Text = **Mark** (OPISW MOU)
Pro:
Con:

Text = Q
Pro:
Con:

Q = **Luke** {(   )}
Pro:
Con:

Q = **Matt** ({OPISW MOU})
Pro:
Con:

10

    Luke = {/} {DE} {/} {O} (//)[8] {ISXUROTEROS MOU}[11] (   )[12], {OU OUK EIMI
IKANOS}[13] [14](/) {[LU]SAI (/)[14] T[ON IMANTA TWN][15] UPODHMAT[WN][15] [AUTOU]}[15]
(//)[14]: {//}[2] {AUTOS {//} }[16]

    Matt = {/} {DE} {/} ({OPISW MOU})[9] /[1] [8]/ {ERX}(OMENOS) /[8] {ISXUROTEROS
MOU}[11] (ESTIN)[12], {OU OUK EIMI IKANOS}[13] //[14] {T}[15](A)[15] {UPODHMAT}[15](A)[15]
[   ][15] [14]/ (BASTA)[15]{SAI}[15] /[14]: {//}[2] {AUTOS {//} }[16]

    Mark = // [(O)] (//)[8] [(ISXUROTEROS MOU)][11] (OPISW MOU)[9], [(OU OUK EIMI
IKANOS)][13] [14]{/} KUYAS [18]/ [LU(SAI) (/)[14] (T)ON IMANTA TWN (UPODHMAT)WN
AUTOU][15] (//)[14]. **1:8** [2]/ [(EGW)][3] (//)[4] [//][5] E[(BAPTI)][3]SA [4](/)
[(UMAS)][3] (/)[4] [5][/] [(UDATI)][3] [/][5] /[2], [(AUTOS / DE /

    Pap Q = {/} {DE} {/} {O} //[8] {ISXUROTEROS MOU}[11] (   )[12] {OU OUK EIMI
IKANOS}[13] [14]/ [(   )][15]{SAI}[15] /[14] {T}[15][(   )][15] {UPODHMAT}[15][(   )][15][
][15] //[14] {//}[2] {AUTOS {//})][16]

    Q =

Text = **Mark 1:7** // [(O)] (//)[8] [(ISXUROTEROS MOU)][11] (OPISW MOU)[9], [(OU OUK
EIMI IKANOS)][13] [14]{/} KUYAS [18]/ [LU(SAI) (/)[14](T)ON IMANTA TWN (UPODHMAT)WN
AUTOU][15] (//)[14]. **1:8** [2]/ [(EGW)][3] (//)[4] [//][5] E[(BAPTI)][3]SA [4](/)
[(UMAS)][3] (/)[4] [5][/] [(UDATI)][3] [/][5] /[2], [(AUTOS / DE /)][16]
Pro:
Con:

Text = **Q** The order in Luke and Matt agrees; the Lucan wording: {/} {DE} {/}
{O} //[8] {ISXUROTEROS MOU}[11](   )[12], {OU OUK EIMI IKANOS}[13] [14]/ {[LU]SAI
/[14] T[ON IMANTA TWN][15] UPODHMAT[WN][15] [AUTOU]}[15] (//)[14]: {//}[2] {AUTOS {//}
Pro:
Con:

11

    Luke = {ISXUROTEROS MOU}
    Matt = {ISXUROTEROS MOU}
    Mark = [(ISXUROTEROS MOU)]
    Pap Q = {ISXUROTEROS MOU}
    Q =

Text = **Mark** [(ISXUROTEROS MOU)]
Pro:
Con:

Text = **Q** Luke and Matt agree {ISXUROTEROS MOU}.
Pro:
Con:

12

    Luke = (   )
    Matt = (ESTIN)
    Pap Q = (   )
    Q =

Q = **Luke** (   )
Pro:
Con:

Q = **Matt** (ESTIN)
Pro:
Con:

13

    Luke = {OU OUK EIMI IKANOS}
    Matt = {OU OUK EIMI IKANOS}
    Mark = [(OU OUK EIMI IKANOS)]
    Pap Q = {OU OUK EIMI IKANOS}
    Q =

Text = **Mark** [(OU OUK EIMI IKANOS)]
Pro:
Con:

Text = **Q** Luke and Matt agree {OU OUK EIMI IKANOS}.
Pro:
Con:

14

    Luke = (/) {[LU]SAI (/) T[ON IMANTA TWN]^{15} UPODHMAT[WN]^{15} [AUTOU]}^{15} (//)
    Matt = // {T}^{15}(A)^{15} {UPODHMAT}^{15}(A)^{15} [   ]^{15} / (BASTA)^{15}{SAI}^{15} /
    Mark = (/) KUYAS ^{18}/ [LU(SAI) (/) (T)ON IMANTA TWN (UPODHMAT)WN AUTOU]
^{15} (//)
    Pap Q = / [(   )]^{15}{SAI}^{15} / {T}^{15}[(   )]^{15} {UPODHMAT}^{15}[(   )]^{15}
[   ]^{15} //
    Q =

Text = Mark (/) KUYAS ^{18}/ [LU(SAI) (/) (T)ON IMANTA TWN (UPODHMAT)WN
AUTOU] ^{15} (//)
Pro:
Con:

Text = Q
Pro:
Con:

Q = Luke (/) {[LU]SAI (/) T[ON IMANTA TWN]^{15} UPODHMAT[WN]^{15} [AUTOU]}^{15} (//)
Pro:
Con:

Q = Matt // {T}^{15}(A)^{15} {UPODHMAT}^{15}(A)^{15} [   ]^{15} / (BASTA)^{15}{SAI}^{15} /
Pro:
Con:

15

    Luke = ^{14}/ {[LU]SAI /^{14} T[ON IMANTA TWN] UPODHMAT[WN] [AUTOU]} //^{14}
    Matt = //^{14} {T}(A) {UPODHMAT}(A) [   ] ^{14}/ (BASTA){SAI} /^{14}
    Mark = ^{14}(/) KUYAS [LU(SAI) /^{14} (T)ON IMANTA TWN (UPODHMAT)WN
AUTOU] (//)^{14}
    Pap Q = ^{14}/ [(   )]{SAI}^{15} /^{14} {T}[(   )] {UPODHMAT}[(   )]^{15} [   ] //^{14}
    Q =

Text = Mark ^{14}(/) KUYAS [LU(SAI) (/)^{14} (T)ON IMANTA TWN (UPODHMAT)WN
AUTOU] (//)^{14}
Pro:
Con:

Text = Q
Pro:
Con:

Q = Luke ^{14}/ {[LU]SAI /^{14} T[ON IMANTA TWN] UPODHMAT[WN] [AUTOU]} //^{14}
Pro:
Con:

Q = Matt //^{14} {T}(A) {UPODHMAT}(A) [   ] ^{14}/ (BASTA){SAI} /^{14}
Pro:
Con:

16

    Luke = {AUTOS {//}^{10} ^{17}{/} UMAS {/}^{17} BAPTISEI {//}^{17} EN PNEUMATI AGIW}
    Matt = {AUTOS {//}^{10} ^{17}{/} UMAS {/}^{17} / BAPTISEI {//}^{17} EN PNEUMATI AGIW}

Mark = [(AUTOS)] ^{10}/ [(DE) /^{10} //^{17} BAPTISEI ^{17} UMAS /^{17} EN PNEUMATI AGIW)]
Pap Q = {AUTOS {//}^{10} ^{17}{/} UMAS {/}^{17} BAPTISEI {//}^{17} EN PNEUMATI AGIW}
Q =

Text = Mark + 'minor agreement' [(AUTOS)] ^{10}/ [(DE)] /^{10} [(//^{17} BAPTISEI ^{17}/UMAS /^{17} EN PNEUMATI AGIW)]
Pro:
Con:

Text = Q
Pro:
Con:

Q = Luke {AUTOS {//}^{10} ^{17}{/} UMAS {/}^{17} BAPTISEI {//}^{17} EN PNEUMATI AGIW}
Pro:
Con:

Q = Matt {AUTOS {//}^{10} ^{17}{/} UMAS {/}^{17} / BAPTISEI {//}^{17} EN PNEUMATI AGIW}
Pro:
Con:

17
Luke = {/} UMAS {/} BAPTISEI {//}
Matt = {/} UMAS {/} BAPTISEI {//}
Mark = // BAPTISEI / UMAS /
Pap Q = {/} UMAS {/} BAPTISEI {//}
Q =

Text = Mark + 'minor agreement' // BAPTISEI / UMAS/
Pro:
Con:

Text = Q Luke and Matt agree {/} UMAS {/} BAPTISEI {//}.
Pro:
Con:

Luke 3:17 OU TO PTUON EN TH XEIRI AUTOU (   )^1 DIAKAQAR[A]^{1}I THN ALWNA AUTOU KAI SUNA[GAG]^{1}EI[N]^1 TON SITON ^{2}/ EIS THN APOQHKHN /^{2} AUTOU //^{2}, TO DE AXURON KATAKAUSEI PURI ASBESTW.

Matt 3:12 OU TO PTUON EN TH XEIRI AUTOU (KAI)^1 DIAKAQAR(IE)^{1}I THN ALWNA AUTOU KAI SUNA(C)^{1}EI[   ]^1 TON SITON //^{2} AUTOU ^{2}/ EIS THN APOQHKHN /^{2}, TO DE AXURON KATAKAUSEI PURI ASBESTW.

Pap Q 3:17 OU TO PTUON EN TH XEIRI AUTOU (   )[1] DIAKAQAR[(   )][1]I THN ALWNA
AUTOU KAI SUNA[(   )][1]EI[   ][1] TON SITON [2]/ EIS THN APOQHKHN /[2] AUTOU //[2], TO
DE AXURON KATAKAUSEI PURI ASBESTW

Q 3:17

1

    Luke = (   ) DIAKAQAR[A]I THN ALWNA AUTOU KAI SUNA[GAG]EI[N]
    Matt = (KAI) DIAKAQAR(IE)I THN ALWNA AUTOU KAI SUNA(C)EI[   ]
    Pap Q = (   ) DIAKAQAR[(   )]I THN ALWNA AUTOU KAI SUNA[(   )]EI[   ]
    Q =

Q = Luke (   ) DIAKAQAR[A]I THN ALWNA AUTOU KAI SUNA[GAG]EI[N]
Pro:
Con:

Q = Matt (KAI) DIAKAQAR(IE)I THN ALWNA AUTOU KAI SUNA(C)EI[   ]
Pro:
Con:

2

    Luke = / EIS THN APOQHKHN / AUTOU //
    Matt = // AUTOU / EIS THN APOQHKHN /
    Pap Q = / EIS THN APOQHKHN / AUTOU //
    Q =

Q = Luke / EIS THN APOQHKHN / AUTOU //
Pro:
Con:

Q = Matt // AUTOU / EIS THN APOQHKHN /
Pro:
Con:

Luke 3:21 (   )[1] [{E]G[E]NET[O}][2] [DE][3] ({   })[4] ({   )}[5] (   )[6] [{EN}][7]
T[W][8] [9]/ {BAPTI}SQHNAI /[9] [10]/ [A]{PA}[NT]{A} [TON LAON] /[10]
[{KAI}][11] (   )[12] [13] (/) (O)[13] {IHSOU(   )} (/)[13] {BAPTISQ}[15]E[NTO][15]S (//)[13]
({   })[16] ({   }   {   }   )[17] (   )[18] ({   })[19] {KAI}[20] ({   }   )[21] [PROSEU
XOMENOU][22] [A][23]NEWXQH[N][23]A[I][23] (   )[24] [{T}][25]{O}[25][N][25] {OURANO}[25][N][25] (
//[9] Matt 3:13 concerning Jesus' baptism here at Luke 3:21a, but Matt 3:6
{EBAPTIZONTO} concerning John's general baptism is after Luke 3:6. //[10] Matt 3:5 after
Luke 3:6.

Matt 3:5,6,13,16a TOTE {ECEPOREUETO PROS AUTON [10][/] {//} {IEROSOLUM}A
{/} ({KAI}) {PA(S)A (H IOUDAIA}) {/} [/][10] / KAI PASA H PERIXWROS TOU

IORDANOU /[3]:3.9 , **3:6** [9][/] ({KAI EBAPTIZONTO {/} EN TW IORDANH POTAMW {/}
UP' AUTOU {//} ECOMOLOGOUMENOI TAS AMARTIAS AUTWN.}) [/][9]... **3:13**
(TOTE)[1] (PARA)[2]{G}[2](I)[2]{NET}[2](AI)[2] [   ][3] //[7] [//][9] [//][10] (O {IHSOUS})[4] ({APO
}) NAZARET ({THS GALILAIAS})[5] (EPI TON IORDANHN PROS TON
IWANNHN)[6] [{   }][7] T(OU)[8] [9][/] BAPTISQHNAI (UP' AUTOU) [/][9]... **3:16a**
[{   }][11] [//][13] {BAPTISQ}[15]E(I)[15]S (DE)[12] [13]/ (O)[14] IHSOU{S} /[13] {//}[20] {EU
QUS}[16] ({AN}E{B}H)[17] (APO)[16] {TOU
UDATOS.})[19] [20]{/} KAI {/}[20]({ID}OU)[21] [   ][22]
(H)[23]NEWXQH(S)[23]A(N)[23](AUTW)[24][{   }][25]{O}[25](I)[25] {OURANO}[25](I)[25] /,
(//[3]:3.9 Luke 3:3.9 after Matt 3:1.)

Mark 1:5,9-10a KAI (ECEPOREUETO PROS AUTON [10][/] (/) (PASA H IOUDAIA)
XWRA (KAI) (/) OI (IEROSOLUM)ITAI [PANT]ES (//) [/][10] ,
[9][/] (KAI) (E)[(BAPTI)](ZONTO (//) UP' AUTOU (/) EN TW IORDANH POTAMW (/)
ECOMOLOGOUMENOI TAS AMARTIAS AUTWN.) [/][9] **3:9** KAI [E(G)E(NET)O][2] [EN][7]
EKEINAIS TAIS HMERAIS [//][9] [//][10] HLQEN [13][/] [(IHSOU)S][4] /[13] (APO)[5] NAZARET
(THS GALILAIAS)[5] [KAI][11] [//][13] E[(BAPTISQ)][15]H EIS TON IORDANHN UPO IWANNOU.
1:10a [20](/) [(KAI)] (/)[20] (EUQUS)[16] (AN)[17]A(B)[17]AINWN EK (TOU
UDATOS)[19] (//)[20] E(ID)[21]EN SXIZOMENOUS [T(O)][25]US [(OURANO)][25]US

Pap Q 3:21 (   )[1]
[{(   )}][2]{G}[2][{(   )}][2]{NET}[2][{(   )}][2] [   ][3] ({   })[4] ({   })[5] (   )[6] [{
}][7] T[(   )][8] [9]/ {BAPTI}SQHNAI / [9]   [10]/ [   ] {PA}[   ]{A}
[   ] /[10] [{   }][11] (   )[12]
[13](/) (O)[14] {IHSOU(   )} (/)[13] {/}[4] {BAPTISO}[15]E[(   )][15]S (//)[13] ({   })[16] ({
}   {   })[17] (   )[18] ({   })[19] {KAI}[20] ({   }   )[21] [   ][22] [(   )][23]NEW
XQH[(   )][23]A[   ][23] (   )[24] [{   }][25]{O}[25][(   )][25] {OURANO}[25][(   )][25]
(//[9] Matt 3:13 concerning Jesus' baptism here at Luke 3:21a, but Matt 3:6
{EBAPTIZONTO} concerning John's general baptism is after Luke 3:6. //[10] Matt
3:5 after Luke 3:6.)

Q 3:21

1
    Luke = (   )
    Matt = (TOTE)
    Pap Q = (   )
    Q =

Q = Luke (   )
Pro:
Con:

Q = Matt (TOTE)
Pro:
Con:

2
    Luke = [{E]G[E]NET(O}]
    Matt = (PARA){G}(I){NET}(AI)
    Mark = [E(G)E(NET)O]
    Pap Q = [{(   )}]{G}[{(   )}]{NET}[{(   )}]
    Q =

Text = **Mark** [E(G)E(NET)O]
Pro:
Con:

Text = **Q**
Pro:
Con:

Q = **Luke** [{E]G[E]NET[O}]
Pro:
Con:

Q = **Matt** (PARA){G}(I){NET}(AI)
Pro:
Con:

3
    Luke = [DE]
    Matt = [ ]
    Pap Q = [ ]
    Q =

Q = **Luke** [DE]
Pro:
Con:

Q = **Matt** [ ]
Pro:
Con:

4
    Luke = ({ })
    Matt = (O {IHSOUS})
    Mark = [(IHSOU]S)
    Pap Q = ({ })
    Q =

Text = Mark [(IHSOU]S)
Pro:
Con:

Text = Q
Pro:
Con:

Q = Luke ({   })
Pro:
Con:

Q = Matt (O {IHSOUS})
Pro:
Con:

5

    Luke = ({   )}
    Matt = ({APO}) ({THS GALILAIAS})
    Mark = (APO) NAZARET (THS GALILAIAS)
    Pap Q = ({   })
    Q =

Text = Mark (APO) NAZARET (THS GALILAIAS)
Pro:
Con:

Text = Q
Pro:
Con:

Q = Luke ({   )}
Pro:
Con:

Q = Matt {APO} {THS GALILAIAS}
Pro:
Con:

6

    Luke = (   )
    Matt = (EPI TON IORDANHN PROS TON IWANNHN)
    Pap Q = (   )
    Q =

Q = **Luke** (   )
Pro:
Con:

Q = **Matt** (EPI TON IORDANHN PROS TON IWANNHN)
Pro:
Con:

7

    Luke = [{EN}]
    Matt = [{   }]
    Mark = [EN]
    Pap Q = [{   }]
    Q =

Text = **Mark** [EN]
Pro:
Con:

Text = **Q**
Pro:
Con:

Q = **Luke** [{EN}]
Pro:
Con:

Q = **Matt** [{   }]
Pro:
Con:

8

    Luke = T[W]
    Matt = T(OU)
    Pap Q = T[(   )]
    Q =

Q = **Luke** T[W]
Pro:
Con:

Q = **Matt** T(OU)
Pro:
Con:

9

    Luke = / {BAPTI}SQHNAI / (// Matt 3:13 concerning Jesus' baptism here at
Luke 3:21a, but Matt 3:6 {EBAPTIZONTO} concerning John's general baptism is
after Luke 3:6.)

    Matt 3:6 = [/] ({KAI {EBAPTIZONTO {/} EN TW IORDANH POTAMW {/} UP' AUTOU
{//} ECOMOLOGOUMENOI TAS AMARTIAS AUTWN.}) [/] **3:13**
$(TOTE)^1$ $(PARA)^2${G}$^2(I)^2${NET}$^2(AI)^2$ [ ]^3 //^{7} [//] [//]^{10} (O {IHSOUS})^4 ({APO}
)^5 ({THS GALILAIAS})^5 (EPI TON IORDANHN PROS TON
IWANNHN)^6 [{ }]^7 T(OU)^8 [/] BAPTISQHNAI (UP' AUTOU) [/]

    Mark 1:5 = [/] (KAI) (E)[(BAPTI)](ZONTO (//) UP' AUTOU (/) EN TW IORDANH
POTAMW (/) ECOMOLOGOUMENOI TAS AMARTIAS AUTWN.) [/] **3:9** KAI
[E(G)E(NET)O]^2 [EN]^7 EKEINAIS TAIS HMERAIS [//]

    Pap Q = / {BAPTI}SQHNAI / (// Matt 3:13 concerning Jesus' baptism here
at Luke 3:21a, but Matt 3:6 {EBAPTIZONTO} concerning John's general baptism
is after Luke 3:6.

    Q =

Text = **Mark 1:5** [/] (KAI) (E)[(BAPTI)](ZONTO (//) UP' AUTOU (/) EN TW IORDANH
POTAMW (/) ECOMOLOGOUMENOI TAS AMARTIAS AUTWN.) [/] **3:9** KAI
[E(G)E(NET)O]^2 [EN]^7 EKEINAIS TAIS HMERAIS [//]
Pro:
Con:

Text = **Q**
Pro:
Con:

Q = **Luke** / {BAPTI}SQHNAI / (// Matt 3:13 concerning Jesus' baptism here at
Luke 3:21a, but Matt 3:6 {EBAPTIZONTO} concerning John's general baptism is
after Luke 3:6.)
Pro:
Con:

Q = **Matt 3:6** [/] ({KAI {EBAPTIZONTO {/} EN TW IORDANH POTAMW {/} UP' AUTOU
{//} ECOMOLOGOUMENOI TAS AMARTIAS AUTWN.}) [/] **3:13**
$(TOTE)^1$ $(PARA)^2${G}$^2(I)^2${NET}$^2(AI)^2$ [ ]^3 //^{7} [//]
[//]^{10} (O {IHSOUS})^4 ({APO})^5 ({THS GALILAIAS})^5 (EPI TON IORDANHN PROS TON
IWANNHN)^6 [{ }]^7 T(OU)^8 [/] BAPTISQHNAI (UP' AUTOU) [/]
Pro:
Con:

10

    Luke = / [A]{PA}[NT]{A} [TON LAON] / (// Matt 3:5 after Luke 3:6.)

    Matt 3:5 = [/] {//} {IEROSOLUM}A {/} ({KAI}) {PA(S)A (H IOUDAIA})
{/} [/]... **3:13** $(TOTE)^1$ $(PARA)^2${G}$^2(I)^2${NET}$^2(AI)^2$ [ ]^3 //^{7} [//]^9 [//]

Mark 1:5 = [/] (/) (PASA H IOUDAIA) XWRA (KAI) (/) OI (IEROSOLUM)ITAI
[PANT]ES (//) / ... **3:9** KAI [E(G)E(NET)O]^2 [EN]^7 EKEINAIS TAIS HMERAIS
[//]^9 [//]

   Pap Q = / [   ]{PA}[   ]{A} [   ] /

   Q =

Text = **Mark 1:5** [/] (/) (PASA H IOUDAIA) XWRA (KAI) (/) OI (IEROSOLUM)ITAI
[PANT]ES (//) / ... **3:9** KAI [E(G)E(NET)O]^2 [EN]^7 EKEINAIS TAIS HMERAIS
[//]^9 [//]
Pro:
Con:

Text = **Q**
Pro:
Con:

Q = **Luke** / [A]{PA}[NT]{A} [TON LAON] / (// Matt 3:5 after Luke 3:6.)
Pro:
Con:

Q = **Matt 3:5** [/] {//} {IEROSOLUM}A {/} ({KAI}) {PA(S)A (H IOUDAIA)}
{/} [/]... **3:13** (TOTE)^1 (PARA)^2{G}^{2}(I)^2{NET}^{2}(AI)^2 [   ]^3 //^{7} [//]^9 [//]
Pro:
Con:

11

   Luke = [{KAI}]
   Matt = [{   }]
   Mark = [KAI]
   Pap Q = [{   }]
   Q =

Text = **Mark** [KAI]
Pro:
Con:

Text = **Q**
Pro:
Con:

Q = **Luke** [{KAI}]
Pro:
Con:

Q = **Matt** [{   }]
Pro:
Con:

12

    Luke = (   )
    Matt = (DE)
    Pap Q = (   )
    Q =

Q = Luke (   )
Pro:
Con:

Q = Matt (DE)
Pro:
Con:

13

    Luke = (/) (   )^{14} {IHSOU(   )} (/) {BAPTISQ}^{15}E[NTO]^{15}S (//)
    Matt = // {BAPTISQ}^{15}E(I)^{15}S (DE)^{12} [/] (O)^{14} IHSOUS /
    Mark = / [(IHSOU]S)^{4} / (APO)^{5} NAZARET (THS GALILAIAS)^{5} [KAI]^{11} //
    Pap Q = (/) (   )^{14} {IHSOU(   )} (/) {BAPTISQ}^{15}E[(   )]^{15}S (//)
    Q =

Text = Mark / [(IHSOU]S)^{4} / (APO)^{5} NAZARET (THS GALILAIAS)^{5} ^{X}/ [KAI]^{11} //
Pro:
Con:

Text = Q
Pro:
Con:

Q = Luke (/) (   )^{14} {IHSOU(   )} (/) {BAPTISQ}^{15}E[NTO]^{15}S (//)
Pro:
Con:

Q = Matt // {BAPTISQ}^{15}E(I)^{15}S (DE)^{12} / (O)^{14} IHSOUS /
Pro:
Con:

14

    Luke = (   )
    Matt = (O)
    Pap Q = (   )
    Q =

Q = Luke (   )
Pro:
Con:

Q = Matt (O)
Pro:
Con:

15
    Luke = {BAPTISQ}E[NTO]S
    Matt = {BAPTISQ}E(I)S
    Mark = E[(BAPTISQ)]H
    Pap Q = {BAPTISQ}E[(   )]S
    Q =

Text = Mark E[(BAPTISQ)]H
Pro:
Con:

Text = Q
Pro:
Con:

Q = Luke {BAPTISQ}E[NTO]S
Pro:
Con:

Q = Matt {BAPTISQ}E(I)S
Pro:
Con:

16
    Luke = ({   })
    Matt = ({EUQUS)}
    Mark = (EUQUS)
    Pap Q = ({   })
    Q =

Text = Mark ({EUQUS})
Pro:
Con:

Text = Q
Pro:
Con:

Q = Luke ({   })
Pro:
Con:

Q = Matt ({EUQUS)}
Pro:
Con:

17

    Luke = ({ } { })
    Matt = ({AN}E{B}H)
    Mark = (AN)A(B)AINWN
    Pap Q = ({ } { })
    Q =

Text = Mark (AN)A(B)AINWN
Pro:
Con:

Text = Q
Pro:
Con:

Q = Luke ({ } { })
Pro:
Con:

Q = Matt ({AN}E{B}H)
Pro:
Con:

18

    Luke = ( )
    Matt = (APO)
    Pap Q = ( )
    Q =

Q = Luke ( )
Pro:
Con:

Q = Matt (APO)
Pro:
Con:

19

    Luke = ({ })
    Matt = ({TOU UDATOS})
    Mark = ({ })

Pap Q = ({   })
Q =

Text = **Mark** (TOU UDATOS)
Pro:
Con:

Text = **Q**
Pro:
Con:

Q = **Luke** ({   })
Pro:
Con:

Q = **Matt** ({TOU UDATOS})
Pro:
Con:

20

Luke = {KAI}
Matt = {//} ({EUQUS})^{16} ({AN}E{B}H)^{17} (APO)^{18} {TOU UDATOS.})^{19} {/} KAI {/}
Mark = (/) [(KAI)] (/) (EUQUS)^{16} (AN)^{17}A(B)^{17}AINWN EK (TOU UDATOS)^{19} (//)
Pap Q = {KAI}
Q =

Text = **Mark** (/) [(KAI)] (/) (EUQUS)^{16} (AN)^{17}A(B)^{17}AINWN EK (TOU UDATOS)^{19} (//)
Pro:
Con:

Text = **Q**
Pro:
Con:

Q = **Luke** {KAI}
Pro:
Con:

Q = **Matt** {//} ({EUQUS})^{16} ({AN}E{B}H)^{17} (APO) {TOU UDATOS.})^{19} {/} KAI {/}
Pro:
Con:

21

Luke = ({   })(   )
Matt = ({ID}OU)
Mark = E(ID)EN

    Pap Q = ({   })( )
    Q =

Text = **Mark** E(ID)EN
Pro:
Con:

Text = **Q**
Pro:
Con:

Q = **Luke** ({   })( )
Pro:
Con:

Q = **Matt** ({ID}OU)
Pro:
Con:

22
    Luke = PROSEUXOMENOU]
    Matt = [   ]
    Pap Q = [   ]
    Q =

Q = **Luke** [PROSEUXOMENOU]
Pro:
Con:

Q = **Matt** [   ]
Pro:
Con:

23
    Luke = [A]NEWXQH[N]A[I]
    Matt = (H)NEWXQH(S)A(N)
    Pap Q = [( )]NEWXQH[( )]A[( )]
    Q =

Q = **Luke** [A]NEWXQH[N]A[I]
Pro:
Con:

Q = **Matt** (H)NEWXQH(S)A(N)
Pro:
Con:

24

    Luke = (   )
    Matt = (AUTW)
    Pap Q = (   )
    Q =

Q = **Luke** (   )
Pro:
Con:

Q = **Matt** (AUTW)
Pro:
Con:

25

    Luke = [{T}]{O}[N] {OURANO}[N]
    Matt = [{   }]{O}(I) {OURANO}(I)
    Mark = [T(O)]US [(OURANO)]US
    Pap Q = [{   }]{O}[(   )] {OURANO}[(   )]
    Q =

Text = **Mark** [T(O)US [(OURANO)]US
Pro:
Con:

Text = **Q**
Pro:
Con:

Q = **Luke** [{T}]{O}[N] {OURANO}[N]
Pro:
Con:

Q = **Matt** [{   }]{O}(I) {OURANO}(I)
Pro:
Con:

Luke 3:22a {KAI}[1] ( )[2] [3]/ {KATAB}[1][HNAI][4] /[3] {TO PNEUMA}[1] T[O AGION SWMATIKW EIDEI][5] (//)[3] {WS( )[6] PERISTERAN {//}[3] ( )[7] E}[1]P' {AUTON}[1],

Matt 3:16b {KAI}[1] (EIDEN)[2] { [//][3] TO PNEUMA}[1] T(OU QEOU)[5] [3]/ {KATAB(AINON}[4] /[3] WS}[1](EI)[6] {PERISTERAN}[1] {//}[3] (KAI ERXOMENON)[7] {E}[1]P' {AUTON}[1]:

Mark 1:10b [(KAI [//][3] TO PNEUMA (//)[3] WS PERISTERAN [3]/ KATAB]AINON[4] /[3] [E)]{1}IS [(AUTON)][1]:

Pap Q 3:22a {KAI}^{1} (   )^2 ^{3}/ {KATAB}^{1}[(   )]^4 /^{3} {TO PNEUMA}^{1} T[(   )] //^{3} ^{5}
{WS(   )^6 PERISTERAN (   )^7 E}^{1}P' {AUTON}^{1}

Q

1

    Luke = {KAI} (   )^2 ^{3}/ {KATAB}[HNAI]^4 /^{3} {TO PNEUMA} T[O AGION SWMATIKW
EIDEI]^5 (//)^3 {WS(   )^6 PERISTERAN {//}^{3} (   )^7 E}^{1}P' {AUTON}
    Matt = {KAI} (EIDEN)^2 { [//]^3 TO PNEUMA} T(OU
QEOU)^5 ^{3}/ {KATAB(AINON)^4 /^{3} WS}(EI)^6 {PERISTERAN} {//}^{3} (KAI
ERXOMENON)^7 {E}^{1}P' {AUTON}:
    Mark = [(KAI [//]^3 TO PNEUMA (//)^3 WS PERISTERAN
^{3}/ KATAB]AINON^4 /^{3} [E])]IS [(AUTON)]:
    Pap Q = {KAI} (   )^2 ^{3}/ {KATAB}[(   )]^4 /^{3} {TO PNEUMA} T[(   )]^5 //^{3}
{WS(   )^6 PERISTERAN (   )^7 E}P' {AUTON}
    Q =

Text = Mark [(KAI [//]^3 TO PNEUMA (//)^3 WS PERISTERAN
^{3}/ KATAB]AINON^4 /^{3} [E)]^{1}IS [(AUTON)]:
Pro:
Con:

Text = Q
Pro:
Con:

Q = Luke {KAI} (   )^2 ^{3}/ {KATAB}[HNAI]^4 /^{3} {TO PNEUMA} T[O AGION SWMATIKW
EIDEI]^5 (//)^3 {WS(   )^6 PERISTERAN {//}^{3} (   )^7 E}P' {AUTON}
Pro:
Con:

Q = Matt {KAI} (EIDEN)^2 { [//]^3 TO PNEUMA} T(OU
QEOU)^5 ^{3}/ {KATAB(AINON)^4 /^{3} WS}(EI)^6 {PERISTERAN} {//}^{3} (KAI
ERXOMENON)^7 {E}^{1}P' {AUTON}:
Pro:
Con:

2

    Luke = (   )
    Matt = (EIDEN)
    Pap Q = (   )
    Q =

Q = Luke (   )
Pro:
Con:

Q = Matt (EIDEN)
Pro:
Con:

3

    Luke = / {KATAB}[1][HNAI]⁴ / {TO PNEUMA}[1] T[O AGION SWMATIKW EIDEI]⁵ (//)
{WS(   )⁶ PERISTERAN {//}
    Matt = { [//] TO PNEUMA}[1] T(OU QEOU)⁵ / {KATAB(AINON)⁴ / WS}[1](EI)⁶
{PERISTERAN}[1] {//}
    Mark = [([//] TO PNEUMA (//) WS PERISTERAN / KATAB]AINON)⁴ /
    Pap Q = / {KATAB}[1][( )]⁴ / {TO PNEUMA}[1] [( )]⁵ //
    Q =

Text = Mark [([//] TO PNEUMA (//) WS PERISTERAN / KATAB]AINON⁴ /)
Pro:
Con:

Text = Q
Pro:
Con:

Q = Luke / {KATAB}[1][HNAI]⁴ / {TO PNEUMA}[1] T[O AGION SWMATIKW EIDEI]⁵ (//)
{WS(   )⁶ PERISTERAN {//}
Pro:
Con:

Q = Matt { [//] TO PNEUMA}[1] T(OU QEOU)⁵ / {KATAB(AINON)⁴ / WS}[1](EI)⁶
{PERISTERAN}[1] {//}
Pro:
Con:

4

    Luke = {KATAB}[1][HNAI]
    Matt = {KATAB[1](AINON})
    Mark = [(KATAB][1]AINON)
    Pap Q = {KATAB}[1][( )]
    Q =

Text = Mark [(KATAB][1]AINON)
Pro:
Con:

Text = Q
Pro:
Con:

Q = **Luke** {KATAB}[1][HNAI]
Pro:
Con:

Q = **Matt** {KATAB[1](AINON})
Pro:
Con:

5

    Luke = T[O AGION SWMATIKW EIDEI]
    Matt = T(OU QEOU)
    Pap Q = T[(   )]
    Q =

Q = **Luke** T[O AGION SWMATIKW EIDEI]
Pro:
Con:

Q = **Matt** T(OU QEOU)
Pro:
Con:

6

    Luke = {WS}[1](   )
    Matt = {WS}[1](EI)
    Mark = [(WS)][1]
    Pap Q = {WS}[1](   )
    Q =

Text = **Mark** [(WS)][1]
Pro:
Con:

Text = **Q**
Pro:
Con:

Q = **Luke** {WS}[1](   )
Pro:
Con:

Q = **Matt** {WS}[1](EI)
Pro:
Con:

7

  Luke = ( )
  Matt = (KAI ERXOMENON)
  Pap Q = ( )
  Q =

Q = **Luke** ( )
Pro:
Con:

Q = **Matt** (KAI ERXOMENON)
Pro:
Con:

Q 4

Leif Vaage

Institute for Antiquity and Christianity
Claremont, CA 91711

Luke 4:1-2 (   )[1] IHSOUS [DE PLHRHS PNEUMATOS AGIOU UPESTREYEN APO TOU IORDANOU KAI][2] (   )[3]H[GETO][3] [4]/ [EN][5] {T}[5][W][5] {PNEUMA}[5]T[I][5] /[4] {E}[6][N][6] {TH ERHM}[6][W][6] ·//[4].[8] **4:2** [7]{/} HMERAS {/}[7] TESSERAKONTA {//}[7] [8]/ {PEIRA[ZOMENOS] UPO TOU}[9] DIABOLOU. {KAI}[9] /[8] [OUK EFAGEN OUDEN][10] [EN TAIS HMERAIS EKEINAIS KAI SUNTELESQEISWN AUTWN][11] EPEINASEN.

Matt 4:1-2 (TOTE O)[1] IHSOUS [   ][2] (AN)[3]H(XQH)[3] //[4] {E(IS) TH(N) ERHM(ON)}[6] [4]/ (UPO)[5] {T(O)[5]U)[5] {PNEUMA}[5]T(OS)[5] /[4] [8]/ {PEIRA(SQHNAI) UPO TOU}[9]DIABOLOU. **4:2** {KAI}[9] /[8] (NHSTEUSAS)[10] [7]{/} HMERAS {/}[7] TESSERAKONTA //[{7}].[8] (KAI NUKTAS TESSERAKONTA, USTERON)[11] EPEINASEN.

Mark 1:12-13a KAI EUQUS [(T]O [PNEUMA)][5] AUTON EKBALLEI [(E]IS [TH]N [ERHM]ON)[6]. **1:13a** KAI HN EN TH ERHMW //[7] TESSERAKONTA [7]/ HMERAS /[7] [(PEIRA)ZOMENOS (UPO TOU)][9] SATANA, [(KAI)][9] HN META TWN QHRIWN,

Pap Q 4:1-2 (   )[1] IHSOUS [   ][2] (   )[3]H[(   )][3] [4]/ [(   )][5] {T}[5][(   )][5] {PNEUMA}[5]T[(   )][5] /[4] {E}[6][(   )][6] {TH}[6](   )[6] {ERHM}[6][(   )][6] //[4].[8] **4.2** [7]{/} HMERAS {/}[7] TESSERAKONTA {//}[7] [8]/ {PEIRA[(   )] UPO TOU}[9] DIABOLOU {KAI}[9] /[8] [(   )][10].[11] EPEINASEN

Q 4:1-2 [1] IHSOUS [2] (AN)[3]H(XQH)[3] [EN][5] {T}[5][W][5] {PNEUMA}[5]T[I][5] {E}[6][N][6] {TH}[6] {ERHM}[6][W][6] //[4] {PEIRA(SQHNAI) UPO TOU}[9] DIABOLOU **4:2** {KAI}[9] HMERAS TESSERAKONTA //[{7}].[8] [OUK EFAGEN OUDEN][10] (USTERON)[11] EPEINASEN

---

1   **Luke** = (   )
     Matt = (TOTE O)
     Pap Q = (   )
     Q = omit

Q = Luke (   )

Pro: 0: Luke is not adverse to use of the definite article before the name, Jesus. The use is normal Greek style. The name, Jesus, appears with the definite article before it otherwise here in Q (4:4[5], 8, 12). No reason can be given why Luke would delete the definite article here. Matt has added the definite article as harmonization of style.

Q = Matt (TOTE O)

Con: TOTE: according to Schulz (178) TOTE is Matthean redaction. Matt alone has TOTE three other times elsewhere in this pericope: Matt 4:5, 10, 11.

2   **Luke** = [DE PLHRHS PNEUMATOS AGIOU UPESTREYEN APO TOU IORDANOU KAI]
     Matt = [   ]
     Pap Q = [   ]
     Q = omit

Q = Luke [DE PLHRHS PNEUMATOS AGIOU UPESTREYEN APO TOU IORDANOU KAI]

Con: According to Schulz (178) Luke is redactional. Albertz and Bussmann agree (Schulz 178:10). According to Schulz (178:10) PLHRHS PNEUMATOS is used redactionally by Luke once (1) in the gospel and four times (4) in Acts. UPOSTREFEIN is used redactionally 9 in the gospel and 11 in Acts. Motivation for the redaction in Luke is perhaps the parallel passage in Mark. PLHRHS PNEUMATOS AGIOU corrects the exorcistic crudity of EKBALLEI in Mark. Jesus' retreat from the Jordan stems from interior motivation in Luke; it is not exterior compulsion as Mark has it.

3   **Luke** = (   )H[GETO]
     Matt = (AN)H(XQH)
     Pap Q = (   )H[(   )]
     Q = (AN)H(XQH)

Q = Luke (   )H[GETO]

Pro: Schulz (178) notes that ANAGEIN is otherwise common in Luke. A redactional motive on the part of Luke here is apparent only if one assumes that the subtlety of Conzelmann's middle versus a passive Christology is accurate (see below, **Con**). The Lukan addition in 4:1-2[2] is, perhaps, support for such a view. Luke has then, however, not actually corrected qua changed his source over against Matt's reading but indicated via 4:1[2] that he **reads** EGETO as middle where Q read the very same form as passive. Luke is, furthermore, interested in mountains as places of prayer and points of esoteric epiphanies and communication with the higher world (Schulz [180] quoting Conzelmann). It is not clear, then, why he would want to excise ANAGEIN.

Con: Conzelmann (28) apparently understands HGETO in Luke not to be passive but middle: "according to Luke Jesus is not 'led by' the Spirit, but himself acts 'in the Spirit.'" A footnote (28:1) calls this a "correction of the source." Schulz (178:11) follows Conzelmann and thinks that Luke is redactional. HGETO in Luke is a fusion of Matt = Q and Mark. The passive voice of the verb in Matt is preserved in the passive voice of HGETO. To be full of the Holy Spirit does not oppose being led in the Spirit. Luke changed the tense of the verb from aorist as Matt has it to imperfect as a reflection of the continuous character of the historical present (EKBALLEI) in Mark. The historical present is not used by Luke because of its rudeness (see 4:9[1]). This constitutes a second motivation for the correction of the verb, EKBALLEIN, here in Mark by Luke (the first motivation is suggested in 4:1-2[2]).

Q = Matt (AN)H(XQH)

Pro: PARALAMBANEIN in Matt 4:5, 8 is not typical of Matthean redaction otherwise. In fact, in Matt 4:8 PARALAMBANEI seems to be Q together minimally with the prepositional phrase, EIS OROS (see 4:5[1]). A redactional motive on the part of Matt is unclear. ANHXQH = Q as lectio difficilior insofar as to be led **up** into the wilderness is not apparently necessary or clear; i.e. how does one know that the wilderness is higher?

Con: The mountains and the desert are synonymous notions in Palestine: higher = drier. One might see redactional motivation on the part of Matt, furthermore, in the use of ANAGEIN here, given Matt's apparent interest in mountains otherwise in his gospel. It is only in Matt that the climax of the temptations occurs on "a very high mountain." Luke has no such phrase in his corresponding passage (Luke 4:5). However, the verb, ANAGEIN, does occur here in Luke (4:5). Matt has apparently removed the verb, ANAGEIN, from its original position in Q (Luke 4:5) to the beginning of the pericope (4:1) and replaced it in 4:5 (Matt 4:8) with the verb, PARALAMBANEIN (used only by Matt in Matt 4:5, 8), and the phrase, EIS OROS UYHLON LIAN. The aorist tense of the verb in Matt recalls the aorist participle in Luke 4:5; the passive voice reflects the passive voice of HGETO in Q.

4   **Luke** = / [EN]^5 {T}^{5}[W]^5 {PNEUMA}^{5}T[I]^5 / {E}^{6}[N]^6 {TH ERHM}^{6}[W]^6 //
     Matt = // {E(IS)^6 TH(N)^6 ERHM(ON)}^{6} / (UPO)^5 {T(O}^{5}U)^5 {PNEUMA}^{5}T(OS)^5/
     Pap Q = / [(   )]^5 {T}^{5}[(   )]^5 {PNEUMA}^{5}T[(   )]^5 / {E}^{6}[(   )]^6
                {TH}^{6}(   )^6 {ERHM}^{6}[(   )]^6 //
     Q = {E}^{6}[(   )]^6 {TH}^{6}(   )^6 {ERHM}^{6}[(   )]^6 [(   )]^5 {T}[(   )]^5
            {PNEUMA}^{5}T[(   )]^5

Q = Luke / [EN]^5 {T}^{5}[W]^5 {PNEUMA}^{5}T[I]^5 / {E}^{6}[N]^6 {TH ERHM}^{6}[W]^6 //

Pro: The original order in Q here would presumably follow the evangelist who otherwise seems to preserve the wording of the two prepositional phrases in Q. This would be Luke in the present instance (see 4:1-2[5,6]).

Con: Luke, however, seems to be responsible for altering the order of the subsequent phrases, HMERAS TESSERAKONTA and PEIRASQHNAI UPO TUO DIABOLOU (see 4:2[2]). Here, Luke may alter the order of the two prepositional phrases in order to correct as much as possible the parallelism which Matt preserves quite forcefully, namely, that the leading up of Jesus by the Spirit equals (this is the effect of the purposive infinitive, PEIRA-SQHNAI) the temptation by the devil.

5   **Luke** = [EN] {T}[W] {PNEUMA}T[I]
     Matt = (UPO) {T(O}U) {PNEUMA}T(OS)
     Mark = KAI EUQUS [(T]O [PNEUMA)] AUTON EKBALLEI

Pap Q = [(   )] {T}[(   )] {PNEUMA}T[(   )]
Q = [EN] {T}[W] {PNEUMA}T[I]

Text = Mark

Con: In Mark, the Spirit is the active subject of the sentence whereas both Matt and Luke agree that the Spirit is the agency of a passive construction. Likewise, the Spirit in Mark hurls Jesus out into the wilderness in the same way that Jesus casts out demons otherwise in Mark (EKBALLEIN) whereas both Matt and Luke agree that Jesus is led (AGEIN) in(to) the wilderness via the Spirit.

Q = Luke [EN] {T}[W] {PNEUMA}T[I]

Pro: 4:1-2[2] makes clear that Luke in this verse imagines the Holy Spirit in a quite personal way. The instrumental preposition, EN, in Luke seems thus somewhat incongruous and, therefore, as lectio difficilior, originally Q. The definite article before PNEUMATI further underscores the incongruity. The instrumental character of the preposition, EN, cannot be seen as a reflection of the character of the Spirit qua exorcist in Mark. The Spirit qua exorcist in Mark is presumably as personal as Jesus qua exorcist is personal otherwise in Mark. UPO plus the genitive in Matt is, in this regard, much more a reflection of the character of the Spirit in Mark than is Luke.

Q = Matt (UPO) {T(O}U) {PNEUMA}T(OS)

Con: UPO plus the genitive is classically the proper way to show personal agency. Matt seeks to show the agency of the **person** of the Spirit by his use of UPO plus the genitive.

6   **Luke** = {E}[N] {TH ERHM}[W]
     Matt = {E(IS) TH(N) ERHM(ON)}
     Mark = [(E]IS [TH]N [ERHM]ON)
     Pap Q = {E}[(   )] {TH}(   ) {ERHM}[(   )]
     Q = {E}[N] {TH ERHM}[W]

Text = Mark

Pro: One might assume that originally Mark had both phrases and Matt and Luke have each chosen differently one of the two.

Con: The assumption that Luke and Matt are dependent upon Q here does not assume any knowledge of Q at this point on the part of Mark. It also does not explain how it is that Matt and Luke put their respective phrases in such similar constructions, lacking any such model in Mark.

Q = Luke {E}[N] {TH ERHM}[W]

Pro: There is a certain real tension between the circumstantial preposition, EN, and the singular transition of the aorist verb, ANHXQH = Q (see 4:1-2[3]). Use of the imperfect verb

HGETO, by Luke relieved this tension in Luke. Matt relieved the tension by using the similar but rather more appropriate phrase in Mark: EIS THN ERHMON. Q = {E}[N] is attested somewhat further in Mark 1:12, 13. Mark has both phrases, EIS THN ERHMON and EN TH ERHMW, one after the other. The first phrase, EIS THN ERHMON, is the final piece of the exorcistic scenario which is Mark 1:12. The second phrase, EN TH ERHMW, immediately subsequent in Mark 1:13, seems redundant. Where else would Jesus be after he was hurled **into** the wilderness? The second phrase remains in Mark 1:13 because it is the phrase originally in Q after which the first phrase, EIS THN ERHMON, in Mark 1:12 was modeled.

Con: Luke at this point has Jesus led **within** the wilderness by means of the Spirit. The circumstantial character of the preposition, EN, fits well the repetitious force of the imperfect verb, HGETO, in Luke. One might suppose Lukan redaction here in this direction.

Q = Matt {E(IS) TH(N) ERHM(ON)}

Con: Mark and Matt agree here; Matt is derived from Mark. Mark knows from Q that the temptations of Jesus begin in the wilderness. The preposition, EIS, is due to Mark's use of the verb, EKBALLEIN.

7   **Luke** = / HMERAS / TESSERAKONTA //
    Matt = / HMERAS / TESSERAKONTA //
    Mark = // TESSERAKONTA / HMERAS /
    Pap Q = / HMERAS / TESSERAKONTA //
    Q = HMERAS TESSERAKONTA

Text = Mark

Con: It is difficult to explain why both Luke and Matt would "change" Mark identically at this point.

8   **Luke** = / $[EN]^5$ ${T}^5[W]^5$ ${PNEUMA}^5T[I]^5$ $/^4$ ${E}^6[N]^6$ {TH ERHM}$^6[W]^6$ $//^{4.8}$
      4:2 $^7{/}$ HMERAS ${/}^7$ TESSERAKONTA ${//}^7$ / {PEIRA[ZOMENOS] UPO
      TOU}^{9} DIABOLOU. ${KAI}^9$ / [OUK EFAGEN OUDEN]^{10}
    Matt = $//^4$ {E(IS) TH(N) ERHM(ON)}^{6} $4/$ (UPO)^5 ${T(O}^5U)^5$ {PNEUMA}$^5T(OS)^5$ $/^4$
      / {PEIRA(SQHNAI) UPO TOU}^{9}DIABOLOU.   **4:2** ${KAI}^9$ / (NHSTEUSAS)^{10}
      $^7{/}$ HMERAS ${/}^7$ TESSERAKONTA $//^{{7}.8}$
    Mark = $[(E)IS [TH]N [ERHM]ON)^6$.   **1:13a** KAI HN EN TH ERHMW $//^7$
      TESSERAKONTA ^{7}/ HMERAS $/^7$ [(PEIRA)ZOMENOS (UPO TOU)]^9 SATANA,
      $[(KAI)]^9$ HN META TWN QHRIWN,
    Pap Q = ^{4}/ [(   )]^5 ${T}^5[($ $)]^5$ {PNEUMA}$^5T[($ $)]^5$ $/^4$ ${E}^6[($ $)]^6$
      ${TH}^6($ $)^6$ {ERHM}$^6[($ $)]^6$ $//^{4.8}$ **4.2** $^7{/}$ HMERAS ${/}^7$
      TESSERAKONTA ${//}^7$ / {PEIRA[($ $)] UPO TOU}^{9} DIABOLOU
      ${KAI}^9$ / [($ $)]$^{10.11}$
    Q = ^{4}/ [(   )]^5 ${T}^5[($ $)]^5$ {PNEUMA}$^5T[($ $)]^5$ $/^4$ ${E}^6[($ $)]^6$ {TH}^{6}
      (   )^6 {ERHM}$^6[($ $)]^6$ $//^4$ {PEIRA[($ $)] UPO TOU}^{9} DIABOLOU
      4:2 ${KAI}^9$ $^7{/}$ HMERAS ${/}^7$ TESSERAKONTA ${//}^7$ // [($ $)]$^{10.11}$

Q = **Luke** ^{4}/ [EN]^5 {T}^{5}[W]^5 {PNEUMA}^{5}T[I]^5 /^{4} {E}^{6}[N]^6 {TH ERHM}^{6}[W]^6 //$^{4.8}$
4:2 ^{7}{/} HMERAS {/}^{7} TESSERAKONTA {//}^{7} / {PEIRA[ZOMENOS] UPO TOU}^{9}
DIABOLOU. {KAI}^{9} / [OUK EFAGEN OUDEN]^{10}

Con: Luke agrees with Mark and is most likely dependent upon him here.

Q = **Matt** //^{4} {E(IS) TH(N) ERHM(ON)}^{6} ^{4}/ (UPO)^5 {T(O}^{5}U)^5 {PNEUMA}^{5}T(OS)^5 /^{4} /
{PEIRA(SQHNAI) UPO TOU}^{9}DIABOLOU. **4:2** {KAI}^{9} / (NHSTEUSAS)^{10}
^{7}{/} HMERAS {/}^{7} TESSERAKONTA //$^{\{7\}.8}$

Pro: Matt need not have moved the designation, forty days, in order to build his Moses-typology **around** the designation, forty days. On the other hand, it is difficult to conceive that Matt would have been content to create (by removing the expression, forty days, from an original position between the Spirit and the devil) the parallelism which exists now in Matt 4:1, namely, that the leading up of Jesus by the Spirit equals the temptation of Jesus by the devil (see 4:1-2[4]).

Con: Schulz (178) thinks that Matt is interested here to construct a parallel with Moses and so has altered the original position of "forty days," thus causing the statement that Jesus was tested by the devil to follow directly the leading by the Spirit. (Schulz [178:13] cites Hahn, Baumbach, and Dupont as thinking similarly.)

9   **Luke** = {PEIRA[ZOMENOS] UPO TOU} DIABOLOU {KAI}
     Matt = {PEIRA(SQHNAI) UPO TOU} DIABOLOU {KAI}
     Mark = [(PEIRA)ZOMENOS UPO TOU)] SATANA [(KAI)]
     Pap Q = {PEIRA[(   )] UPO TOU} DIABOLOU {KAI}
     Q = {PEIRA(SQHNAI) UPO TOU} DIABOLOU {KAI}

Text = Mark

Pro: According to Schulz (178) the summary conclusion of the "Versuchtswerdens" of Jesus is dependent upon Mark. This applies, according to Schulz, both to Matt and to Luke.

Con: Both Matt and Luke agree that Jesus is tempted UPO TOU DIABOLOU where Mark states UPO TOU SATANA. Neither Matt nor Luke otherwise shows a particular aversion to use of the name, SATANA. Matt uses the name shortly in Matt 4:10 and in Matt 16:23 preserves the use of the name in the correlate passage in Mark (8:33). (The agreement between Matt 12:26/Mark 3:23, 26/Luke 11:18 regarding use of the name, SATANA, is unclear in its significance, given the possible use of Q here by Mark. Attested then is the real possibility of the use of the name, SATANA, otherwise in Q.) Luke uses the name, SATANA, independently in Luke 10:18; 13:16; 22:3, 31. In Mark 4:15, SATANA is used by Mark and replaced with another name by both Matt and Luke. In this case, however, neither Matt nor Luke in their respective passages substitutes the same term. Matt 13:19 has O PONHROS; Luke 8:12 has O DIABOLOS. The agreement between Matt 4:1 and Luke 4:2 in this regard is, therefore, noteworthy and warrants the supposition that UPO TOU DIABOLOU = Q.

Q = Luke {PEIRA[ZOMENOS] UPO TOU} DIABOLOU {KAI}

Con: The participle, PEIRAZOMENOS, in Luke is exactly what is found in Mark 1:13. Derivation from Mark is, thus, the most probable explanation of the participle here in Luke.

10   Luke = [OUK EFAGEN OUDEN]
     Matt = (NHSTEUSAS)
     Pap Q = [(   )]
     Q = [OUK EFAGEN OUDEN]

Text = Q

Pro: Both NHSTEUSAS and OUK EFAGEN anticipate the verb with which both Matt and Luke end this verse: EPEINASEN. He hungered; the presupposition is that he ate nothing = fasted.

Con: Exod 34:28 describes the fasting of Moses on Mt. Sinai when Moses received the law. Schulz (178) claims that the association of forty days and nights with fasting in Matt is "dependent upon a Moses-typology." Yet it is Luke who apparently makes this explicit, according to Schulz, by citing most subtly (?) the two single words, OUK EFAGEN. Schulz is not unaware of the problems here and so says that it is more than likely that neither Matt nor Luke preserves Q. The crux of the problems in Schulz at this point is the assumption by Schulz that OUK EFAGEN assumes Exod 32:28 LXX.

Q = Luke [OUK EFAGEN OUDEN]

Pro: Luke presumably preserves Q insofar as the notion that Jesus did not eat is attested by both Matt and Luke and Matt does not preserve Q.

Con: According to Schulz (179) Luke here is referring to Exod 34:28. OUK EFAGEN is an instance of the "preference of Luke for Septuagintisms."

Q = Matt (KAI NHSTEUSAS)

Con: Schulz (179) thinks that Matt is redactional here. Schulz (179:14) cites Matt 6:16-18 as evidence of "a certain interest" of the community of Matt in fasting. According to Schulz, Matt "removes" a citation from Exod 34:28 LXX at this point in favor of the technical expression, NHSTEUW.

11   Luke = [EN TAIS HMERAIS EKEINAIS KAI SUNTELESQEISWN AUTWN]
     Matt = (KAI NUKTAS TESSERAKONTA, USTERON)
     Pap Q = [(   )]
     Q = (USTERON)

Text = Q

Pro: Both Matt and Luke precede the final verb, EPEINASEN, with some expression of finality: USTERON and SUNTELESQEISWN AUTWN.

Q = Luke [EN TAIS HMERAIS EKEINAIS KAI SUNTELESQEISWN AUTWN]

Con: EN TAIS HMERAIS EKEINAIS: Schulz (179) thinks that EN TAIS HMERAIS EKEINAIS is Lukan redaction because of its relation to the designation of forty days in the first half of the verse which Schulz claims that Luke derived from Mark. It is not clear, however, that Luke derived the designation of forty days in the first half of the verse from Mark (see 4:1-2[7]). The expression, EN TAIS HMERAIS EKEINAIS, is not necessary for intelligibility, though it is helpful for clarity and, therefore, probably Lukan redaction. KAI SUNTELESQEISWN AUTWN: according to Schulz (181:55) the verb, SUNTELEIN, occurs only 6 in the entire New Testament; in addition to this use, the verb is used 1 in Luke (4:13!) and 1 in Acts.

Q = Matt (KAI NUKTAS TESSERAKONTA, USTERON)

Pro: USTERON: one might take Matt to preserve Q on the basis of rudeness; the genitive absolute in Luke is a more sophisticated construction than the adverb, USTERON, in Matt.

Con: KAI NUKTAS TESSERAKONTA: the added designation of forty nights is Matthean redaction, given the construction of a Moses-typology here on the part of Matt (see Schulz 178).

Luke 4:3 (   )[1] [2]/ EIPEN [DE][1] AUTW /[2] O [DIABOLOS][3] //[2]: EI UIOS EI TOU QEOU, EIPE [4]/ [TW][5] LIQ[W][5] [T][5]OUT[W][5] /[4] INA //[4] [6]/ GEN[H][5]TAI /[6] ARTO[S][5] //[6].

Matt 4:3 (KAI PROSELQWN)[1] //[2] O (PEIRAZWN)[3] [2]/ EIPEN [   ][1]AUTW /[2]: EI UIOS EI TOU QEOU, EIPE //[4] INA [4]/ (OI)[5] LIQ(OI)[5] OUT(OI)[5] /[4] //[6] ARTO(I)[5] [6]/ GEN(WN)[5]TAI /[6].

Pap Q 4:3 (   )[1] [2]/ EIPEN [   ][1] AUTW /[2] O [(   )][3] //[2] EI UIOS EI TOU QEOU EIPE [4]/ [(   )][5] LIQ[(   )][5] [   ][5]OUT[(   )][5] /[4] INA //[4] [6] GEN[(   )][5]TAI /[6] ARTO[(   )][5] //[6]

Q 4:3 (KAI)[1] EIPEN [1] AUTW O [DIABOLOS][3] //[2] EI UIOS EI TOU QEOU EIPE //[4] INA (OI)[5] LIQ(OI)[5] [5]OUT(OI)[5] //[6] ARTOI(I)[5] GEN(WN)[5]TAI

1   **Luke** = [DE]
     Matt = (KAI PROSELQWN)
     Pap Q = (   ) /[2] EIPEN [   ]
     Q = (KAI) /[2] EIPEN

Q = Matt (KAI PROSELQWN)

Pro: KAI: according to Schulz (179) KAI as a semiticizing conjunction is more original than DE in Luke.

Con: PROSELQWN: according to Schulz (179:17) PROSELQEIN is used redactionally ca 35 in Matt and often in precisely the construction found here: participle plus a finite verb.

2   **Luke** = /EIPEN [DE]^1 AUTW / O [DIABOLOS]^3 //
     Matt = // O (PEIRAZWN)^3 / EIPEN [   ]^1 AUTW /
     Pap Q = / EIPEN [   ]^1 AUTW / O [(   )]^3 //
     Q = EIPEN [   ]^1 AUTW O [(   )]^3

Q = Matt //O (PEIRAZWN)^3 / EIPEN [   ]^1 AUTW /

Con: The Matthean addition, PROSELQWN, at the beginning of the verse (see 4:3[1]) displaced the quotation formula, EIPEN AUTW, to the end of the phrase.

3   **Luke** = [DIABOLOS]
     Matt = (PEIRAZWN)
     Pap Q = [(   )]
     Q = [DIABOLOS]

Q = Luke [DIABOLOS]

Pro: The term, DIABOLOS, is used otherwise in the temptation accounts.

Q = Matt (PEIRAZWN)

Con: According to Schulz (179) PEIRAZWN in Matt is redactional. PEIRAZEIN is used once redactionally in Matt 22:35.

4   **Luke** = EIPE / [TW]^5 LIQ[W]^5 [T]^{5}OUT[W]^5 / INA //
     Matt = EIPE // INA / (OI)^5 LIQ(OI)^5 [   ]^{5}OUT(OI)^5 /
     Pap Q = EIPI / [(   )]^5 LIQ[(   )]^5 [   ]^{5}OUT[(   )]^5 / INA //
     Q = EIPE INA [(   )]^5 LIQ[(   )]^5 [   ]^5

Q = Luke EIPE / [TW]^5 LIQ[W]^5 [T]^{5}OUT[W]^5 / INA //

Con: The order in Luke means that the stone is addressed directly. According to Schulz (179) this direct address is "stilistisch gewandter" than the construction in Matt and, therefore, secondary. There does seem to be a certain heightening or focusing of the first temptation in Luke. The temptation in Luke is not only to change a stone into bread in the way that John 2 has Jesus change water into wine but, by virtue of the direct address in Luke, to prove a certain cosmic status after the fashion of Mark 4:41 where the disciples ask following the calming of a storm: "Who then is the man, because both the wind and the sea obey him?"

5   **Luke** = [TW] LIQ[W] [T]OUT[W] GEN[H]TAI ARTO[S]
     Matt = (OI) LIQ(OI) OUT(OI) GEN(WN)TAI ARTO(I)
     Pap Q = [(   )] LIQ[(   )] [   ]OUT[(   )] GEN[(   )]TAI ARTO[(   )]
     Q = (OI) LIQ(OI) OUT(OI) GEN(WN)TAI ARTO(I)

Q = Luke [TW] LIQ[W] [T]OUT[W] GEN[H]TAI ARTO[S]

Con: The single stone in Luke is due to the direct address which is Lukan redaction (see 4:3[4]). The singularity of the stone compares to the singularity of the wind and sea in Mark 4:41 where the issue is likewise one of the obedience of the elemental forces to Jesus. Schulz (179) agrees "possibly," citing (179:20) Harnack.

Q = Matt (OI) LIQ(OI) OUT(OI) GEN(WN)TAI ARTO(I)

Con: According to Schulz (179:20) this is the opinion of Spitta, Albertz, Schmid.

6   **Luke** = // GEN[H]^{5}TAI / ARTO[S]^5 /
     Matt = ARTO(I)^5 / GEN(WN)^{5}TAI //
     Pap Q = // GEN[(   )]^{5}TAI / ARTO[(   )]^5 /
     Q = ARTO[(   )]^5 GEN[(   )]^{5}TAI

Q = Matt / ARTO(I)^5 / GEN(WN)^{5}TAI //

Pro: The order originally in Q here is determined by faithfulness otherwise in the preservation of the saying per se. Matt is the evangelist most faithful here (see 4:3[4,5]).

Luke 4:4 //^{3} [KAI]^1 AP[E]^{2}KRIQ[H PROS AUTON]^2 ^{3}/ O [IHSOUS]^4 /^{3}: GEGRAPTAI [OTI]^5 OUK EP' ARTW MONW ZHSETAI O ANQRWPOS (   )^6

Matt 4:4 ^{3}/ O [   ]^4 /^{3} (DE)^1 AP(O)^{2}KRIQ(EIS EIPEN)^2 //^{3}: GEGRAPTAI (   )^5: OUK EP' ARTW MONW ZHSETAI O ANQRWPOS, (ALL' EPI PANTI RHMATI EKPOREUOMENW DIA STOMATOS QEOU)^6.

Pap Q 4:4 //^{3} [(   )]^1 AP[(   )]^{2}KRIQ[(   )]^2 ^{3}/ O [   ]^4 /^{3} GEGRAPTAI [   ]^5 OUK EP' ARTW MONW ZHSETAI O ANQRWPOS (   )^6

Q 4:4 ^{3} [KAI]^1 AP(O)^{2}KRIQ(EIS EIPEN)^2 O [IHSOUS]^4 GEGRAPTAI ^{5} OUK EP' ARTW MONW ZHSETAI O ANQRWPOS^6

1   **Luke** = [KAI]
     Matt = (DE)

Pap Q = $//^3$ [( )] AP[( )]^{2}KRIQ[( )]^2
Q = $//^3$ [KAI] AP[( )]^{2}KRIQ[( )]^2

Q = **Luke** [KAI]

Pro: The situation is the reverse of 4:3[1]. The criterion of decision remains the same, however, according to Schulz (179). The semiticizing KAI = Q.

2   **Luke** = AP[E]KRIQ[H PROS AUTON]
     Matt = AP(O)KRIQ(EIS EIPEN)
     Pap Q = AP[( )]KRIQ[( )]
     Q = AP(O)KRIQ(EIS EIPEN)

Q = **Luke** AP[E]KRIQ[H PROS AUTON]

Con: The preposition, PROS, together with the verb, APOKRIQHNAI, is used redactionally 1 in Luke and 3 in Acts, according to Schulz (179:21).

Q = **Matt** AP(O)KRIQ(EIS EIPEN)

Pro: The combination, APOKRIQEIS EIPEN, occurs 1 unambiguously in Q (Luke 7:22//Matt 11:4). The same combination appears also shortly in Luke 4:8, 12.

3   **Luke** = // [KAI]^1 AP[E]^{2}KRIQ[H PROS AUTON]^2 / O [IHSOUS]^4 /
     Matt = / O [ ]^4 / (DE)^1 AP(O)^{2}KRIQ(EIS EIPEN)^2 //
     Pap Q = // [( )]^1 AP[( )]^{2}KRIQ[( )]^2 / O [ ]^4 //
     Q = [( )]^1 AP[( )]^{2}KRIQ[( )]^2 O [( )]^4

Q = **Luke** // [KAI]^1 AP[E]^{2}KRIQ[H PROS AUTON]^2 / O [IHSOUS]^4 /

Pro: No reason can be given why Luke would displace O IHSOUS to the end of the quotation formula. Luke 4:8 betrays a lack of necessity on the part of Luke to put the personal name, Jesus, at the end of the quotation formula here.

Q = **Matt** / O [ ]^4 / (DE)^1 AP(O)^2 KRIQ(EIS EIPEN)^2 //

Pro: Conceivably, O IHSOUS began the sentence in Q after KAI. This is attested by the initial definite article, O, in Matt, which stands now in the first position rather than in the second position due to the postpositive particle, DE, used by Matt in place of both KAI and IHSOUS.

Con: The location of the definite article in Matt depends upon the use of the postpositive particle, DE, and the non-use of the name, Jesus, in Matt. Insofar as DE is Matthean redaction (see 4:4[1]) alterations in order dependent upon the particle seem likewise to be the handiwork of Matt. Similarly, if Q originally had the name, Jesus, as Luke has it, the definite article would not begin the sentence, as Matt has it, but immediately precede

the name, as in Luke. If Matt has excised the name, Jesus, from the quotation formula
(see 4:4[5]) grammatically speaking he must remove the definite article to the front of
the sentence in order to signify together with the redactional particle, DE, the changed
speaker in the conversation.

4   **Luke** = [IHSOUS]
     Matt = [   ]
     Pap Q = [   ]
     Q = [IHSOUS]

Q = Luke [IHSOUS]

Pro: No reason can be given why Luke would add the name, Jesus, here when the same
name is missing in the similar quotation formula in Luke 7:22. The originality of the
name, Jesus, here in Q depends upon the utter impossibility of the definite article
otherwise here in Luke. The definite article is shared with Matt and so attested to be Q.
Schulz (179) thinks that the name, Jesus, is "primary." He notes (179:23) that the name
occurs in the other two similar quotation formulae in the narrative of the temptations:
Matt 4:7, 10 par.

Q = Matt [   ]

Pro: No obvious reason can be given why Matt would excise the name, Jesus, here when
the same name is included in the similar quotation formula in Matt 11:4.

Con: Matt may have excised the name, Jesus, in the interests of brevity, sharpening the
antithetical character of the exchange, permitted to do so by his replacement of the
narrative conjunction, KAI, with the adversative particle, DE.

5   **Luke** = [OTI]
     Matt = [   ]
     Pap Q = [   ]
     Q = omit

Q = Luke [OTI]

Con: Schulz (179) following Harnack (179:24) thinks that OTI is Lukan redaction "for
clarification."

Q = Matt [   ]

Pro: The absence of the conjunction is lectio difficilior.

6   **Luke** = (   )
     Matt = (ALL' EPI PANTI RHMATI EKPOREUOMENW DIA STOMATOS QEOU)

Pap Q = (   )
Q = omit

Q = Matt (ALL' EPI PANTI RHMATI EKPOREUOMENW DIA STOMATOS QEOU)

Pro: Rabbinic practice does not require full citation of the verse in view. That Matt cites the full verse is, therefore, not necessarily attributable to him.

Con: Schulz (179) following Harnack, Spitta, Schnackenburg (179:25) thinks that Matt here is redactional. Matthean interest in the literal fulfillment of earlier scripture motivates the full quotation.

Luke 4:5 [KAI ANAGAGWN]^1 AUTON (   )^1 [E]^{2}DEI[CE]^{2}N AUTW PASAS TAS BASILEIAS T[HS OIKOUMENHS EN STIGMH XRONOU]^3

Matt 4:8 (PALIN PARALAMBANEI)^1 AUTON (O DIABOLOS EIS OROS UYHLON LIAN KAI)^1 [   ]^{2}DEI(KNUSI)^{2}N AUTW PASAS TAS BASILEIAS T(OU KOSMOU KAI THN DOCAN AUTWN)^3

Pap Q 4:5 [(   )]^1 AUTON (   )^1 [   ]^{2}DEI[(   )]^{2}N AUTW PASAS TAS BASILEIAS T[(   )]^3

Q 4:5 [KAI]^1 (PARALAMBANEI)^1 AUTON (O DIABOLOS EIS OROS KAI)^1 ^{2}DEI(KNUSI)^{2}N AUTW PASAS TAS BASILEIAS T(OU KOSMOU KAI THN DOCAN AUTWN)^3

1   **Luke** = [KAI ANAGAGWN] AUTON (   )
     Matt = (PALIN PARALAMBANEI)^1 AUTON (O DIABOLOS EIS OROS UYHLON LIAN KAI)^1
     Pap Q = [(   )] AUTON (   )
     Q = [KAI]^1 (PARALAMBANEI)^1 AUTON (O DIABOLOS EIS OROS KAI)

Q = Luke [KAI ANAGAGWN] AUTON (   )

Pro: KAI: Schulz (180) thinks that KAI = Q. The situation here is repeated in Luke 4:9/Matt 4:5. In both instances Matt has PARALAMBANEIN; Luke has ANAGEIN and AGEIN. The woodenness of the repetition in Matt suggests redactional correction.

Con: According to Schulz (180) PARALAMBANEIN is "für Mt nicht typisch." The wooden composition in Matt (= Q) has been improved by the simple and compound verbs in Luke. According to Schulz (180:38) ANAGEIN is used redactionally 1 in Luke and 17 in Acts. The isolated use of the verb, ANAGEIN, here is peculiar. In Luke, the devil has simply led Jesus up . . . Luke uses the participle, ANAGAGWN, presumably in remembrance of the phrase (minimally) in Q: PARALAMBANEI EIS OROS. (The participle is, thus, a king of "Reminiszenz" but not recalling 4:1[4] as Schürmann states according to Schulz [180:36].) Luke has deleted explicit reference to a mountain in favor of the temporal phrase, EN STIGMH XRONOU (so Schulz [180]; see 4:5[3]). The setting of the mountain which functions as the physical presupposition of this temptation in Matt (= Q) is deleted for the more metphysical (and, thus, cosmically or historically weightier) temptation which Luke describes.

Also it may be, according to Schulz (180), that the functions otherwise characteristic of mountains in Luke—prayer and epiphany (see 4:1 [4])—do not welcome a mountain here as the place of temptation.

Q = Matt (PALIN PARALAMBANEI) AUTON (O DIABOLOS EIS OROS UYHLON LIAN KAI)

Pro: O DIABOLOS: Luke lacks the personal subject here but has it in the immediately subsequent verse where Matt lacks it (see 4:6[1]). Presumably, Luke has deleted O DIABO-LOS here together with the rest of the phrase which Matt alone preserves. Luke 4:5 par introduces a change in the speaking subject, however, and so Luke is required in the subsequent verse to state explicitly what is here deleted. (Schulz [180] reaches the same conclusion; however, the grounds are different: "Das Fehlen des DIABOLOS bei Lk könnte durch die Umstellungen der Versuchungen bedingt sein.") UYHLON: Schulz (180) thinks that this was in Q. KAI: the conjunction at the end of the phrase is necessary, given that the finite verb, PARALAMBANEI, is Q (see above, **Q = Luke Con**). Luke has removed the con-junction by virtue of his election of the participle, ANAGAGWN. According to Schulz (180) the "semitisierende Parataxe bei Mt ist sicher ursprünglicher als die hypotaktische Kon-struktion bei Lk."

Con: PALIN: the adverb here seems to be editorial intensification. UYHLON LIAN: there is no way to conclude whether or not the mountain in Q was either "high" or "very high." If one sees **all** the kingdoms of the world from the mountain, the mountain would be understandably "high" or, just as understandably, "very high." Just as easily, in Q the mountain may have been simply "a mountain" which subsequently was elevated by Matt to a "very high mountain," presumably in the interests of accentuation and plausability.

2 **Luke** = [E]DEI[CE]N
   Matt = [   ]DEI(KNUSI)N
   Pap Q = [   ]DEI[(   )]N
   Q = DEI(KNUSI)N

Q = Luke [E]DEI[CE]N

Pro: Schulz (180) thinks that Matt has replaced the aorist tense of the verb with the historical present.

Q = Matt [   ]DEI(KNUSI)N

Pro: No reason can be given why Matt would replace the aorist tense of the verb with the historical present. Luke, on the other hand, might replace the historical present with the aorist tense as the proper or less rude tense in which to narrate a history. PARALAMBA-NEI (see 4:5[1]) at the beginning of the verse is an historical present.

3 **Luke** = T[HS OIKOUMENHS EN STIGMH XRONOU]
   Matt = T(OU KOSMOU KAI THN DOCAN AUTWN)

Pap Q = T[(   )]
Q = T(OU KOSMOU KAI THN DOCAN AUTWN)

Q = Luke T[HS OIKOUMENHS EN STIGMH XRONOU]

Con: OIKOUMENH is the more refined and typically Greek word for"world." It also appears to be a clarification or reduction for the sake of plausability on the part of Luke insofar as OIKOUMENH makes better political and geographical sense over against "all the kingdoms" than does the rather excessive KOSMOS in Matt. EN STIGMH XRONOU: according to Schulz (180) the phrase is Lukan redaction because "XRONOS ist gut lk." XRONOS is used redactionally ca 3 in Luke and 17 in Acts (Schulz 180:42; Baumbach is cited here as thinking similarly).

Q = Matt T(OU KOSMOU KAI THN DOCAN AUTWN)

Pro: The phrase, KAI THN DOCAN AUTWN, absent here in Luke, appears per se (as a "Reminiszenz") in the immediately subsequent verse (Luke 4:6) where the phrase is absent in Matt (4:9a). Luke excised the phrase in Luke 4:5 as he is responsible otherwise in this verse for radical edition. EN STIGMH XRONOU in Luke displaces the second member of the hendiadys in Q. Further evidence noted by Schulz following Schnackenburg (181:47) that the phrase, KAI THN DOCAN AUTWN, belongs here in Q as Matt has it is the lack of a "Beziehungswort" for the plural personal pronoun, AUTWN, in Luke 4:6. Referring originally in Q to "all the kingdoms," the plural personal pronoun now lacks any antecedent in Luke 4:6, "ein Anzeichen dass Lk eine schriftstellerische Vorlage unachtsam umgearbeitet hat."

Luke 4:6 KAI EIPEN AUTW [O DIABOLOS][1]: [2]/ SOI /[2] [3]/ DWSW /[3] [THN ECOUSIAN][4] TAUT[HN][4] //[2] [A][5]PA[S][4]A[N][4] //[3] [KAI THN DOCAN AUTWN, OTI EMOI PARADEDOTAI KAI W EAN QELW DIDWMI AUTHN][6]:

Matt 4:9a KAI EIPEN AUTW [   ][1]: //[2] //[3] [   ][4] TAUT(A)[4] [2]/ SOI /[2] [   ][5]PA(NT)[4]A[   ][4] [3]/ DWSW /[3] [   ][6]

Pap Q 4:6 KAI EIPEN AUTW [   ][1] [2]/ SOI /[2] [3]/ DWSW /[3] [   ][4] TAUT[(   )][4] //[2] [   ][5]PA[(   )][4]A[   ][4] //[3] [   ][6]

Q 4:6 KAI EIPEN AUTW [O DIABOLOS][1] //[2] //[3] [4] TAUT(A)[4] SOI [5]PA(NT)[4]A[4] DWSW [6]

1   **Luke** = [O DIABOLOS]
     Matt = [   ]
     Pap Q = [   ]
     Q = omit

Q = Matt [   ]

Pro: Luke has displaced O DIABOLOS here from the preceding verse (see 4:5[1]).

2   **Luke** = / SOI / ^{3}/ DWSW /^{3} [THN ECOUSIAN]^4 TAUT[HN]^4 //
     [   ]^{5}PA[(   )]^{4}A[   ]^4 //^{3}

Matt = // //^{3} [   ]^4 TAUT(A)^4 / SOI / [   ]^{5}PA(NT)^{4}A[   ]^4 ^{3}/ DWSW /^{3}

Pap Q = / SOI / ^{3}/ DWSW /^{3} [   ]^4 TAUT[(   )]^4 //[   ]^{5}PA[(   )]^{4}A[   ]^4
     //^{3}

Q = //^{3} [   ]^4 TAUT[(   )]^4 SOI [   ]^{5}PA[(   )]^{4}A[   ]^4 ^{3}/ DWSW /^{3}

Q = Matt // //^{3} [   ]^4 TAUT(A)^4 / SOI / [   ]^{5}PA(NT)^{4}A[   ]^4 ^{3}/ DWSW /^{3}

Pro: The order of SOI previous to DWSW is mutually attested in Matt and Luke. The question here is whether or not part of the direct object of the verb precedes SOI as in Matt or follows the entire construction as in Luke. The evangelist whose direct object = Q presumably preserves the word order of Q here as well (see 4:6[4]). Luke has moved everything functioning as the direct object of the verb behind DWSW due to the considerable expansion of the number of words which now constitute the direct object in his sentence.

3   **Luke** = ^{2}/ SOI /^{2} / DWSW / [THN ECOUSIAN]^4 TAUT[HN]^4 //^{2}
     [   ]^{5}PA[(   )]^{4}A[   ]^4

Matt = //^{2} // [   ]^4 TAUT(A)^4 ^{2}/ SOI /^{2} [   ]^{5}PA(NT)^{4}A[   ]^4 / DWSW /

Pap Q = ^{2}/ SOI /^{2} / DWSW / [   ]^4 TAUT[(   )]^4 //^{2} [   ]^{5}PA[(   )]^{4}A[   ]^4
     //

Q = //^{2} [   ]^4 TAUT[(   )]^4 ^{2}/ SOI /^{2} [   ]^{5}PA[(   )]^{4}A[   ]^4 DWSW

Q = Matt //^{2} // [   ]^4 TAUT(A)^4 ^{2}/ SOI /^{2} [   ]^{5}PA(NT)^{4}A[   ]^4 / DWSW /

Pro: The situation is essentially the same as 4:6[2]. Luke has moved DWSW from its original position in Q at the end of the sentnece as Matt has it due to the additional direct object, KAI THN DOCAN AUTWN, inserted into Q at this point by Luke (see 4:5[3]).

4   **Luke** = [THN ECOUSIAN] TAUT[HN] [A]^{5}PA[S]A[N]

Matt = [   ] TAUT(A) [   ]^{5}PA(NT)A[   ]

Pap Q = [   ] TAUT[(   )] [   ]PA[(   )]A[   ]

Q = TAUT(A) [   ]^{5}PA(NT)

Q = Luke [THN ECOUSIAN] TAUT[HN] [A]^{5}PA[S]A[N]

Con: According to Schulz (180f.) ECOUSIA is used redactionally 1 in Luke and 7 in Acts. Luke has added THN ECOUSIAN here perhaps as specification regarding "all the kingdoms of the world" and certainly in keeping with the words, KAI THN DOCAN AUTWN, which he appends immediately (see 4:5[3], 4:6[5]). As such, THN ECOUSIAN is an anticipatory interpretation of "their glory"; i.e., "their glory" is precisely political power. The singular form of the word and subsequent singularization of OUTOS and PAS is likewise an anticipatory assimilation to the singular form of DOCAN.

5   **Luke** = [A]PA[S]^{4}A[N]^4
     Matt = [   ]PA(NT)^{4}A[   ]^4
     Pap Q = [   ]PA[(   )]^{4}A[   ]^4
     Q = PA[(   )]^{4}A[   ]^4

Q = **Luke** [A]PA[S]^{4}A[N]^4

Con: According to Schulz (181) "APAS is ausgesprochen lk." The word is used redactionally ca 8 in Luke and 10 in Acts (Schulz 181:45).

6   **Luke** = [KAI THN ECOUSIAN AUTWN, OTI EMOI PARADEDOTAI KAI W EAN QELO DIDWMI
              AUTHN]
     Matt = [   ]
     Pap Q = [   ]
     Q = omit

Q = **Luke** [KAI THN ECOUSIAN AUTWN, OTI EMOI PARADEDOTAI KAI W EAN QELW DIDWMI
             AUTHN]

Pro: The possibility of the occurrence of such a Johannine-sounding phrase in Q is attested in Luke 10:22 par where virtually the same meaning is expressed.

Con: KAI THN ECOUSIAN AUTWN: see 4:5[3]. OTI EMOI PARADEDOTAI KAI W EAN QELW DIDWMI AUTHN: there is no hint of any such clause in Q at this point in Matt. Luke has presumably expanded Q at this point on the model of what he read elsewhere in Q.

Luke 4:7 [SU OUN]^1 EAN (   )^2 PROSKUNHSHS [ENWPION]^3 [E]^{4}MO[U]^3, [ESTAI SOU PASA]^5.

Matt 4:9b [   ]^1 EAN (PESWN)^2 PROSKUNHSHS [   ]^3 [   ]^{4}MO(I)^3 [   ]^5.

Pap Q 4:7 [   ]^1 EAN (   )^2 PROSKUNHSHS [   ]^3 [   ]^{4}MO[(   )]^3 [   ]^5

Q 4:7 ^{1} EAN ^{2} PROSKUNHSES ^{3} ^{4}MO(I)^3 ^{5}

1   **Luke** = [SU OUN]
     Matt = [   ]
     Pap Q = [   ]
     Q = omit

Q = **Luke** [SU OUN]

Con: SU: the personal pronoun here is unnecessary emphasis and so likely Lukan redaction. OUN: the logical particle both sharpens the process of reasoning which constitutes the temptation of Jesus and is helpful here in Luke syntactically to renew the original line of reasoning in Q which Luke has interrupted with his expansion of Luke 4:6[4,6].

2   **Luke** = (   )
    Matt = (PESWN)
    Pap Q = (   )
    Q = omit

Q = Matt (PESWN)

Con: According to Schulz (181) Matt has an especial fondness for this verb. The verb is used "traditionally" ca 14 and redactionally ca 4; it is used together with the verb, PROSKUNEIN, in Matt 2:11 and 18:26 (Schulz 181:48; Harnack, Albertz, Schnackenburg are cited here as thinking similarly). The verb is somewhat redundant vis-a-vis PROSKUNEIN.

3   **Luke** = [ENWPION] [E]^{4}MO[U]
    Matt = [   ] [   ]^{4}MO(I)
    Pap Q = [   ] [   ] ^{4}MO[(   )]
    Q = [   ]^{4}MO(I)

Q = Luke [ENWPION] [E]^{4}MO[U]

Con: According to Schulz (181) ENWPION is a Luka "Vorzugswort." It is used redactionally ca 5 in Luke and 13 in Acts (Schulz 181:46). The preposition is somewhat redundant here vis-a-vis PROSKUNEIN. Can one do obeisance behind or beside the object of obeisance?

4   **Luke** = [E]MO[   ]^3
    Matt = [   ]MO(   )^3
    Pap Q = [   ]MO[(   )]^3
    Q = MO[(   )]^3

Q = Luke [E]MO[(   )]^3

Con: The emphatic form of the personal pronoun is here due to the intrusion of the preposition, ENWPION, between the personal pronoun and the verb (see 4:7[3]) which places an emphasis now upon the personal pronoun as the object of the preposition. Matt otherwise shows no aversion to the emphatic form of the pronoun.

5   **Luke** = [ESTAI SOU PASA]
    Matt = [   ]
    Pap Q = [   ]
    Q = omit

Q = Luke [ESTAI SOU PASA]

Pro: According to Schulz (180:43) Schürmann thinks that Luke is not redactional here.

Con: According to Schulz (180) the sentence is due to the secondary expansion of Luke 4:6f. by Luke. Albertz and Baumbach apparently agree (Schulz 180:43). Like the logical particle, OUN (see 4:7[1]), the sentence is needed here in Luke to renew the chain of thought interrupted by the expansion of Luke 4:6. Together with SOI DWSW which Luke received from Q but removed to the beginning of the direct statement in Luke 4:6 (see 4:6[2,3]), the sentence here forms a bracket around the new material which constitutes the Lukan expansion of Luke 4:6.

Luke 4:8 [KAI APOKRIQEIS][1] [2]/ O IHSOUS /[2] [EIP][3]E[N][3] AUTW //[2]: (   )[4]
GEGRAPTAI (   )[5]: KURION TON QEON SOU PROSKUNHSEIS KAI AUTW MONW LATREUSEIS.

Matt 4:10 (TOTE)[1] //[2] (LEG)[3]E(I)[3] AUTW [2]/ O IHSOUS /[2]: (UPAGE, SATANA)[4]:
GEGRAPTAI (GAR)[5]: KURION TON QEON SOU PROSKUNHSEIS KAI AUTW MONW LATREUSEIS.

Pap Q 4:8 [(   )][1] [2]/ O IHSOUS /[2] [(   )][3]E[(   )][3] AUTW //[2] (   )[4] GEGRAPTAI
(   )[5] KURION TON QEON SOU PROSKUNHSEIS KAI AUTW MONW LATREUSEIS

Q 4:8 [KAI APOKRIQEIS][1] O IHSOUS [EIP][3]E[N][3] AUTW //[2] [4] GEGRAPTAI [5] KURION
TON QEON SOU PROSKUNHSEIS KAI AUTW MONW LATREUSEIS

1   Luke = [KAI APOKRIQEIS]
     Matt = (TOTE)
     Pap Q = [(   )]
     Q = [KAI APOKRIQEIS]

Q = Luke [KAI APOKRIQEIS]

Pro: KAI APOKRIQEIS = Q in Luke 4:4[1,2].

Q = Matt (TOTE)

Con: Schulz (181) is "sure" that TOTE is Matthean redaction.

2   Luke = / O IHSOUS / [EIP][3]E[N][3] AUTW //
     Matt = // (LEG)[3]E(I)[3] AUTW / O IHSOUS /
     Pap Q = / O IHSOUS / [(   )][3]E[(   )][3] AUTW //
     Q = O IHSOUS [(   )][3]E[(   )][3] AUTW

Q = Luke / O IHSOUS / [EIP][3]E[N][3] AUTW //

Pro: The faithfulness of the evangelist otherwise in the preservation of the quotation formula here determines whose order is to be assumed as Q. Luke is in this instance the most faithful (see 4:8[1,3]). This is the order in which the name, Jesus, occurs in Matt 11:4 whose quotation formula otherwise parallels exactly Luke 7:22 (the name, Jesus, does not appear in the quotation formula in Luke 7:22).

3   **Luke** = [EIP]E[N]
     Matt = (LEG)E(I)
     Pap Q = [(   )]E[(   )]
     Q = [EIP]E[N]

Q = **Luke** [EIP]E[N]

Pro: EIPEN = Q here on the basis of the use of this word in the same construction elsewhere in Q (see 4:4[2], 4:12[1]).

Q = **Matt** (LEG)E(I)

Con: Matt has changed the verb here on the basis of 4:9[5].

4   **Luke** = (   )
     Matt = (UPAGE, SATANA)
     Pap Q = (   )
     Q = omit

Q = **Matt** (UPAGE, SATANA)

Pro: According to Schulz (181) UPAGE SATANA is "sprachlich nicht mt." Schulz assumes that Matt preserves the order of the temptations originally in Q and supposes, therefore, that Luke has striken the injunction here because "die Aufforderung zur Teufelsanbetung nicht mehr den Höhepunkt darstellt."

Con: If it is Matt who has rearranged the order of the temptations originally in Q, then Matt has added the injunction here precisely because Matt has made this incident the climax of the temptations. The climactic response of Jesus in Luke (4:12) shows no reminiscence of any such corresponding injunction. The matthean addition, GAR (see 4:8[5]), postulated by Schulz (181) makes sense if one assumes Matthean redaction here. What was originally in Q Jesus' actual reply, as Luke has it, becomes in Matt the **ground** for the actual reply in Matt. UPAGE SATANA is Jesus' reply in Matt; what is written (GEGRAPTAI) is the reason for this reply rather than the reply itself as in Luke.

5   **Luke** = (   )
     Matt = (GAR)
     Pap Q = (   )
     Q = omit

Q = Luke (   )

Pro: Schulz (181) following Schnackenburg (181:52) supposes that Luke here = Q. Luke earlier (4:4[5]) was held responsible for adding OTI at this point in the sentence.

Q = Matt (GAR)

Con: Insofar as UPAGE SATANA is Matthean redaction on other grounds, the insertion of the injunction by Matt is then motivation for the insertion of GAR here by Matt.

Luke 4:9 [HGAGEN DE][1] AUTON (   )[2] EIS [IEROUSALHM][3] KAI ESTHSEN (   )[4] EPI TO PTERUGION TOU IEROU KAI [EIP][5]E[N][5] AUTW: EI UIOS EI TOU QEOU, BALE SEAUTON [ENTEUQEN][6] KATW:

Matt 4:5-6a (TOTE PARALAMBANEI)[1] AUTON (O DIABOLOS)[2] EIS (THN AGIAN POLIN)[3] KAI ESTHSEN (AUTON)[4] EPI TO PTERUGION TOU IEROU **4:6a** KAI (LEG)[5]E(I)[5] AUTW: EI UIOS EI TOU QEOU, BALE SEAUTON [   ][6] KATW:

Pap Q 4:9 [(   )][1] AUTON (   )[2] EIS [(   )][3] KAI ESTHSEN (   )[4] EPI TO PTERUGION TOU IEROU KAI [(   )][5]E[(   )][5] AUTW: EI UIOS EI TOU QEOU BALE SEAUTON [   ][6] KATW

Q 4:9 (PARALAMBANEI)[1] AUTON [2] EIS [IEROUSALHM][3] KAI ESTHSEN (AUTON)[4] EPI TO PTERUGION TOU IEROU KAI (LEG)[5]E(I)[5] AUTW: EI UIOS EI TOU QEOU BALE SEAUTON [6] KATW

1   **Luke** = [HGAGEN DE]
     Matt = (TOTE PARALAMBANEI)
     Pap Q = [(   )]
     Q = (PARALAMBANEI)

Q = Luke [HGAGEN DE]

Pro: HGAGEN: according to Schulz (179) Luke is responsible for the verb, AGEIN, here but preserves the tense of the verb in Q. The assumption is, apparently, that the historical present does not occur in Q. DE: according to Schulz (180) TOTE = Q and thinks, following Harnack and Schmid (180:32), that, therefore, DE = Q.

Con: HGAGEN: according to Schulz (179) Luke is responsible for the verb, AGEIN. Regarding the tense of the verb, Schulz (179:29) himself notes that Harnack "meint allerdings, dass Lk das Praesens historicum meide." Luke may do this here to mirror the tense of the aorist verb, ESTHSEN, shortly following and attested to be Q in both Matt and Luke. DE: the adversative particle is redactional in 4:3[1], 4:4[1]. The appearance of the particle here may be linked to the subsequent non-appearance of the subject, O DIABOLOS, in Luke (4:9[2]). DE assumes the change in subject otherwise not expressed in Luke 4:9. Perhaps KAI was the first word of this sentence in Q as in 4:5[1].

Q = Matt (TOTE PARALAMBANEI)

Pro: PARALAMBANEI: it was decided in the similar situation in 4:5[1] that PARALAMBANEI = Q.

Con: TOTE: according to Schulz (180) TOTE = Q.

2   **Luke** = (   )
     Matt = (O DIABOLOS)
     Pap Q = (   )
     Q = omit

Q = Luke (   )

Pro: Luke was held responsible for excising O DIABOLOS from the similar quotation formula in Luke 4:5[1]. In the subsequent quotation formula in Luke 4:6[1], however, the excision is then recalled. There is no recollection of a possible excision here by Luke in the subsequent quotation formula. O DIABOLOS is not unneeded here (i.e., redundant). Whereas AUTON in 4:9[4] is an actual redundancy of the same word in the first half of the sentence, O DIABOLOS is here otherwise only implicitly supplied. The explicit denomination in Matt is not semitic repetition but rhetorical clarity. It is for this reason that it is more likely that Matt has added the name here than that Luke removed it. Luke dealt with the lack of clarity by using the adversative particle, DE, in place of an original (?) KAI (see 4:9[1]).

Con: According to Schulz (179) Luke has excised O DIABOLOS here because he expressly used the noun in Luke 4:3, 6. Just as Luke excised the "semitisierende Wiederholung" or AUTON in 4:9[4], according to Schulz (180), so similarly, perhaps, O DIABOLOS was excised as redundant.

Q = Matt (O DIABOLOS)

Con: It would be most consistent if here Q originally had O DIABOLOS for the third time in the introduction to the third temptation. It is for this reason that one might assume that Matt has added the name here. Matt here may be mindful of his excision of DIABOLOS in favor of PEIRAZWN in 4:3[4].

3   **Luke** = [IEROUSALHM]
     Matt = (THN AGIAN POLIN)
     Pap Q = [(   )]
     Q = [IEROUSALHM]

Q = Matt (THN AGIAN POLIN)

Con: According to Schulz (179f.) only Matt uses the description, "the holy city," for Jerusalem.

4   **Luke** = (   )
     Matt = (AUTON)
     Pap Q = (   )
     Q = (AUTON)

Q = Luke (   )

Con: According to Schulz (180) Luke has removed the characteristically semitic repetition of the direct object, presumably in the interests of a tighter style.

5   **Luke** = [EIP]E[N]
     Matt = (LEG)E(I)
     Pap Q = [(   )]E[(   )]
     Q = (LEG)E(I)

Q = Luke [EIP]E[N]

Pro: In 4:8[3] the decision was EIPEN = Q.

Q = Matt (LEG)E(I)

Pro: The decision in 4:8[3] that EIPEN = Q rested upon the appearance of the formulaic combination, APOKRIQEIS EIPEN, elsewhere in Q. The situation is different here. The decision in favor of the historical present, PARALAMBANEI, as Q in 4:9[1] makes plausible here the similarly historical present, LEGEI, as Q. It was the present tense of the verb here, perhaps, which was the model for Matt's alteration of the verb in 4:8[3].

6   **Luke** = [ENTEUQEN]
     Matt = [   ]
     Pap Q = [   ]
     Q = omit

Q = Luke [ENTEUQEN]

Con: Schulz (180) following Harnack and Schnackenburg (180:31) thinks that ENTEUQEN = Luke. The adverb here is unnecessary and added for the sake of a certain symmetry.

Luke 4:10 GEGRAPTAI GAR OTI TOIS AGGELOIS AUTOU ENTELEITAI PERI SOU [TOU DIAFULACAE SE][1]

Matt 4:6b GEGRAPTAI GAR OTI TOIS AGGELOIS AUTOU ENTELEITAI PERI SOU [   ][1]

Pap Q 4:10 GEGRAPTAI GAR OTI TOIS AGGELOIS AUTOU ENTELEITAI PERI SOU [   ][1]

Q 4:10 GEGRAPTAI GAR OTI TOIS AGGELOIS AUTOU ENTELEITAI PERI SOU [1]

1   **Luke** = [TOU DIAFULACAI SE]
     Matt = [   ]
     Pap Q = [   ]
     Q = omit

Q = Luke [TOU DIAFULACAI SE]

Con: Schulz (180) following Spitta and Harnack (180:35) thinks that Luke is redactional
here. Harnack noted rightly that the Lukan addition is exactly the subsequent three
words of Psalm 91:11 LXX. Luke is doing here essentially what Matt did in 4:4[6].

Luke 4:11 KAI [OTI][1] EPI XEIRWN AROUSIN SE, MHPOTE PROSKOYHS PROS LIQON TON
PODA SOU.

Matt 4:6c KAI [   ][1] EPI XEIRWN AROUSIN SE, MHPOTE PROSKOYHS PROS LIQON TON
PODA SOU.

Pap Q 4:11 KAI [   ][1] EPI XEIRWN AROUSIN SE MHPOTE PROSKOYHS PROS LIQON TON
PODA SOU.

Q 4:11 KAI [1] EPI XEIRWN AROUSIN SE MHPOTE PROSKOYHS PROS LIQON TON PODA SOU.

1   **Luke** = [OTI]
     Matt = [   ]
     Pap Q = [   ]
     Q = omit

Q = Luke [OTI]

Con: According to Schulz (180) following Harnack and Schnackenburg (180:34) OTI =
Luke. Given Luke's immediately preceding expansion of the Old Testament quotation in Q
(4:10[1]) in terms of the LXX, this non-Septuagintal expansion is perhaps a bit surprising.
However, the conjunction, KAI, at the beginning of the sentence in both Matt and Luke is
also not in the LXX. Luke has added OTI, accentuating the separation of the two verses
already begun in Q by the use of the conjunction, KAI, at the beginning of the sentence.
OTI functions here as a second set of quotation marks otherwise lacking in Q.

Luke 4:12 [KAI APOKRIQEIS EIPEN][1] AUTW O IHSOUS [OTI EIRH][2]TAI: OUK
EKPEIRASEIS KURION TON QEON SOU.

Matt 4:7 (EFH)[1] AUTW O IHSOUS: (PALIN GEGRAP)[2]TAI: OUK EKPEIRASEIS KURION TON
QEON SOU.

Pap Q 4:12 [(   )][1] AUTW O IHSOUS [(   )][2]TAI OUK EKPEIRASEIS KURION TON QEON
SOU.

Q 4:12 [KAI APOKRIQEIS EIPEN]¹ AUTW O IHSOUS (GEGRAP)²TAI OUK EKPEIRASEIS
KURION TON QEON SOU

1   **Luke** = [KAI APOKRIQEIS EIPEN]
     Matt = (EFH)
     Pap Q = [(   )]
     Q = [KAI APOKRIQEIS EIPEN]

Q = Luke [KAI APOKRIQEIS EIPEN]

Pro: KAI APOKRIQEIS EIPEN = Q on the basis of KAI APOKRIQEIS EIPEN elsewhere in Q
(see 4:4[1,2], 4:8[1,3]).

2   **Luke** = [OTI EIRH]TAI
     Matt = (PALIN GEGRAP)TAI
     Pap Q = [(   )]TAI
     Q = (GEGRAP)TAI

Q = Luke [OTI EIRH]TAI

Con: OTI: the conjunction constituted Lukan redaction in 4:4[5], 4:11[1]. Presumably
the same conclusion is pertinent here, although the indirect statement introduced here is
not the quotation per se as in the previous two instances but is rather Jesus' reply as a
whole. Schulz (180) following Harnack (180:36) thinks that OTI = Luke. EIRHTAI: Schulz
(180) hypothesizes that EIRHTAI = Luke after the fashion of TO EIRHMENON in Acts 2:16;
13:40. This expression might be seen to be particularly significant for Luke insofar as it
introduces the first section of Peter's thetic sermon on Pentecost and introduces the conclusion of Paul's sermon in Antioch of Pisidia.

Q = Matt (PALIN GEGRAP)TAI

Pro: PALIN: according to Schulz (180:37) Harnack thinks that PALIN = Q. GEGRAPTAI:
this is the verb used otherwise in the temptations in Q (see Luke 4:4, 8, 10 par).

Con: PALIN: the adverb constituted Matthean redaction in 4:8[1]. Schulz (180) following
Schnackenburg (180:37) thinks that PALIN = Matt.

Luke 4:13 [KAI SUNTELESAS PANTA PEIRASMON]¹ ²/ O DIABOLOS /² A[PE]³S[TH
AP']³ AUTO[U]³ //² [AXRI KAIROU.]⁴

Matt 4:11 (TOTE)¹ //² A(FIH)³S(IN)³ AUTO(N)³ ²/ O DIABOLOS /² ({KAI} IDOU
{AGGELOI} PROSHLQON KAI {DIHKONOUN AUTW.})⁴

Mark 1:13b (KAI)⁴ OI (AGGELOI DIHKONOUN AUTW.)⁴

Pap Q 4:13 [(   )]^1 ^{2}/ O DIABOLOS /^{2} A[(   )]^{3}S[(   )]^3 AUTO[(   )]^3 //^{2}
[(   )]^4

Q 4:13 [KAI]^1 //^{2} A(FIH)^{3}S(IN)^3 AUTO(N)^3 O DIABOLOS ^{4}

1   Luke = [KAI SUNTELESAS PANTA PEIRASMON]
     Matt = (TOTE)
     Pap Q = [(   )]
     Q = [KAI]

Q = Luke [KAI SUNTELESAS PANTA PEIRASMON]

Pro: KAI: one might assume that the conjunction was in Q here due to its general appearance otherwise at the beginning of a sentence in the narration of the temptations.

Con: SUNTELESAS PANTA PEIRASMON: according to Schulz (181:55) the vocabulary here is Lukan. The verb, SUNTELEIN, appeared to be Lukan redaction in 4:1-2[11]. Conzelmann (28) claims that the Lukan interest in this phrase "can scarcely be overemphasized" and provides a rationale: "It really means that henceforth there will be no temptations in the life of Jesus. Thus his life as a whole is not regarded as a temptation either."

Q = Matt (TOTE)

Con: According to Schulz (181) TOTE = Q. This was the decision also in 4:1-2[1], 4:8[1], 4:9[1].

2   Luke = / O DIABOLOS / A[PE]^{3}S[TH AP']^3 AUTO[U]^3 //
     Matt = // A(FIH)^{3}S(IN)^3 AUTO(N)^3 / O DIABOLOS /
     Pap Q = / O DIABOLOS / A[(   )]^{3}S[(   )]^3 AUTO[(   )]^3 //
     Q = A[(   )]^{3}S[(   )]^3 AUTO[(   )]^3 O DIABOLOS

Q = Matt // A(FIH)^{3}S(IN)^3 AUTO(N)^3 / O DIABOLOS /

Pro: Matt is the evangelist most faithful otherwise in this part of the sentence.

3   Luke = A[PE]^{3}S[TH AP']^3 AUTO[U]^3
     Matt = A(FIH)^{3}S(IN)^3 AUTO(N)^3
     Pap Q = A[(   )]^{3}S[(   )]^3 AUTO[(   )]^3
     Q = A(FIH)S(IN) AUTO(N)

Q = Luke A[PE]^{3}S[TH AP']^3 AUTO[U]^3

Con: According to Schulz (181:55) AFISTANAI is used redactionally 1 in Luke and 6 in Acts. Insofar as Conzelmann is correct (see 4:13 [1]) the devil in Luke canot actually let

Jesus go (AFIENAI) but backs off (AFISTANAI) "until an opportune moment" (AXRI KAIROU; see 4:13[4].

4   **Luke** = [AXRI KAIROU]
     Matt = ({KAI} IDOU {AGGELOI} PROSHLQON KAI {DIHKONOUN AUTW.})
     Mark = (KAI) OI (AGGELOI DIHKONOUN AUTW.)
     Pap Q = [(   )]
     Q = omit

Q = Luke [AXRI KAIROU]

Con: According to Schulz (181:55) the vocabulary is Lukan. According to Conzelmann (28) the phrase is part of Lukan theology: "It is not until the moment indicated by AXRI KAIROU that temptation recurs. Luke xxii, 3 and the prompt reappearance of the PEIRASMOS motif in the farewell speeches in Luke show how important it is to emphasize this."

Q = Matt [{KAI} IDOU {AGGELOI} PROSHLQON KAI {DIHKONOUN AUTW.})

Con: According to Schulz (181) Matt assumes Mark here "fertig formuliert." PROSHLQON is, according to Schulz, "für ihn typisch." It was decided that PROSELQWN constitutes Matthean redaction in 4:3[1].

Bibliography

Conzelmann, Hans. *The Theology of St. Luke.* Translated by Geoffrey Buswell. Philadelphia: Fortress Press, 1961.

Schulz, Siegfried. *Q: Die Spruchquelle der Evangelisten.* Zürich: Theologischer Verlag, 1972.

Q 3-4

Ulrich Luz

[Prefatory note by James M. Robinson: In the Summer Semester of 1978 Ulrich Luz prepared and circulated to his class in Göttingen a reconstruction of Q prior to those published in 1979 by Athanasius Polag and in 1981 by Wolfgang Schenk. Though the reconstruction by Luz has not been published, he has been kind enough to put it at our disposal.]

Sigla:

( )   Text supported by only one evangelist; probable form of the text [in distinction from instances where the text is supported by only one evangelist but no parentheses are used, in which case the text is considered practically certain]

(( ))   Text supported by only one evangelist; fully hypothetical

. . .   Lost text

[ ]   Sequence of words uncertain

JOHN THE BAPTIST

1. The Emergence of the Baptist.
     The text cannot be reconstructed. Details: . . . πᾶσα ἡ περίχωρος τοῦ 'Ιορδάνου . . . (The OT quotation from Isa 40:3 without Mal 3:1 is *after* the presentation of the emergence of John.)

2. The Baptist's Preaching of Repentance. Luke 3:7-9 // Matt 3:7-10

     7 (("Ελεγεν οὖν τοῖς ἐκπορευομένοις . . .))
     Γεννήματα ἐχιδνῶν, τίς ὑπέδειξεν ὑμῖν φυγεῖν ἀπὸ τῆς μελλούσης ὀργῆς;
     8 ποιήσατε οὖν καρπ(ὸν) τῆς μετανοίας· καὶ μὴ (δόξητε) λέγειν ἐν ἑαυτοις·
     πατέρα ἔχομεν τὸν 'Αβραάμ· λέγω γὰρ ὑμῖν ὅτι δύναται ὁ θεὸς
     ἐκ τῶν λίθων τούτων ἐγεῖραι τέκνα τῷ 'Αβραάμ.

9 ἤδη δὲ (( )) ἡ ἀξίνη πρὸς τὴν ῥίζαν τῶν δένδρων κεῖται·
πᾶν οὖν δένδρον μὴ ποιοῦν καρπὸν καλὸν ἐκκόπτεται καὶ εἰς πῦρ βάλλεται.

3. The Announcement of the Messiah/Judge. Luke 3:16-17 // Matt 3:11-12

16 Ἐγὼ μὲν [ὑμᾶς] βαπτίζω [(ἐν) ὕδατι] (( ))
(ὁ δὲ ((ὀπίσω μου)) ἐρχόμενος ἰσχυρότερός μοῦ ἐστιν,)
οὗ οὐκ εἰμὶ ἱκανὸς (τὰ ὑποδήματα βαστάσαι)·
αὐτὸς ὑμᾶς βαπτίσει ἐν (πνεύματι (( )) καὶ) πυρί·
17 οὗ τὸ πτύον ἐν τῇ χειρὶ αὐτοῦ
(καὶ διακαθαριεῖ) τὴν ἅλωνα αὐτοῦ
καὶ (συνάξει) τὸν σῖτον εἰς τὴν ἀποθήκην ((αὐτοῦ)),
τὸ δὲ ἄχυρον κατακαύσει πυρὶ ἀσβέστῳ.

4. The Baptism of Jesus
The form of the text cannot be reconstructed. The existence of pieces can only be conjectured due to agreements between Matt//Luke: ἀνοίγω and ἐπ᾽ αὐτόν (Matt 3:16) and the occurrence of the title Son of God in Matt//Luke 4:1ff.

THE TEMPTATION: LUKE 4:1-13 // MATT 4:1-11

5-7. The text of the introduction cannot be reconstructed with certainty. What may belong to Q is: A passive formulation that Jesus was led by the Spirit into the desert, the catchwords διάβολος and ἡμέραι τεσσεράκοντα, his fasting, and ἐπείνασεν.

3 ((ὁ πειράζων)) [εἶπεν αὐτῷ]· εἰ υἱὸς εἶ τοῦ θεοῦ, εἰπὲ
(ἵνα ((οἱ)) λίθ((οι)) οὗτ((οι)) ἄρτ((οι)) γέν((ωνται))).
4 ((καὶ ἀπεκρίθη)) (( ))· γέγραπται ((ὅτι)) οὐκ ἐπ᾽ ἄρτῳ μόνῳ
ζήσεται ὁ ἄνθρωπος.
9 (( )) (παραλαμβάνει) αὐτὸν (ὁ διάβολος) εἰς (᾽Ιερουσαλὴμ)
καὶ ἔστησεν ((αὐτὸν)) ἐπὶ τὸ πτερύγιον τοῦ ἱεροῦ καὶ (λέγει) αὐτῷ
εἰ υἱὸς εἶ τοῦ θεοῦ, βάλε σεαυτὸν ( ) κάτω.
10 γέγραπται γὰρ ὅτι τοῖς ἀγγέλοις αὐτοῦ ἐντελεῖται περὶ σοῦ
11 καὶ ((ὅτι)) ἐπὶ χειρῶν ἀροῦσίν σε, μήποτε προσκόψῃς
πρὸς λίθον τὸν πόδα σου.
12 (ἔφη) αὐτῷ ὁ ᾽Ιησοῦς (ὅτι) (γέγραπται)· οὐκ ἐκπειράσεις κύριον
τὸν θεόν σου.
5 (( )) ((παραλαμβάνει)) αὐτὸν ((εἰς ὄρος ὑψιλὸν λίαν)) (καὶ
δείκνυσιν) αὐτῷ πάσας τὰς βασιλείας (τοῦ κόσμου) [καὶ
τὴν δόξαν αὐτῶν],
6 καὶ εἶπεν αὐτῷ· (ταῦτά) σοι (πάντα) δώσω,
7 ἐὰν ( ) προσκυνήσῃς (μοι).
8 λέγει αὐτῷ [ὁ ᾽Ιησοῦς]· (ὕπαγε, σατανᾶ· γέγραπται ((γάρ))·
κύριον τὸν θεόν σου προσκυνήσεις καὶ αὐτῷ μόνῳ λατρεύσεις.

John and the Coming One
(Matt 3:11-12//Luke 3:16-17)

Harry Fleddermann

The saying about John and the Coming One occurs in all four gospels (Matt 3:11-12; Mark 1:7-8; Luke 3:16-17; John 1:26-27).[1] Matthew and Luke agree against Mark in using the particle μέν and the preposition ἐν, in placing the sentence about the Coming One between the two parts of the baptism sentence, in using the present tense for John's baptism, in announcing a fire baptism, and in adding the image of the man with the winnowing-fan.[2] Since these agreements against Mark are significant, they indicate that the saying appeared in Q, so we must consider at least five forms of the saying—the Q form and the forms found in each of the four gospels. We begin by comparing the Matthean and Lucan forms and reconstructing the Q saying.

Matt 3:11-12	Luke 3:16-17	
11a ἐγὼ μὲν ὑμᾶς βαπτίζω ἐν ὕδατι εἰς μετάνοιαν,	ἐγὼ μὲν ὕδατι βαπτίζω ὑμᾶς·	16a
b ὁ δὲ ὀπίσω μου ἐρχόμενος ἰσχυρότερός μού ἐστιν	ἔρχεται δὲ ὁ ἰσχυρότερός μου,	b
c οὗ οὐκ εἰμὶ ἱκανὸς τὰ ὑποδήματα βαστάσαι·	οὗ οὐκ εἰμὶ ἱκανὸς λῦσαι τὸν ἱμάντα τῶν ὑποδημάτων αὐτοῦ·	c
d αὐτὸς ὑμᾶς βαπτίσει ἐν πνεύματι ἁγίῳ καὶ πυρί·	αὐτὸς ὑμᾶς βαπτίσει ἐν πνεύματι ἁγίῳ καὶ πυρί·	d
12a οὗ τὸ πτύον ἐν τῇ χειρὶ αὐτοῦ	οὗ τὸ πτύον ἐν τῇ χειρὶ αὐτοῦ	17a
b καὶ διακαθαριεῖ τὴν ἅλωνα αὐτοῦ	διακαθᾶραι τὴν ἅλωνα αὐτοῦ	b
c καὶ συνάξει τὸν σῖτον αὐτοῦ εἰς τὴν ἀποθήκην,	καὶ συναγαγεῖν τὸν σῖτον εἰς τὴν ἀποθήκην αὐτοῦ,	c
d τὸ δὲ ἄχυρον κατακαύσει πυρὶ ἀσβέστῳ	τὸ δὲ ἄχυρον κατακαύσει πυρὶ ἀσβέστῳ	d

---

[1]Echoes of the saying are found in John 1:15, 30, 31, 33, and Acts 1:5; 11:16; 13:25; 19:4.

[2]See P. Hoffman, *Studien zur Theologie der Logienquelle* (NTAbh 8; Münster: Aschendorff, 1972) 18-19; R. Laufen, *Die Doppelüberlieferungen der Logienquelle und des Markusevangeliums* (BBB 54; Königstein/Bonn: Hanstein, 1980) 93-94.

In the ἐγώ-clause (Matt 3:11a//Luke 3:16a) Matthew reflects Q in the position of ὑμᾶς and ὕδατι and in the use of the preposition ἐν. This is easily verified by comparing the αὐτός-clause (Matt 3:11d//Luke 3:16d) where Matthew and Luke agree. Luke has adopted a more normal word order as he does elsewhere,[3] and he omitted an awkward ἐν.[4] Matthew's εἰς μετάνοιαν is an interpretative addition to the Q text.[5] The phrase is absent in Luke; there is no parallel expression in the αὐτός-clause; and repentance is a Matthean concern. Matthew emphasizes repentance in his summaries of the preaching of both John (3:2) and Jesus (4:17). Since repentance is also a concern of Q (Matt 3:8//Luke 3:8), with the addition εἰς μετάνοιαν Matthew brings together his own concern with repentance (3:2) and the emphasis he found in Q (3:8), and at the same time he also brings John's baptism (3:16) into line with his preaching (3:8).[6]

Matthew probably preserves the Q text of the second clause (Matt 3:11b//Luke 3:16b), for his clause, ὁ δὲ ὀπίσω μου ἐρχόμενος ἰσχυρότερός μού ἐστιν, shows some characteristics of Q. The sentence structure is similar to that of another Q passage, ὁ δὲ μικρότερος ἐν τῇ βασιλείᾳ τοῦ θεοῦ μείζων αὐτοῦ ἐστιν (Luke 7:28b; compare Matt 11:11b); and Q elsewhere refers to the Coming One (Matt 11:3//Luke 7:19; Matt 23:39//Luke 13:35). Luke ἔρχεται δὲ ὁ ἰσχυρότερός μου is an assimilation to Mark. Luke's introduction to the saying states that the people were wondering whether John might be the Christ (3:15). Mark's clause which emphasizes the coming of the stronger one fits Luke's context better than the Q clause, preserved in Matthew, which emphasizes the superiority of the Coming One rather than the coming itself.[7] The echo of the saying in Acts 19:4 (εἰς τὸν ἐρχόμενον μετ' αὐτόν) is further evidence that Luke is secondary, for this passage shows that Luke knew the Matthean form. Luke has omitted the phrase ὀπίσω μου because he does not want to give the impression that Jesus is a disciple of the Baptist. Both in Q and in Mark the preposition ὀπίσω means "after" in a temporal sense as it commonly does in the Greek OT,[8] but for Luke the phrase ἔρχεται ὀπίσω μου is too closely associated with the concept of discipleship for him to apply it to Jesus and the Baptist (compare Luke 9:23; 14:27). This is confirmed by Acts 13:25 and 19:4 where Luke

---

[3]Compare Luke 5:14 with Mark 1:44; Luke 19:36 with Mark 11:8; Luke 20:9 with Mark 12:1; Luke 20:19 with Mark 12:12; Luke 20:25 with Mark 12:17. See H. J. Cadbury, *The Style and Literary Method of Luke* (Cambridge: Harvard University, 1920) 152-53.

[4]Compare Luke 4:33 with Mark 1:23; Luke 8:4 with Mark 4:2; Luke 8:27 with Mark 5:2; Luke 20:9 with Mark 12:1. See H. J. Cadbury, *Style*, 204-5. Luke always avoids ἐν with ὕδατι (see especially Acts 11:16). See further C. F. D. Moule, *An Idiom-Book of New Testament Greek* (2d ed.; Cambridge: Cambridge University Press, 1959) 77. While not impossible Greek, the use of ἐν in an instrumental sense reflects Hebrew syntax. See BDF §195, §219.

[5]S. Schulz, *Q—Die Spruchquelle der Evangelisten* (Zürich: Theologischer Verlag, 1972) 368; W. Schenk, *Synopse zur Redenquelle der Evangelien: Q-Synopse und Rekonstruktion in deutscher Übersetzung mit kurzen Erläuterungen* (Düsseldorf: Patmos, 1981) 19.

[6]P. Hoffman, *Studien*, 22.

[7]R. Laufen, *Doppelüberlieferungen*, 94-95.

[8]Compare 3 Kgdms 1:6, 24; Neh 3:16, 17; Eccl 10:14 (LXX) and Dan 2:39; 7:6 (Theodotion). See V. Taylor, *The Gospel according to St. Mark* (2d ed.; London: Macmillan, 1966) 156-57; R. Laufen, *Doppelüberlieferungen*, 113-14.

twice substitutes the preposition μετά for ὀπίσω to make it clear that he means a temporal succession rather than a spatial following that might suggest discipleship.[9]

The first οὗ–clause (Matt 3:11c//Luke 3:16c) is difficult. Matthew and Luke agree in the wording of the first part of the clause (οὗ οὐκ εἰμὶ ἱκανός),[10] but they diverge in the wording of the infinitive construction. Hoffman, Schulz, Laufen, and Schenk prefer Matthew's expression,[11] but H. Schürmann claims that Matthew has simplified the diction.[12] Schürmann is on the right track, although it is probably more accurate to say that Matthew has simplified the image. There are other instances of this redactional procedure in Matthew. In his version of the Salt Saying (5:13) Matthew describes the fate of the salt with the expression (εἰς οὐδὲν ἰσχύει ἔτι εἰ μὴ βληθὲν ἔξω καταπατεῖσθαι ὑπὸ τῶν ἀνθρώπων) that simplifies the image found in Luke 14:35 (οὔτε εἰς γῆν οὔτε εἰς κοπρίαν εὔθετόν ἐστιν, ἔξω βάλλουσιν αὐτό).[13] The same phenomenon is apparent in the Faith Saying (Matt 17:20//Luke 17:6). Although he switches from the image of the sycamore to Mark's mountain (compare Mark 11:23), Matthew's μετάβα ἔνθεν ἐκεῖ appears to be a simplification either of the Lucan image (ἐκριζώθητι καὶ φυτεύθητι ἐν τῇ θαλάσσῃ) or the Marcan image (ἄρθητι καὶ βλήθητι εἰς τὴν θάλασσαν).[14] To this main consideration some minor ones can be added. First, no other version of the saying reflects Matthew's infinitive construction. Second, there are two stylistic features of Luke's phrase that indicate primitiveness. The noun ἱμάς is rare in the NT, occurring in the singular only in the various versions of this saying.[15] Luke's redundant αὐτοῦ, while not impossible Greek, is more congenial to Semitic syntax, and along with the preposition ἐν it adds to the Semitic color of the saying.[16]

Matthew and Luke agree in the wording of the αὐτός–clause (Matt 3:11d//Luke 3:16d). However, Schulz maintains that the words πνεύματι ἁγίῳ were not part of the original Q text but were inserted from Mark.[17] But the use of ἐν[18] and the identical placement of the words in Matthew and Luke indicate that the words stood in Q. They probably indicate, though, that the Q saying is not the earliest recoverable form of the saying, but we will delay the discussion of this point until the Q saying has been reconstructed.

Matthew and Luke are very close in the second οὗ–clause (Matt 3:12//Luke 3:17). Matthew's features, διακαθαριεῖ and συνάξει, preserve the Q wording. Luke's infinitives are an attempt to improve the Greek by subordinating instead of coordinating, but Luke

---

[9]R. Laufen, Doppelüberlieferungen, 96.

[10]For another occurrence of the phrase οὐκ εἰμι ἱκανος in Q compare Matt 8:8// Luke 7:6.

[11]P. Hoffman, Studien, 23; S. Schulz, Q, 368; R. Laufen, Doppelüberlieferungen, 95; W. Schenk, Synopse, 19.

[12]H. Schürmann, Das Lukasevangelium: Erster Teil: Kommentar zu Kap 1,1-9,50 (HTKNT 3; Freiburg/Basel/Vienna: Herder, 1969) 173 n. 79.

[13]See S. Schulz, Q, 471.

[14]Compare also Matt 5:25 with Luke 12:58 and Matt 7:24 with Luke 6:48.

[15]The plural appears once in Acts 22:25.

[16]BDF §297; on ἐν see n. 4 above.

[17]S. Schulz, Q, 368.

[18]Many manuscripts read an ἐν before πνεύματι ἁγίῳ in Mark but this obviously harmonizing reading should be rejected with B L b t vg.

agrees with Matthew in the final future κατακαυσει (Matt 3:12d//Luke 3:17d). The position of the final αὐτοῦ (Matt 3:12c//Luke 3:17c) is extremely difficult. The other two occurrences of αὐτοῦ in the second οὗ-clause (Matt 3:12a//Luke 3:17a; Matt 3:12b//Luke 3:17c) both come at the end of a phrase. Since the saying is so strongly characterized by parallelism, it is likely that the third occurrence follows suit which means that the position of the pronoun in Luke is original. What is decisive is that Matthew uses "wheat" as a symbol of the elect in the parable of the Weeds among the Wheat (Matt 13:24-30, 36-43), so Matthew had a reason to change the position of αὐτοῦ, whereas Luke had no reason to shift it. By moving the pronoun Matthew has allegorized.[19] It is, of course, quite likely that the wheat and the chaff should be understood as allegorical in the original Q saying. In this case Matthew by shifting the pronoun has simply emphasized an allegorical feature of the original text because it coincided with his own thought in much the same way as his εἰς μετάνοιαν develops a focus of Q that he is particularly interested in.

The reconstructed saying would look like this:

Q 3:16-17

16a ἐγὼ μὲν ὑμᾶς βαπτίζω ἐν ὕδατι,
  b ὁ δὲ ὀπίσω μου ἐρχόμενος ἰσχυρότερός μού ἐστιν
  c οὗ οὐκ εἰμὶ ἱκανὸς λῦσαι τὸν ἱμάντα τῶν ὑποδημάτων αὐτοῦ·
  d αὐτὸς ὑμᾶς βαπτίσει ἐν πνεύματι ἁγίῳ καὶ πυρί·
17a οὗ τὸ πτύον ἐν τῇ χειρὶ αὐτοῦ
  b καὶ διακαθαριεῖ τὴν ἅλωνα αὐτοῦ
  c καὶ συνάξει τὸν σῖτον εἰς τὴν ἀποθήκην αὐτοῦ
  d τὸ δε ἄχυρον κατακαύσει πυρὶ ἀσβέστῳ

In the following discussion we will call this saying the Q saying, meaning that this was the form of the saying in the source Q that was available to Matthew and Luke. This saying offers no support to any theory that Matthew and Luke used different versions of Q because the differences between Matthew and Luke all result from Matthean and Lucan redaction of the Q saying. Before discussing the pre-history of the saying, it might be helpful to summarize Matthew's and Luke's redaction.

Although Matthew undoubtedly knew Mark's saying, he chose simply to rewrite Q. At two points Matthew has developed aspects of Q that coincide with his own emphases. His addition εἰς μετάνοιαν draws out the repentance motif that is important both to Q (Matt 3:8//Luke 3:8) and to Matthew himself (Matt 3:2; 4:17). While it is possible that Q understood the wheat and the chaff allegorically, Matthew emphasizes this allegorical understanding of the wheat by shifting the position of the pronoun αὐτοῦ. In the first οὗ-clause Matthew has simplified the imagery.

Most of Luke's changes are stylistic. He has lightly retouched the Q saying at several places, rearranging the word order and dropping the ἐν in the ἐγώ-clause and twice substituting infinitives for Q's finite verbs in the second οὗ-clause. For his only major change, Luke substituted Mark's ἔρχεται ὁ ἰσχυρότερός μου for the second Q clause to

---

[19]P. Hoffmann, *Studien*, 19.

adapt the saying to the context of his introductory verse (3:15), and in the process he has dropped an offensive ὀπίσω μου.

The Q saying has also been redacted by the addition of the words πνεύματι ἀγίῳ καί. Since there is no corresponding phrase in the ἐγώ-clause and the saying is so strongly dominated by parallelism, it is probable that ἐν πυρί was originally opposed to ἐν ὕδατι. This is confirmed by the second οὗ-clause which develops the fire, but not the spirit, imagery. So the earliest saying looked like this:

ἐγὼ μὲν ὑμᾶς βαπτίζω ἐν ὕδατι,
ὁ δὲ ὀπίσω μου ἐρχόμενος ἰσχυρότερός μού ἐστιν,
οὗ οὐκ εἰμὶ ἰκανὸς λῦσαι τὸν ἰμάντα τῶν ὑποδημάτων αὐτοῦ·
αὐτὸς ὑμᾶς βαπτίσει ἐν πυρί·
οὗ τὸ πτύον ἐν τῇ χειρὶ αὐτοῦ
καὶ διακαθαριεῖ τὴν ἅλωνα αὐτοῦ
καὶ συνάξει τὸν σῖτον εἰς τὴν ἀποθήκην αὐτοῦ
τὸ δὲ ἄχυρον κατακαύσει πυρὶ ἀσβέστῳ

In the following discussion we will call this saying the pre-Q saying. At some stage in the development of the saying the words πνεύματι ἀγίῳ καί were interpolated between ἐν and πυρι, but it is not possible to determine when this was done. It could have happened prior to the incorporation of the saying into Q or the words could have been added by the Q redactor. The general reason for the addition is relatively easy to see, but it is quite difficult to describe the thought exactly. The pre-Q saying is dominated by the concept of the stronger one—the Coming One is stronger than John. In the pre-Q saying the strength of the Coming One is in his fire baptism which is then explained by an image of definitive judgment. Whoever added the reference to a holy spirit is further developing the concept of the stronger one. Now the stronger one introduces a whole new order—the spirit. We now compare Mark and Q.

Q 1:16-17	Mark 1:7-8
16a ἐγὼ μὲν ὑμᾶς βαπτίζω ἐν ὕδατι	
b ὁ δὲ ὀπίσω μου ἐρχόμενος ἰσχυρότερός μού ἐστιν,	ἔρχεται ὁ ἰσχυρότερος 7a μου ὀπίσω μου,

c οὗ οὐκ εἰμὶ ἰκανὸς
   λῦσαι τὸν ἰμάντα
   τῶν ὑποδημάτων αὐτοῦ·
	οὗ οὐκ εἰμὶ ἰκανὸς b
	κύψας λῦσαι τὸν ἰμάντα
	τῶν ὑποδημάτων αὐτοῦ·
	ἐγὼ ἐβάπτισα ὑμᾶς 8a
	ὕδατι,

d αὐτὸς ὑμᾶς βαπτίσει ἐν
   πνεύματι ἀγίῳ καὶ πυρί·
17a οὗ τὸ πτύον ἐν τῇ χειρὶ
    αὐτοῦ
b καὶ διακαθαριεῖ τὴν
   ἅλωνα αὐτοῦ
	αὐτὸς δὲ βαπτίσει ὑμᾶς b
	πνεύματι ἀγίῳ.

c καὶ συνάξει τὸν σῖτον
  εἰς τὴν ἀποθήκην αὐτοῦ
d τὸ δὲ ἄχυρον κατακαύσει
  πυρὶ ἀσβέστῳ

What is the relationship of these two similar, yet different, texts? Are they variant forms of the oral tradition? Did one of them develop from the other? Is there an even older text that lies behind them? R. Laufen wants to separate the two sentences and see them as two originally distinct units, but to do this he must make several assumptions. In the originally separate sentences he assumes that the subject of βαπτίσει was ὁ ἐρχό- μενος, that there was no reference to a fire baptism, that there was no direct address so the pronouns ὑμᾶς were not present, and that ὁ ἰσχυρότερος was the subject of the verb ἔρχεται and not a predicate qualifying ὁ ἐρχόμενος. In this way he arrives at two origi- nally independent sentences that together form the hypothetic ancestor of both Q and Mark:[20]

ἔρχεται (ὁ) ἰσχυρότερός (μου ὀπίσω μου), οὗ οὐκ εἰμὶ
ἱκανὸς λῦσαι τὸν ἱμάντα τῶν ὑποδημάτων αὐτοῦ
(or: ὑποδήματα βαστάσαι).

ἐγὼ βαπτίζω ἐν ὕδατι, ὁ δὲ ἐρχόμενος βαπτίσει
ἐν πνεύματι (ἁγίῳ).

But Laufen's procedure heaps hypothesis on top of hypothesis. Just because we can imagine that the sayings developed in this way is no proof that they did. On the contrary, two observations make Laufen's reconstruction unlikely. First, with the exception of the reference to a holy spirit, the Q saying gives the impression of being a finely wrought original unit. The parallelism of the two baptism clauses, the intertwining of the baptism statement and the statement about the stronger one (note μὲν . . . δὲ . . .), and the two οὗ-clauses present a carefully constructed, complex statement in which John and his baptism are first introduced, then John is contrasted with the stronger one whose bap- tism is then described. Second, there is nothing in Mark which is not in Q except the word κύψας. Mark is really closer to Q than either Q or Mark is to Laufen's hypothetical ancestor.

Before positing a third text behind Mark and Q, it is methodologically sounder to compare Mark and Q to see if one of them can be shown to be prior to the other, and, if so, whether the prior one is the source of the other. Comparing Mark and Q, we find several signs that Mark is secondary. First, Mark's finite verb ἔρχεται looks forward to the coming of Jesus in v. 9, and his aorist ἐβάπτισα looks back to the activity of the Baptist in vv. 4-5. These two features of Mark's text are secondary adaptations of the saying to the historicizing gospel genre.[21] Q's participle ἐρχόμενος and present verb βαπτίζω are more likely to be original. Second, Mark's statement emphasizes Christian spirit baptism more strongly than Q does because the reference to a fire baptism has

---

[20]R. Laufen, *Doppelüberlieferungen*, 97-116.
[21]R. Laufen, *Doppelüberlieferungen*, 108.

dropped out. This Christian emphasis is a sign of further development.[22] Third, Mark's two separate sentences focus attention on Jesus even more than the Q saying does. This Christological concentration is also a sign of further development.[23] Fourth, Q's preposition ἐν in the baptism statement reflects Semitic idiom; Mark's instrumental dative is Greek. Fifth, Mark's baptism sentence refers to a holy spirit. We have seen that the reference to a holy spirit was the last element to be added to the Q saying. Since Mark's baptism sentence depends on this final development, it cannot be earlier than the Q saying. These arguments show that Mark is later than Q.

Since Mark is later than Q, we must examine the differences between them to see if they could result from Marcan redaction of the Q saying. As we noted above, the only element in Mark that is not Q is the word κύψας. Mark likes to use redundant participles,[24] and there is a fairly close analogy to κύψας in Mark's redundant use of ἀναστάς (1:35; 2:14; 7:24; 10:1), so the participle can be easily understood as a Marcan redactional addition to the saying. Instead of Q's carefully intertwined sentences Mark has two separate sentences. Since he wants to begin immediately with the story of Jesus, Mark has reduced the Baptist's role to that of a forerunner. He eliminates any mention of an independent mission of John or anything that would distract from the coming of Jesus. Even the reference to John's preaching in v. 4 ("baptism of repentance for the forgiveness of sins") is directed toward Jesus, for it prepares his way (vv. 2-3). Because he has reduced John to the forerunner of Jesus, Mark wants the only actual quotation of John's preaching to begin with a proclamation that Jesus is coming. For this reason he separates the intertwined Q sentences, draws the saying about the Coming One forward, and transforms it into a proclamation of Jesus' coming by changing Q's participle ἐρχόμενος into a finite verb ἔρχεται. Instead of stating that the Coming One is stronger than he is as in Q, John now proclaims that one stronger than he is coming. This prepares directly for Jesus' coming in v. 9. Mark retains the first οὗ–clause, adding only the participle κύψας. After separating out the saying about the Coming One, Mark now draws the two parts of the baptism sentence together. He straightens out the word order by placing the objects ὑμᾶς after the verbs, and he improves the syntax by dropping the preposition ἐν. He also changes Q's present βαπτίζω to the aorist ἐβάπτισα because this sentence is a turning point for him. It brings to a close the public activity of the Baptist and provides the transition to the work of Jesus. The aorist points back to the description of John's baptism in vv. 4-5 and shows that John's work is over. It is significant that Mark does not mention the people in his portrayal of Jesus' baptism (vv. 9-11).[25] From v. 8 on all that remains for John is to baptize Jesus privately; then he disappears from the stage (v. 14) and is afterwards always referred to in the past (6:14-29; 8:28; 9:11-13; 11:27-33). Mark

---

[22]P. Hoffmann, *Studien,* 19.

[23]R. Pesch, "Anfang des Evangeliums Jesu Christ: Eine Studie zum Prolog Markus-evangeliums (Mk 1,1-15)," in *Die Zeit Jesu: Festschrift für Heinrich Schlier* (ed. G. Bornkamm and K. Rahner; Freiburg/Basel/Vienna: Herder, 1970) 121.

[24]Compare Mark 1:35; 2:14; 7:24; 8:28; 9:5; 10:1, 24, 51; 11:14; 12:26, 35; 14:48; 15:12. See V. Taylor, *Mark,* 63; E. J. Pryke, *Redactional Style in the Marcan Gospel: A Study of Syntax and Vocabulary as Guides to Redaction in Mark* (Cambridge: Cambridge University, 1978) 99-103.

[25]P. Hoffmann, *Studien,* 20.

drops the reference to a fire baptism and with it the entire judgment motif of the second
οὖ–clause because he intends to define Jesus' person and mission in three short scenes
that recount Jesus' baptism (vv. 9-11), temptation (vv. 12-13), and preaching (vv. 14-15).
Thus the differences between Mark and Q can all be explained as resulting from Marcan
redaction. We conclude that Mark knew and used the Q saying.
We now turn briefly to John's form of the saying:[26]

John 1:26-27

ἐγὼ βαπτίζω ἐν ὕδατι·
μέσος ὑμῶν ἔστηκεν ὃν ὑμεῖς οὐκ οἴδατε,
ὁ ὀπίσω μου ἐρχόμενος,
οὖ οὐκ εἰμὶ ἄξιος ἵνα λύσω αὐτοῦ
τὸν ἱμάντα τοῦ ὑποδήματος.

John's saying shows a bewildering set of agreements and disagreements with the Synoptics and Acts. John agrees with Acts 13:25 in the singular "sandal" and in the adjective
ἄξιος, but with Matthew and Mark in the prepositional phrase ὀπίσω μου. He is closest
to Luke in the wording of the clause about unfastening the sandal strap, but he agrees
with Mark in dropping the reference to fire baptism. It is not surprising, then, to find
scholars who claim that John's form of the saying is an independent version that goes
back to the oral tradition.[27] This judgment may well be correct, but some things need to
be noted. First, some peculiarities of John's saying are minor. For example, the singular
"sandal" could easily be suggested by the singular ἱμάντα, and the adjective ἄξιος is a
much more common word that could easily be substituted for ἱκανός. Second, there are
obviously redactional elements in the various versions of the saying in John. For example,
John interprets the superiority of the Coming One in terms of pre-existence in John 1:15,
30. The clause μέσος ὑμῶν ἔστηκεν ὃν ὑμεῖς οὐκ οἴδατε is Johannine in diction and
thought.[28] Third, John 1:26-27 is really closer to the reconstructed Q saying than it is to
any other form of the saying, especially if John 1:33 is drawn into the picture because it
refers to baptism with a holy spirit which was the last element added to the Q saying.
We can now summarize the tradition history of the saying. The earliest recoverable
form of the saying is the pre-Q saying. Sometime before the final Q the words πνεύματι
ἀγίῳ καί were inserted to form the Q saying. Mark radically redacted the Q saying.
Matthew's saying is a less radical rewriting of Q. Luke both redacts the Q saying and
conflates it with Mark. John also depends on Q. At the beginning of this rich development
in the gospels stands the Q saying.

---

[26]Compare also John 1:15, 30, 31, 33.

[27]P. Gardner-Smith, *Saint John and the Synoptic Gospels* (Cambridge: Cambridge
University Press, 1938) 3-4, 10; R. E. Brown, *The Gospel according to John* (2 vols.; AB
29 and 29A; Garden City, NY: Doubleday, 1966-70) 1. 52.

[28]The expression ὃν ὑμεῖς οὐκ οἴδατε recurs in John 7:28 (compare also John 4:32).

Prophecy, Property and Politics

J. Andrew Dearman

The relationship between the subject of prophecy, property, and politics is the focus of this paper. The outline of the paper is as follows. Relevant texts from the prophetic corpus are arranged in three charts for easy reference in the belief that the important issues emerge from the texts themselves and that, therefore, they are the proper starting point. After introductory remarks, a brief discussion ensues of Amos, Isaiah of Jerusalem, and Micah. What is crucial to these figures of the 8th century will be so for the most part in the 7th century as well. Two specific topics are then analyzed: land tenure and the royal administrative/judicial system. Finally, concluding remarks are offered with questions for further discussion.

Very little information about property is provided by the pre-exilic prophets. Most of the references occur in polemical contexts concerned with the misappropriation of property, demonstrating that the subject was intensely debated.

Chart One lists references made to property in the context of accusations against either the nation or segments of its population. In a large number of references the misappropriation of property is the stated reason for the announcement of judgment. There are, of course, other references to property in the prophetic literature than are included in these lists, but perhaps the majority of *all* the references where property itself are a major issue of the speech is found in Chart One.[1]

Chart Two divides the perceived crimes into four categories. Obviously there is some overlap among them. The fourth category (D), especially, is a general one, and the misappropriations listed there probably have reference back to the type of infractions listed in the first three categories. What is called debt slavery clearly is a major element among the accusations. The term refers to an institution in antiquity whereby a man and/or his family became the property of a creditor. Mendelsohn's comparative studies suggested to him that indebtedness was the chief cause of slavery in the ancient Near East.[2] The institution is known in the Hebrew Bible (Exod 21:2-11; cf. Lev 25:39; Deut 15:12; 2 Kings 4:1-7; Neh 5:1-5), although the legal obligations and assumed rights are often unclear. How the institution may have functioned in the 8th century in Israel has been discussed quite helpfully by Lang in a series of articles, and the details will not be

---

[1] A number of references refer to the looting of property by foreign powers (e.g., Isa 10:14; Jer 5:15-17; Nah 2:2; Hab 2:6-11) or to their selling of people (Amos 1:6, 9).

[2] I. Mendelsohn, *Slavery in the Ancient Near East* (NY: Oxford, 1949) 43.

repeated here.[3] It should be stressed that the various categories of Chart Two presuppose a process whereby the indebted persons gradually forfeit what they own until the only thing left to sell is themselves.

Finally, the processes leading to debt slavery also presuppose the failure of the administrative/judicial system to mitigate the harshness of indebtedness, foreclosure, and eviction. *Chart Three* contains references to this system which come as part of the accusations against property misappropriation (marked with an asterisk) or as part of the general social critique of the prophets.

In comparing the various charts several issues emerge into prominence.

(1) As noted above, the various references in Chart One taken together presuppose a process of several stages whereby the effects of indebtedness move almost inexorably to the state of debt slavery.

(2) These same references demonstrate that land tenure and the alienability of landed property are important issues (discussed below).

(3) Chart Three demonstrates that the general critique of the administrative/ judicial systems often reflects specifically the accusations of misappropriation of property. Therefore, any discussion of the process whereby persons are dispossessed of their property must consider the administrative/judicial procedures and institutions with which the credit must normally operate.

(4) A large number of those persons addressed in charts one and three are named by title or office. In many instances, therefore, those who are involved as creditors and dispossessors and who are accused of thievery, robbery, extortion and "blood"[4] are using their office and authority for gain.

AMOS

The crimes ($p^e \check{s}\bar{a}\,^c\hat{i}m$) of 2:6-8 involve the relationship between debtor and creditor and also the role of the administrative/judicial system. Selling and buying (cf. 8:5) of persons must refer to the acquisition of both them and their possessions. As to a father and son having sexual relations with the same female, some commentators conjecture that the two men have broken the laws of consanguinity and that this is the crime to which Amos pointed. However, the use of the term $na\,^c\bar{a}r\bar{a}h$ and the context of property infringements suggest something else. A list of "rights" is provided in Exod 21:7-11 for a daughter sold into slavery. One of the rights she should have is that she may become the wife of her master *or* his son, but not both.[5] Amos 2:7c, with its reference to the maiden

---

[3]B. Lang, "Slaves and Unfree in Book Amos (11:6, VIII 6)," *VT* 31 (1981) 482-86; "The Social Organization of Peasant Poverty in Biblical Israel," *JSOT* 24 (1982) 47-63 = Chapter 4, *Monotheism and the Prophetic Minority* (Sheffield: Almond, 1983).

[4]Blood (*dām*) stands for the vitality of life and death. The "shedding of blood" is often a metaphor for actions which, in effect, rob one of the vitality of life. Cf. Mic 3:10; Jer 22:17; Ezek 22:6.

[5]Mendelsohn, (*Slavery*, 13) writes that Exod 21:7-11 probably represents "a fragment of a series of enactments that originally dealt with all cases of conditional sales of young girls."

having sexual relations with a father and son, is best understood as an accusation that the *na ʿārāh* has become the sexual property of both individuals.

Objects taken in pledge is a transaction known from the legal codes (Exod 22:25; Deut 24:6, 12-13, 17) and refers to property given by a debtor to a creditor as collateral for a loan. The final crime concerns a payment in kind (wine). The participle of the verb *ʿnš* in 2:8 defines the wine consumed by the prophet's opponents as acquired through exactions. The term *ʿnš* is used in the legal traditions to refer to compensation measures (Exod 21:22; Deut 22:19) and occurs in similar form as a reference to taxation (2 Kings 22:33).[6] Thus it is likely another example of the forced "exchange" of property between debtor and creditor, or perhaps a tax.

The setting for the last two crimes is a temple. A possible explanation of this setting is the fact that in antiquity temples were often lending institutions and centers of banking.[7] Recently published administrative documents from Neo-Assyrian temples illustrate such a banking system at a time contemporary with pre-exilic Israel and Judah.[8] Money and property deposited at the temple were received under the name of the deity *and* the depositor. It seems no interest accrued to the depositor, but the money could be lent out, and any interest which accrued apparently went to the creditor. In this way a person could have a "safe house" for working capital, prestige, and the temple would benefit from the pool of funds it administered. In the case of Amos 2:8 the garment taken in pledge and the wine exacted would be dedicated at the temple and thus removed from profane use. If the goods were still technically the property of the debtor, they would no longer be so once deposited in the sacred center by the creditor.

A temple banking system could work in different ways; my proposal is that *part* of Amos's critique of worship centers (2:8; 3:14; 4:4-5; 5:4-5, 21-24; 7:17) comes from their involvement in what he perceives to be social crimes. As a priest who also owned property, Amaziah's interest in Amos would be understandable.[9]

The phrase "to turn aside the way of the afflicted" in 2:7b is a metaphor[10] signifying the failure of the administrative/judicial system to mitigate the circumstances of property loss. Indeed, as an accusation it points the finger of responsibility for the failure

---

[6]Cf. 1 Kings 10:15, LXX, where the better reading *ʿōnešê,* "exactions," is found for the *ʾanešê,* "men" of MT. The verse is a description of Solomon's sources of wealth. Also note *ʿnsm,* "taxes," "tariffs," in R. S. Tomback, *A Comparative Semitic Lexicon of the Phoenician and Punic Languages* (SBLDS 32, Missoula: Scholars Press, 1978) 253.

[7]Cf. Judg 9:4 and E. Newfield, "The Prohibition Against Loans at Interest in Ancient Hebrew Laws," *HUCA* 26 (1955) 376-83 for the many references to temple documents from antiquity.

[8]B. Menzel, *Assyrische Temple* (Studia Pohl; Rome: Biblical Institute Press, 1981) vol. I, II. Cf. the detailed review of J. N. Postgate, *JSS* 28 (1983) 155-59.

[9]Is the banking system behind the reference to a "den of robbers" in Jer 7:11? Note also that archaeological research shows Arad and Beersheba were both worship and administration centers. The *archaeological* evidence is less decisive for either Dan or Bethel. There is an intimate relationship between religion, urbanism, and administrative practice as made clear by G. Ahlström, *Royal Administration and National Religion in Ancient Palestine* (Leiden: E. J. Brill, 1983).

[10]The use of the verb *nṭh* in the context of perverting justice can be found in 1 Sam 8:3; Amos 2:7, 5:12; Exod 23:2, 6; Isa 10:2, 29:21, 30:11; Deut 16:19.

at the system. Elaboration on the process can be found in 5:10-12, where justice in the gate is denied, exactions from property owners[11] are forced, and bribes (disguised as fees?) seal the fate of those taxed.

Amos's attack on the mountain of Samaria in 3:9-11 provides one institutional setting for the crimes of robbery and violence which are stored in the city. Kenyon's excavations in Sebeste concluded that "the capital was administrative only,"[12] and that the common people lived on the eastern slope of the hill where the present Arab village is located. The robbery and violence stored up in the ʾarmānôt of Samaria would then refer to the governmental buildings of the enclosed acropolis.[13]

ISAIAH

Land accumulation is an activity obviously opposed by the prophet (3:14; 5:8-10; probably 10:1-2). Elders and officials are held responsible for this perceived injustice in the first reference, as are the latter for the ruin of widows and orphans in 1:23. Most interesting is the woe oracle of 10:1-4, where injustice is done through statutes (ḥqq) and written documents. Robbery (gzl, as in 3:14) by statute is a description of the process by which the property of persons is appropriated. The word pair ḥqq/ktb is found in Job 19:23 and Isa 30:8 in the context of preparing a written document. Ancient equivalents of loan agreements, mortgage deeds, purchase statements, and service contracts would be recorded[14] and witnessed in the gate of the appropriate municipality. If a suit arose over noncompliance, the proceedings would be witnessed there as well. Apparently the statutes of 10:1 were written and enforced in such a way that appeal seemed fruitless. Those addressed as statute-writers may be referred to in an official capacity. Hentschke's study of the word group ḥōq concluded that an old tribal office dealing with the levy and land apportionment (Judg 5:9, 14; Deut 33:21; Num 21:18; cf. Ps 60:8-11) is behind the accusations of 10:1-2, though under the monarchy such persons who performed these tasks would be responsible to the royal administration.[15]

---

[11]The hapax bōšaskem of Amos 5:11a may be related to an Akkadian cognate to take payment from fields. For philological details, H. R. Cohen, *Biblical Hapax Legomena in the Light of Akkadian and Ugaritic* (SBLDS 37; Missoula: Scholars Press, 1978) 49. That exactions are the point of the prophetic accusation is clear from parallelism and context.

[12]The quote is from K. Kenyon, *Royal Cities of the Old Testament* (London: Barric and Jenkins, 1971) 82.

[13]The ʾarmānôt were not private homes but palaces, strongholds, and public buildings. Cf. Amos 1:4, 7, 10, 12, 14, 6:8; 1 Kings 16:18; 2 Kings 15:25; Lam 2:7; Hos 8:14.

[14]E.g., J. N. Postgate, *Fifty Neo-Assyrian Legal Documents* (Warminster: Aris & Phillips, 1976). Cf. Jer 32:9-15.

[15]R. Hentschke, *Satzung und Setzender* (BWANT 3; Stuttgart: W. Kohlhammer, 1963) 11-20.

MICAH

Like his urban contemporary, Micah viewed with horror the practice of land accumulation (2:1-2, 9). Those responsible for this are named as heads and rulers in 3:1, 9. These are general titles from the premonarchic period (Judg 11:11) but must have been applied in Judah to regional officials with ties to the royal administration. The legal authority for foreclosure on landed property is perhaps reflected in 2:1b, "they do it in the light of morning because there is ʾēl in their hand." Morning was the accepted time of assembly in gates for judicial affairs, and the reference to having ʾēl in the hand seems to signify right or authority in a legal sense (cf. Gen 31:29). The Hebrew equivalent of eviction (grš) occurs in 2:9 demonstrating the activity of foreclosure.

LAND TENURE

The prophetic opposition to landed property accumulation raises the issue of land tenure rights. A widely held reconstruction[16] of the issue finds in the premonarchic tribes of Israel some land held in common by the tribes and clans, and other plots held by clans and families in inalienable trust for posterity. Undergirding this system was the theological conviction that Yahweh had granted the land to the tribes and was the actual "owner"; an Israelite family was simply the steward of this gift.

The more commercially oriented and socially stratified Canaanites used land as a form of capital, buying and selling it for profit. Kings held large tracts of land, which they distributed to officials as grants in return for loyalty and service. Israel may have prevailed politically and militarily through David, but this Canaanite political economy was incorporated into the workings of state, and as the national government grew in Israel or Judah, so did its reliance on aspects of this system. By the 8th century conflict was inevitable between these two systems. On the one hand, kingship and its attendant bureaucracy required a political economy along the lines of neighboring states with increasingly urban classes of people. On the other, the Israelite heritage was rooted in a different social order. A short schema can illustrate this.

Canaan	Israel
king, family, city-state	tribe, clan, village
urban, merchant	agrarian, pastoral
centralized bureaucracy	decentralized leadership
land = capital	land = inheritance

---

[16]E.g., A. Alt, "Der Anteil des Königtum an der sozialen Entwicklung in den Reichen Israel und Juda," *KS* (Munich: Beck'she, 1953-59) 3. 348f.; G. von Rad, "The Promised Land and Yahweh's Land in the Hexateuch." *The Problem of the Hexateuch and Other Essays* (New York: McGraw Hill, 1966) 79-93.

This model is helpful in understanding some of the social issues raised by the prophets, but problems remain. To begin with, the dichotomy between the two entities is cast in absolute terms with the characteristics of each stated in monolithic terms. From the perspective of sociological analysis it has been proposed that "early Israel originated in a socio-economic and religio-political revolution among native Canaanites of the lower and disprivileged classes."[17] If this conclusion is even close to the truth, than Canaan had no single, monolithic political economy but a dominant system opposed for various reasons by some Canaanites. And by definition, what is genuinely Israelite is also native Canaanite.

Heltzer's study of the rural community at Ugarit[18] showed some elements of an agrarian, village-based economy operating with more conservative tendencies in land tenure. While such an economy was dominated by the nearby urban center, it was a functioning system and perhaps illustrative of the village-based economy posited for the tribes of Israel.

Something similar to this tension between competing systems in a state political economy can be shown for the developing city-states in Greece.[19] Asheri's study of this issue showed the tension between what he called a "conservative and agrarian" system based on independent households, a certain "equality" in land distribution and strict inheritance laws. The other system he termed "unprejudiced and liberal," which favored immovable property to be of individual ownership to promote freedom of trade and the accumulation of wealth. While urban Canaan of the Amarna period would favor the latter type of system described by Asheri, what became early Israel would favor the former. It may not be helpful to label the latter system Canaanite, since not all Canaanites supported it and not all Israelites opposed it.

Alt has suggested that Mic 2:2b, "a man and his house, a man and his inheritance (naḥālāh)," represents the Israelite social ideal.[20] The "ideal" does represent what Micah wished to preserve for Judean families, and perhaps the view can be applied as well to Isaiah, Amos, Jeremiah, and others. But it is also a common ideal for an agrarian, village-based, tribal society and would find support in a number of societies of antiquity.

Royal land grants are an issue related to land tenure and to the social conflicts of the pre-exilic period. This should not be considered a "Canaanite" practice and therefore foreign to Israel. According to 1 Sam 22:7, Saul asked a rhetorical question of his servants concerning the outlaw David's ability to grant fields and vineyards to his followers or to make them *śārîm* over thousands and hundreds. Implied, of course, is that he could do so as the legally constituted ruler. According to the visionary account of Ezek 46:16-18 (a post-exilic text), when the prince of the reconstructed community makes a land grant to his servants, it shall not be in perpetuity, nor shall people be dispossessed to add to the royal holdings. Such a reform implies previous abuse in the national history. These

---

[17]N. Gottwald, "Early Israel and the Canaanite Socio-economic System," *Palestine in Transition* (ed. Freedman, Graf; Sheffield: Almond Press, 1983) 25.

[18]M. Heltzer, *The Rural Community in Ancient Ugarit* (Wiesbaden: Ludwig Reichert, 1976).

[19]D. Asheri, "Laws of Inheritance, Distribution of Land and Political Constitutions in Ancient Greece," *Historia* 12 (1963) 1-21.

[20]A. Alt, "*Ges Anadasmos* in Juda," *KS* 3. 379-81.

two texts stand like bookends to the 8th and 7th centuries where the practice must have been one factor in the issue of land accumulation.[21]

One could point to the text of 1 Sam 8:11-17 where it is assumed that a king in Israel will take land and give it to his servants, and also that he will take sons and daughters for royal projects. The passage is difficult to date, but it does not show the editorial hand of the Deuteronomist and is probably as old as Solomon.

Royal grants in antiquity often included tax-exempt status or other "perks" which were instrumental in providing support for the king's allies and officials. Armed with such an economic base, it is easy to understand how an official might have both the opportunity and the working capital to accumulate yet more property.

THE ADMINISTRATIVE/JUDICIAL SYSTEM

Several recent studies have traced the development of such a system from its tribal setting through the period of the divided monarchy.[22] What follows, therefore, is based on the conclusions of these studies and attempts to apply them to the specific subject of the prophetic social critique.

Under the monarchy an administrative/judicial system was developed whereby judges were appointed by the crown in regions throughout the realm. For Judah this system is attributed to Jehoshaphat (described with some post-exilic additions in 2 Chr 19:4-11). Included is a type of supreme court located in Jerusalem. Pentateuchal texts attribute the development of a similar system to Moses during the wilderness wanderings (Exod 18:13-27; Num 11:16-27; Deut 1:9-18; 16:18-20; 17:8-13). The most important point to be made is that some form of royally appointed system is *presupposed* by the pre-exilic prophets, and this is clearly demonstrated by charts one and three where the elders, heads, judges and officials are intimately involved in the accusations of property abuse. These same titles are found in the narratives mentioned above as Mosaic or royally appointed officers. Both the system and its staff are included in the prophetic critique.[23]

---

[21]M. Weinfeld, "The Covenant of Grant in the Old Testament and the Ancient Near East," *JAOS* 90 (1970) 184-203; 2. Z. Ben-Barak, "Meribaal and the System of Land Grants in Ancient Israel," *Bib* 62 (1981) 73-91. I think the Samaria Ostraca from 8th century Samaria show the receipts from goods of land grant property sent to "owners" in the capital. The *lmlk* stamps from 8th century Judah show, I believe, evidence of containers used for goods collected from crown estates and from taxes.

[22]Two recent dissertations have covered the territory. Cf. K. Whitelam, *The Just King. Monarchical Judicial Authority in Ancient Israel* (Sheffield: JSOT, 1979); E. Davies, *Prophecy and Ethics: Isaiah and the Ethical Tradition of Israel* (Sheffield: JSOT, 1981) 90-112.

[23]Lang (*Monotheism,* 126) does not reckon with the influence of a royal judicial system, as he believes judicial affairs were always decentralized. I think he misses the point that local officials were (often) appointed by the crown. His oversight weakens considerably his helpful analysis.

Also to be stressed is the link between these officials and both the military levy and the royal land-grant system. Jehoshaphat's appointees went to the fortified cities (2 Chr 19:5). In fact the "judges" may also have been military commanders and responsible for regional security.[24] The semantic range of the word *špṭ* includes both military and administrative activity (cf. 1 Sam 8:6, 20), and the appointees of Exod 18:13-27 and Deut 1:9-18, just like the *śārîm* of 1 Sam 8:12 and 22:17, are leaders arranged according to military status. Such leaders, with their crucial roles in the national army and the royal administration, would have substantial influence in the regions where they served. They would be entitled to royal land grants, exemption from certain services, perhaps tax collection privileges, along with authority in judicial affairs. It is a system without enough checks and balances to maintain equilibrium in a rural community where those with the most official duties answer primarily to the crown rather than local custom.

CONCLUSIONS

When one works from the internal evidence of biblical texts in the area of reconstructing a political economy, it quickly becomes apparent that there are serious gaps in the materials for the task. It is the lack of administrative texts which is especially limiting. The application of sociological theories may be helpful if one uses them as a heuristic device, but one must always be careful that they are not imposed on texts.

There are several approaches to the issue of the prophetic social protest that I think do not assist us in the investigation. One is to say that the prophets opposed Canaanite economic practices.[25] We do not find the prophets *themselves* complaining that land speculators and creditors are Canaanite, or even Canaanized. Such a criticism is perhaps more relevant to some aspects of the cult and problem of syncretism. In spite of their harsh rhetoric most of what is opposed is assumed to be Israelite and (unfortunately) legal.

Nor is it useful to apply the label "capitalism" to the system opposed by the prophets.[26] This label is anachronistic and misleading and should not be used of a non-western, pre-industrial society in antiquity. Some scholars are now using the term *Rentenkapitalismus*[27] to describe the various forms of the absentee landlord system in the ancient Near East with indebted peasants working plots of land as service to their creditor. This

---

[24]Cf. the letter of appeal from Yavneh Yam where the worker appeals to the *śār* of a corvée team. *ANET,* 568.

[25]The following quote is an extreme example of a widespread analysis. "Die Bescheltungen der Propheten richten sich ausschiesslich gegen die kanaanische oder kanaanisierte Oberschicht und Beamtschaft." H. Donner, "Die soziale Botschaft des Propheten im Lichte der Gesellschaftsordnung in Israel," *OrAnt* 2 (1963) 243.

[26]I have collected numerous examples, many with qualifiers, such as "early" capitalism. Cf. H. W. Wolff, *Joel and Amos* (Hermeneia; Philadelphia: Fortress, 1977) 69; H. J. Kraus, "Die Prophetische Botschaft gegen dar soziale Unrecht Israel," (*EV T* 15 (1955) 298; R. B. V. Scott, *The Relevance of the Prophets* (New York: Macmillan, 1944) 30.

[27]So Lang (note 3 above) and O. Loretz, "Die prophetische Kritik des Rentenkapitalismus," *UF* 7 (1975) 271-78.

term, too, because it contains the modern term "capitalism," is suspect, though the system described is helpful for understanding its inner workings. Much of what Gott-wald[28] described as the Asiatic mode of production, including his use of the term "absentee landlord," is virtually identical to *Rentenkapitalismus.*

I would prefer the general term *Redistribution System,* used by some analysts of antiquity[29] to describe the political economy of Iron Age Israel or Judah under the monarchy. It is a descriptive, functional term and emphasizes the central role of the national government in redistributing goods and services in a pre-industrial society. A redistributing economy under kingship depended heavily on the role of the upper classes, which are usually a very small percentage of the total population in such a society. Such persons rarely acted only as private citizens, since most of them were intimately related to the royal administration and held various appointed offices. As I have indicated in this paper, the relationship to and acitivities in regional affairs by royal officials are the major catalysts for the conditions decried by the prophets.

In conclusion I would like to propose that Neo-Assyrian society provides a good historical and cultural analogy for Israel or Judah of the pre-exilic age. *Every aspect* of the political economy and role of officials identified in this paper from the difficult prophetic texts can be demonstrated in detail from the *hundreds* of Neo-Assyrian administrative documents from the 9th through the 7th centuries. In these documents one finds material on:

1. The taxation and conscription system of the empire.[30]
2. Contracts detailing the sale of landed property, the function of pledges and the sale of people as well.[31]
3. Royal officials in the 8th century, including their various state duties, their taxation efforts, their activities as creditors, and their pattern of collecting landed property in scattered parts of the countryside.[32]
4. The royal practice of land grants.[33]
5. The role of temples as banking institutions.[34]

Analyses of the Assyrian countryside conclude that even under Essarhaddon more revenue was produced from internal provinces than was collected through conquest. Regardless of the wealth of the empire, the economic conditions of the peasant in the

---

[28]Cf. note 17 above.

[29]T. F. Carney, *The Economics of Antiquity* (Lawrence: Coronado Press, 1973) 21-22, 36, 64-70; M. Nash, *Primitive and Peasant Economic Systems* (San Francisco: Chandler, 1966) 26-33. Note the use of the term in T. McClellan, "Towns and Fortresses: The Transformation of Urban Life in Judah from 8th to 7th Centuries B.C." *SBLASP* (Missoula: Scholars Press, 1978) 1. 281.

[30]J. N. Postgate, *Taxation and Conscription in the Assyrian Empire* (Rome: Biblical Institute Press, 1974).

[31]Cf. note 14 above.

[32]J. V. Kinnier Wilson, *The Nimrod Wine Lists, A Study of Men and Administration at the Assyrian Capital in the Eight Century B.C.* (London: British School of Archaeology in Iraq, 1972).

[33]J. N. Postgate, *Neo-Assyrian Royal Grants and Decrees* (Rome: Pontifical Biblical Institute, 1969).

[34]Cf. note 8 above.

countryside never improved,[35] but if anything became worse as the empire expanded. The question was not one of the supply of goods and services but of the demand of a central administration which claimed the right to acquire and redistribute them.

It is too much to claim that Israel or Judah simply adopted Neo-Assyrian practices. The former were not empires. That they had many practices in common should not be surprising to anyone who has studied the fragile nature of nation building in Iron Age Syria-Palestine.

CHART ONE

PROPERTY		ACCUSATION AGAINST

Amos

2:6-8	debt slavery, foreclosures	--
3:9-10	"robbery"	Mt. Samaria
5:11	forced exactions	--
7:1	royal tax	tax is not object of the accusation
8:4-6	fraud, debt slavery	merchants

Hosea

4:2	theft	nation
5:10	territorial expansion	Judah
8:14	palaces and fortifications	Israel, Judah
12:8-9	fraud	Israel

Isaiah

1:23	thievery, corruption	officials (śārîm)
3:14-15	theft of land, produce	elders (zekānîm), officials (śārîm)
5:8-10	landed property accumulation	--
10:1-2	"robbery" of poor	statute makers

Micah

2:1-2	landed property accumulation	--
2:8	theft of pledge?	--

---

[35]J. N. Postgate, "Some Remarks on Conditions in the Assyrian Countryside," *JESHO* 17 (1974) 225-43, with references; G. van Driel, "Land and People in Assyria," *BiOr* 27 (1970) 168-75.

2:9	property eviction	--
3:1-2	"robbery"	heads (*rōʾšîm*), leaders (*qāṣîn*)
3:9-10	debt slavery, corvée	heads, leaders
6:10-12	fraud	rich men, statute makers? (cf. 6:16)

Zephaniah

| 1:9 | fraud, property acquired by violence | officials (*śārîm*) sons of the king? (cf.1:8) |

Jeremiah

5:26-28	debt slavery, misappropriation	wicked men
7:9	theft	nation
7:11	robbery	temple
21:11-12	robbery, oppression	king should protect against such deeds
22:11-17	debt slavery, corvée	Jehoiakim
34:8-22	debt slavery	officials(*śārîm*), people

Ezekiel

| 22:6-12 | extortion, usury, sexual violation (cf. 18:7-8) | princes (*nᵉśîʾîm*) |
| 46:16-18 | unjust land grants, eviction | the prince (*nāśîʾ*) |

CHART TWO

A.	Debt Slavery		B.	Landed Property	
	Amos	2:6-8		Amos	2:6-8
		8:5			5:11 (cf. 3:15)
	Isa	10:2 (prob.)		Hos	8:14
	Mic	3:2, 10		Isa	3:14
	Jer	5:26			5:8
		22:13		Mic	2:2
		34:8-22			2:9
	Ezek	22:6-7			3:1-2 (prob.)
				Jer	22:13-15 (prob.)
				Ezek	46:16-18

C.   Movable Property   D.   Fraud, Theft, Robbery
     Amos 2:7   Amos 8:5-6
           5:11   Hos   4:2
           7:1 (royal tax)   12:8-9
     Isa   3:14   Isa   1:23
           10:2 (prob.)   10:2
     Mic   2:7   Mic   3:2-3
     Zeph 1:9   6:10-12
     Ezek 21:12   Jer   7:9, 11
                                                     21:12
                                               Ezek 22:7

CHART THREE

Text	Person Addressed	Circumstance
Amos		
2:7a *	--	perversion (nṭḥ) of justice
5:7, 10 *	(tax collector, creditor?)	corruption at the gate
5:12 *	--	bribery, perversion (nṭḥ) of justice
5:15	--	necessity for justice in the gate
Hosea		
13:10	king, judges, officials	sarcasm over their ineffectiveness
Isaiah		
1:17	Judah	need for justice
1:21-26 *	Jerusalem, officials, judges, counsellors	thievery, bribery, corruption
3:2	judge	need for removal
3:14 *	elders, officials	robbery of the poor
10:1-2 *	statute makers (ḥqq)	perversion (nṭḥ) of justice, robbery
29:21	--	perversion of justice
Micah		
2:1-2 *	--	seizure of property
3:1, 9 *	heads, leaders	injustice

| 3:11 | heads | bribery |
| 7:3 | officials, judges | bribery |

Zephaniah

| 3:3 | officials, judges | accused as predators |

Jeremiah

| 5:28 * | wicked men | injustice |
| 21:11-12 * | house of David | call for justice |

Ezekiel

| 22:6 | princes | shedding blood |

Habakkuk

| 1:3-4 | Judah | injustice |

*Signifies the passage concerns the subject of the misappropriation of property and may be found in Charts One or Two as well.

Huldah and the Men of Anathoth: Women in Leadership in the Deuteronomic History

Duane L. Christensen

American Baptist Seminary of the West and G. T. U.

One of the fruits of the struggle for the liberation of women within biblical studies has been a fresh look at familiar passages of Scripture from a new perspective. We are consequently deeply in debt to scholars like Phyllis Trible for helping us see that Adam was not in fact a male figure as such until after woman was removed from him in the creation of Eve.[1] Thus the familiar arguments for the subordination of women based on the order of creation have no actual basis in the biblical text. Male and female are created together as Adam is transformed in the story of Genesis 2—from "human-kind," on the one hand, to the male counter-part of a remarkable "help-mate" who is in fact Adam's equal.

In a similar manner the current interest in the so-called "new literary criticism" of the Bible, with its focus on the integrity of the biblical text in its received form, has brought new depths of meaning to familiar passages as well.[2] This paper is an attempt to combine these two impulses in contemporary biblical studies to take a fresh look at the role of women in leadership in ancient Israel as preserved in the Deuteronomic tradition.

Within the Deuteronomic tradition there are only two women who are designated "prophets" (נביאה)—namely, Deborah (Judg 4:4) and Huldah (2 Kgs 23:14). It is interesting to compare these two persons who form an inclusion of sorts around the Deuteronomic History of life in the Promised Land. And since, as Frank Cross has argued, the first edition of the Deuteronomic History (Joshua through 2 Kings) was written in Josiah's reign, that inclusion in fact frames the whole of the original literary work as such.

Cross has identified the two major themes of the original composition of the Deuteronomic History, namely the sin of Jeroboam I, on the one hand, and the faithfulness of Josiah, on the other.[3] It is the interplay of these two parallel themes which gives the work its peculiar Deuteronomic flavor. If one keeps the terms of the covenant as David and Josiah did, the blessings are in effect. On the other hand, if one follows the example of Jeroboam I or the wicked Manasseh the covenant curses are inevitable. For Cross the sin of Manasseh is a secondary theme introduced by an exilic redactor to explain the

---

[1]Phyllis Trible, *God and the Rhetoric of Sexuality* (Philadelphia: Fortress Press, 1978) 12-21

[2]For a convenient bibliography of this growing body of literature see Adele Berlin, *Poetics and Interpretation of Biblical Narrative* (Sheffield: Almond Press, 1983) 159-170.

[3]Frank M. Cross, Jr., *Canaanite Myth and Hebrew Epic* (Cambridge, Mass.: Harvard University Press, 1973) 274-289.

death of Josiah. Be that as it may, it seems likely that an additional theme should be added to the list—the role of the prophet in ancient Israel, especially in relation to kingship. It may well be that this theme is consciously developed as an exposition of the laws of the king and prophet in Deuteronomy 17-18.

The central stories within the Deuteronomic History which explore the role of the prophet in ancient Israel are as follows:

> A - 1 Kings 13 Kingship and Prophecy: the Way of Obedience
>   B - 1 Kings 18 Elijah on Mt. Carmel: vs. Prophets of Baal
>   B'- 1 Kings 19 Elijah on Mt. Horeb: the Mosaic Prophet
> A'- 1 Kings 22 Kingship and Prophecy: Prophet against Prophet

Elijah is the focus of attention and is presented as a Moses-figure who defeats the "false" prophets of the first kind as presented in Deut 18:9-14—namely, the Canaanite or pagan prophets who are an abomination. The contest between Elijah and the prophets of Baal on Mount Carmel in 1 Kings 18 is set over against Elijah's theophanic experience on Mount Horeb in 1 Kings 19. In this latter instance Elijah's experience is clearly patterned after that of Moses who not only experienced God in the awesome "thunderstorm" on the mountain (Exod 19:16-24), but who also had the privilege of a glimpse of Yahweh's glory from a "cave" on that same holy mountain (Exod 33:17-23). But Elijah's experience is not oriented only toward the past. It clearly foreshadows a new phase of prophetic activity within the canon of both the Former Prophets and the Latter Prophets in imagery which is particularly evident in the story of Jonah.[4]

But what is important for our purposes here is to note the role of Jezebel, both here and in the larger structure of 1 and 2 Kings. It is Jezebel who forms the link between these two contrasting stories of Elijah. The resultant structural pattern of "prophet" and "king" in the Deuteronomic rendition of the history of ancient Israel is indeed provocative.

> A - Deborah and Barak (Judges 4-5)
>   B - Jeroboam I and Prophetic Conflict (1 Kings 13)
>   C - Elijah on Mount Carmel (1 Kings 18)
>   D - Jezebel (1 Kings 16:31 - 2 Kings 9:37)
>   C'- Elijah on Mount Horeb (1 Kings 19)
>   B'- Ahab and Prophetic Conflict (1 Kings 22)
> A'- Huldah and Josiah (2 Kings 22)

In the opening story Barak, the son of Abinoam, clearly foreshadows the Deuteronomic conception of what constitutes a good king. Like Saul and David, Barak is primarily a war lord who is commissioned by the "prophet" to lead Israel in fighting Yahweh's wars. And whatever his historical role may have been in ancient Israel, Barak is clearly

---

[4]See my article on "The Song of Jonah: A Metrical Analysis," *JBL* (forthcoming). Whereas Moses and Elijah ascend the mountain of God to experience a theophany, Jonah descends to "the roots of the mountains" where he also encounters Yahweh. The fact that details in the story of Elijah as recorded in 1 Kings 19 are also reflected within the narrative of the book of Jonah has been noted by numerous scholars.

presented in the story as subject to the word of God as delivered through Deborah.

In a similar fashion Huldah plays a role of great importance over against that of king Josiah. It was to Huldah that Josiah sent Hilkiah the high priest to authenticate the "book of the Torah" which was found in the Temple (1 Kings 22:13-14). And it was Huldah the prophetess who pronounced a word of judgment, blessing, and instruction to both the people of Judah and their king (2 Kings 22:16-20). Besides these two stories there are only two other kings who recognize the authority of the prophet in ancient Israel and thus are deemed good kings from a Deuteronomic point of view—namely, David who recognized the authority of Nathan, and Hezekiah who installed Isaiah as royal prophet in Judah after the fall of the northern kingdom of Israel. It is curious to note that Isaiah's wife is also singled out as a "prophetess" (נביאה) in Isaiah 8:3. The only other time this term is used in the first two sections of the Hebrew canon (the Law and the Prophets) is to designate Miriam, the sister of Moses, as a "prophetess" (Exod 15:20).

The parallel stories dealing with prophetic conflict in 1 Kings 13 and 22 present all three of the major themes of the Deuteronomic historian. The story of the unnamed man of God who is slain by the lion of Judah is set against the sin of Jeroboam at the very moment of the building of the detested altar of Bethel (1 Kings 13). And Josiah is named explicitly in perhaps the most glaring *vaticinum ex eventu* in the Bible (1 Kings 13:2). The primary focus of the story, however, is on prophetic conflict which takes on still deeper meaning when seen over against the story of Micaiah and Zedekiah in 1 Kings 22. Both stories deal with two prophets in conflict, both of whom presume to speak the word of Yahweh (cf. Deut 18:20-22). In one case the two prophets are anonymous while in the other they are clearly identified. In one instance the prophetic word is described as coming from a "messenger" (angel) of Yahweh (1 Kgs 13:18). On the other hand, Micaiah describes a vision of the very proceedings of the heavenly court with Yahweh Himself presiding over the host of heaven (1 Kgs 22:19). The description of what Micaiah observed throws unexpected light on an ambiguous statement in the earlier story. In Micaiah's account it is clearly Yahweh Himself who sends the "lying spirit" to entice Ahab to go up to his own death. In the previous story the narrator added the simple statement, "He lied to him" (1 Kgs 13:18). Though the commentaries are almost unanimous in assuming that it was the old prophet from Bethel who deceived the man of God from Judah, it is quite possible to see the "angel" as the author of the lie. The old prophet would then have lied unwittingly. Such an interpretation would make it easier to understand the old prophet's grief over the death of his "brother" (1 Kgs 13:30) and the curious instructions he gave his "sons": "When I die, bury me in a grave in which the man of God is buried; lay my bones beside his bones" (1 Kgs 13:31).

By far the most interesting feature of the structuring device observed in this nesting of parallel stories in the Deuteronomic History is the actual center. It is the wicked Jezebel who forms the bridge between the two mountain-top experiences of Elijah. And the structure itself invites a comparison of Jezebel with Deborah and Huldah. In the account of Josephus, Jezebel's father Ethbaal king of the Sidonians was a priest in the Phoenician cult of Baal and Astarte.[5] Be that as it may, she certainly is responsible in the biblical story for advancing the cult of Baal in Israel; as her daughter Athaliah is subsequently in Judah (2 Kings 2:18).

---

[5] *Antiquities*, VIII, xiii, 2.

It is particularly instructive to examine closely the account of the death of both Jezebel and her daughter Athaliah. When Jehu came to Jezreel for Jezebel she was in an upper room where "she painted her eyes, and adorned her head, and looked out of the window" (2 Kgs 9:30). What a splendid woman! Though she knew her death was imminent, she was going to make her exit in style. But of even greater interest to the careful reader is the wording here which reminds one of the ending of the "Song of Deborah," where:

> Out of the window she peered;
> The mother of Sisera gazed through the lattice (Judg 5:28).

In Canaanite mythology the god Mot ("Death") found entrance to Baal's palace through a window which the latter had been urged not to construct. As Grace Lorenz has recently noted, "Through the window/lattice" is a vivid metaphor for the way in which death enters a building. As she put it:[6]

> Death has not only come to Sisera, but it is simultaneously entering into Sisera's dwelling and his mother with such clarity that the action of the woman is a stark reality. She does not see her son's body, but in the act of looking and/or shrieking she is already mourning without fully knowing why. The first view of entering Death is unobstructed. The second view of death comes through a veiled or latticed window.

The text in the Song of Deborah continues by quoting the mother of Sisera:

> Why is his chariot so long in coming?
> Why tarry the hoofbeats of his chariots? (Judg 5:28b)

The imagery here is perhaps a foreshadowing of the curious description of the death of Jezebel's daughter Athaliah who was taken out of the Temple "through the horse's entrance to the king's house" where she was slain (2 Kgs 11:16).

But it is not just repetition of words or imagery as such that ties together these four dominant women in the Deuteronomic account of the history of ancient Israel. The presentation of these four women also takes up the three central themes of the Deuteronomic historian already noted, while at the same time introducing something more.

> A - Deborah: a "Prophetess" of Yahweh alongside Barak
> B - Jezebel: a Royal Advocate of Baal in Israel
> B'- Athaliah: a Royal Advocate of Baal in Judah
> A'- Huldah: a "Prophetess" of Yahweh alongside Josiah

Huldah brings an added dimension to the theme of Josiah's faithfulness. In place of the sin of Jeroboam we have explicit pagan practice that centers in the worship of Baal. And

---

[6]The paper in question was presented under the title "Judges 5:24-31, Propaganda for Yahweh at its Best," at a meeting of the Society of Biblical Literature / Pacific Coast Region on March 30, 1984, at Golden Gate Baptist Seminary. The quotation is taken from p. 13 of her unpublished manuscript.

though the two "prophetesses" here are not in conflict with each other, they are clearly set in sharp contrast over against the two royal feminine personages to illustrate the inherent tension between "prophet" and "king" in ancient Israel.

But why did the Deuteronomic historian focus on four dominant women in this structural schema? How are we to explain the fact that in the Deuteronomic tradition which crystalized at the end of the national history of ancient Israel, women are singled out to occupy major roles in both the royal and prophetic offices? The answer to these questions is perhaps to be found in placing the Deuteronomic tradition in its proper social location in ancient Israel. And this brings us to the "men of Anathoth."

It is perhaps going too far to see Huldah as Jeremiah's aunt, as suggested by Robert Wilson.[7] But it is clear that the circle of persons mentioned by name in 2 Kgs 23:3-14 includes members of the Anathoth priesthood, descendants from Abiathar, who were part of the central political establishment in Jerusalem under Josiah.[8] The "men of Anathoth" who subsequently plotted against Jeremiah are probably to be identified "as some of Jeremiah's priestly relatives who were still occupying positions in Jerusalem's religious establishment" after Jeremiah's removal from the royal court.[9]

The Levitical establishment at Anathoth, a suburb of modern Jerusalem, was probably the social location which preserved the so-called Northern or Ephraimite tradition in ancient Israel. The prophet Jeremiah was born in Anathoth. Josiah's reform thus included a religious compromise which brought back the "Moses group" which stemmed ultimately from premonarchic Shiloh, and canonized their perspective alongside that of the royal Zadokite priesthood long established in Jerusalem. It was this alternative view of Israel's ancient story that was in fact the more archaic. In fact, the very description of Josiah's great passover celebration in 2 Kgs 23:22 is instructive: "For no such passover had been kept since the days of the judges who judged Israel, or during the days of the kings of Israel or of the kings of Judah."

It was the institution of the monarchy in ancient Israel, at least from the point of view of the "men of Anathoth", which was ultimately responsible for all that was wrong in ancient Israel—including the subordination of women. The social stratification introduced by a new economic and political order, and the royal harem in particular, as introduced by Solomon, were responsible for subtle and far-reaching changes in the status of women. The so-called Northern perspective, as preserved among the "men of Anathoth," was more archaic in nature, rooted in agrarian values of a pre-monarchic era where the sexes were treated with relative equality. It was to this Moses-group in Anathoth that both Huldah and Jeremiah belonged. Among the agrarian values they brought to the canonical process in the time of Josiah was a high regard for the place of women in roles of leadership, both religious and political.

It should be noted that the treatment of women on the part of the Deuteronomic historian is simply part of a larger concern for the powerless in ancient Israel. The "men of Anathoth" were excluded from political power from the time of Solomon to Josiah and again after the fall of Jerusalem. The book of Deuteronomy represents their point of

---

[7]Robert R. Wilson, *Prophecy and Society in Ancient Israel* (Philadelphia: Fortress Press, 1980) 223.

[8]Ibid., 234.

[9]Ibid., 245, where Wilson is citing S. Dean McBride.

view in its constant concern for the widow, the orphan, and the alien within the social structure of ancient Israel. For the most part, women in general were among the powerless whose rights were protected by Deuteronomic legislation. They also apparently provided an appropriate symbol around which to structure some of the central theological concerns of the Deuteronomic historian.